France

A geographical, social and economic survey

✥ France

A geographical, social and
economic survey

Philippe Pinchemel
Professor of Geography in the University of Paris I
with Chantal Balley, Nicole Mathieu, Geneviève Pinchemel and Denise Pumain

Translated by DOROTHY ELKINS with T. H. ELKINS

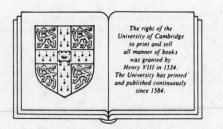

*The right of the
University of Cambridge
to print and sell
all manner of books
was granted by
Henry VIII in 1534.
The University has printed
and published continuously
since 1584.*

CAMBRIDGE UNIVERSITY PRESS
Cambridge
London   New York   New Rochelle   Melbourne   Sydney

EDITIONS DE LA MAISON DES SCIENCES DE L'HOMME
Paris

Published by the Press Syndicate of the University of Cambridge
The Pitt Building, Trumpington Street, Cambridge CB2 1RP
32 East 57th Street, New York, NY 10022, USA
10 Stamford Road, Oakleigh, Melbourne 3166, Australia
and Editions de la Maison des Sciences de l'Homme
54 Boulevard Raspail, 75270 Paris Cedex 06

Originally published in French as *La France*
by Armand Colin 1980 and 1981
and © Libraire Armand Colin
First published in English by Editions de la Maison des Sciences de
l'Homme and Cambridge University Press 1986 as *France: a geographical,
social and economic survey*
English translation © Maison des Sciences de l'Homme and
Cambridge University Press 1987

Printed in Great Britain at the University Press, Cambridge

British Library cataloguing in publication data

Pinchemel, Philippe
France: a geographical, social and
economic survey.
1. Anthropo-geography – France.
2. France – Historical geography.
I. Title.   II. La France. *English*
304.2′0944   GF571

Library of Congress cataloguing in publication data

Pinchemel, Philippe.
France: a geographical, social, and economic survey.
Bibliography.
Includes index.
1. France.   I. Balley, Chantal.   II. Title.
DC17.P5513 1986   911′.44   85–31385

ISBN 0 521 24987 2 hard covers

ISBN 2 7351 0175 4 hard covers (France only)

WV

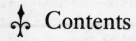 Contents

Part IV: Resources, economic activity and economic enterprises

Part V: The infrastructure of spatial interaction

Part VI: Landscape and environment in rural France

Part VIII: Conclusion

✧ Illustrations

⚜ Tables

⚜ Translators' preface

The first edition of this book, published in 1963, was translated by Christine Trollope and Arthur J. Hunt.[1] By 1980, however, the French version had reached a substantially rewritten and reorganized form, in which the principal author was assisted by four collaborators, and it was evidently felt that this entirely new English translation should be commissioned. The translation is based on a somewhat reduced and considerably amended version of the 1980/1 French text, which was further amended by the author in the course of translation, so that effectively a unique new edition has emerged.

Some explanation is needed with regard to the treatment of place-names. There was initially no doubt in our minds that the proper procedure required that they should all be rendered in the form current in the country in which they were located rather than in familiar English versions, but problems emerged in practice. The French departments presented no problem, as they have acquired no English-language equivalents. They are accordingly given their official French names as they stood at the time of going to press. In practice, the use of departmental names for the purpose of conveying locational information has been minimized in the text, since only those who have received the benefit of a French education know where they are. Who, for example, can unhesitatingly point to the Departments of Ain or Aude on the map of France? So far as possible, where the original text uses departmental names, more general regional names have been substituted.

[1] *France: a geographical survey* (Bell, London, 1969).

The principle of using the native form has also been maintained for towns; Lyon is preferred to Lyons, Marseille to Marseilles. For the sake of uniformity this involved the reluctant acceptance of the form 'Dunkerque' for a town which in its anglicized form is not without a place in British history. Towns outside the borders of France present greater difficulty; clearly the use of French forms where French is not the local language is not acceptable, so Bâle, Trèves and Aix-la-Chapelle have to be rejected. After considerable hesitation, especially when faced with bilingual Brussel–Bruxelles, we decided in the interest of simplicity to anglicize them. French regional names also present great difficulties; it seems unnecessarily pedantic not to use forms such as Brittany, Normandy, Picardy or Burgundy, some of which were once English possessions, and which are embedded in British history and consciousness; one might say that too much British blood has been shed in Flanders' fields for the correct French name to be easily assimilable. An exception to this rule is the use of the French form 'Aquitaine', which is close enough to the English for the difference to be almost imperceptible. Matters are even more difficult where traditional regional names are also the official titles of the new administrative regions of France. Our initial intention was to use only the French form in this case, but in practice this involved further confusion, and we decided to settle so far as possible for a consistent inconsistency, using the English regional names wherever they are well established, and French forms otherwise.

We wish to thank a number of friends and colleagues for their patience and goodwill in responding to strings of queries about the translation of specialist terms. Particular thanks are due to Dr A. Potts, Dr D. A. Robinson and Dr R. B. G. Williams (University of Sussex) for help in respect of physical geography, Dr A. J. Fielding (University of Sussex) in respect of economic and population geography, Mr C. Flockton (University of Surrey) in respect of urban and regional planning, and to Ms Beryl T. Atkins (one of the editors of the Collins–Robert dictionary) for help with various neologisms, but there were many others. Nevertheless, it must be stressed that responsibility for any defects in the translation rests solely with ourselves.

Finally, we wish to record that the translators enjoyed a particularly close relationship with Philippe Pinchemel, the principal author. Each chapter has been sent to him on completion, together with a string of queries and suggestions, to be returned amended, improved and (where appropriate) updated by the inclusion of additional material. We feel privileged to have been able to enter into this enjoyable, stimulating and, we trust, fruitful interchange.

Dorothy Elkins
T. H. Elkins

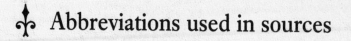

Abbreviations used in sources

CNASEA	Centre National d'Aménagement des Structures d'Exploitations Agricoles
DATAR	Délégation Générale à l'Aménagement du Territoire et à l'Action Régionale
INED	Institut National d'Etudes Démographiques (Paris)
INSEE	Institut National de la Statistique et des Etudes Economiques
PUF	Presses Universitaires de France
SCEES	Service Central des Enquêtes et Etudes Statistiques (Ministère de l'Agriculture)
SEGESA	Société d'Etudes Géographiques, Economiques et Sociales Appliquées (Paris)

1

⚜ General characteristics

How did it happen that a fragment of the earth's surface, which is neither a peninsula nor an island, and which physical geography cannot properly regard as a unified whole, evolved into a state, became, in fact, the home of a nation?

P. Vidal de la Blache

1 Historical formation

The 551,695 sq km (213,009 sq miles) of metropolitan France, delimited by boundaries which are conventionally simplified into an elegant hexagon, have not endured without modification over the centuries; throughout its entire history the territorial extent of France has undergone dynamic change. If some boundaries were fixed at a very early stage, others are of much more recent origin (Fig. 1.1).

After the absorption of Brittany and Auvergne into the kingdom of France in the reign of Francis I, and after the treaties of Vervins (1598) and Lyon (1601), territories in the royal domain and the private holdings of the royal family were united by an edict of Henry IV (1607), giving the country a cohesion that had formerly been lacking (Fig. 1.2). At this stage, only the northern and eastern boundaries of France still remained to be settled. Apart from some minor enclaves such as Warneton, which disappeared in 1769, the present northern boundary from the North Sea to the river Sambre dates from the Treaty of Utrecht (1713), while the alignment between the Sambre and the Rhine was finally settled by the second Treaty of Paris (1815), when France lost Philippeville, Marienbourg and Bouillon in the Ardennes, and also Sarrebourg and Landau.

In the east, the Rhine was attained throughout its whole length in Alsace by the Treaty of Rastadt (1714) (the 1648 Treaty of Westphalia had given France only the Sundgau and the control of ten Imperial cities, not including Strasbourg and Mulhouse). The duchy of Lorraine was only finally annexed in 1766, on the death of Stanislas Leczinski, and it was not until 1793 that Montbéliard became French. Alsace and the part of Lorraine corresponding to the Department of Moselle were detached from France for a period of half a century between the

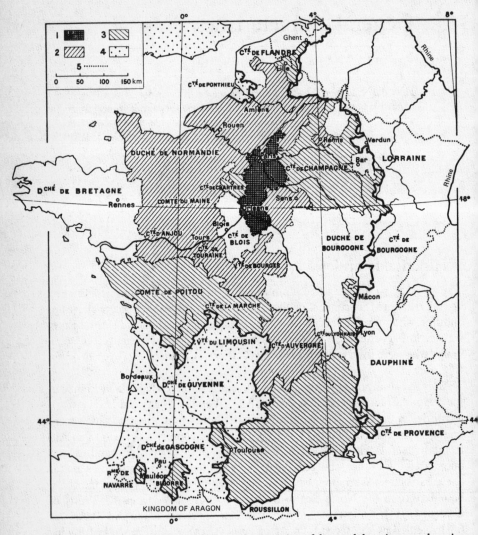

Figure 1.1 Historical evolution of France's expansion of the royal domain up to the reign of Philip the Fair. 1. Royal domain at the beginning of the reign of Henry I 2. Acquisitions in the reign of Philippe Auguste 3. Acquisitions from the reign of Louis VIII to that of Philip the Fair 4. English possessions 5. The boundary of France in 1945. Source: A. Demangeon, *Géographie universelle* (A. Colin, Paris, 1948), vol. 6, part II (2), Fig. 273.

Treaty of Frankfurt (10 May 1871) and the Treaty of Versailles (28 June 1919).
In the south, Roussillon was added to France under the terms of the Treaty of
the Pyrenees (1659). Corsica, which had already been in French hands on four
occasions from the reign of Charles VI to that of Henry II, finally became French
in 1768, while the Papal possessions of Avignon and the Comtat Venaissin (the

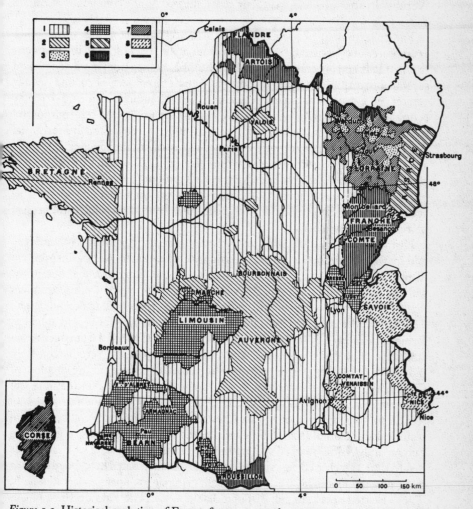

Figure 1.2 Historical evolution of France from 1515 to the present. 1. Royal domain in
1515 2. Acquisitions under Francis I 3. Acquisitions under Henry II 4. Acquisitions
under Henry IV 5. Acquisitions by the Treaty of Westphalia (1648) 6. Acquisitions
following the Treaties of the Pyrenees (1659), of Aachen (1668) and of Nijmegen
(1678) 7. Acquisitions during the reign of Louis XV 8. Acquisitions during the late
eighteenth and nineteenth centuries 9. The boundary of France in 1945. Source:
Demangeon, *Géographie universelle*, vol 6, part II (2), Fig. 274.

present Vaucluse Department) were transferred in 1791. Savoy and the County of Nice, annexed at the Revolution but lost after the Napoleonic Wars, were regained under the terms of the Treaty of Turin (1860). Roquebrune and Menton were ceded to France by the Prince of Monaco in 1861.

The latest modifications to the boundaries of France date from the Second World War, after which in 1947 Italy ceded the two Alpine communes of Brigue and Tende.

The political unity of France was thus achieved long before that of any other great power of continental Europe apart from Spain. In contrast to the fragmentation of Italy and of central and northern Europe, France from the sixteenth and seventeenth centuries was a great political unity. The country, becoming steadily greater in extent, was solidly organized by an authoritarian and strongly centralized monarchy, which pursued a policy of unification and purposeful planning, even before the latter term was invented. These distinctive territorial and political characteristics were among the sources of the influence, attraction and dynamism of France in the past; they also explain the early emergence and power of its centralizing forces. Nevertheless it must not be forgotten that certain provinces were late additions to French political and administrative space. This accounts for certain peculiarities of structure and mentality which still persist, more or less consciously.

Historical evolution still plays an important role in the present-day landscape and spatial organization of France. It is impossible to understand the distribution of population, settlement and some forests, or the siting of numerous towns without reference to the political history of France, to the network of frontiers that formerly crossed the country, and to the walled cities built to defend it. The frontiers of the ancient city-states of Gaul and the provinces and duchies, formerly delineated by forests, have not completely disappeared from the French landscape. The Arrouaise forest, which used to separate the Veromandui from the Atrebates and the Nervii and which served as a boundary to the kingdom of Charles the Bald at the partition made by the Treaty of Verdun (843), is still clearly visible in the landscape between Saint-Quentin and Cambrai.

The continued existence of vast forests is similarly due to a combination of historical and natural factors; for example, the forests of the west of France, in Perche and Maine, marked the frontier of Brittany. The land of France was divided into vast cleared areas based on fertile soils, separated by wooded areas or by heaths and moors on areas of poor soil, generally on uplands or watersheds. These cleared areas are still distinguishable today. The Pays de Bray and its surroundings manifest sharp contrasts in settlement pattern: the dividing line between the area of dispersed settlement and the area of grouped village settlement coincides with the former frontier of Normandy, which ceased to exist at the Treaty of Saint-Clair-sur-Epte (911).

This gradual political shaping of French geographical space makes it easier to understand that the concept of a France bounded by 'natural' frontiers is a highly contingent one. It is true that there is no shortage of natural underpinning for these boundaries: out of a total of 5,500 km, more than 2,700 are coastlines; 1,000 km are based on mountain ranges, generally but not invariably following their crest-lines (Pyrenees, Alps); 195 km follow the course of a single river, the Rhine. However, there is in fact nothing more artificial than a boundary allotting to different states the two banks of a river, with their adjoining lowlands. Only the northern boundary is not aligned on natural features; its peculiar characteristic is to cut across numerous rivers and river basins, from the Moselle to the Yser.

The land on which France has been imposed was in no way predestined by natural configuration to give rise to a state. It could have nourished a completely different political entity, either extending beyond the present boundaries, or not reaching them. The constantly emphasized French hexagon, with all its connotations of symmetry and balance, belongs more to geometry than to geography.

The France thus created covers 551,695 sq km, or 5 per cent of the European continent, or 0.428 per cent of the land area of the globe. France has the largest land area of any state of Europe outside the USSR, being larger even than Spain (449,000 sq km).

2 Geographical advantages
2.1 Advantages of situation

France is situated between latitudes 42°30′ and 51°N, approximately equidistant between the equator and the north pole (the southern tip of the island of Corsica touches 41°24′). No other European country has this range of latitude, which allows France to participate in both the subtropical world of the Mediterranean and the temperate climate of northwest Europe. The Etang de Lacenau in the Landes, the Bec d'Ambès (confluence of the Dordogne and the Gironde), the confluence of the Rhône and the Isère and the summit of the Meije (in the Oisans Alps) are all situated on the 45th parallel. As regards longitude, France lies between 4°W and 8°E (but Bastia, on the east coast of Corsica, is at 9°30′E).

France thus appears as territorially compact, without excessive elongation in any direction. The distance from Dunkerque to Le Canigou in the Pyrenees, and from Ouessant (Ushant) at the western extremity of Brittany to Strasbourg, is 950 km; from Hendaye on the Spanish frontier to Lauterbourg on the Rhine 1,000 km; from Brest to Menton 1,050 km. No point in the whole country is more than 500 km from the sea as the crow flies. Such proportions provide France with truly remarkable geographical advantages.

2.1.1 At the centre of the world's land masses

The unique centre of the hemisphere containing the greater part of the world's land masses lies near Nantes, constituting for France, and for western Europe in general, a most valuable advantage. This explains the advantages of centrality that France and western Europe offer, for example, to the world network of airlines or to international congresses and world organizations. The inhabitants of the east-coast towns of North America are as near to the Alpine resorts as they are to the mountains of the west coast of their own country. Moreover France, like western Europe as a whole, is situated at the centre of the vast zone of humid temperate and subtropical climates, bounded on the periphery of the land hemisphere by an arid crescent isolating them from tropical Africa and from eastern and southern Asia.

2.1.2 At the western extremity of Europe

Lying within this temperate and humid zone, France is both firmly tied to the mainland of the European peninsula and open to the Atlantic Ocean. It is thus in a state of tension between two climatic tendencies: a continental influence, with effects felt mainly in the east of the country, and a maritime influence, predominant especially in the west. But there are other complicating factors. France faces three very different seas: the land-locked Mediterranean, the vast Atlantic Ocean, with its links to the distant Americas, and the North Sea, which took over from the Mediterranean as a focus of civilization. It is by way of France that these seas can most easily communicate one with another. Across Aquitaine, by way of the Carcassonne gap and Languedoc, the Atlantic is a mere 400 km from the Mediterranean, which is also linked to the North Sea either by the Rhône–Rhine axis or by a route from the Rhône through Champagne and Flanders.

It is evident that eastern and western France present contrast in the direction of movement. In the east, movements are predominantly north–south, linking centres of advanced economy and at the same time centres of continental type. In the west, by contrast, movements are east–west and link areas of continental type with the Atlantic ports. France has always had difficulty in integrating west and east, as well as north and south.

2.2 Advantages of relief

France combines advantages of situation and relief in a unique way. Many countries are advantageously situated but have their potential richness reduced to nothing by high mountain ranges which make communication difficult and which minimize opportunities for developing agriculture and centres of population; an example of such a disfavoured region is the west coast of north America. Such is not the case in France, where more than 60 per cent of the country is below 250 m above sea level. On a comparable scale, only the British Isles have a lowland area of comparable extent, but combined with a different advantage of situation, insularity.

The disposition of lowlands makes France more open to the outside world than most other countries. Lowlands predominate in the northern half of the country, where only the Vosges and the Morvan interrupt the plains and plateaus of the Paris basin and of the Armorican massif. In the southern half of the country there are widespread lowlands from Poitou and the Vendée to the Pyrenees, but from the Central massif to the Alps and Mediterranean they are represented by extensive coastal plains (as in Languedoc), broad corridors (such as the Rhône–Saône valley) or reduced to intermontane basins (such as the Limagne) or narrow valley corridors, as in the Alps. In terms of relief, France thus falls into two distinct sectors.

2.3 Climatic advantages

France is for the most part situated in the temperate zone; its southern regions are on the northern fringe of the Mediterranean subtropical zone. Situation and relief provide France with a climate unique in Europe, a mixture of oceanic, continental and Mediterranean influences. The result is a range of climates of generally moderate characteristics, rarely running to extremes. Of continental climates, with seasonal contrasts that are so often extreme, that of France is the least continental; of Mediterranean climates, with their dreaded summer droughts, that of France is the least Mediterranean. This generally moderate climate has many advantages, being one of the most favourable in the world, and even one of the most favourable within the temperate and subtropical zones.

This threefold advantage of situation, relief and climate has, from the earliest times, made France a crossroads, a meeting place of numerous influences: maritime, continental, Nordic, Anglo-Saxon and Mediterranean. France is a melting-pot which has absorbed with ease the most diverse influences, out of which have sprung a way of thinking, a civilization and universal values acknowledged by every other nation.

3 The human factor in the development of France
3.1 A country of early human impact

The most characteristic feature of the geography of France is the extent to which its landscape has been modified by man's activities. Natural landscapes of forest, heathland and rocks occupy only a minor part of the total area. It is the multicoloured mosaic of cultivated fields, meadows, villages and urban areas that predominates, the product of the intense activity of man since ancient times.

Unexpected features of this humanized landscape include the small size of its basic unit of cultivation (the parcel) and the extreme diversity of its agricultural structures and forms of agricultural organization. Open fields and *bocage*, ploughland and meadow, mingle irregularly to form a complex whole. Various archaic elements are also readily apparent, most obviously the generally small size of parcel in a world where agricultural mechanization requires large fields if cultivation is to be economic. The old and worn-out fabric of settlement, both rural and urban, is another characteristic.

Human impact on the landscape of France is in fact of very early origin, whether the clearing of the waste, the establishment of routes or the founding of towns. This early origin provides a cultural heritage and a historical content of inestimable value; the other side of the coin, however, is represented by an archaic spatial organization and a cumbersome and outmoded infrastructure, difficult to adapt to present-day conditions.

3.2 An underpopulated country

At the census of March 1982 France had 54,257,300 inhabitants. Table 1.1 gives for a number of states of Europe and other continents both overall density of population and density per sq km of agriculturally used land (excluding forests, uncultivated land and built-up land). The comparison reveals the low population density of France as compared with all her European neighbours except Spain. This low density is one of the essential characteristics of the country, clearly presenting major problems when contrasted with the richness of natural resources. Other problems are implied. Is France underpopulated? If so, is this underpopulation responsible for a poverty of organization, a defective planning of French geographical space? How has this low population affected French economy and development?

Nevertheless, if France has only 1.6 per cent of the world's population, it has 2.7 per cent of all industrially occupied people and 2.6 per cent of all those engaged in the tertiary sector. Such figures indicate a high level of economic and social development.

3.3 A developed country

In 1977 the World Bank put France in the tenth place among the 160 countries included in its statistics. Whatever reservations there may be regarding the detailed reliability of these relative placings, there is no doubt that they put France in the first division of developed and industrialized states. A fertile soil and variety of climate have always made agriculture one of the bases of French economic development, while the availability of mineral resources and the many links with countries supplying raw materials have favoured the development of industry.

3.4 Growth and change

The demographic and economic data (Tables 1.1 and 1.2) point to profound changes in the population and economy of France initiated in the years 1945–50. Between 1946 and 1975, population rose from 40.5 million to 52.6 million, an

Table 1.1 *Population Density*

Country	Per sq km	Per sq km of agricultural land
Belgium	322	641
France	96	163
German Federal Republic	248	463
Italy	186	320
Japan	303	1,940
Netherlands	338	662
Spain	72	129
United Kingdom	229	302
USA	23	49

Source: L'Observateur de L'OCDE, March 1978.

Table 1.2 *Significance of French output at world level and in the European Community of the Nine (1977)*

Commodity	France (000 tonnes)		Percentage world production	Percentage output of EUR 9
Wine	58,799		20.0	44.5
Cars	3,559	(000 units)	10.9	34.0
Synthetic rubber (1974)	479		7.3[a]	26.2
Barley	10,262		5.8	27.2
Oil-refining capacity	172,740		5.2	20.3
Commercial vehicles	450	(000 units)	4.7	33.6
Wheat	17,349		4.5	45.1
Sugar	4,020		4.4	...[b]
Aluminium	546		4.0	20.8
Cement	28,956		3.8	22.2
Iron and ferro-alloys	18,719		3.7	...
Oats	1,901		3.7	29.7
Crude steel	22,094		3.3	...
Meat	3,414		3.3	23.3
Potatoes	7,803		2.9	20.1
Electricity	210,845	(million kWh)	2.9	...
Bauxite	2,059		2.6	98.3
Iron ore (1976)	13,792		2.6	83.6
Maize	8,505		2.4	54.6
Cattle	23,898	(000 units)	2.0	30.2
Wood pulp	1,926		1.7	35.4
Pigs	11,638	(000 units)	1.6	16.4
Roundwood (1974)	33	(million m³)	1.3	4.0
Fish (1976)	806		1.1	15.9
Coal	22,996		0.9	9.4
Natural gas	71,507	(teracalories)	0.6	4.9

[a] Excluding USSR.
[b] Data not available.
Source: United Nations statistical yearbook.

increase of 29.8 per cent that was all the more remarkable in that it followed a long period of stability (the population was already 40.7 million as long ago as 1901).

On the eve of the Second World War the French economy was close-circuited within the boundaries of a vast colonial empire, shielded by customs protection against external competition. By comparison with neighbouring Germany and Britain, French industrial power was modest.

By the end of the Second World War the French economy was partially destroyed; in 1945, production was 20 per cent below that of 1929. Within a few years France was to find herself in a radically different world: one of decolonization, of European integration (Coal and Steel Community in 1951, the European Community of the Six in 1957, of the Nine in 1977), of the rise of multinational capitalism, of a developing market economy, and of significant scientific and technical change.

In the context of these events, the economy of France underwent changes, the impact of which is often unrecognized. The volume of production, which had taken the fifty years 1889–1939 to double, proceeded to triple in the twenty years 1946–66. Gross national product per head multiplied 2.3 times between 1955 and 1974, and the gross production per head of the economically active population increased almost threefold. Between 1950 and 1975, industrial production doubled every seven years, and between 1966 and 1976 imports and exports registered a fourfold increase in value. This economic growth was achieved by an economically active population that scarcely increased; it was 20.5 million in 1946, 20.2 million in 1968, and 21.8 million in 1975. A tripling of productivity between 1945 and 1974 was thus achieved.

Changes in international trade provide a valuable indication of the transformation of the economy. France survived the nineteenth century and the first part of the twentieth century without having to resolve the problems of employment and change that afflicted its neighbours. In Germany, Britain and the Netherlands the nature of economic development was determined by the need to export manufactured goods on a massive scale in order to pay for imports of foodstuffs.

France was in a different position, and this explains the particular nature of French overseas trade. Statistics reveal the growth in the French share of world trade, both absolutely and relatively. Imports in 1972 were 5.5 per cent of total world trade, exports 6.2 per cent (5.3 per cent in 1968). Since 1972 France has been the fourth most important trading nation, following the USA, the German Federal Republic and Japan. Nevertheless the economy is still heavily dependent on the internal market; in 1974, exports accounted for only 17.5 per cent of gross national product (8 per cent in 1953), a proportion lower than that of other industrial countries (German Federal Republic 25.5 per cent, Netherlands 48 per cent).

The changing composition of external trade is also highly significant (Table 1.3). In 25 years, due to the influence of decolonization, the European Com-

Table 1.3 *Foreign trade composition*

Percentage of total imports or exports, by value

Product	Imports				Exports			
	1934	1950	1965	1980	1934	1950	1965	1980
Foodstuffs	32.3	17.7	19.9	9.3	14.4	10.8	16.4	15.5
Energy resources		15.6				6.1		
	49.3		33.0	33.0	28.8		12.5	8.3
Other raw materials		31.1				10.1		
Manufactures	18.4	24.3	46.6	57.7	56.8	66.9	71.1	76.3

Source: INSEE, statistical yearbooks.

munity and the liberalization of international trade, there has been a considerable change in both import and export markets. In 1949, 41 per cent of French exports were destined for the colonies (31 per cent in 1934), but in 1974 less than 10 per cent went to the franc monetary zone. In 1977, 70 per cent of French business turnover was concentrated within a radius of 1,500 km from Paris and more than half of all foreign trade was with the countries of the European Community.

These demographic and economic changes resulted in a fundamental transformation of French society. Between 1959 and 1974 the purchasing power attributable to the average income per head increased by 4.4 per cent per year, the national income per inhabitant increased from $1,155 in 1960 to $4,427 in 1947 and the gross national product per inhabitant increased from $1,920 in 1965 to $5,760 in 1970. Table 1.4 uses a range of indicators to show the extent of these changes.

Geographical mobility is one of the essential characteristics of this new French society, whether it be the daily journey to work, tourist or vacation travel, the successive movements that reflect professional career development, or ultimate migration on retirement. Between 1968 and 1975, 4.3 million French people moved to another region and nearly 9 million to another commune. During the same period 50.5 per cent changed house, 32 per cent changed to another commune, 24 per cent moved to another town and 8.7 per cent to another region.

3.5 Structural weaknesses and economic vulnerability

The changes which took place between 1950 and 1980 were imposed on structures characterized by their permanence and rigidity. The grafting of new upon old was a difficult and delicate operation; it was inevitable that the new urgency and dynamism would have to confront the sluggish weight of inherited structures, and even active resistance. The problem of adaptation or lack of adaptation was and still is an acute problem for France.

Table 1.4 *Selected indicators of socio-economic change*

	Period 1950–5	Period 1970–5
Urban population (millions)	23 (1954)	34 (1975)
Vehicle registrations (thousands)	173 (1950)	1,525 (1974)
Domestic consumption of electricity (million kW)	3,551 (1950)	34,100 (1974)
Pupils in secondary education (millions)	1,100 (1950)	4,700 (1974)
Students (thousands)	135 (1950)	780 (1974)
Second homes (thousands)	447 (1954)	1,685 (1975)
Economically active female population (thousands)	6,683 (1954)	8,132 (1975)

Source: INSEE, statistical yearbooks.

Weaknesses include: the sparsity of population and limited urban development; the small number of technologically advanced growth industries compared with traditional industries; the inadequacy of traditional agriculture and the limited indigenous resources of energy and minerals. In 1974 the agricultural sector employed 10.1 per cent of the national work force, but accounted for only 6 per cent of the total value of internal production. By contrast, industry with 30 per cent of the work force accounted for 52 per cent of production.

The modernization of France has not followed the common pattern of most other countries; it has been heterogeneous, varying greatly from one sector to another. For two decades growth overcame structural inertia but in the longer term, with the deterioration of the general economic climate, the dead weight of inherited structures came more and more to predominate. In the economic context of France, inflation has during the last few years come to appear as a structural feature in its own right. This endemic inflation – apart from particular factors such as the level of public expenditure – can be explained by the specificity of French demographic structures, by the excessive expenditure involved in the servicing of sparse populations, by policies regarding retirement and by an insufficiency of productive investment.

These weaknesses of economic and demographic structure make France susceptible to the various hazards of development, whether derived from climate, economics or politics. Since 1940 these have been numerous. First there has been the heavy toll of wars, especially the Second World War, with 600,000 dead and 300,000 wounded, as well as 215,000 industrial or commercial enterprises destroyed or damaged, entire cities in ruins, and marshalling yards and railway networks disrupted. The Korean war of 1951 and the Suez crisis of 1956 had their effects. Other hazards have been decolonization (1960), the return of the French from Algeria (1962–3), the student unrest of 1968, the 1974 oil crisis, and various severe winters or summer droughts (1974).

Since 1974–5 France has had to face a twofold crisis affecting the mainsprings of its spectacular growth: a population crisis (since 1973 the birth rate has dropped sharply) and an energy crisis (quadrupling of the price of oil in 1973).

External trade performance also witnesses to the weakness and fragility of the French economy. From 1928 to 1954 inclusive, the balance of trade was more or less permanently in deficit; since 1954 it has only intermittently been in surplus.

France is increasingly unable to live on its own resources. The achievement of a balance in external trade is a necessity. While exports have become the principal creator of employment, the economy remains fragile, vulnerable to international competition and to decisions taken abroad.

The defective composition of external trade reveals that France has not yet reached the level of other great industrial nations, nor has it succeeded in optimizing the use of its own resources. Commodities are imported that French industry and agriculture could and should produce in greater quantity. In the light of the natural advantages of France, agricultural exports are small, consisting primarily of cereals and other products where the value added in production is low. In 1977 the balance of trade in agricultural products registered a deficit of 3,700 million francs. If a deficit is inevitable in relation to the tropical products, it is not so for pork, beef, fish or wood, and even less so for vegetables, processed food and frozen products, which are often derived from French raw materials. It seems paradoxical that France should import 80 per cent of high-protein animal feedstuffs.

Similarly in the industrial field, exports have included a higher proportion of finished products with low value added – cast iron, iron and steel products – than metallurgical products, machinery or finished products with high value added. French deficiency in the production of capital goods and especially of machine tools has often been stressed. Dependence on foreign sources of energy is a particularly adverse factor, while 55 per cent of raw material must also be imported. A major and doubtless increasing proportion of foreign trade now consists of 'linked' or 'captive' payments between multinational firms and their subsidiaries in other countries, or between one subsidiary of such a company and another.

3.6 Diversity

The fact that geographically and historically France can be considered as a unity does not imply uniformity – quite the reverse. France is a mosaic of regions and *pays*, whose features find clear expression in the landscape, spatial structures, attitudes and human activities. Nature and man have played an equal role in creating this diversity. Differing conditions of geology, morphology, climate, soil and vegetation are responsible for widely differing natural habitats. Out of these habitats man has made regions, accentuating natural diversity by differences of organization and use. France cannot be understood except by using as a point of departure this long-established regional marquetry, progressively revealed throughout the ages. The lengthy history of France, however, and the strength of its administrative and political centralization have extinguished ethnic, linguistic and cultural differences that could have threatened national unity. This process has acted to the advantage of yet smaller regions, the *pays*: there are, for example, 600 officially defined agricultural regions.

3.7 Inequality

The new wealth arising from economic development has been very unevenly distributed. A 1977 study estimated that average family wealth varied between 87,000 and 200,000 francs. However, a mere 1.56 per cent of households possessed a quarter of the nation's wealth, 10 per cent of households shared half the total wealth, while the poorest 25 per cent of households had to make do with a mere 6 per cent. In terms of income rather than wealth, the richest 10 per cent of households disposed of 33 per cent of total national income. Equally significant divergences can be seen in salary scales and in the payments made to men and women.

These inequalities are repeated in the disparities of family, social and professional structure; between large and childless families, between manual and white-collar workers, between skilled and unskilled workers, or between students of the elite *grandes écoles* and those of other forms of higher education. However, recent evidence points to a certain diminution in the range of inequality, first becoming apparent from 1962, and more particularly from 1976.

3.8 The new geography of France

Demographic and economic growth, together with changes in the nature and levels of consumption, has had a major impact on the differentiation and organization of French geographical space. It was impossible to move from a static to a dynamic population, from a peasant rural society to an industrial–urban one, or from a closed colonial-type economy to a competitive market economy without geographical changes of the highest significance in such fields as the construction of housing (with related infrastructure), the transformation of transport networks, urban growth and industrial expansion. These demographic and economic changes have affected the spatial distribution of people and their activities. Changes are even more noticeable in that they have been imposed on inherited geographical structures that had been relatively stable for at least half a century.

A range of questions then presents itself. How have rural areas been affected by a process of modernization that went hand in hand with the departure of tens of thousands of agricultural workers, and what has been the impact on the age-old geographical patterns of rural settlement, field systems and routeways? How did an urban network that had scarcely changed for centuries sustain a growth of 11 million town dwellers in the space of 25 years? What has been the impact of the new industrialization on the low-density pattern of traditional manufacturing?

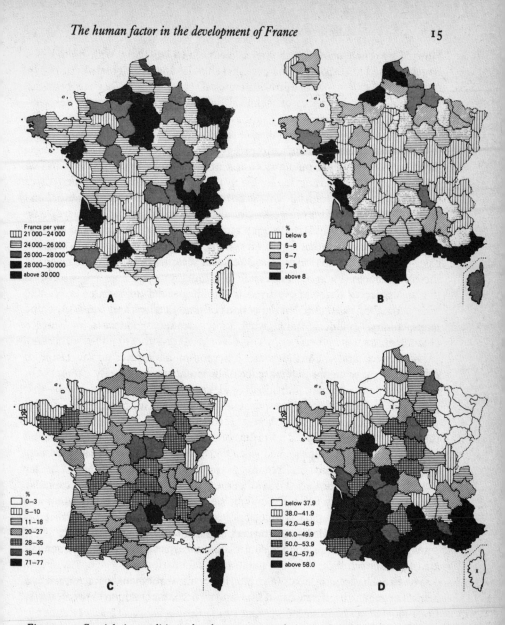

Francs per year
21 000–24 000
24 000–26 000
26 000–28 000
28 000–30 000
above 30 000

A

%
below 5
5–6
6–7
7–8
above 8

B

%
0–3
5–10
11–18
20–27
28–35
38–47
71–77

C

below 37.9
38.0–41.9
42.0–45.9
46.0–49.9
50.0–53.9
54.0–57.9
above 58.0

D

Figure 1.3 Spatial inequalities. A. Average annual net earnings, 1975. Source: Statistiques INSEE. B. Percentage of work force unemployed, 1979. Source: *Le Monde*, 13 March 1979. C. Rural communes 30 km or more distant from a *lycée* (grammar school) in 1970. Source: A. Delamarre *et al.*, 'L'accès aux équipements scolaires dans la France rurale: approche géographique', *Bulletin Sté. Neufchateloise de Géographie*, no. 22, 1977. D. Proportion per 1,000 population of medical practitioners in rural areas. Source: D. Lévy, *Les Médecins dans les zones rurales*, Thèse de 3e cycle, Paris, 1980. × = information not available.

How did French geographical space, centralized on Paris, with boundaries largely created to keep out real or potential enemies adapt itself both to European unity and to the demands of a growing regionalist movement? What have been the geographical consequences of technical innovation? To what extent have the various geographical regions of France reacted differentially to these changes?

The theme of regional inequality, of regional contrast, has of late been widely studied, providing one of the mainsprings for programmes of regional development, a subject on which public opinion is increasingly sensitive. The regions and *pays* of France have participated in highly differing degrees in the demographic, social and economic transformations of recent decades. These transformations have often served only to increase disparities between rich and poor regions, between innovative and traditional regions, between dynamic and passive regions, and between urban and rural regions. A simple examination of a range of basic indicators at departmental and regional scale will underline the extent of these differences (Fig. 1.3). The extent of inequality often comes as a surprise to the unsuspecting observer, so fixed is the image of a homogeneous France, bound together by an efficient network of communications and consolidated by long-standing political unity with its associated political–administrative centralism.

Differences and inequalities are inherent in all nature; to lay claim to egalitarianism, to an absolute absence of differentiation, is purely Utopian. On the other hand, human individuals and groups do not readily accept that politicians and administrators responsible for the well-being of regions contained within one and the same state should fail to suppress, reduce or at least palliate these regional inequalities. This claim for spatial justice and equality goes hand in hand with the claim for social justice and equality in a more general sense.

The transformations of French geographical space were effected under specific political conditions. To say that the French economic system is capitalist does not take us very far. All economic development implies the creation and accumulation of capital, the source of necessary investment in the various sectors of activity. The attitudes of the owners and users of capital, the quality of the agents of political and economic control, and the overall economic environment are of greater significance than capitalism as such.

The French economy exists in an international environment characterized by a market economy, by private capitalism, and by fierce competition between states. For about twenty years now this private capitalism has above all been embodied in great multinational companies, the most powerful of which are based in North America. It is essential to understand the consequences of decisions taken by multinationals on the establishment or closure of industrial plants, and on the location of industry.

Of all western nations, France is one of the few to favour a state capitalism which controls large sectors of the economy and which has adopted comprehensive planning policies. The French planning system originated after the end of the Second World War and embraces both economic planning and the more specifically geographical, regional or spatial planning. There are those who see in the French systems of state capitalism and economic planning a search for a mixed economy combining economic liberalism with a degree of state control, and free enterprise with the machinery to control its worst excesses. The interaction between planning and the free market must be a prime subject of consideration in this book, as must the evolution over time of the practices of economic and spatial planning.

The political changes which took place in May and June 1981 (the election of a socialist President of the Republic, a socialist majority in the National Assembly (Lower House of Parliament), and a socialist–communist coalition government) were reflected in an increase in state intervention in all spheres of activity. Policies were designed to lessen inequalities, help underprivileged social groups, assist economic activities or regions in crisis, reduce the power of foreign economic interests, and change administrative and management structures. It has to be said that the thrust of these policies (other than administrative reform) was blunted by subsequent economic difficulties. It remains to be seen to what extent they will find expression in the future geography of France.

✢ The natural environment

France is without doubt one of the least isolated, least 'enclosed' of the countries of Europe.

A. Demangeon

2

⚜ Relief

---

1 Elevation and predominant relief trends

Taken as a whole, France is a country of moderate elevation, in which plains, low plateaus and mountains of only modest height predominate over areas of high mountains. This characteristic is clearly shown by the average elevation of mainland France (Corsica excluded), which is 342 m (European average 297 m). Table 2.1 gives a division of France into six altimetric zones.

One quarter of mainland France is situated below 100 m and more than 60 per cent is below 250 m. Surprisingly only 17.8 per cent of mainland France (not including Corsica) is higher than 500 m, and only 6.8 per cent above 1,000 m. These figures are difficult to reconcile with what we know about the presence of Hercynian massifs and young mountain ranges, which include Europe's highest summit.

A first indication of the location of lowlands is given by the pattern of contour lines. The 100 m contour line outlines some major embayments, notably the Aquitaine basin, the lower Loire valley and the region of Rennes, Laval and Le Mans in Armorica (Fig. 2.1). The 250 m contour is a convenient dividing line between lowland France and the France of high plateaus and mountains; it follows a sinuous course from the Belgian frontier near Fourmies southwards through Saint-Dizier, Auxerre, Nevers, La Châtre, Confolens, Cahors and Toulouse to Pau, at the foot of the Pyrenees. To the west of this line only two areas of high ground are of any significance. One consists of the uplands of

Table 2.1 *Altimetric zones*

Altimetric zones	Area (sq km)	Percent
0–100	135,524	25.4
100–250	192,301	36.4
250–500	110,453	20.4
500–1,000	64,730	11.0
1,000–2,000	28,830	5.3
over 2,000	8,425	1.5

Source: E. de Martonne, *Annales de Géographie*, no. 284, 1941, p. 245.

Perche (where Mont d'Amain reaches 309 m) and their continuation in the hills of Normandy (Mont Pinçon 365 m) and in the uplands of Maine, which reach 417 m at the Signal des Avaloirs in the Forêt d'Ecouves. The other consists of the uplands of interior Brittany, where Tuchenn Gador in the Monts d'Arrée reaches 384 m. Elsewhere in this lowland sector the height of 200 m is reached only exceptionally, for example in the hills fringing the Boulonnais and the Pays de Bray.

In upland France, by contrast, to the east of the 250 m contour, lowlands are rare; they occur on the Mediterranean coast, in the Rhône valley and the plains of the Saône and the Rhine. But this contour is merely a conventional line, having no topographical significance. The real topographical differentiation is indicated by the 500 m contour, which marks the beginning of the mountains; Figure 2.1 indicates how they are distributed in discontinuous massifs of very unequal size.

1.1 A fundamental dividing line

However, the key to the disposition of relief features in France is not provided by a contour line but by a major physical divide, to which structure, relief and hydrology all contribute. The line appears in the south, with the first spurs of the Montagne Noire, the southwestern promontory of the Central massif. It then follows the southern and eastern borders of the Central massif, by way of the Monts de l'Espinouse, the great escarpment of the Cévennes, the Vivarais, the summit line of the Monts du Lyonnais, the Monts du Beaujolais and the Monts du Maconnais. From there it continues through the plateaus of the Côte d'Or, the Plateau of Langres and the so-called Monts Faucilles (the watershed between the Saône and the Meuse) to reach the southern end of the Vosges near the Ballon d'Alsace.

This great S-shaped divide, running generally north–south, marks the boundary between two fundamental divisions, Hercynian France and Alpine-Pyrenean France. Along this divide are found the greatest elevations of the entire area between the line itself and the western coast of France. Crystalline blocks fringing the divide were caught up in the intense upthrust characteristic of the eastern side of the Central massif, attaining 1,640 m at Pierre-sur-Haute in the Monts du Forez. The even higher altitudes reached in Auvergne result from the piling of rocks of volcanic origin on to the massif (Plomb de Cantal 1,858 m).

This divide is broken by occasional cols and lowland corridors, for example the Seuil de Langres, the Seuil du Charolais and the Seuil de Jarez, on the latitude of Vienne. From the maximum elevations along the divide there is an abrupt eastward descent to the wide corridor of plains and plateaus extending from the

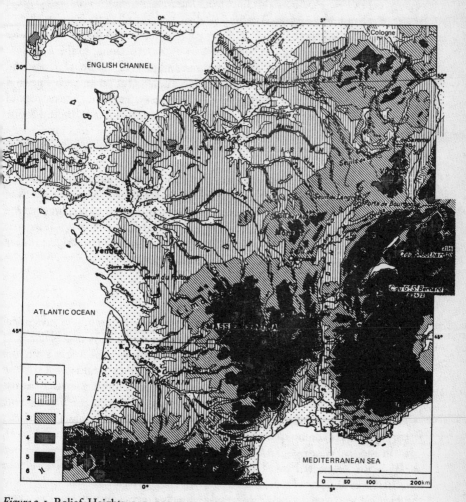

Figure 2.1 Relief. Heights: 1. 0–100 m 2. 100–250 m 3. 250–500 m 4. 500–1,000 m 5. Above 1,000 m 6. Passes. Source: A. Demangeon, *Géographie universelle* (A. Colin, Paris, 1946), vol. 6, part II(1), Fig. 8.

Porte de Bourgogne (which leads into Alsace) to the Seuil de Lauregais (which gives access to the Aquitaine basin). The fall to the plains of Bas-Languedoc and the Rhône–Saône corridor is considerable, frequently exceeding 1,000 m. The extent and steepness of this change of elevation isolate the uplands west of the divide from the bordering depressions, making it difficult for them to benefit from the easy flow of traffic along the low ground, since transverse links are sparse or absent over long stretches, especially between the Montagne Noire and Mont Pilat, south of Lyon.

The barrier effect of this great dividing line relates to its role as the major watershed of France. Along this line, from the Moselle southwards, rise a great many of the country's rivers. Asymmetrically situated well to the eastern side of the country, it divides the extensive river basins draining outwards towards the Atlantic, the Channel and the North Sea from those draining to the Mediterranean. To the west, the well-articulated river systems of the Seine, Loire and Garonne occupy basins on the broad slope descending gently to the sea. The land east of the divide is mainly occupied by the Rhône system, where a complex of streams from the Jura, Alps and Cévennes converge in the Rhône–Saône corridor.

To the west, the valleys of the main streams heading at the divide are incised to a greater or lesser extent into a relief of plateaus and plains. Apart from the disturbance caused to the upper Loire by volcanic activity and by the collapse of the Limagne basins, these plains and plateaus broadly correspond to a series of surfaces declining westwards and northwards from the divide. To the east the rivers are less well articulated, their sinuous courses taking advantage of the line of fault troughs and depressions of predominantly structural origin. These characteristics reflect the very recent origin of the divide.

1.2 Hercynian France and Alpine France

This major divide separates two divisions of quite different morphological development. Western France is a land of widespread plains and plateaus of mature relief, and of valleys incised into a landscape which still bears in varying degree evidence of a sequence of earlier erosion surfaces reaching back to the Hercynian orogeny. Plains and plateaus are developed indiscriminately across the sedimentary basins and the massifs of Hercynian France. The average elevations in this part of France clearly indicate the generally low relief: Paris basin 178 m, Aquitaine basin 135 m, Armorican massif 104 m, Central massif 715 m and the Vosges 530 m.

By contrast, eastern France is a land of young mountains, of recent subsidence and of marked variety of relief; mountains, secondary ranges, escarpments, plains and subsidence troughs exist side by side. This is a more youthful France, where Tertiary mountain-building has produced major upwarpings of rock. It is a region where, because of the multiplicity of folds and faults, structural morphology plays a much more important role than in Hercynian France to the west. The explanation of the relief of Alpine France is to be looked for not in hydrological evolution but in the geological map. Average elevations are obviously greater: Alps 1,121 m, Pyrenees 1,008 m, Jura 660 m or Corsica 570 m, but these mountain areas exist side by side with extremely low-lying regions, such as Lower Languedoc (average 122 m) or the Rhône valley (279 m).

2 The morphological evolution of Hercynian France

The Hercynian massifs are traditionally contrasted with the sedimentary basins, occupying depressed areas which are themselves part of the general Hercynian structure.[1]

2.1 The ancient massifs

The ancient massifs are veritable palimpsests, bearing the more or less legible traces of a complex tectonic, sedimentary and morphological history. The present relief forms are the expression, admittedly incomplete, of this history.

2.1.1 *Geological structure and the post-Hercynian surface*

The Hercynian massifs originated in the Palaeozoic era, and consist of geologically complex massifs including crystalline, metamorphic and Palaeozoic sedimentary rocks. Most of the massifs date from the Hercynian folding, which was extremely violent, with much faulting and overthrusting. However, some parts of the ancient massifs may be fragments of Caledonian or even Precambrian massifs.

The geological structure of the ancient massifs is highly diverse. Vast areas consist of crystalline rocks, with granite batholiths and aureoles of gneiss and micaschist. Also to be found is a banded structure corresponding to folds in the Hercynian chain which have been eroded to their roots; crystalline rocks formed in the cores of the anticlines alternate with Palaeozoic sediments preserved in the synclines, as in southern Brittany or in the hills of the Bocage Normand. Alternatively folded Palaeozoic sediments may completely mask the crystalline rocks, as in the Ardennes.

From the end of the Palaeozoic era, beginning in the Permian period, the massifs were subjected to considerable erosion, resulting in the formation of the post-Hercynian peneplain. This was formed during varying periods of time, as is borne out by the markedly differing extent of lagoonal or marine sediments under which it is preserved. The morphology of the post-Hercynian surface is highly variable, but in some places it is a perfectly levelled surface, which can be traced

---

[1] The reader not requiring the rather technical content of the following pages can proceed to section 5 of this chapter.

in areas such as the fringe of the Vosges, in spite of being affected by later deformations.

In many places the erosion surfaces resulting from terrestrial action have been further trimmed by marine transgressions. Elsewhere the Hercynian surface is characterized by a relief of mature or senile valleys, preserved by deposits derived either from infill or from marine transgression, as in the Vendée. Finally, in regions of appropriate structure and lithology unbevelled quartzite ridges persist, emerging for example through the Triassic or Liassic sediments of the Cotentin peninsula and the Collines de Normandie.

2.1.2 *Subsequent evolution of the post-Hercynian surface*

Since the peneplanation at the end of the Palaeozoic era, the Hercynian massifs have been affected by three interdependent phenomena: marine transgression with association deposition; structural deformation; and cycles of erosion of varying effect.

(i) Marine transgressions. It is difficult to determine the existence and extent of marine transgressions in the absence of significant sedimentary residues. The Vosges–Black Forest area was completely covered by the Jurassic seas, as is proved by the limestone deposits of the downfaulted and fragmented Vosges foothills belt, overlooking the Alsace plain. The southern part of the Central massif was affected by a Jurassic transgression, which left behind massive geosynclinal-type Triassic, Liassic and Jurassic deposits in the Causses (1,500 m thick in the Grands Causses). The continuity of these limestone deposits from Quercy to the Causses of Rodez is only broken by a 'bridge' of ancient rocks some 20 km wide south of Decazeville.

In the second half of the Tertiary era, the Armorican massif, in common with all western France, was affected by extensive Miocene and Pliocene transgressions. A vast extension of the sea spread over Anjou, Touraine, Vendée and part of Brittany, depositing Mio-Pliocene sands, limestones and the shelly marl (crag) deposit known in French as *faluns*. The deposits are preserved in depressions, both erosional and structural in origin. This first tectonic phase was followed by a marine regression.

(ii) Structural deformation. Since the formation of the post-Hercynian peneplain and between periods of marine transgression, the Hercynian massifs were subjected to deformations of tectonic origin which continued until comparatively recent times. The degree of distortion has been uneven, depending on the distance of the massifs from the orogeny, and also on their composition. The rocks of which the massifs are composed are brittle and liable to fracture rather than being subject to plastic deformation (Fig. 2.2). These distortions occur in a number of forms.

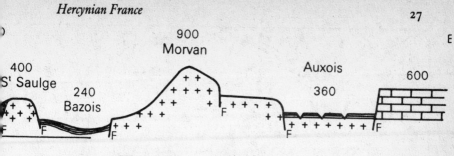

Figure 2.2 Diagrammatic cross-section illustrating large-scale deformation of the post-Hercynian surface. 1. Ancient rocks of the Hercynian massif 2. Liassic strata 3. Later Jurassic strata. (Altitudes in metres.) Source: J. Beaujeu-Garnier, *Le Morvan et sa bordure* (PUF, Paris, 1957), Fig. 11.

(a) Generalized movements. Uplift, warping, asymmetrical tilting and subsidences give rise to the great sedimentary basins (also to more local areas of subsidence, such as the basins of Velay and the Allier valley, with their Miocene and Villafranchian deposits). The Armorican massif has two areas of upwarping, one represented by the Breton peninsula (Basse Bretagne), the other by the hills of the Bocage Normand (Collines de Normandie) and their continuation into Perche. Between the two lies a depressed zone stretching southwards from the Bay of Mont-Saint-Michel by way of Rennes to the Loire at Nantes. Subsequently the whole of Brittany was tilted from north to south, thereby giving rise to the orographical and hydrographical asymmetry of the peninsula.

(b) Faulting. The southern edge of the Rennes basin is made up of a system of faults originating or renewed in quite recent times. The upthrusting of the Vosges began as early as the Oligocene epoch and the movement continued, and even, according to some authors, increased in the Quaternary era, at the same time as the Rhine rift valley was being formed. The subsidences and faults occurred during periods when intermission in the Alpine folding resulted in a relaxation of pressure.

(c) Minor folding. These deformations, according to their size and nature, are responsible for three different types of ancient massifs.

The Armorican type. Here the Hercynian structure remains predominant. Tertiary structure appears only in the form of widespread warping and of isolated faults which never constitute a major fault zone but create a structure of tilted blocks. The fault lines are marked by fault-line scarps, which separate extensive plateau surfaces; the fractures also control the directions of the river systems. This relief type is characteristic of Armorica, the Ardennes and the western part of the Central massif (Fig. 2.3).

Vosges type. The structure is basically of Tertiary origin, and is characterized by strongly tilted blocks, the fault systems disrupting the continuity of the post-Hercynian surface. The Hercynian structure is incorporated in a system of

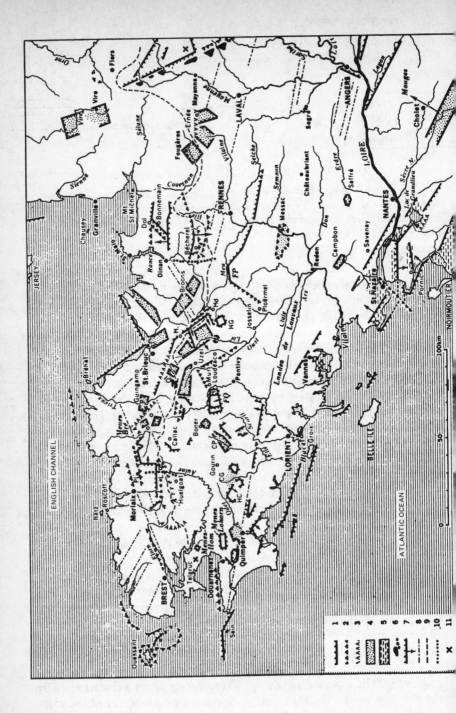

inclined structural surfaces of Tertiary age. This type is represented in the Vosges, caught up in the great Vosges–Black Forest upwarping and fractured along its eastern side overlooking the plain of Alsace. The type is also found in the south of the Central massif, which clearly reflects the impact of the Alpine–Pyrenean mountain-building movements.

The Forez type. Tertiary structure is again dominant, even in detail. The massif is broken up by extensive fault systems – whether new faults from the Tertiary period or reactivated Palaeozoic faults – producing stepped structures, horsts and grabens. The east of the Central massif is of this type, the vast faulted zone stretching from Sancerrois southwards by way of the Limagne basins to the Causses.

In the parts of the Central massif which were most affected by Tertiary deformation, volcanic eruptions took place. Volcanic activity ranged in time from the late Palaeocene (Menat basin) to the Holocene, although within this period there were times of greater activity: Mont-Dore (1,884 m) and Cantal (1,858 m) date from the late Miocene and early Pliocene; the Velay volcanoes are of Villafranchian (late Pliocene–early Pleistocene) age.

These various volcanic eruptions added a whole range of different relief forms to the morphology of the ancient massifs, including minor cinder cones in the Chaîne des Dômes, the shield volcanoes of Cézallier, the vast composite Cantal volcano, fissure flows and widespread lava sheets with either rough or smooth surfaces, as in Aubrac and Velay. The action of erosion on these relatively young deposits has further increased the variety of forms. It has attacked the cones, dividing their flanks into separate segments (*planèzes*), eroded out the lava plugs from the enveloping masses of scoria and ashes of Le Puy, and also freed linear lava flows from the softer materials over which they spread, leaving them as ridges, as in the lava flows of the Limagne. Volcanic morphology introduced unaccustomed variations into the relief of the massifs, raising elevations to unexpected levels, or disrupting drainage systems by the creation of volcanic barrier lakes or the diversion of rivers such as the Truyère. Volcanicity has also created vast uniform tracts, permeable and without valleys, repellent in aspect.

(iii) Cycles of erosion and erosion surfaces. Since the formation of the post-Hercynian

---

Figure 2.3 Tertiary tectonics of the Armorican massif. 1. Fault 2. Presumed fault 3. Fold 4. Fault trough (graben) 5. Marshes of the Nantes region 6. Depressions (E = infilled by Eocene deposits) 7. Tilted block (arrow indicates direction of tilting) 8. Structural line controlling river direction 9. English Channel/Atlantic watershed 10. Downsag in fold axis 11. Deposits of sands and gravels at abnormal altitudes. Pl.: Plouigneau L.: Lannéanou Q.: Quintin HG: Horst de Gommené HC: Horst de Coadri CG: Cuvette de Guiscriff CP: Cuvette de Plouray FQ: Forêt de Quénécan FP: Forêt de Paimpont. Source: M. Gautier, 'La tectonique tertiaire dans le Massif Armoricain' *Annales de Géographie*, no. 414, 1967, p. 177.

surface of erosion, the alternation of marine transgressions and tectonic deformation unleashed a series of cycles of erosion, relating to the varying base levels
and acting on hill masses of differing elevation. There were accordingly many
possible ways in which the initial surface of the ancient massifs could be
destroyed or altered, as witnessed today by the complexity of the surviving
surfaces and the difficulties attending their reconstruction.

The Eogene surface is one of the most important of the surfaces cutting the
ancient massifs. Under the influence of the Eocene tropical climate the massifs
were subjected to intense weathering, and the crystalline rocks were decomposed
into great thicknesses of sands of more or less lateritic type. Characteristic
deposits of this surface are sideritic sands, lateritic clays, sheets of detritus and
basin deposits. The morpho-climatic conditions of the time suggest that this was
a surface of pediplain type, with residual inselbergs, rather than a surface
resulting from erosion under temperate conditions. This sharply planed-off
relief was initiated in the Jurassic and the Cretaceous, when the ancient massifs
began to emerge from the sea as islands, peninsulas or archipelagos. The surface
was sometimes temporarily reoccupied by the sea, which through wave action
further contributed to its planation. This Eogene surface occupies a predominant
place in the present structural morphology of the Central massif.

After the Eogene, the erosion surfaces were more localized and less clearly
marked, for they were formed between phases of mountain-building, which
restricted both in time and space the stable conditions necessary for the complete
formation of an erosion surface.

Frequently the post-Hercynian surface remains the master surface of the
ancient massifs. Some authors have shown that the sum of all the cycles of
erosion subsequent to that which produced the post-Hercynian surface resulted
in the removal of only a very thin layer of material. The situation most frequently
found is the juxtaposition of fossilized deposits of various ages on a composite
polycyclic surface.

(iv) Structural morphology and differential erosion in the ancient massifs. Even though
the ancient massifs are cut by surfaces of erosion, this does not mean that all
structural morphology is absent. Occasionally a line of hills or a ridge will break
the uniformity of the surface, separating two plateau areas or linking two stepped
surfaces.

Appalachian ridge and valley morphology has long been recognized in the
ancient massifs: ridges formed of quartzites or Palaeozoic limestones, normally
running in straight lines across the massifs but occasionally twisted into hairpin
bends, alternate with depressions eroded in the less resistant foliated slates or
shales. This type of relief is particularly well developed in the Armorican massif.

Recent research has emphasized the impact of recent tectonic movements in
the ancient massifs. These movements resulted in the creation of escarpments
along the line of Tertiary faults, in warping, in tilted blocks, tilted surfaces, or

Table 2.2 *Stream and valley densities in the ancient massifs*

1 Region	2 Rock type	3 Stream density (km/sq km)[a]	4 Valley density (km/sq km)[b]	5 Column 3 / Column 4
Limousin	granite	1.94	2.61	0.74
Morvan	granite	0.35	2.54	0.13

[a] Stream density = total length of watercourses in a basin (or other defined area).
[b] Valley density = total length of valleys, with or without a stream, in the basin (or other defined area).

more structural guidance of the river systems (Fig. 2.3). Some of these deformations are of Tertiary age following Tertiary structures; others, while of Tertiary age, involve reactivation of Hercynian structures. Moreover, laboratory studies have demonstrated the unequal degree of resistance to erosion of the various crystalline and metamorphic rocks. Granite, for example, according to its chemical composition, porosity, frequency of joints, the slopes on which it is found and the type of erosion attacking it, may be either a very resistant rock, producing prominent relief, as in Sidobre (southwest Central massif), or a soft one, eroded into depressions as in the Vénazès, south of Aurillac. In Corsica, the true granite landscapes with their rounded summits, convex slopes and slow rate of decomposition contrast with the granulitic landscapes, with their relief fretted into ridges and sharp peaks. The landscapes of rounded and tumbled blocks for which the Sidobre and Huelgoat regions are famous are explained by the separation on the surface or at depth of blocks of coarse-grained granite delimited by a rectangular joint system.

These detailed studies lead to the recognition in the ancient massifs of patterns of considerable subtlety. The relief of crystalline regions, too often described as confused, can be broken down into basins of very varied sizes, hollowed-out depressions, pinched out on the downhill side, mantled with a varying thickness of detritus alternating with ridges.

Nor must we forget that the basic relief of the ancient massifs consists of valleys rather than escarpments and ridges, which are comparatively rare. In the impermeable terrain of these Hercynian massifs the density of valleys is particularly high, dissecting the surfaces into rounded ridges and interfluves (Table 2.2).

In complete relief contrast to the ancient massifs are the areas of subsidence and fault troughs, such as the Causses or the plain of Alsace (Fig. 2.4).

2.2 Sedimentary basins

Like the ancient massifs, the basins experienced successive cycles of erosion, periods of planation, marine transgression and deformations. Gradually each took on its own individual character according to the degree of uplift on its fringes

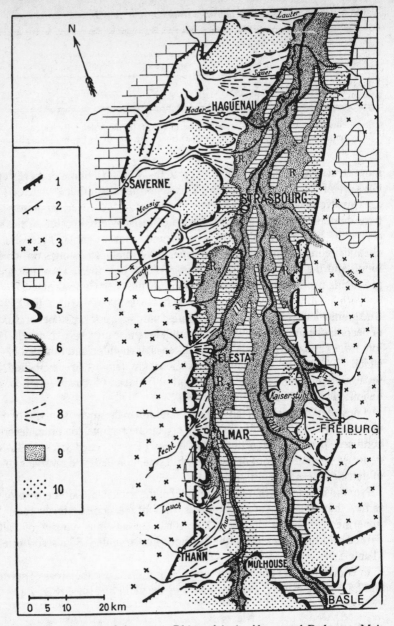

Figure 2.4 Geomorphology of the upper Rhine plain in Alsace and Baden. 1. Main boundary fault 2. Other faults affecting relief 3. Hercynian massif 4. Overlying sedimentary rocks 5. Hill margin 6. Low terrace with sharp edge 7. Low terrace without sharp edge 8. Alluvial fan merging with low terrace 9. Present flood plain and *Ried* (zone of accumulation of recent alluvium with high water table): R_1, Ried de Hoerdt R_2, Ried

and the degree of subsidence of the underlying basement rocks, as well as the extent of erosion operating in the sedimentary cover of the uplifted ancient massifs.

The sedimentary regions of Hercynian France are divided into two great basins: the basin of Aquitaine and the Paris basin. Flanders, however, being situated north of the Artois axis which marks the northern boundary of the Paris basin, belongs to the Anglo-Franco-Belgian basin.

2.2.1 Sedimentation

The history of sedimentation is relevant to the morphological analysis of the basins, as it determines the lithology and thickness of the strata.

The Paris basin is characterized by the large scale of its subsidence, the migration over time of its centre of maximum subsidence and the preponderance of limestones and chalk. In Lorraine and Champagne the Jurassic is more than 1,000 m thick, but the subsidence took place gradually, in line with the slow depression of the sea bed, largely under the weight of the sediments deposited. The result was that the depth of the sea remained relatively constant, as did the conditions of sedimentation. That is why limestones, especially reef-limestones, predominate in the Jurassic sedimentation (Fig. 2.5). After a period of regression and emergence at the end of the Jurassic and the beginning of the Cretaceous, the Cretaceous seas covered the entire Paris basin. The typical sediments of this period consisted of great thicknesses of chalky rocks, mainly chalk proper, but including chalk marl, glauconitic chalk, sandy chalk and even micaceous chalk.

After a long period of emergence at the end of the Cretaceous, the sea again invaded the Paris basin, this time advancing more unevenly, then receding, leaving lakes and lagoons. Eocene and Oligocene sedimentation produced alternations of sand, clay and limestone in a sequence that has become a classic example of geological succession. In the centre of the Paris basin, the Oligocene sequence ends with the lacustrine limestone of Beauce (Fig. 2.6). Then in the Mio-Pliocene period, the sedimentation moved southwest, where shelly crag (*faluns*) deposits were laid down in a synclinal trough along the line of the lower Loire. The extent of Pliocene transgression in the Paris basin is still uncertain, although deposits have been dated in Haut Perche and in the Pays de Caux.

The geological history of the Aquitaine basin is more varied, reflecting the greater variety of its upland frame, with the Central massif to the north and east, and the Pyrenees to the south. In the northern half of the basin, between the Garonne and the Central massif, moderate subsidence of the basement rocks persisted throughout the Mesozoic and Tertiary eras, so that the sea remained

de l'Andlau R$_3$, Ried de Sélestat R$_4$, Ried de Rouffach 10. Loess cover. Source: E. Juillard, 'Une carte des formes de relief dans la plaine d'Alsace-Bade', *L'Information Géographique*, May–June 1949, p. 117.

shallow. Accordingly, deposition in the Jurassic consisted predominantly of limestones, as in Quercy and Périgord, similar to those of the Paris basin. Cretaceous sediments consisted of sands, clays and alternations of limestones and less resistant beds.

In the south of the Aquitaine basin, on the other hand, geological history is determined by the rise of the Pyrenean chain. A foredeep was initiated in the Cretaceous and accentuated in the Tertiary, and in it were accumulated deposits of flysch, sandstone, shales and limestone, derived from the erosion of the mountains. Tertiary sedimentation subsequent to the Pyrenean folding took three forms. Firstly there were marine deposits from seas that entered the basin along its wide ocean front. They were particularly extensive in the Stampian and Burdigalian (Miocene), but did not spread east of the meridian of Bordeaux. Secondly, lacustrine deposits, either limestone or detrital (sandstones, molasse, conglomerates), were laid down under tropical conditions, usually in basins of interior drainage. Finally, there were deposits of continental type, either fluviatile

PRINCIPAL ROCK TYPES

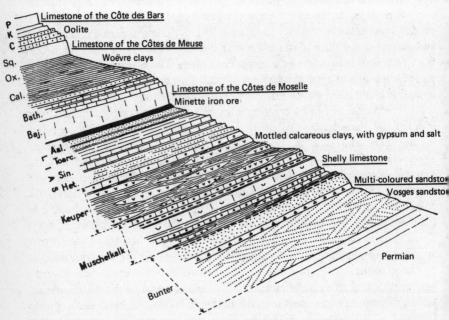

Figure 2.5 Diagrammatic cross-section of the Secondary rocks of the eastern Paris basin. P: Portlandian   K: Kimmeridgian   C: Corallian   Sq.: Sequanian   Ox.: Oxfordian Cal.: Callovian   Bath.: Bathonian   Baj.: Bajocian   Aal.: Aalenian   Toarc.: Toarcian Sin.: Sinemurian   Het.: Hettangian. The principal scarp-forming rocks are underlined. Source: E. de Martonne, *Géographie universelle* (A. Colin, Paris, 1942), vol. 6, part 1, Fig. 17.

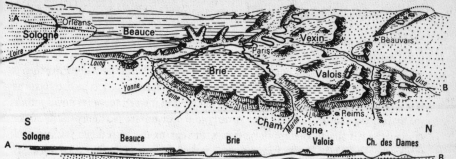

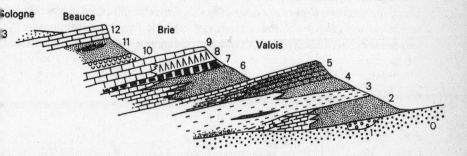

Figure 2.6 Rock outcrops and geomorphological features of the Paris basin. Above: Perspective view showing the relationships of the principal structural surfaces; also diagrammatic cross-section along line A–B. Below: Diagrammatic cross-section. O: Chalk. 1. Earliest Tertiary marine deposits in depressions of the sub-Palaeocene surface 2. Palaeocene: Thanetian (Landenian) (Bracheux Sands) 3. Eocene: Sparnacian (plastic clays with lignite) 4. Eocene: Cuisian (Ypresian) (sands with nummulites) 5. Lutetian (massive limestone or Calcaire Grossier) 6. Bartonian (Beauchamp Sands, with limestone intercalations; Saint-Ouen Limestone) 7. Oligocene: Sannoisian (clays, gypsum and travertine) 8. Sannoisian (calcareous clays capping gypsiferous deposits) 9. Sannoisian (Brie Limestone) 10. Stampian (calcareous clays with oyster shells) 11. Stampian (Fontainebleau Sands) 12. Aquitainian (lacustrine Beauce Limestone) 13. Miocene (trails of fluviatile sand). Source: J. Goguel, *Géologie de la France* (PUF, Paris, 1975), p. 443.

or detrital, in the form of debris fans or detritic material transported gravitationally by mass-movement, represented for example by the Pliocene sands underlying the Landes. The deposits are derived both from the Central massif and the Pyrenees, but predominantly the latter, source of the vast mass of material forming the Lannemezan plateau, made up of a number of fans between the valleys of the Aspe and the Salat, burying the sedimentary surface of the Aquitaine basin and forming a remarkable piedmont.

2.2.2 *Deformations and the structure of the basins*

Deformation of the rocks of the sedimentary basins is closely related to deformation of the underlying basement rocks and their distance from the surface. Where the sedimentary cover is thin, it is likely to reflect deformation of the basement. The latter being rigid, its deformations usually take the form of faults. Reactivation of the faults may be reflected in the sedimentary cover either in the form of faults or of folds, according to the degree of plasticity of the rocks concerned. In the northeast Paris basin, for example, the intense folding and faulting of the Triassic and Liassic strata follow Variscan (northeast–southwest) trends; the same is true of the Nivernais, Artois and the Boulonnais. Most of the Artois faulting, however, reflects faults of Armorican (northwest–southeast) direction, which were reactivated in the Tertiary, breaking the Cretaceous cover. Where on the other hand the sedimentary cover is very thick, the overlying sediments behaved autonomously, and any folding is independent of events in the basement rocks. The sedimentary basins thus each have a major structure determining the basin as a whole, on which secondary structures are superimposed.

2.2.3 *Recent cycles of erosion and erosion surfaces*

Like the ancient massifs the sedimentary basins experienced numerous episodes of planation interspersed between episodes of marine transgression and emergence and deformation. The erosion surfaces which are visible in the present-day morphology of these basins date essentially from the Tertiary era. The main Alpine mountain-building movements divide the surfaces into two groups: an earlier group of pre-Tertiary and Palaeogene surfaces and a later Neogene (Mio-Pliocene) group.

(i) Pre-Tertiary and Palaeogene surfaces. Even more than in the ancient massifs, the upper Cretaceous and early Tertiary surfaces appear as the master element in the morphology of the basins. This complex of planations cut across Jurassic and Cretaceous rocks between the end of the Cretaceous transgressions and the beginning of the Eocene transgressions. The surface is identified by the presence of Eocene deposits, relics of its burial and subsequent exhumation, which are unconformable with the Mesozoic sedimentary rocks on which they lie. The deposits were derived from Eocene seas and lagoons. The surface is particularly well developed in the chalk plains of Picardy and Normandy.

Clay-with-flints is often considered to be a deposit characteristic of this early Tertiary surface, evidence of subaerial decalcification of the chalk. In fact the term 'clay-with-flints' covers several different formations. The thin layer of black clay-with-flints found between the chalk and the Tertiary rocks is a true product of subaerial decalcification, but the deposit can also be formed at depth. Red clay-with-flints, often re-sorted into bief (residual clay-with-flints), is never found under Tertiary rocks and incorporates Eocene sedimentary clay and Tertiary gravel. It is generally held to have been laid down from the end of the Cretaceous and the Eogene, spreading over the flanks of anticlinal zones as they were uplifted, but other interpretations favour a more recent origin.

(ii) Neogene planation. In the Paris basin, after the middle Oligocene sea had receded, leaving behind the Fontainebleau sands, and following deformation in the Oligocene, a new cycle of planation was initiated. It took place in a rather arid tropical or subtropical climate, giving rise to savanna or steppe conditions. The Aquitanian (late Oligocene) deposits of the Beauce lake date from this period. The upper part of the Beauce limestone was silicified and transformed into *meulière* (burrstone or millstone, much used locally in building). In the west of the Paris basin the Miocene surface is marked by vast spreads of decomposed granitic material (Lozère sands).

In the Aquitaine basin, the Aquitanian surface, marked by surface silicification, clearly relates to planation developed indifferently across Cretaceous and Tertiary limestones, deriving its silica from the Périgord sands.

(iii) Older surfaces. Traces of older surfaces are to be found on the periphery of the basins. At the end of the Portlandian (Upper Jurassic), there was a general recession of the seas, which were succeeded on the emerging land surface by a series of Purbeckian and Wealden lakes and lagoons. The transgressive Cretaceous deposits stretch uncomfortably across the various horizons of the Jurassic. This post-Jurassic and pre-Cretaceous surface is found fringing sedimentary basins in the Barrois, the eastern Paris basin, and the Jurassic limestone plateaus surrounding the Morvan. It also has a fundamental role in the cores of the breached anticlinal structures of the Pays de Bray and the Boulonnais.

In the centre of sedimentary basins, planation surfaces are well separated and the oldest ones are buried by intercalated sedimentary deposits resulting from intervening transgressions. When these surfaces are projected to the fringes of the basin, however, they intersect each other at very low angles and are more difficult to distinguish. For this reason, the further these surfaces are traced outwards from the centres of the basins, the greater is the tendency to interpret them as polycyclic. This intersection of erosion surfaces, combined with uplift in the fringe areas, has exposed the older rocks which surround and limit the sedimentary basins.

2.2.4 Structural and lithological morphology

Recent cycles of erosion have emphasized the lithological and structural contrasts between the various sedimentary rocks in the basins. In the Jurassic and Tertiary areas of the Paris basin the structural morphology is particularly well

Table 2.3 *Stream and valley densities in sedimentary rocks*

1 Region	2 Rock type	3 Stream density (km/sq km)	4 Valley density (km/sq km)	Column 3 / Column 4
Houtland (Interior Flanders)	clays and sands	0.58	0.80	0.72
Beauce	limestone	0.0	0.83	0.0
Champagne	white chalk	0.17	1.10	0.15
Picardy plateau	chalk	0.08	0.95	0.08
Woëvre	clays	0.78	1.67	0.47

For notes on calculations see Table 2.2.

developed owing to the frequent alternation of resistant and weak rocks (Figs. 2.5 and 2.6). The structural surfaces, which have been tilted to a greater or lesser degree, survive as plains (Beauce), plateaus (Soissonnais) or systems of cuestas. The Cretaceous rocks, on the other hand, show few contrasts; the slight lithological differences between chalk and clays produce an unimpressive structural morphology.

In the Aquitaine basin the structural morphology is much less clearly marked, because friable sediments predominate and because limestone facies are often discontinuous. Structural forms appear mostly in the limestone of Quercy and Périgord or are associated with certain Tertiary limestone formations, as in the Agen region. There is nothing comparable in scale to the structural morphology of the Paris basin. A similar morphology of sand and clay, without a stiffening of limestone, predominates in Flanders.

Independently of structural conditions, lithological differences are also responsible for morphological contrasts within the sedimentary basins. Lithological variations are reflected in a diversity of hydrological development: valley density and the number of dry or intermittently occupied valleys vary considerably from one outcrop to another. In addition to lithology, slope and climatic conditions are complementary factors. For example, in the Landes region of southwest France, the Haute-Lande region, lacking slopes, has developed no stream networks, although benefiting from a humid climate. The lowest valley density is found in the subhorizontal limestone of Beauce; valleys are either nonexistent over large areas or exist only in the form of dry valleys, scarcely incised on the surface. On the Jurassic plateaus variable degrees of disruption to normal hydrographic organization can be observed. Dry valleys predominate on the limestones of the eastern Paris basin, with dolinas (closed depressions) on the interfluves. Karstic features are much more important in Quercy and Périgord. Mesozoic and Tertiary sands and clays have more highly developed valley systems. Contrasts stand out clearly on the map, which shows a great variety of topographical forms. The stream-bearing valleys are of varying density and varying average length, while interfluve length varies also.

2.3 Morphological interdependence of the ancient massifs and the sedimentary basins

In the preceding pages the close interrelationship between the morphological development of the ancient massifs and the sedimentary basins has been noted. The broad outlines of their relief were determined by the same deformations, erosion surfaces and river systems. The radiation of drainage from the Central massif played an important part in the landscape history of Hercynian France, particularly during the Tertiary. The weathering of the massif was the source of waste sheets which spread unevenly over the sedimentary rocks of the basins (such as the Lozère, Sologne or Brenne formations), even burying subsequent depressions and cuestas of Palaeogene or pre-Tertiary age.

2.3.1 *Hydrological unity*

Hercynian France has a remarkable degree of hydrological unity; the main rivers and their tributaries – the Loire, Seine, Meuse, Moselle, Garonne with its right-bank tributaries and Charente – ignore the differences between basins and massifs. The great river axes run northwest, west and southwest from the major divide of France that was defined at the beginning of the chapter. A major share of run-off is collected by the Seine, occupying the Tertiary depression of the Paris basin, by the lower Loire, born in the depression of the Faluns (Crag) sea, and by the Garonne, in the central depressions of the Aquitaine basin. The overall picture is that of a single vast slope which had already begun to develop in the Eogene (Palaeogene) and which became more pronounced in the Neogene. The slope was, however, affected by local disturbances, for example the formation of north–south grabens and volcanic activity in the Central massif, creating a secondary node of river radiation.

It is remarkable that there are so few 'water towers' (nodes from which streams radiate) in Hercynian France. Those that exist are the Monts d'Arrée (Brittany), Perche (western fringe of the Paris basin), the Pays de Bray (Normandy), the Artois ridge, the Cantal (Central massif), already mentioned, and the crystalline Vosges, which prolong the main French watershed. These nodes correspond to axes of recent uplift, probably Pliocene in age.

2.3.2 *Zones of contact between massifs and basins*

These contact zones have a great variety of morphological types, since many factors are involved; the lithology of the basement rocks, the lithology of sedimentary rocks, variations in dip, structural complications and the nature of erosion surfaces affecting the area.

Three main morphological contact types are found in Hercynian France:

(1) The glacis (uninterrupted slope) type has continuity of relief from massif to basin rocks, with no differential erosion, either because the rocks on both sides are equally resistant, as on the fringe of the Armorican massif, or because the unconformity has been buried beneath waste sheets, as with the ferruginous sands of Eocene age in the Brenne, on the northwest border of Limousin (Central massif).

(2) The classic type has a peripheral depression excavated in weak Permo-Triassic rocks, bounded on the massif side by the eroded slope of the exhumed post-Hercynian surface and on the basin side by a cuesta formed by the first limestone horizon of the Jurassic, as on the northern border of the Morvan. The small sedimentary basins situated on the edge of the massifs show an identical morphological arrangement, for example the Brive basin fringing the Central massif, or the Saint-Dié basin fringing the Vosges.

(3) The contact type, where the division is provided by structural features, either folds or faults. Beyond a depression which may be no more than a fault-line valley, a fault-line scarp faces the ancient massif, as on the southwest border of the Central massif, or in Auxois and Bazois, east and west of the Morvan (Fig. 2.2).

2.4 The morphological heritage of the Quaternary
2.4.1 Climatic conditions

Only three areas of Hercynian France were directly glaciated: the mountains of Auvergne (Cantal and Forez) in the Central massif, the Vosges and Corsica. Between two and four glaciations have been identified in the Central massif. Examples of glaciated relief are few, but some are beyond dispute: the U-shaped glacial valley of Haut-Fossat in Forez, the ice-smoothed 'roches moutonnées' and confused relief of Artense, which ice moving down from the neighbouring volcanoes covered with a piedmont glacier, or the umbilical of Bort-les-Orgues. The extensive Vosges glaciation covered the whole of the crystalline Vosges; streams of ice carved the valleys into U-shaped troughs, and thrust their terminal moraines as far west as Epinal.

The other regions of Hercynian France experienced periglacial conditions, being very close not only to the Pyrenean and Alpine glaciers, but also to the ice sheets covering part of England and the Netherlands.

During periods of glacial advance climatic conditions were similar to those of the present-day taiga and tundra: cold climates of oceanic type with abundant falls of snow, causing great fluctuations in the position of the ice fronts. Violent winds blew mainly from the north and east, and the ground was frozen to a considerable depth, only its surface thawing in summer or in periods of glacial retreat. Vegetation was sparse, although with differences between northern and southern France, and with periodic variations reflecting fluctuating glacial conditions. Periglacial conditions did not continue uninterruptedly throughout the older Quaternary; periods of warmer weather alternated with cold spells, corresponding to the advance and retreat of the ice sheets.

The chronology of the Quaternary in France is normally related to four glaciations identified in the Alps: Gunz, Mindel, Riss and Würm; a problem is presented, however, by the fact that a different number of glaciations is normally identified in Britain and the Netherlands. Each glacial and interglacial period is estimated at between 200,000 and 250,000 years, and can be divided into a series of lesser climatic swings known as stadials and interstadials of several tens of thousands of years, each with its own individual scale and character, for example Würm I and Würm II. The curve of each stadial and interstadial then shows still shorter oscillations. This theoretical hierarchy multiplies the opportunities for differences of interpretation between specialists, as outside the Alpine regions directly affected by glaciation it is possible to confuse glaciations and stadials.

2.4.2 Periglacial modification of relief

The influence of Quaternary history on the relief of Hercynian France is undeniable and highly original. Except for constructional forms, periglacial morphology is characterized by erosional remodelling of existing relief features.

Periglacial erosion involves a number of processes:

(1) Freeze–thaw, which splits solid rocks into fragments through which water can circulate.
(2) Permafrost (tjäle), which consolidates loose deposits and encourages solifluction, the slipping of thawed surface material over the frozen subsoil.
(3) Variations in river flow, which are linked to climatic oscillations, and changes in the sea level, which are linked to the alternation of glacial and interglacial phases.

(i) Periglacial deposits and their formation. Gravity plays an essential role in the periglacial system of erosion; slopes were covered with material disintegrated by freeze–thaw processes and set in motion by solifluction, including screes, block fields (as in Margeride and Montagne Noire), various slope deposits ranging from clayey gravels to limon (silt), mud flows, coastal heads and layered series in which the alternation of fine and coarse material relates to the succession of seasons or years with varying temperature conditions and varying snowfall. The chalk region of Champagne, thanks to the ease by which the rock is disintegrated by freeze–thaw processes, became buried beneath waste sheets which moved down slope from the interfluves or which were transported by rivers.

Table 2.4 *The Quaternary era (about 2,500,000 years)*

Time before present[a]	Marine stages (Mediterranean and northern Europe)	Glaciations	Climate and fauna	Human cultures	
3,000–700–800	Dunkerquian transgression	Postglacial	Climatic optimum	Age of metals	
10,000–6,000	Flandrian transgression			Neolithic	
				Mesolithic	
15,000–6,000		Late glacial	Cold fauna of Lauscaux (15,500 BP)		
38,000–17,000	Succession of minor advances and retreats	Würm III	*Homo sapiens*	Magdalenian Solutrean Aurignacian }	Upper Palaeolithic
	—				
	Grimaldian regression				
About 45,000		Würm II Amersfoort Würm I	Neanderthal man Warm fauna	Mousterian and Levalloisian }	Middle Palaeolithic
About 62,000					
About 100,000	Tyrrhenian II:Eemian Retreat of more than 100m	Riss		Acheulean Abbevillian (Chellian) }	Lower Palaeolithic
	Tyrrhenian I: Holstein sea	Mindel Gunz	*Homo erectus* Cold fauna		
	Sicilian				
	Calabrian	Donau Biber	*Australopithecines* Villafranchian	Pebble culture	

[a] Before present = before 1950.
Source: P. Bellair and C. L. Pomerol, *Eléments de géologie* (A. Colin, Paris, 1965), p. 459.

Periglacial deposits are, however, unevenly distributed; although they are conspicuous, their spatial extent must not be exaggerated. They carpet minor tributary valleys, fill preglacial valleys or valley-heads which have been modified to form nivation hollows, and occur on slopes which because of their orientation were frequently thawed, while the opposite slopes may be free of drift.

(ii) Asymmetric valleys are one of the most widespread legacies of the periglacial system of erosion. This asymmetry, which chiefly affects valleys running north–south (and especially northwest to southeast) contrasts west-facing hillsides with steep slopes, and east-facing hillsides with gentle slopes. The phenomenon is to be attributed to the combined action of westerly winds and snow.

(iii) Limon is another type of superficial deposit. It was formerly held that limon was derived from minute particles picked up by the wind from morainic material and dropped in the form of loess when checked by vegetation or by areas of more abundant rainfall, occasionally accumulating to a depth of several metres. Limon covers large areas of the Paris basin and some areas in the Armorican massif, in particular the north coast of Brittany; the Léon region owes its fertility to limon (Fig. 4.1). Not all limon is of aeolian origin; recent analyses have shown the important part played in its formation by friable Tertiary sediments. The vast sandy covering of the Landes is also believed to be an aeolian deposit laid down during a recent Quaternary cold spell. The material probably came from the continental shelf uncovered by the sea during a phase of marine regression.

(iv) Constructional relief forms. In the downstream sections of river basins, variations in sea level brought about the formation of alluvial spreads, subsequently dissected into terrace systems. Such eustatic terraces are found along valleys such as the Somme and the Garonne, at constant relative intervals, so that it is possible to distinguish high, middle and low terraces (Table 2.4). Periglacial material carried by rivers were deposited whenever there was a break in the long profile of the stream or where valleys narrowed. This explains how consequent river gaps in Champagne and Picardy were often blocked by these deposits, which built up some very remarkable plains, sometimes dissected into terraces at a later date (Figs. 2.7 and 2.8).

These events in the Quaternary played an important geographical role. They mantled the hillsides, creating gentler slopes related to the angle of rest of frost-shattered waste, and filled in the valleys. Occasionally they added new topographical features, and they always sculpted the surface so as to modify pre-existing relief forms. This periglacial remodelling led to the creation of a prematurely 'senile' landscape.

The Quaternary has left a legacy of alluvium-choked valleys, with between their gentle sides widths of anything from a few dozen metres to several kilometres of waterlogged soil, marsh and peat bog, bearing sluggish streams and ox-bow lakes. These valleys introduce a highly individual landscape into Hercynian France. The events of the Quaternary have superimposed upon the solid geology a drift geology of unconsolidated deposits, providing a patchy

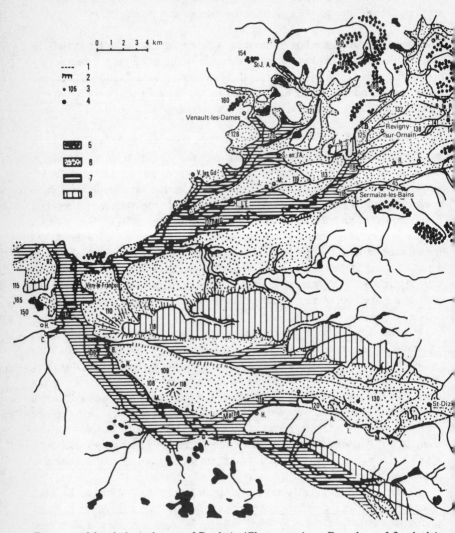

Figure 2.7 Morphological map of Perthois (Champagne). 1. Boundary of flood-plain alluvium 2. Terrace edge 3. Spot heights 4. Village 5. Highest drift deposits (First Interglacial) 6. Upper surface of sand and gravel train II 7. Upper surface of sand and gravel train III 8. Slopes incised in Stage II deposits during the deposition of III. Source: J. Tricart, *Le Bassin parisien oriental* (Société d'Edition et d'Enseignement Supérieur, Paris, 1952), vol. 2, p. 313.

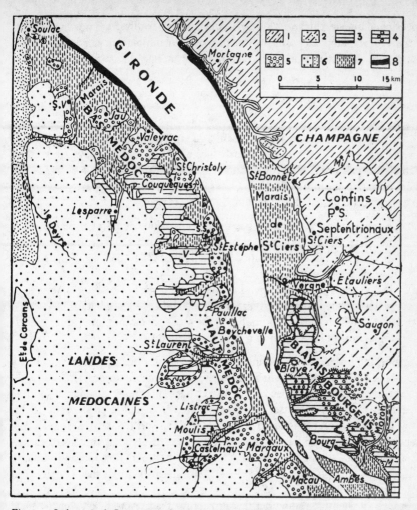

Figure 2.8 A typical Quaternary landscape: the Gironde and the northern Bordelais (Bordeaux region). 1. The *champagnes* (open landscapes) of the Charentes region (soft Upper Cretaceous limestones) 2. The northern fringes of the Bordelais (continental Eocene sands) 3. Tertiary limestone domes of Listrac and Couquèques-en-Médoc 4. Tertiary limestone plateaus of the Blayais and Bourgeais 5. *Graves* of Médoc (laterally coalescing alluvial fans of early Quaternary age) 6. *Landes* (heathlands) of Médoc (Landes Sand) and coastal dunes 7. Fluvio-marine silts and lowland peats of the Bordelais 8. Recent coastal accretion in the Mortagne and Jau regions. M: Marcamps Mi: Mirambeau PS: Pleine Selve SS: Saint-Seurin-de-Cardourne SV: Saint-Vivien V: Valeyrac. Source: P. Barrère, H. Enjalbert, L. Papy and G. Viers, *Annales de Géographie*, no. 370, 1959, p. 495.

covering of uneven thickness nearly everywhere, especially in the northern half of France. These slope deposits provide the parent material from which has evolved the soil that has been worked and improved by man.

2.4.3 *Present-day erosion*

There remains the question as to whether plains, plateaus and hills are undergoing active erosion at the present time. In a temperate climate, and under forest or grass cover, erosion is clearly limited. Many authors have stressed its virtual non-existence, pointing out that carpets of dead leaves in forests are still there from one autumn to the next. Other factors explain this apparent resistance to erosion of the present-day relief:

(1) The recent rise in sea level has moved upstream the point at which rivers reach base level, thus reducing their erosive power. The filling of rias, estuaries and valleys has reduced the length of valley slopes and the relative relief available for attack.

(2) Most of the slopes correspond to the gentle angles of rest characteristic of Quaternary deposits and are, moreover, stabilized by vegetation.

(3) Linear erosion by rivers is limited by the presence of undrained areas in their basins, not yet integrated into the river systems.

Further, the progressive lowering of the water-tables means that springs break out lower down on slopes, which limits the area available for erosion.

Nevertheless erosion goes on, its effects becoming more obvious as altitude and available relief increase. The load carried by rivers is clear proof of this erosive action, even though part of the material transported derives from alluvial deposits previously laid down further upstream. Every year the Loire carries 700,000 tonnes of solid matter and the Seine between 150,000 and 200,000 tonnes, not counting the much greater quantity of material that is carried in solution.

Above all we must remember that erosion works spasmodically, for the most part in bursts of activity as brief as they are intense, closely related to exceptional weather conditions. A storm or exceptionally heavy rain will fill the drainage network with the load of sediment being transported, and will temporarily restore the flow of dry valleys. Heavy rain also tears at the earth in fields unprotected by vegetation. Similarly, exceptionally cold winters prepare the way for the instability that sets in with the thaw, causing countless landslips. These forms of erosion are a useful reminder that equilibrium rather than stability is character-istic even of areas of temperate climate.

3 The morphological evolution of Alpine–Pyrenean France

The evolution of this structural province is entirely dominated by the formation in the Tertiary era of young mountain ranges, movements which also affected their forelands and surrounding regions.

3.1 Tectonics and structure

3.1.1 The Pyrenees

The Pyrenees, although abutting on the highlands of the Iberian peninsula, are nevertheless lithologically and structurally distinct, constituting a young mountain chain of distinctly individual character. The chain is the result of differential movements of the Iberian and European plates. In the greater part of the range the rocks are derived from the Hercynian chain, Primary sediments metamorphosed by contact with vast granitic masses which have been levelled by erosion and covered by an incomplete and not particularly thick succession of Mesozoic sedimentary rocks.

Embryonic mountain-building movements appeared as far back as the Cenomanian, as is shown by abundant orogenic deposits such as breccias and conglomerates. The Hercynian basement was then shattered, great fractures dividing it into blocks, which moved differentially. The sedimentary cover was also faulted, and depending on local circumstances was folded, pinch-folded or affected by gravity flows, resulting in a highly complex structure. This paroxysmal phase of the Pyrenean folding is normally attributed to the upper Eocene; it also affected parts of Languedoc and Provence, where folds of Pyrenean type are found.

In the western Mediterranean the collapse of the Pyrenean–Provençal massif took place slowly and intermittently between the Oligocene and the Quaternary. In the eastern Pyrenees the thickness of the marine Pliocene of Roussillon (780 m) and the angles of dip are evidence of a post-Pontian, probably post-Villafranchian, uplift of 1,000 m, confirming the recent nature of fault escarpments in this region.

3.1.2 The Alps

The history of the Alpine orogeny begins with the vast Mediterranean geosyncline, which originated as far back as the Precambrian. Mountain ranges produced by the Hercynian earth movements were again deformed in the Lower Permian, when the coal deposits were apparently trapped in the synclines of the basement rocks. From the Permian – or at latest the Triassic – period onwards the Alpine area was divided into a geosyncline in the east and a zone of shallows on the present site of the crystalline massifs of Belledonne and Mont-Blanc.

During the Mesozoic era, the geosyncline was characterized by a very fluid alternation of troughs in which massive sediments were accumulated, and upfolded cordilleras where sedimentation was reduced. One of these cordilleras was the Briançon ridge, which separated the great geosyncline in the east from a subsiding foredeep.

Preliminary orogenic movements began in the Upper Cretaceous, continuing in the Lower Eocene (pre-Lutetian) and affecting mainly the external non-geosynclinal zone, where during the Upper Cretaceous the sub-Alpine massifs were thrust upwards.

The second phase of folding occurred in the Oligocene. The mass of sedimentary rocks contained in the geosyncline rose in an enormous upwarping, sometimes called a 'geotumour' or 'undation', which was progressively displaced from east to west. This development can be classified as the fundamental tectonics of Alpine mountain-building. The upwarping consisted of a core of rocks derived from the substratum, with a cover of sedimentary rocks. The continuing upwarping of the 'geotumour' caused the sedimentary cover to be displaced and to slip by gravity on its flanks. This development may be classified as appertaining to the superficial tectonics of Alpine mountain-building, and was the origin of the overthrust nappes. These were detached from underlying rocks along a thrust plane at the level of the Trias, which acted as a lubricating layer.

Only the internal zone, however, was affected by orogenesis during the Oligocene; the external regions were not involved until later, during a third phase of folding, of Ponto-Pliocene age. This affected the Pre-Alps (arcs of Digne, Castellane and Nice). The external zone was also affected by the late uplift (early Pliocene) of the crystalline massifs, their sedimentary cover displaced to form the pre-Alpine folds.

These external movements did not happen independently of the main Alpine paroxysm. They can be regarded as the last stage of the east–west displacement of the major axis of Alpine upwarping (geotumour). Between the first upwarping in the east during the Eocene and its most westerly manifestation during the Miocene, there was a period of something like 20 million years during which the nappe structures were developed. The slow displacement of the axis of major upwarping explains the stratigraphical complexity of the nappes, for example the breaks which have been observed in their continuity; the passage of the wave of upwarping generated forward displacement of nappes on its advancing face and counter-displacement as the crest passed. The crossing of the external massifs by these nappes is easily explained by the fact that at the time these were not sufficiently uplifted to provide serious topographical barriers.

In the maritime Alps, during the Pontian, the sedimentary cover slid in the process of upwarping, pushing before it strata displaced at the Triassic level. These were piled up in festoons against the ancient Tyrrhenian-Maures-Esterel massif, which was in process of subsiding to the south.

After the long tectonic history of the formation of the Alps, there was a readjustment during the Plio-Quaternary which raised the Alpine orogen as a whole. That this deformation has continued into very recent times can be demonstrated geologically in the maritime Alps. Similarly, a comparison of successive geodetic levelling from 1884 to 1892 and from 1961 to 1968 showed a general uplift in the Alpine chain as a whole of between approximately 1.0 and 1.8 mm a year.

3.1.3 *The Jura and Provence*

The Jura could easily be regarded as a third sub-Alpine chain bordering the Alps to the northwest, but it differs from the preceding chains by the fact that it is not continuous with the Alpine system. Between the Pre-Alps and the Jura is the wide crescent of molasse which widens out in Switzerland. This is a belt of thick, continuous sedimentation, a sort of pre-Alpine foredeep. It was probably the enormous weight of these Oligo-Miocene conglomerates on the Swiss plain which prevented the folding of the underlying rocks, thereby causing the folding to occur to the west of the Tertiary basin.

The tectonic history of the Jura can be summarized in four phases:

(1) A period of deformation in the Oligocene, affecting a sedimentary basin abutting on the Vosges–Black Forest massif and the Central massif, its fringe corresponding symmetrically with the Paris basin on the other side of the Langres plateau. The basin with its basement rocks was then shattered into a mosaic of fault blocks which interacted one with another, distorting and folding the sedimentary cover. At the same time subsidence formed the Bresse depression.

(2) A phase of Miocene deformation followed, which reached its maximum in the late Miocene; a wave of uplift spread from east to west, resulting in a very complex tectonic structure of small nappes caused by localized gravity flows. The western edge of the Jura was thus thrust forward over the Bresse depression. The Bresse Tertiary deposits were covered for between 10 and 15 km by a true nappe with a thrust plane at Triassic level.

(3) A phase of post-Pontian and pre-Plaisancian folding, causing new tectonic slips.

(4) A final phase of Plio-Quaternary deformations with uplift and reactivation of the folds; in particular a general uplift in the Upper Pliocene.

To the south of the Alps, Provence experienced a similar development, punctuated by many episodes of orogenic activity. An initial orogenic phase took place in the Albian period of the Cretaceous, giving rise to the 'Durance isthmus'. At the end of the Upper Cretaceous a phase of folding shaped the great synclinal basins and anticlinal zones which make up the major structural lineaments of present-day Provence. At the end of the Middle Eocene, a Provençal orogenic phase brought about first the sliding of the sedimentary cover and then the subsidence of the basins, which were filled with an Oligocene sedimentation sequence. At the end of the Oligocene a pre-Aquitanian phase re-emphasized the older structures and thrust up the Maures massif. Finally, in the Pontian, powerful movements distorted the whole of Provence, downwarping it in a southerly direction, so that the Maures massif in part collapsed beneath the Mediterranean Sea.

Corsica is a distinct structural unit with both Hercynian and Alpine elements. Isolated from the continent from the Miocene period onwards, it consists of a vast granite mass (Hercynian Corsica), to the east of which is a group of foliated rocks of sedimentary origin which abut and impinge on the older basement rocks. These foliated rocks were for a long time said to date from the Palaeozoic, but now geologists place them in the much later Mesozoic and Tertiary eras.

3.1.4 Plains in the forelands of young mountains

From Alsace to Roussillon, plains of varying forms and dimensions fringe the mountains or lie between the various Alpine chains. Successively from north to south are to be found the Alsace plain (upper Rhine plain), the Belfort gap, the plains of the Saône, the plains and basins of the Rhône (Valence, Montélimar), the plains of the lower Rhône, the plain and plateaus of Languedoc and the triangular plain of Roussillon. Their formation is linked to the rise of the Pyrenean and Alpine chains and the simultaneous development of areas of subsidence. As depressions fringing the outer face of the Alpine–Pyrenean orogen, they show the effects of a complex morphological history, with a great variety of developments compressed into a short distance, showing a sequence of transgressions, deformations, deposition of waste sheets derived from the erosion of young chains, and phases of emergence.

In advance of the Alpine zones, there was, in the Mesozoic era, a development of epicontinental seas similar to that of the Paris and Aquitaine basins; transgressions alternated with periods of regression during which planation took place.

After the Stampian, the Eogene seas laid down thick layers of molasse, gravels and conglomerates in the depressions. In the Oligocene, with the end of the Alpine–Pyrenean movements, the fringe of the Alps was affected by a series of north–south orientated areas of subsidence. They were occupied by lakes, which deposited a thick sequence of sedimentary rocks: it was at this time that the depressions of the Saône plain and Bresse, of Bas-Dauphiné and Gard were initiated. The collapse of the central sector of the Pyrenean–Provençal chain and the formation of the Golfe du Lion took place in the Miocene, precipitating a vast marine transgression in the Burdigalian and Vindobonian.

The Rhône depression has a great diversity of structural features which are partly hidden by recent morphological developments.

As the Alps rose and the axis of maximum upwarping (geotumour) approached, the sediments deposited in the circum-Alpine piedmont zone became ever coarser: Miocene conglomerates and debris cones are evidence of the onset of the disintegration of the chain. Further to the west the Miocene sea (Vindobonian transgression) deposited several hundreds of metres of sandy molasse, burying along its shores the upper chains of the Jura and the fringe of the Central massif, of which the uplifted edge was already well marked.

Further tectonic activity introduced a continental phase in the Rhône corridor (Pontian regression), initiating the excavation of the Rhône ria to below the present sea level. This continental phase ended with the filling of the ria by fluvio-lacustrine deposits. During the Pliocene, Roussillon, Languedoc, the lower Rhône and the Rhône corridor were affected by a Pliocene (Plaisancian) transgression linked with a deformation of the continental margin; this transgression created a branching gulf more than 200 km long. The Pliocene transgression deposited unconformably on all strata from Jurassic to Tertiary a thick deposit of grey clay, with sand and limestone appearing only at the top of the sequence. The transgression drowned a vigorous relief of escarpments and mountain chains. In the Camargue 1,500 m of Pliocene deposits were accumulated; today the maximum elevation reached by the deposits is 180 m. Lake Bresse, upstream from Lyon, was filled with deposits of the Middle and Upper Pliocene to a thickness of 200 m. Large amounts of gravel and fluvio-continental waste from the destruction of the surrounding mountains were intercalated with the marine deposits and also covered them.

Similar forms to the vast coalescent debris fans of the Pyrenean piedmont are not found fringing the Alps because of the arrangement of the structured units, the complex history of sedimentation and the size of the pre-Alpine limestone massifs. The Alpine piedmonts are more fragmented and varied, all the way from Dombes north of Lyon to the enormous Pliocene debris fan of the Crau, formed by the Durance, which plunges beneath the alluvium of the Rhône delta.

During these periods of sedimentation the eastern edge of the Central massif continued to rise in successive stages; the great fault bounding the Vivarais and the Cévennes must have been strongly reactivated during the Middle or Upper Pliocene; the formation of the escarpment in this sector probably dated from after the Plaisancian. In the case of the Cévennes, analysis of the heavy minerals and sediments of Languedoc has made it possible to date the major part of their uplift to the Oligocene and Miocene, with a continuation on a reduced scale into the Pliocene.

3.2 Morphology

Throughout the Alpine–Pyrenean region, folding has created relief forms on a grand scale; subsidence and faulting increased the contrasts within the structural units, juxtaposing massifs and depressions in a 'piano-key' type of tectonics and multiplying the number of escarpments, all of very recent origin. The intensity of erosion is thus understandable. There have been countless modifications of the hydrological system, such as the captures made by the mountain streams of the Cévennes. During the Quaternary, denudation was continued by agents which today are confined to high mountain areas where frost, snow and ice still occur regularly.

3.2.1 Cyclical morphology

In these regions of youthful relief, the extent and chronology of erosion surfaces are clearly very different from those of Hercynian France. It is still possible, although difficult, to identify the post-Hercynian surface on the blocks incorporated in or affected by the Tertiary folding. Certain fragments of this surface, such as the Chamrousse plateau in the Alps, play a secondary but by no means negligible role in the present relief.

In the Jura, erosion surfaces are more important, the morphology of the plateaus and folds bearing evidence of numerous periods of planation. Pre-Pontian surfaces were created in relation to the base-levels of the molasse sea in the east and of Lake Bresse in the west; they were bevelled by more localized Pliocene planations (Fig. 2.9).

In Provence there are also traces of a polygenetic and complex Pontian surface and of a surface dating from the end of the Cretaceous and the beginning of the Eocene, associated with the development of bauxite deposits. These surfaces are well preserved because they are on limestone, which is little affected by fluviatile erosion.

3.2.2 Lithological and structural morphology

The young fold mountains are characterized by the variety of conditions under which sedimentation took place, the incorporation of ancient massifs within the youthful folds, the complexity and detail of structure and the scale of erosion by torrents, rivers and ice. These characteristics make the young fold mountains into veritable museums of the forms of lithological and structural morphology.

Granite may give rise to massive domes, fretted by glaciers, as in the Maladetta and the Mercantour, where faulting plays a major role in determining the direction of the drainage pattern. Alternatively, granite may form areas of low relief, or peaks and crest lines, as in the Mont-Blanc massif.

Weak strata, which are frequent because of the conditions of sedimentation, are an easy prey to erosion. Both inside and outside the mountains, shales, clays, sands, flysch and molasse are gullied into spectacular 'badlands'. Limestone, however, is the master rock in this structural morphology, in the Alps, the Jura and the Pyrenees as well as Provence and Languedoc. Where it is preserved in extensive outcrops, it forms high limestone plateaus, profoundly affected by karstic erosion, as in the Jura, Parmelan, Vercors, Vivarais and Provence. When it is sandwiched in beds of variable thickness it can, according to the angle of dip,

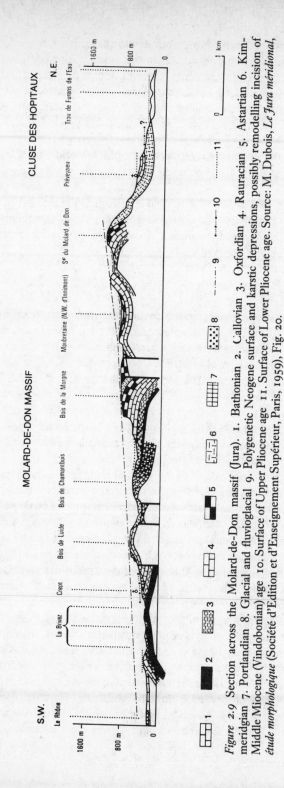

Figure 2.9 Section across the Molard-de-Don massif (Jura). 1. Bathonian 2. Callovian 3. Oxfordian 4. Rauracian 5. Astartian 6. Kimmeridgian 7. Portlandian 8. Glacial and fluvioglacial 9. Polygenetic Neogene surface and karstic depressions, possibly remodelling incision of Middle Miocene (Vindobonian) age 10. Surface of Upper Pliocene age 11. Surface of Lower Pliocene age. Source: M. Dubois, *Le Jura méridional, étude morphologique* (Société d'Edition et d'Enseignement Supérieur, Paris, 1959), Fig. 20.

all conceivable structural forms, from gentle cuestas to vertical hogs-backs, from normal relief to total inversion. In the interior Alps, differential erosion of various strata in the extremely complex superficial tectonics has produced a bewildering array of such structural and pseudo-structural forms, bearing little relationship to the fundamental tectonics of overthrusts and unconformities. In the pre-Alps, massive Upper Jurassic and Lower Cretaceous limestones, separated by beds of clay and calcareous clay, create the structural forms which provide the characteristic splendour of high vertical rock faces, massive mountain summits, soaring escarpments and synclines left perched by inversion of relief.

In the Pyrenees, the most common structural landscape is the product of the combination of bands of Urgonian (Lower Cretaceous) limestone, sometimes, as in Béarn, reinforced by Jurassic dolomites, dominating lengthy longitudinal depressions excavated in clays and shales.

3.2.3 *Climatic morphology*

(i) Glaciations, glaciers and periglacial activity. Within the Alpine chain only two glaciations are recognizable. In the northern Alps, the ice cover was almost complete, whereas in the southern Alps there were only a few valley glaciers, of which the largest advanced as far as Sisteron.

The great Alpine ice sheet radiated furthest at the beginning of the Riss glaciation, reaching the neighbourhood of the Mont-Blanc massif, where the Rhône glaciers met the glaciers emerging from the transverse valleys (cluses) of the Pre-Alps. The ice reached the Rhône at Lyon, covered the Dombes as far as Bourg-en-Bresse and invaded the southern Jura; a tongue of ice also advanced along the Isère valley as far as Saint-Marcellin.

The Pyrenean glaciers, unlike those of the Alps, only exceptionally advanced beyond the chain. The absence of major glaciers in the Pyrenees during the Quaternary is explained by the lower altitude, the narrowness of the chain and the small catchment areas. Most authorities can find evidence of only one glaciation in the Pyrenees. Würm glaciations also affected the mountains of Haut Var and Corsica. At the present time, glaciers cover only a relatively small area: 21 sq km in the Pyrenees and 300 sq km in the Alps. Nevertheless there are a great many different types which create high mountain landscapes of indescribable beauty, a great attraction for tourists.

The mountain massifs show a very highly developed glacial morphology, which can be divided into glaciated valley features and glacial drift features. The glaciated valleys of the northern Alps are made up of a sequence of U-shaped sections linked by glacial steps corresponding with rock bars. Glacial forms of great freshness are revealed by the continuing retreat of the glaciers, which leave behind magnificent terminal moraines, through which the meltwater torrents must cut their way, as at Bossons. Moraines and glacial drift features cover large areas and carpet the valley sides, creating favourable conditions for settlement and cultivation. Terminal moraines where valleys leave the mountains are characteristic of the Alps, but less so of the Pyrenees. The glaciers have also spread their drift deposits outside the mountains. Between the Dombes and the Dauphiné plateau there are three sequences of terminal moraines, with associated fluvioglacial outwash plains.

(ii) Periglacial slope development. The most significant forms of relief associated with the periglacial climate in the young mountains are the pediments (*glacis d'érosion*), which developed under periglacial conditions on the soft rocks at the foot of escarpments. These features can be seen in the interior of the southern Alps (Durance valley), on the upland shoulders fringing the lower Rhône, in the Corbières (eastern Pyrenees), the Basque country and Languedoc.

(iii) Present-day erosion. In this highly accidented region of France with slopes and abrupt changes of elevation everywhere, present-day erosion takes on many different forms, including rock falls, rotational slips, gullying and subsidence. The intensity of present-day erosion is explained by the frequency of steep slopes, the great variation in relief, the liability to snow accumulation, and rainfall of continental or Mediterranean type. The most precise information on the intensity of erosion can best be acquired by measuring the load carried by rivers and streams. Figures for the mountain basins are very high: those for the Drac at Grenoble indicate the removal each year of 615 tonnes for each sq km of its basin.

In Mediterranean France, erosion is more vigorous than in the temperate zone, heightening the contrasts between slopes and flats, exposing the limestone bones of the hills and spreading the eroded waste over the plains and in the beds of seasonal torrents. Gullying of 'badlands' type appears on the soft rocks of the Limagne basins immediately south of Clermont-Ferrand and increases in frequency southwards, to become spectacular in the shale and clay terrains of the Alps. However, glacial and periglacial erosion persists at high altitudes, due to heavy snowfalls and seasonal changes of climate.

Present-day erosion is commonly accentuated by human activities, which are often responsible for disrupting the balance of the natural environment. Erosion processes which are difficult to reverse are often unleashed by the bringing of land into cultivation, by the clearing of the forests, or by the extension of fields and vineyards on excessively steep slopes. Equally adverse effects may be initiated by the neglect of cultivation terraces or drainage systems, by land abandonment, or by the replacement of crops such as olives and vines by crops such as flowers, which do not bind the soil.

3.2.4 Hydrological systems

In the young mountains there has been a succession of very different drainage networks. These may reflect changing shorelines, relating to the advance and retreat of the sea. They may also reflect episodes of complex deformation, highly diverse lithological and structural distributions, and the disruption caused by the superimposition of river systems upon structures other than those on which they were initiated.

The river systems of the young mountains are more recent (pre-Pontian) than those of Hercynian France and less well integrated in the form of their basin, types of drainage network and the detail of their courses. The numerous tilting movements have often caused complete reversals of drainage direction, as in Provence. In this region of miniature chains and basins with its slopes and backslopes, river systems were formed by linking up successive segments, according to the random opportunities offered by the possibility of avoiding obstacles of relief, by proximity to an inlet of the sea, by a low col or a temporary and local base-level. In detail, minor streams are adapted to structure, following the maximum angle of slope offered by the initial relief.

Only the largest rivers could retain a measure of integration through all the tectonic changes, which explains why there are so many examples of superimposition and antecedence. The extent of the sedimentary infilling of the Rhône trough, burying the relief of its bordering uplands, explains the importance of superimposition in the Central massif: the courses of the Rhône and the Saône provide a number of examples.

4 Coastal relief

The 2,700 km of French coastline offer a tremendous variety of forms, often providing landscapes of great beauty, such as the *calanques* of Provence, the cliffs of Corsica and Normandy, the capes and peninsulas of Brittany, the dunes of the Landes and the North Sea, the estuaries of the Atlantic coast and the delta of the Rhône. This variety is a reflection of the structural and morphological variety described in the preceding pages. However, the erosive or regulating action of the sea accentuates lithological and structural contrasts and exposes rocks which on land are covered with regolith and soil.

The seas which bathe these shores are equally varied with regard to their depths, currents and tides. The latter are almost non-existent in the Mediterranean but in the Atlantic range from 4 to 12 m with a maximum of 15 m in the Bay of Mont-Saint-Michel.

The present-day coastlines date from the changes in sea level produced in the last episodes of the Quaternary. The Normanian (Tyrrhenian II or Eemian) transgression, which was contemporary with the last interglacial period, raised the level of the sea by 15–20 m. The pre-Flandrian (Grimaldian) regression, during the Würm glaciation, reduced the level of the sea by 120 m, while the post-Würmian or Flandrian transgression continued until the fifth century AD (Dunkerquian transgression). At present the level of the sea is about 2 m lower than it was in the Flandrian period (Table 2.4).

These movements have resulted in a predominance of coasts of submergence, following transgressions which have had varying effects on the displacement of the shoreline. In regions without a continental shelf, where slopes plunge without interruption into the sea, the coastline has hardly changed (in Provence or the west of Corsica variations are more often caused by very recent tectonic deformations).

In the regions where there is a continental shelf – and these are in the majority – the shoreline has been subjected to great changes. The coastal topography reveals the state of the relief at the time of its submergence, for example the archipelagos of the north coast of Brittany, the Breton rias, the *calanques* of Provence or estuaries such as that of the Seine and the gulf of Morbihan which bring the sea and its agents of erosion far inland. On low-lying coasts the advance of the sea has created gulfs, sometimes cut off by offshore beach bars, which fluvial sedimentation has transformed into marshes. Maritime Flanders was built in this way, in advance of a coastline which ran west–east from Cape Blanc-Nez to north of Saint-Omer, then curved round in the direction of Bergues. The link between England and the continent of Europe was probably broken when a proglacial lake of the North Sea ice sheet overflowed over the Boulonnais–Wealden uplift.

On coasts of submersion, modifications by accumulation are evidently rare; the Rhône delta is all the more exceptional in this respect, although some rivers flowing into the Atlantic, such as the Gironde and the Loire, have submarine deltas.

Structural conditions and the degree of morphological evolution on land play a greater part than marine erosion in shaping coastal relief. The headlands and islands fringing the Armorican peninsula correspond to uplands which are often thought to be of structural origin (fault-blocks), while the Charente islands are anticlines continuing the structures of the mainland.

The differential nature of marine erosion can be seen at every level, whether in the general outline of the coast, with bays corresponding to soft rocks, capes to resistant ones, or in detailed sculpture, with dykes left prominently standing and joints opened up. The significance of cliff development in coastal morphology varies greatly: it is prominent on the sedimentary coasts of Picardy, Boulonnais and Normandy, whereas in the less exposed and more recently submerged coasts of the crystalline rocks it is minimal. Rocky coasts and cliff coasts are far from identical; often the rocky coast sinks into the sea without marine erosion having had the time or the strength to cut a cliff. There are very few examples of cliffs which have receded to any great extent: those which have done so include the Vaches Noires in Normandy, the chalk cliffs of the Pays de Caux and the Jurassic sandstone cliffs of the Boulonnais. In such examples, marine erosion has operated faster than normal erosion, truncating the valleys and leaving them above the beach as notches.

No less important is the role of the sea in transporting and accumulating sediments: along the low-lying coasts of Languedoc, the Landes, the Cotentin

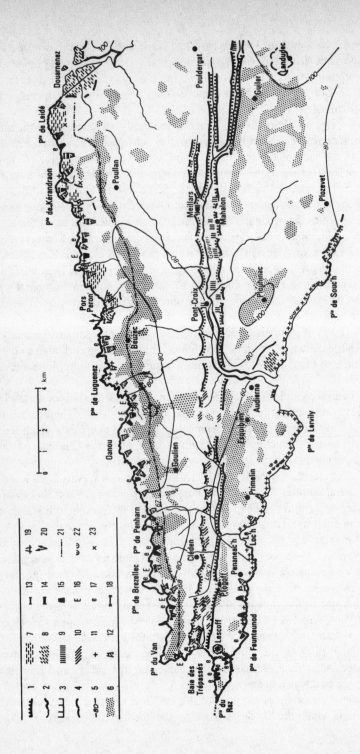

Légende:

1 — 7 — 13 I — 19 ⊥
2 — 8 — 14 II — 20 V
3 — 9 ||||| 15 ■ — 21 ———
4 — 10 — 16 E — 22 ⌣⌣
5 -80- 11 + 17 e — 23 ×
6 — 12 ⚏ 18 I

Douarnenez
P⁽ᵉ⁾ de Leidé
P⁽ᵉ⁾ de Kérandraon
Poullan
Pors Peron
Beuze
P⁽ᵉ⁾ de Luguenez
Oanou
P⁽ᵉ⁾ de Penharn
P⁽ᵉ⁾ de Brezellec
Goulien
Cléden
Penmarc'h
P⁽ᵉ⁾ du Van
Lescoff
Baie des Trépassés
P⁽ᵉ⁾ du Raz
P⁽ᵉ⁾ de Feunteunod
Loc'h
Plogoff
Primelin
Esquibien
Audierne
P⁽ᵉ⁾ de Lervily
Plouhinec
Pont-Croix
Mahalon
Meillars
Plozevet
Guiler
Pouldergat
Canduglec

0 1 2 3 4 km

peninsula and Picardy, the sea has built long beach bars, mostly crowned by sand dunes; these stretch for 200 km between Bayonne and the Gironde estuary. The dunes migrate laterally in the direction of the coastal currents, displacing river mouths, as in the estuaries of Picardy, forming lagoons as in Languedoc, and joining islands to the shore as at Quiberon, Betz and Hyères. But the sea accumulates sand and creates beaches in every bay and inlet.

Saltmarsh is an important coastal feature, both in size (the Marais Poitevin extends for 9,500 sq km) and because it offers a landscape of great originality. Saltmarsh develops in the sheltered part of an estuary, such as the Gironde (Fig. 2.8), behind a beach bar as in the coastal plain of Picardy, or in the inner reaches of a bay, as with the Marais Poitevin. Since the Flandrian transgression the play of tidal currents and the double sedimentation from the sea and from rivers flowing into it have favoured the accumulation of mud. The saltmarsh, like the margins of estuaries, consists of a zone of halophitic (salt-loving) vegetation (*schorre*), which is only exceptionally submerged by the sea, and an outer zone of mudflats (*slikke*) with no vegetation, regularly covered by the tides.

Variations in sea level have produced complex types of coastal morphology. The recession of the sea during the Würm glaciation left behind Normanian cliffs and estuaries which were differentially remodelled by terrestrial erosion and buried by waste sheets and periglacial dune deposits. These unconsolidated deposits were particularly vulnerable to erosion by the returning seas, which rapidly cut new cliffs. This explains why present-day marine erosion appears to be more active in certain well-sheltered bays than on exposed headlands (Fig. 2.10).

Apart from regions of recent tectonic activity and coasts which have receded particularly rapidly, analysis of the relief often reveals the existence of former coastal features at higher elevations. Fossil cliffs, former shore platforms and

Figure 2.10 Geomorphological map of Cape Sizun area, Southwest Brittany. 1. Steep slopes in resistant rocks 2. Coastline (thickened line indicates high cliffs) 3. Fault, apparently reactivated in the Tertiary 4. Inland limit of former marine surface, with former cliff line more or less degraded 5. Contours of sub-Eocene surface 6. Surviving remnant of Eocene surface, in places somewhat remodelled and incorporated in a more recent surface 7. Sainte-Anne surface (50–65 m) 8. 30–35 m surface 9. Benches of Goayen valley 10. Benches of Loc'h and Lacal valleys 11. Monasterian beaches 12. Coastal valley infilled with head deposits, in process of exhumation 13. Coastal hanging valley accordant to Monasterian level 14. Coastal hanging valley accordant to the 30–35 m level 15. Coastal valley infilled with head deposits, not in process of exhumation 16. Superimposition on to head deposits of coastal valley 17. Embryonic coastal valley 18. Interruption of structural origin in long profile of coastal valley 19. Hanging valley caused by cliff recession 20. Beached watershed 21. Watershed in northern part of Cape Sizun 22. Dunes 23. Residual quarzitic sandstone boulders of Eocene age. Pte: Pointe (Point). Source: A. Guilcher, *Le Relief de la Bretagne méridionale* (H. Poitier, La Roche sur Yon, 1948).

raised beaches maintain constant elevations. These relate to higher sea levels during the Quaternary. Their most widespread occurrence is at about 2–5 m above present sea level, corresponding to a retreat stage of the Normanian transgression.

The coasts provide a particularly vulnerable environment, a meagre, precarious legacy. On the one hand, natural processes such as cliff erosion, movement of beach bars and the deposition of sand and silt, all still very active, make it a very mobile, dynamic environment. On the other hand, the coastal area is the meeting point for marine and terrestrial processes, concentrating at the mouths of rivers the transported sediments and pollution loads derived from their basins. It is on this complex and living environment of dunes, marshes, estuaries and cliffs that human societies impinge, in concentrations that are today particularly large, dense and complex in their nature. Coasts and maritime regions have always offered a favourable environment for human activities. Until recent times, apart from the creation of dykes and polders, human influence was mainly limited to the creation of ports by the adaptation of such natural features as estuaries, rias or bays. Important changes in maritime transport since the 1960s have, however, brought about a change of scale in coastal development. The creation or extension of ports involves gigantic infilling in front of the former shoreline, as at Antifer (Seine estuary) and Dunkerque, the building of long jetties perpendicular to the coast (Antifer), and the excavation of approach channels; all these operations modify the coastal currents.

The tourist industry, which is essentially coastal, has also transformed and changed the shorelines by building embankments for the creation of yachting harbours and marinas and by bringing in sand to create or extend beaches. Other activities such as the working of sand and gravel play their part in disturbing the fragile balance of the coastal environment.

5 Morphological regions

If we disregard structural divisions, which should never influence attempts at classifying geographical environments, and consider only types of relief or combinations of forms which result from the morphological history of France, we can distinguish three principal morphological types: the plains and plateaus of Hercynian France; the uplifted, faulted or folded types of Hercynian France and the Alpine fringe; and the high mountains and their valleys.

5.1 Plains and plateaus of Hercynian France

This type consists of all Hercynian France which does not bear visible morphological traces of the intense deformation associated with Tertiary mountain-building. Because of distance from Pyrenean and Alpine orogenesis this type of terrain is structurally tranquil, affected only by deformations of wide radius and gentle warping; more vigorous structures have only a strictly local and isolated occurrence.

This is a morphology of plains and plateaus, found in the sedimentary basins as well as on the ancient massifs; both bear witness to the number and extent of the cycles of erosion which had bevelled an earlier relief massively eroded and rejuvenated only to a minor degree. The plains and plateaus are formed on rocks which outcrop over vast areas and which are relatively uniform: the Cretaceous (given uniformity by the predominance of its chalk facies and by the extent of its covering by clay-with-flints), crystalline rocks, or the limestones and weak Tertiary rocks of the Aquitaine basin. In these regions escarpments are rare and ridges even rarer. Usually they appear as isolated morphological features: hill slopes which mark the boundary of interior Brittany, the Artois anticline, the inward-facing scarps of the Pays de Bray, the cuesta of the Pays d'Auge, and the Appalachian relief of the Armorican massif. Such features often occur where erosional surfaces developed as plains or plateaus meet at different levels; only rarely are they associated with contrasts in structural morphology.

There are, it is true, some morphological differences of lithological or structural origin, for example basins large and small interposed within upland areas, and depressions set into plateaus, but these contrasts are only relative. The Rennes basin and the basin of Châteaulin in the Armorican massif differ from their surroundings by characteristics which have been only gradually acquired; it is often only on one side of such basins that there is a marked discontinuity with the surrounding terrain.

In such homogeneous regions, the relief is essentially determined by the network of valleys, which, however, are insufficiently incised to destroy the general surface. There is a markedly hierarchical drainage network with large, well-integrated drainage basins. Regional contrasts derive from the differences in valley density. The morphology of the valleys has fashioned the detailed relief of plains and *bocages* in Hercynian France. The interfluves, well drained and therefore drier, more windswept but relatively easy to cultivate, contrast with the damp valley bottoms where water is more accessible, where the soil is heavier but more fertile and occasionally marshy. Between the two are the varied hillsides, with their alternation of benches and gentle slopes broken by minor tributary valleys. Traditional rural toponymy has given a precise vocabulary for these features of the landscape, emphasizing their particular characteristics: the valley, the valley side, the high ground, the plain, the bottom. The repetition by the thousand of these 'sites' or 'ecotopes' provides the framework for the spatial organization of these regions. The mesh that contains them is a very unequal one, highly dependent on the density of the valley network; differences are of degree rather than kind. There are innumerable cultivated and occupied sites, providing an infinity of environmental relationships.

Although there are differences between natural regions in this part of France, we must not exaggerate their significance. There are, of course, contrasts between Valois and Soissonnais, Vimeu and the plateau of Picardy, Trégorrois and Léon, but they are not very marked; lithological differences are responsible for major regional contrasts, while historical differences are often more significant than physical ones in the definition of smaller regions or *pays*.

5.2 Uplifted, faulted and folded types of Hercynian France and the Alpine fringe

As we leave the plains of western France and move eastwards, altitudes increase; we encounter a second major relief division, which has many common features, although its actual boundaries are difficult to define. Its backbone is provided by the great French divide described earlier. This morphological division embraces the eastern Paris basin, most of the Central massif, Languedoc, Provence (except for the maritime Alps), the Rhône–Saône corridor, the Jura plateaus, the Vosges and Alsace and part of the folded Jura and of the Pre-Alps.

Its most significant characteristic lies in the importance of morphological contrasts of structural origin. All these regions, whether structurally old or young, were distorted, faulted and folded during the various orogenic phases of the Tertiary. From the fault belt of Saverne at the northern end of the Vosges to the tilted block of the Montagne Noire at the southwestern extremity of the Central massif there is a continuous succession of fault troughs and horsts, upland plains and scarps, areas of subsidence and faulted ridges, massifs and depressions. Corresponding to the mosaic of the geological map there is a morphological mosaic consisting of sharply contrasting topographical features. The incised relief of the valleys plays an important part in the limestone plateaus or on the uplifted crystalline massifs of the Central massif, but it is abruptly broken by escarpments and breaks of slope, which are not to be found in northern and western France. Limestone plateaus and long dip slopes are also characteristic, stretching from Lorraine to the Grands Causses, by way of the Langres, Haute-Saône and Jura plateaus, the fragmented limestone segments of the Maconnais, the plateaus and folds of the Pre-Alps, the plateaus of Vivarais and the plateaus of Provence. These limestone plateaus are affected to varying degrees by karst phenomena and are situated at varying heights above their crystalline or sedimentary settings, but they play a major role in determining regional characteristics and contrasts.

The hydrology of this division of France is unusual in several respects: on both sides of the main divide the direction of rivers is more or less southerly; valleys, corridors, depressions and troughs all have the same direction.

The array of relief forms contrasts with that of northern and western France, reflecting the greater scale of available relief. Mountain summits, hitherto non-existent, appear, together with crest lines, dome-shaped mountains (*ballons*), *puys* and the elongated ridges (*serres*) of the Cévennes. A compartmented morphology is characteristic, in which major structure predominates over minor forms of relief, which are, however, always present in detail. Relief contrasts are more marked than in the previous division; particularly privileged sites and *pays* emerge, regions whose attraction lies in their aspect, soil or microclimate. The most common forms of relief involved are hill slopes, cuestas and fault escarpments, at the foot of which human settlements were established, attracted by the more varied, fertile land and the sheltered, sunny climate available there.

In addition, therefore, to the contrast between upland and lowland we also have the contrast between agriculturally productive and poor regions, something which does not exist so markedly in western and northern France. The morphological environment favours the development of clearly defined *pays*, minor regions with sharply contrasting characteristics. The pattern of relief also exerts an overwhelming influence on the system of communications: the main lines are restricted to the valleys or the interfluves; transverse links across the grain of the country are correspondingly difficult and limited.

5.3 The high mountains and their valleys

This third region is of limited extent; it consists of young mountains of high and intermediate elevation, and the valleys that dissect them. Its two distinguishing characteristics are:

(1) Altitude, which increases the available relief and results in an altitudinal zoning of relief forms, climatic conditions, vegetation and soils. This zoning has a marked influence on the pattern of land use.

(2) The morphological predominance of valleys and vast mountain slopes. Except along the major valley floors, flat surfaces are rare; where they do exist, they are either too high or too inaccessible from the valleys to be used and developed for human occupance. The geographical environment has thus a twofold division into valley bottoms and the great slopes which rise above them. Human occupance is concentrated in the valleys, is predominantly linear and characterized by exploitation of the altitudinally zoned environment. Whereas in the previous morphological type there are still stretches of terrain not directly linked with an organized hydrological system, here the domination of the valleys is total; this is in every sense the domain of the great intermountain valley. This morphological type does not correlate spatially with geologically or structurally 'Alpine' units, which in the Alps and Pyrenees are of much wider extent.

Lucien Gachon has analysed with great subtlety the contrast between the last two morphological types, a contrast between a type of relief compartmented into innumerable minor interfluves isolated by valleys incised to a greater or lesser extent, and the type of the great Alpine valleys:

In the Alps the physical unit is the valley . . . men have taken refuge in these narrow, deep troughs. In the Alps the improved land (*ager*) as strictly defined is narrowly localized, circumscribed and confined by altitudinal and hydrological differentiation. In the Central massif, on the other hand, the *ager* can spread or contract to a remarkable degree . . . essentially because of the limited orographical and hydrological differentiation.[2]

The geographical sites of these mountain regions contrast markedly in terms of altitude, exposure and slope with those of the plains and plateaus.

[2] L. Gachon, 'The French Alps and the Central massif', *Revue de Géographie Alpine*, part IV, 1955, pp. 685–96; the term *ager* is defined as the cultivated part of the land belonging to a settlement.

3

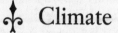 Climate

1 A favourable climate

France is generally regarded as having an equable climate, lacking in extremes. These characteristics can be related to the country's geographical situation and relief.

1.1 The consequences of situation

France lies for the most part in the southern half of the temperate zone (as strictly defined), extending into the northern fringe of the subtropical zone. The boundary between the temperate and the subtropical zone (defined for western continental margins by 12 months with a temperature above 6 °C and a July temperature of 20 °C) crosses southern France, leaving Aquitaine and Mediterranean France within the subtropical region. It is often forgotten that France belongs to two distinct climatic zones, because the subtropical climate is often perceived as a subdivision of the temperate zone.

The possession of two coasts at no great distance from each other gives France a climate unique in Europe. In the west the latitude is high enough to give the country the benefit of the warm waters of the North Atlantic Drift. In the south, the Mediterranean basin brings its reserves of humidity and its moderating influence to latitudes which would otherwise experience the rigours of a desert climate.

1.2 The effect of relief

The disposition of relief lays France open to the penetration of western climatic influences. In this respect the country has the advantage over the Iberian peninsula, with its generally high relief, and over the British Isles and the United States, with their western mountain barriers. But the country is also open to the penetration of climatic influences from north, east and south.

In spite of these advantages, however, the French climate is neither regular nor uniform. By the very fact of its advantageous latitudinal situation, France is almost always in the path of depressions originating along the polar front. The country is subjected to the influence of air masses of varying provenance, each bringing its distinctive meteorological characteristics. The result is a climate consisting of a succession of different types of weather, marked by sudden changes and even dramatic accidents. Although on average the French climate is a moderate one, the daily, weekly and monthly reality is rich in variety and contrast.

2 Climatic elements
2.1 Temperature

Three influences are clearly discernible in the map of temperature (Fig. 3.1), although they are not of equal significance.

(1) The influence of latitude is seen in the northward decline in average annual temperatures, from 15 °C (Côte d'Azur) to 9 °C (Lille). In the intermediate seasons (spring and autumn) the isotherms also reflect the influence of latitude, except in coastal regions.

(2) The interrelationship between maritime influences and latitude varies according to the seasons. The oceanic influence is at its maximum in winter, counterbalancing the effects of latitude so that the 6 °C to 8 °C isotherms run parallel with the coast from the Cotentin peninsula to the Basque country. The Channel has a less marked effect, because of its epicontinental character. The oceanic influence is more persistently apparent in the average annual range of temperature, which increases inland as distance from the Atlantic increases (Brest 10 °C, Nice 14 °C, Paris 16 °C, Strasbourg 19 °C). France thus experiences neither the limited range of the pure oceanic climate (Valentia Harbour in the Republic of Ireland 4.7 °C), nor the extreme contrasts of the true continental climate (Warsaw 21.3 °C).

(3) In detail, relief is the predominant influence shown by the maps of actual temperatures, although the overall impact of latitude and of the sea can still be detected (Fig. 3.1, A–B). In January, the greater part of the country west of the Pre-Alps, the Jura and the Meuse has an average temperature of 0 °C or above; only the high ground of the Central massif provides an exception to this rule. In July most of the country has temperatures above 15 °C, exceptions being

provided by the Alps, the Pyrenees, the Jura and the Central massif; the maximum mean monthly temperature is 22 °C.

This sensitivity of actual temperatures to relief provides the basis for broad

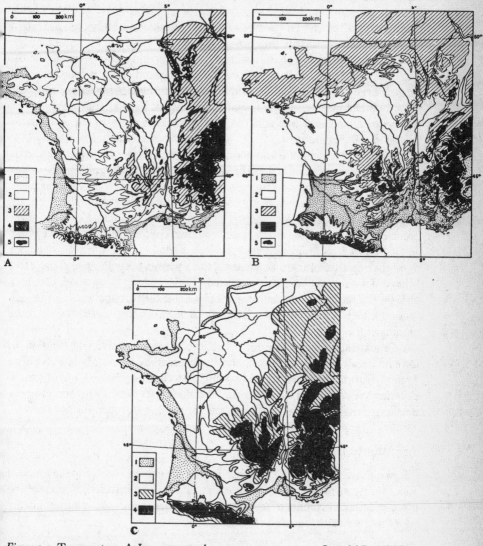

Figure 3.1 Temperature. A. January, actual average temperature. 1. Over 6 °C 2. 6 °C to 0 °C 3. 0 °C to −5 °C 4. −5 °C to −10 °C 5. Below −10 °C. B. July, actual average temperature. 1. Over 20 °C 2. 18 °C to 20 °C 3. 15 °C to 18 °C 4. 10 °C to 15 °C 5. Below 10 °C. C. Number of days with frost. 1. Fewer than 40 days with frost 2. 40 to 80 days 3. 80 to 100 days 4. More than 100 days. Source: E. de Martonne, *Géographie universelle* (A. Colin, Paris, 1942), vol. 6, part 1, Fig. 104A.

regional contrasts. In the plains of the north and west the isothermal lines are uncomplicated. Temperatures tend to be uniform over wide areas and are not markedly affected by relief. On the other hand, in highly dissected and mountain regions the isotherms are closer and interdigitated, emphasizing the valleys and lowland corridors, such as the Rhône–Saône corridor, where the 20 °C July isotherm reaches as far north as Chalon-sur-Saône. Regions of varied temperature conditions are thus brought into close proximity, with conditions in the uplands contrasting sharply with those of adjoining valleys and lowlands. Regional differences in temperature, of minor significance in northern and western France, are here very important; even in Lorraine, temperature contrasts occur between the cuestas and the intervening vales. In addition, the valleys and the isolated, enclosed basins of the Central massif are affected at night by inversions of temperature.

The number of days of frost is another important element in regional climatic contrast. The frost period reflects the degree of continentality and altitude rather than latitude. Only the coastal regions of the Atlantic and the Mediterranean average less than 30 days of frost. Above 1,000 m the ground and the rivers are frozen and snow settles for a period of at least three months. Frost and snow preclude all agricultural activity, make communication difficult and necessitate adaptation to ways of life suited to this long period of cold. Even Lorraine has more than 80 days of frost. By contrast, the lowlands of southern and southeast France stand out as climatically favoured. These include Languedoc, Provence and the Rhône valley, especially south of Valence; they are sheltered by the high ground which surrounds them and which itself experiences three or more months of frost.

Of equal importance to the duration of the frost is its seasonal distribution. In lowland areas bordering the sea, and more generally in the whole of western France, frost is strictly confined to winter. By contrast, days with frost can be experienced even in summer at inland locations, especially above 800 m in the northern parts of the Central massif, and from 1,000–1,200 m further south.

2.2 Atmospheric circulation

The western Europe in which France is set is too small an area, and too much of an intermixture of land and sea, to generate air masses. Instead it is the meeting place and field of conflict of rapidly moving and frequently changing circulatory systems originating thousands of kilometres away.

2.2.1 *Types of atmospheric circulation*

(i) *Low-pressure systems.* The most permanent and important feature is the Icelandic low, a complex zone of depressions of dynamic origin intensified, especially in winter, by the warm waters of the North Atlantic Drift. It draws in disturbances and air currents of northern (polar), western (polar front) and southern (tropical) provenance, revitalizes the depressions and channels them on a westerly course towards Europe. The Genoa or Ligurian depression is another persistent feature. It is especially active in winter, spring and autumn, giving way in summer to subtropical high pressure originating from further south. In summer a depression periodically develops over an overheated central Europe.

(ii) High-pressure systems. Western Europe comes under the influence of high-pressure systems of both oceanic and continental origins. Of the systems of oceanic origin, the most important is the Azores high, part of the belt of high pressure of dynamic origin which rings each hemisphere, separating the trade-wind belt from that of the westerlies. More precisely, western Europe is affected by an offshoot of the Azores anticyclone developed in a modified polar air mass. The movements of this system have a great influence on the climate of France. In winter it does not go beyond the 35° parallel, leaving the western Mediterranean open to air masses and cyclonic circulation of westerly origins. In summer it moves up to the 48th parallel, reaching the Loire and covering the western Mediterranean. The whole of southern France thus falls under its protective influence and is shielded from the mild wet winds of Atlantic origin. This protection is further strengthened by the existence of a zone of high pressure in the upper air over the western basin of the Mediterranean. The fine warm dry weather of the summer months is directly linked to the scale of the Azores anticyclone.

Independent of the Azores high, but often a clear extension of it, there are Atlantic anticyclones which correspond to outbreaks of polar air between two families of depressions. After several sizeable outbreaks of such air a true Atlantic anticyclone may develop, replacing the Icelandic low. Continental high-pressure systems are formed in winter over the cold land and ice surfaces of Scandinavia, central and eastern Europe or Greenland. Such continental high-pressure systems may develop independently, but are often the westernmost extension of the high pressures which persist throughout the winter over Asia and European Russia. Under certain favourable barometrical conditions the continental anti-cyclone may be joined to the oceanic Azores anticyclone by a col of high pressure separating the Atlantic from the Mediterranean. When continental anticyclones predominate, they send extremely cold and dry air over France.

2.2.2 *Fronts*

The air masses are separated by fronts along which hot and cold air meet, causing atmospheric disturbances.

The polar front marks the meeting of polar air with air of tropical origin or, frequently, with returning polar air that has been warmed during a southward movement over the sea.

The arctic front is formed where air from the Arctic basin meets the polar air.

This front is not confined to high latitudes: it may extend down to the Mediterranean, juxtaposing arctic and tropical air.

The Mediterranean front in winter separates cold continental polar air from warm Mediterranean air.

Other secondary fronts appear spasmodically, with varying effects on France. They include the trade-wind front between the maritime trade winds and the continental trade winds from the Sahara, and in summer the Aquitaine front over the Gulf of Gascony, between Atlantic and continental air.

The paths followed by the depressions associated with these fronts sweep over the whole of France, bringing winds successively from the northwest, west, southwest, southeast and east. Wind trajectories are determined by location of the pressure systems at the time. The mobility of the pressure systems and fronts subjects western Europe to extremely varied meteorological situations, which are a familiar feature of the daily weather maps.

2.2.3 Weather types

A weather type consists of the sum of meteorological conditions over a defined period corresponding to a clearly defined barometrical situation. Each weather type relates to particular conditions of temperature and humidity; a summer hot-weather type, for example, is determined by a high-pressure system over the Mediterranean and a depression over northern Europe or Iceland, whereas a mild, wet weather pattern in winter is caused by south or southwest winds coming from the Azores anticyclone.

Mezin[1] listed a succession of 519 weather types between 1926 and 1935, dividing them into 26 categories. The average length of a type is ten days, but it may be prolonged by periods of anticyclonic blockaging. In winter, for example, cold dry weather may last for several weeks.

The variability index is derived from the number of monthly changes in weather types in relation to the annual number of changes. The most variable months are September, December (index 0.098) and April (0.091); September and April are transition months, during which there is a rapid succession of different patterns. The months of greatest stability are July (0.070), February (0.072) and January (0.076), months during which the predominance of high pressure from either the Azores or the continent restricts changes.

The diversity index is derived from the number of distinct weather types experienced in any one month in relation to the total number of categories. The months showing the greatest diversity are March (index 0.61), April and November (0.57), which once again are months of climatic transition. This index clearly underlines the old French saying: 'Ne'er cast a clout till April is out!' Conversely, the months which experience the least diversity in weather types are July (0.14), August (0.25), January and February (0.26).

[1] M. Mezin, 'Evolution des types de temps en Europe occidentale', *Association Française pour l'Avancement des Sciences, Congrès* (1945), vol. 2, pp. 171–82.

The statistical analysis of weather types thus allows us to understand all the subtleties of climatic factors. Pédelaborde[2] has defined the climate of the Paris region according to categories of weather types revealed by the daily weather maps over a period of six years. During this period continental weather patterns (anticyclones or indeterminate barometric situations) accounted for 22.35 per cent of the days, and oceanic situations for 77.64 per cent, with the following origins:

25.3 per cent of north and northeast cyclonic origin;
22.87 per cent of west cyclonic origin;
15.61 per cent of southwest and southeast origin;
13.81 per cent of oceanic anticyclonic origin.

2.2.4 Winds

France is a meeting point of winds from many different directions; the nature of the relief features that they must overcome or bypass gives them further individuality. The inhabitants have long since given traditional names to the winds that may freeze their crops, ruin their tree-fruit crops, melt the snow or bring eagerly awaited rain. The cold wind that blows from the north or east is called the *bise*. In the Aquitaine basin the *cers* brings rain, and the *autan*, blowing down from the Pyrenees or the Lauragais, disperses the clouds. The *mistral* is a north wind channelled down the Rhône corridor. It has formidable consequences: in winter it is a cold, violent wind that from January to April can blow continuously for between three and nine days, causing intense evaporation. In summer, it dries up the overheated atmosphere, raising clouds of dust.

2.3 Precipitation

In an average year, France receives 450,000 million cu m of precipitation in the form of rain or snow. Almost every part of the country receives more than 500 mm annually; the limited areas receiving less than this figure include the coasts of Provence and Languedoc, the Illiers-Combray district on the margins of Beauce and Perche, and Alsace. At the other end of the scale, only the highest peaks of the Pyrenees and of the northern Alps, and a few summits in the Jura and the Central massif have a precipitation of more than 2,000 mm.

The rainfall closely follows the map of relief (Fig. 3.2). As the rain is brought mainly by westerly winds, the disposition of relief features and their orientation affect the amount received. Where the direction of relief is north–south, a rain-shadow effect is created on plains and depressions further east. Once more a contrast emerges between the uniform regions of western France and the more varied terrain of eastern France and the mountains, where basins, valleys and lowland corridors receive less precipitation than the heights that surround them.

[2] P. Pédelaborde, 'Un exemple de circulation atmosphérique régionale: la circulation sur l'Europe occidentale', *Annales de Géographie*, no. 334, 1953, pp. 401–17.

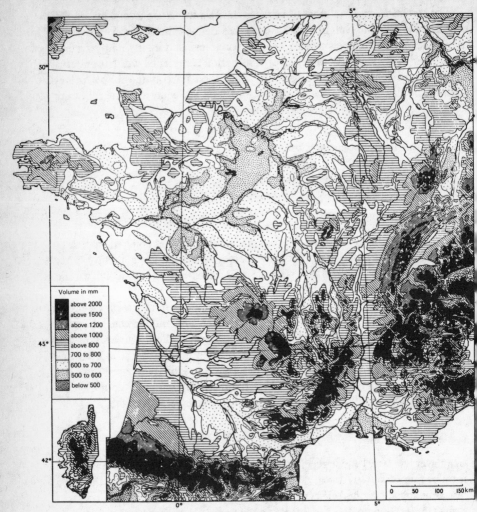

Figure 3.2 Average annual precipitation. Source: de Martonne, *Géographie universelle*, vol. 6, part I, Fig. 107 (after H. Gaussen).

2.3.1 *The seasonal distribution of precipitation*

In the whole of France, autumn is the wettest season, followed by summer and spring. A simplified version of the classification of the seasonal distribution of rainfall allows three distinct categories to be determined (Fig. 3.3):

   Maximum in autumn and winter, in that order. This is a maritime type found in both the Mediterranean coastlands and along the Atlantic coast and the western Channel coast. In the latter area, however, precipitation characteristically takes the form of a fine drizzle which can last for days at a time, whereas on the Mediterranean coast sudden, concentrated downpours are typical.

Maximum in summer and autumn, with either season predominant. This type is characteristic of most of France. As distance from the coast increases, the oceanic influence, with its tendency to an autumn maximum, is progressively overlain by the continental influence with its summer maximum and dry winters. The penetration of oceanic influences far into France is explained by the nature of relief, which rises only gently to maximum heights situated well to the eastern side of the country. These summer and autumn rains are stormy in nature, being caused by the convection of air of high humidity over overheated land.

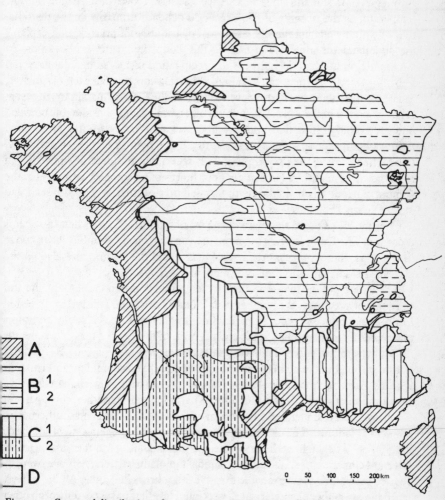

Figure 3.3 Seasonal distribution of precipitation. The seasons of high precipitation are: A. Autumn (followed by secondary peak in winter) B. Summer and autumn (B1 autumn maximum, B2 summer maximum) C. Spring and autumn (C1 autumn maximum, C2 spring maximum) D. Other types of seasonal distribution. Based on R. Musset, *Annales de Géographie*, no. 292, 1943 (separate map not included in pagination).

Maximum in spring and autumn, in that order. This type is found over much of southern France. It is characteristic of the northern fringe of the Mediterranean subtropical zone; the dry summers relate to the predominance of the subtropical high-pressure systems, the dry winters to the extension over France of the continental high-pressure system.

2.3.2 Snow

Although snowfall and the persistence of snow cover are related to low temperatures, the quantity of snow received depends primarily on the distribution of winter precipitation. The seasonal distribution of precipitation explains the abundance of snow which falls on the mountains in the cold seasons. At Chamonix, more than 80 per cent of precipitation in December, January and February is in the form of snow; at high altitudes snow may fall even in summer, as late as mid-June at heights above 1,000 m in the Central massif, in August at 1,800–2,000 m in the Alps. The amount of snowfall varies considerably between one meteorological station and another, and also varies from year to year. Average figures for 1940–9 in the Alps are 2.8 m at Saint-Pierre-de-Chartreuse, one of the resorts of the Pre-Alps regularly recording considerable snowfall, 5 m at Megève, 10 m at the Hameau du Tour (north of Chamonix), and 47 m at the summit of Mont-Blanc. In the Central massif there were falls of 1.55 m recorded at La Chaise-Dieu (1,075 m).

Over most of France there are only a small number of days when snowfall is recorded. The figure increases to more than 20 days on high ground above 500 m in the Alps, the Pyrenees, the Central massif and the Vosges, and also on the plateaus of Lorraine and the headwaters of the Saône.

The length of time that snow lies on the ground is as important to the life and economy of a region as the number of days on which it falls. This is clearly related to the temperature regime. In mountain areas above 1,000–1,500 m the snow cover lasts from December to the end of April. In the Central massif it generally lies only from the end of January, and may melt and be replaced several times before spring, but the highest parts of the massif are snowbound for three to four months. Although the Central massif has fewer days with snowfall than the Alps, the duration of snow cover is the same. What is more, the southernmost parts of the massif have a longer period under snow than the Pre-Alps and southern Alps at a similar latitude, the latter being more exposed to the penetration of southerly influences. The high surfaces of the Central massif are a meeting place of different climatic types. Lacking substantial mountain barriers, they are swept by sudden snowstorms more terrible than the falls channelled along Alpine valleys.

All these weather characteristics, associated together or succeeding each other as the seasons unfold, combine to produce a particular climatic type, whose biotic significance is at least as great as that of soil or slope. In particular, cold weather with its various expressions in the form of frosts and snow determines the length of the growing season and so plays its part in differentiating fruitful from poor land. Areas of strong oceanic influence, and the plains generally, have the benefit of a long growing season, which locally, as on the Mediterranean coast, may even be uninterrupted, but in the mountains the growing season may last for only three to six months, their soils lying sterilized by snow and cold for the remainder of the year. This shortness of the growing season applies just as much to the young fold mountains as to the upland surfaces of the Hercynian massifs; it does not exceed 150 days in the uplands of Limousin, Haut-Livradois and Forez, and is between 100 and 125 days in Cantal, Aubrac and Margeride. It is clear that these natural conditions influence the potential agricultural exploitation of these areas, and thus their human occupance and land use.

3 Regional types of climate

The prime climatic contrast in France, fundamental for the whole human geography of the country, is between north and south. Northern France belongs to the temperate zone; here, oceanic and continental influences confront each other throughout the year. Southern France belongs to the northerly part of the subtropical zone, and is subject in summer to the extension of subtropical high-pressure systems which shield it from oceanic influences. The pattern of relief is such, however, that the higher parts of the Central massif, the Alps and the Pyrenees introduce into southern France 'northerly' climatic characteristics of both temperate and oceanic type. The typical southern type of climate, marked by summer drought and high temperatures, is restricted to the Atlantic coastal lowlands south of the Loire, the Aquitaine basin, and the whole of the Mediterranean south, including the south of the Central massif and the southern Alps. In both northern and southern France there is a gradation of climate from the predominantly oceanic influences of the west to increasingly clear continental influences in the east.

The regional climatic contrasts of France will become apparent in an examination of climograms of representative stations (Figs. 3.4 and 3.5).

3.1 Climates of northern France

Brest and Strasbourg represent the two extreme types of climate found in this part of France, and Paris an intermediate type.

Brest. The entire climogram is situated above 50 mm average monthly precipitation. It is circular in shape, showing a contrast between the colder months (September to February), which all receive more than 75 mm precipitation, with the absolute maximum of more than 90 mm in October and November. By contrast, the months of the hot season (March to August) receive less than 60 mm. The transition between the two distinct precipitation regimes is very abrupt. Variations in temperature are much less pronounced, although they

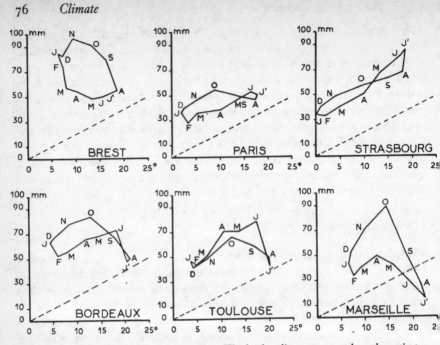

Figure 3.4 Climograms of lowland stations. The broken line corresponds to the ratio $p = 2t$, where p = the total of monthly precipitation and t = mean monthly temperature. Following the idea put forward by H. Gaussen, months falling below the broken line are considered as 'dry'.

exist; the marked cooling that takes place between August and November is to be explained by the amount of precipitation received at this period.

Strasbourg. In contrast to the circular climogram of Brest, that for Strasbourg is elongated diagonally and lies nearer to both axes. This pattern is similar to that of true continental climate but differs from it in the steep slope of the graph and the amount of precipitation in the winter months. The graph divides into two branches, with increasing temperature and precipitation from January to July and a decline of both thereafter. Oceanic influence is apparent only in the October–December rainfall, which is higher than that of spring. The temperature range is almost 20 °C, but the range of precipitation is not much greater than that of Brest.

Paris is an example of a mixed type of climate; the climogram shows the interaction between continental and oceanic influences. The left-hand side from October to April is essentially oceanic, with a clearly marked autumn precipitation maximum. Continental influence is shown on the right-hand side of the graph from May to September, with a second rainfall peak in June–July equal to the autumn maximum. The temperature range of 15 °C is intermediate between oceanic and continental figures, but the range of monthly precipitation totals is particularly small at about 30 mm.

3.2 Climates of southern France

In this part of the country, it is essential to distinguish between lowland and upland stations. Bordeaux, Toulouse and Marseille represent three types of climate found on the plains and coasts. Their climograms have in common the pronounced 'hook' which pulls down the right-hand side of the graph and which reflects the dryness of the summer season, in complete contrast to the temperate continental-type climate of Strasbourg. In these three stations maximum precipitation is received in spring and autumn. The low rainfall in summer is to be attributed to the influence of the Azores anticyclone, and the low winter rainfall to the extension of the continental anticyclone.

Bordeaux. The left-hand side of the Bordeaux climogram is similar to that of Paris, showing the strong oceanic influence over western Aquitaine during the cold season; the autumn precipitation maximum stands out very clearly, after which the establishment of the anticyclonic conditions checks any further increase. Summer on the other hand shows the influence of Mediterranean conditions, as does the moderate January average temperature of 4.9 °C.

Toulouse. Being further inland, oceanic influence is weaker and spring rather than autumn is the period of maximum precipitation. Nevertheless even in this easterly location some oceanic influence still results in the absence of the torrential rains and high winds of the Mediterranean: 'paler skies, less sharply defined outlines in a less transparent atmosphere, are the characteristics of this peaceful, in some way incomplete, south'.[3]

Marseille. The climogram does not indicate a true Mediterranean climate of dry summers associated with winter maximum rainfall. Here, spring and autumn are the periods of maximum precipitation. The climate is purely Mediterranean only between April and September, when rainfall is extremely low. The range between the annual extremes of rainfall is very high.

High-altitude stations. Unlike the previous stations these climograms do not give a picture of a regional type of climate but reflect local conditions of situation, altitude and exposure. It is particularly difficult to generalize about the climatic regions and types of the Central massif, which extends over such a wide area between the plains of northern France and the narrower lowlands of southern France, and which is the meeting place of so many climatic influences. The contrasts that can exist within even a short distance are illustrated by the climograms for the Puy-de-Dôme in the mountains of Auvergne and for Clermont-Ferrand. Puy-de-Dôme, exposed to all the winds of heaven, has an extremely high precipitation (no month below 120 mm), a winter precipitation maximum and only minor variations between the remaining months of the year. Clermont-Ferrand, by contrast, situated in the Limagne lowland a few kilometres to the east, in the rain-shadow of the Puy-de-Dôme, has a completely

---

[3] D. Faucher, *La Vie rurale vue par un géographe* (Institut de géographie de la Faculté des Lettres et Sciences Humaines, Toulouse, n.d.).

different climogram. There is an overall continental pattern, with a July and August 'hook' indicating some Mediterranean influence in summer. Even in the western part of the massif the elevation is sufficiently high to shift southwards the area of summer drought, which appears only south of the river Lot. The main high-mountain axis of the massif, provided by the volcanic massifs of Auvergne from the Chaîne des Dômes southwards to the Aubrac, creates a sharp division between the oceanic influence to the west and the continental influence to the east. The limit of Mediterranean climatic influence is more difficult to define, despite the sudden physical contrast between the Central massif and the lowlands of the Mediterranean region.

In the Alps, Chamonix too has its own particular characteristics. From April to October there is abundant summer rainfall, which is a continental feature; but there is also plentiful cold-season precipitation, with a maximum in autumn, an oceanic feature. In contrast, Embrun, in the southern Alps, has a climogram which is almost identical to that of Bordeaux, with an autumn maximum and July–August 'hook' of dry weather.

It follows that in areas of mountainous or highly diversified relief local climates should be considered before the regional climate. In such areas local winds – mountain and valley winds, pseudo-föhns – and local variations in temperature, even temperature inversions, are more important than the overall climatic pattern of a station, which it would be wrong in any case to consider as in any way representative of a regional climate. For example, the intramontane basins and the wider valley floors of the Pyrenees or Alps, together with the sunny slopes (*adrets, soulanes*), enjoy favourable climatic conditions. By contrast adjacent high plateaus, the upper slopes and peaks towering above, and the north-facing

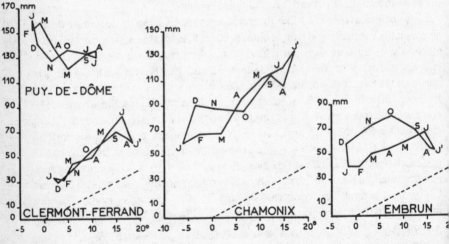

Figure 3.5 Climograms of upland stations.

shaded *ubacs* are climatically disadvantaged. There is obviously a close relationship between this detailed climatic geography and the basic facts of biogeography
and human geography.

4 Climatic irregularities and climatic accidents

Although France enjoys temperate climatic conditions, every region is subject to
climatic irregularities of varying forms and varying duration.

4.1 Climatic accidents

These may take such forms as torrential rain concentrated in a restricted area,
thunderstorms, fierce gales with driving rain, very heavy snowfalls and cold
spells. They are spectacular in their suddenness, their concentration in limited
areas and their repercussions on the economy and life of the region.

4.1.1 Drought

A prime example of the effects of drought is provided by the summer of 1976,
which began with an exceptionally hot, dry June over virtually the whole country.
Instead of a normal monthly precipitation of approximately 50–70 mm, rain
gauges registered zero or at most a few millimetres (Limoges: 0 instead of a
monthly average of 65 mm; Rennes: 0.4 instead of 45; Strasbourg: 21 instead of
77).

The drought had a wide range of consequences. The number of forest fires
increased and there were water shortages in both towns and the countryside,
particularly severe in the normally high-rainfall western France, the traditional
area of stock-rearing. There was a fall in electricity production from thermal
power-stations which were affected by the unusually high temperatures of rivers
used as sources of cooling water, from run-of-stream hydroelectric plants and
also from plants which were unable to draw on depleted reservoirs to meet peak
morning demand. The Canal du Centre had to be closed prematurely to traffic as
its normal water supply from the Etang de Torcy had to be diverted to keep the
Le Creusot heavy industry going. The Nantes–Brest canal was also closed.

The drought forced the authorities to take a range of measures. The price of
straw (used as an emergency feedstuff for animals) was fixed, to curb speculation.
In some areas there were bans on the use of water for washing cars and watering
lawns; in more extreme cases the water supply was cut off or rationing
introduced. Many departments were declared disaster areas in respect of cereals,
fodder crops or fish-farming. To pay for measures to assist those hardest hit, a
'drought tax' was introduced in the name of national solidarity. Paris bus drivers
even went on strike to protest against working in such heat and the transport
authority suggested a 'heat bonus'.

4.1.2 *Severe winters*

The winter of 1962–3 was one of the worst ever known in France, even worse than February 1956, owing to the combination of persistent cold and very heavy falls of snow. It had considerable repercussions on agriculture. Almost all the autumn-sown barley and more than one-sixth of the autumn wheat (800,000 ha) were ruined and had to be replanted. Half of the vegetable crop was also destroyed in the ground. The delayed onset of the vegetative period caused a bunching in the normally staggered maturation of fruit and vegetable crops, which all came on the market together, causing a collapse of prices.

Many other branches of the economy were affected, notably transport. Canals were frozen for several weeks and roads blocked by ice and snow. Even after the thaw, frost damage was such that they were unable to provide normal transport, especially of coal. In building and construction, employees were forced into a period of unemployment which exceeded the 42 days of compensation normally allowed for bad weather.

Severe conditions were also experienced at the end of 1970, when the Rhône valley motorway was blocked by snow for four days; 60 cm of snow fell within a few hours, cutting off thousands of cars. Special trains had to be used to evacuate 10,000 people, and wagon-loads of emergency supplies were sent to Montélimar and the surrounding districts. Similar falls of snow had previously occurred in 1901 and 1941, and snowfall accompanied by violent winds brought much of France to a standstill in January 1979.

The climatic accidents of recent years, which have had a particularly severe impact upon agriculture, have led to proposals for the setting up of a national fund for agricultural disasters. Because agriculture is developing in the direction of specialization, farmers are more vulnerable to climatic irregularity than under the old system of subsistence polyculture, where it was unlikely that all crops and animal enterprises on a farm would be equally affected.

4.2 Climatic fluctuations

These climatic accidents are sudden and violent manifestations of 'normal' climatic variations, which are usually masked by the use of average figures. In fact variability of temperature and rainfall from one year to the next is the rule. Pau, for example, received 250 mm precipitation in April 1918, 0.2 mm in April 1958; Versailles, with an annual average precipitation of 600 mm, had 249 mm in 1921, 382 mm in 1949 and 417 in 1953. These variations are in turn contained within long-term climatic fluctuations which are difficult to establish with certainty because of the lack of statistical observations in the past. The historian Le Roy Ladurie has proposed the following sequence:

the 'sunny millennium' of the Campignien;

the sub-Atlantic deterioration;
the warm period around 1000 AD (ninth–twelfth centuries);
the 'Little Ice Age' of the seventeenth and eighteenth centuries;
the rise in temperature during the nineteenth century;
the present-day wet period.[4]

Southern France, which has in the normal course of events to endure extremely dry conditions every summer, is also more exposed than northern France to climatic hazards because it is subject to a succession of sharply contrasted climatic conditions. Major climatic disasters apart, these seasonal anomalies of temperature or rainfall are not exceptional; abnormally dry or wet summers and severe winters occur throughout a climatic history which has little relationship to average climatic data. Yet these exceptional climatic events can have a major impact on the life of the people, despite the high degree of technical progress characteristic of the present day. Installations and protective measures designed for 'average' situations, or for only moderate variations of temperature or climate, can be quite inadequate in the face of extreme and prolonged anomalies. For example, despite its advanced technology, French energy production is not completely independent of climatic crises. On 19 December 1978 the whole of France was blacked out for several hours: the reason was a sudden excess consumption of electricity caused by a sharp overnight drop in temperature.

Reference to broad climatic categories does not go far towards explaining the variety of actual natural environments that are the concern of the geographer. Monthly averages and totals or numbers of days during which particular conditions are established give only a highly generalized picture of climatic reality. In the field of local climate, statistics on such vital matters as duration of insolation or amount of evaporation exist for only a very small number of stations. Only detailed studies can reveal the actual variations of local climate and show contrasts in local and regional geography which are smoothed out of existence by generalized data. In the Central massif, for example, Fel has calculated the actual effective precipitation at ground level, between December and May, clearly bringing out the contrast between the upland grasslands of the west and the eastern regions where there is very little grassland.[5]

Climatic accidents apart, the climate of France must be considered as an invaluable asset with regard to agriculture, industry and tourism alike.

[4] E. Le Roy Ladurie, *Histoire du climat depuis l'an mil* (Flammarion, Paris, 1967).
[5] A. Fel, *Les Hautes Terres du Massif Central* (Publication de la Faculté des Lettres et Sciences Humaines, Clermont-Ferrand, 1962).

4

⚜ Soils

___

The physiographical and geological diversity of France and its situation at a crossroads of climatic influences account for the variety of its soils.

1 Climatic control: zonal soil types

On a global scale, soil types are grouped in major zones corresponding to the major world climatic regions. On this scale, almost the whole of France belongs to the zone of brown forest soils. This zone gives way northwards to the podzol zone and southwards to the zone of Mediterranean soils.

Brown earths develop beneath a deciduous forest cover in areas of temperate climate, with mild winters, warm summers and annual precipitation between 500 and 700 mm. The warm summers ensure a high degree of decomposition of organic matter, more marked than with podzols, leading to a lesser degree of acidity in the upper horizon. On the other hand, the moderate rainfall results in less extensive leaching; the colloids (iron-clay) remain; only the carbonates are almost or completely leached out. Soil profiles are homogeneous, varying in colour from pale yellow to dark brown, with an alluvial horizon that is inconspicuous apart from a lower layer with a few nodules. Exceptionally when the water-table is close to the surface and drainage is impeded, this lower horizon may develop into a true iron-pan, as illustrated by the *alios* of the Landes and *grep* in the Toulouse region. *Alios* is a sandstone formed from quartz sand bonded by a humo-ferric cement representing 4–16 per cent of the whole. This unevenly distributed formation derives from material brought in laterally or which was raised by root action according to variations in the water-table. Most of the formation, however, is doubtless an inherited feature, dating from before the continental dune formation of the Landes.

French climatic variety undoubtedly explains the diversity of brown-earth types. Climatic contrasts between Lorraine and Brittany, for example, are sufficiently striking for typical brown earths to be found in the east of the Paris basin, whilst in western France they experience a greater degree of leaching, producing a podzolic or degraded brown-earth structure. In western France, however, podzolization is not purely a reflection of climate; it is encouraged by changes in the plant cover, especially the planting of coniferous forest and the degradation of the initial vegetation into heathland. Brown earths are, of course, admirably suited to agricultural use.

Mediterranean soils cover only a small part of France. They have a characteristic red or reddish colour which in Mediterranean landscapes contrasts with the whitish colours of the limestone outcrops. This *terra rossa* (red earth) is found in depressions and on the surface of plateaus; it is a decalcified red clay mixed with coarse quarzitic elements. Under Mediterranean climatic conditions it also develops on non-calcareous parent rocks. Its origin is still the subject of much debate; it may be a clay still in process of formation by present-day decalcification or it may be a former soil horizon, the result rather of tropical than subtropical conditions. But it cannot in itself be considered as a true soil; more precisely it is to be regarded as a point of departure for the development of present-day soil profiles. The redness of Mediterranean soils is caused by the concentration of iron oxides, which are subject to upward migration during the dry season. The red earths of the Mediterranean are not to be confused with their lateric tropical equivalents; they can be fertile, yielding fine crops, and can produce soils which stand up well to summer droughts.

2 Control by geology and relief: azonal soils

This overriding zonal pattern, already modified by variations of local climate, altitude and relief, is further modified by important azonal differences introduced by rock type. Under similar climatic conditions soils formed on limestone, clay, granite and basalt will have differing characteristics and properties (Fig. 4.1).

A soil is not formed directly from bedrock, whether an outcrop of limestone or of granite, but on an intervening layer of physically and chemically altered material known as regolith. This may take the form of sands produced by the decomposition of granite or of a decalcified layer over limestones. Under present-day climatic conditions, these physical and chemical changes take place only on a small scale and very slowly. The nature of soil change was very different in the climatic conditions of the Quaternary period. In the cold periods, periglacial action broke down the bedrock, mantled slopes with solifluction deposits and broke up the upper layers of the rocks by cryoturbation. It was on this superficial mantle that soils were developed; to the extent that they extend into areas that now have a Mediterranean climate, they must be related to past climatic conditions, not those of today.

Limestone outcrops produce characteristic modifications of soil types. On pure limestone, rendzinas develop, ranging from the classic type through various degraded types to calcareous brown forest soils. Rendzina soils are characterized

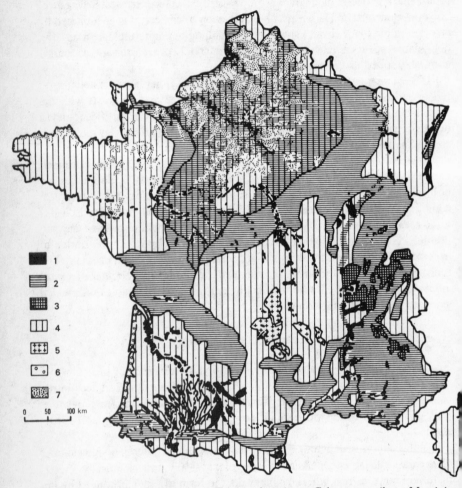

Figure 4.1 Soil-parent materials. 1. Terrace deposits 2. Calcareous soils 3. Morainic material 4. Siliceous or silicated material 5. Volcanic soils 6. Dune Sands 7. Loess and plateau limon (brick earth). The superimposition of shadings 2 and 4 indicates areas where calcareous soils and siliceous or silicated soils form a mosaic. Source: G. Plaisance, *Guide des forêts de France* (La Nef de Paris, 1961).

by the presence of calcium, which prevents the leaching of colloidal elements; they form particularly on the softer limestones and calcareous marls of the Jurassic and Cretaceous formations.

On the extensive chalk outcrops, intercalated clay horizons and superficial clay-with-flints deposits introduce a measure of variety, with deeper and more developed soil profiles. But the great contrast within the group of limestone soils is that between northern and southern France. The limestone regions of southern France are all to a greater or lesser degree *causses*, their fissured karstic surfaces riddled with dolinas (solution hollows) and swept periodically by the torrential rainstorms characteristic of the Mediterranean region. Soils of any depth tend to be restricted to the valleys and dolinas, contrasting with the much more continuous soil cover on the limestones further north.

Limon or loess is a particular type of parent rock, formed under periglacial conditions (see chapter 2, 2.4.2). The principal constituent is silt (average grain size 0.025 mm), with strictly limited clay and sand content. Like the *terra rossa* of the Mediterranean, loess or limon is strictly a soil-parent material, not a soil. The upper horizon of loess when bleached and decalcified is transformed into loam or brickearth.

The lithological characteristics of the parent rock strongly influence the quality of the soil. On clay and marl the soils are heavy and poorly aerated, producing tenacious mud when wet; for cultivation they need to be dressed with lime. Limestone, on the contrary, produces light, warm, easily worked soils which from earliest times attracted farmers. Loess, loess-loam and brickearth, although producing somewhat heavier soils, have been similarly attractive. Sands, in particular granitic sand (itself a residual formation), provide friable but hungry soils, which rapidly lose their humus and plant nutrients. Older superficial deposits, such as those of the Palaeogene erosion surfaces, give rise to particularly infertile soils. The deposits strewn on the Palaeogene surfaces of the Central massif, for example, positively repel attempts at agricultural utilization. The same is true of the cold soils of some of the debris cones of the mountain piedmonts, such as the Lannemezan fan, which is derived from the granitic massifs of the Pyrenees and is devoid of limestone.

The quality of the alluvial deposits of river valleys as soil-parent materials depends on their composition, that is to say on the nature of the rocks from which they are derived. Alluvial deposits of the Alsace plain, which are derived from the crystalline Vosges, have been left under forest cover, whereas the alluvium of the Limagne basin of the Central massif, being derived from the volcanic mountains of Auvergne, produces fertile black earths.

In mountain regions the necessarily slow process of soil formation has been hindered and is still being hindered by the relative youth of the mountains themselves, by the action of the glaciers that have only recently retreated, by the vigour of erosive activity and by the short duration of the warm season. Soils are characteristically skeletal, more like regolith than soils. Mountain soils are very variable, depending on the nature of the parent rocks; unconsolidated and relatively heterogeneous material, such as fluviatile or morainic deposits, produce soils more rapidly than solid rock. The two chief characteristics of mountain soils are the slowness with which they form and their tendency to accumulate acid humus, giving them profiles similar to podzols.

The regularity of zonal and lithologically related soil types is modified by slope characteristics. The typical soil profiles develop only on level ground; on slopes, soil creep results in the downhill movement of the finer particles and the truncation of soil profiles. Secondly, chemical processes do not operate only vertically but also horizontally, with the down-slope movement of water. At the foot of slopes, where these movements cease, decomposed material accumulates, humidity is greater and fertility is constantly enriched by further movement from above. This explains the reputation and continuing attraction of soil formed in such slope-foot positions.

3 Human influences on the soil

In a country of very early settlement such as France, human influence on the soil has been powerful. Manuring and agricultural improvements have modified the structure and composition of the soil. The originally heavy and marshy soil of interior Flanders, for example, has been enriched over the centuries by the tenacity and toil of the Flemish peasants. Improved drainage, whether surface or underground, has also modified hydrological conditions. Irrigation can raise the water-table and change the conditions of soil development.

Conversely, man can damage soils and exhaust them, either by intensive cultivation with insufficient use of fertilizers or by practices which encourage erosion. Examples are not restricted to the Mediterranean area; research has shown that the practice of fallowing under the three-field system accelerated erosion by leaving a large and continuous area of arable land exposed to rain and run-off for a whole year. This erosion is frequently referred to in the lists of grievances drawn up in 1789. Similarly, the loss of agricultural land which has been going on in the last hundred years, and the consequent extension of waste land, have brought about profound pedological changes through compaction, diminished aeration and the establishment of a permanent sward. Finally, the balance of the soil can be destroyed by artificially raising the water-table (chapter 2, 1).

4 The diversity of French soil types

The soil map has a far more intricate pattern than the corresponding geological map; an outcrop which on the latter is represented by a single colour becomes on the soil map a finely divided mosaic of soil types, differing according to the degree of modification and decomposition of the parent material, according to slope and according to soil moisture conditions. The nature and fertility of soils change very rapidly from one field to another, occasionally within the same field. In only a very few regions without pronounced slopes or valleys, such as Beauce and Santerre, are the soil types uniform over large areas.

Out of the experience of generations of those who have cultivated this incredible variety of soils and topographical sites have emerged the popular assessments of local land quality that are expressed in the traditional names of fields, soils and hillsides. They sum up in evocative and pithy fashion the characteristics of light sandy soils, lime-rich soils, stony soils, heavy damp soils, soils that are easy to work and soils that are difficult. In western France, for example, the heathland soil (*terre de lande*) – black, cold, wet and heavy – is contrasted with the open, well-drained field land (*terre des champs*).

It is difficult to give a detailed assessment of the value of French soils. It has been estimated that soils of the highest quality cover between one-sixth and one-eighth of France. Included in this category are the loess- (limon-) covered plains of the Nord region (Cambrésis), Picardy and the central Paris basin (Beauce), as well as the smaller limon patches in Normandy and Brittany. Soils of this type are also characteristic of the marls of Lorraine, Normandy and Charolais (northeast Central massif), many alluvial soils of the coastal marshes or valley infloors, the soils of basaltic lava flows (*planèzes*) of the Auvergne, and the black earths of the Limagne basin.

Particularly poor soils cover about a quarter of the country. These include the soils of steep mountain slopes, the skeletal soils of the limestone *causses* and the leached siliceous soils of many superficial deposits. Between the two extremes there is a tremendous variety of intermediate types of soil, which through human effort over thousands of years have been made more suitable for agriculture, thanks to the evolution of techniques for fertilizing the soil and helping it to recover its richness.

5

✤ Vegetation

The plant cover of France is not to be explained solely in terms of natural causes, however fundamental these may be. In a country of such ancient human occupation, cultivated for thousands of years, the influence of nature must be put strictly in its place; a large part of the present-day plant geography must be related to human influences.

1 Climatic factors

Plant associations are to a large extent adapted to present-day climates, which are on the whole favourable to vegetative life. The growing season lasts according to region from six to ten months, given the criterion of a minimal average monthly temperature of 10 °C. However, straightforward climatic statistics do not always indicate the necessary requirements for plant growth. Minimum periods of sunshine, for example, are required for plant growth: the evergreen oak needs an average of 2,800 hours of sunshine a year, the mountain pine (*Pinus mugo*) 2,700 hours, the Scots pine (*Pinus sylvestris*) 2,000 hours, the spruce 1,800 hours and the beech 1,700 hours. Other important limiting factors are early frosts, wide variations in temperature, and winds which dry the soil, accelerate transpiration and even blow down trees, especially on the forest margins.

The present-day climate, however, like the current vegetation cover, represents a mere stage in a long sequence of changes; the vegetation map undoubtedly owes more to the legacy of the palaeoclimates than to the conditions of the present day (Table 2.4). France has always stood at a climatic crossroads, a meeting point for warm influences from the south and cold influences from the north, where oceanic and continental tendencies also met and mingled. The migration into France of species of northern boreal type was favoured during the periods of Quaternary ice advance, whereas the movement of subtropical xerophytic types reflected warm interglacial periods. A major role in these exchanges was played by the Atlantic coastlands and the Saône–Rhône corridor, which enabled the obstacle of the Central massif to be bypassed (Fig. 5.1).

Local climatic and site conditions, for example particularly sheltered areas with favourable soils, have made possible the survival of relict botanical species. It is therefore not surprising to find isolated relics of Mediterranean species in the Paris basin. The Montpellier maple (*Acer monspessulanum*), the box and the pubescent (downy) oak (*Quercus pubescens*), all essentially Mediterranean species, are found as far north as Lyon and on the Poitou gate. Conversely, the beeches surviving in southern and western France are relics of colder periods.

In mountain regions, these climatic changes had even more important consequences, since all vegetation disappeared from the peaks during glacial periods, either as a direct result of the glacial action, or because of severe climatic conditions. Plant species withdrew to the foot of the mountains and to

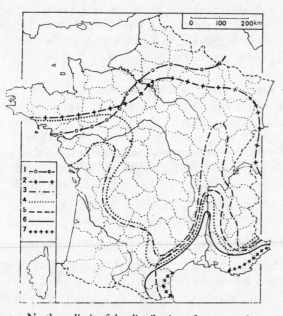

Figure 5.1 Northern limit of the distribution of some southern plant species. 1. Vine 2. Sweet chestnut 3. Maize (corn) 4. Evergreen oak 5. Mulberry 6. Olive 7. Citrus fruits. Source: G. Goujon, 'Les relations entre la végétation française et le climat' in *Géographie universelle* (A. Colin, Paris, 1946), vol. 6, part II (1), Fig. 4.

neighbouring plains, but in warmer periods, when the ice retreated, they were again able to colonize the mountain slopes. The history of mountain vegetation is thus a very short one, dating from after the Würm glaciation.

2 Human factors

The present-day plant geography of France can only be understood in the context of human intervention. Forests which once stretched without a break over almost the whole of the land have now been cleared and cover less than one-fifth of the total area. The degradation of the forests has been brought about not only by their clearance for agricultural purposes but also by the effects of grazing animals. In modern historical periods they have also had to support the charcoal iron industry and supply timber for shipbuilding and other forms of construction, as well as for domestic firewood. Over large areas high forest has given way to coppice and scrub.

Botanists distinguish a threefold sequence in the degradation of a sere: forest, heath and finally grassland. For example, on the slopes of the Corbières (foothills of the eastern Pyrenees), the natural forest climax is evergreen oak. Deforestation produces a heath association of Mediterranean type known as *garrigue*, and the further degradation of the *garrigue* results in a form of grass-steppe known locally as *erm*. These various stages constitute the evergreen oak sere. Although environmental characteristics determine what particular botanical sere will predominate, human action controls its transformation, whether in a progressive or regressive direction, and so determines the vegetational stage that will actually be present.

Human intervention is also seen in the selection of some species at the expense of others. As agricultural utilization and timber working let more light into the forests, the shade-loving beech was replaced by the oak. The extension of the sweet chestnut owes much to human propagation, as it was valued not only because it provided food but because its timber was used for vine stakes. Human action has also been responsible for the introduction of new species such as the orange, the agave, various kinds of palm and the eucalyptus. In Brittany the Scots pine has been introduced for the reafforestation of heathlands.

3 Phytogeographical regions

France can be divided into two major but unequal phytogeographical provinces: the Holarctic province, characterized by northern species, and the Mediterranean province. These in turn are subdivided into sub-provinces and sectors (Fig. 5.2).

3.1 The Holarctic province

This is subdivided into three sub-provinces.

3.1.1 *The Atlantic sub-province*

This is further divided into sectors.

The *Armorico-Franco-Atlantic* sector covers a large part of France, including the whole of western France north of the Charente, most of the Paris basin and central France with the exclusion of those highlands of the Central massif above 1,000 m. Predominant species include the oak in forests which have been subjected to earlier clearance, the beech in areas of more than 600 mm rainfall, and the birch which, together with the oak and the beech woods, plays an important part in the vegetation succession of heathland and waste. Conifers are also present.

The *boreal-Atlantic sector* north of the Somme has, generally speaking, the same composition of forest species as the previous sector, but in different proportion; the Atlantic species are less dominant than northern ones.

The *Aquitanian sector* has more clearly defined characteristics because of its subtropical climate. Atlantic and Mediterranean species are here mingled, including pubescent (downy) oak, Pyrenean oak (*Quercus pyrenaica*) and (in areas nearest the sea) cork-oak, chestnut and maritime pine.

All the original forest types of this Atlantic area degrade into heathland. Broom, gorse, bracken and heather constitute one of the most characteristic landscapes of western France; heathland is a pseudo-natural formation produced by clearing or accidental deforestation. Sun-loving plants such as heather and gorse spread, and as they decompose they acidify the soil, making it difficult, especially on poor soils, for trees to be re-established. In the Aquitaine sector, the heathlands (*touya*) have a slightly different composition. Like the Mediterranean *garrigues*, they show some degree of adaptation to the relatively dry summers; box, wild rose and blackthorn are some characteristic species to be found there.

On the hills and intermediate mountain slopes of the Basque country, oakwoods of Atlantic type degrade into three types of heathland. The most widespread is dominated by bracken and asphodel, often mingled with brambles. In the second type, on lowlands nearer the coast, gorse predominates, while a third type, confined to porous and siliceous soils, is dominated by heather.

On permeable limestone or chalk soils, shrubs and trees are uncharacteristic. Rough pastures with short sparse grass predominate, such as the *Savarts* of Lorraine.

In the Atlantic region, plant associations are determined by the interrelationship of altitude and distance from the sea. The Central massif is cooler and wetter than Brittany, with more sharply defined winters. Oakwoods give way to beechwoods and the hardy Scots pine. The massif does not have a natural

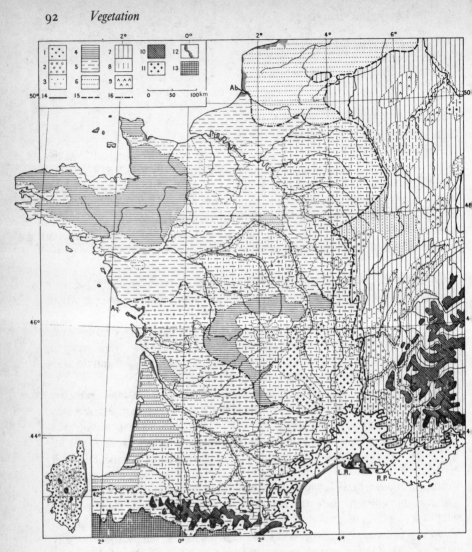

Figure 5.2 Floristic regions and combinations of floristic elements. 1. Characteristic Mediterranean flora 2. Abundant Mediterranean elements 3. Some Mediterranean or sub-Mediterranean elements 4. Atlantic flora 5. Less characteristic Atlantic flora, or Atlantic elements mingled with others 6. Northern type of Atlantic flora 7. Central European flora 8. Central European elements mingled with others 9. Arctic elements mixed with others in the Jura and in the higher parts of the Hercynian massifs 10. Alpine flora of higher parts of Alps and Pyrenees 11. Arctic elements (with sub-Alpine elements near to summits) in the higher parts of the Central massif 12. Coastal flora (Atlantic and Mediterranean) on saline soils and dunes 13. Iberian flora 14. Boundary of Mediterranean region 15. Boundary between the Atlantic and central European regions 16. Limits of floristic sectors in the Atlantic region. Aq.: Limit of Aquitanian sector Ab.: Boundary with northern sector. In the Mediterranean region: LR: Boundary between the

altitudinal zoning of vegetation. Climatically it is as a whole suitable for forest growth, as is demonstrated by the success of the many schemes of reafforestation using either Douglas fir or spruce, a ubiquitous species that can adapt to the most varied conditions of altitude and climate. The upland pastures of the higher parts of the Central massif (Cantal, Chaîne des Dômes, Aubrac, Margeride, Forez and Lozère) are not natural subalpine grasslands but are the result of forest clearing.

3.1.2 *The central European sub-province*

This is confined to eastern France. It is subdivided into two sectors. The *Baltic sector* includes northern Lorraine and the Ardennes; here the Norway maple, beech, hornbeam and the pedunculate oak (*Quercus robur*) mix with ash, birch, sorbus and larch. The *intermediate mountain sector* includes the Vosges, Jura and northern Pre-Alps, beech forests giving way in the higher mountains to firs and spruces.

3.1.3 *The mountain sub-province*

This domain replaces the other domains at heights above about 1,000 m, and is notable for the altitudinal zoning of vegetation. Climatically the mountain zone has cloudy, wet and cold conditions; characteristic species are beech and fir. *The sub-Alpine zone* has a cold but clear climate, with a very great amount of sunshine; characteristic species are mountain pines and larches. Spruce, which is also found in the domain below, accounts for up to 90 per cent of new planting. *The Alpine zone* consists of meadows and high mountain pastures; the only species of trees are of the dwarf variety, such as dwarf willows, clinging to the rocks which give them protection against the wind and some reflected warmth.

The upper limit of forest varies considerably in altitude. The present tree-line is not, moreover, a natural one but reflects human utilization of both the forests and the Alpine pastures. In the Alps, the upper limit of the forest varies from 1,800 m in the Chartreuse to 2,300 m in the Haute-Maurienne, reaching 2,500 m for isolated trees. In the Pyrenees, the trees disappear at about 2,300 m, but the height of the tree-line varies from the Atlantic to the Mediterranean. The youthful relief and vigorous erosion characteristic of the high mountains result in impeded drainage, favouring the development of sphagnum-peat bogs, marshes, reeds and moss.

The botanical contrasts between Alps and Pyrenees can be related to differences of latitude, climate and general ecological environment. The contrasting extent of Quaternary glaciation is also significant. The Pyrenees have a

western or Languedoc sector and the Rhône sector RP: Boundary between the Rhône sector and the Provençal sector. Source: E. de Martonne, *Géographie universelle* (A. Colin, Paris, 1942), vol. 6, part I, Fig. 158 (after H. Gaussen).

greater number of endemic species than the Alps, and more Mediterranean species or species derived from the vegetation of the Tertiary era.

There are also numerous contrasts within each of the mountain ranges, reflecting local conditions of rainfall, slope and exposure. On the outer chains of the northern Alps, where the rainfall is high, fir and spruce predominate, the upper limit of the montane forest is low, and pseudo-Alpine pasture occupies the sub-Alpine zone. In the southern outer Alps, which are drier, the original forest cover consisted of beech and Scots pine, but these have disappeared, having degenerated into *garrigue* and dry pasture. The climate of the inner Alps is drier and sunnier, with the Scots pine dominating the montane zone and the larch the sub-Alpine zone. The Scots pine is also much used for afforestation; many pinewoods in the central Pyrenees, the inner Alps and the east of the Central massif were planted in the nineteenth and twentieth centuries on fallow land, heathland and abandoned meadows. As well as in the higher parts of the fold mountains, upland grasslands are to be found in the Vosges (*chaumes*) and the highest parts of the Central massif, where their presence is to be explained either by exceptional natural conditions (the permeability of volcanic deposits) or in relation to human pastoral activities.

3.2 The Mediterranean province

This province contrasts sharply with the remainder of France. Summer is the adverse season because of the severity of its drought, destroying plants unable to tolerate months of fierce heat and no rain. This explains the predominance of annuals which die off in the summer, of tuberous and bulbous plants, of xerophytic plants which reduce transpiration by means of their spiny, woolly or glossy leaves, and of aromatic species. There are thousands of endemic species: stone pines (*Pinus pinea*), Aleppo pines (*Pinus halepensis*), evergreen or holm oaks (*Quercus ilex*), known in southern French as *yeuse*, kermès oak (*Quercus coccifera*), olive and all the heathers, cistuses and lavenders. It should perhaps be added that the island of Corsica, isolated since the Pliocene era, has a highly individualistic Mediterranean flora.

In the rare wooded areas, the pines or evergreen oaks stand widely spaced, with an undergrowth of prickly shrubs. On the hills and plateaus of Mediterranean France the predominant vegetation is *maquis* and *garrigue*. *Maquis* consists of dense thickets of shrubs, 2 m or more in height, brightened in spring by flowers of cistus, broom and tree-heather: some *maquis* may be a natural climax vegetation, but in most cases it is the result of human activity. The more open rock-heath known as *garrigue* can be regarded as a degraded form of *maquis*.

Where there is a permanent supply of water, whether at the surface or underground, the vegetation changes and the trees – poplars, willows, alders and maples – growing among green meadows, form landscapes of lush beauty which reflect the association of heat and adequate water.

Paradoxically, it is not easy to lay down a precise boundary to this Mediterranean province. This reflects the legacy of palaeoclimates and the effect of contrasting site factors, particularly of the border regions, where mountains alternate with lowland corridors and projecting ridges with valleys. Botanists somewhat reluctantly acknowledge the value of the olive as an index in defining this boundary (Fig. 5.1).

4 The present-day forest cover

It is obvious that forests today do not occupy as great a surface area as would exist if natural conditions prevailed. Otherwise they would cover the whole of France, with the exception of a few particularly arid Mediterranean areas, a few windswept stretches of the Atlantic coast and some waterlogged soils.

The present-day rural landscape has emerged from the clearance of this original forest landscape. It is even uncertain whether the forest from which the original medieval landscape emerged was primeval forest. Some clearances certainly reoccupied second-growth areas subsequent to the Germanic invasions, following the end of the Gallo-Roman period. A parallel phenomenon was seen as a result of the Hundred Years War, when 'the forests came back with the English'.

This is not the place for retracing in detail the stages in the clearing of this vast forest cover. The most intense clearances took place in the tenth–thirteenth centuries, the fifteenth century, the second half of the eighteenth century (following the edict of 13 August 1766) and the nineteenth century. Between 1828 and 1908 an estimated 489,000 ha of forest were cleared; this was very largely made possible by the disposal of large areas of state forests, which declined in extent from 117,000 ha in 1831–5 to 72,000 ha in 1868. Since the Second World War, clearances have continued in regions such as eastern Champagne and Berry as part of a drive to increase the area available for cultivation. Sometimes clearances have permitted the introduction of new crops, such as strawberry-growing in Périgord. Clearances have averaged 10,000 ha annually.

Reafforestation has always gone hand in hand with clearance. Notable stages in this development include the afforestation of the Landes of Gascony with pines from 1857 onwards, the reafforestation of the Sologne from 1859, and of mountain areas from 1860. There has also been a general tendency to replant existing low-grade woodland and waste land with conifers and to transform areas of scrub into high forest.

The policy of reafforestation has assumed increasing importance since the Second World War. The National Forest Fund, initiated in 1946, has planted or replanted more than 1.1 million ha in twenty years. But the official reafforestation policy may in certain regions conflict with official policies for the improvement of farm structure and with the needs of particular agricultural systems.

At present, forest covers 14 million ha, in other words nearly one-quarter of the whole of France (Fig. 5.3). The largest areas are found in northeast France, on the scarps of the eastern Paris basin, the Ardennes and the Vosges massifs, and the Jura chains. Here most departments have high proportions of their area under forest, some over 35 per cent. In the area of the Vosges massif, Vosges Department records 42 per cent and Haut-Rhin 37 per cent under forest. Jura Department has 36 per cent, while in the scarps and vales between the massifs, Haute-Saône and Haute-Marne each have about 37 per cent. Other densely forested areas include the Landes (Landes Department 60 per cent, Gironde 45 per cent), the Alpine and Pyrenean chains, with a forest cover of 20–30 per cent,

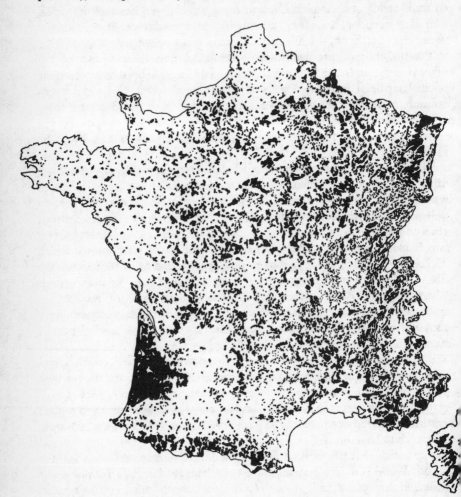

Figure 5.3 Distribution of forests and woodland in France. Source: G. Plaisance, *Guide des forêts de France* (La Nef de Paris, 1961).

and some massifs bordering the Mediterranean (Var 49 per cent). The lowest rates are to be found in the Armorican massif and the Nord region. The Central massif also has relatively few forests.

The present distribution of forests can in the first place be related to natural conditions, above all to areas of poor soil. These include sandy soils, as on some outcrops of the Paris basin, on the sandstone Lower Vosges, the Sologne and the Landes. Skeletal limestone soils bear forests on the dip-slope plateaus of the Lorraine scarplands and on the Langres plateau. Heavy clay soils are often left under forest, as in the Argonne or on the clay-with-flints of Normandy, while the Hardt forest of Alsace grows on gravel spreads along the Rhine. Tertiary planation surfaces, characterized by poor soils developed on sandy-clay deposits, with frequent occurrence of hardpan, play an important role in forest location. Among areas of this type are the forests of upper Perche (southwest fringe of the Paris basin), of the plateaus of Touraine, and of the Landes.

Human action has also been significant; indeed forest and human occupance are to a large degree mutually exclusive, forest being found only in areas of low population. Forests very often survived because they formed frontier marches between different peoples or regions, such as the forests of Eu, Bray and Lihons separating Normandy and Picardy.

Forest locations also correspond to differences of function. Some are purely 'wood-producing machines', but multiple functions are more characteristic. As well as being sources of timber, forests may serve to limit gullying in mountain areas, to fix coastal dunes against wind erosion, or to help exhausted soils recover. The use of forests for hunting by the elite few is a long tradition, but increasingly they are coming to serve a recreational function for the many, especially on the fringes of great cities, like Fontainebleau and other forests of the Ile-de-France.

Some forests are of positively regional extent: the Landes forest covers 1 million ha, the Ardennes forest 100,000 ha, the Vosges 95,000 ha, the Maures 67,000 ha. Even the forests which form only one element in a regional landscape can be very extensive: the forest of Orléans covers 45,500 ha, Fontainebleau 25,000 ha, Compiègne 14,500 ha. Frequently, however, forests and woods are fragmented, distributed according to differences of soil, slope, shape of parcels and basic rural structure; fragmentation of parcels is accompanied by a corresponding fragmentation of the woodland cover. The position has been made worse by scattered plantations on former agricultural parcels by owners who have left the land, a form of social fallow. Such planting was initially encouraged by the National Forest Fund. As early as 1954 there was a legislative attempt to forbid such piecemeal reafforestation. In order to avoid the intrusion of small parcels of forest into the cultivated land, a decree passed in 1960 made provision for the defining of zones in which the planting of trees would be either banned or strictly controlled.

Like other agricultural products, forest production has to adapt to variations in demand, but by its nature it is unable to adapt quickly or even within the space of a few years. This explains the almost constant disequilibrium that exists between forests and economic realities. A third of forests are either unproductive or not regularly exploited. Another third consists of high forest, properly managed for regular timber production. The remaining third is worked as coppice or coppice-with-standards, producing firewood, pit-props and second-grade hardwood timber, which is in decreasing demand. How a forest is exploited is closely related to ownership. Communal and private forests have a much smaller proportion of high forest than state forests, which correspondingly have only 17 per cent of their area in coppice or coppice-with-standards. Broadleaved species occupy 67 per cent of the forest area in France, as compared with only 30 per cent in the German Federal Republic. The productivity of French forests is also lower than that of neighbouring countries. Thus paradoxically France, in spite of its great area of forest land, has to import 57 per cent of its needs of wood and wood products, in particular softwoods for the manufacture of wood-pulp.

There is clearly a need for a major and necessarily lengthy transformation of the French forests, which would involve the afforestation of a further million hectares, the conversion of coppice and scrub into high forest, and the substitution of conifers for broadleaved species; the optimum rate of afforestation would be in the order of 27 per cent. To attain these objectives a law was passed in 1963 'for the improvement of production and of the basic structure of forests in France'. To the private individuals who own 65 per cent of French forests, the communes which hold 21 per cent and the foresters of the 14 per cent in the hands of the state, it assigned the task 'of ensuring the biological balance of the country and of satisfying its needs for wood and other forest products'. It set up Regional Centres for Forest Properties (Centres Régionaux de la Propriété Forestière) to encourage new developments and to lay down the direction of advance. In 1966 both state and communal forests were placed under the management of the National Forest Service (Office National des Forêts).

These laws and institutions are merely the latest manifestation of a long tradition of forest protection which is said to go back to an edict of Philippe Auguste in 1219. Subsequent stages included an edict by Francis I in 1515, Colbert's edict on rivers and forests in 1669, and the national Forest Code of 1827.

Today, protection of forests and wooded areas in both urban and rural areas is governed by an increasingly comprehensive body of laws and regulations (circular of 1 August 1977). The effectiveness of these measures varies, however, according to whether the forests are owned by the state or by private individuals, and whether or not they are located in communes which have a communal land-use plan (*plan d'occupation des sols – POS*). A particular problem of forest conservation is that the forest area is inevitably seen as offering much less contentious sites than agricultural land for major construction projects such as motorways, railways and power lines. Forests are also constantly under the threat of residential development. It must also not be forgotten that forest fires destroy on average 35,000 ha of forest a year (90,000 ha in 1976), with the Mediterranean forests the worst affected.

It has to be accepted that in spite of all the regulations and exhortations, there is a lack of real commitment, both on the part of individuals and the state, to the modernization of the French forest, and rapid progress is not to be expected.

6

⚜ Hydrology and water supply

1 Hydrogeology and groundwater sources

Very large parts of France are underlain by sedimentary deposits, in particular by permeable chalk, limestone, sandstone, sand and gravel. The country is in consequence well supplied with groundwater from alluvial, perched and underground aquifers.

It is difficult to imagine the enormous quantities of water which seep into the aquifers; the chalk in northern France receives 102,000 cu m daily, while the figure for the carboniferous limestone in the same region, fed from an area of 290 sq km, is 153,000 cu m. In crystalline areas also, not all precipitation is lost by run-off into the rivers. Much is absorbed into localized water-tables, their extent determined by the thickness of sandy, weathered material. Even the unweathered crystalline rocks do not provide an impermeable barrier to water, which is able to penetrate along joints and fissures.

The characteristics of aquifers depend on the way in which they are fed, but above all on their size. Large aquifers are little affected by fluctuations, being able to smooth out variations due to drought and to recover losses rapidly because of their extensive catchment areas. On the other hand, in areas of crystalline rocks, a three-month drought exhausts the reserves of the localized water-tables, and it takes three months after the return of rainy conditions to refill them.

The water-table is drained by springs. These may be at outcrop, where the base of the aquifer is in contact with an impermeable layer, or they may occur where valleys cut down far enough to intersect the water-table. Springs are particularly important geographically, with their own distinctive morphology. A characteristic flush vegetation develops round them, and their soils are distinguished by intense chemical decomposition and biological activity.

Springs are closely linked to the fluctuations of the water-table, especially along the superficial valleys cutting down into the aquifer. The downstream movement of springs is one of the transformations of the natural environment that can be perceived in the span of a lifetime. There is widespread evidence of these movements in place-names, and in the sites of villages once grouped round a spring which is now situated several kilometres downstream.

Not all limestone areas have major and coherent aquifers, which are found only in rocks that are sufficiently fissured and provided with bedding planes to allow a single interconnecting body of water to develop. Often there are perched or local water-tables, independent of each other, or unconnected stretches of underground circulation. In such cases the depths from the surface at which water can be reached vary greatly from one commune to another. In karstic regions underground water-tables are replaced by whole networks of underground circulation.

Human activity, whether deliberate or not, increasingly impinges on the characteristics of aquifers. This is particularly true of major civil-engineering works; the building of the Donzère–Mondragon canal alongside the Rhône seriously disturbed the behaviour of underground water. In some places the water-table rose to the surface; elsewhere inflow to the aquifer was reduced, lowering the water-table and producing desiccation of the soil. Growing needs for water have resulted in increasing demands on underground supplies. In some regions the cumulation of withdrawals by village wells, for industrial uses and to supply nearby towns, has reached a critical point in relation to available groundwater supplies. Major urban and industrial needs have increasingly to be met by drawing on distant sources outside the region concerned.

In the meantime, regional water-tables are rapidly falling to a critical threshold. In northern France the surface of the chalk water-table fell from 17 m to 8 m above sea level between 1945 and 1959. Between February 1959 and February 1960, there was a further fall from +8 m to +4.8 m. Fortunately the mass exodus at weekends and holiday periods from Paris and other large cities makes it possible for the aquifers to recover, so avoiding the exhaustion of supplies in the height of summer.

2 Surface hydrology

The flow characteristics of French rivers reflect on the one hand their courses and long-profiles, on the other their climatic and hydrological conditions.

2.1 River regions and flow characteristics

Flow characteristics reflect a range of factors, notably the longitudinal and cross-profile of the stream concerned, the geological and physiographic characteristics of its catchment area, and the seasonal distribution and nature of precipitation.

France can be broadly divided into two hydrological regions by drawing a line from the Basque country to the Vosges. North and northwest of the line, relief is subdued, river basins are extensive, and long-profiles are extremely gentle. Precipitation is abundant, falling mainly in autumn and winter; the existence of widespread areas of permeable limestone, chalk and sand means that much of the precipitation infiltrates into the ground. When combined with losses by evaporation this means that the proportion of precipitation entering the river is relatively low, giving flow coefficients below 0.6 and even 0.4 over much of the region (the flow coefficient is the ratio between total precipitation and the volume of river flow). River regimes tend to be very regular throughout the year with no period of extremely low flow. Similarly, periods of extremely high flow are also rare, and flood peaks are low.

In southern and southeastern France, by contrast, a much more accentuated relief results in steep profiles. Characteristically, basins combine mountainous areas upstream with contrasting lowland sections. The distribution of precipitation throughout the year is much more irregular, particularly in the Mediterranean area. A large part of this precipitation is accumulated during the cold season in the form of snow and ice, to be released in spring and summer. Flow coefficients are high, averaging 0.6 to 0.7, but reaching 0.8 in mountain catchments. Flow characteristics are highly irregular, reflecting not only the distribution of rainfall but other influences such as snow melt.

Measurement of the relationship between stream flow and the area of river basin concerned (expressed in litres/second per sq km) shows clearly the difference between the two major regions: figures for the Seine (6.7) and the Loire (7.5) contrast with those of the Tarn (14.3), the Hérault (17.8), the Ain (35.4) and the Arve at Chamonix (70.0). Types of river regime are illustrated in Table 6.1

2.1.1 Regimes of northern and western France

These are almost entirely pluvial in nature (that is, derived from rainfall), either of oceanic type or, more rarely, of a very regular continental type.

2.1.2 Regimes of southern and eastern France

Here there is much more variation.

Mediterranean pluvial (the Hérault at Montagnac), as illustrated by the mountain streams of the Vivarais and the Cévennes, which are as dry as Saharan wadis in summer and are raging torrents in autumn and spring.

Table 6.1 *Types of river regime*

Regime	Jan.	Feb.	Mar.	Apr.	May	June	July	Aug.	Sept.	Oct.	Nov.	Dec.
Oceanic pluvial												
Saône at Auxonne	1.58	*1.95*	1.50	1.01	0.85	0.57	0.42	0.34	0.38	0.76	1.14	1.56
Mediterranean pluvial												
Hérault at Montagnac	1.06	0.94	*1.75*	1.24	0.86	0.48	0.20	0.13	0.65	1.04	1.73	*1.89*
Mountain nival												
Romanche at Chazeaux	0.25	0.23	0.33	0.73	2.14	*2.49*	2.04	1.52	0.98	0.56	0.42	0.32
Nivo-pluvial												
Fier at Val-de-Fier	0.92	0.94	1.24	*1.52*	1.44	0.82	0.68	0.62	0.68	0.88	1.12	1.14
Oceanic pluvial–nival												
Dordogne at Argentat	1.39	1.41	*1.53*	1.40	1.07	0.69	0.47	0.35	0.40	0.63	1.11	1.42
Mediterranean pluvial–nival												
Ardèche at Vallon	1.20	1.25	1.50	1.42	0.90	0.42	0.15	0.17	0.45	1.37	*1.67*	1.51
Complex regimes:												
Rhône at Lyon	0.78	0.78	0.95	1.10	1.14	1.21	*1.25*	1.11	0.93	0.92	0.91	0.88
Rhône at Givors	1.09	1.07	*1.16*	1.15	1.03	0.96	0.93	0.82	0.73	0.85	1.05	*1.12*
Rhône at Valence	0.95	0.95	1.07	1.14	*1.17*	1.16	1.02	0.84	0.74	0.87	1.02	*1.04*
Rhône at Beaucaire	0.99	0.95	1.08	1.15	1.20	1.14	0.90	0.73	0.70	0.93	*1.12*	1.07

Note: The figures are coefficients of monthly flow, that is to say the ratio of average monthly flow to average annual flow. Months of peak flow are given in italic.
Source: M. Pardé, *Fleuves et rivières* (A. Colin, Paris, 1968).

Pluvio-nival, oceanic type (the Dordogne at Argentat, on the boundary of the two major regions), where cold season rain of oceanic type combines with snow melt in March and April.

Pluvio-nival, Mediterranean type (the Ardèche at Vallon), with a pluvio-nival maximum in spring and a pluvial maximum in autumn. In the mountains the flow is predominantly derived from melted snow and ice.

Nival, mountain type (the Romanche at Chazeaux). In the interior basins of mountain regions, regimes are almost exclusively of this snow-melt type.

Nivo-pluvial (Fier), where the cold-season pluvial maximum is prolonged into the spring by snow melt.

The great river systems obviously have more complex types of regime; the Garonne and the Rhône are two good examples. The Garonne unites two types of regime, since it derives its flow both from the pluvio-nival rivers of the Central massif and the nivo-glacial rivers and mountain streams of the Pyrenees.

The Rhône shows an even more remarkable series of influences (Table 6.1). When it enters France it has a glacial or approximately pluvio-nival regime, with a hot-season maximum (Lyon). Downstream from Lyon, the Saône introduces a very different element: coming from northern France, it adds a cold-season pluvial maximum to the spring–early summer nival maximum that the Rhône derives from the Alps. At Valence, the Isère introduces a powerful nivo-glacial influence, once more accentuating the warm-season maximum. Finally, the Rhône is joined by a number of tributaries of Mediterranean regime, including the Durance and right-based tributaries such as the Gard and the Ardèche. Their spring and autumn maxima help to produce a somewhat more balanced regime in the main river. At its mouth at Beaucaire the Rhône has two maxima, in spring and late autumn, a pronounced summer minimum in the Mediterranean dry season, and a secondary minimum in January, reflecting the locking-up of mountain precipitation in the form of snow and ice.

2.2 High-flow characteristics

Particularly high flows, leading to flooding, have a range of possible causes. They may derive from a climatic accident such as exceptionally heavy rain, or the sudden arrival of warmer weather which melts the snow, especially if such an accident coincides with one of the normal high-flow periods. Sometimes two climatic accidents are combined, for instance when very heavy rainfall coincides with a period of rapid and intense thaw (Fig. 6.1).

The extent of flooding is related to the long-profiles and cross-sections of river valleys, that is to say to the speed with which the flood develops, and to the possibilities for flood water to spread out both within the normal river banks and over the flood plain; the same areas are covered at each flood.

The speed at which the flood peak is attained varies considerably from basin to basin. It is only a few hours on mountain streams in the Cévennes, between 20

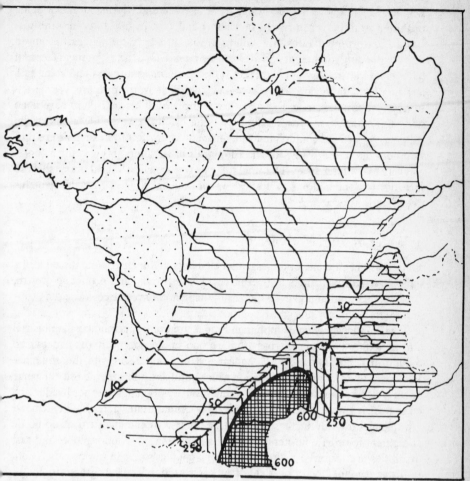

Figure 6.1 Severity of flooding of French rivers. The figures indicate the ratio between average flow and the highest recorded flood. Source: J. Corbal, 'Érosion et grands cours d'eau en France', *L'Information Géographique*, May–June 1962, p. 115.

and 30 hours on the Garonne at Toulouse, and from eight to nine days on the Seine at Paris. In normally tranquil regions such as the Paris basin, catastrophic floods occur only when flood peaks from two or three major tributaries coincide. If, on the other hand, the peaks from the various tributaries arrive in succession, the result is an extended period of high flow but no actual flooding.

Vulnerable areas such as towns may be protected by the building of dykes, and bridges can be strengthened by increasing the number of piers. Such measures, however, may raise flood peaks and cause even greater flooding upstream. Each river has its own type of flood. The Garonne has the biggest floods, rising to a height of 11 m above the low-water mark at Agen and Marmande. The Seine upstream from Paris can rise by between 3 and 5 m. In July 1977 in southwest France, a torrential rainstorm falling on an already saturated earth caused terrible flooding to a height of 8 m along the Gers. Since the beginning of April it had rained for two days out of three: 'At first the earth absorbed all the rain,' said a farmer from the region, 'but very soon it couldn't absorb any more. We started to worry about our crops. Last year it was drought. This year there have been non-stop cloudbursts. Just lately, everything has been washed away down the valley, as the ground couldn't hold anything any more.' It only needed 24 hours of rain between 7 and 8 July for the tributaries of the Gers to burst their banks, carrying everything away. The final toll was very heavy: 18 dead, more than 20 missing, tens of millions of francs' worth of damage, and four departments declared disaster areas.

3 Water-resource problems

Water has become one of the essential elements in the environment, one of the most rare and most fragile of resources. Demographic and economic growth, urban concentration and ever-increasing depletion of resources raise the problem of the adequacy of water resources.

Total annual water consumption in France, for domestic, municipal, industrial and agricultural purposes, rose from 19,000 million cu m in 1955 to 35,000 million in 1970. These figures appear low by comparison with the 165,000–180,000 million cu m of precipitation which annually infiltrates the soil of France or runs off into the rivers. Average annual consumption of water per head is 458 cu m (Great Britain 225, Netherlands 964, United States 2,720). The demand for water constantly increases: urban needs rise as the standard of domestic equipment improves, farmers are turning more and more to irrigation, and vast quantities are required by industry and as cooling water in power generation. Industry accounts for 43 per cent of all water used in France; agriculture for 34 per cent; public use for 14 per cent and domestic use for 9 per cent.

The water consumed in France is derived from a range of sources: by pumping from underground sources (31 per cent), by abstraction of surface water (52 per cent) and from springs (17 per cent). The corresponding percentages for the first two categories in the German Federal Republic are 75 and 9, and in Belgium 71 and 29. The average cost per cubic metre is basically higher for surface water than for underground supplies. In an average year, the French population uses only a little more than 4 per cent of total rainfall for economic purposes and only a little more than 1 per cent for domestic consumption. These percentages could appear reassuring were it not for the spatial discordancy between the distribution of annual average rainfall and the distribution of demand (heavily concentrated in the low-rainfall Paris region). Above all, there is the problem of the seasonal variation and of the considerable variation in the quantity of rainfall received from year to year.

Problems also arise in relation to effluent disposal, involving organic, physical and chemical pollution. In 1975, for example, half of the effluent of the Paris sewers was discharged untreated into the Seine. Forms of pollution include organic or suspended matter and toxic or nitrogenous substances; the latter group involves toxic products such as chromium, cadmium, lead and cyanide. These dangerous chemical pollutants are derived from the waste products of the chemical industry and other industrial plants, and from metallic ore treatment. Waste salt from potash mines is a particular problem in the Alsace water-table and the Rhine. The increasing use of agricultural fertilizer is a source of pollution of both groundwater and river waters; some herbicides and insecticides are particularly dangerous.

4 Water policy

Measures against floods and against the kind of pollution that might lead to epidemics are of long standing; Paris itself was too often the victim of flooding for the government to ignore the problem. As early as the eighteenth century it had been suggested that the Cure, a tributary of the Yonne (one of the Seine headwaters), should be regulated by a system of reservoirs. After the 1924 flood, a first generation of flood-retention reservoirs was built on the Cure and the Yonne. Then after 1949 a second emergency programme led to the building of the Seine reservoir on the Morge, another headstream of the river (completed 1966), and the Marne reservoir, covering 4,800 ha and able to retain 350 million cu m of water (completed in 1974). But only in recent years has there been a real attempt to draw up a coherent water policy for France as a whole. Legislation in 1964 laid down regulations for the use of water, set up a National Water Committee, and created six regional Water Authorities (Agences de Bassin) covering Seine–Normandy, Artois–Picardy, Rhine–Meuse, Rhône–Mediterranean France–Corsica, Loire–Brittany and Garonne–Adour. Each authority has three institutions: the Basin Committee, which is an assembly representing all interests in the region concerned, the Basin Mission, consisting of representatives of all official bodies concerned with water-supply and utilization, which co-ordinates research and new developments, and finally the Financial Agency, a public body which receives the dues paid by those who consume water or discharge effluent.

The fight against pollution began in 1969; between 1971 and 1976, 3,000 million francs were invested in the fight against industrial pollution by financing water-treatment plants and special installations for dealing with heavily polluted effluent from industrial plants. Aid is also directed towards the development of 'clean' technology such as the recycling of water, the recovery of industrial pollutants for recycling, and pollution-free methods of manufacture. Plans are now established for each branch of industry, laying down the standard to be applied and the time-limits within which they must be achieved. French rivers have been classified into four categories according to their degree of pollution.

Between 1975 and 1995, 13,000,000,000 francs are to be spent under a 'clean rivers' programme. In 1976, the government adopted a 15-year plan whose aim was to restore the quality of the waterways by the systematic purification of industrial and domestic effluent, to ensure a minimum rate of river flow at all times of the year, and generally to assist the fight against pollution. This was mainly to be achieved by the building of about 60 reservoirs which would retain 2,000 million cu m of water to add to the 8,000 million cu m already retained in reservoirs constructed for electric power generation. Clearly a construction programme on this scale raises major problems of management and finance. In addition, proposals for reservoir construction are opposed by conservationists, owners whose land would be flooded, farmers and residents of villages who would be made homeless. On the other hand it is a general experience that reservoirs, once established, can become of considerable local benefit through the development of leisure activities and the attraction of tourists.

It is clear that water policy, because it affects the most widespread and dynamic element of the environment, is necessarily one of the most difficult aspects of spatial planning. It is inevitably beset with clashes of interests and controversies of all kinds.

7

✣ The environment and environmental policies

1 The diversity of natural environments

The purpose of a geographical study lies not in the successive analysis of the individual natural elements such as relief, climate, soil and hydrology, but in the consequences of their combination. The distribution and spatial differentiation of each element are determined both by its own genetic and developmental processes and by interaction with the patterns of the other elements.

Climatic types and botanical regions have their own distinctive limits, defined by purely climatic or purely botanical factors, but the first is also affected by variations in relief, the second by both relief and soil. Relief factors tend to produce a threefold division: northern and western France; central France; eastern and southern France. The climatic pattern clearly and simultaneously contrasts northern with southern France, and oceanic western France with continental, mountainous eastern France. The combination of these patterns produces five landscape types whose boundaries are not clearly drawn, but whose characteristics are well defined.

The northwest, stretching from Vendée to Champagne, is the France of plains, climatically dominated by oceanic influences, with a plentiful rainfall. This is a France of great agricultural potential, of uniform environment; its peaceful landscapes bear the mark of centuries of human activity. Outcrops of bare rock are seldom seen; nearly everywhere it is covered with thick, moist fertile soil on which grow forests, meadows and crops.

The northeast is clearly defined by the survival of an extensive forest cover, except in Alsace. This is the France of plateaus and wooded limestone cuestas; except in a few favoured *pays* and regions the soil is poor. Climatically, continental characteristics become more marked.

The southwest, Aquitanian in the broad sense of the term, is a type of western France differentiated by its own distinctive climatic conditions. It is a country of plains, hills and plateaus; D. Faucher called it 'an unfinished Midi', but greener, richer in plant and tree species, less dotted with scree and skeletal soils than the true Midi.

The southeast stretches from the Limagne basins of the Central massif to the plains of Provence, and from Roussillon to the Saône trough. This part of France is a patchwork full of natural contrasts between escarpments and basins or between snow-covered or arid plateaus and fertile valleys. Soil and plant cover is discontinuous, broken by the stony expanses of limestone plateaus, by precipitous faces where the limestone gleams white, and by mountain slopes gullied by erosion. Good cultivable land is found only in small, fragmented and isolated patches.

The mountains constitute a separate and distinctive region of their own. Within each of these major landscape types, however, local combinations of natural factors have created a great number of different *pays*. The extreme landscape diversity of France is the essential lesson to be learned from this analysis. Throughout the country there are 'good' and 'bad' regions, districts lashed by winds and others that are sheltered, slopes that are favourable, regions that attract occupance and others that repel it. This diversity of natural environments explains both the importance in France of the concepts of natural region and *pays* and their persistence despite the intensity of human intervention. In fact, any talk of 'natural environment' in France is an abuse of language. The natural environment in the strict sense of a stable ecological climax unaffected by human intervention has been almost non-existent over the whole of France since the early Middle Ages, and in many regions such as the limon plateaus of the Paris basin and various limestone plateaus, even since Neolithic times.

The natural environment has been humanized for centuries, but the natural processes, whether physical or chemical, which produced it continue to operate. The previous chapters have shown their power, their occasional excesses, and the fragility of the ecological balance in spite of the position of France in the most tranquil sector of the zone of temperate climate. In the short term, not a year goes by without at least one climatic, hydrological or geological disaster to remind us of the active presence of these natural elements. Their consequences are all the more serious in a populated, humanized country such as France, which is not prepared for such disasters, since they are always perceived as exceptional.

In the long term, there is also the problem of the conservation of plant, soil and water resources, which it is essential to preserve from damage or exhaustion. The greatest human influence on environment is doubtless the least visible, the product of the drive for greater agricultural productivity by means of an increasing degree of interference in the natural, biological and physico-chemical processes. Over the 15 years 1954–69, for example, farmers multiplied their use of fertilizers sixfold and of pesticides elevenfold. The suppression of hedges in *bocage* areas causes the disappearance of small burrowing animals which prey on field-mice, with the result that the latter have to be killed by poisoned bait. The suppression of hedges also modifies microclimates, dries the upper soil horizons and encourages wind erosion.

2 Environmental policies

In France, as in other developed countries, concern for the protection of nature has a long history. As early as 1853, a group of French painters called for the creation of a nature reserve in the forest of Fontainebleau; in 1901 a society was founded for the protection of the landscape, and in 1930 the Commission des Sites came into official existence.

2.1 The awakening of public opinion

Beginning in the late 1960s, when the results of economic growth bore witness to the unquestionable transformation of France and the world-wide rise in standards of living and human welfare, French society, like all others in the developed countries of the West, became open to trends of thought which had hitherto affected only a minority. There was widespread concern at the excesses of a type of progress and growth measured exclusively in economic terms, at the excesses of the consumer economy and of an urbanization typified by the megalopolis, with its millions of inhabitants, the vast housing project (*grand ensemble*) and the tower block.

Population, because of its growth, increasing concentration and excessive density, has pushed well beyond the thresholds up to which the ecological balance is maintained by self-regulating mechanisms. For example, the seasonal concentration of people in tourist resorts has led to dysfunctions such as the failure of the food distribution system or the breakdown of waste-disposal mechanisms.

The student-led unrest of 1968 accelerated these trends in public conscious-ness. People looked with a new eye at the landscapes in which they lived, and the deterioration of the environment came as a shock to them; they were made aware of the absurdity of the daily round of travel–work–sleep (*métro–boulot–dodo*) and the artificiality of a life lived in two distinct compartments, one devoted to work, the other to leisure.

There was a growing perception of a vital need to preserve the heritage of landscape and buildings and to ensure the protection and improvement of the environment and the quality of life. The term 'ecology' came to be applied to a varied range of movements concerned with community control of decision-making, public participation in administration, the quality of life, the defence of the environment, public transport, town planning, pedestrianization, nuclear power-stations and bio-degradable packaging. This tide of opinion was powerful enough to bring about changes in administrative and ministerial structures. At ministerial level the first move was the creation in 1971 of a new Ministry for the Protection of Nature and the Environment. After many changes – State Secretariat for the Environment (Secrétariat d'Etat à l'Environnement) and Ministry for the Quality of Life (Ministère de la Qualité de la Vie) – it was, symbolically, eventually subsumed into the powerful ministry which since the war had successively drawn its title from Reconstruction, from Town Planning and from Equipment, and which between 1978 and 1981 became the Ministry for the Environment and the Quality of Life (Ministère de l'Environnement et du Cadre de Vie). An independent Ministry of the Environment was re-established in 1971.

In 1972 an interministerial group for the evaluation of the environment (Groupe Interministériel d'Evaluation de l'Environnement) was set up. The titles of the working parties and the published reports are indicative of the acknowledgment of new factors grouped together under the ecology banner: they included the concept of the quality of life, the use of space, natural resources, energy and environment, and the mathematical evaluation of the environment. It was succeeded in October 1978 by a Commission for Evaluating the Benefits of the Natural Heritage (Commission des Comptes du Patrimoine Naturel). Its task was to integrate into the national accounting system those elements of the natural heritage which had hitherto been disregarded. Many public agencies and organizations were created, including in 1979 an agency in Metz to fight air pollution, 16 Regional Delegates for the Environment, acting as contacts of the ministry, 9 regional workshops (*ateliers*) dedicated to the landscape, and a national institute in Angers directed to the recycling of waste.

Private initiatives have often been the first to emerge, with the establishment of pressure groups whose actions were sometimes generously motivated but too impulsive. Such organizations included the private foundation Space for Tomorrow, founded in 1977, and the Foundation for Nature, launched in 1979. At the same time laws relating to the protection of buildings (1975), the disposal and recycling of waste (1975) and the protection of nature (1976) were passed.

2.2 The protection of the environment

At the same time the environmental policy took on a more all-embracing aspect, being concerned with the impact of environmental change and applying specific regulations to sites of outstanding importance. A new spatial classification was introduced, with the object of protecting some regions from human impact deemed to be harmful, and identifying areas which have been damaged but which

:ould be restored to their natural condition for educational or recreational
purposes.

2.2.1 Nature parks and reserves

The creation of nature parks and reserves has a threefold objective: firstly, to
protect nature at its most picturesque and with regard for its most valuable

NATIONAL PARK (with peripheral zones)

NATIONAL PARK proposed or in preparation

REGIONAL NATURE PARK

REGIONAL NATURE PARK proposed or in preparation

•3   NATURE RESERVE

Figure 7.1 National parks, nature parks and nature reserves. Source: Ministère de
l'Environnement et du Cadre de Vie.

associations of flora and fauna; secondly, to preserve pockets of wild nature in a world in which people normally spend both their working days and their leisure time shoulder to shoulder. Thirdly, to make possible a rural revival in areas where both agricultural and industrial development have proved inadequate.

(i) National parks. These were set up under legislation in July 1960. Legally speaking, a National Park is a state establishment under ministerial control. It must have its own administrative council, advised by a scientific committee. The first to be created, the Vanoise National Park in the Alps (60,000 ha) dates from 1963; it was succeeded by the parks of Port-Cros island in the Mediterranean (1963), Western Pyrenees (1967), Cévennes (1970), Ecrins (1973) and Mercantour (1979) (the latter two both in the Alps); these six parks cover approximately 344,000 ha.

In theory the concept of a national park envisages a rural peripheral zone surrounding an uninhabited central zone, which would be under government control and in which both agriculture and tourism would be encouraged as joint activities. The peripheral zones cover 750,000 ha and house 125,000 permanent residents. In tourist seasons they serve as holiday centres and bases for those wishing to visit the central zone. But this very clear-cut division has meant that the peripheral zones have in holiday periods been under very great pressure from overcrowding, raising the problem of over-saturation by visitors and above all the problem of pressure from property developers and investors who wish to make a profit out of the rise in property values which comes from proximity to the parks.

Ideas are developing in the direction of a modification of this rigid division; but the change could either be for the better or for the worse. France does not have vast uninhabited natural reserves; even the Cévennes park has several hundred inhabitants. It is difficult to apply to closely settled France the ideal of a completely uninhabited nature park such as Yellowstone, the prototype of the national parks of the United States (1872). The result is that the few existing national parks suffer from an excessive number of visitors.

(ii) Regional parks. The division into central and peripheral zones does not apply to regional parks, whose creation dates from 1967. These are parks where the preservation of rural life is quite explicitly linked with efforts to attract the public; they are places of tranquillity and relaxation, where nature is protected but where provision is made for educating the public and offering facilities for sport and sailing. Saint-Amand Regional Park (Nord) of 10,000 ha was created in September 1968; 18 others followed between 1969 and 1978, covering a total of 2,200,000 ha. Since 1975 the final decision to create a 'regional' park has belonged to the new regional administrations, subject to governmental approval. Both national and regional parks have experienced difficulties of management and finance due to the diversity of bodies involved, whether at national, regional or local level.

(iii) Sites of special scientific interest. These were conceived in 1973, created in 1975 and given legal status in July 1976. They consist of small areas deserving of protection by virtue of their flora, fauna, situational or archaeological import-ance; among them are the reserves of the Sept Iles off Perros-Guirec (Brittany), Sixt (near Samoens) and Roc de Chère (Lac d'Annecy). The largest site of this type is at Vaccarès (10,000 ha) in the Camargue.

2.3 Impact studies

Impact studies relating to the environment were made obligatory following the 1976 law on the protection of nature. The planning process of large-scale developments had to include a detailed analysis of the consequences of their environmental impact. In particular, works undertaken by a public body or which required administrative authorization were to be preceded by an impact study.

The 'impact file' must first describe the condition of the site and its natural riches prior to development. It must then analyse the consequences of the plan for the landscape, animals, vegetation, natural environment, ecological balance, neighbourhood and public health. Such a study must furthermore indicate for what reason one particular variant of the plan has been adopted rather than another. An account must also be given of the measures provided for eliminating, reducing or compensating the harmful consequences of the project, and an estimate provided of the cost of these precautionary measures. The impact study has to be paid for by the developer.

2.4 Protection of coastal regions

The public was made aware of the deterioration of the maritime and coastal environment by the gigantic scale of the expansion of industrial port areas, such as Marseille–Fos and Dunkerque, and the extent of urbanization of the coast, whether planned as in Languedoc, or unplanned as in the case of marinas and resorts built by property developers, by the private appropriation of sections of the coast and by disasters caused by oil spills.

It emerged from surveys that very little of the coast was still under the control of the state and local authorities. In 1973 the government launched the experimental use of plans for the protection and utilization of the sea (*schémas d'aptitude et d'utilisation de la mer* – SAUM). In March 1974 it was decided to create coastal and leisure resorts which would unite the protection of nature with the provision of tourist amenities.

In 1975 a body was set up concerned with the preservation of the shores of the sea and of lakes (Conservatoire du Littoral et des Rivages Lacustres). Its objectives included the ecological aim of safeguarding the areas of the coast or lake shores which are still unspoilt, together with their flora, fauna and landscape. Economic objectives included the channelling of building developments in new directions, since linear coastal urbanization had reached crisis point. With regard to tourism, the objective was to preserve and improve what was already attractive on the coasts of France.

3 Conclusion

A total of 8 per cent of the area of France is protected in the form of 6 national parks, 19 regional parks, 48 nature reserves, 2,160 classified sites and 4,440 less strongly protected registered sites. While these places are protected from excessive settlement, they are at the same time exposed to the dangers of too many visitors. Conceived as nature reserves, areas free of any kind of pollution, each year such areas attract increasing numbers of tourists whose conduct does not always match ecological aspirations. Some of these 'protected' areas are thus threatened with exceeding their capacity of absorbing visitors; the provision of paths and other facilities far exceeds initial intentions.

It may also be questioned whether, out of a desire for protection, the real nature of the environmental problem has been overlooked. The demands of the ecological lobby appear to be highly negative. In the name of ecology and the protection of the environment, they oppose all progress, modernization and development. All space appears to be seen as inevitably an arena of conflict between economic development and the preservation of the ecological balance. The solutions and compromises between the parties involved are ultimately of a geographical nature, that is to say, relating to spatial organization: location, networks, dimensions, interactions. The new consciousness of the environment and the new awareness of ecology are rapidly leading to the emergence of a new type of ecological planning.

II

⚜ People

If a Christopher Columbus were to discover an uninhabited France, he would people it in a very different fashion from that of today.

A. Sauvy

8

✧ Population growth since the beginning of the nineteenth century

Population change is an essential element of geographical analysis, because changes in total population trends and in population structure have different expressions and a different impact according to the time and place in which they occur.

1 General evolution of the population

Since the beginning of the nineteenth century, the population of France has almost doubled, rising from a total of about 28.3 million in 1800 to 54.3 million on 4 March 1982. This increase came about, however, in a manner peculiar to France, with extremely slow growth during the whole of the nineteenth century and the first half of the twentieth, followed by an abrupt upward reversal of this tendency soon after the Second World War (Fig. 8.1 and Table 8.1). Whereas in the fifty years ending in 1914, during which the urban and industrial revolutions took place, neighbouring European states maintained or even increased their rates of growth, French growth declined and total population stagnated at less than 42 million in 1911, a figure which was to stand as the maximum population throughout the first half of the twentieth century. This demographic crisis was doubtless both the cause and the consequence of the relatively low rate of economic development between 1850 and 1914. Lacking a large labour force, France did not experience an industrial revolution comparable with that of other European countries; conversely, this relative economic stagnation did not encourage demographic growth.

Table 8.1 *French population change since 1821*[a]

	Total population (thousands)	Percentage variation
1821	31,161	
1831	33,218	+6.6
1841	34,911	+5.1
1851	36,472	+4.5
1861	37,386	+2.5
1872	37,653	+0.1
1881	39,239	+4.2
1891	39,946	+1.8
1901	40,681	+1.8
1911	41,415	+1.8
1921	39,108	−5.6
1926	40,581	+3.8
1931	41,524	+2.3
1936	41,502	0
1946	40,503	−2.4
1954	42,577	+5.1
1962	46,520	+9.3
1968	49,779	+7.0
1975	52,666	+5.8
1982	54,335	+3.2

[a] France within its present-day limits. Until 1921 figures are for decades; from 1921 onwards for intercensal periods.
Source: INSEE, censuses.

1.1 Natural variation

The slowing of demographic growth during the first half of the twentieth century was due above all to a decline in fertility. This decline had set in before the end of the eighteenth century, long before that of the majority of other European countries (1880 in England and Wales, Belgium and the Netherlands, still later in Germany).

1.1.1 From the beginning of the nineteenth century to 1939

A comparison of birth rates for European countries reveals the unusual position of France, especially in the period 1801–1911. From a crude birth rate of 32.0 per thousand in 1801–10 the figure dropped to 26.3 per thousand in 1851–60 and to 20.6 per thousand in 1901–10, whereas the figures for neighbouring states show a less rapid decline. The number of births per year stabilized at about 1 million until 1884, then dropped steadily; by 1902 it had fallen below 900,000 and in 1911 below 800,000. The lowest figures understandably coincide with the First World War, varying between 380,000 and 480,000 per annum. After a slight recovery in 1920 and 1921 (834,000 and 812,000), the number of births again fell, until by 1933 it was lower than 700,000.

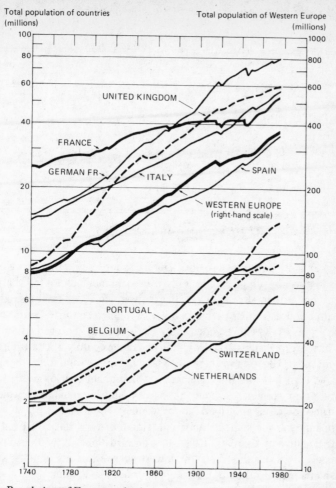

Figure 8.1 Population of France and selected European countries, 1740–1976. Source: *Population*, no. 2, 1977, p. 257.

The decline in fertility is revealed even more clearly in the net reproduction rate. While this remained constant between 1806 and 1890, assuring the replacement of the generations – except between 1854 and 1859 – it then fell below replacement rate until just before the Second World War. If the natural balance of population (births in relation to deaths) remained positive in spite of the continuing decline in fertility, it was thanks to the existence of a structurally young population; the high number of young people in the age groups likely to have children compensated for a while for the decline in fertility. It related also to a fall in the death rate, particularly marked from 1895–1900 onwards.

The annual number of deaths throughout the nineteenth century remained

Table 8.2 *Changing birth rates: selected European countries*

Percentages

Period	France	Germany	England and Wales	Belgium	Netherlands	Sweden
1801–10	32.0					30.9
1811–20	31.9					33.4
1821–30	31.0					34.6
1841–50	27.4	36.1	32.6	30.9	33.0	31.1
1861–70	26.4	37.2	35.2	32.0	35.8	31.4
1881–90	23.9	36.8	32.5	30.2	34.2	29.1
1901–10	20.6	32.9	27.2	26.1	30.5	25.8
1920–4	19.8	23.1	21.3	21.1	26.7	20.3
1935–9	14.8	19.4	14.9	15.5	20.3	14.5

Source: *Annuaire statistique de la France*, Résumé retrospectif, 1966.

constant at about 900,000–950,000, a figure slightly below that of the birth rate. After 1895 (as a result of Pasteur's discoveries in medicine) it fell sharply, from 24.0 per thousand in 1851–5 to 13.3 per thousand in 1911–13. This reduction in the death rate was similar to that in other developed countries, but it happened later in France (1875 in Sweden, 1880 in England). The reduction of infant mortality was especially marked after the end of the century; the rate fell from 170 per thousand in 1891–5 to 139 per thousand in 1901–5, and to 124 per thousand in 1911–13. As a result, life expectancy, which in about 1865 was 39 years for men and 41 for women, rose about 1900 to 45 years for men (49 for women), and about 1920 to 52 years for men (56 for women).

In the interwar years, the demographic situation was critical. Natural variation became negative in 1929 and from 1935 onwards, not only because of the low birth rate – 14.8 per thousand, the lowest France had ever known – but also because of a high death rate reflecting an ageing population.

Much has been written about the reasons for this critical decline in fertility, which has been ascribed to a host of (no doubt interrelated) characteristics of the French people and of French society: individualism, the conservatism of the wealthy classes, the decline in the influence of religion, the emancipation of women, the centralization which devitalized the provinces, the requirement under Article 832 of the Civil Code of equal division of inheritance among all heirs (an invitation to couples to have only one child), and the long absence of family legislation. More generally, the changes in living conditions imposed by urbanization and industrialization were of the greatest significance.

Many voices were raised to encourage the limitation of population. In the 1820s, Jean-Baptiste Say exhorted people 'to save money rather than have children', and forty years later Guizot accompanied his exhortation to 'make money' with the advice to 'exercise caution in conjugal union'. One cannot fail to be astonished by the indifference to population developments shown by the rulers of France during this long period. Not one of them was willing to acknowledge the seriousness of the demographic stagnation of the country. Doubtless they feared overpopulation rather than underpopulation, and doubtless they were afraid of any increase in the working classes (the 'dangerous classes'). One can only say that they were lacking in foresight and had an inadequate appreciation of the facts of the situation.

1.1.2 Population change since 1945

After the Second World War, French population made a spectacular recovery. The upsurge in the birth rate, allied to the continuing decline in the death rate, made the population graph soar upwards. This recovery no doubt related to the legislation pertaining to the family (Family law of 29 July 1939), but doubtless also to a change of mentality among the postwar generation, who no longer refused to have children. The sudden increase in fertility, which seems to have been more marked in France than in neighbouring countries, enabled the annual birth rate to remain at 800,000–875,000 until 1973, after which it dropped sharply.

The high birth rate of the postwar years slowed down from 1955 and more especially from 1964, but this tendency was for a few years partially masked by the increase in the number of couples of child-bearing age, reflecting the large numbers of births between 1944 and 1954. The net reproduction rate has fallen steadily; since 1974 it has again been below replacement level. (Given the present rate of mortality, a generation of women must give birth to 2.1 children each to maintain a stable population, but in 1983 it was estimated that the rate was only 1.8 children.) As a result of the decline in fertility, the birth rate still continues to drop, from 20.9 per thousand in 1946 to 17.6 in 1965 and 14.8 in 1982. This development is comparable with that of the majority of west European countries.

During the same period the death rate has also shown an appreciable decline, from 13.1 per thousand in 1946–50 to 10.1 in 1982. Infant mortality has been considerably reduced, from 63.4 per thousand in 1946–50 to 23.4 in 1964 and 9.5 in 1982. These trends reflect progress in the prevention and treatment of illness (notably the widespread use of antibiotics), the general improvement in standards of living, and rising educational standards. In recent years, however, the death rate has remained constant; methods of combating the remaining causes of death (ageing, cancer, cardio-vascular disease) are slow to emerge.

To sum up, population overall has continued to grow, in spite of its feeble rate of natural increase. The fundamental demographic weakness of France is only partially revealed in the fluctuating figures of total population, which have been sustained by another dynamic element, the product of migratory exchanges with foreign countries.

1.2 The impact of international migration

At certain periods, net international migration has contributed substantially to the growth of the French population. In general, periods of high immigration coincide with periods of rapid economic growth, the achievement of which depends on a plentiful supply of labour. For France, where natural population growth was insufficient to supply an adequate labour force, the importation of foreign workers became a necessity.

Not much is known about international migratory movements between 1800 and 1851, but they were important during at least two periods: 1831–6 and 1841–6. During the whole of the second half of the nineteenth century and up to the First World War, there was massive immigration from bordering countries. At the 1851 census, there were 379,000 foreigners, and in 1891, 1,130,000.[1] From 1881 to 1911 an average of 30,000 people a year entered France; net immigration accounted for about half of population growth.

Immigration reached a very high level after the First World War. Foreigners, who constituted 1 per cent of the population in 1851 and 3 per cent in 1911, had increased to 6 per cent in 1926. The economic crisis of the 1930s then caused a drop in numbers. In 1946 the government made it easier for foreign families to enter the country and immigration soared once more. After the oil crisis of 1973, a new policy was established, and in 1974 the entry of foreign workers was provisionally suspended. Following a period of renewed liberalization initiated by the 1981 Mitterrand government, economic difficulties once more caused a more restrictive policy to be adopted.

In 1954, foreigners represented 4.1 per cent of the population; by 1982 the percentage was fairly stable at 8.0. For about twenty years after 1950 the positive balance of international migration constituted 40 per cent of the total population increase. The excess of immigration over emigration was 585,000 between 1947 and 1954, rising to 1,150,000 between 1954 and 1962, 1,325,400 between 1962 and 1968, and 847,700 between 1968 and 1975. These immigrants, moreover, with their higher birth rate, helped to raise the rate of population growth. From 1946 to 1956, 5 per cent of births were to foreign parents; this figure rose rapidly, reaching 10 per cent in 1973. On 31 December 1982 there were 4.5 million foreigners living in France, to whom must be added about 815,000 French North Africans who were repatriated from 1962 onwards. Their establishment, for the most part in southern France, had a major impact on population change and on the demographic vitality in this region.

---

[1] Foreigners are recorded in the censuses from 1851 onwards. Since the 1945 decree regulating the status of foreigners resident in France, the Ministry of the Interior regularly publishes the relevant statistics, derived from the number of valid residence permits. These statistics exclude, however, Algerians and resident nationals from countries such as the former French dependencies in sub-Saharan Africa and member-countries of the EEC, although the Ministry provides estimates of the numbers contained in these categories.

Table 8.3 *Changing population densities: selected European countries*

Year	Persons per sq km			
	France	Germany[a]	United Kingdom	Italy
1800	51.3	69.6	43.0	60.1
1850	66.2	100.8	85.2	80.7
1900	73.8	158.4	151.6	108.0
1950	76.4	196.3	207.3	153.0
1975	95.0	250.0	230.0	180.0
1983	100.0	247.5	229.5	186.9

[a]From 1950, German Federal Republic and West Berlin only.
Sources: Censuses and yearbooks.

1.3 A relatively underpopulated country?

In 1750 France, with approximately 21 million inhabitants, was the most densely populated country in Europe, but as a result of the country's peculiar demographic development this lead progressively disappeared. The French proportion of the total population of Europe has continually declined.

An examination of changing population densities confirms the uniqueness of the French position (Table 8.3). The contrast between France and the neighbouring countries is increasing; whereas the present density of 100 inhabitants per sq km is twice that at the beginning of the nineteenth century, other countries have at least trebled their population densities during the same period. If France had a population density comparable with those of its neighbours it would have a vastly different total population. If it had the density of Switzerland it would have a total population of 86 million, of the United Kingdom 126 million, and of the Netherlands 184 million.

At the present time France, in common with Spain, is one of the relatively underpopulated countries of Europe (Fig. 8.2). Population density only reaches the normal level for industrialized and urbanized northwest Europe in a few areas, such as the Nord region, Alsace, the Paris (Ile-de-France) region and the urbanized regions of Lyon and Marseille (with its eastern extension along the Côte d'Azur).

2 Population growth and distribution
2.1 Changes at national and local level

Over the long term, although for varying periods of time, there is a general correspondence between the scale of population variation at national level, and the proportion of national territory showing a parallel variation. In other words, any acceleration of general demographic growth tends to be accompanied by an increase in the number of growth areas; any decline brings about the emergence or extension of zones of demographic stagnation, if not of absolute depopulation.

In the period 1801–51, for example, there was an increase in population in all departments of metropolitan France during the first two decades, which were characterized by a general rise in the country as a whole.

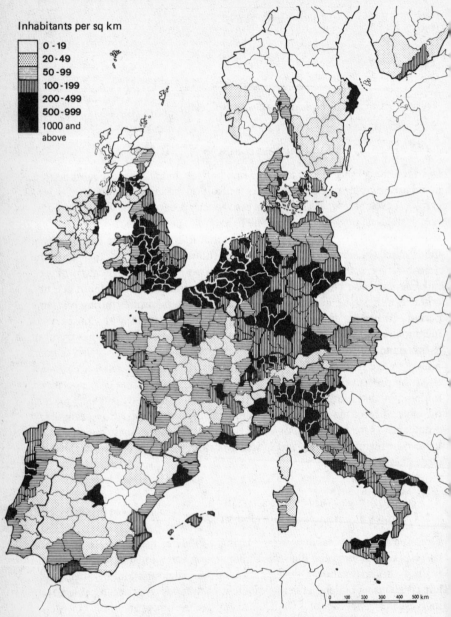

Figure 8.2 Western Europe: population density, 1971. Source: INED.

Between 1851 and 1911, a period characterized by an increasingly marked decline in population growth, only 48 departments increased their population, and 26 of these had a growth rate lower than the national average (+13.8 per cent). The situation after the Second World War was completely different, since the increase affected all departments with the exception of 11 situated exclusively in the Central massif. This renewed population growth contributed greatly to the expansion of urban centres.

The link between the intensity of growth and its territorial extension has consequences for territorial planning. Indeed, the problems raised by population change have differing characteristics, according to whether they relate to an acceleration of growth (pressure on the housing stock and on social equipment), to demographic stagnation (affecting particular categories of people, the old for example), or to a sudden reversal of growth either in the positive or the negative sense (failure of the spatial spread of employment opportunities to correspond with the availability of labour). At a time when problems are changing in scale and/or nature, the consequences of their geographical diffusion must also be faced.

Fig. 8.3 shows the different forms of population change both spatially and over time. Comparison of the rate of development of each department with the national average (+13.8 per cent in 1851–1911, +30.0 per cent in 1946–75) permits a division into seven categories. This classification throws into prominence the duration and extent of population decline in mountain areas (the Central massif in particular), in the whole of the southwest, and in parts of western and eastern France. It also reveals the concentration of the highest population growth in an area of limited territorial extent beginning in Normandy and swinging eastwards in an arc to end eventually on the Mediterranean coast.

2.2 Changes in population distribution

The extent to which population growth in particular departments diverges from the national average underlines the changes which for more than a century have affected the distribution of population in France. From 1866 to 1975, this distribution has been affected simultaneously by a twofold movement of concentration and thinning out (Fig. 8.4). A comparison of the proportion of the total population residing in each department at the two dates reveals that the changes have taken place to the detriment of two-thirds of the country. The population has fallen in the whole of interior France, notably on the western and southern fringes of the Central massif, in the Aquitaine basin and the southern half of the Paris basin, whereas the highest densities of population are to be found essentially in the north, the Ile-de-France (Paris) region, the Departments of Rhône (Lyon agglomeration) and Bouches-du-Rhône (Marseille agglomeration).

Figure 8.5 summarizes all the changes by differentiating three broad cat-

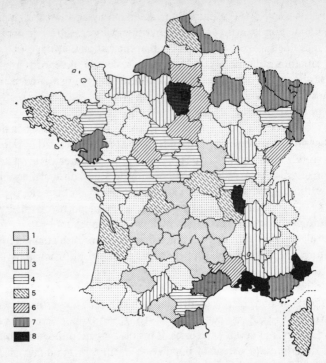

Figure 8.3 Characteristics of population change in the periods 1815–1911 and 1946–75 by department. 1. Decline in both periods 2. Decline in first period/no growth or low growth in second period 3. Decline/high growth 4. Low growth in both periods 5. High growth/low growth 6. Low growth/high growth 7. High growth in both periods 8. Very high growth in both periods. Definitions: low growth – below French average for period concerned; high growth – above French average for period concerned; French average 1851–1911 +13.8 per cent; 1946–75 +30.0 per cent.

egories of department. The first includes those whose population has changed little, precisely because of the similarity of their growth to the national figure; they are to be found dotted across the country. A second category consists of departments whose ranking has fallen. For 22 of them, the decline is only relative: their populations have actually increased between 1866 and 1975, while declining relatively to that of France as a whole. The departments concerned are mostly situated in western France. By contrast, in 36 departments, situated for the most part in southern France, relative decline in 1866–1975 was accompanied by absolute population loss, which in half of them was still continuing as late as 1968–75. The third category consists of departments where population has increased relatively and absolutely. According to the degree o

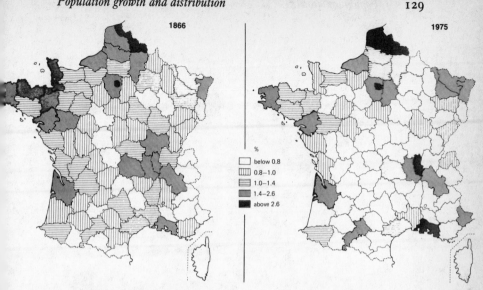

Figure 8.4 Distribution of population by department, as percentage of total French population. One per cent of total French population: 1866 – 380,000 inhabitants; 1975 – 526,000 inhabitants.

growth, three types may be distinguished. Departments where growth is moderate yet higher than the national average are widely dispersed geographically, except for some degree of concentration in northern and northeastern France. There is then a limited number of departments of rapid growth, where the population has increased by at least half, and finally the departments of very high growth: Alpes-Maritimes (Nice region), Bouches-du-Rhône (Marseille region), and the former Departments of the Seine and of Seine-et-Oise in the Ile-de-France (Paris) region.

The growth of Paris and the Paris agglomeration constitutes a phenomenon unique in France in terms of scale, rapidity and spatial spread. The city of Paris in the first place, and subsequently its suburban extensions, essentially grew by draining off the population of provincial France. From 1876 to 1936, whereas the population of France increased by 3,473,900 inhabitants, that of the Ile-de-France region (within its present-day boundaries) alone increased by 3,465,000! From 1876 to 1975, that is to say during a century, the population of France was multiplied by only 0.4, while that of the Ile-de-France region increased by threefold. At the present time, growth is rather more evenly distributed across the country as a whole; since 1946 only a quarter of the national increase has been absorbed by the Ile-de-France region. The population of this region, always preeminent in France, has increased so that it makes up almost one-fifth of the total

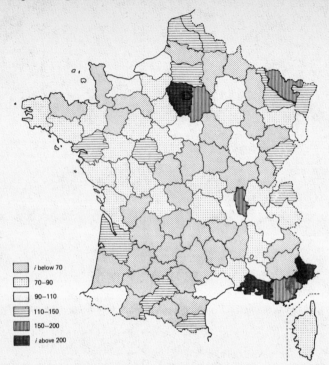

Figure 8.5 Population change 1866–1975, by department. The index of change is calculated according to the formula: i = percentage of total population 1975/percentage of total population 1866. Source: Statistiques INSEE.

population of the country today: the share of the national total was 3.7 per cent in 1801, 6.5 per cent in 1901, 15.3 per cent in 1946, 18.8 per cent in 1975 and 18.5 per cent in 1982.

9

⚜ The changing distribution
of urban and rural
population

In a country of long-established population and ancient civilization, such as
France, it would be pointless to try to understand the present demographic
pattern without turning to the past to trace the development of the present map of
population, itself representing only a passing phase in a continuing process of
evolution. Over the past hundred years the spatial variation in French population
has been derived from the interaction of two movements: rural depopulation and
urbanization. Some countries have been able to urbanize without a disturbing
decline in rural population, by relying on the natural increase of their populations. In the demographic context of France this possibility was not available; it
was therefore from the rural areas that France recruited people to carry out its
twofold urban and industrial revolution.

1 Rural and urban population change

In 1861, 62.1 per cent of the French population lived in communes of fewer than
2,000 inhabitants; by 1982 the figure had fallen to 23.3 per cent. Until about
1846–51, rural and urban populations both increased.[1] Thereafter only urban
growth continued, even accelerating after the Second World War. Rural
population first stagnated, then started a process of uninterrupted decline which
has lasted to the present day (Fig.9.1). The countryside has thus progressively

---

[1] The terms 'rural population' and 'urban population' refer to definitions adopted by statisticians
to differentiate the two types of population for census purposes.

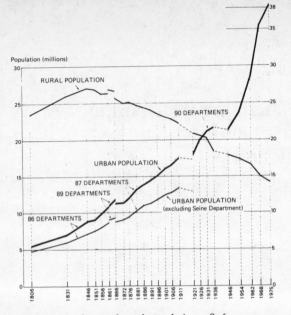

Figure 9.1 Change in urban and rural population, 1806–1975.

lost part of its population to the towns. Towards the end of the 1920s there were as many urban as rural residents, since which period the urban proportion has increased rapidly: 53.2 per cent of total population in 1946, 67.3 per cent in 1962 and 73.4 per cent in 1982.

The growth of urban population affected all types of towns but especially the largest, those with a population of between 100,000 and 1 million. In 1851 there were 4 towns in this category, accounting for 1.7 per cent of the population, in 1975 there were 38 (13.7 per cent of total population).

2 Factors in changing population distribution

Causes of change included:

(i) The industrialization of the towns and mining areas. This required the concentration of a massive labour force, and also led to the disappearance of many rural craftsmen and numerous industries based on the use of wood. All the surveys and monographs record the brutal collapse or the slow decline of a whole range of occupations: textiles, wood, glassworking and charcoal iron-working, which at the time were widely dispersed in many regions. Thousands of spinners, seamstresses, weavers, blacksmiths and woodworkers were unable to continue working at home or in small workshops; the youngest and most enterprising left

Table 9.1 Distribution of population by size-category of commune, 1851–1975

Size category of commune	Characteristics of category	1851[a]	1921	1954	1975	1982
Below 500 inhabitants	N[b]	15,504	21,715	23,803	22,731	5,932
	P[c]	4,839.4	5,556.3	5,691.6	5,046.9	4,085.9
	%[d]	13.5	14.2	13.3	9.3	7.5
500–999	N	11,955	9,065	7,594	6,454	2,916
	P	8,445.8	6,242	5,212.0	6,639.1	4,006.5
	%	23.6	15.9	12.2	8.2	7.3
1,000–1,999	N	6,517	4,350	3,726	3,561	
	P	8,943	5,946.4	5,093.0	4,894.7	
	%	25.0	15.2	12.0	9.1	
2,000–4,999	N	2,262	1,828	1,841	2,153	
	P	6,592.6	5,350.8	5,480.0	6,519.7	
	%	18.4	13.6	12.9	12.1	
5,000–9,999	N	271	397	518	728	
	P	1,939.1	2,658.6	3,550.7	4,969.7	
	%	5.4	6.8	8.3	9.3	
10,000–19,999	N	93	174	250	381	
	P	1,393.8	2,438.3	3,492.7	5,242.4	
	%	3.9	6.2	8.2	9.8	
20,000–49,999	N	38	92	146	277	
	P	1,272.3	2,718.6	4,359.4	8,375.8	
	%	3.5	6.9	10.2	15.6	
50,000–99,999	N	10	33	39	70	
	P	692	2,306.1	2,689.5	4,589.9	
	%	2.0	5.9	6.2	8.6	

Table 9.1 cont.

Size category of commune	Characteristics of category	1851[a]	1921	1954	1975	1982
100,000–199,999	N	4	14	23	28	
	P	607.3	3,085.9	4,355.0	3,848.5	
	%	1.7	7.9	10.1	7.2	
200,000–1 million	N				10	
	P				3,501.4	
	%				6.5	
Over 1 million	N	1	1	1	1	
	P	1,053.9	2,906.5	2,850.2	2,317.2	
	%	3.0	7.4	6.6	4.3	
Total	N	36,655	37,669	37,991	36,394	36,433
	P	35,783.8	39,209.5	42,774.1	53,696.8	54,334.8
	%	100	100	100	100	100

[a] France within present-day boundaries with the exception of Nice and Savoie.
[b] N: Number of communes in category.
[c] P: Total population of all communes in category (thousands).
[d] %: Total population of all communes in category as a percentage of the total population of France.
Source: INSEE.

for the towns, whilst the others fell back on the small family farm or became day labourers. At the same time the service sector declined, adjusting to lower numbers of customers and to their new needs; the farrier and the blacksmith gave way to the mechanic and the dozens of small shopkeepers were replaced by travelling salesmen from the nearby towns.

(ii) Changes in agriculture. Rural depopulation did not stem merely from the lure of the town and employment possibilities in industry; it was also impelled from within the rural areas by changes in agriculture. In quick succession came the disappearance or contraction of crops employing a large labour force: viticulture, sericulture and industrial crops (linen and hemp). The extension of grassland at the expense of arable also reduced the demand for labour. By the end of the nineteenth century the widespread use of agricultural machinery condemned farm labourers to unemployment.

Consideration must also be given to the disappearance of the communal practices which before the Revolution allowed rural people who owned neither land nor plough animals to subsist by making use of common grazing land. More particularly, it was at this time that subsistence farming had to adapt to the massive exchange of commodities permitted by the advent of the railways and stimulated by urban demand, and on the other hand to competition from overseas grain. This transformation of agriculture spelled ruin for small subsistence farming, which was incapable of providing normal standards of living comparable to those of the towns. Modernization called for heavy investment, without which the holding was doomed to collapse, and its occupier obliged to leave and seek employment in the town.

(iii) Natural conditions clearly had an influence on rural depopulation. Regions of poor soil and the most deprived mountain areas were the most affected. From 1906 to 1954, Haut-Limousin lost 50 per cent of its population, the Causse Noir 49 per cent, the Larzac Causse 51 per cent and the Cévennes 42 per cent. It is significant that all these districts are in the Central massif. It was the same on the limestone plateaus of the eastern Paris basin and in mountain areas generally.

(iv) Additional and random influences. Once the migratory movement had been set in motion, the new urban civilization, with its gaslamps, its availability of piped water in proximity to the dwelling, its trams, its entertainments, its values and reputation, justified or otherwise, steadily expanded its sphere of influence and drew in people from the rural areas. Rural–urban migration was also stimulated by economic crises, both general and specific to agriculture: the 1848 crisis in particular contributed to the ruin of rural industries. The fall in demand for agricultural products, linked to the slump in prices between 1880 and 1896, and the economic crisis of the 1930s, intensified depopulation.

The nineteenth-century countryside was also hard hit by a range of diseases:

potato blight at mid-century; diseases of the silkworm, which brought about the decline of many communes in the Midi through the disappearance of sericulture; and phylloxera, which, from 1865, affected most of the vineyards, considerably reducing the total area planted with vines and completely changing traditional agrarian structures. Another factor was the First World War. Out of 3,700,000 farmers who had been mobilized, 673,000 were killed and 500,000 invalided out. The death-blow was given to many villages by the loss of only ten or twenty soldiers whose names, engraved on a simple monument, watch over the abandoned houses of a village, itself at the point of death.

(v) Multiple secondary causes also hastened rural depopulation. Railways, as they spread across the country, recruited construction workers in rural areas, who were subsequently drawn away to urban destinations as the railways advanced. On the other hand, the attraction of inhabitants into communes which had a railway station tended to concentrate rural population along the main railway lines, at the expense of communes not served by rail.

The spread of state education also encouraged rural depopulation to some extent, since, once educated, rural dwellers had no place in traditional country life. After 1880, compulsory military service also recruited young men from the country and housed them in urban barracks, thus introducing them to the towns and the opportunities of employment they afforded. Information about urban opportunities was passed on to those remaining in rural areas by the increasing number of family members and acquaintances who were already settled in the towns.

In more general terms, there was a confrontation between two different civilizations, two ways of living, existing at two different stages of development, the older and more traditional giving way before the innovations of the newer. Irrespective of factors stemming from changes in the agricultural economy, the emigrants were not so much fleeing from the countryside as from the conditions of life, of housing, of work and of leisure opportunities to be found there. Women, who suffered particularly from hardships, often took the lead in the decision to abandon rural life.

3 The uneven rate of rural depopulation

The behaviour of populations differs not only on a sub-regional scale but from one commune to another; it also varies over time. In a given region, some communes may have been quite unaffected for a whole century while neighbouring communes experienced a torrential emigration. This astonishing diversity can be attributed to the way in which rural communities developed greatly differing characteristics over the centuries. Even if the development of a craft or industrial tradition as a differentiating factor is excluded, nevertheless variations in farm structure, size of holding, cropping systems, or even the temperament of the people explain the juxtaposition of demographically 'strong' and 'weak' villages.

3.1 The initiation of the depopulation process

In the first half of the nineteenth century, France was essentially a rural country (Fig. 9.2). In 1851, with the exception of the Seine Department (Paris region) and the Bouches-du-Rhône Department (Marseille region), the proportion of rural population was very high, sometimes overwhelming (more than 85 per cent in 19 departments). But already population growth in the smaller communes was slowing down, and in several regions the predominant urban system of small market towns (10,000–20,000 inhabitants) lacking specialized activities was already showing signs of inability to absorb growing emigration from the countryside. Between 1836 and 1851, communes of fewer than 3,000 inhabitants lost 1.8 per cent of their population, while the total population of France increased by 6.6 per cent.

From the middle of the nineteenth century, rural depopulation intensified and

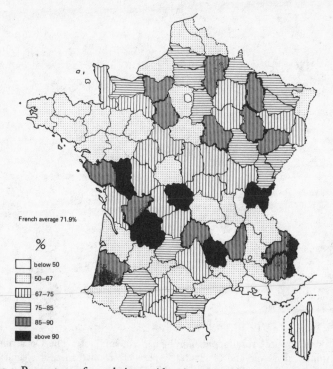

Figure 9.2 Percentage of population resident in rural communes, 1851, by department. Source: Ch. Pouthas, *La Population française pendant la première moitié du XIXe siècle* (PUF, Paris, 1956), p. 71.

became irreversible, but the time-scale varied from place to place. The dates at which particular rural departments attained maximum population extend over the entire century (Fig. 9.3).

3.2 The extent of rural depopulation

In the space of a century, rural population was almost halved, falling from 26.5 million in 1866 to 14.2 million in 1975. But just as movements began at different times, so also their scale varied according to the region (Fig. 9.4). In general, no close correlation can be observed between the rates of decline from the point of population maximum and the length of the period during which the decline takes place. Nevertheless in the majority of the departments where decline was 40 per cent or more, it lasted for at least a hundred years.

Rural population remained stationary for a few years following the Second World War, but decline began again in 1954, lasting until 1968, since when it has

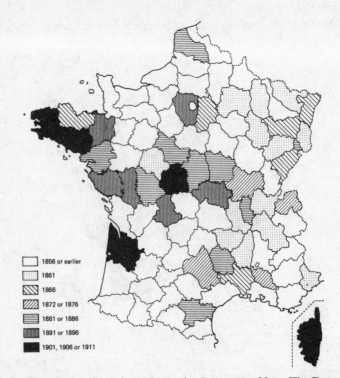

Legend:
- 1856 or earlier
- 1861
- 1866
- 1872 or 1876
- 1881 or 1886
- 1891 or 1896
- 1901, 1906 or 1911

Figure 9.3 Period of peak rural population, by department. Note: The Departments of Alpes-Maritimes, of Savoie and of Haute-Savoie were created in 1860; Meurthe-et-Moselle and the Territory of Belfort in 1871. The Departments of Bas-Rhin, Haut-Rhin and Moselle were part of Germany between 1871 and 1918, the last two with some changes in their boundaries. Source: P. Merlin, *L'Exode rural* (PUF, Paris, 1971).

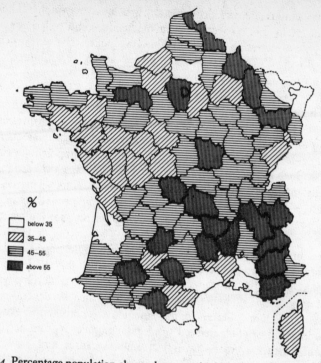

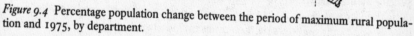

Figure 9.4 Percentage population change between the period of maximum rural population and 1975, by department.

slowed down (17.2 million rural people in 1954 and 14.3 million in 1975). Factors tending to stabilize rural populations include the decline in the rate of natural increase, the ageing of the residual population, the revitalization of the countryside through the diffusion of various economic activities and the emergence of attitudes more favourable to nature and the rural way of life, and the urbanization of communes located in the rural–urban fringe. Between 1975 and 1982, the rural population once more increased, reaching 14.5 million.

3.3 The relationship between rural emigration and rural depopulation

The most important factor in the demographic history of rural France since the beginning of the nineteenth century was not that emigration was continuous – for emigration normally sets in well before actual population decline and can, moreover, exist independently of it – but that it was counterbalanced neither by return migration nor by a continuing high birth rate. In certain regions, however, birth rates did remain high enough, sometimes for long periods, to compensate for the effects of emigration, thus retarding the emergence of depopulation; the Nord region, Brittany and Alsace are the best examples. But as soon as natural increase falls, emigration and depopulation become synonymous. There is a marked contrast in this respect between nineteenth-century Brittany, which experienced heavy migration loss but remained overpopulated because of its high birth rate, and the Central massif or Aquitaine, which were drained of their human capital by emigration.

Emigration took several forms according to the categories of people mainly affected. There was, first of all, migration unrelated to occupation, resulting either from the excess of deaths over births or from the many departures of young people prior to taking up work. Alternatively, migration might relate to occupational change, thus affecting only the economically active population (with their dependants). Such groups included farmers whose holdings had been rendered economically marginal by technical progress, farm workers displaced by the introduction of machinery, craftsmen unable to compete with rising urban industries, and shopkeepers affected by a reduction in the number of their customers.

Of these different types of migration, some are quite normal, relating to general causes; rural areas could not expect to keep all the children resulting from a high birth rate, or the craftsmen attracted into developing urban industries, or people working in the service sectors, which are dependent on the total level of population. This type of movement is a response to the existence of surplus population, whether derived from demographic or from occupational developments. Other types partly reflect general causes and partly involve individual decisions, that is to say they include categories of people who could have stayed in the countryside. Examples include the sons of small farmers who, by the very fact of their departure, condemn the family farm to extinction, or the small farmers themselves who choose to leave the land.

At the present time, rural regions are being more and more sharply differentiated according to their levels of population. Below a certain threshold the population cannot hold its own; social life disappears, land is abandoned, houses fall into ruin. A region in the throes of depopulation inevitably ceases to attract investment. Only a very limited part of rural France can attract some new developments and play a part in the dissemination of a new way of life in which urban amenities and the benefits of nature are more closely associated.

3.4   The effect of rural population change on population density

Changing population density gives a useful indication of the transformations which, in the course of time, have affected rural populations (Fig. 9.5). Towards the middle of the nineteenth century, high rural densities were characteristic of the whole of northwest France, northern and central Aquitaine, the Limagne lowlands in the Central massif, the Lyon region and eastern France. The Nord Department broke the records for rural density with more than 112 inhabitants per square kilometre. The Department of Haut-Rhin followed with 91, Côtes-du-Nord with 81, Puy-de-Dôme with 61 and Ardèche with 58. On the other hand, a crescent-shaped zone of low population crossed France to the east and south of the Paris region, branching out into southern France. The Departments of Lozère, Hautes-Alpes and Alpes-de-Haute-Provence were generally

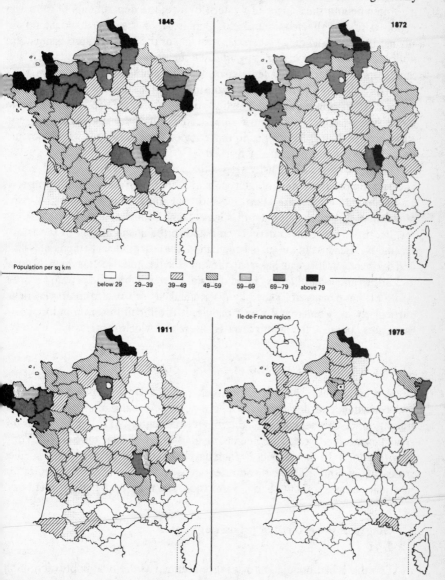

Figure 9.5 Density of rural population in 1845, 1872, 1911 and 1975, by department. Note: In 1975, the Departments of Seine, Hauts-de-Seine, Seine-Saint-Denis and Val-de-Marne had no rural population. Source: Statistiques INSEE.

regarded as deserts, with 25, 21 and 19 inhabitants per square kilometre respectively. Rural depopulation spread progressively through western France, eastern France, the Central region, the Alps and southwest France. The map of rural population densities for 1872 shows the rapid extension of the phenomenon in Aquitaine and the fringes of western France; the departments of the Lyon region were also affected. The Breton peninsula, on the other hand, stood out against the trend, as did the two departments of the Nord region. From 1872 until 1911, four zones were greatly affected: the Paris basin, the Aquitaine basin, the central Pyrenees, and a few departments in southeast France. From 1911 until 1975, density fell in the whole of the interior of the country and in mountain regions. At the present time, the highest rural densities are to be found either in those regions which combine a rural tradition favouring a high birth rate (Brittany, the Nord, Alsace), or in those regions where the postwar urban and economic boom was particularly marked.

The areas of lowest density (Fig. 9.6) constitute a specific spatial entity, covering almost 45 per cent of metropolitan France at an average rural density of 22 inhabitants per square kilometre and containing a third of the total rural population; they pose particular problems. Diminishing interest in rural life has resulted in an increase in derelict land and in the abandonment of the family farmhouse. Because of the sparse population, the cost of social equipment is high and tax income is low, causing great difficulties in territorial management by local authorities and a more or less rapid deterioration in public and private services. Areas of low density are generally disadvantaged with regard to employment, particularly for women and young people. It is difficult to set up industries in these areas because the labour force is sparse and widely dispersed.

4 The unequal distribution of urban population

At the present time, urban population is characterized by an unprecedented scale and consistency of development. The process of urbanization has been continuous since the beginning of the nineteenth century (Table 9.2), while the spatial expansion of cities has been particularly marked since the Second World War (Fig. 9.7). In this respect French development has mirrored, on a smaller scale, that of other European countries, whose periods of greatest urbanization took place between about 1830–40 and 1900, and from 1946 to the present day.

4.1 Stages in the growth of urban population
1806–51

In 1806 the urban population of France (defined as the total population of all communes in France, within its present boundaries, having at least one agglomeration of 2,000 inhabitants or more) was 5.6 million. Only two departments had a very high concentration of urban inhabitants: Seine (Paris region)

Table 9.2 *Changes in the urban population*

	1806[a]	1851[b]	1886[b]	1911[b]	1931[a]	1954	1975	1982
Urban population millions	5.6	9.4	13.8	17.5	21.1	23.9	38.4	39.8
Percentage of total French population	18.8	28.1	36.0	44.1	50.8	56.0	72.9	73.4

[a] France within its present-day limits.
[b] France within the limits of the year concerned.
Sources: Censuses

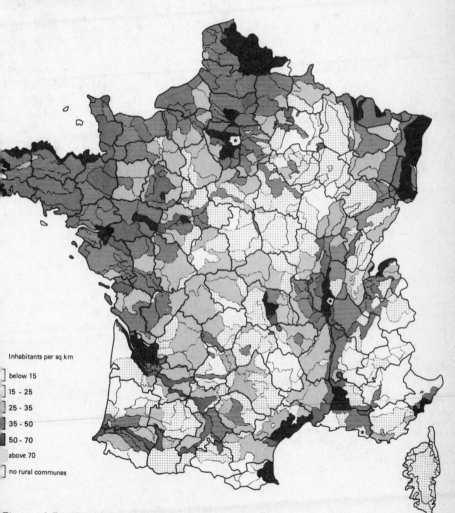

Inhabitants per sq km

] below 15
] 15 - 25
] 25 - 35
] 35 - 50
] 50 - 70
] above 70
] no rural communes

Figure 9.6 Population density by minor agricultural regions.

with 89.3 per cent, and Bouches-du-Rhône (Marseille region) with 67.7 per cent. The Lyon region as well as part of the Mediterranean coastlands could also be regarded as urbanized. Everywhere else, urban life was represented by only a scatter of small towns, which, however, were of great significance for local life. At this time the departments were a relatively new institution, and were in the process of creating administrative structures based on the prefectures and sub-

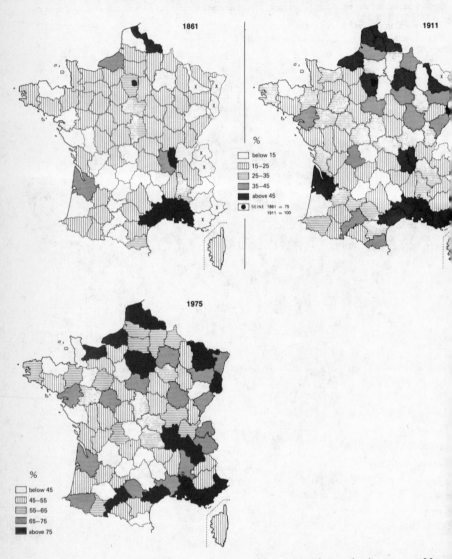

Figure 9.7 Percentage of urban population in 1861, 1911 and 1975, by department. Note: Average for France as a whole: 1861 – 28.8 per cent; 1911 – 44.2 per cent; 1975 – 73.0 per cent. ×: Data not available. Source: Statistiques INSEE.

prefectures. The towns selected to fulfil these functions increased their population by nearly 2 million in the period 1801–5, giving a growth rate of 50 per cent, well above the national rate of increase of urban population (31.8 per cent).

The first great surge of urban growth took place from 1831 to 1846, during the reign of Louis-Philippe, when the towns grew twice as fast as the population of France as a whole. Expansion was then checked by the political and economic crisis of 1846–50, which affected the towns as well as rural areas.

1851–1911

Urban residents increased from 28.1 per cent of the total French population in 1851 to 36 per cent in 1886 and 44.1 per cent in 1911. Whereas the increase in the total urban population was 86.2 per cent in this period, that of towns of more than 20,000 inhabitants was 114.4 per cent, their population more than doubling, from 3,414,000 to 7,320,000. The highest growth rates were in areas affected by industrial expansion, notably the Nord region, the Central region (extending from the middle Loire valley to Bourges and Châteauroux), the coalfields of Saint-Etienne and Le Creusot, and a few port areas. Within the space of a few years, many formerly small settlements acquired thousands of inhabitants. This period also saw the establishment of the inner suburban ring around Paris, where villages which perhaps had only 2,500 inhabitants in 1851 had by 1911 expanded into substantial urban agglomerations, often exceeding 30,000 inhabitants.

1921–36

There was a marked increase in the growth of the urban population in the years following the First World War, which was also the period when urban population overtook rural population. But the rate slowed down progressively after 1930, due to the combined effects of the economic crisis, the reduction of foreign immigration, and reduced building activity in the towns.

1946–82

It had taken almost a century, from 1836 to 1931, for the urban population to increase from 25 per cent to 50 per cent of total population; it took less than half that time for it to increase by nearly another 25 per cent, to reach 72.9 per cent in 1975. The years from 1939 to 1945 provided a marked break between two periods of contrasting demographic development, with urban growth subsequently profiting greatly from the sharp rise in population that followed the war. This great increase in urban population was not only typical of departments that were already urbanized. One of the characteristics of this period was undoubtedly the emergence of medium-sized towns which had hitherto barely grown, indeed had even stagnated; Grenoble is a classic example.

Each of the intercensal periods since 1954 has given a very different picture of the rate and pattern of urban growth in France. The period 1954–62 (+19.5 per cent) witnessed a great increase in eastern France, from Lorraine to Provence–Côte d'Azur. In the period 1962–8 (+18.4 per cent) a contrast developed between the southern regions, where the arrival of the repatriates from North Africa gave a great impetus to urban growth, and the Lorraine and Nord regions, where growth rates were very much below average. The growth during this period of towns in the Centre (Loire valley) region and in Lower Normandy doubtless corresponds to the first stage of decentralization of industrial employment from the Paris region. The period 1968–75 (+10.1 per cent) maintained (in a period of lower overall growth) greater regional disparities than those of the first intercensal period. There was a great increase in urban population in central France (Pays de la Loire and Burgundy regions) and also on the fringe of the Paris basin (Lower Normandy and Picardy), which partly reflects the diffusion of growth from Paris. The towns of the Nord and Lorraine regions continued to grow much more slowly than those of other regions. In southern France, only the Provence–Côte d'Azur region maintained a level of urban growth distinctly above average, showing the continuing attraction of the sun as a factor in migration.

In the period 1975–82, urban growth fell to 3.8 per cent, but the reduction was more apparent than real, reflecting the diffusion of urban growth outside the limits of the officially defined urbanized areas. This took the form of the urbanization of rural communes on the fringes of the towns, the growth of non-agricultural activities in rural communes, and the migration of retired people to the country.

4.2 Growth of the Paris agglomeration

The speed of the growth of the City of Paris in the nineteenth century and the creation of a surrounding ring of high-density suburban population provided the most original feature of the distribution of population in metropolitan France (Table 9.3). At all periods there has been a major disparity in size between Paris and the next largest French town. In 1851, Marseille had 195,000 inhabitants, whereas Paris had already more than a million. By 1982 the Lyon agglomeration had 1.2 million inhabitants, while the Paris agglomeration, with 8.7 million, was seven times as great.

From the middle of the nineteenth century, growth was so great that it overran the capital's boundaries. Even as late as 1860 the city of Paris was an identifiable unit within a Department of the Seine which still included numerous other distinct communes, often very small; out of a total of 80 communes, 60 were still classified as rural in 1836 and 54 in 1851. Until this stage an urban area consisting of only 12 of the present 20 arrondissements, bounded outwards by the present *Boulevards extérieurs*, was sufficient to contain the growth of a population which, between 1806 and 1851, rose from 580,600 to more than a

Table 9.3 *Population of Paris and of the Ile-de-France 1876–1982*

Population in thousands

Year	City of Paris	Petite couronne[a]	Grande couronne[b]	Ile-de-France region
1876	1,988.8	483.2	848.4	3,320.4
1896	2,536.8	895.8	936.2	4,368.8
1911	2,888.1	1,412.4	1,035.1	5,335.6
1921	2,906.5	1,691.5	1,084.8	5,682.8
1936	2,829.7	2,481.3	1,474.9	6,785.9
1954	2,850.2	2,730.8	1,736.2	7,317.2
1975	2,299.8	3,976.8	3,602.0	9,878.6
1982	2,168.3	3,899.2	3,988.6	10,056.1

[a] Petite couronne: inner ring of older suburbs: Departments of Hauts-de-Seine (92), Seine-St-Denis (93) and Val-de-Marne (94).
[b] Grande couronne: outer ring of newer extensions: Departments of Seine-et-Marne (77), Yvelines (78), Essonne (91) and Val d'Oise (95).
Source: INSEE.

million. After that date, the flow of population moved not only into Paris but also into neighbouring communes. In spite of the addition of a further eight arrondissements in 1860, bringing the city to its present limits (marked approximately by the *Boulevard périphérique*), the average annual growth rate of the city of Paris proper dropped (3.9 per cent in 1851–66, 1.41 per cent in 1872–96, 0.9 per cent in 1896–1911), whilst that of the suburbs rose (0.6 per cent in 1851–66, 4 per cent in 1872–96, and 3.2 per cent in 1896–1911).

The greatly increased population outside the walls of Paris was concentrated into suburban agglomerations which in this relatively restricted area were of high average density. This was the origin of the phenomenon of suburbanization, a tendency reinforced by the arrival of the first railway lines. The population growth index for the city of Paris rose from 100 in 1876 to 145 in 1911, whilst that for the inner suburban ring (the Petite couronne as currently defined) rose to 292. From 1911 to 1936, the index stagnated for the city of Paris, whilst that for the Petite couronne soared to 513.5. Since 1946, the pattern of growth has been reversed. The population of the city of Paris has been decreasing; the Petite couronne at first continued to grow, although more slowly, but by 1982 had joined the city of Paris in decline, while the Grande couronne (the outer ring of recent suburbs and new towns) shows a marked increase (Table 9.3).

5 The impact of population change on spatial structure

The changes in the numbers of rural and urban people that have gone on for more than a century have also brought about modifications in their spatial distribution. In some areas, such as parts of western France or the Ariège Department, an existing 'rural' character has become even more marked than before, whereas elsewhere existing urban characteristics have been accentuated (northern Alps, part of the Paris region, the Pas-de-Calais Department and a few isolated coastal departments). In other regions, on the contrary, we notice a weakening either of a previously predominant rural character (the Lyon region west of the Rhône, the Vosges, the Puy-de-Dôme Department), or of urban characteristics (Languedoc, the northern fringe of the Paris basin, several departments of eastern France, Normandy, and the Departments of Nièvre and Gironde). Only a limited number of regions have been affected from both points of view: the Seine-et-Oise and Isère Departments (rural decline and urban growth), the Nord Department (both rural and urban decline), the Moselle and Oise Departments (both rural and urban growth) and the Bas-Rhin Department (rural growth, urban decline).

The movement of population between country and town has above all refashioned spatial distributions. The mountain areas have been drained, with people preferring to regroup on the lowlands. An analysis of the Lyon region, the Aquitaine basin, Lorraine or the northern parts of the Central massif underlines the extent of the changes and shows to what degree depopulation has affected the interfluves, with the valleys remaining as the resistant framework of population distribution. In more general terms, population has become concentrated in the basins of interior France, on the coastal plains, and in the interior valleys of the Alps and the Pyrenees.

From the point of view of the geographical distribution of population, three major geographical divisions stand out.

(1) Western France. In this region of plains, contrasts between interfluves and valleys are not very marked: the plains, hills and plateaus which lie between the only slightly incised troughs of the rivers are themselves attractive to population. Contrasts in density are lessened by the relative uniformity of the environment.

(2) In eastern and southern France, areas of high density are more scattered; the influence of relief is much more marked, whether in the Lyon region or in the Aquitaine basin. A second characteristic lies in the multiplicity and extent of contrasts in density. From a densely populated coastal region, valley or inland basin, there is often a sudden change to an almost empty hinterland or to a mountain fringe; in Provence, rural communes which in a hundred years have lost more than half their population are to be found only a few kilometres away from urban or suburban communes whose population has more than doubled in the same period. This juxtaposition of contrasting geographical milieux is not to be found to the same extent in western France. Links between the various high-density zones of eastern and southern France, where they exist at all, are linear in nature, following the valleys.

(3) Between the two major divisions there is a third, difficult to delimit precisely, but with easily discernible characteristics. It roughly corresponds to the zone of very low population shaped like an inverted S, stretching from the edge of the Cévennes to the Ardennes. Against this background, individual communes

stand out as scattered islands of denser population. The linear arrangement of population, following valleys or other lines of relief, is less apparent, and the contrasts of density are also less important; this is a population thinly dotted across the face of the land.

10

 Geographical mobility and migration

1 Changing mobility
1.1 Quantitative aspects

Thanks to the improvement in census statistics, it has become possible to measure the intensity and development of geographical mobility, either by comparing a person's place of residence with the place of birth or, using material available only in more recent censuses, comparing the place of residence at the time of two successive censuses. It has thus been calculated that male geographical mobility doubled in 120 years, and female mobility in 90 years. At each census, the proportion of people living away from the department of birth has risen from 15.4 per cent in 1881 to 20.8 per cent in 1911, 25.6 per cent in 1936 and 50.5 per cent in 1975.

The geographical field within which residential change takes place is also expanding; movement occurs over ever-longer distances. In the hundred years between the intercensal periods 1850–60 and 1954–62, the rate of movement from one department to another increased two and a half times, whereas during the same period the rate for change of commune within the same department remained constant. During the period 1954–75 geographical mobility was increasingly taking place at regional, even national, level. Between 1954 and 1962, 12 million people changed their place of residence, of whom 4.9 million moved to another department and 3.3 million to another region. Between 1962 and 1968, a shorter period than the preceding one, the proportions stayed the same: 11.5 million changed communes, of whom 5.4 million went to another department and 3.2 million to another region. For 1968–75, the figures were respectively 15.5, 7.4 and 4.6. The proportion of inter-regional migrants, 27.5 and 27.8 per cent in the first two intercensal periods mentioned, rose to 30 per cent in 1968–75.

The high geographical mobility of young people is a normal phenomenon at any period and whatever the mobility rates at the period concerned. Age-specific mobility increases rapidly between ages 15 and 25–29, then lessens between 30 and 40, and thereafter declines steadily. Geographical mobility now increases again at the age of retirement, which is often marked by a change in place of residence. More than age, however, it is the context in which people live that allows us to understand the growth and variations in geographical mobility. The decision as to whether or not a person migrates is made in differing circumstances, according to the period in which a person is born and that in which he is living during his years of greatest mobility.

1.2 Factors relating to geographical mobility

Usually it is a combination of factors at a given place and time which triggers off the mechanism leading to migration. Economic factors are normally preponderant, but are not in themselves a sufficient explanation of the migratory process. The more economic constraints are relaxed, the greater becomes the weight of sociological and psychological factors.

As a general rule, migratory movements flow from economically depressed zones to more favoured areas; for a century and a half, movements of this kind have been in progress between country and town, and between the provinces and Paris. The same movement is to be observed today between economically depressed areas, such as the Nord region and Lorraine, and regions of continuing economic progress, such as southeastern France. Labour migration is a response to the redistribution of economic opportunities, to regional wage differentials and to specific local employment requirements in terms of skill and the particular industrial and tertiary 'mix'.

There is also a general relationship between the degree of mobility (measured, for example, by the rate of initial migration) and the rate of economic growth. In general, economic growth at only average level is accompanied by considerable internal migration, but by rather low immigration from other countries. When economic growth becomes rapid, internal migration is intensified and there is also a substantial rise in the number of foreign immigrants. A slowing down or a sudden decline in economic growth is followed by a reduction of internal and more particularly of international migratory movements.

Social impacts on the decision to migrate include events such as marriage or the search for better living conditions. Marriage tends to involve a change of residence for one partner at least, if not for both. In traditional rural societies, migration related to marriage usually involved movement over only small distances, but when marriage coincided with the search for employment, the move could be much more decisive. The search for a new dwelling can also occasion a change of place of residence. This may be a move to an area with the same type of environment, but if the desire to change residence signifies aspiration towards a new way of life, it may bring about a complete uprooting of the individual or the family. This occurs, for example, in the transfer from a rural to an urban environment, or in the change from an apartment to a detached house.

The likelihood of migration from one place to another depends on the relative sizes of the populations of the places concerned and the distance separating them. It also appears that the distance over which major migration takes place towards a particular urban centre increases with the size and rate of that centre's growth. While small towns recruit their immigrant population from the department in which they are situated, major agglomerations such as Lyon, Marseille and Bordeaux attract migrants from their surrounding regions and even beyond. The Ile-de-France (Paris) region draws its immigrants from the whole of France.

2 Migration duration and migrant characteristics

Reference to duration permits a distinction to be made between temporary and permanent migration.

2.1 Temporary migrations

These are of limited duration, but can nevertheless be as long as several months.

2.1.1 *Nineteenth-century migrants in search of work*

Until the economic transformation caused by technical progress and industrial development in the last quarter of the nineteenth century, temporary migration was, for many rural people, a way of augmenting inadequate returns from land which was under constant pressure from rising population. The migrants left poor regions for more prosperous ones, either during the seasons of high agricultural activity in other rural areas (harvest work, grape-picking), or alternatively during the off season, when they would go into the towns as vendors, to carry on some craft, or to work as labourers in the building trade. At the end of winter they would return home, bringing any money they had made, in order to take part in the normal work on the land.

Mountainous areas were most affected by these seasonal movements, notably the Central massif, from which whole networks of occupational migration were organized. Each year thousands of migrants left the Departments of Creuse and Haute-Vienne to go and work on building sites, most heading for Paris.

With changes in the organization of the economy during the latter part of the nineteenth century, temporary migration tended to become permanent. The town, and especially the great city, became more and more attractive to rural dwellers. In spite of the introduction of new machinery into building and construction, much work at this period was still largely done by hand, and the opening of large construction sites necessitated the recruitment of a substantial labour force working throughout the year. The new industrial plants were also unable to operate with a seasonally fluctuating labour force. More and more of the temporary migrants decided to settle in the towns either for a few years before returning home, or even permanently. By the beginning of the twentieth century, work migration had become an affair for the whole family, a clear indication of the will to take up a completely new way of life.

2.1.2 Present-day migratory movements

The current organization of the labour supply has produced changes in the scale of geographical mobility. Temporary migration for work purposes now mainly takes place across national boundaries, while internally, at least in western countries, this type of migration has given way to daily commuting.

(i) The daily journey to work. At the present time, the spatial discordance between home and workplace gives rise to daily commuting or journey-to-work flows. These have tended to increase in intensity with the growth of towns, the spatial diffusion of industry and population out of the older urban centres, the improvement in means of transport, and the organization of systems of assembling workers, for example collection by works buses. The daily migration of labour affects millions of people. Although it may not be desirable that managers and workers should live next door to their place of work, it is equally undesirable for there to be a separation of home and workplace necessitating a long, unpleasant journey: this is likely to have adverse sociological, economic and psychological consequences.

Even national boundaries are no barrier to these daily flows, which reflect inequalities in the labour market, in earnings and in conditions of work. Every day thousands of Belgians come to work in the textile mills of Lille–Roubaix–Tourcoing. French workers from Alsace commute to Baden-Württemberg and Switzerland, and inhabitants of Lorraine living near the German boundary cross into the Saarland.

(ii) Leisure migration. There has also been a great increase in temporary migration for purposes of leisure (considered in its widest sense), particularly associated with the holiday periods punctuating life at school and at work. This marked increase in the number of holidaymakers obviously reflects the progressive reduction in hours of work and the securing of the right to holidays with pay. Also

of importance are the general rise in the standard of living, the development of the mass tourist industry, the need to escape from the stresses of urban life, and improvements in transport. The proportion of French people going away on holiday rose from 44 per cent in 1964 to 54.3 per cent in 1978. With the development of winter sports, the seasonal summer exodus is now tending to be joined by a parallel winter movement. The intensity of movements for holiday purposes varies according to the size of the commune of residence, to the type of dwelling and to socio-economic status. Of all French people, the inhabitants of the city of Paris travel most frequently for holiday purposes, journeys by inhabitants of rural communes being 2.5 times fewer. Vacation migration is essentially an urban phenomenon: for at least one month of summer, Paris is no longer the overcrowded centre of French life. The rate of departure varies also with the socio-economic status of the head of the household. It is extremely high for senior managers and members of the professions, but particularly low for persons not in employment, farmers and agricultural workers. Holiday migration is thus closely linked to income and status.

During the holiday seasons, above all in summer, population takes up a markedly peripheral distribution, reflecting the attraction of the sea and also of the young mountains (Alps and Pyrenees), which are more popular than the ancient massifs in the interior of the country.

These holiday movements have a considerable spatial impact. They have required investment in a new spatial structure to support resort activities. They have called into existence a mass of new building: second homes, hotels, holiday homes for families and holiday villages. The process has included the transformation of farm buildings into self-catering accommodation (*gîtes ruraux*), and the provision of sports grounds, play areas and related roads. The sums spent by holidaymakers contribute significantly to the local economic base, while, for some, seasonal visits may result eventually in the establishment of a permanent residence.

2.2 So-called 'permanent' migrations

These are movements followed by a phase of geographical stability of some duration. Because of improved statistics, more is known about this type of migration in the recent period 1945–75 than for earlier periods.

2.2.1 *Inter-regional population exchanges*

Figures 10.1 and 10.2 show the quantitative and spatial extent of population exchanges in the period 1954–75 between the 21 regions (excluding Corsica). In addition to the strong growth in mobility, the figures throw into prominence profound changes in the relations between the French provinces and the Paris region. The average annual number of migrants from one region to another has progressively increased: 411,270 in 1954–62, 540,240 in 1962–8 ad 651,660 in 1968–75. But these figures are merely the net balance, resulting from two contrary flows, in-migration and out-migration, and provide only an imperfect understanding of the total volume of exchanges. In the Ile-de-France (Paris) region, for example, the net balance of entries and exits for the period 1962–8 was positive at 37,880, but this relatively modest figure was the result of the arrival of 721,736 persons and the departure of 683,856.

For the most part, these migratory movements take place either between neighbouring regions or between the provinces and the Paris region. Four regions (Nord–Pas-de-Calais, Lorraine, Champagne–Ardennes, Franche-Comté) had net losses of population by migration throughout the period 1954–75. At the same time, the net increase by migration in Provence–Côte d'Azur reached unparalleled proportions; between 1968 and 1975, the migratory gain for this region amounted to 43 per cent of the total for all 13 regions showing migratory gain. In the Provence–Côte d'Azur region, the average annual intercensal figure gain by migration was 11,000 in 1954–62, 14,050 in 1962–8, and 30,200 in 1968–75. The Ile-de-France (Paris) region occupies a place of its own in the general picture; from a migratory gain of 41,890 over the rest of France in 1954–62, it moved through a period of relative balance (+6,313) in 1962–8 to a loss of 23,885 in 1968–75.

In any event, whatever the net balance or even the absolute figures for a particular region, the composition of inward and outward migratory flows differs, sometimes fundamentally, according to age, occupation and sex. Those who arrive are not the same as those who leave: this is why it is important to know the characteristics, in order to have a better understanding of the changes caused by their arrival and their departure.

Migration is in the first place linked to occupation. The activity rates of migrants oscillate around 40 per cent, with often marked variations between immigrants and emigrants showing the great imbalance between the Ile-de-France (Paris) region and the provinces as employment zones. The Ile-de-France region is the only one in France to exercise a powerful attraction over members of the active working population, to the detriment of the provinces. It receives migrants who are, or become, blue-collar or white-collar workers, and

---

Figure 10.1 Migratory exchanges between regions, 1954–62 and 1968–75 (Ile-de-France region excluded). Each circle is proportionate to the migratory balance of the region concerned with all regions other than the Ile-de-France (Paris) region. The length of the arrows is proportionate to the total migratory movement between the two regions concerned. In the 1968–75 map the additional thickness of the arrows linking the Rhône-Alpes and Provence–Côte d'Azur regions indicates that they should be twice as long accurately to represent the migratory flows concerned. The difference between the length of the black arrow and that of the white arrow gives an indication of the migratory balance. Movements of fewer than 8,000 persons have been ignored.

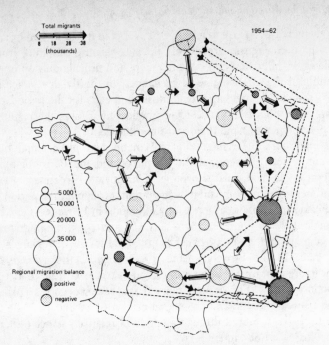

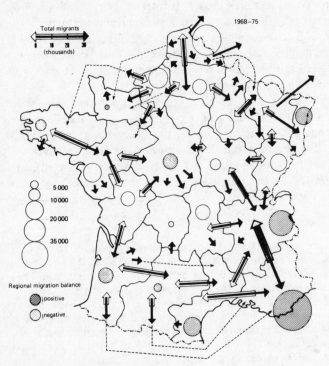

Figure 10.1

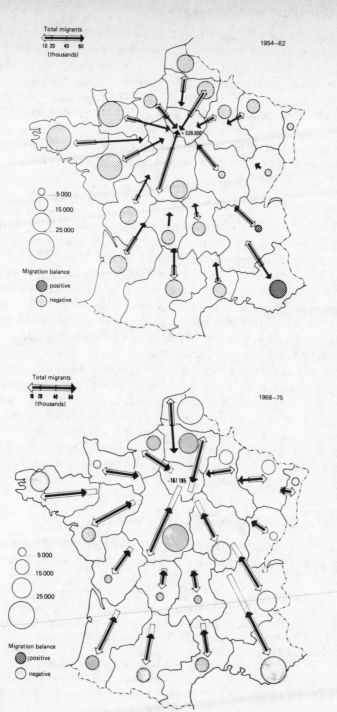

Total migrants

10 20 40 60

(thousands)

1954–62

+ 326,000

○···· 5 000
○ 15 000
○ 25 000

Migration balance

● positive
○ negative

Total migrants

10 20 40 60

(thousands)

1968–75

− 167 195

○···· 5 000
○ 15 000
○ 25 000

Migration balance

● positive
○ negative

Figure 10.2

employees in the service industries; it loses owners, managers and members of the professions. Women are well represented in the flow of economically active migrants; occasionally they outnumber men in migrating to attractive regions, doubtless because of the greater range of employment, which allows them to fill posts in the tertiary sector. On the other hand, they are always over-represented in emigration flow, because of their disproportionately high numbers in age-groups over 50. Young adults are also inclined to settle in the most attractive regions, and especially in the Ile-de-France region, whilst adults of mature age, as well as retired people, prefer to move to the southern half of France.

2.2.2 *Population exchanges between communes*

The behaviour of migrants becomes clearer when we study their distribution according to the size and type of communes of origin and destination. The more a rural commune is dominated economically by agriculture, the greater the tendency for inhabitants to leave it for one of the larger towns. A quarter of rural emigrants settle in towns of more than 100,000 inhabitants (Paris agglomeration excluded). The emigrants from towns of fewer than 100,000 inhabitants are divided more or less in the same fashion; the favoured destinations are in the first place the rural communes, then the larger towns (excluding Paris). A very different behavioural pattern is found in the migratory movement from Paris and the larger cities, more than a third of which is directed towards rural communes.

There is frequently a discrepancy in age structure between emigrants and immigrants. Young adults aged between 20 and 34 are lost by rural communes and gained by towns, especially large towns. For old people over 65 the figures are reversed, rural communes and especially small towns receiving more migrants in this age group than they lose. Net migration gain diminishes as the size of the town increases, becoming negative for the largest agglomerations and especially for the Paris agglomeration.

2.2.3 *Migration to the Paris agglomeration*

Paris has long been a powerful magnet for population flows from almost the whole of France, the only French city to have so vast an area of attraction. In

---

Figure 10.2 Migratory exchanges between the Paris region and other regions, 1954–62 and 1968–75. The circles are proportionate to the migratory balance between the region concerned and the Ile-de-France (Paris) region, except that the circle for Brittany in respect of 1954–62 corresponds to 60,000 migrants. The length of the arrows is proportionate to total migratory movement between the region concerned and the Paris region. The difference between the length of the black arrow and that of the white arrow gives an indication of migration balance. Movements of fewer than 10,000 persons have been ignored.

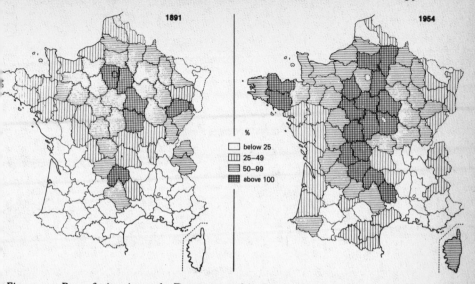

Figure 10.3 Rate of migration to the Department of the Seine, 1891 and 1954. The maps show the total number of persons from the department of origin resident on the day of census in the Department of the Seine as a percentage of the remaining population of the department of origin. Source: Y. Tugault, *Fécondité et urbanisation* (PUF, Paris, 1975), pp. 52–3.

1891, the zone of attraction covered two-thirds of the country; since then it has continued to expand, except in southeastern France (Fig. 10.3).

2.2.4 Retirement migration

The end of working life may be accompanied by a change of residence. At present, however, more than two-thirds of elderly retired people continue to live in the place where they ended their working lives. In spite of this relatively low percentage of departures, the absolute number of retired migrants tends to grow with the increase in size of the population aged 60 or above, and is now estimated at 2.5 million. The most mobile age bracket is between 60 and 64.

The amount of retirement emigration varies according to the size of the places of original residence and their geographical characteristics. The proportion of retired people moving away varies by department between 1.3 per cent and 17 per cent (Fig. 10.4). These variations may be related to the level of income, living conditions at the place of origin, family structure and the quality of opportunities for social life. Retirement migration reaches its greatest intensity in the Ile-de-France (Paris) region, and is at its lowest in Alsace, the Nord region, western France and in part of the Central massif (Fig. 10.4). The propensity to move varies in relation to sex, matrimonial status and occupation immediately prior to

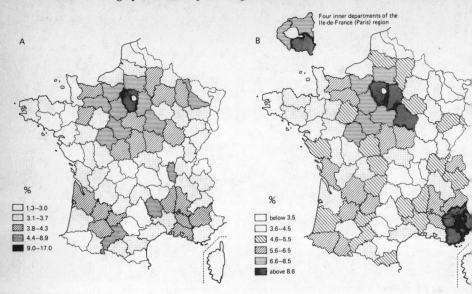

Figure 10.4 Migration of persons aged 65 years and above, 1962–8. A. Emigrants of 65 years and above as percentage of total population of 65 years and above. B. Immigrants of 65 years and above as percentage of total population of 65 years and above. Source: F. Cribier, *La migration de retraite* (CORDES, Paris, 1973).

retirement. Married couples, salaried employees in the public sector and business people are the most mobile on retirement, while single women, retired men without spouses and agricultural workers are the least likely to move.

Retirement migration brings about a spatial redistribution of the elderly population, and often involves long distances. It may involve a return to the region of origin; according to surveys carried out among Paris workers, 30–50 per cent of retired people who leave the agglomeration go back to the department where they or their spouses were born. Retirement migration from the Paris area involves the whole of France to a greater or lesser degree. It also takes place over shorter distances, within and around the agglomerations of origin.

The proportion of retired migrants in the total retired population at the point of destination varies, however, from one region to another (Fig. 10.4). There is a high concentration in the south of the Paris basin and on the Côte d'Azur. Large urban regions are not as a rule attractive to retired migrants, who prefer in general to settle in rural communes, especially in small towns.

2.2.5 Structural consequences of population redistribution

Increased geographical mobility, the large number of people involved and the increasingly specific nature of current migratory flows modify existing populations in a manner that may be found surprising with regard to both speed and changes observed within a short period of time. Migratory movements have a direct influence on the age structure of the population, the relationship of each age group to the total population being modified by arrivals and departures.

11

⚜ Population structure

The population of present-day France and the various groups of which it is made up differ according to demographic structure, a diversity which is as much a consequence of the past as of recent changes. The structural characteristics of the population provide an essential part of the basic data required in the process of French territorial planning.

1 Age structure
1.1 General characteristics

The increasing average age of the population has been observed since the beginning of the nineteenth century (Table 11.1), and relates essentially to declining fertility. The increase in the birth rate after the Second World War for a time put a check on the ageing of the population, but the resumption of decline is once more resulting in an inexorable erosion of the base of the age pyramid. The division of the French population into very unequally sized age groups has changed markedly over time, in particular reflecting the ageing process. From 1861 to 1975 the under-twenties increased by only 25.7 per cent (from 13.4 million to 16.8 million); the 20–64 age group by 34.0 per cent (from 21.5 million to 28.8 million) and those over 65 by 180.5 per cent! In 1861 members of this group numbered 2.5 million, but at present there are more than 7 million. According to the INSEE forecasts, the distribution of the population between these three main age groups in the year 2000 is likely to be 29 per cent under 20,

Table 11.1 *Percentage age distribution of the population,*
1851–1982

Age group	1851	1901	1936	1962	1975	1982
0–19	36.1	34.2	30.0	33.1	30.7	29.6
20–64	59.4	57.3	60.0	55.1	55.1	57.2
65 and above	4.5	8.5	10.0	11.8	14.5	13.2

Source: INSEE.

Table 11.2 *Percentage age distribution of the population in selected*
member-countries of the European Community, 1 January 1975

Country	Under 20 years	20–64 years	65 years and above
Belgium	30.5	55.7	13.8
German Federal Republic	28.9	56.8	14.3
Italy	31.4	56.6	12.0
Netherlands	34.2	55.1	10.7
United Kingdom	30.8	55.3	13.9

Source: European Communities, demographic statistics (Eurostat).

57 per cent 20–64 and 14 per cent aged 65 and above, on the assumption that births will be high enough to assure a replacement of the generations, and 26.0 per cent, 59.5 per cent and 14.5 per cent on the assumption that births will be of the order of 1.8 children per woman, insufficient to ensure the replacement of the generations.

Women are more strongly represented in the oldest age group than men. They were less affected than men by the losses of two world wars, and they have a life-expectancy which is greater than that of men, but by contrast tend to be under-represented in the economically active population because of the predominance of males among immigrants.

For France, as for all western societies (Table 11.2), the ageing of the population is not a new phenomenon, but it is becoming a matter of pressing concern by its very size, by the social and economic problems it presents, and by its marked spatial variation.

1.2 Spatial distribution of the population according to age groups

The maps of the spatial distribution in 1975 of the population aged below 20 and over 65 (Fig. 11.1) look like a photographic positive and negative of the map of gross reproduction rates (Fig. 11.2). The departments with a high percentage of young people form a sort of cone in the northern half of France corresponding quite closely with the area of highest fertility. Conversely, the departments with a high percentage of old people correspond closely with the area of low fertility. But if fertility is a dominant factor in the age distribution of a population, it does not explain everything; a careful scrutiny of the maps reveals the importance of other factors. In Brittany, for example, the lower proportion of young people in the Departments of Finistère and Côtes-du-Nord is in part a reflection of emigra-

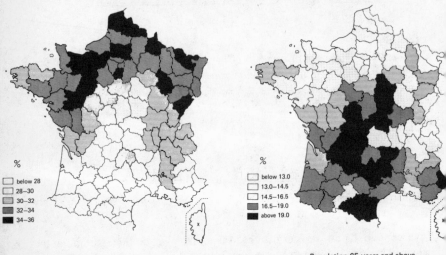

%

☐ below 28
▨ 28–30
▤ 30–32
▦ 32–34
■ 34–36

Population below 20 years

%

☐ below 13.0
☐ 13.0–14.5
▤ 14.5–16.5
▦ 16.5–19.0
■ above 19.0

Population 65 years and above

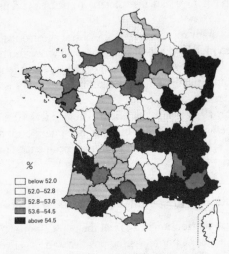

%

☐ below 52.0
☐ 52.0–52.8
▤ 52.8–53.6
▩ 53.6–54.5
■ above 54.5

Population 20–64 years

Figure 11.1 Distribution in 1975 of the three main age divisions, by department. ✕: Data not available. Source: *Economie et Statistique*, no. 90, 1977.

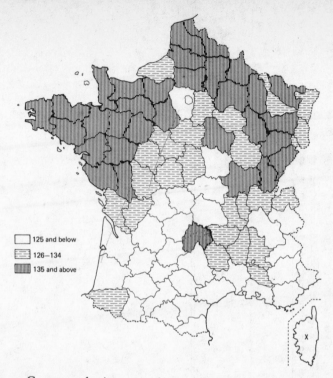

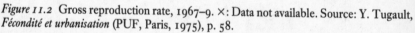

Figure 11.2 Gross reproduction rate, 1967–9. ×: Data not available. Source: Y. Tugault, *Fécondité et urbanisation* (PUF, Paris, 1975), p. 58.

tion. The main impact of migratory flows, however, is on the intermediate group of persons in the economically active years. The proportion of adults in the total population is generally higher in the southern half of France, but above all in the zones where high economic activity provides a powerful attraction to the labour force.

The relative significance of the three main age groups also varies according to whether communes are rural or urban, and according to the size of the latter. These contrasts can be seen within departments, in which urban agglomerations very often have a younger population structure than rural communes. Contrasts are also to be observed between size-categories (Table 11.3). Paris is the urban agglomeration with the smallest number of young people and the largest number of adults, chiefly because of the strong attraction of the employment opportunities it has to offer. The rural communes which do not belong to the zones of industrial and urban population (*zones de peuplement industriel et urbain* – ZPIU) have fewer young people than the national average, partly due to emigration; they form virtual 'reservations' of the old, 20 per cent of their population being aged 65 or above.

Table 11.3 Percentage division of the population into principal age groups, according to type and size-category of commune, 1975

	Rural communes		Within urbanized areas (size-categories in thousands)								
	Within ZPIU	Outside ZPIU	Below 5	5–10	10–20	20–50	50–100	100–200	Above 200	Paris agglomeration	France
0–19	29.2	32.7	32.0	32.2	32.8	32.1	32.1	33.1	30.6	27.2	30.7
20–64	50.9	52.0	52.4	53.2	53.8	54.8	55.6	55.7	56.7	60.5	55.0
65 and over	19.9	15.3	15.6	14.6	13.4	13.1	12.3	11.2	12.7	12.3	14.3
Total	100.0	100.0	100.0	100.0	100.0	100.0	100.0	100.0	100.0	100.0	100.0

Source: *Economie et Statistique*, no. 90, 1977.

2 The structure of the employed population

Since 1946 the size of the employed population at national level has increased only slightly, reflecting the raising of the school-leaving age, the lowering of the age of retirement, the decline in the number of farmers' wives recorded as in agricultural employment, and the arrival on the labour market of the *classes creuses* (the age groups depleted by war deaths or low natality). Between 1954 and 1962 the increase would have been even less, or there could even have been a decline, but for the immigration of foreign workers (Table 11.4). This stability of the employed population stands in marked contrast to the scale of postwar economic growth, demographic recovery and the transformation of the French economy in the last 25 years. The problem is a different one: the population has to meet a growing burden of investments, taxation and social security charges to support the young, the unemployed and the aged. Expansion and economic progress are now based on productivity gains, not on increased labour inputs. More recently, a further problem emerged with the arrival of the postwar generations on the labour market; development now risks being seriously hampered by the effects of the economic crisis on the employment rate.

2.1 Distribution of the working population by sector of employment

From 1954 to 1981 the proportion of the working population engaged in the primary sector (for the most part in agriculture) fell from 26.8 per cent to 9 per cent. The proportion of those occupied in the tertiary sector rose from 37.9 per cent to 56 per cent, whilst the share of industry and of building and construction remained almost constant, registering only a small decline. This profound change in the occupational structure has demanded changed attitudes, changed methods of work, a continuous adaptation to new kinds of work, and a constant emphasis on the importance of vocational training. Changes no less profound will undoubtedly continue to be required in the future. The transformation of agricultural employment has been particularly striking. Since the end of the Second World War, the agricultural work force has declined at a hitherto unprecedented average annual rate of 3 per cent, reflecting the large number of farmers and farm workers who have left for other occupations, the fall in the number of new entrants into farming, as well as retirement and death. The numbers in agriculture fell from 6.2 million in 1946 to 5.1 in 1954, 3.9 in 1962, 3.0 in 1968, 2.0 in 1975 and 1.8 in 1981.

Table 11.5 permits a comparison between the occupational structure of France and a number of other countries. France is situated between the two extremes of countries as different as Italy and the Netherlands. In France the agricultural sector is still relatively large, whereas it is proportionally much less important in countries of more advanced economic development. The secondary sector appears less strong than in the other European states, while the tertiary

Table 11.4 *Changes in the employed population, 1954–75*

Year	Total (thousands)	Percentage of total population	Male (thousands)	Female (thousands)	Percentage foreign	Available for, and seeking, employment (per cent)
1954	19,185	44.8	15,502	6,683	...a	...
1962	19,251	41.4	15,587	6,664	5.7	1.2
1968	20,398	41.2	13,272	7,126	6.3	1.6
1975	21,175	41.4	13,643	8,132	7.3	3.4

a Not available.
Source: INSEE.

Table 11.5 *Employment by main sectors, 1979*

Country	Total Thousands	Agriculture Thousands	%	Industry Thousands	%	Other Thousands	%
Belgium	3,754	119	3.2	1,334	35.5	2,301	61.3
Canada	10,369	589	5.7	2,994	28.9	6,786	65.4
France	21,127	1,897	9.0	7,670	35.3	11,560	54.7
German Federal Republic	25,041	1,558	6.2	11,233	44.9	12,250	48.9
Italy	20,187	3,012	14.8	7,546	37.7	9,629	47.5
Japan	54,790	6,130	11.2	19,140	34.9	29,520	53.9
Netherlands	4,632	279	6.0	1,481	32.0	2,872	62.0
United Kingdom	24,803	631	2.5	9,669	39.0	14,503	58.5
USA	96,945	3,455	3.6	30,402	31.4	63,088	65.1

Source: OECD.

sector in France is close to the German Federal Republic but far behind Britain, the Netherlands and the United States. Unfortunately this comparison, instead of providing explanations, merely raises questions. Is it, for example, the retention of millions of French workers in the primary sector that is responsible for the relative weakness of the other two sectors, or is it the inadequate demographic growth of the last hundred years?

The major study regions used for French strategic spatial planning (*zones d'étude et d'aménagement du territoire* – ZEAT) all reflect these changes but to varying degree, each having a characteristic 'mix' of agricultural, industrial and tertiary activities. The variety of employment opportunities available to the working population will therefore vary according to the region in which they live (Fig. 11.3).

The proportion of agricultural workers in the total active population has everywhere shown a marked decrease, but there is nevertheless a considerable range between the extremes of the Paris region (0.9 per cent) and the West (20.6

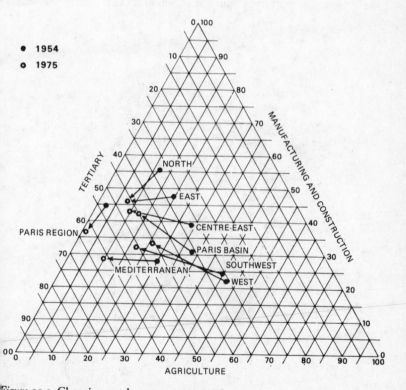

Figure 11.3 Changing employment structure of study regions for strategic spatial planning (ZEAT). Note: 'ZEAT' stands for *Zone d'étude et d'aménagement du territoire*. Source: Statistiques INSEE.

per cent). The Southwest, with 10.1 per cent in agriculture, is also above the national average. The map showing those engaged in agriculture as a percentage of the total work force shows a clear division of France along a northwest-southeast diagonal from the mouth of the Seine to the mouth of the Rhône (Fig. 11.4).

The development of the tertiary sector has been more uniform. In most regions the proportion of workers in this sector, which in 1954 represented about 30–35 per cent of the total working population, increased until as late as 1975, when it reached between 45 and 50 per cent. The Paris and the Mediterranean regions stand out from this general trend: the extremely high levels of tertiary activity which characterized them in 1954 were still to be found in 1975.

It is perhaps in the industrial sector that regional differences are most sharply defined, not only with regard to differences in the percentages of industrial employment, but also with regard to the variation of this sector in relation to the other two. Not only were there considerable differences in the percentage of industrial employment within individual regions in the period 1954–75, but the direction of change often varied from one region to another. Industrial employ-

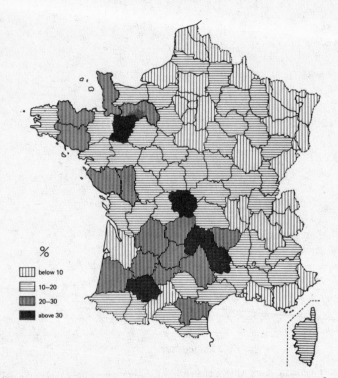

Figure 11.4 Active population engaged in agriculture, as a percentge of total active population, 1975. Source: SEGESA.

ment increased only slightly in the West and Southwest, but more markedly in the Paris basin. In the Mediterranean region the proportion fell, whilst in the industrialized regions (especially Paris and Nord) the percentage of industrially occupied population either remained stable or suffered a decline.

2.2 Division of the working population according to socio-economic status

Two important changes have affected the socio-economic division of the working population. In the first place there was the extraordinary reduction in the numbers employed in agriculture. Between 1954 and 1975, the number of farmers fell from 20.7 per cent to 7.6 per cent of the total occupied population and farm workers from 6 per cent to 1.7 per cent. Secondly, there was a considerable increase in the numbers and percentage of members of the professions, executives and senior managers, middle managers and white-collar workers. Two other socio-economic categories have also changed their importance. Owners of industrial and commercial enterprises have proportionately declined, while manual workers have slightly increased in relative importance (Table 11.6). The result of these various movements is that the salaried and wage-earning element in the economically active population has risen sharply from 63.7 per cent in 1954 to 82.7 per cent in 1975.

There are also marked regional contrasts in the relative importance of the socio-economic status groups. In any region, one of the socio-economic categories is generally found to be present in proportions above the national average: its combination with other groups is also often distinctive. For example, an over-representation of farmers is generally accompanied by a clear under-representation of industrial workers (a phenomenon very apparent in Brittany and southwest France), and by a high proportion of persons not in employment. Thus the dividing line mentioned above between an agricultural and a less agricultural France contrasts, in fact, two quite different types of economic development. Another very distinctive feature of socio-economic structure at regional level is that the categories of owners of industrial and commercial enterprises, members of the professions and senior managers are dominant only in the Ile-de-France (Paris) region and in Provence–Côte d'Azur.

2.3 Foreign workers

In 1962 there were 1.1 million foreign workers. The figure rose to 1.3 million in 1968, and to 1.8 million in 1981. The proportion of foreign workers in the total employed population is also increasing. Foreign workers are heavily concentrated in a limited number of branches of employment, where their contribution is of considerable economic importance. Because the great majority of them come from countries with a low standard of living, and have no vocational

Table 11.6 *Employed population by socio-economic category*

Category	Total in category, 1975	Average annual change			Percentage of employed population			
		1954–62	1962–8	1968–75	1954	1962	1968	1975
Farmers	1,650,865	−3.3	−3.5	−5.6	20.7	15.8	12.1	7.6
Farm workers	375,480	−4.2	−5.6	−6.1	6.0	4.3	2.8	1.7
Owners of industrial and commercial establishments	1,708,925	−1.5	−0.7	−1.9	12.0	10.6	9.6	7.8
Professions and higher management	1,459,285	4.1	4.5	5.6	2.9	4.0	4.9	6.7
Middle management	2,764,950	3.8	4.9	4.7	5.8	7.8	9.8	12.7
Clerical and supervisory	3,840,700	1.9	3.8	3.6	10.8	12.5	14.7	17.7
Manual workers	8,207,165	1.1	1.5	0.9	33.8	36.7	37.8	37.7
Service occupations	1,243,490	0.4	1.8	0.9	5.3	5.4	5.7	5.7
Others (creative workers, clergy, armed forces, police)	524,000	1.2	−1.2	−0.1	2.7	2.9	2.6	2.4
Total for France	21,774,860	0.04	0.97	0.84	100.0	100.0	100.0	100.0

Source: Thévenot, 'L'extension du salariat', *Economie et Statistique*, no. 91, 1977.

qualifications, they find unskilled work as agricultural labourers, miners, dockers, forestry workers, labourers in the building, construction, steel, chemical and vehicle industries. Of all the foreign workers, 49 per cent are unskilled or labourers, accounting for 20.5 per cent of all workers in this category, and 22.9 per cent are foremen, skilled workers or apprentices, 11.5 per cent of the category. Typically foreign workers are young men (25–40) who have immigrated without their families, which gives this group its very individual social characteristics. They are chiefly concentrated in the industrial regions of eastern France and in the Paris region (Fig. 11.5).

2.4 Women

The increasing importance of female employment is a major recent change in the economic organization of the country. In the period 1962–8 female employment

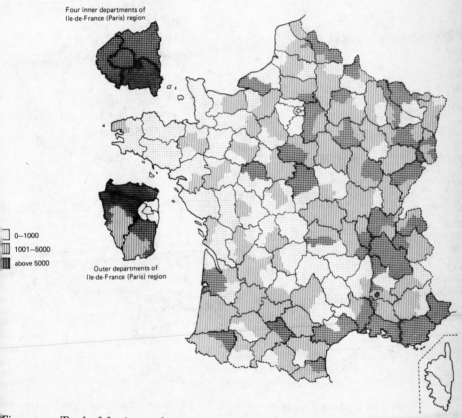

Figure 11.5 Total of foreign workers, 1975, by *arrondissement*. Data for Corsica not available. Source: DATAR.

increased annually by an average 77,000. By 1968–75 the average annual increase had doubled to 143,700, resulting in a total female work force of 8.1 million by the end of the period. It was the rapidly increasing contribution of women that enabled the overall French activity rate to remain constant (41.2 per cent in 1968, 41.4 per cent in 1975). There was, in fact, a twofold development. Until the 1950s, women worked chiefly on family farms in the agricultural sector but increasingly the growth of opportunities for paid employment, especially in the tertiary sector, offered them new possibilities of work. The female element in the agricultural work force fell rapidly from 41.4 per cent in 1946 to 8.6 per cent in 1975, while women's share of tertiary employment rose from 44.8 per cent in 1954 to 65.9 per cent in 1975. Female activity rates, which had at first fallen when

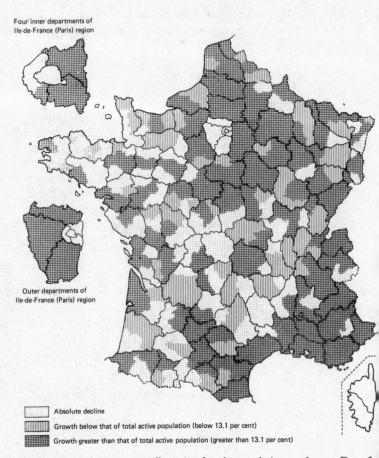

Four inner departments of
Ile-de-France (Paris) region

Outer departments of
Ile-de-France (Paris) region

Absolute decline
Growth below that of total active population (below 13.1 per cent)
Growth greater than that of total active population (greater than 13.1 per cent)

Figure 11.6 Changes in the economically active female population, 1962–75. Data for Corsica not available. Source: DATAR.

Table 11.7 *Proportion of women in the working population by socio-economic category*

Category	1954	1962	1968	1975
Farmers	41.5	39.2	38.1	34.3
Farm workers	15.0	11.5	10.3	11.6
Owners of industrial and commercial establishments	37.2	36.7	35.2	33.4
Professions and higher management	13.8	15.9	19.1	23.2
Middle management	36.7	39.6	40.6	45.2
Clerical and supervisory	52.8	58.8	61.0	63.9
Manual workers	22.7	21.6	20.4	22.4
Service occupations	80.7	80.9	79.1	77.9
Others	26.1	23.4	20.7	19.1
Total	34.8	34.6	34.9	37.3

Source: Thévenot, 'L'extension du salariat'.

so many women left agricultural work, subsequently rose to 36.8 per cent in 1968 and 40.2 per cent in 1975.

Characteristic female occupations have greatly changed in recent years (Table 11.7). As compared with 1954, more women in 1975 were occupied in teaching, administration, higher management, middle management, and in clerical occupations. The proportion of women among manual workers has remained much the same, but with a significant redistribution wthin the category. Women are now less strongly represented as foremen, skilled workers and unskilled workers, but more strongly represented among labourers, where their share rose from 21.6 per cent in 1954 to 38.1 per cent in 1975.

Regional differences in female activity rates are also marked, ranging from 31.9 in Languedoc–Roussillon to 41.8 per cent in the Ile-de-France (Paris) region. Between 1962 and 1975 the growth of female employment was particularly rapid in the eastern half of France (Fig. 11.6).

2.5 The unemployed

The changing structure of economic activity has not been of unmitigated benefit to the working population. Changes often take place imperceptibly, until businesses unable to stand up to competition are driven into bankruptcy or restructuring. These structural difficulties, accentuated in the context of international economic crisis, explain the present extremely tense situation of the labour market and the growing number of people out of work. The unemployment figure rose steadily from 1967 onwards, with women and young people under 25 most affected.

12

 Contrasting mentalities and civilizations

Landscape is an expression of civilization, reflecting a nation's character quite as much as its literature, its art or its history. The landscape, however, is difficult to 'read', because it is not made anew in every century; instead, each century leaves its mark on what remains from the past, a mark sometimes imperceptible, sometimes confused. Yet it is undeniable that the way the land is used is linked to the psychology of its inhabitants and to their social, legal and political traditions.

1 French culture and civilization

Both landscape and geographical structure bear witness to the influence of pre-industrial cultures and civilizations existing prior to the creation of French geographical space. The diversity of the traditional elements within the provinces of France is an essential component of French geography, corresponding to specific ethnic and cultural differences reaching back to the very origins of the French people. These differences are to be seen in the varying characteristics of consumption, customs and behaviour and persist despite population mobility, migration and considerable intermixing. Occupying a unique position within Europe, France is at the crossroads of Atlantic, northern and Mediterranean civilizations. There are four different faces of France: a northern France which contrasts with a southern France, and an Atlantic France which is opposed to a continental France.

1.1 France north and south

The contrasts between north and south are so numerous and so distinct that the division has long been recognized (Fig.12.1). It is based on the fundamental opposition between the customary law of Germanic tradition and the codified Roman law, between the *langue d'oïl* and the *langue d'oc*, and between peoples of Frankish and Mediterranean origin.

These essential differences are not alone in distinguishing northern from southern France. The contrast is reinforced by the distinction between openfield and *bocage*, between a triennial rotation of crops in the north and a biennial rotation in the south, and by the presence of trees growing in the arable fields in the south. In terms of settlement, the most striking difference is in roof forms: in northern France the roofs slope steeply at an angle of about 45 degrees and are covered with flat tiles nibbed on the underneath for suspension; in southern France the rounded Roman tiles give a gentle 30 degrees slope to the roof.

This boundary between north and south in France doubtless coincided originally, except on the Atlantic coast, with a forest barrier. Brenne, Sologne, Bourbonnais, Nivernais, Bresse and the central Jura constituted a group of wooded regions, often marshy and infertile, although interspersed with more favourable open areas. It was the northerners who, at the beginning of the second millennium, cleared and populated these wooded areas, with the result that the linguistic frontier came to be situated on their southern fringes. With the revival of regionalist movements in France, this north–south division has often been analysed in psychological and political terms. The Occitan movements, for example, which were formerly purely cultural, now accuse the state of the 'colonialist exploitation' of southern France.

1.2 France west and east

The north–south contrast is complicated by differences between east and west. These are of a different order, relating to the distinctive character of Atlantic coastal regions. Pierre Flatrès has drawn attention to the existence of an Atlantic civilization whose common characteristics are to be found from the northwest of the Iberian peninsula through Aquitaine, Brittany, Ireland, Cornwall, Wales and Scotland to Norway.[1] These are for the most part Celtic lands, which unquestionably share the same civilization, despite differences of climate and soil arising from a great spread of latitude. But the sea has also played a unifying role, moderating climatic extremes, providing seaweed for fertilizer and offering facilities for transport and exchange. It is the essential role of the sea that explains the limited penetration into the land of this civilization.

[1] P. Flatrès, *Géographie rurale de quatre contrées celtiques* (Rennes, 1957), and 'Les structures rurales de la frange atlantique de l'Europe' in *Géographie et Histoire Agraires* (Proceedings of conference held 2–7 September 1957, Faculté des Lettres de l'Université de Nancy, 1959), pp. 193–202.

A unity of agricultural system marks this Atlantic fringe. Thanks to the use of manures derived from the sea, the same land can be cultivated year after year. Rotations, instead of being rigid, are subtly adapted to the quality of the land. Moorland also has a distinctive role, both for extensive grazing (Basque *touya*, Breton *landes*) and for cultivation in temporary breaks. Another common

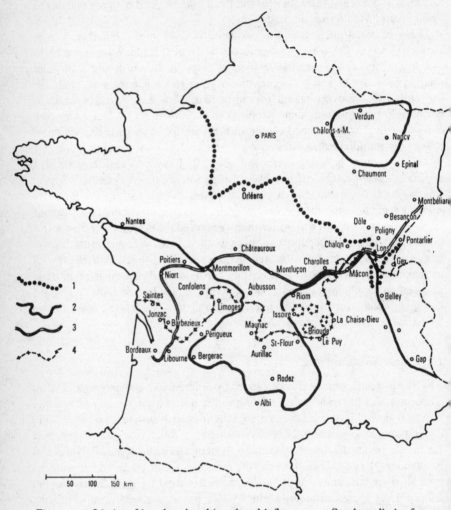

Figure 12.1 Limits of 'northern' and 'southern' influences. 1. Southern limit of open-field 2. Northern limit of low-pitched roofs with Roman tiles 3. Boundary between 'langue d'oïl' and 'langue d'oc' 4. Boundary between the area of written law and the area of customary law. Note on linguistic terms: '*Langue d'oïl*: the group of regional languages and dialects north of dividing line (3), such as Picard or Walloon; *langue d'oc*: the group of regional languages and dialects south of dividing line (3), such as Limousin, Auvergnat, Gascon or Provençal. Source: R. Lebeau, *Revue de Géographie de Lyon*, 1948.

characteristic is the small scale of the basic agricultural cell, typically the dispersed, isolated farmhouse or very small groups of farms; rural settlements do not reach the size of the grouped villages of Lorraine. The traditional rural settlement structure of the Atlantic fringe, which is still characteristic of today's landscapes, is in fact a dual one, combining dispersed farms with service hamlets (the so-called *villages* of Brittany).

Above all, it is the sea that has shaped the character of this Atlantic fringe. Its people have learned to combine the ways of life of farmer and sailor. The existence of numerous ports and the early links with foreign countries have contributed to the formation of distinctive, outward-looking and inquiring attitudes among the population.

In more general terms, the west–east division reflects the contrast between maritime and continental France. Maritime France is a world of rivers, long used for transport, of estuaries and ports turned towards colonial possessions in the Indies and Africa. Here a bourgeoisie grew rich on the sale of spices and tropical produce, nourishing a maritime capitalism orientated more towards the maintenance of trading interests than to the development of manufacturing. Eastern France, by contrast, if the Mediterranean seaboard is excluded, was marked by a long-standing political attachment to Germany and Italy, and economic links with the capitalists and entrepreneurs of the Rhinelands, Switzerland and Piedmont. This continental France was commercial and industrial, more 'European' than maritime in its interests.

Upon this framework of indigenous cultures, more powerful civilizations were superimposed, permeating and diffusing into the older structures. They offered or imposed their own languages, laws and ways of life and thought. This was the case both with the Gallo-Roman civilization and with the Christian civilization of the Middle Ages. But the uniqueness of France lay in the precocious formation of a state, a centralizing power favouring the early development of an indigenous civilization which itself acted as a powerful unifying force.

2 The French mind

People and their societies do not interact with environment in a direct, value-free and objective way. Interaction depends on the perception of environments and on the evaluation of their potential in terms of the advantages and difficulties that their utilization presents. This process of perception and evaluation is not neutral, but varies with the temperaments and characteristics of each individual society, which in their turn are not independent of environment. The temperaments of the people of Brittany, Provence or Alsace vary because they are rooted in geography as well as in history.

A distinction must be made between the range of popular and regional cultures and the culture of France itself. On a regional scale, the relationship of societies to their environment is age-old, dating from pre-industrial times. These were little-urbanized peasant societies, which could be differentiated into groups of cattle breeders, arable cultivators, mountain pastoralists, wine-growers and fishermen. All these developed an intimate knowledge of their environments which often exceeds that gained from scientific investigation. The results of observation, experience, the knowledge transmitted from past generations, and the fruit of personal experience produced an authentic 'geographical wisdom'.

At the national level, France is the opposite of an isolated society, in contact with all the cultural regions of Europe, absorbing many different influences and in return disseminating its own ideas and philosophies. In the eyes of its inhabitants, France is a person, a land, a territory, an idea to be admired, possessed and defended, not primarily a space, a territorial organization. It is an anthropomorphic concept rather than a spatially and geographically defined nation; a nobly endowed person, blessed by the gods, who is immortal and who will emerge victorious from all difficulties. Such a personal identification hardly favours an attitude of curiosity with regard to territorial or geographical problems. The French tend to believe in miracles; they do so because their history consists of a series of astonishing recoveries and revivals. This concept of France, linked to its wealth, its low population and an ingrained Christianity leads to the notion that all problems can be miraculously solved.

The civilization of France has not spread beyond its borders in visible, geographical ways; it has exported ideas, not life-styles or models of territorial planning. Man cannot be content, however, with idealizing his own country, nor reducing it to a complete abstraction; he is inevitably driven to manipulating the given space, to humanizing it. Certainly some of the characteristics of the French temperament and civilization are permanently present in man–environment relations; others are rather the legacy of history.

2.1 Intellectualism

The French temperament is essentially intellectual: it has a liking for abstract thought, theory and reflection (to which any other consideration must be sacrificed), for a rigorously ordered structuring of ideas, for logic and a degree of analysis reflecting more a striving for intellectual satisfaction than for the truth about the real world. A Frenchman is more interested in the moments before and after an event than in the event itself, for these are more rich in intellectual possibilities. 'The French mind always rates the formula, the arbitrary, the *a priori*, the abstraction, the artificial more highly than the real, and prefers clarity to truth, words to facts and rhetoric to knowledge' (H. Amiel).

Consequently the Frenchman is not inclined towards concrete thought, or the adjustment of ideas to the demands of reality; nor is he inclined to prefer a partial reform that is capable of implementation to an attractive but impracticable overall theory. This explains the paradox of the French style of planning. It was the French who evolved a theory of comprehensive planning which was to attract world attention by its guiding concepts, the ways in which these were developed in practice, and the flexibility of their implementation. The French, however, satisfied with this first stage of the 'intellectual' development of the plan, are less concerned to verify whether the planning proposals are transformed into concrete reality and whether the means of application and control are as advanced as the theoretical conception.

It would perhaps be an exaggeration to say that the French are content to live their lives on a fictional plane, but as people of thought rather than action they are often content to create a single, unique work; all too often others are left to profit from French creativity.

2.2 Legalism

The legalistic mentality of the average Frenchman is well known: he feels that he has the law on his side, and that he has the protection of a whole battery of regulations which constitute the ordered framework of existence. Salvadore de Madariaga has given an excellent definition of this trait of the French temperament:

Order in France is imposed from above, although it is accepted from below. It is intellectual, artificial, regulated, prefacing action by a complicated system of rules formulated in anticipation of every possible contingency. This tendency towards intellectualism immediately comes into play, limiting and defining the available field of action, over which it casts a network of principles to which all future acts must conform. So much is enshrined in legislation. Naturally these principles with their perfect consistency are excessively remote from the irregularities of real life. In order to lessen the gap between the actual situation and the action permitted by law, the French mind inserts an even more subtle network of implementing orders and regulations into the network of the law.[2]

This dual network of laws and regulations clearly encourages routine and inertia; it confines space and its organization within the shackles of orders and regulations which make a normal evolution and adaptation difficult if not impossible. To the extent that new situations bring the regulations into question, the principles of the law itself may seem to be challenged: that is why the Napoleonic Code is still the legal dinosaur of twentieth-century France.

The necessary proposals for the reform of territorial structures – regrouping of communes, administrative bodies for urban agglomerations, modifications to the system of land holding – are not considered in relation to present needs but in relation to great political and legal principles, such as individual freedom and the rights of private property.

These two traits – intellectualism and legalism – explain the world-wide success of French concepts and examples; by virtue of their very generality and abstraction they appear universally applicable. One can also understand the French predilection for clear-cut categories, for vertical administration in

[2] *Anglais, Français, Espagnols* (Gallimard, Paris, 1952), pp. 52–3.

homogeneous sectors. The French are less at ease in a horizontal organization on the geographical plane, where elements of the vertical sectors interact, although it is here that we find the very essence of the organization of space and the global and regional understanding of problems.

2.3 Individualism

There is no need to stress the individualism of the French temperament. It is apparent in the landscape, with its scattered little plots of land, and houses which show the striving whenever possible for individuality of design and layout. The Frenchman is deeply attached to individual initiative and individual responsibility.

André Siegfried saw in this individualism one of the reasons for the weakness of the industrial revolution in France: 'The industrial revolution was accepted reluctantly in France . . . Tradition and routine counselled individual production in small businesses where initiative could give of its best. Tradition and routine similarly counselled the peasant not to specialize, and to preserve his complete and intimate knowledge of the land.'[3]

The same characteristic is found in the Frenchman's relationship with nature. He does not blend into the natural environment in the same way as the Englishman; logical to a fault, he will level the ground and wipe out all trace of original vegetation in order to create, out of nothing, parks and gardens 'in the French manner', so forming an entirely artificial setting.

2.4 Egalitarianism

The French have a highly developed sensitivity towards injustice and inequality. Their passion for justice finds expression in the wish to suppress inequalities or at very least to lessen them and to equalize differences. This attitude manifests itself in the field of geography. The whole policy of territorial strategic spatial planning (*aménagement du territoire*) rests on the desire to redress the balance of the different regions of France, wiping out the differences between rich and poor regions, between Paris and the provinces. Harmony and balance are the two words which express this feeling. This egalitarian attitude, however, takes little account of differences in spatial structure, of historical or geographical contingences, nor of inequalities of temperament and capacity for enterprise. It explains the reliance on state action to achieve equality for all.

2.5 Conservatism, protectionism and Malthusianism

Other characteristics may appear less permanent, being the more immediate legacy of recent historical and economic conditions. From a combination of

[3] Preface, P. Combe, *Le Drame français* (Plon, Paris, 1959), p. iii.

individualism and legalism sprang attitudes which have permeated French thinking in recent centuries. Conservatism and Malthusianism are not permanent features of the French temperament, as the history of France proves; they are the logical result of a century of demographic stagnation. The almost one-to-one replacement of the population from one generation to another posed no problems of growth, expansion of investments or creation of employment. The French could delude themselves into thinking that they were being governed when in reality they were merely being administered.

This period had a profound psychological impact. Attitudes became protective, devoted to the defence of established rights. In the economic field, from 1800 onwards protectionism had decreed that France should be a national reservation, shielded from the winds of competition; for decades (and still today in certain domains) all government action was directed to the protection of small-scale enterprise: the small shopkeeper, the small farmer, the small or medium-sized firm. There was no recognition of the inevitability of change, no response sufficient to minimize its adverse effects.

2.6 Attachment to place

The French have always been reluctant to uproot themselves; in recent times there has been none of the pioneering tradition that in America takes migrants perpetually across the continent in search of more satisfactory employment and living conditions. Even so, there are contrasts between regions, some of which have a tradition of emigration.

More often, however, movement is imposed by the economic situation, because no other solution is possible. Each closure of a mine or a factory reveals the difficulty and occasionally the impossibility of providing alternative employment within reasonable travelling distance. The Frenchman is deeply attached to his native village; if he moves away, he returns with increasing frequency during the holidays or on retirement.

All these characteristics are far from being entirely negative; it would be foolish to refuse to recognize that they are associated with such values as a sense of justice, respect for the individual, love of the place where one was born, reticence and unease when faced with the dehumanization of present-day conditions of life. At a time when frontiers have opened, when populations have increased at a rate unknown to previous generations, and when every economic and territorial structure is subject to review, these values are being severely tested.

2.7 Centralization

Though lacking physical and ethnic unity, France has been subjected to an unparalleled political and administrative centralization. This was doubtless the price paid for the unification of a territory open to the influence of so many different worlds and civilizations, steeped in so many regional conflicts and contrasts in those lively peripheral areas along the coasts and frontiers. But in France the tendency encountered well-prepared ground: the two characteristics of intellectualism and legalism favoured the establishment of a bureaucracy in Paris monopolizing and controlling all initiatives. From Paris emerged all the laws and regulations implementing them, drawn up in the most minute detail, irrespective of the differing characteristics of the regions of France.

Grafted on to the image of France as a person, this centralization gave rise to the concept of a government power, an abstract state, which the French shower simultaneously with criticism and requests for favours. The power of this state has become to some extent detached from its territorial foundation and appears as a godsend capable of subsidizing, investing, compensating and bailing out without any return being required. This duality of mind to some extent explains the success of French planning.

The administrative centralization and bureaucratic control exercised from Paris have serious consequences:

(1) France has come to be treated as a completely uniform entity, since all laws and regulations emanating from Paris were regarded as applicable to each commune, without taking regional differences into consideration.

(2) Vertical, sector-based administrative divisions – agriculture, industry and education – have been privileged at the expense of the horizontal administration of districts and regions.

(3) Responsible persons at regional and local level have come to abandon all spirit of enterprise, to consider all thought and initiative as useless because they are likely to lead nowhere. The exchange of ideas between centre and region was rendered impossible by the lack of a truly responsible local elite.

(4) All the most enterprising individuals have been drawn from the provinces into Paris, which also controls the employment of capital derived from provincial and rural France. In this way France was long deregionalized; the French were vertically organized into group and professional associations having only rare contact with members of other groups living in the same town or region. They were not even aware that common problems could arise, let alone be solved, at regional level.

3   The two faces of France

The recent book by E. W. Fox is entirely based on the identification throughout the history of France of its two faces: the France of the urban periphery, a trading nation, liberal and pragmatic, and interior France, rural, administrative and centralized.[4] The former consists of the Mediterranean ports and the Atlantic seaboard, the towns of Artois and Flanders and those of the Rhine–Rhône corridors. The latter is continental France, unable to enjoy the benefits of long-

[4] E. W. Fox, *History in geographic perspective: the other France* (Norton, New York, 1971).

distance trading brought by proximity to seas and rivers, and equally unable to engage in specialized agricultural production. The economic integration of this France was assured by the evolution of the nation-state, by the periodic visits of royal officials and troops, and by the circulation of a common currency.

According to Fox, the nineteenth century and the first half of the twentieth century saw the supremacy of internal, Jacobin, bureaucratic and protectionist France over mercantile France, which had fallen victim to blockades and wars; since the 1960s, however, it was this other France which took control of the levers of power. This analysis agrees with that of many other observers who have long stressed the permanence of the twofold division of France.

For some observers this division can also be seen within every Frenchman. The association of conservative and progressive instincts has often been noted:

The French are arrant conservatives who were so irritated by the idea of a change of currency in 1960 that they succeeded, with tacit general agreement, in securing the permanent coexistence of the old and the new franc. They are also revolutionaries who in spite of confusing revolt with revolution, a passion for liberty with libertarianism, have nevertheless given the world exemplary principles which, whatever people may say, still have a very powerful influence. In each French citizen, therefore, there are two people. One wants nothing to change, the other wants everything to be transformed.[5]

This combination doubtless explains the constant search for a third way between the unbridled capitalism of the West and the totalitarian socialism of the East.

The French temperament reveals a close fusion between traditional qualities derived from a peasant background and more intellectual attitudes of mind. The peasant background explains the success of ecological ideas, the attraction of a return to the land, the symbolics of space on a human scale (the little house with garden) and the taste for a humanized landscape. Individualism, on the other hand, accounts for the enthusiasm displayed in the cultivation of differences and peculiarities, the personalization of ideas and events, and the identification with heroes and saviours. If France occasionally gives the impression of being a profoundly divided country both politically and ideologically, it is also capable of national unity and great outbursts of solidarity and common sense, rallying supporters from both camps. Present-day difficulties stem from the fact that French society is undergoing intense and rapid change after a long period of immobility; much of that society, however, is still deeply rooted in the past.

Certain of these characteristics have found it hard to resist demographic and economic change; according to observers a new French society began to emerge in the decade 1960–70. It is characterized by the destruction of individualism by widespread socialization, by the rejection of formal authority, by the demand to be informed and to participate in decision-making, and by an openness to innovation and creativity; the arts are being replaced by science, and philosophy by technology.

[5] Jean-Pierre Moulin, *Comment peut-on ne pas être Français?* (J. C. Lattès, Paris, 1978), p. 150.

III

⚜ Actors and policies in the
spatial structuring of France

13

Administrative geography

All political power is power over territory.

Roman Schnur

The division of a state into administrative units provides one of the fundamental links between society and the territory that it occupies and exploits. The operations of government – the transmission, diffusion and implementation of decisions – are transmitted through an administrative infrastructure.

The territories delineated by this administrative division have characteristics of size, shape and hierarchy which condition their effectiveness. French administrative units bear the strong imprint of the past. Established for the most part at the beginning of the nineteenth century, they often mirror more ancient divisions, the parishes, bailiwicks, *généralités* or provinces of the *Ancien Régime*, or even the *civitates* or *pagi* of ancient Gaul. Their extent and boundaries are a mixture of natural frontiers and purely artificial limits, corresponding to the possibilities of movement of the time. This administrative infrastructure tends to change only slowly, in marked contrast to the rapid change in population, technology, means of communication and human attitudes.

Until 1972 the administrative hierarchy was that established by the Constituent Assembly about two centuries ago, consisting of four levels: commune, canton, arrondissement and department, of which the first and the last were the most important. On to these was superimposed a new administrative level, the region, its powers and responsibilities established in three main stages (1964, 1972 and 1982).

1 The communes

The communal network corresponds to most ancient divisions. Each commune is a functional historical unit, rooted in the primitive communities which originally cleared and cultivated the land of France. These units provided the basis for the formation of parishes, delineated for the most part before AD 1000, at the end of the great movement of Christianization which took place in the early Middle Ages. Further parishes were created at a later date in the hitherto uncleared forests, but these were limited in both time and space. It is within the framework of the commune that people live and that their activities are organized. It is also by way of the commune that public investment is distributed spatially. French society is divided into as many rural and urban communities as there are communes.

1.1 Large and small communes

In 1975 France was divided into 36,394 communes, with an average area of 1,492 ha. The two largest communes occupy the Rhône delta, Arles with 76,908 ha and Les Saintes-Maries-de-la-Mer with 37,445 ha. The smallest commune, Plessis-Balisson in the Department of Côtes-du-Nord (Brittany) has only 8 ha. The size-distribution of communes in 1968 was as follows:

Communes below 100 ha	104
100–249	1,050
250–499	5,291
500–999	11,994
1,000–1,499	7,630
1,500–1,999	4,336
2,000–4,999	6,707
5,000–9,999	768
Over 10,000	119

It was only in 1958 that an exact picture of the network of communes was provided, thanks to the 1 : 2,000,000 map drawn up by the cartographical laboratory of the Ecole Pratique des Hautes Etudes. It is evident that a line running from the bay of Mont-Saint-Michel by way of Orléans, the Morvan and the Rhône lowland to Grenoble divides a France of small communes to the north from a France of larger communes to the south. The prime interest of the map (Fig. 13.1) lies in the extraordinary variation in the size of communes recorded.

1.1.1 Very large communes

Comprising more than 2,000 ha, these correspond to:

(1) forest areas, either where forested communes extend into neighbouring communes (Fontainebleau, Locquignol-Forêt de Mormal, Hagenau) or

where the forest has a regional extent (Landes, Sologne, Vosges, Morvan, Dombes or Bresse);

(2) mountain regions, where forest is also important (northern part of Hautes-Alpes Department, Provence, Pyrenees, Vosges);

(3) urban communes (Marseille, Nîmes, Toulouse, Paris), but also less important towns which formerly included a 'suburban agricultural belt' within their limits;

(4) alluvial zones, coastal wetlands and polders.

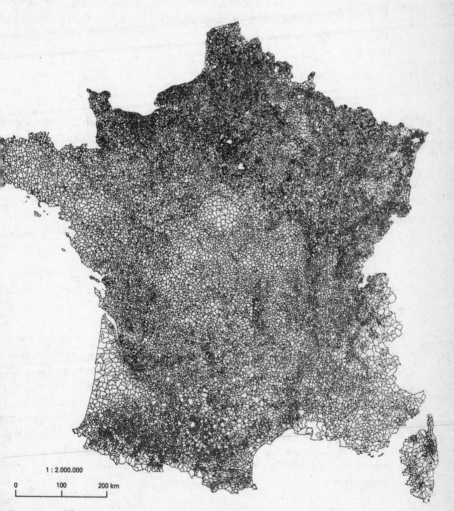

1 : 2.000.000

0   100   200 km

Figure 13.1 The communes of France. Map drawn by the Laboratoire de cartographie de l'École Pratique des Hautes Études. Source: P. Bernard, *Le Grand Tournant des communes de France* (A. Colin, Paris, 1969).

1.1.2 Large communes

These are on the whole typical of areas of dispersed settlement, especially in Armorica and the Central massif. They provide administrative groupings where there is not the same feeling of unity as that which exists in areas of grouped settlement, where a single village may contain the whole population of the commune. The large commune is typically an amalgam of Breton-type villages (not wholly devoted to agriculture), of hamlets and isolated farms. In Brittany the parishes made their appearance only after the establishment of a settled population, while the *bourgs* (low-order rural service towns) are even more recent than the commune.

1.1.3 Small communes

These are characteristic of:

(1) mountain valleys (Grésivaudan); fertile depressions set within plateaus or mountains less favourable to agriculture, such as the depressions fringing the Morvan, the Limagne, the Balagne (Corsica) and the basins fringing the Central massif;

(2) wine-producing regions (Burgundy, the Jura fringe, Languedoc, Champagne, Cognac and Saintes);

(3) particularly fertile regions of limon (loess or loess-loam) soils;

(4) the *bon pays* of early agricultural occupation, that is to say areas of light, easily worked soil.

These small communes correspond to the France of grouped village settlement, forming a 'cellular tissue in the fullest sense of the term' (E. Juillard), with one nucleus to each cell.[1] The commune was the fundamental unit of agricultural life, while each commune had only one centre of social life.

However, the generalization that large communes are to be associated with poor land, and small communes with rich land, must be treated with great caution and discrimination. Exceptions are numerous; for example the minuscule communes of the Norman *bocage* contrast with the extensive Breton communes, although conditions of physical geography are similar. In Aquitaine large communes were created by the union of several parishes, while in other provinces a direct correspondence between commune and a single antecedent parish is more common. Nevertheless, when the map of France is considered as a whole, the major geological units such as the Central massif or Vosges stand out with surprising clarity.

---

[1] A. Meynier, A. Perpillou, E. Juillard, H. Enjalbert, P. Barrère, G. Duby and A. Piatier, *Annales*, no. 4, 1958, pp. 447–87.

1.2 The shape and boundaries of communes

The network of communes can be regarded as providing an initial division of French geographical space into basic units of human spatial organization. Theoretically, and assuming the absence of environmental constraints, the requirements of accessibility to the communal administrative centre, equality of size and the need for contiguity with neighbouring communes would dictate a hexagonal structure. Communes of circular, polygonal and even hexagonal form are indeed frequently found in undissected lowlands of uniform soil conditions. Many of these regular forms are also found where villages occupy forest clearings. But the diversity of environment and the frequent use of boundaries inherited from earlier historical periods explain the numerous departures from the hexagonal model. The greater the variety of relief and hence of the terrain features of the local region, the more eccentric the forms and the more unequal the sizes of communes. For example, in scarpland areas such as Lorraine communes are elongated, extending right across an escarpment from scarp-foot to dip-foot, thus uniting an area of forest on the plateau, slopes with a favourable exposure along the escarpment, good arable land at the scarp-foot and meadow-land along the stream following the strike vale.

Certain features directly determine the shape of a commune by fixing one or more of its boundaries. These may be a shoreline, an estuary, a break of slope, a rock face, a plateau edge or a crest line. The rich communes of the valleys contrast with poorer ones on the plateaus, which are often on limestone. Hydrography plays a decisive role. Small rivers flow through communes, but as the valley grows wider and the river becomes an obstacle to passage it becomes a dividing line. The courses of a great many rivers accordingly stand out on the map of French communes (Fig. 13.1). The courses of the Loire and Allier can be traced between Roanne and Clermont-Ferrand, as well as stretches of the Rhône. The same is also true of parts of the Saône and of the Garonne. In marshy regions drainage channels give communes a regular shape. In mountain regions the communes tend to coincide almost exactly with stream catchments. On the ancient massifs communes are centred on the plateaus and are naturally bounded by the rivers flowing in deeply incised valleys. These controlling lines frequently give rise to regular chains of communes, easily picked out on the map, strung along such features as the coast of Normandy, the Garonne estuary, the banks of the Rhine or the scarps of Lorraine. Occasionally a commune will throw out a corridor of land to link it with some desirable feature such as a river, a belt of pastures (Blénod in Lorraine) or a forest (Villaincourt near Blénod). Natural features are not alone in determining the shape of a commune. Boundaries often follow roads; the straightest communal boundaries in all France follow the roads of the Gallo-Roman period.

1.3 Changes in the pattern of communes

The network of communes is far from static. Communes may disappear as a result of war; the wars at the close of the Middle Ages and the Thirty Years War brought about the total destruction of villages in northern and eastern France. Villages in Lorraine and Champagne destroyed in the First World War have not been rebuilt. In such areas the network of communal boundaries was formerly more finely drawn than at present. Communes may also disappear through municipal incorporation; urban growth may bring about a remodelling of the communal network by the absorption of suburban communes into the core city (the outer arrondissements of the city of Paris were independent communes until 1869).

New communes may be formed out of existing ones in tourist areas. Coastal or winter-sports resorts, which have grown from a hamlet or even in an uninhabited area, claim their autonomy as communes when their interests diverge from those of the traditional commune centre (an example is the new resort of La Grande-Motte on the coast of Languedoc). New communes are also formed in industrial areas. In Lorraine new communes have been created to serve tracts of industrial housing, for example in 1957 at Saint-Nicholas-en-Forêt, near Thionville. A need for the creation of new communes may also arise in urbanized areas, through the creation of major urban-fringe housing projects (*grands ensembles*) and new towns. Their inhabitants may not identify with the administrative centres of the existing communes, which are frequently remote and poorly equipped with services.

Changes in the number of communes are not very perceptible, occurring as they do over long periods of time. The greatest changes have been in areas of very large communes and dispersed settlement, either through subdivision or by the elevation of hamlets to the status of parish or commune. The greatest upheaval took place during the Revolution, when each commune was granted the right of local self-government. New communes were established, many of them very small; the Arrondissement of Rodez, for example, which had 140 communes in 1936, had 326 in 1793, a time when the number of French communes reached its maximum of 44,000. As early as 1800, however, the number had been reduced to about 37,000.

Considered as a whole, the communal system shows remarkable stability. The French temperament, the antiquity of the communes and the consequent accentuation of their individual characteristics have acted as a brake on merger attempts. Only an intimate knowledge of the communes makes it possible to understand the differences between them. The inhabitants of a village are often known by a nickname, a more or less good-humoured expression coined by the inhabitants of neighbouring communes. Over the centuries each commune has acquired its own distinctive personality, having been in the hands of particular administrators, and taught by particular elementary school teachers and priests, of very differing temperaments. Political affiliations also vary from village to village; in such conditions, it is easy to understand the difficulties and resistance which face any plan to reform the system of communes.

1.4 Ossification of the communal pattern

This administrative fragmentation of France appears archaic; in other European countries the communal network is looser, and there is no hesitation, in similar situations, in carrying out modernization of the system, as in the German Federal Republic at various dates from about 1969, the London region in 1965 and the remainder of the United Kingdom in 1974. The archaic nature of the division in France is all the more apparent in a country that is sparsely peopled and in which urbanization and rural exodus have completely changed population distribution. In 1975, out of the 36,394 communes of metropolitan France, 16,732 (more than 45 per cent) had fewer than 300 inhabitants, 2,978 had fewer than 100, and 989 fewer than 50. There is a complete discordance between size, shape and function. The commune is decreasingly capable of serving as an appropriate spatial unit for the provision of public investments and services, whether secondary schools, postal or banking services, or leisure facilities. The smaller communes have no real capacity for management or administration. The divorce between administrative unit and socio-economic functional area becomes ever more pronounced.

Communal fragmentation is further accentuated by the existence of more than 35,000 'sections', subdivisions of large communes containing several nuclei of population, the inhabitants of which have obtained a kind of semi-autonomy in electoral and occasionally in administrative matters. Problems are no less apparent in urban communes. Urban agglomerations which extend over the territories of a number of communes suffer from a multiplicity of administrative bodies, from the difficulty or impossibility of their reaching agreement with each other, and from the parallel establishment of quite separate plans for each commune.

Attempts to encourage the fusion or regrouping of communes in 1968 and 1971 came to nothing. Between 1971 and 1978 only 2,025 communes amalgamated to form 832 new ones, while during the same period 13 communes which had previously amalgamated reclaimed their autonomy. A transformation of the communal system must nevertheless come in the end, whether the change takes a radical form (in 1962 the 'Club Jean Moulin' advocated a reduction to 2,000 communes) or a disguised form (the Guichard Report of 1976 proposed communities of communes', consisting of 750 urban communities and 3,600 other communities'): E. Pisani proposed between 3,500 and 4,000 federations of communes based on existing cantons in rural areas, and on urban agglomerations.[2]

As rapid change appears impossible, solutions involving voluntary associations have been encouraged:

(1) The formation of *intercommunal associations* (*syndicats intercommunaux*) under a law of 22 March 1980, either with a specific object, for example relating to water supply, education or fire services, or for more general purposes (*syndicats intercommunaux à vocations multiples* – SIVOM), of which there were more than 1,738 in 1975, affecting 16,940 communes and 19.4 million people.

(2) The creation of *Districts*, grouping the communes of an urban agglomeration without suppressing them. A District council is then put in charge of the planning, implementation and administration of common services. There were 67 Districts in 1967 and 148 in 1975, affecting 1,269 communes with 4.6 million inhabitants.

(3) The Urban Community (Communauté Urbaine) provides a different and more flexible formula than that of the District for use in major cities. This solution was indeed made obligatory in 1966 for four regional capitals, Bordeaux, Lille, Lyon and Strasbourg, remaining optional for all other cities of more than 50,000 inhabitants. Urban Communities are legally recognized bodies under French administrative law, in charge of services and amenities affecting the agglomeration as a whole. All communes are represented on the administrative council of the Community concerned, which thus provides a first step towards a two-tier administration in agglomerations. By 1980, 252 communes with about 4 million inhabitants had been grouped into nine Urban Communities.

Official action which is shaping the geography of France for years to come has necessarily to be taken within the existing framework of the commune. This is the case with land-use plans, with agricultural land consolidation and the siting of much social equipment. The spatial pattern of investment continues to be contained in this archaic framework, thus providing a degree of resistance to changes in the existing settlement pattern. Demographic and economic changes, and changes in the location of housing and services, have increased the distance between home and work, thus tending to divide communes into two categories: communes which are centres of economic activity on the one hand, and dormitory communes on the other. There is also a fundamental contradiction between decentralization policies aimed at increasing powers and resources at local level, and the continuing existence of more than 30,000 communes.

[2] O. Guichard, *Vivre ensemble, Rapport de la Commission de Développement des responsabilités locales* (Documentation Française, Paris, 1976).

2 The departments

The division of France into departments originated in 1790, when the Constituent Assembly created 83 departments. The aim was to create an equal division of territory; the delineation of the departments even started off from a theoretical concept of a rectanglar network with sides each of a length of 18 leagues. In practice the Constituent Assembly often re-used the boundaries of the former Gallo-Roman dioceses, which in turn frequently corresponded with the limits of the Roman *civitates*. In this way, they often resurrected former provinces such as Rouergue, Quercy or Périgord.

The departments are now the object of much criticism for their arbitrary boundaries and inadequate scale in relation to modern needs (Fig. 13.2). The resultant anomalies are the cause of excessive costs and conflicts of interest. Lyon, for example, the largest city of provincial France, is contained in the 2,859 sq km of the Rhône Department, one of the smallest in France. Isère Department, which stretches right up to the city, has no interest in seeing Lyon extend into its territory. It is true that, in 1968, 23 communes from Isère and 6 from Ain Department were transferred to the Rhône Department, but Vienne, only 25 km from Lyon, is still subject to a departmental administration based on Grenoble. The shape of certain departments is also particularly irregular, notably the long, thin and wasp-waisted Nord Department. Communal and cantonal enclaves also complicate the situation; thus three communes of Nord Department form an enclave within Pas-de-Calais, while the Canton of Valréas of the Department of Vaucluse forms an enclave in the Drôme, an anachronistic survival of an exclave of the former Papal territory of Avignon within the then Dauphiné.

The division into departments has had important geographical consequences. The existence of departments was responsible for a process of urban selection involving the privileged growth and expansion of tertiary functions in the prefectures (departmental capitals). If France regrets the lack of major regional capitals, the responsibility must lie with the 90 departments that have created so many small central places of limited regional influence. It is on the poles represented by the prefectures that human networks and human movements have organized themselves. Despite their small surface area, averaging 6,130 sq km, not all parts of the departments have enjoyed the same attention from the administrators at the prefecture. Lacking intermediate centres, and in the absence of a powerful local advocate in the person of a particularly influential Deputy to the National Assembly or member of the departmental council, outlying sectors of the departments have frequently received less investment and fewer amenities than areas closer to the prefecture.

The only recent modifications to the departmental network relate to the Paris region, where between 1964 and 1968 two departments gave way to seven, and to Corsica, divided into two departments in 1975. These changes brought the total number of departments to 96.

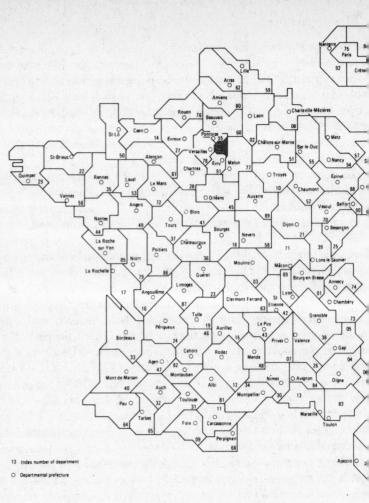

01 Ain
02 Aisne
03 Allier
04 Alpes de Haute Provence
05 Alpes (Hautes-)
06 Alpes-Maritimes
07 Ardèche
08 Ardennes
09 Ariège
10 Aube
11 Aude
12 Aveyron
13 Bouches-du-Rhône
14 Calvados
15 Cantal
16 Charente
17 Charente-Maritime
18 Cher
19 Corrèze
2A Corse-du-Sud
2B Corse (Haute)
21 Côte d'Or
22 Côtes-du-Nord
23 Creuse
24 Dordogne
25 Doubs
26 Drôme
27 Eure
28 Eure-et-Loir
29 Finistère
30 Gard
31 Garonne (Haute-)
32 Gers
33 Gironde
34 Hérault
35 Ille-et-Vilaine
36 Indre
37 Indre-et-Loire
38 Isère
39 Jura
40 Landes
41 Loir-et-Cher
42 Loire
43 Loire (Haute-)
44 Loire-Atlantique
45 Loiret
46 Lot
47 Lot-et-Garonne
48 Lozère
49 Maine-et-Loire
50 Manche
51 Marne
52 Marne (Haute-)
53 Mayenne
54 Meurthe-et-Moselle
55 Meuse
56 Morbihan
57 Moselle
58 Nièvre
59 Nord
60 Oise
61 Orne
62 Pas-de-Calais
63 Puy-de-Dôme
64 Pyrénées-Atlantiques
65 Pyrénées (Hautes-)
66 Pyrénées-Orientales
67 Rhin (Bas-)
68 Rhin (Haut-)
69 Rhône
70 Saône (Haute-)
71 Saône-et-Loire
72 Sarthe
73 Savoie
74 Savoie (Haute-)
75 Seine (Paris)
76 Seine-Maritime
77 Seine-et-Marne
78 Yvelines
79 Sèvres (Deux-)
80 Somme
81 Tarn
82 Tarn-et-Garonne
83 Var
84 Vaucluse
85 Vendée
86 Vienne
87 Vienne (Haute-)
88 Vosges
89 Yonne
90 Belfort (Territoire de)
91 Essonne
92 Hauts-de-Seine
93 Seine-St-Denis
94 Val-de-Marne
95 Val d'Oise

13 Index number of department

O Departmental prefecture

Figure 13.2 The departments of France. The index numbers of departments form the first two digits of the French postal address codes (thus making it unnecessary to name the department in addressing a letter) and the last two digits of vehicle registration numbers (thus indicating the department in which the vehicle was registered). Source of diagram boundaries: INSEE.

Until 1982, the two administrative authorities of the department were the Prefect, appointed by the government and exercising complete executive power, and the council (*conseil général*), composed of representatives of cantons, having an essentially consultative role with limited powers.

Administration at departmental level was revolutionized by the 1982 reforms, aimed at implementing the socialist government's widespread decentralization policies. Executive power was vested in the departmental council (*conseil général*), with the council's president taking precedence over the Prefect, renamed Commissaire de la République. Thus the decisive power of decision at departmental level was transferred from a high-grade civil servant to an elected politician.

The number and size of the departments have been repeatedly questioned, and plans for reform submitted. Departments were originally conceived so as to ensure that all the communes could be reached in a day's journey from the prefecture. The same distance today can be covered in an hour's drive, a shrinking of distance that gives some indication of the present relevance of this level in the administrative hierarchy. The city of Paris is a special case, being both in its territorial extent and its administrative machinery simultaneously a commune and a department. Legislation in 1977 allowed Paris to have an elected mayor (previously, direct government control through the Prefect had been considered essential for this potentially turbulent city), in addition to an elected council. At the same time a certain amount of administrative devolution to the city's constituent arrondissements was instituted.

3 The regions

Individual ministries have long been accustomed to circumvent the disadvantages of the departmental system by the creation of larger units suited to their particular requirements. The extraordinary administrative jigsaw-puzzles that resulted from these uncoordinated decisions tended to reinforce the independent autonomy and authority of the individual ministries, discouraging any move towards regional government. Yet there has been no shortage of proposals for a division of France into regions; between 1850 and 1950 there were no fewer than ten plans, conceived by such famous names as Auguste Comte (1854), Frédéric le Play (1864), Vidal de la Blache (1910) and Yves Chataignau (1945). It was not until 1955, however, that proposals came to fruition in the creation of 20 programming regions (*régions-programmes*) formed from groups of departments ranging in number from two (Nord and Alsace regions) to eight (Midi-Pyrénées). These regions were far from perfect, but had two advantages. In the first place, they restored an economic significance to the regions which had descended from the ancient provinces. Secondly, they provided a regional framework on to which the various administrative divisions that had grown up over the years could be grafted, giving for the first time a certain cohesion to the administrative map of France.

In 1964, regions entered the official administrative hierarchy of France (F
13.3). Each was headed by a regional Prefect (Préfet de Région), advised b
Commission for Regional Economic Development (Commission de Dévelop
ment Economique Régional – CODER), which gave advice on the impleme
tation of economic and social development, and on strategic spatial planning.

Regional policy represented an important change of official attitudes towa
the spatial organization of France, particularly with regard to the relations|
between Paris and the rest of the country. As de Gaulle remarked in 1968: 'T
age-old striving towards centralization, which was for so long necessary in or
to achieve and maintain unity, in spite of the differences between the provin

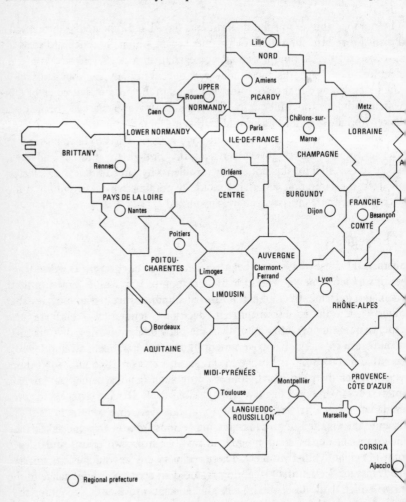

Figure 13.3 The administrative regions of France. Source of diagram of boundari
INSEE.

hat were successively acquired, is henceforth no longer necessary. On the
ontrary, it is action on a regional basis that now appears as the mainspring of the
conomic power of the future.'

Until as late as 1968–70, regional proposals involved only the provision of a
new level in the administrative hierarchy. Thereafter a number of factors played
heir part in changing ideas and in developing a real trend towards a more
comprehensive view of regionalism. These included:

1) The entry of France into the European Community, highlighting the
   regional aspects of development, redeployment and relations with other
   states. Frontier regions in particular discovered a new solidarity with regions
   in neighbouring countries; at the same time they were made aware of the
   obstacles to communication arising from the centralization of the French
   administrative system in Paris.
2) The rapid development subsequent to the student riots and strikes in May
   1968 of a whole range of ideas relating to participation, co-management,
   joint control and dialogue, stimulating the wishes of people in the French
   provinces to have a larger control over their destinies.
3) The revival of regional consciousness, especially in Brittany and southern
   France (Occitanie), in opposition to the dominance of Paris. The regional
   factor thus became the basis for the demands of a range of intellectual,
   cultural and even political movements.

After the failure of de Gaulle's own proposals for regional devolution in the
1969 referendum, a first decisive step towards the creation of regional government for France was taken by the law of 5 July 1972. To the 20 regions of 1955
were added Corsica, detached from Provence–Côte d'Azur, and (on 1 July 1976)
the Paris region (subsequently renamed Ile-de-France region). The region as
conceived in 1972 was not a level of local government but simply a government
office, closely controlled by the regional Prefect, with no independent
administrative authority. In addition to the executive under the Prefect, each
region had a deliberative council (*conseil régional*) and a consultative council
comité économique et social). An important innovation was to allow the region to
have an income of its own, the product of various taxes. But the prefects, as
representatives of the central power, continued to be the only authorities
empowered to allocate funds derived from the centre. This regionalization was
more a deconcentration than a decentralization of power.

The decisive phase in regionalization was reached with the reforms of 1982. In
parallel with developments in the departments, executive power was transferred
from the regional Prefect to the president of the regional council. Members of
his body are directly elected, thus adding the region to the French hierarchy of
democratically elected political bodies.

The effectiveness of a division into as many as 22 regions is often questioned; a
division into between five and ten larger regions has been proposed. Division into

a smaller number of regions is already foreshadowed in the selection of ten cit
outside Paris for development into regional metropolises (*métropoles d'équilib*
in the nine French regions originally proposed as part of possible regio
division of the European Community; in the eight study regions for strate
spatial planning (*zones d'étude et d'aménagement du territoire* – ZEAT); the regio
economic observatories of INSEE (the government statistical office) or
regional managements of various public services such as the national elec
supply service (Electricité de France – EDF) and French Railways (SNCF).

Regionalization is a contemporary necessity, but France, because of the nat
of its structure and history, is without doubt one of the most difficult countrie
regionalize. A region is not created by legislation, it exists because it
recognizable in every aspect of social and economic life; it is regionalized by
investment in social equipment and polarized by some great city, its centre
communications, which it recognizes as its capital, its intermediary with Pa
Prior to the 1982 reforms, at any rate, France has over the centuries become l
regionalized, a tendency reinforced by the development of communications a
by the growth of Paris. The low density of population of the French space,
weakness of the urban network and in particular the dearth of large regio
capitals make real regionalization very difficult to achieve. This explains v
regional consciousness remains much more apparent at the level of the *pays*,
small local region, and is weak in the larger regions. Only Paris and Lyon h
generated real city regions for themselves.

Any regional reorganization poses difficult problems of dimension and delii
tation, beginning with the need to define a Paris region. Within a radius of 1 (
150 km around Paris, the only possible region is based on Paris itself. This is
region that Paris dominates directly, by means of industrial and terti
decentralization, by the leisure-time activities there of its inhabitants, by
creation of second homes, and by an extensive pattern of commuting. As in
past, everything today seems to contribute to strengthening the importance a
extending the influence of Paris, notably the increasing speed of travel and
progressive dispersion of industrial and tertiary activity.

Elsewhere, the financing, location and function of major development proje
– canals, motorways, national parks or tourist attractions – are increasingly int
regional, even international, in nature. It is difficult to strike the right bala
between the interests of the region and the national, or even the Europe
interest.

14

✤ Political geography and geographical policies

If intervention by the state is necessary anywhere, it is in relation to [geographical] space.

G. Dessus

Political geography should not be reduced, as is commonly done, to the study of political entities and the frontiers which divide them. Every policy finds its expression in a landscape and has a direct or indirect geographical significance. Every decision of a demographic, educational, social, economic or even political nature inevitably has a spatial effect. A determination of the rate of economic growth, a decision to increase incomes, an inflationist or deflationist economy, all have geographical repercussions. Membership of a political entity therefore places every piece of geographical space into a system which gives individual characteristics to its geographical structures because the forces which shape them are themselves individual. There are also policies which have specifically geographical results, for example policies of spatial planning whose intention is to reduce regional imbalance, create new infrastructures or encourage urban development.

These two aspects of political geography have long been significant in France. Because of the early formation of the French nation and state, because of the strength of central power and centralizing tendencies, the land of France has for centuries been marked by the geographical consequences of decisions taken by those in power. Policies having a specifically geographical effect have existed throughout the history of the French state. Intervention has reflected not only political considerations but economic ones; frequently, both have gone hand in hand. For example, there has been continuity from Sully (1560–1641) to Freycinet (1828–1923) in the establishment of the road and rail networks whose

routes, radiating from Paris, are a clear and visible representation
centralization.

Since the end of the Second World War, these activities and their spati
effects have developed considerably, on the one hand as a result of the mixe
economy, at once free-market and interventionist, on the other as a result of tl
growing importance of actions of specifically geographical significance, as part
the development of a system of structural spatial planning.

1 National plans for modernization and development

'The plan is an act by an administrative authority which imposes coherent aim
and a timed programme on the decisions of individuals and corporate bodies'

Planning found in France a more favourable land and climate of opinion tha
in other European states. The land was that of postwar France, drained an
ruined, but rich in its soil and its people. For the first time in decades, plans fo
the future had to be made: for the construction of schools and housing, fo
budgetary allocations or the creation of employment. As to the climate of opinio
the quest for long-term objectives, the successful co-ordination of the growth
dozens of economic and social sectors and the combination of economic an
social objectives, these could only be found in an intellectual nation with
passion for ideas and ideals.

French planning stemmed directly from the wartime Resistance moveme
and from the political circumstances of the immediate postwar period: it w
written into the proposals of the Conseil National de la Résistance (the suprem
body grouping the various Resistance movements) and into the programmes
the three parties of the post-Liberation coalition government (Popular Republ
can Movement, socialists, communists). On 3 January 1946 a decree was passe
setting up a Planning Council (Conseil du Plan) and a Central Planni
Commission (Commissariat Général du Plan de Modernisation et d'Equip
ment) under Jean Monnet. The assigned objectives were numerous an
ambitious: 'To increase production in metropolitan France and the overse
territories and their trade with other countries, to raise productivity generally
equal the highest levels that have been attained, to ensure full employment,
raise the standard of living of the population, and to improve housing conditio
and the general life of the community'.

1.1 The sequence of plans

From 1947 to 1980 there were seven plans.

(i) The First plan (1947–53) was devoted to postwar reconstruction. Efforts we
concentrated on sectors judged to be most critical for the nation: mines, ste

[1] Pierre Bauchet, *La Planification française: du premier au sixième plan* (Seuil, Paris, 1971).

agricultural machinery, electricity, transport and cement. These sectors were also those in which public intervention was easiest, since the government could control them, either directly because they were nationalized or indirectly through tariffs, subsidies or tax concessions. The plan also made it possible to control and direct the considerable aid provided after the war by the United States under the Marshall Plan, which made possible 7,000 million francs of public investments.

(ii) The Second plan (1954–77) was approved belatedly in March 1956. Its objectives were much wider, concerning the whole of the national economy, and were designed to reconcile the need for expansion with monetary stability. It focused attention on the ossification from which the whole of the French economy suffered. The plan gave special emphasis to housing, agriculture, processing industries and colonial products. Measures were proposed relating to the development of regions designated as 'deprived' or 'in a state of crisis': the Landes in southwest France, Languedoc, the Durance basin in the southern Alps, and the marshlands of the west coast.

(iii) The Third plan (1958–61), designed to last for five years, fell victim to the political events of 1958 (the return of General de Gaulle and the creation of the Fifth Republic) and was not published until February 1959. It set out to respond to two pressing and closely connected needs, to restore the balance of international payments and to respond to new political and economic circumstances. The European Community, launched by the Treaty of Rome (1952), was expected to lead to the gradual lowering of trade barriers. At the same time, the movement towards decolonization was depriving French producers of privileged access to important markets. It was therefore imperative to ensure that the national economy was in a fit state to face this growth of international competition. The plan favoured industrial activities likely to lead to a reduction in imports (development of the Lacq natural-gas field) and those which specialized in exporting finished goods (automobile and aircraft industries).

This development of a modernized and more specialized economy had to be carried out without any increase in the working population, indeed with a marked increase in the non-working population. To encourage this economic growth, a liberal policy on the import of foreign capital was adopted. The Third plan foundered under the impact of political and economic events, and was hastily replaced by an interim plan.

(iv) The Fourth plan (1962–5), prepared under the direction of Pierre Massé, is often considered to represent the high point of French planning; it substituted a programme of comprehensive economic and social development for the earlier plans devoted more specifically to modernization and projects of capital equipment. The plan had to be evolved in the context of three fundamental changes. The first was the rise in the number of young people and the increase in the

working population, necessitating the creation of more than a million new jol
The second element was the development of the European Community by t
adoption of new measures of unification between member states. Finally, Fran
was greatly affected by the carrying out of the policy of decolonization, a
particularly by Algeria's attainment of independence.

The plan's global objective was to 'develop the economic resources at t
disposal of France' in order to carry out 'the great national tasks', that is to say
and the order is significant – aid to overseas countries in the franc currency zo
the structural adaptation required by the development of European uni
national defence, East–West competition, aid to the Third World, and improv
ments in the standard of living of the population. The starting point of the Fou
plan was the choice of the relatively ambitious annual economic growth rate of 5
per cent. The allocation of priorities for investment deliberately neglected t
two important sectors of housing and transport.

There was also for the first time an experiment with the 'regionalization' of t
plan. The long-term objectives were to link national and regional plans, to defi
the objectives for regional planning, and to enable decentralized authorities
participate at regional level in the decisions of the plan. This trend fou
expression in regionalized forecasts of anticipated development to the year 196
and especially in statements setting out the distribution between regions of maj
investment projects and the corresponding allocation of investment funds.

A distinction between two types of regional policies dates from this Fou
plan. In regions 'in which agricultural, industrial and commercial expansi
occurs spontaneously and with sufficient vigour' the state confined itself
adapting the social infrastructure, capital projects of all kinds, and the means
financing this 'autonomous' expansion without having recourse to massi
subsidies. A typical example of this kind of action was in relation to the Rhô
valley. On the other hand, the state was more directly interventionist in the le
favoured regions, where it was considered that state action 'must change
character and become a policy of direct impulsion, involving both more ambitio
targets and more significant financial assistance'. The zones where it w
considered that the state must 'fire the first shot' were Nord–Pas-de-Cala
Lorraine, Brittany (with its bordering departments) and the southern fringe
the Central massif (that is to say a sort of crescent of which the ends would be
Angoulême in the west and Valence in the east, and the base in the neighbou
hood of Carcassonne).

(v) The Fifth plan (1966–70) was notable for the way in which its econom
prediction looked forward to a date (1985) well beyond its five-year duratic
The new plan took into account numerous constraints: entry into the Europe
Community, world-wide trade liberalization measures, currency restrictions, t
development of the 'welfare state', the development of the building industry, a
expenditure on defence. The plan envisaged major structural changes in both t

industrial and the agricultural sectors, and insisted on the necessity for mobility of labour.

The close symbiosis between planning at national and regional level was presented as initiating a major change in the system. It was stated that:

the concepts of strategic spatial planning and regional development must in future be taken into account when making decisions which were previously taken on a purely sectoral basis. Thus the unity of the concepts of national planning and strategic spatial planning were affirmed, allowing geographical aspects of development to be included in the process of medium-term planning. In consequence, strategic spatial planning is not restricted to mere reactive measures, ameliorating the adverse effects of spontaneous development, but has its own distinctive objectives and its own dynamism.

The plan made a fundamental distinction between western France, which was in future to receive 35–45 per cent of newly created employment, and a more prosperous eastern France, centred on the Mediterranean–North Sea axis and on the Paris region.

Taken as a whole, the objectives of the Fourth and Fifth plans were achieved, despite the political upheavals of 1968–9.

(vi) The Sixth plan (1971–5) was centred on the restructuring of industrial productive capacity, the basic assumption being that France was essentially under-industrialized. The plan was organized round six basic policies and 25 objectives aiming at the creation of a climate favourable to development. Policies were advocated for employment and professional training, energy, the infrastructures of production (telecommunications, transport), industrial research and finance. Specific proposals were directed at industrial branches deemed to require priority treatment: machine building, chemicals, electronics and computers, the processing of agricultural products, and the food industries.

'Special programmes' (*programmes finalisés*) first appeared in this plan; they related to new towns, road safety, perinatal care, the better functioning of the labour market, and the protection of Mediterranean forests. By putting the emphasis on sectors important for growth and likely to have substantial multiplier effects, the Sixth plan openly sacrificed the building of social equipment. It proposed a more empirical regional policy, stressing the need to achieve a balance between Paris and the rest of France. The spatial development of France was treated under a number of broad themes: the development of western France, improvements in the unfavourable situation of the northern and eastern frontier regions, the planning of the regions of economic growth and highest urban density, and the improvement of rural areas. Regional programmes of capital investment and economic development were drawn up region by region. The first world oil crisis made the objectives of the plan unattainable.

(vii) The Seventh plan (1976–80), which came into effect only on 1 January 1978, was prepared according to new procedures. In October 1974 a central council for

economic planning was established, consisting of seven permanent member meeting with the President of the Republic; the Plan Commission (Commissaria au Plan) became more explicitly the government's technical instrument fo forecasting and medium-term planning. Four major commissions were charge with the task of defining the principal objectives: in the fields of strategic spatia planning and the human environment, social inequality, external economic an financial relations, economic growth, employment and public finance. Th regions were closely associated with this process.

The plan differed markedly from previous plans. It ordained no particula growth rate, although assuming one of 5.2 per cent. Secondly, realizing tha previous plans had been disrupted by the impact of unforeseen developments, i avoided rigidly fixed targets. In the long term only qualitative objectives were lai down, and in the short and medium terms, only priorities.

The preliminary report had only very general objectives, relating to th reduction of inequalities, improvements in standards of living, town planning public transport and the strengthening of economic activity. Above all it had tw priority objectives: redressing the balance of payments and securing fu employment.

The Seventh plan endeavoured to make a clear distinction between objective: predictions and priority programmes. There were first of all 25 priority actio programmes (*programmes d'action prioritaire* – PAP) covering the country as whole. Secondly, there were regional priority action programmes (*programme d'action prioritaires d'intérêt régional* – PAPIR). Regional councils wer empowered to draw up programmes which could lead to contractual agreement with the state. These regional programmes took the most varied forms: the figh against pollution, the rehabilitation of urban centres, the promotion of crafts an small and medium-sized industries, investment in infrastructure and socia equipment, and the improvement of transport. For the first time the authors c the plan discovered that it was not enough to regionalize national perspectives bu that 'location of people and their activities has an impact on development a national level'.[2]

A model known as REGINA (regional–national) was developed from 197 onwards under the leadership of Professor Courbis; its main objective was to tak into account the impact of regional and spatial factors on national development a the level of supply and demand. 'Under these conditions it is no longer a simpl question of industrializing France but of the preferential development of specifi activities in specific regions. The emphasis is on a regional policy which, b achieving a better balance between regions, will foster a higher level of nationa competitiveness and a more rapid rate of growth at national level'.[3]

(viii) The Eighth plan (1980–4) did not survive the political changes of 1981 (th election of François Mitterrand as President of the Republic and of a left-win

[2] Raymond Courbis, *Economie Appliquée*, no. 2–3, 1975, pp. 569–600.
[3] *Ibid.*

majority in Parliament). It was replaced by an interim plan (1982–3), but this had no great impact, due to the economic crisis and the change of policy which followed.

(ix) The Ninth plan 'for economic, social and cultural development' (1984–8) was before Parliament on several occasions. In the spring of 1983 a first law defined general objectives. At the end of 1983 a second law was passed 'to define the legal, financial and administrative measures to be adopted in order to attain these objectives'. Twelve priority action programmes (*programmes prioritaires d'exécution* – PPE) covered the fields of economic development, employment and their consequences, including industrialization, the modernization of firms, education, training, urban life, health and energy.

For the first time in the sequence of plans, financial estimates were prepared to cover the entire five-year period (60,000 million francs for the PPEs alone in the 1984 budget).

The plan also includes the setting up of planning agreements (*contrats de plan*) with both public-sector enterprises and the regions.

1.2 Strengths and weaknesses of the national planning system

The most contradictory opinions have been expressed regarding the French national planning system. Analysis will focus in turn on the achievements of the plans, their ambiguities and the criticism made of them.

1.2.1 The achievements of the planning system

The value of French planning lies firstly in the instruments it forged or inspired, and in the new spirit it fostered at all levels of the social and economic life of the country. It was the Plan Commission which developed the system of national accounting. Without this action under the plan, the present statistical series – national and regional, global and sectoral – would never have been made available. The plan has made people aware of interrelationships and has strengthened solidarity between professions and between social classes at national and regional levels. The plans provide a sense of direction and a rhythm of development which many professional organizations were previously incapable of providing. Seen in this light, the value of French planning is absolute; it offers an information network on the economy as a whole, and 'it reduces uncertainty, acting as a substitute for the market wherever this is unavailable, declining or outmoded', in short 'a foresighted plan for the coherent growth of the economy'.[4]

The second value of the plans lies in their effectiveness. One may justifiably question the link between the existence of national planning and the economic growth of France between 1950 and 1975, since some states achieved higher

[4] Pierre Massé, *Le Plan ou l'anti-hasard* (Gallimard, Paris, 1965).

growth rates without planning. Nevertheless, planning gave impetus and coherent growth not only to the economy but to all sectors of activity, in particular highlighting the importance of a sufficient development of social equipment. It laid down objectives for the future which were beyond the powers of the traditional mechanisms of the French economy and administration to achieve.

1.2.2 *The ambiguities of the system*

The concept of planning, of the existence of a plan, usually involves two assumptions. The first is the existence of an authoritarian organization, commanding the economy: the plan is drawn up with the intention that it shall be implemented and completed. The second assumption is that the objectives of the plan are defined in terms of precise political and economic directions.

Planning

can only exist if it has a certain philosophical and political content stemming from deliberate decisions, for example regarding the direction in which the economy is to move the distribution of incomes, and the attitude to the Third World. It is to be feared that some plans, lacking these decisions, are merely tacked on to existing economic and sociological realities, and are nothing but fictions which degrade the very name of planning.[5]

The first attempt in this direction was made in the preface to the Fourth plan Pierre Massé commented: 'It is possible that the consumer society, foreshadowed by certain aspects of American life, will turn in the end towards trivial gratification, which itself will generate discontent. It would doubtless be preferable to place the coming progressive affluence at the service of a less limited vision of humanity.'[6]

The first ambiguity of French planning lies in its insertion into a free-market economic structure. The reconciliation of economic planning with free enterprise appears to be an attempt to achieve the impossible. The plan in fact varies between being merely indicative or virtually mandatory according to the economic sectors concerned or the methods of pressure or encouragement at the disposal of the state. Confronted with the annual growth rates indicated by the plan, firms, workers and consumers nevertheless keep their freedom of decision on production investment, consumption and the right to apply pressure on government. There is complete state control over coal mining, electricity generation and railways, so that in these branches the achievement of the objectives of the plan poses few problems. In the private sector, state influence depends on the strength of the pressures it can exercise by fiscal means, through financial provision or by government orders. If, however, the particular interest of a firm clash with the general interests, the achievement of the plan's objectives is jeopardized.

[5] Bauchet, *La Planification française.*
[6] Massé, *Le Plan ou l'anti-hasard.*

These ambiguities become more marked as one plan succeeds another. Within the framework of the European Community and of western society, liberal capitalism weaves a web of international investments and overlapping interests; it is difficult to see how these can be expected to adjust to the wishes of French planners. Each year the European Community integrates the French economy ever more completely into a supernational context. The fixing of agricultural prices and the free circulation of capital, goods and workers are progressively depriving the French government of the means of control and intervention required by the plan.

1.2.3 Criticisms of the system

Both the formulation of the French national plans and their implementation have been subject to criticism. Some critics say that the conditions under which the plan is developed liken it to a recording studio, whose objectives are in the end no more than a compromise between the various recipients of the French national income. The plan cannot propose measures which exceed the free interplay of investments and employment and which would require important transfers, particularly of incomes. According to such critics, the plan is in some degree not a plan at all, but an illusion, a blanket for *laissez-faire*, since it has no constraints at its disposal. French planning is also criticized for not being democratic: the various social and professional groups are not given equal representation, while the plan itself is too much tied up with economic rather than social objectives.

The essential problem posed by French planning is that of implementation. Rather than having recourse to direct orders, French planners have, in fact, used psychological and above all financial incentives to secure implementation. These methods remain weak, however, and their degrees of effectiveness vary considerably. Enterprises are differentially affected according to the nature of their product and their financial situation. The plan can have no influence on projects internally financed within the enterprise; it can only oppose sterile competition and decisions to close down factories. More importantly, until the Ninth plan, there was no guarantee that finance for the measures proposed in the plan for any one year would be provided in the corresponding annual national budget. The system of passing legislation providing a framework for planning programmes covering several years, representing a commitment to continuity of investment, was an attempt to remedy this defect.

A major contradiction in the plans is that whereas especially since the Fifth plan the economic recommendations have been on the whole implemented, the investment of capital in construction for social purposes was deliberately sacrificed to the demands of a balanced budget.

As far back as 1963, P. Bauchet made a perceptive comment on French experiments in planning when he wrote:

The French method of planning has, after sixteen years, secured an original place for itself

which in many ways appears satisfactory: it is something more than a counselling bod'
something less than an executive authority. But there is an uneasy balance between th
making of authoritative decisions on the conflicting claims of interest groups and mere
giving advice to them. The centralizing forces of the administration and the pressure
interest groups are continually present, tending to reduce the planning authority to th
level of a simple advisory body to the executive.[7]

What is certain is that over the thirty years during which France has had
central planning system, two contradictory tendencies have emerged. On the on
hand, there has been a marked development of planning theory and practice
involving the increasingly sophisticated forecasting techniques provided by th
computer; on the other, the implementation of the plan has decreasingl
appeared as what the late President de Gaulle once described as a 'burnin
necessity'. From 1965 to 1981, confronted with a deliberate reduction of stat
intervention and evidence of a certain return to reliance on normal mark
processes, many observers spoke of a 'de-planning' of the French economy.

After 1981, a revival of national planning might have been expected from
socialist government which had widened the power of the state by new nation
alization measures directed against banks and additional industrial group
Paradoxically this has not been the case, doubtless because the state is already i
direct command of a substantial part of economic activity and because it ha
ultimate financial control over all sectors through the banking system. Ther
were, however, other reasons for a more hesitant attitude towards nation
planning; the government's ability to control the French economy had bee
limited by entry into the European Community and by an increasing openness t
international economic influences. Acceptance of the requirements of a mark
economy and free enterprise was a further limitation. More generally, there ha
been a change of attitude towards national planning; doubt and scepticism abou
its efficacy have been reinforced by unfavourable economic developments, whic
have prevented the attainment of predicted goals. The very complexity
present-day economy and society has been a deterrent, while the example
states with centrally planned economies has scarcely been encouraging. The ne
policy of administrative and political decentralization has also modified the role
of the state and the regions in the planning process.

2 Policies for strategic spatial planning

Until the 1950s, France officially ignored the existence of regional disparitie
the reality of regional problems, and the necessity for an economic and socia
regionalization of policies, failing to take account of the divergences of interes
and the rivalry between regions. In contrast, recognition of the 'depressed area
(later 'development areas') in the United Kingdom dates from 1931, and the U
Tennessee Valley Authority from 1933.

[7] Bauchet, *La Planification française.*

The prime cause of this attitude lay in political and administrative centralization; from Paris, the seat of all power, France appeared as a homogeneous unit. All grades of the administration and all professional bodies were vertically linked with Paris: there was no meeting with parallel organizations at regional level. Another reason was the demographic and economic stagnation of the interwar years; this absence of growth, together with economic protectionism, meant that many problems relating to development did not arise. Since new industrial plants and related infrastructures were not created, there was no problem of finding appropriate regional locations for them. It was only in the postwar context of economic growth that regional disparities were accentuated.

The first signs of an interventionist policy in the French planning system appeared three years after the initiation of the First plan, but totally independently of it. The initiative came from Eugène Claudius-Petit, then Minister for Reconstruction and Town Planning. In 1949 he created a Directorate of Strategic Spatial Planning (Direction de l'Aménagement du Territoire), and in 1950 formally urged the government to establish a national plan for strategic spatial planning (*aménagement du territoire*). The purpose of such a plan was to ensure 'a better distribution of population in relation to natural resources and economic activities, not only for economic reasons but still more to secure the well-being and prosperity of the nation'.[8] This proposal was the expression of a whole trend of thought inspired by Raoul Dautry, Minister of Town Planning in 1945, by Jean-François Gravier, whose book *Paris and the French desert* (1947) had roused public opinion on the subject, and by architect–planners such as Le Corbusier and Gaston Bardet.

2.1 The evolution of the concept of strategic spatial planning

Over more than a quarter of a century, the framework within which this policy has had to be developed has varied enormously; the facts on which the specialists have based their ideas have been modified or superseded, causing inevitable changes in policy objectives. At first, the disparity between the Paris region and the rest of France was the principal and almost sole reason for intervention. The growth of Paris had to be curbed, therefore the economic development of provincial France must be encouraged, and industrial decentralization from Paris was to assist this process.

The next stage was the arrival of strategic spatial planning in the wake of the demographic and economic boom. Jobs had to be created, new factories located, appropriate facilities of a social nature provided and sited, and the process of runaway urbanization halted. Alfred Sauvy, a voice crying in the wilderness, was one of the first to speak of 'the threefold spatial interaction of school, work and home'. Suddenly, the imbalance and inequalities between regions and between

[8] *Pour un plan d'aménagement du territoire* (Paris, 1950).

different economic and social sectors within the same region were detected and analysed. The fostering of regional development then came into prominence.

A third climate of opinion emerged after 1968, with the rise of regional movements and the 'green' or ecology movement.

Since the middle of the 1970s, the energy crisis, the slowing down of population growth and the increase in economic competition have further modified the environment of strategic spatial planning. To the unease aroused by *Paris and the French desert* was added a further concern with relations between large provincial towns and their own regional 'deserts'. Regional policies predominated until 1974, carried along on a wave of expansion and industrialization: they subsequently had to face the problems of regions with severe unemployment, the problems of factory closures, and the redeployment of workers from declining branches of industry, all in the context of a marked slowing down of demographic growth. The aims set out in the 1950 statement by Claudius-Petit quoted above may be supplemented by those of 1978 marking 15 years of the Delegation for Strategic Spatial Planning and Regional Development (Délégation Générale à l'Aménagement du Territoire et à l'Action Régionale – DATAR): 'to provide a balanced economic development of the regions by the promotion and location of economic activity, as well as by the provision of the necessary infrastructure; to protect and improve the human environment'.[9]

2.2 Methods and institutions of strategic spatial planning

Until 1963 an important role was played by the Directorate-General for Strategic Spatial Planning of the then Ministry for Reconstruction and Town Planning. On 15 February 1963 a decree was passed establishing DATAR: 'This delegation will be charged with co-ordinating activities and stimulating action. On the basis of general objectives outlined by the plan, its role will be to prepare and co-ordinate the information necessary for government decisions concerning strategic spatial planning and regional development.' DATAR was an administrative innovation by reason of its small staff and the youth and diversity of its leadership. Although the head (*délégué général*) of DATAR is responsible for the execution and implementation of spatial planning, the Plan Commission (Commissariat au Plan) 'assisted in this task by a National Commission for Strategic Spatial Planning (Commission Nationale de l'Aménagement du Territoire – CNAT) has the responsibility for basic research concerning spatial planning and for incorporating its findings in the plan for economic and social development'. The first CNAT report was published in September 1964.

---

[9] DATAR, *Nouvelles orientations pour l'aménagement du territoire*, proceedings of conference held in December 1978 (Documentation Française, Paris, 1979).

2.2.1 Sectoral policies

The first measures were directed at the location of economic activity, providing stimulus in some cases, discouragement in others. The methods used were financial and fiscal: subsidies, loans or tax exemptions. They were first aimed at the industrial sector; later the tertiary sector was brought in. The first measures of this kind were spatially extremely limited. Twenty-six critical zones were first selected (January 1956), then eight special conversion zones (March 1959). The criteria for the first were the existence of serious industrial unemployment, either current or imminent, or of surplus labour in agriculture. The second type consisted of zones that were vulnerable in a period of economic recession. The industrial enterprises which were set up, expanded or converted in these zones benefited from various tax incentives and especially from a subsidy amounting to 15–20 per cent of total investment. For a variety of reasons this twofold experiment had little success; the definition of the zones was debatable, criteria were badly chosen, and aid was often given to firms which had no need of it.

In 1964 these zones were replaced by a system of differential assistance to industrialization extending over the whole of France, varying progressively from zones receiving no assistance to those which benefited from the maximum tax exemptions and subsidies for regional development. The map of regional assistance has often been changed, but the total package of available measures has continually increased, including, for example, tax reductions, subsidies for the development of tertiary activities, special rural aid, long-term loans and subsidies for specific purposes (for example, the establishment of small-scale craft industries).

A second group of sectoral measures derives from the local expression of programmes for planned investment in social equipment and infrastructure. These programmes are expressed as maps: maps showing educational provision at various levels, and maps of health facilities; also as structure plans, as for the major road network (1971) or airfield provision (1972).

Since 1982, the seven previously existing forms of assistance have been replaced by three new subsidies: one for strategic spatial planning, financed by the state, and two regional subsidies for the creation of new economic activities and employment, financed by the regions.

2.2.2 Policies at regional level

These policies aim to change the overall organization of a region or to stimulate its general development. An example of the first category was the policy of *métropoles d'équilibre* ('counterbalancing regional capitals') of 1964. It aimed to encourage the growth of large regional capitals which would counterbalance the power of Paris. The Organizations for Research and Metropolitan Development

(Organismes d'Etudes et d'Aménagement des Aires Métropolitaines – OREAM) were called into existence in February 1966. There were to be a maximum of eight, each under the authority of the appropriate regional Prefect. They were charged with drawing up structure plans (*schémas directeurs*) for the 'balancing' metropolitan areas. The parallel OREAV (Organisations d'Etudes et d'Aménagement de Vallées) organizations were responsible for producing structure plans for the highly urbanized valleys of the Oise and the middle Loire.

Another type of regional action concerns particular environments, specific zones and small regions (*pays*). The primary example is provided by the projects of large-scale spatial reorganization (*grands aménagements régionaux*). The model for operations of this type was provided by the National Company for the Rhône (Compagnie Nationale du Rhône – CNR), established between 1922 and 1934: it had three objectives for the development of the valley: to make the Rhône a modern, navigable waterway, to exploit its hydroelectric potential, and to use its water for irrigation.

These major projects of spatial transformation were entrusted to the characteristic French device of 'semi-public companies' (*sociétés d'économie mixte*) whose capital was provided partly from public sources and partly by private shareholders.

La Compagnie Nationale d'Aménagement du Bas-Rhône–Languedoc (1955) was responsible for the regeneration of the wine-producing region of Languedoc by diversifying its rural economy. The key to the operation was to be the irrigation of 200,000 ha between the Rhône and the Pyrenees with water brought by a large-scale canal from the Rhône.

La Société pour la Mise en Valeur Agricole de la Corse (1957) was responsible for the clearing, development and irrigation of 50,000 ha in the malarial plains of eastern Corsica.

La Compagnie d'Aménagement des Landes de Gascogne (1956), succeeded in 1966 by the *Compagnie d'Aménagement Régional d'Aquitaine*, was responsible for reclaiming 200,000 ha of the Landes forests damaged by fire, for draining the marshy areas of the Landes and replacing forest monoculture with a more diversified economy.

La Société du Canal de Provence has constructed a canal from the Verdon to irrigate 50,000 ha, to supplement the water supply of Marseille and Aix, and to supply the industrial and urban developments around the Etang de Berre.

La Compagnie d'Aménagement des Coteaux de Gascogne (1960) had as its task the irrigation of the slopes of the plateau of Lannemezan, using the waters of the Garonne and its tributaries.

La Société des Friches et Taillis Pauvres de l'Est (Company for the Improvement of Disused Land and Scrubland in Eastern France) was responsible for reclaiming and developing 150,000 ha of abandoned arable land in the limestone plateaus of twelve departments in the east of the Paris basin.

La Société d'Economie Mixte et d'Etude pour la Communauté de la Loire et de se

Affluents (1962) covered eight departments. Its aim was to regulate the Loire and its tributaries by the building of reservoirs and to use this water during periods of drought and low water for irrigating, for maintaining the depth of water available for navigation and to assist industrial development.

La Société pour la Mise en Valeur de l'Auvergne–Limousin (1962) was responsible for the modernization of agriculture in some of the most depressed regions of the Central massif.

The success of these large-scale projects has been highly uneven, often rather modest. They have been supplemented by major projects of public investment supervised by interministerial teams (*missions*). The prototype was the Commission for the Planning of the Durance Region (Commission d'Aménagement de la Région de la Durance), set up in 1951, which was to result in the construction of the Serre-Ponçon dam. Among numerous examples are the development of ports and related industries at Fos–Etang de Berre, Verdon, Antifer and Dunkerque, the planned tourist development of the coasts of Languedoc–Roussillon (1963) and Aquitaine (1967); and the new towns.

Next in order come policies which can be related to particular environments. Outline policies have been developed for eight of these, among them areas of particularly low population, industrial conversion zones, frontier regions, areas of high population concentration, and areas of rural renewal. The government appointed special commissioners to implement these policies, for example the commissioners for industrial development and restructuring (Nord, Lorraine, Atlantic coast and Mediterranean regions), and for rural renewal (Auvergne, Brittany, Limousin and the mountain regions).

In April 1975 a major new programme was launched in order to aid the *pays*, the smaller regions of France. The agreements with local interests drawn up under these schemes were known as *contrats de pays*. This return to the old idea of the *pays*, the homogeneous but small-scale geographical region, originated in Brittany. Adopted by the government, the idea becomes a reality in the form of agreements between DATAR and groups of communes round a central place, which are entitled to a range of grants. In three years 198 agreements were made, involving 6,000 communes and 4 million people.

Finally, another very important category of spatial transformation came into existence with the 1967 *Loi d'orientation foncière*, a new urban and rural planning law. In urban environments the drawing up of a structure plan (*schéma directeur d'aménagement et d'urbanisme* – SDAU) provides forecasts of development over the long-term period and serves as a framework for the working out of more detailed local plans. In rural areas, rural development plans (*plans d'aménagement rural* – PAR) define desirable objectives for development and capital investment of a social nature. On 1 October 1977, 170 PARs had been drawn up in metropolitan France; they covered 7,074 communes (19.4 per cent of the total), 8.1 per cent of the population of France and 18.4 per cent of the land area. Some coastal areas are also provided with structure plans.

Neither structure plans nor rural development plans are binding: they have no formal, legal status, and there is no guarantee that resources will be made available to implement them.

2.2.3 Regional planning

In addition to sectoral developments and major projects, there is a third influence on the spatial transformation – what the French call 'regional action'. It has two aspects: administrative regionalization (see chapter 13) and regional planning. The initiative came at first from the regions themselves, with the creation of regional study committees (*comités régionaux d'études*), which first appeared as early as 1943 in Reims, and multiplied during the 1950s. At the beginning of 1958 there were 166, representing areas of greatly varying importance: towns, cantons, departments and even regions.

To these committees, founded on a voluntary basis, goes the credit of having aroused the sleeping provinces. By their research into spatial inequality, the committees made the public aware of the current and future problems of the regions, uniting men who had hitherto worked in isolation, unaware that there could be community of interest at regional level. The disadvantages of these committees stemmed from their merits: their unofficial nature laid them open to attempts at take-over by members of the local establishment, politicians and representatives of particular economic interests, attempts which met with varying degrees of success.

Faced with this proliferation of committees in whose creation it had played no part, the government gave official sanction to the most representative of them in 1961 by recognizing them as committees for economic growth (*comités d'expansion économique*). Throughout their existence these committees have played an essential role by organizing research, providing information, stimulating dialogue and putting forward proposals. They especially contributed in the early days of their existence to the development of regional action programmes (*programmes d'action régionale*).

From 1972 onwards, the progressive development of a formal structure of regional administration faced the committees with delicate problems of adaptation or integration into the new structures. Many did not survive; others have become research organizations for the new regional councils. It is the regional councils, after all, which formulate regional policies by deciding on projects to be financed out of regional revenues, or by putting forward proposals under the PAPIR scheme for financing by the central government (see Seventh plan above).

Nevertheless, it sometimes happens that regions are the direct concern of the central power; such is the case with regard to the Central massif. The unity of the Hercynian massif is only visible on geological maps: administratively it has since 1955 been divided between no fewer than five regions. Although already covered to a great extent by policies relating to mountain areas and rural renewal, it benefited in 1975 from a special development plan. Similar measures were applied to the Paris basin, the Atlantic seaboard, southwest France and Corsica, which in 1975 received a 'charter for economic development'.

Since 1974, regional policies have acquired a European dimension. The European Community has created a European regional fund; financial aid is granted according to programmes submitted by governments.

2.3 The strengths and weaknesses of spatial planning

Opinions on the value of the policy of strategic planning are varied and contradictory. Some praise the positive results of decentralization, the reversal of the migratory flow to the Paris region, and the halting of rural depopulation. Others say that the policy has been almost completely ineffective and see in it merely empty rhetoric concealing the normal free-market striving for cheap labour. Reality doubtless lies between these two extremes of opinion.

In the first place, strategic spatial planning must be given the credit for the introduction and practice of interministerial co-ordination by way of inter-ministerial committees. DATAR played the role of an experimental laboratory for new methods of spatial intervention, which, when proved successful, were absorbed into the normal administrative, legislative or institutional processes.

The development of spatial planning introduced geography into the political and economic administration of France, which was not an easy thing to do. It reintroduced at one and the same time the significance of situation and localization, and the importance of interrelationships, of geographical and spatial interdependence between the different economic sectors and between the different actors on the spatial plane. The spatial, regional or geographic dimensions were discovered and taken into account in economic decision-making, which is a considerable achievement.

The use of strategic spatial planning also introduced a geographical perspective into French planning which had hitherto been completely lacking. Strategic spatial planning has to make predictions with regard to future spatial organiza-tion, an activity very different from tracing the course of a motorway, building a university or extending a priority planning zone (ZUP). It is imposssible to speak of spatial planning without defining the main features of this planned geography or making and justifying the choice between the different possible maps of population density, industrial location, infrastructure or regional agricultural trends in the France of tomorrow. DATAR has several times attempted to define these future scenarios. A national plan for strategic spatial planning was put forward in 1961 but never adopted. At the end of 1968, DATAR formed a small group to provide predictions for the future, known as the Système d'Etude du Schéma d'Aménagement (SESAME); its objective was to draw up a picture of France in the year 2000. The results were published in July 1971, but they

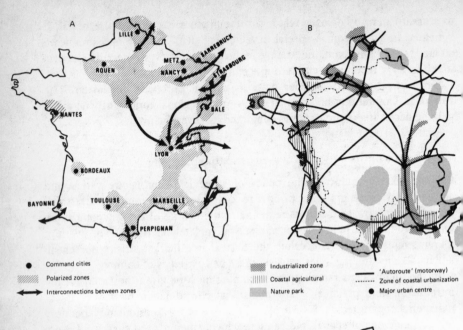

A

- ● Command cities
- ///// Polarized zones
- ◄──► Interconnections between zones

B

- ///// Industrialized zone
- ||||||| Coastal agricultural
- (grey) Nature park
- ——— 'Autoroute' (motorway)
- ------- Zone of coastal urbanization
- ● Major urban centre

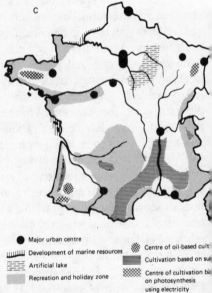

C

- ● Major urban centre
- ||||||| Development of marine resources
- ≡≡≡ Artificial lake
- (grey) Recreation and holiday zone
- (hatch) Centre of oil-based cult
- (bar) Cultivation based on su
- (cross) Centre of cultivation ba
  on photosynthesis
  using electricity

Figure 14.1 Three scenarios of the future spatial structure of France produced by the SESAME study group. The maps show three possible scenarios for the future spatial structure of France, depending on the different policies that might be adopted. A. A 'continental' policy B. A 'coastline' or 'peripheral' policy C. A policy of 'futuristic' agriculture and recreation (leisure activities and tourism). These scenarios were

appeared so 'explosive' that the publication was sub-titled 'Scenario of the unacceptable' (Fig. 14.1). The picture of France as it emerged from this 'essay in geographical science fiction' was described as apocalyptic: a France of extreme contrasts, with strongly polarized zones (the Paris region, the Rhône delta, the border regions), and several large urban regions, separated by vast, almost completely deserted expanses, interrupted by only a few isolated pockets of activity.

Strategic spatial planning has not escaped the controversy aroused by the plans: is it possible to develop a policy of planned locations in a market economy? Is it possible or desirable to reconcile freedom in economic decision-making with planning in the geographical sphere?

These contradictions explain the relative timidity of state intervention throughout the last 25 years. It is all the more understandable because since 1974 demographic recession and the economic crisis have made it no longer possible to rely on population excess and economic surplus, there being few people or activities to redistribute. It is difficult to be concerned with backward regions when the urban and industrial regions themselves are being so badly battered.

Spatial planning policy failed to take full advantage of the demographic and economic growth of the years between 1950 and 1974 so as to move to a redeployment of people and activities. Retrospectively, this policy appears to have been much too timid, too inclined simply to reflect events, insufficiently forward-looking.

These defects and inadequacies bring us back to the central question: what should the real content of strategic spatial planning be? It 'is not to be identified either with town planning, which is its local version, applicable to the limited area of a town or a group of interdependent communes. It is also not to be identified with economic planning, which it uses as an instrument. Nor is it to be identified with decentralization, which is a form of action, or with production, which is an end-product.'[10] It should involve long-term planning for a future geography, derived from decisions of permanent validity and from a steady purpose; this is very different from short-term economic decisions which must of necessity take into account the temporary fluctuations in the national and international economic situation. The immediate gains from short-term profitability and financial profitability might well be preferred to the prospect of more remote advantages, which may partly be measured in terms of social advance and advantages of a non-economic nature.

Strategic spatial planning thus presupposes strength of will and conviction, strong enough to resist the arguments of those who would willingly accept the increasing abandonment of large parts of France as the price of a few poles of

[10] Pierre Randet, mimeo.

---

denounced as unacceptable, but were really only intended to stimulate thought and discussion. Source: DATAR.

urban or regional growth or the development of a few plains or valley corridors. If France really needs growth points and a more solid and modern infrastructure, it does not seem that its past history and its present environments favour a contraction in its inhabited and exploited territory. One reason is that much capital is locked up in even the smallest rural cantons, embodied in fields which for generations have been fertilized and protected against erosion, in buildings and networks of communications. Another reason is that because of the postwar rise in population there are more young people in these regions, and it seems desirable to find a policy which will keep them in the region. A third reason is that it is impossible to foresee the future of a region without knowing how its assets will be assessed in 25 years' time. In the 1950s, for example, no one foresaw the phenomenon of second homes, still less that of the vast extension of the urban–rural fringe.

For lack of a coherent national plan and an overall policy, spatial planning moved in the direction of operations of a very diverse nature, ecological or technological, for example, and towards increasingly short-term assignments, such as acting as 'nursemaid' to ailing enterprises. As a result, resources were dissipated, clearly in consequence of political decisions taken from time to time at government level. Spatial planning was also increasingly drawn into the reaction against short-term economic fluctuations, whereas the very essence of a pro-gramme of spatial planning is that it should be structural and long-term. DATAR has been criticized for being satisfied with the success of spectacular short-term operations. French spatial planning has also been criticized for being more concerned with stimulating economic enterprise as such rather than with transforming environments and regions. Attention has often been drawn to the continued existence of factors responsible for regional imbalance, and to the persistence of the economic advantages or disadvantages of situation. In such cases, the costs of transport or energy discriminate against peripheral regions or regions lacking their own energy resources, such as Brittany. Plans for motorways or new fast railway networks favour the most densely populated and industrial regions.

Since the 1982 legislation on further political and administrative decentraliza-tion, the regions have been given ever-increasing responsibilities. The first planning agreements between the central government and the regions were signed in 1984, allowing the regions to grant employment subsidies, guarantee loans and give direct financial assistance to enterprises. Permitted regional action was, however, limited in scale; a threshold of 30 job creations was frequently imposed. The expansion of regional budgets through the transfer of tax income from the central government has certainly widened the field of action for the regions. But the state still has to act as arbitrator between rich and poor regions and promote inter-regional solidarity. In particular, the government has had to review its attitude to the development of the powerful Ile-de-France (Paris) region.

The role of 'national' planning organizations such as DATAR is inevitably challenged by this process of decentralization; it is not without significance that DATAR is increasingly turning to the long-term view and is relaunching SESAME (Fig. 14.1) with an eye to likely developments in the twenty-first century.

15

 The ownership of land

The state and the communes must be freed from the invisible control that private property exerts on planning decisions.

A. Givaudan

The ownership of land is the fundamental condition for the utilization and transformation of geographical space, at least in a country where private property is regarded as almost sacred, and where the possession of land is regarded as a symbol of liberty and independence. The ownership of land gives power over its utilization, either directly or by concession to others.

Ownership of land is also a source of revenue, hence of the creation of capital. It offers a personal estate which can be transmitted by inheritance and which is a safeguard against currency depreciation. Before the industrial revolution, agriculture was the principal source of income and the basis of land rent. The power of the Lord of the Manor was formerly derived from the sale of the products of the serfs who worked his demesne, or from the rents received from tenants. Frequently the wealth of the burghers of the towns was also derived from rural property. There is also a long history of struggle by the tillers of the soil to lay hands on additional land to extend their holdings.

While land is a possession, it is neither a product nor a commodity; it is in fact finite, limited and incapable of reproduction. Only in very limited circumstances can its surface area be increased, for example by building on more than one level.

The human appropriation of the land entails a fundamental geographical process, the division of the surface into parcels. In both rural and urban areas this division provides the structure from which all human development of the land of France has developed. In 1972, in the 35,933 communes in which the cadastral survey had been revised, that is in 96 per cent of the country, there were 87 million parcels.

1 The owners of land

The land belongs either to individuals or to corporate bodies, private or public. Private ownership predominates; it occupies a far greater area than any other category of ownership. It is estimated that in 1973 there were 12 million landowners.

1.1 Private ownership of agricultural land

The present-day ownership of agricultural land has a complex structure, reflecting the whole history of France since the early Middle Ages. There are five categories of private ownership, by the nobility, the bourgeoisie, the lower middle and working classes, the peasant farmers and private companies (not to mention ownership by the state and public bodies). Not all owners work their land in person.

In 1970, 51.8 per cent of agricultural land was worked directly by the owner (*faire-valoir direct*). The remainder was either tenanted (*fermage*) or worked by share-croppers (*métayage*). All possible combinations of these categories are to be found, from the 39.5 per cent of farmers exclusively working their own land to the 14.6 per cent who are exclusively tenants, while 45.7 per cent cultivate a mixture of their own and of rented land.

1.1.1 Ownership by the nobility

This heritage of pre-Revolutionary France has survived in little-urbanized rural regions, where the nobility has remained powerful, notably the centre of France (Sologne, Berry, Nivernais and Bourbonnais), on the fringe of the Armorican massif (Maine, Anjou), in the central West (Vendée), and in the heart of Brittany. However, some land owned by the nobility is to be found throughout France, for example in the Paris basin or the Boulonnais. Some entire communes are still owned by a single family; such properties typically consist for the most part of forest land.

1.1.2 Ownership by the urban bourgeoisie

French town dwellers have retained a strong attachment to the land, which explains their desire to own and conserve their holdings. This type of land ownership is of long standing, already flourishing under the *Ancien Régime*. The urban bourgeoisie was one of the chief beneficiaries from the distribution of communal property and the sale of the national estate following the Revolution of 1789.

The regions in which urban ownership is important are those where for centuries there has been an old urban bourgeoisie with interests closely bound up with the countryside, deeply attached to the land which is worked through tenant farmers or share-croppers. For example, the agricultural land of the Pays de Caux, fringed by sea and river ports, and accessible from Paris, belongs for the most part to businessmen from le Havre and Rouen, lawyers from Rouen, shipowners from Fécamp and persons of independent means from Paris.

Bourgeois ownership has survived principally in areas where capital available in the towns has not been diverted into industrial development. From 1830, and more especially from 1850, many rural estates were sold to enable their owners to invest in manufacturing industry, but the retreat of the urban bourgeoisie varied from one rural region to another. In Languedoc, for example, the process was reversed. Faced with the rise of competing industrial regions the industrial and commercial bourgeoisie abandoned its traditional textile and chemical industries and also its trading interests to buy land for the cultivation of the vine. The financial and geographical concentration of large-scale industry and business thus impelled the small-town bourgeoisie in the direction of the ownership of rural land.

Rural land ownership by the urban bourgeoisie is particularly concentrated in the Nord region, in the vast wheat-growing plains surrounding Paris, in the Loire valley, the Sologne, Touraine, Languedoc, the Bordeaux region and generally in the spheres of influence surrounding towns. Areas of forest and dunes are particularly sought after by urban bankers and industrialists for the creation of prestige shooting estates. The bankers of the Second Empire took hold of the forests of the Paris region, just as the Lyons bourgeoisie acquired estates in the Dombes. Associated agricultural enterprises were often set up to help meet the heavy cost of maintaining these properties. Urban property owners, however – and the exception confirms the rule – were unable to expand into areas with a deeply rooted and dense peasant population having an assured outlet for their products. This is the situation in Alsace, even though it is a highly urbanized region.

Side by side with the traditional forms of ownership by the urban bourgeoisie is the creation of new agricultural enterprises owned and directed from outside the rural areas. Among the new speculative urban owners are cattle merchants (whose aim is the complete integration of the cycle of meat production), cattle-food manufacturers, food-processing concerns, veterinary practitioners and industrialists or professional people who experiment with farming, putting a professional manager in charge of their property.

1.1.3 *The smaller non-resident proprietors*

In all French communes, as well as properties owned by the nobility, the bourgeoisie and by speculative businessmen, there are properties owned by the vast collection of smaller non-resident proprietors. These may be workers, clerks or members of the lower middle class whose parents, or even great-grandparents a century ago, were once rural dwellers. Their descendants were to join in the rural exodus while clinging on to a few parcels of land.

In many regions a significant part of the area of rural communes consists of land owned by urban non-residents. In 1963 a quarter of the vine-growing area of Languedoc was owned by 3,000 urban dwellers. Some 120,000 ha, including 42,000 ha of vineyards, belonged to the residents of Montpellier, Nîmes and Béziers; another 65,000 ha were owned by 450 Parisians. Property owned by town dwellers is generally concentrated in a fairly well-defined concentric 'land ownership zone'[1] around the urban centre concerned, for example a radius of 18 km around Auch or 80 km around Toulouse. However, Paris and some urbanized regions such as the Nord control 'land ownership zones' situated at a considerable distance.

1.1.4 Property owned by foreigners

The presence of foreigners owning and working land is no new phenomenon. Belgian and Dutch farmers, for example, came to northern France and Picardy after the First World War in search of land available on a larger scale than in their own countries. The low density of the French farming population and especially the existence of fallow and abandoned land attracted agricultural colonists from regions of Europe which had too great a concentration of farmers. Since 1959 the acquisition of land by Germans and Belgians with a view to the installation of tenant farmers has intensified. The purchasers are often companies having access to considerable capital resources; the departments most affected are in the Paris basin. The creation of the European Community reinforced the tendency; nevertheless in absolute terms the movement remains of limited extent: between 1972 and 1978 inclusive, the purchase of agricultural land by foreigners oscillated between 3,200 and 5,750 ha per year.

The international economic and political situation is also reflected in the purchase of land and forests. According to newspaper accounts, Arabs from the Gulf states have since 1975 also been interested in buying land. The Emir of Kuwait purchased 400 ha of Champagne vineyards near Epernay. Entire estates in the Sologne today belong to the 'nouveaux riches' of the oil-producing countries; for example, the Emir of Abu Dhabi has acquired hundreds of hectares of forest land.

1.1.5 Peasant ownership

Even before the French Revolution France had a solid peasant land-owning class, in marked contrast to her European neighbours. Feudal obligations could be a heavy burden; the peasants had constantly to defend themselves against the encroachments and demands of the nobility. Nevertheless they had the right of free transference of their land, whether by sale or through inheritance.

The proportion of land in peasant ownership varied from a third in the north of

[1] R. Dugrand, *Villes et campagnes dans le Bas-Languedoc* (PUF, Paris, 1963).

France to over a half in the south. The hold of the peasants was strengthened by the French Revolution, when the peasant class, already quite prosperous, received the greater part of the land which was distributed or sold. Virtual dynasties of peasant proprietors were created on the basis of holdings put together out of the distributed national lands.

Figure 15.1 shows the very marked contrast between southern France, where two-thirds of the land is owned by the peasants, and the north and northwest, from the Vendée to the Belgian boundary where (Brittany excepted) they have less than 40 per cent of the agricultural land. This peasant property, consisting predominantly of small and medium-sized holdings, is to be found everywhere in France, but especially in:

(1) eastern France (Lorraine, Champagne, Franche-Comté, Burgundy, Alsace), all of which, except Alsace, are regions of little urban development;
(2) southwest France, where Roman law encouraged the division of land on inheritance, and Provence;
(3) the Central massif and its fringes (Velay, Cantal, Limousin, Marche, Limagne, Morvan, Poitou, Quercy);

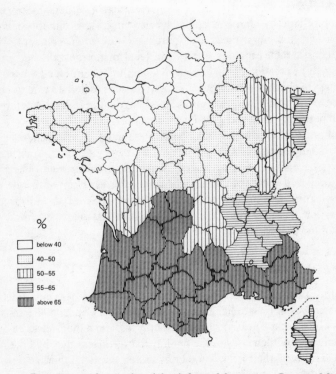

Figure 15.1 Percentage of agricultural land farmed by owner. Source: Ministère de l'Agriculture (CNASEA).

(4) the great river valleys, where rich soil has allowed the proliferation of small-scale but profitable farming enterprises;

(5) mountain regions.

1.1.6 Ownership by private companies

In the great arable regions the land frequently belongs to limited companies, whether family concerns or otherwise. They are usually industrial companies, such as sugar refiners. In southern France the Salins du Midi company is one of the most important landowners. Company ownership is also characteristic of reclaimed marshlands (Compagnie des Polders de l'Ouest).

1.1.7 Ownership patterns and spatial structure

Contrasts in the mosaic of property ownership between one region and another or one commune and another are a reflection of French society and its history, making all attempts at a spatial classification dubious. Clearly, peasant-owned rural Alsace and the Paris region, where town dwellers own a large part of the land, represent opposing extremes, as do the Charentes and Languedoc, but it is at the level of the small region, of the urban sphere of influence, of the individual valley or interfluve that contrasts in ownership structures are most clearly apparent. The diversity of natural environments and land utilization influences the mixture of different types of properties in regions and communes. The valleys are the favoured sites for small properties, whereas medium and large properties are found on the plateaus.

The influence of the physical environment

in fact only becomes apparent as a response to the needs of the occupiers of the land. The most exacting users are ... the peasants ... and this is understandable since of all the methods of working the land, the one they characteristically use, that is direct cultivation by the owner backed by only slender resources, is the one which bears the highest risks. Accordingly, one of the most fundamental and deeply rooted characteristics of the rural settlement pattern of France is the concentration by peasant communities upon sites whose natural advantages minimize the risks of small-scale cultivation. Peasant farmers require an easily worked soil, with sufficient porosity to reduce the effect of both excessive and inadequate rainfall. They also require land offering sufficient alternative possibilities of use for each farmer to find, or to be able to create on the spot all the resources needed to make the holding self-sufficient. The subsequent acquisition of land by members of the bourgeoisie had necessarily to be limited to sites that their peasant rivals had failed to bring into successful and continuous agricultural occupation. Thus there are areas where the owners of small parcels of land readily accepted offers of purchase from bourgeois buyers anxious to build up estates, and areas where they were unwilling to relinquish their property.[2]

[2] R. Dion, 'Réflexions de méthode à propos de "La Grande Limagne" de Max Derruau', *Annales de Géographie*, no. 318, 1951, pp. 28–9.

The land of each rural commune in France is thus fragmented and divided between several hundred owners of whom some, living in far-off parts of the globe, may not even be aware of the fact, having acquired ownership by inheritance from distant relatives. This heterogeneity of ownership clearly does not favour the development of a more rational utilization of the land.

The various rural properties have diverse structures, but their predominant characteristic is extreme fragmentation. The average size of the French agricultural parcel is about 33 acres (3,300 sq m), a unit approximating in size to the former *journal* or day-work, the amount of land that could be ploughed by one man in a day.

Since the beginning of the nineteenth century the parcels have been repeatedly divided. The main factor involved was the Napoleonic Civil Code, which established equal division among all heirs, so multiplying the number of small parcels and small estates. In some cases, subdivision reached the absolute limit at which physical partition was no longer possible, and only notional shares on paper could be legally allocated.

However, not all of France is subjected to the same degree of property fragmentation. It is at its maximum in areas of grouped settlement with openfield divided into strips, in regions of tenant farming, in densely populated cantons, and on islands. Even in such regions, however, parcels belonging to one owner may be contiguous, providing isolated blocks under single ownership. The fragmentation of ownership is least in regions of dispersed settlement, where land is farmed directly by the owner, and where the farmhouse and the land around it form a single uninterrupted block. The west of the Central massif, Limousin and Cantal have long remained faithful to maintaining the estate entire, without fragmentation. Some provinces, such as the Basque country and Béarn, have avoided fragmentation on inheritance by maintaining primogeniture, which explains the greater average area of their estates and, where cultivation by the owner predominates, of holdings.

All land-ownership structures are to be found in France, from total dispersal in small parcels to the large estate with its land in a single uninterrupted block. The factors determining the type of territorial organization of ownership are as much human as physical. The territorial structure of properties varies according to their historical origins. Some were from the beginning intended for direct cultivation, with land in one continuous block. In the seventeenth and eighteenth centuries, for example, monastic orders and the nobility grouped parcels of land together in order to create continuous estates. Other estates, on the contrary, have been created purely for investment purposes, consisting of collections of parcels that are not necessarily contiguous. Below a certain size, of course, the unit of ownership is no longer sufficient to make up a viable unit of cultivation on its own.

1.2 Private ownership of built-up land

As with agricultural land, ownership of urban land is highly fragmented, shared between many different owners. Owner–occupier households were 35.5 per cent of all households in 1954, 43 per cent in 1968 and 46.6 per cent in 1975. The town is an arena of competition between various economic, political and social forces; the struggle for control over land is keen. Urban land also provides the greatest speculative gains, or at any rate offers the greatest hopes of gain to speculators. The struggle for the possession of land is much more intense than in rural areas. Urban land is also covered by buildings of varied industrial, administrative, service or other functions, activities which are either the source of considerable capital appreciation, or demand central locations in towns. The two characteristics are far from being mutually exclusive. The requirements for land in urban areas, and the consumption of urban space, thus combine to produce a formidable demand. This demand has been magnified by overall urban growth, which, however, arrived later and in a less acute form in France than in other developed countries.

Urban land ownership is accordingly subject to rapid diversification and change. Alongside the category of small-scale urban property, consisting essentially of the private dwellings of individuals, there developed during the course of the nineteenth and twentieth centuries an essentially bourgeois type of property destined for letting. This category is not entirely new; under the *Ancien Régime* nobles, merchants and professional men owned urban property in addition to their palaces or town houses. With industrialization and migration to the towns, ownership of property by the bourgeoisie increased, reaching a first peak between 1870 and 1920. Apart from private individuals, today's large urban landowners are industrial and commercial companies, financial institutions, banks, insurance companies and other corporate bodies.

Another type of land ownership made its appearance between 1950 and 1975: acquisitions by the big banks in anticipation of future urban expansion or to provide for property development schemes. For example, as soon as development of the industrial port of Fos became likely, banking groups bought land or gained control of companies that already owned land in the area. Land ownership of this type is only temporary, pending resale once the property development process is complete, at which stage the costs of the operation are passed on to the property developer, and thus to the consumer. In this way, under the co-ownership legislation introduced in the 1950s, purchasers of dwellings become joint owners of the land on which their apartment block is built.

Foreigners also participate in the French market in housing land. They buy five out of every hundred second homes sold in France. In addition, foreign-based companies buy land for subdivision and sale as building plots in regions of high tourist demand, such as the Alps, Corsica, the Côte d'Azur and Hérault.

1.3 Public ownership

In 1977 the state owned 4 per cent (2,060,000 ha) of the surface area of France; this does not include the so-called 'public domain' reserved for transport activities by land, river and sea. State-owned land may be divided into the following categories:

State forests	1,428,000 ha
Land belonging to the armed forces	248,000 ha
of which military camps	110,000 ha
training grounds	32,000 ha
airfields	35,000 ha
barracks	18,000 ha
Non-military land outside built-up areas	100,000 ha
Land in built-up areas	150,000 ha

In this large proportion of state-owned land, France differs markedly from other European countries, where local authorities are the principal public landowners.

The French communes own 2,567,000 ha of forests, as well as grazing land, mountain pastures, heathlands and common marsh. Communal forests are particularly extensive in the east of the country and in Corsica. In addition to the holdings of the communes, land is also held by intercommunal associations, particularly in the Alps and Pyrenees. These associations, covering a particular valley or district, are of long standing, owning mountain pastures in common.

A third category of landowner consists of public bodies of all kinds, the nature of property owned clearly reflecting their functions. Electricité de France, the nationally owned electric power supplier, owns 180,000 ha, three-quarters of which lie beneath the waters of the reservoirs of hydro-power schemes. The SNCF (French Railways) owns 115,000 ha, of which 75,000 ha are covered by track, and the remaining third by stations and workshops. Charbonnages de France (French Coal Board) owns 36,354 ha, including 4,553 ha forest, 8,037 ha agricultural land, 7,503 ha of mine and industrial land and 8,829 ha built-up land. Hospitals, savings banks and similar organizations are also important landowners.

The various ministries, local authorities and public bodies tend to behave just like private landlords with respect to the land that they own. Losing sight of the specifically 'public' nature of 'their' property, they tend to react to requests to release extensive areas of land to provide for large-scale public projects by becoming 'speculators', only reluctantly releasing land, and then at a high price, neglecting the general interest of the public. In the course of urban expansion many areas of land in public ownership, such as barracks, railway goods yards or redundant gasworks, formerly on the fringe of the town, turn out to be in a most desirable location and are therefore much sought after.

The greed of private investors has not spared even the public domain. From the 1950s onwards, parts of the coastline, formerly in the public domain, were appropriated by property developers in order to construct yacht marinas by building on land reclaimed from the sea. The government authorized these concessions of the coastal public domain under a law of 16 September 1807.

2 The property market
2.1 The transfer of property

During the course of the single year 1976, 5,853,758 parcels changed ownership. The buying and selling of land, whether built on or not, is the consequence of a mutual decision of the interested parties. A transfer of property may be a free decision, or required by special circumstances, most commonly the need for sale as part of the inheritance process.

Property transfers are numerous because they are the basis of all changes in the organization and use of land. The building of a motorway, airport or university must begin with the acquisition of land. The availability of land, the willingness to sell and the price of agricultural or building land are at the source of geographical change. The impact of property transfer, however, varies according to whether it takes place within the same category, that is from agricultural use to another agricultural use, or from one urban use to another, or whether it involves transfer from one category to another, especially from agricultural use to building land. There are in fact two separate property markets, the agricultural and the urban, each with its own internal logic.

2.1.1 *The market in agricultural land*

Historically the struggle between different groups for possession of the land took on different aspects according to the period and the region in which it took place, but was progressively reduced to the conflict between the peasant class and the nobility and urban bourgeoisie. With the development of towns there emerged an affluent class of rural origin but independent of the nobility, ready to dispute the ownership of rural land with nobility and peasantry alike. From the fourteenth to the eighteenth centuries, nobles and bourgeois acquired numerous small peasant properties and created estates consisting of one or more holdings let to tenants or share-croppers. From the nineteenth century onwards, however, the peasants had their revenge, doubling their possessions in the course of 150 years. Population growth and subsequent rural overpopulation in some regions brought about a division of estates and the creation of small peasant holdings, made viable by agricultural intensification.

To the peasant, the purchase of the land he cultivates gives priceless confidence and security, which he often prefers to investing in the land that he rents. The purchase of land allows him not only to expand his farm but to ensure that his children will inherit it. For many farmers the purchase of land is the only way of setting up sons as farmers.

External factors may shake the structure of ownership and holdings in any region. The most recent example of a sudden change of this kind is provided by the return of French settlers from North Africa. From 1952 they settled in the Toulouse region, buying holdings formerly let to share-croppers and regrouping them into large estates.

The agricultural property market is relatively stable: 600,000 to 670,000 ha changed hands annually from 1968 to 1973, 500,000–530,000 ha since 1974 which represents 1.5–2 per cent of the total agricultural area. Purchases made by farmers and the SAFER (see section 3.2.1) represent 75–78 per cent of the total.

Overall, and in the long term, agricultural land is increasingly the property of those who cultivate it; from 1971 to 1977 inclusive, the net gain of the farmers was 1,338,000 ha. The agricultural property market is thus dispersed and fragmented. Transactions are concerned less with complete properties than with individual parcels. In 1977, fewer than 3,000 properties of more than 20 ha were sold, an indication of how difficult it is for young people to set up in farming. Eighty per cent of the purchasers lived in the department where the transaction took place, and 64 per cent in the same canton. Farmers and in particular tenant farmers were the principal purchasers, the principal sellers being residents of the towns and especially of the Paris region.

2.1.2 *The agro-urban property market*

In a normal year, the average area of land which changes from the rural to the urban land market is estimated at 200,000 ha. Applications for building permits alone amount to 120,000 ha per year. The transformation of agricultural land into built-up land, or land on which building can take place, depends on satisfying a range of conditions, notably of servicing (the provision of roads, water, drainage and so on), of town planning or zoning (so that areas to be built on may be defined) and of land division (specification of minimum plot size, subdivision into building plots).

By changing from the agricultural into the urban category, land acquires speculative value, which is determined by the anticipated return on investment and not by the value of agricultural production.

Every change in land use creates an economic rent, based on the difference between the economic value of the ultimate use and that of the initial use, or on the imbalance between supply and demand. An economic rent may even be created by the existence of public investments facilitating development to the ultimate usage of the land, or by an attractive natural environment.[3]

Hence capital gains from land speculation have in France become superior to profit: more money can be made by buying land and waiting than by investing in industry and risking loss.

[3] M. E. Chassagne, 'Aspects fonciers de l'aménagement de l'espace rural', *Economie Rurale*, no. 117, 1977, pp. 35–47.

Until the 1950s the property markets in urban and agricultural land were, for various reasons, stable and quite distinct from each other. Subsequent developments that have brought the two markets closer together include urban growth, the diffusion of urbanization, the creation of industrial zones and new towns, the demand for second homes, and transport developments such as motorways, canals and high-speed rail lines.

An economic rent due to situation may be created by the transformation of the environment, for example by the arrival of a Métro extension, the construction of a motorway and its interchange system, the establishment of an administrative complex, or of a university. The diffusion of major constructional projects and new forms of infrastructure linked to the town has an impact far beyond the urban fringe, breaking down the division between the urban and the rural land markets.

Agricultural buildings acquired together with rural land may be resold as second homes; the consolidation of holdings and the provision of means of access to the new parcels may produce potential building plots. Even the process of town planning itself, by drawing up local structure plans and anticipated zoning arrangements, may make known in advance anticipated transformations from agricultural to urban use, and so alert investors to development opportunities. Communal land-use plans (*plans d'occupation des sols* – POS) in rural areas give rise to speculative ways of thinking or at the very least to the expectation of gain from increased land values, which explains the bitterness of the discussions over the delineation in the plans of areas allocated for building development. In such areas there is increasing conflict between farmers and non-farmers over the acquisition of land, generally at the expense of the former.

A. Givaudan has attempted to define the 'hot spots' of property speculation. He locates them in 58 departments of France, 24 of them on the coast, 17 in mountain areas and 9 on the Rhône–Rhine axis, together with the eight departments of the Paris region. In all 300,000 sq km of land are involved, or 38 million inhabitants. Within these departments, the areas most affected are those where local structure plans and Communal Land-use Plans have been established. Such areas constitute 25 per cent of the surface area of France, comprising 60 per cent of the population.

There remain all those who own undeveloped land and who find themselves caught between two societies; on the one hand the France of cities, of the developing coasts, of the great route axes, of the nodes of economic activity and of the tourist centres; on the other hand, rural France. For the most part owners are anxious to benefit from the general rise in economic prosperity. Probably just over a million people own unbuilt land in the 5,343 communes covered by communal land-use plans in the hot-spot areas, and no more than 2 million people in the whole of France. Numerous though they may be, those who hold a sizeable share in controlling the future physiognomy of a quarter of French territory are only a minority. Their interests, however understandable or evident, must not take precedence over the general interest.[4]

---

[4] A. Givaudan, 'La question foncière', *Revue d'Economie et de Droit Immobilier*, no. 67, 1976, pp. 32–80.

The property market is made up of the behaviour and decisions of hundreds of thousands of owners. They may sell their land either because they are obliged to, or in order to free capital for further investment elsewhere. Alternatively they may hold on to their property, waiting for a favourable moment to sell on a rising market, using the land as a tried and tested hedge against inflation. Where land is subject to joint ownership, it may also lie unused for long periods.

2.2 The price of land

The outcome of a completed negotiation between the purchaser and the vendor of land is agreement on a price. This will be fixed by compromise at some point between the minimum price in the mind of the vendor and the maximum price acceptable by the purchaser. Differences in price between apparently compar- able transactions reflect the complexity and diversity of the land market. It is clear that price differences are more to be attributed to the purchaser than the vendor, the price acceptable to the former being determined by the anticipated return on the cost of purchasing the land once a certain amount of capital has been invested in it. The unit of land in relation to which price determination takes place varies according to the category of land concerned, being made by the hectare for agricultural land, forest or vineyard, but by the square metre for building land, in other words in a ratio of 1:10,000.

2.2.1 *The price of agricultural land*

Land values provide an extremely sensitive barometer whose fluctuations are determined by a wide range of factors which may be natural (soil, climate, aspect, relief or the proportion of arable land in the total land area of the region), spatial (ease of access, distance from large towns), economic (gross productivity of the land concerned), demographic (population pressure, size of holding) or geographical (whether a parcel or a complete holding changes hands, the parcels selling at a higher price). In 1977 the average price per hectare was about 17,000 francs, arable being more expensive (17,600 francs) than grassland (15,600 francs). Land costs vary from region to region, from parcel to parcel even (Fig. 15.2).

All evidence confirms that the real value of agricultural land declined for the greater part of a century (1880–1950). The extent of depreciation between 1862 and 1939 has been estimated at two-thirds for grassland and four-fifths for arable land. In 1908 the price of a hectare of arable land was equivalent to the price of 60 quintals of wheat; by 1953 it was equivalent to the price of only 35 quintals (the metric quintal is 100 kilograms). There are many reasons for this decline, including the dismantling of the rights of ownership brought about by legislation on agricultural tenancies, the increase in conveyancing charges, the widening of the gap between the prices of agricultural and industrial products, the increased costs of building and of property repairs, the growing scale of working capital needed when compared with land costs and the ever-increasing attraction of investment in securities.

Since 1950 the decline in real value has been reversed: between 1950 and 1975 the cost of agricultural land trebled; between 1960 and 1975 its price increased by 44 per cent at current prices, corresponding to an average annual increase of 4.5 per cent at constant prices.

2.2.2 *The price of urban land*

In urban areas, the market in land is a function of the market in built property. The price of land is all too often a residual value derived from the estimated cost at which a square metre of built property can be offered to a client without risk of being left on the vendor's hands. It is only in theory, and very schematically, that the price of land varies in space–time relationship to the urban core; many factors complicate this simple rent-gradient model. On the edge of the town the price of building land does not grade into that for agricultural land; instead there is a

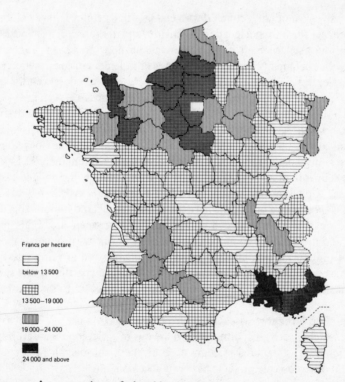

Francs per hectare

below 13 500

13 500–19 000

19 000–24 000

24 000 and above

Figure 15.2 Average prices of ploughland and permanent pasture, 1978. Source: *Le Nouvel Économiste*, no. 207, 5 November 1979.

sudden upsurge from rural levels as soon as the first signs of urban development appear. It is in this rural–urban fringe that land prices increase most rapidly, while remaining relatively attractive by comparison with those of central districts. It has been said that towns have exported their appreciated land values to the rural–urban fringe, the new prices being established step by step by outward movement from the centre. Recent tendencies towards a more dispersed urbanization and the acquisition of second homes have caused these sudden price increases to occur also in country areas beyond the rural–urban fringe.

Between 1956 and 1968 the price of building land increased 4.3 times, or 2.66 times at constant prices. Since 1969 property values have been increasing by an average of 14 to 15 per cent yearly, with particularly marked increases from time to time, at periods of marked economic upswing. Pressure from rising land prices fuels inflation, because of the discrepancy between the high price at which land changes hands, and its true use-value.

3 Problems and policies with regard to land
3.1 Land problems

The excessive cost of land, coupled with changes in its control, have deplorable consequences. The rational location of activities and the appropriate allocation of land to various uses are made impossible. Available floor-area has to be reduced, while the price of land becomes an ever-increasing element in construction costs. For example, the element of land cost has increased from one-seventh to one-quarter of the total cost of new housing. The consequences are seen in excessive residential densities, enforced social segregation and relegation to undesirable locations. Spatial organization can be regarded as determined by the cost of land.

In rural areas, owners who do not farm their own land are decreasingly interested in investment in agricultural land for the sake of rent income. Farmers are practically forced to buy rather than to rent land, thus being obliged to carry unaided the capital burden of land provision, and to get heavily into debt.

There is inevitably a problem where the ownership of land inhibits social and economic development, where there is a conflict between the rights of the landlord and the needs of community and society. A further problem is that the growth of tourism, the emphasis on outdoor activities and growing interest in ecology have focused attention on the monopolization of coastlines, lake shores, river banks and forests by private owners, who deny access to these attractive areas.

Yet another difficulty arises from the fragmented nature of French land holdings, which places great difficulties in the way of agricultural modernization, the development of rational systems of cultivation, the overall protection of forests and of large-scale projects of urban development.

3.2 Policies for land

A national policy for land involves all actions of public bodies relative to the use or ownership of land, with a view to imposing on these the acceptance of general objectives previously fixed by the government.

All property policies are the expression of previous political choices. Faced with the problems posed by the property market, there are two possible attitudes. One is total liberalism, giving free rein to the market mechanisms of supply and demand. This approach, whose characteristic expression could be 'everything can be urbanized', is specifically urban; rural areas are considered as reserve land available to investors. By contrast is the interventionist attitude, which is necessarily restrictive; its objective is to protect the agricultural property market and to reserve it for farmers, while at the same time allowing for urban expansion. In the first case the policy strengthens the rights and prerogatives of owners, in the second it limits them. The effects of these policies may favour either private property or the forms of collective ownership. Property policies have existed in France for a long time, even though they were not always called by that name.

3.2.1 The growth of owner-occupation

Successive governments have encouraged the growth of owner-occupation in housing or land. In towns this policy, dating from the First World War, had numerous advantages; it ensured security of tenure, encouraged people to settle in the towns, and integrated the working class into the social system. At national level, the growth of owner-occupation curbs the mobility of the working population.

In rural areas the basic principle of government policy from 1945 to 1970 was to facilitate the acquisition of land by farmers. The chief measures have been:

(1) The law giving the right of pre-emption to the agricultural tenant and share-cropper.

(2) Government assistance for the purchase of land by farmers. The first significant example was the aid given to farmers repatriated from North Africa in 1962. Then, by a procedure introduced in 1965 and modified in 1973, the government aided farmers to secure ownership of their land (since 1978 there has been particular emphasis on the purchase of land by sitting tenants).

(3) The encouraging of elderly farmers to retire. Under the provision of the Social Action Fund for the Improvement of Agricultural Structure (Fonds d'Action Sociale pour l'Amélioration des Structures Agricoles – FASASA), elderly farmers who voluntarily gave up their farms in such a way as to favour agricultural restructuring could benefit from the system of Indemnités Viagères de Départ (IVD), a supplementary pension. This policy had very significant consequences: from 1964 to 1975 inclusive it applied to 508,000 farmers working 8,854,000 ha (29.5 per cent of the agriculturally used area), thereby

permitting the expansion of 556,000 holdings. The system had its maximum impact between 1969 and 1972. It accounted for 85 per cent of transfers in 1975, but only 40 per cent in 1977, reflecting a decline in the attractiveness of the system due to a failure to adjust pension rates.

(4) The establishment of the Organizations for Land Restructuring and Rural Resettlement (Sociétés d'Aménagement Foncier et d'Etablissement Rural – SAFER) under the agricultural legislation of 3 August 1960 (*Loi d'orientation agricole*). The aims are clearly stated: 'to encourage the expansion of family holdings which are too small or uneconomic in order to make them viable and to give them stability of employment as well as of income; in the long term to create new, stable and profitable family holdings'. When land that is either in agricultural use or is potentially cultivable is offered for sale, the SAFER have the right of pre-emption, that is, they may step in and buy the land over the heads of other possible purchasers. The SAFER operate as property companies, buying plots of land (if necessary using the right of pre-emption) and regrouping them in order to sell blocks of land back to those who may be saved by the addition of a few extra hectares. The SAFER are provided with funds to oppose the concentration of land in the hands of big farmers or persons from outside the agricultural profession. However, when the reserve prices go beyond the ceiling fixed by the SAFER, they lose the land, something that happens particularly when land is sold by auction.

From 1961 to 1977 the SAFER acquired more than 800,000 ha. SAFER acquisitions represented 10 per cent of the land changing hands by sale in 1968–9, and 15 per cent in the period since 1974. Retroceded land is above all used to expand existing holdings, and in a lesser degree to create new ones. It is in fact difficult to create viable new holdings out of the random offerings of the property market.

Since the 1970s, agricultural land policies have been appreciably modified, reflecting changing conditions in agriculture:

(1) Rising agricultural indebtedness, which acts as a brake on investment in modernization and intensification.
(2) The tendency for farmers to retain ownership of their land after retirement.
(3) The spread of attitudes favouring the retention of land for speculative purposes.

In consequence, official land-finance policies have moved towards a reduction in the financial burdens of farmers by enrolling non-agricultural investors. The Agricultural Finance Groups (Groupements Fonciers Agricoles – GFA), set up under a law of 3 December 1970, have as their objective the mobilization of savings from outside the farming world to buy land and to give farmers security without obliging them to become owners. In 1974 the SAFER were authorized to intervene in the formation of GFA by actively seeking non-agricultural investors. In 1977 the rights of pre-emption of the SAFER were redefined to favour the installation of young farmers.

3.2.2 *The development of public ownership*

In the 1950s various measures were introduced to enable local authorities and public bodies to acquire land destined for the establishment of industrial estates (by Chambers of Commerce) and of housing projects. Subsequent developments included the system of priority planning zones (*zones à urbaniser en priorité* – ZUP) under the decree of 31 December 1958, followed by zones of deferred development (*Zones d'aménagement différé* – ZAD). Until very recently, however, local authorities had almost no financial resources to build up land reserves, but since 1977 they have received grants for this purpose.

The French government has encouraged a greater flexibility with regard to land owned by the state and its various dependent bodies by allowing the government department or other public body concerned to retain the proceeds of land sales by setting up a system of 'compensatory exchanges', whereby in return for the release of an area of land the organization concerned is allowed to acquire a greater area elsewhere. These measures have freed key areas vital for the success of major town-planning schemes. An example is the Part-Dieu project at Lyon, built on land formerly owned by the army. Social housing and projects of public-sector investment are often facilitated by transfers between the various organs of central and local government. This explains the building of universities on sites whose only merit is that they could be acquired quickly and at reasonable cost.

3.2.3 *Control of urban land and land suitable for building*

France has gradually acquired a whole arsenal of laws and regulations relating to the acquisition of land for urban development.

(1) Compulsory purchase for public purposes. The procedure was formerly reserved for the acquisition of land for bridges and similar civil-engineering projects, for road and rail lines, and for other projects of benefit to the public. Since the 1940s it has been progressively extended, first to cover reconstruction following war damage, and then the construction of social housing and industrial estates. The law of 6 August 1953 authorized expropriation for the creating and putting into operation of town-planning schemes. Finally the urban and regional planning legislation known as the *Loi d'orientation foncière* (1969) allowed compulsory purchase to be used in the assembling of land reserves without prior notification as to their intended use.

(2) Pre-emption. This right, which through the SAFER applies generally in rural areas, is in urban areas strictly limited since 1958 to the ZUPs and since 1962 to the ZADs. Under the ZUP procedure, local authorities and associated construction concerns had the right of pre-emption for from four to six years over land within the defined area. Such zones on the urban fringe were destined for large public housing projects (*grands ensembles*) which were intended to be the answer to the enormous postwar housing demand.

The ZADs are created by order of the Prefect of the department concerned. Within these zones, the organs of central and local government and even Chambers of Commerce and semi-public companies (*sociétés d'économie mixte*) may exercise a pre-emptive right on land offered for sale. The object of the ZAD procedure was to control land prices in areas where development in the medium term is anticipated. In 1977 there were approximately 2,000 ZADs in areas as widely different as the urban fringe, the coasts of Aquitaine or Languedoc, or along motorways; in the Paris region alone, 128,000 ha have been 'zadés'. In fact, normal property transactions have been distorted. Property transactions are infrequent in the ZAD, while speculation is rife in the immediately surrounding areas.

The zones of controlled urban development (*zones d'intervention foncière* – ZIF), established under the law of 31 December 1975, are similar to the ZAD, but their full application is only to the urbanized area of communes of more than 10,000 inhabitants and to communes with a valid land-use plan (POS). The duration of the ZIF is unlimited and its objectives specifically restricted to the creation of urban open spaces, social housing, public infrastructure, the restoration of individual buildings, area restoration, or the creation of land reserves.

(3) The control of land use. This is one of the key policies with regard to land; it is also one of the most controversial, since every measure taken reduces the freedom of the owner.

(4) The law of 31 December 1975 relating to the reform of property policies reiterates that 'the right to build is attached to the ownership of land', but introduces the idea of a 'legal plot ratio' (*plafond légal de densité* – PLD) specifying that any construction exceeding the legal plot ratio is the concern of the local authority. The aim of the legal plot ratio is to limit property speculation and to combat excessive building densities, while at the same time generating additional income for local authorities.

The legal plot ratio is fixed at 1.0 for the whole country except for Paris, where the figure is 1.5. A plot ratio of 1.0 allows the building of a total floor area equal to the total area of the plot concerned. Any exceeding of the permitted area involves the payment to the local authority of a sum equivalent to the cost of the additional land that would be necessary to allow the construction of the floorspace concerned at the proper plot ratio. In provincial towns building reaches the maximum plot ratio of 1.0 only in very limited areas. The fixing of a legal plot ratio is the first step in a policy whose principles, according to many specialists, represent the only means of solving the property problem, that is by the separation of the right to build from the ownership of land.

(5) Zoning is the other important method of controlling land use. In theory it is satisfactory, but it discriminates arbitrarily between owners. The lottery of a line drawn on a map divides land which may be profitably developed from land which must remain agricultural. No procedure for adjustment or compensation has yet been found which can completely meet the desire for equity in this situation.

(6) Land taxation is another method which allows the state to control the use of land. The law of 19 December 1963 introduced a betterment charge on appreciated land values, levied at the time of sale. The *Loi d'orientation foncière* (urban and regional planning law) of 30 December 1967 introduced a local tax levied when items of infrastructure are provided. The purpose of the tax is to restore to the local community some of the appreciation in property values occasioned by public investment.

The land policy followed since the Second World War has been progressively extended by the addition of new measures, but always within the framework of the maintenance and even extension of private property. The results of this policy are not always commensurate with its objectives, and other measures have been proposed. One extreme proposal is land nationalization. In future the state would be the sole purchaser of land. Ownership of land would be separated from that of buildings, the owners of which would lease the land on which they stood from the state. A decentralized version of this proposal would involve giving control of the land to the municipalities, by creating local property offices at communal or departmental level which would make land available to users either on leases for 64 years or for an unlimited term.

4 The changing structure of ownership

The morphology and structure of the pattern of parcels are an important element in the utilization and transfer of land. It is possible to speak of a determinism derived from ownership which is superimposed on financial determinism. In rural areas, the influence is clear: the size and shape of parcels aid or impede cultivation, motorization and mechanization. Parcels which are too small or excessively fragmented involve additional expenditure of time and energy.

In urban areas, the type of utilization tends to be determined by the shape and size of parcels, rather than by any concern for a rational and harmonious organization of space. The parcel is largely responsible for the nature, shape, size and layout of buildings. Depending on the intended use, the texture of parcels can attract or repel potential purchasers. A public authority responsible for a vast project of urban development or the provision of infrastructure will by sheer force of conditions be obliged to abandon an area of complex and fragmented ownership structure in favour of a site made up of large parcels concentrated in the hands of very few owners, even if it is less suited to the intended purpose. Generally on the immediate outskirts of towns one could find, and can still find today, a highly fragmented system of parcels with such uses as market gardens, leisure gardens and orchards. From medieval times areas of this type have evolved into suburbs, many of which, as a result of urban expansion, are now located in the central parts of the town. With an urban tissue such as this, there is a risk that progressive urban renewal and increased density of occupation will take the form of a random scatter of projects, their location determined by the chance availability of parcels becoming available for redevelopment.

Large parcels of building land attract the developers of housing estates and other major building projects, while small parcels are used by individuals building for themselves. The 1924 law that made it more difficult to subdivide large areas of land for resale as building plots led in the Paris area to the sale of small vineyard plots for individual house-building. Since the 1960s, however, the trend in housing policy has radically transformed conditions for the transfer of land from the agricultural to the urban category by the purchase of enormous areas for such large-scale developments as *grands ensembles* (major public housing projects) and new towns.

In the past there was a distinct harmony between the typical structure of parcels on the developing rural fringes of towns and the relatively low and modest buildings erected there. But modern buildings are markedly incompatible with the traditional rural pattern. Either the inherited structural tissue must be totally recast, or else redevelopment must preserve the scale of building inherited from the past. Wise town planning would adopt the second solution, rejecting the increased densities made possible by modern technology. The worst possible solution is to build in the present-day idiom in accordance with a structure of parcels inherited from a bygone age, which is an easy option and therefore the one most commonly adopted. This ancient structure of ownership, which implicitly determines urban form, is responsible by its anachronism and its lack of adaptation to present-day requirements for the incoherent relationships now existing in the different sectors of the urban whole.

A few decades ago, the system of land parcels in rural France, fragmented by successive division, had reached a critical stage; this so-called 'cadastral fossilization' was the chief obstacle to the modernization of agriculture. Understandably a policy of land consolidation was developed to counter the trend to fragmentation. The first consolidation took place in 1770 at Neuville-sur-Moselle, but it is only since the end of the nineteenth century that the process has been given serious legislative backing. Consolidation is, in fact, only one element in a more general policy of agricultural and rural reconstruction, which has as its aim the provision of a structure of ownership and holdings that will allow a rational use of land and buildings. The process has, of course, to pay due regard to the quality of the soil and its conservation, to agricultural techniques and their development, to the human environment, to the general economic conditions of the country and to the appropriate economic development of the area concerned. This rural reconstruction is achieved by a redistribution of parcels of land and buildings in the context of a general process of land consolidation. The process includes the necessary civil-engineering work to make possible a rational cultivation of the land; the bringing into cultivation of abandoned land, especially in order to enlarge agricultural holdings too small to be profitable; the creation of new enterprises; and afforestation.

The principle of consolidation is simple: all the land of a village is redistributed among all the owners in such a way that each receives back land of the same value to that originally held. Parcels are reduced to the minimum number possible consistent with optimum accessibility from the economic buildings of the holding concerned. All parcels are provided with vehicular access. It is a principle of consolidation that the smaller holdings are grouped near to the village, and the larger ones at a distance. Parcels which are owned by residents of adjoining villages are reallocated to the boundary with the commune concerned.

It is estimated that 15 million ha of land in France are in urgent need of consolidation, the equivalent of 40 per cent of cultivated land (excluding heath and woodland). At the end of 1977, over 10 million ha had been consolidated, as compared with 5.7 million ha at the end of 1967. In recent years the state has made an increasing contribution to consolidation, meeting 80 per cent of the cost involved, the proprietors finding the rest. The impact of consolidation has varied regionally, being most apparent in regions of predominantly arable cultivation with grouped village settlement, for example in the Paris basin, where 19 departments have each over 100,000 ha of consolidated land.

Departments in which few communes have been subjected to consolidation are those with little or no cultivable land (Seine, Alpes-Maritimes, Corsica, Lozère), and departments dominated either by forest (Landes, Dordogne, Var) or by grassland (Manche, Aveyron). It is important not to overlook the fact that land consolidation has been limited by delicate problems of relief or type of land use in mountain regions, in very isolated regions and generally in districts where vines, bush and tree crops, and special crops such as hops are grown. Similar difficulties occur in respect of pasture land and more generally everywhere that relief introduces a great diversity of soil, slopes and sites. Although the consolidation of orchards and vineyards presents great problems, they are not impossible of resolution. In general, forest land is not consolidated; the Vosges area is among very few exceptions.

Obstacles due to attitudes of mind are even more significant, explaining why in the same region communes accepting consolidation and communes hostile to it can exist side by side. The agreement of all proprietors affected is needed before a consolidation scheme can be put into effect, which explains the slowness of operations of this type. As it stands, the uneven progress of consolidation, so clearly revealed on the map, is not without its dangers, accentuating the economic gap between the farmers of northern and southern France, further disadvantaging regions which are already backward.

Consolidation is not permanent; after 15 or 20 years the uneven development of holdings, the process of concentration of holdings and the continuance of changes due to inheritance tend to break up the orderly patterns that have been created with such difficulty. While consolidation represents undeniable progress, it cannot escape from serious internal contradictions. Its aim is to improve the efficiency of agriculture by rearranging the structure of agricultural ownership. It is therefore at its most effective in regions where the units of ownership and the units of agricultural operation coincide, which is not normally the case. Consolidation is only effective when it is part of a policy of the total reorganization of agrarian structures and rural space.

Schemes for the restructuring of urban parcels do not exist on the same scale. They have been carried out as part of the process of rebuilding towns destroyed in the last war, and are also facilitated by the procedures allowing the grouping of landowners (*copropriété*). It is perhaps a matter of regret that there is no legal requirement, whether in urban or rural areas, that proposals for changes in the utilization of parcels should necessarily be preceded by a restructuring procedure.

5 Conclusion

Up to now, government policies with regard to land ownership have had three objectives:

(1) to fight against the unearned wealth that urban development brings to the owners of land;
(2) to provide land at reasonable prices for developers, particularly for the building of social housing;
(3) to provide ways of land acquisition other than by the operation of the land market.

The extent to which these objectives have been attained is questionable. It is fair to say that policy with regard to land has up to now not been governed by the needs of town planning; instead, the taxation of unearned incremental value has been governed rather by moral considerations. Legislation passed in 1963 even had a harmful effect on town planning because the tax imposed on incremental values became incorporated in the price at which land was offered for sale. It is true that the government's systematic efforts to increase opportunities for building can be regarded as a justifiable response to present-day needs for urban development, yet such measures can be disastrous if they lead to the use of badly located sites or to building at excessive densities. In short, all policies with regard to property ownership should have proper regard for the requirements of urban and regional planning; hitherto this has hardly been the case in France.

16

⚜ Agents of geographical change

---

1 Powers and decisions

1.1 Agents

The term 'geographical agent' is often applied incorrectly to the factors affecting geographical location and land use, and as an explanation of the areal differentiation of the earth's surface. More precisely, the term should be restricted to any person or institution with the power or ability to intervene in the use, organization or transformation of the earth's surface.

This 'geographical power' has varying effects. The actions of geographical agents spring from decisions which may be consciously or unconsciously taken. Decisions of spatial significance are consciously taken by those responsible for town planning, for strategic spatial planning, for channelling decentralization, for drawing up Structure Plans, for creating new towns and industrial estates, or for developing legislation on the protection of the environment. Decisions of spatial significance are unconsciously taken where the object is not the deliberate geographical transformation of a region but where a proposal or action have inevitable geographical consequences.

The geographical effects of decisions and actions are too often neglected, even completely forgotten. An economic decision does not have exclusively economic consequences; it is likely to have a spatial impact by, for example, modifying the flows of people and commodities, or affecting the cost of land and buildings.

The spatial effects of decisions and actions may also be influenced by geographical inertia; a decision sets the administrative machine in motion, and it is only after an interval, sometimes a very long one, that there is any consequent change in the landscape or spatial structure.

Actions which have geographical consequences – and few have not – are expressed in phenomena such as roads, airports or buildings which, once imprinted on the earth's surface, are difficult to erase. In the context of the history of France, every part of the land surface is a palimpsest of social equipment, the result of decisions and investments spread out sometimes over several centuries, which are only partially represented in present-day functional reality.

The investment decisions of public bodies as well as private individuals have an irreversible effect for years to come, leaving an indelible impact on the land. We measure the responsibility of governments and local authorities towards present and future generations as much by the investments that they themselves make as by the constraints they impose on investments by others.[1]

The numerous geographical agents include the state, local authorities, private companies, public bodies, semi-public organizations and private individuals. The agents play a part in the transformation of the geography of France in a variety of differing ways. They differ firstly in spatial scale, by the area within which their actions have effect, whether local, regional, national or international. They differ also on a time-scale, according to whether the programmes have short-term, medium-term or long-term objectives.

Geographical agents differ also in their objectives; their actions may be sectoral or global, may have economic aims or social aims, or be quantitative or qualitative. There is clearly a very unequal geographical impact between the decision of the owner of a small parcel of land who decides to use it to build his own house and that of the large-scale property developer, between the peasant who flattens the banks of a hollow way crossing his land, and French Railways bulldozing thousands of hectares of agricultural land to construct a new line for the high-speed train. But none of these categories can be ignored, for if the number of agents is inversely proportionate to their power, the proliferation of numerous small actors can have a profound impact on a landscape. The nibbling away at rural areas through dispersed urbanization is the result of the action of thousands of small proprietors, of hundreds of local authorities agreeing to the division of land into building plots, and of dozens of private housing-estate developers.

The possibilities of action, decision and guidance derive from a range of types of power:

(1) Political power, from which stem the powers of legislation and the issue of regulations and orders.

[1] J. Lesourne and R. Loué, *L'Analyse des décisions d'aménagement régional* (Dunod, Paris, 1979).

(2) The technocratic power of the specialists, possessors of technological expertise.

(3) The financial power of those who hold the purse strings, whether of the national budget, private capital or individual savings.

(4) Power based on the ownership of land or buildings.

(5) The power of pressure groups, anxious to impose their views in the service either of self-interest or ideology.

These agents and powers are organized into a hierarchy; at each level there are appropriate roles, responsibilities and means of action. Secret, unofficial networks, moreover, may exist behind the official hierarchies, constituting complex systems with relationships that may be either interdependent or conflicting.

1.2 Information availability and decision-making

The various bodies concerned make their decisions in the light of a range of factual information, but also in the light of their past experience, their political motivations and their ideological positions. A negative decision, or a failure to reach a decision, can be geographically as important as a positive one: there are towns in France which have paid heavily, and are still paying, for having failed to welcome the passage of a railway line or more recently a motorway, others from having rejected the establishment of industry.

Factual information is only useful if absorbed and understood by sufficiently informed minds. In the case of France, the postwar problems followed a period of zero growth and protectionism in the interwar years. It was only some years after the war, when the first signs of an increase in the birth rate had become apparent, that the administrators of towns and departments were convinced that circumstances had changed, and were willing to take the effects of population growth into consideration.

Decision-making thus largely depends on the quantity and quality of information, not only on its existence and reliability, but also on its accessibility and diffusion. Until just after the end of the Second World War, statistical information in France – the national censuses of population apart – was extremely difficult to come by. It is only in the last thirty years that France has acquired institutions providing statistical information in adequate quantity. The deficiency was still more pronounced at regional level, until the formation of committees for regional economic expansion, and later the establishment of the Regional Economic Observatories of the National Statistical Office, the Economic Missions attached to offices of the prefects, and the statistical offices attached to the Chambers of Commerce and Industry.

The arrival of the computer and the creation of data banks made the possession and processing of information essential cogs in the machinery of administration and planning, offering increasingly sophisticated procedures of budgetary allocation, modelling and simulation. Forecasting and the presentation of alternative scenarios of future development have played an increasingly important role in strategic spatial planning. Plans for modernization, regional development programmes, local structure plans and proposals for new towns were drawn up according to forecasts of economic and demographic growth. These forecasts had to be frequently amended in the light of more recent information, changing economic conditions, or simply policy changes. The fact is that the gathering of statistical information and the making of forecasts on the basis of that information do not constitute an exact science. As the basic information is far from exhaustive and objective, the decisions based on such information must necessarily be biased and imperfect.

1.3 The environment of decision-making

Decisions are made by politicians, financiers and entrepreneurs within the framework of the economic, social and political system, which is itself in process of evolution. Since the last war, French policies have been marked by two apparently contradictory trends. One is the liberal–capitalist trend, based on the free play of market mechanisms. Under it every holder of capital has the widest freedom to invest innovatively in the creation of new enterprises. The second trend is that of state intervention, aiming to plan and control market mechanisms. Since 1945 France has lived in this curious dual economy, half liberal, half interventionist, but with the balance of advantage towards the private interests favouring the development of private capitalism but in a national climate where the risks of free enterprise are minimized. The results are sometimes curious, reflecting the chance play of political pressures. For example Air France, the national airline, may find itself faced by competition from private companies which are receiving direct or indirect help from the state.

This alliance of the public and the private sectors may be regarded in the long term as uniting two tendencies which have existed throughout the history of France. The tendency towards state intervention in the economy was already evident under the *Ancien Régime* in the seventeenth-century policies of Sully, Colbert and Vauban, subsequently during the Revolutionary period and the Empire of Napoleon I. The other tendency, towards economic liberalism, was the traditional ideology of the commercial and industrial bourgeoisie, but one which was never completely independent of the state. This dualism complicates the development of spatial policies: all too often the geographical landscape reflects the juxtaposition, the succession or the mingling of economic liberalism and interventionism, and the subsequent compromises between the two that changing political circumstances have dictated.

Under the socialist–communist government (May 1981), intervention by the state has been reinforced by the nationalization of the entire financial sector and the major steel, chemical and engineering companies.

The relationships of the various decision-makers to geographical environment and space also vary. The landowner, the farmer, the financier, the ski instructor, the housing developer, the executive in search of a second home or the labourer holidaying on a camp site do not perceive the landscape in the same way. The interests of landowners are not necessarily those of developers, nor are those of farmers the same as those of visitors from the town.

Those responsible for decisions often make them according to their personal views, according to examples observed elsewhere to which they respond positively or negatively, to models presented to them by 'experts' or to whatever is in vogue at the moment. Accordingly, not only does the fashion in projects vary from one period to another (the industrial estate gives way to the swimming pool, the university supplants the major industrial project in desirability), but the detailed nature of particular types of development, their layout and their siting, may also vary as fashions change. Alternatives include concentration or dispersion of settlement, high-rise apartment blocks of *grand ensemble* type or single-family detached housing, private or public transport, linear or grouped development, high-density or low-density urban development, exclusive land zoning or a mixture of uses, and a quest for the monumental or 'development on a human scale'.

2 Financial resources

Money is often seen to symbolize power: the Treasury is perceived as the supreme seat of power in the state, while in the private sector the bank is the very symbol of the capitalist system. Yet initially money is merely a means of translating into action the decisions of political and economic agents, ranging from the household to the multinational company, from the mayor to the prime minister, but nothing can be accomplished except by recourse to money. It is amassed to provide capital, and it is laid out in investments. Every decision and every achievement of the agents of geographical change are clearly dependent on the existence of the necessary financial resources.

2.1 Savings

The financing of investments is at its most fundamental level a function of savings, the mobilization of available capital, although the process can be manipulated by government action. For individuals and households the amount of money saved is an indication of the capacity for self-financing, which makes borrowing unnecessary or provides the security on which borrowing may be based. Self-financing is the characteristic investment mechanism of private firms; it involves the allocation of part of the profits to the acquisition or replacement of plant, the construction of buildings or the purchase of new factories. Self-financing has the advantage of leaving complete freedom of investment decsion to the entrepreneur. The rate of self-financing for firms varies greatly, depending on the volume of profit and the investments that are to be made.

The aggregate contribution of French households is far from negligible, whether by way of savings or investment. The French are born savers; moneyboxes and savings banks are closely linked with their style of living and way of thinking. The French view of wealth, hence of savings, is more static than dynamic, more Latin than Anglo-Saxon. It is not created wealth in the form of factories and businesses which interests the French, but rather money as such. They prefer monetary deposits giving a regular return to speculative investments. The accumulation of wealth coupled with this attitude of mind explains why the French before 1914 were the universal moneylenders and why the accumulation of capital by private individuals was one of the greatest in the world. The attitude was symbolized by the traditional coin-filled woollen stocking of the peasant, and the fluctuations in the price of the old twenty-franc gold coin known as the 'Napoleon', a favourite with hoarders.

Counter-inflationary investments in gold, precious stones or works of art are negative in the sense that they are outside the productive sector. Rather more positive are investments by private individuals in property and housing, investments which are also considered to be resistant to erosion by inflation. These attitudes have significant geographical consequences, as shown by the scale of investment in built property and the growing popularity of second homes.

Savings are channelled into the financial institutions by means of networks of agencies which have expanded considerably since the 1960s. It has long been commonplace to depict the draining of the savings of provincial France through a centralized banking system into the hands of the state, Paris financiers and overseas investors. This extreme centralization is reinforced by the take-over of regional banks, a situation further underlined by the weakness of the provincial stock exchanges. This major opposition between Paris and the rest of France is illustrated by the statistics of borrowing and lending, which also bring out the regional contrasts within provincial France (Fig. 16.1).

2.2 Investments

Not all investments are alike; some are directly productive, leading to the creation of wealth and governing the pace and direction of economic development. These productive investments are not uniform in their effect. Some increase productive potential and create employment, while others are predominantly aimed at increasing productivity, thus making it possible to reduce the use of labour (under the system of free enterprise the provision of employment is not the main object of investment). Other investments are not directly productive but are of a derived or supportive nature; this particularly applies to investment in social equipment, such as housing, schools or crèches.

From the point of view of the geographical environment, investment has a structuring effect, organizing space by the creation or reinforcement of poles of activity, or facilitating movement towards or between such poles. Investments of this type include industrial estates, new towns, motorways, airports and large office complexes, and they have a considerable spread effect. They can revolutionize the geographical scene by introducing new elements into previously existing spatial structures.

Notions about the rate of return to be expected on capital invested, and the acceptable degree of risk, will vary with the investor. The expectation that investments will in fact yield an adequate return is nevertheless always present, and can be ignored only as the result of a political decision taken at the highest level. However, the notion of what is profitable can be a very relative one.

Power to change the geography of France thus depends on control of monetary flows, on the relationship between income and expenditure, on the total volume of capital resources, and on the control exercised over their use.

The industrial and urban changes of the last century reflected a major investment effort. The great period from 1860 to 1913 saw the opening of mines and the construction of railways and canals, of industrial plant and urban housing. Already, however, French savings were being channelled abroad;

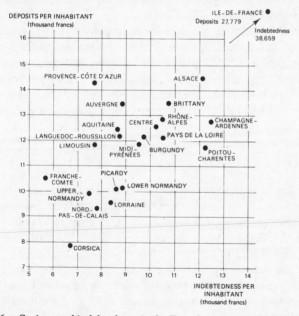

Figure 16.1 Savings and indebtedness in the French regions, 1 January 1978. Source: *La Vie Française*, 17 April 1978.

Russian, South American and other foreign loans absorbed a large part of the available liquid assets, to the detriment of French internal development and ultimately of many of the lenders. It has been estimated that from 1892 to 1913 between a third and a half of French savings were invested abroad. In 1913 French assets abroad were valued at 45,000 million francs.

This was the beginning of a process of under-investment in France, which reached its lowest point between 1929 and 1936. Social equipment and infrastructure were not replaced or modernized while rent-control legislation discouraged the renewal of the housing stock. In a climate of demographic stagnation and economic protectionism, any policy of growth and thus of investment appeared unnecessary.

Immediately after the Second World War the widespread destruction of industrial plants, cities and infrastructure, added to the neglect of the interwar period, called for an immediate and large-scale investment programme. The Marshall Plan, from which the majority of European nations profited, brought France $3,000 million in cash or equipment such as ships and locomotives. Only $209 million took the form of loans, which were repaid by 1962. This aid was a lifeline, whose importance and salutary effect cannot be denied.

The total volume of investments in any country is calculated either in relation to the total national product or to the gross internal product. On average, between 1949 and 1955 France devoted less than 20 per cent of its gross internal product to investment; from 1956 to 1963 the proportion was just above this figure. In the same period in the German Federal Republic, Italy and the Netherlands the proportion varied between 22 and 25 per cent, reaching 35 per cent in Japan. French investment exceeded 25 per cent by 1970, the proportion rising above 26 per cent in 1972 and 1974. The period of maximum productive investment lay between 1970 and 1975, thereafter declining slightly (1970: 11.7 per cent; 1975: 11.1 per cent). The share of industrial investments declined from 4.7 per cent in 1970 to 3.5 per cent in 1975, which represented a sharp decline in outlay on plant.

3 The state

In France, the state is an almost exclusive system of power, a privileged repository of all means of action. The state intervenes in a variety of ways, most obviously through legislation, orders and regulations. To a great extent the landscape is the expression of the decrees promulgated in the *Journal officiel*, the French government's official gazette!

The state also intervenes in the economy directly. The nationalization measures of 1945 gave the state full or partial ownership of industries such as fuel and power, aeronautics and aerospace. Until 1982 the nationalized sector accounted for between 10 and 12 per cent of French industrial production and employed 12 per cent of the working population. In 1982 a new wave of nationalization measures further increased the control of the state over the economy.

Another way in which the state intervenes is through financial policies and decisions. State expenditure amounted to 11.4 per cent of the gross internal product in 1913, 17.5 per cent in 1935, 31.9 per cent in 1953, 23.8 per cent in 1970 and 20.6 per cent in 1976. The financial power of the state is not limited to the budget: the banks (all nationalized since 1982), the nationalized insurance companies and the money collected through the Savings Banks (Caisses d'Epargne) considerably augment the state's capacity for intervention.

The state also makes use of its ability to control credit, to encourage lending on less economic projects by topping up interest payments, and to fix tariffs charged to consumers in the sectors where it has direct control, such as fuel and power, or transport. In addition it can influence decisions in a desired direction by the use of aids and financial inducements such as subsidies, loans, tax relief and the placing of government orders and contracts.

The role of the state has continued to grow, particularly since the Second World War, extending not only into health, education, culture and housing but into production and commerce.

3.1 Instruments of state power

The state exercises its powers through intervention by the government and its ministries, relayed by a swarm of government agencies, special funds and financial bodies, which under various names but with similar objectives have continued to proliferate since the 1950s. Examples include:

(1) The Social and Economic Development Fund (Fonds de Développement Economique et Sociale – FDES) provides loans for the financing of certain types of productive equipment, essentially in the nationalized industries.
(2) Intervention Fund for Strategic Spatial Planning (Fonds d'Intervention pour l'Aménagement du Territoire – FIAT).

Two recently created funds reflect a desire for simplification and systematization:

(3) Urban Planning Fund (Fonds d'Aménagement Urbain – FAU) in 1976 consolidated state funds previously allocated through various channels for slum clearance, urban renewal and urban renovation.
(4) Rural Development and Planning Fund (Fonds de Développement et d'Aménagement Rural – FAR), set up in June 1979.

French industrial policy, dating from 1969, was embodied in the creation of the Industrial Development Institute (Institut de Développement Industriel – IDI) in 1970. Its aim is to 'encourage an increased rate of growth in French industry by contributing to the strengthening of the financial base of enterprises with inadequate resources of their own'. As time has gone on, and particularly after the arrival in power of the Mitterrand government, a great number of additional committees, institutes and special funds for industrial assistance have been set up.

Alongside these purely governmental organizations there exists a whole series of institutions which are either under state control or are in greater or lesser degree subject to the influence of the state. By their activities and their capacity to channel investment, they are in possession of powers which may have considerable geographical impact. A particularly important institution of this type is the Caisse des Dépôts et Consignations, which occupies a powerful financial position as the recipient of the deposits in the Savings Banks (Caisses d'Epargne) and of the funds of the social security organization. It operates through the intermediary of very important subsidiaries, such as the Central Company for Territorial Equipment (Société Centrale d'Equipement du Territoire – see section 6.1) or organizations for which it has managerial responsibility, such as the Equipment Fund for Local Authorities (Caisse d'Aide à l'Equipement des Collectivités Locales). In 1978 the National Agricultural Credit Bank (Caisse Nationale de Crédit Agricole) was according to its balance sheet the third largest bank in the world. The Crédit Agricole has a monopoly in the distribution of government aid to agriculture; it is also one of the major French sources of housing finance.

In more specialized sectors, organizations such as the nationalized industries (energy, transport, Renault) or the Paris Transport Organization (Régie Autonome des Transports Parisiens) are economic and financial agents of considerable power. In addition there is a range of semi-public bodies operating in the economic sphere, such as independent port or airport authorities, motorway concessionaires, companies for the implementation of urban improvements and administrations of markets of national importance (Marchés d'Intérêt National).

Each of these bodies has a share in the authority of the state while retaining a margin of independence, sometimes a considerable one. Through them the action of the state as a geographical agent is dispersed among hundreds of officials, directors, departmental heads, technocrats, financiers and administrators. Their actions are guided by government policies but also by their own geographical strategies. Each body has its own independent policies and strives to be profitable, or at least to break even. For example, when French Railways closes down lines, it does not take into account the consequences for strategic spatial planning, but only the cost to the organization of continuing to run unprofitable lines. It is only at government level that subsidies can make up for deficits and maintain costly services; the subsidizing of suburban commuter fares is a perfect example.

3.2 Concentration and centralization

The totality of state powers provides an extraordinary concentration of the means of geographical transformation, and the control over these means is also geographically centralized. All the organizations mentioned above 'naturally' have their headquarters in Paris. The effect of excessive centralization has been to encourage, side by side with the rise of political power, the growth of a bureaucratic and technocratic power, springing from the expansion of the central services of the state and the division of the administration into specialist sectors. Too much power is concentrated into the hands of the same small group of people: 'It is unacceptable that the same civil servants should prepare, give advice on, control, implement and provide finance for our projects . . . and at the same time profit from them.'[2]

The concentration and centralization of powers and their almost exclusive location in Paris have significant geographical consequences. The effect has been to reinforce the perception and the depiction of France as a uniform territory; regional differences have been ironed out. Yet it seems that concentration and centralization may have reached their limit. As early as 1967 this was clearly stated: 'Whenever possible it is better that the state should cause others to take action rather than take action itself. Excessive centralization does not lead . . . to the strengthening but to the weakening of state power' (Nora Report).[3]

In the last twenty years the state's share of tax revenue has steadily declined (85.2 per cent in 1959, 79.9 per cent in 1973), while the share of the local authorities has correspondingly increased.

The regional legislation introduced in 1982 was the product of a government with the political will to decentralize powers of decision, a process to take place over the period 1983–5. The intention was that the various activities and related buildings or other equipment would be divided between communes, departments and regions as their nature and scale dictated. The communes, for example, would look after primary schools or yacht marinas. The departments would have control of secondary schools (*collèges*), school buses or small commercial ports, while *lycées* (grammar schools), inland harbours or major commercial ports would be a regional responsibility. The communes have also received the responsibility of issuing building permits and drawing up communal land-use plans (POS). The state, however, has kept control of activities it considers essential, such as technical education and, more generally, all operations deemed to be of 'national interest'.

In fact, as soon as a project reaches such a large scale that it demands extraordinary means of financing and the short-cutting of normal administrative procedures, the state takes over from the local authorities and intervenes directly.

---

[2] M. Lucotte, 1977. For example, engineers of the Ponts et Chaussées, responsible for civil-engineering projects, receive a fee based on the cost of the works supervised.
[3] *Rapport sur les entreprises publiques* (Documentation française, Paris, 1967).

The development of the new towns, for example, was the responsibility of an interministerial group at government level; the communes affected lost their control over the sections of their territory required for new-town development.

4 Local and regional government
4.1 The communal level

Until as late as the 1950s mayors of communes were essentially administrators, concerned with the registration of residence, births, marriages and deaths, with the running of public services such as primary schools and with the public assistance (welfare) system. To these legal responsibilities were recently added de facto responsibilities regarding housing, employment and economic development. The demographic and economic changes of the recent decades have transformed mayors into entrepreneurs, builders and planners. In order to help communal administrators to deal with these new functions a whole series of public, semi-public and private institutions made their appearance: semi-public companies, local agencies set up for particular tasks, state-owned or locally owned companies, franchises, research organizations, subsidiaries of banking groups or organizations derived from political parties. All of these hold some share in the powers and resources of local government.

The communal budgets are characterized by their slender tax base and by the large volume of their investment expenditure (communal expenditure amounted to 200,000 million francs in 1982). In 1977 the president of the Nord–Pas-de-Calais regional council stated: 'In France, out of each 100 francs of direct taxation paid by the citizens, only 19 francs go to the local authorities and 81 to the state. In no other European country is this discrepancy so marked.' Yet these local authorities, however poor in direct income, undertake more than half of all investment in social equipment in the country, and their significance in this respect is increasing. It must, however, be accepted that local taxation, in spite of recent improvements, still bears the imprint of an age when the geographical extent of areas of common interest was much more limited than in the conditions of the present day.

Until as late as 1974 the resources of the communes were based on four local taxes: the taxes on built property, landed property, the number of residents and the *patente*, a tax paid by businesses and members of the professions. In 1975 the *patente* was replaced by the 'professional' tax on numbers employed, and since 1979 the communes have also received from the state a general grant (Dotation Générale de Fonctionnement – DGF), based on the value-added tax (VAT).

Whether or not a commune can command substantial resources depends on the presence or otherwise of economic activities on its territory. The prosperity or poverty of a commune therefore depends on random decisions regarding the location of economic activity and the use of land, which may produce a very uneven distribution. For example, a purely residential suburban commune, lacking any significant income derived from the presence of industry or commerce, may be hard put to finance large-scale investments in social equipment to meet the needs of its population. By contrast a commune having on its territory a power-station, large industrial plant or hypermarket receives the considerable 'professional' taxes paid by these establishments, although its residential population may be quite small.

The professional tax provides on average 50 per cent of the tax income in urban communes of more than 30,000 inhabitants. In 224 of these communes, however, the percentage lies between 75 and 88, and it is still higher in small rural communes containing major industrial establishments such as power-stations. The property taxes paid by industrial firms are also considerable. The finely drawn nature of the communal network accentuates the contrasts in revenue derived from these sources.

Urban growth has created another contrast in the distribution of communal income and expenditure. Until as late as the 1950s the central commune of an urban agglomeration benefited from the presence on its territory both of economic activities yielding substantial tax income and of numerous residents; since that time economic activity has dispersed or decentralized and has moved outside the towns. At the same time people were leaving their homes in the central city, partly impelled by the high taxes there, in order to settle in the outer suburbs. Yet the expenditure needs of the central commune have not been reduced in proportion to the movement of population, since it still provides essential amenities and services for the whole of the agglomeration. Taxes in the central commune therefore rise yet higher, accentuating the tendency for inhabitants to move out, and increasing the degree of social segregation within the agglomeration. This degree of geographical inequality can only be resolved by bypassing the commune as a basis for tax assessment.

The government intervenes in the investment programmes of the communes by the device of long-term loans from the Caisse des Dépôts (see section 3.1). Investments by the communes are financed through equipment grants given by the central government or by the department, by loans and by internal financing out of tax revenue. Through its policies on grant allocation, the state had until 1983 an opportunity for repeated intervention in the affairs of the commune. The granting or otherwise of such selective subsidies had clear electoral implications. Moreover these government grants, being derived from different ministries, were strictly sectoral in their impact.

The 1982 administrative reform introduced a new system of allocating government funds to the communes, whereby the existing general grant towards current expenditure (Dotation Globale de Fonctionnement) was supplemented by a general grant towards capital expenditure (Dotation Globale d'Equipement) which was not earmarked for use only in specified sectors. That additional administrative costs would be involved in taking up new functions was recognized by the allocation of a special decentralization grant (Dotation Générale de Décentralization).

Until 1982, communes had been subjected to the *tutelles* (close government scrutiny of administrative, legal and technical matters, both prospective and retrospective). Obtaining approval for new projects involved lengthy delays. The 1982 administrative reforms abolished all the *tutelles*, allowing communes much greater freedom of decision, including the possibility of intervening to stimulate economic activity, subject only to retrospective control to see that legal powers had not been exceeded. The main problems continue to be financial; there are fears that the financial resources transferred will be insufficient to meet the new responsibilities, so that the communes, departments and regions will be faced with greater financial burdens.

Initially, under the law of 1884 governing the administration of communes, all were regarded as of equal status, without regard for any specific characteristic. Progressively, however, differences in population size have had to be taken into account. For example, the drawing up of a Land-Use Plan is compulsory for communes of more than 10,000 inhabitants, and a special tax for financing public transport is levied on communes of more than 300,000.

The differences between communes with regard to the provision of social equipment, as revealed in the marked disparities in their investment rates, are attributable to the inequality of their resources, the varying degrees of dynamism of their municipal councils, and differences in their strategies, which may be either social or economic, conservative or progressive.

In fact, because the French communes are so numerous and their populations so low, the vast majority have only derisory resources at their disposal and will continue to depend on subsidies.

4.2 The regions

Two categories of policy are pursued at regional level. One involves the deconcentration to the regions of certain government powers and corresponding financial resources, or (since 1982) a genuine decentralization. The other involves policies carried out by public administrative agencies set up at regional level for specific purposes.

4.2.1 The powers of the regions

Initially the competence of the regional assemblies was limited to such areas as regional parks or recreational and socio-educational facilities. But since their creation in 1972 the regions have received other powers and responsibilities transferred from the centre, for example responsibility for departmental and communal roads, and primary schools. The regions also received the right to draw up their own integrated transport plans, and to participate in joint schemes for local development (*contrats de pays*).

The limited role of the regions before 1982 can be seen from the size of their budgets. Regional income from taxation was restricted by a legal ceiling imposed by the government; it was 25 francs per inhabitant in 1972, 45 francs in 1978, and 120 francs in 1983. Other sources of finance included grants from the central government and local authorities. By 1979 the budgets of the regions of provincial France amounted to 3,043 million francs, with a further 2,083 million francs for the Ile-de-France region. Each region has a different investment strategy. Possibilities include an even territorial sprinkling, so as to give each department its share; an even division according to sector, or concentration in an area or sector considered to have priority. Some regions distribute their funds so as to make up the deficiencies in allocations from the state, while others reject this attitude and concentrate their investment on specific projects considered to be of particular regional importance.

In October 1975, the regional assemblies voted their regional plans, complete with financial estimates, not only allocating to each region its own resources, but for the first time expressing preferences with regard to the allocation of government grants at departmental and regional levels. The learning process of the new regional authorities has been a slow one. However, not all regions have been deterred from innovation. For example, in 1979 a tripartite convention was signed between the Nord–Pas-de-Calais region, the French government and French Railways, envisaging the establishment of an integrated transport plan and also the modernization of the rolling stock of local trains by means of a grant made from regional funds to French Railways.

As with departments and communes, the 1982 administrative reform gave the regions new responsibilities, powers and resources. The region of Corsica, where militants seeking autonomy had been active, was allowed a somewhat greater degree of independent action than the other regions.

4.2.2 *Other agents at regional level*

Side by side with the regional administrative structures, and frequently antedating them, other bodies exercised powers on a regional basis in the past, and continue to do so. There are about a hundred Chambers of Commerce and Industry. They have been officially recognized since 1898 and play an increasingly important role in the equipping and development of French regions. They run 65 seaports, 33 inland ports, 38 long-distance bus stations and 200 industrial estates and are concessionaires for 84 airports; they participate in the drawing up of Land-use Plans and local Structure Plans. Also of significance are the Regional Development Companies (Sociétés de Développement Régional) which appeared in the 1950s. They were legally constituted as limited companies under private law, but in reality functioned as public agencies. Their aim was to provide part of the capital of firms in the region concerned, the necessary finance being derived from banks and institutional investors. But as contributions from these sources proved inadequate, they were reduced to borrowing, and have not fulfilled the role expected of them. More recent, and of increasing importance, are the Regional Institutions for Industrial Participation (Instituts Régionaux de Participation) which give grants to industrial firms or take shares in them.

5 The private sector

This term covers all private agents, whether individuals or corporate bodies.

5.1 Changes in the private sector

This sector has gone through a major transformation. Formerly there was a close identity between the place of origin of capital and its place of use.

Since the 1950s there has been a retreat from the local level, a 'deregionalization' of capital, a growing separation between the place of origin of capital and the place where it is used. Regions whose development for more than a century has been assured by a local capitalism by means of regional banks and a local commercial bourgeoisie, as in the north, the east and the Lyon region, have seen their economic activities pass under the control of 'foreign' companies from outside the region. These changes occurred through new investment from outside the region, mergers, take-overs or the buying of a participant shareholding. Changes have also been brought about by local firms resorting to the national capital market, either when requiring additional capital in a climate of expansion, or in a crisis situation demanding the injection of additional capital in a struggle for survival. This transformation of capitalism does not stop at frontiers; the work of private geographical agents is now international.

At the same time, the scale of units of production and service provision has grown, under the influence of technical evolution and the search for economies of scale. Capital requirements have never ceased to grow, capital being more and more substituted for labour. The inability of firms to finance the advance to the necessary scale of operations out of internal resources led to heavy indebtedness.

The increase in capital requirements and the widening of the capital market have occasioned a growing influence of the banking sector. The banks, faithful to their aim of ensuring the maximum return on capital and the maximum security for the funds invested, practise a complex strategy for the creation of new plants, closures, mergers, restructuring, the choice of new locations or the abandonment of old ones, guided solely by their expectations of profit or hopes of cutting losses. In the view of these financial decision-makers, towns and regions are anonymous non-places, of interest only as sources of profit.

Banks thus invest in sectors that appear promising, but are just as likely to withdraw their support from sectors that appear unprofitable. Among sectors that have particularly attracted investment from the banks in recent times have been tourism (the 'white gold' of the winter-sports resorts), major retailing centres, motorways and the property market. Until the 1960s the banks steered clear of the property market; thereafter they associated with property developers or even engaged themselves in development directly.

This large-scale banking capitalism introduces a separation between the owners of capital and the decision-makers; the effective management of large industrial firms depends more on efficient management than on possession of capital. Shareholders have progressively lost their powers of decision to the managers. These are the real masters of the companies; they control the finance of a company whether or not they have any stake in its capital. The fact that investment comes from very large banks or holding companies reinforces the tendency for investment to be concentrated into large-scale projects. The consequence is the creation of a limited number of development poles into which capital investment is concentrated, to the detriment of other regions and cities. The spatial structure of the economy thus takes on a completely new dimension, at odds with what existed before.

The position was changed somewhat by the almost total nationalization of the banking system in 1981. The rules of the game were changed, with the banks obliged to comply with government policies, investing in officially designated industrial sectors and participating in the rescue of industrial branches or individual plants facing closure.

5.2 Investments from abroad

Investments from other countries are a normal element in a liberal–capitalist economy. The ability to draw capital investments from abroad is a sign of monetary health, testifying to the economic attractiveness of a country. Foreign capital represents a considerable reinforcement of investments derived from national sources, but at the same time has its dangers. Every take-over of a French firm, every foreign participation in a firm's capital structure represents an alienation of the nation's agricultural, industrial or commercial capacity. Because of the lack of appropriate legislation, the fruits of this foreign investment may be lost to the community through repatriation to the country that provided the capital in the first place. This has particularly been the case since 1958 when, in order to attract foreign capital, France liberalized the legislation regarding the repatriation of income derived from the sale of goods and services, the yield of investments and interest from deposited funds.

Although the presence of foreign capital has become more evident since the Second World War, because of the massive scale of the influx and some spectacular take-overs of French firms, it has always been one of the characteristic elements of the French economy (cf. chapter 24, 2.4.2). For example, iron mines in Lorraine have long been owned by foreign interests, notably Belgian steel companies such as Providence or Cockerill-Ougrée, and companies from Luxemburg and the Saar. Similarly firms such as Aluminium Company of Canada (ALCAN) and the Swiss AIAG hold large interests in French bauxite deposits.

Until 1967, foreign capital invested in France was essentially American; thereafter capital from the other countries of the European Community claimed an increasing share. Since the oil crisis of 1974, Middle Eastern capital has become important.

As late as the 1970s, foreign penetration of the French economy was not globally significant; only 10.7 per cent of workers were dependent on industrial companies where foreign participation exceeded 50 per cent (the calculation relates to firms employing 200 workers or more, and excludes agriculture, building and construction, and the food industry). But in some sectors, and in some regions, the presence of foreign firms appears to be above the threshold of tolerance, reaching 80 per cent in the agricultural machinery industry of the Nord region, 90 per cent in the electronic industry of Languedoc–Roussillon and Auvergne, 75 per cent in the rubber industry of Picardy and 65 per cent in the chemical industry of Champagne–Ardennes. Foreign participation is not restricted to industry; foreign capital is invested in office construction, housing (particularly the building of single-family housing estates) and tourist activities. In August 1979 the winter-sports resort of Isola 2000 was sold by its English investors to a Lebanese company!

Faced with the risk that foreign capital could take control of key sectors of the economy, the state sometimes intervenes to keep firms in French hands, as happened in 1975 with Honeywell-Bull and LMT, a subsidiary of the American company ITT. Such intervention has principally involved firms deemed to be of strategic importance, in the computer, nuclear or telecommunications industries. This policy has been reinforced since 1981.

With regard to locational choice, mergers, the opening or closing of branches, or the transfer of head offices, the spatial consequences of foreign investments are no different from those of other capitalist-type agents in the private sector. There is, however, an even greater degree of remoteness in the making of decisions, which may be taken with insufficient knowledge of the local environment within which the firm operates and with less concern for their local consequences. Managers thousands of miles away clearly do not have the same conception of the realities of regional and urban life as people on the spot. On the other hand, foreign investment can be considered as a positive element when it is used to set up new plants or for the revival of existing firms which are in difficulty.

By offering spatially varying inducements the government can direct the choice of location by foreign firms towards regions in crisis or peripheral regions. Foreign investors may also have the advantage of being less overwhelmed than their French equivalents by the attractions and dominance of Paris. But the internationalization of investments is matched by an internationalization of locational choice. Decisions by foreign concerns are no longer made solely in the context of France but in relation to the European market as a whole and with regard to their own internal strategies regarding branch-plant structure. Multinational firms do not choose between a number of French towns as a location, but between a number of European ones. In the European Community the suppression of customs barriers and the free circulation of capital and goods greatly increases the range of possible locations. Firms have taken advantage of this situation to bargain for the maximum advantages in terms of inducements to locate. France, for example, used such inducements to try to ensure the location of branch plants of giant American automobile companies, which might otherwise have gone to other countries.

On the whole, the locations chosen by foreign firms have not greatly contributed to improving the spatial structure of France. With few exceptions, foreign firms have gone to locations that were already favoured, in the Ile-de-France (Paris) region, the Paris basin, the north and the east.

6 Results
6.1 Overlapping agents

The spatial pattern of present-day France is thus the product of the activities of a great diversity of agents. But these agents, endowed with powers and resources of very varied nature and size, do not intervene without an impact on each other. The administration and spatial planning of France appear increasingly complex and difficult because of the considerable degree of overlapping and entanglement of the decision-makers, the financiers, political leaders and officials. French geographical space, a single entity, is the subject of competition between the various agents, each perceiving a different possibility for the development of the same land. By comparison with the first half of this century, the pressures associated with growth and change have been transformed both in nature and scale; they expose the whole country to repeated conflicts and bitter confrontations between the various agents.

The politico-economic organization of France is characterized by the overlapping of the public and private sectors and by the different levels and categories of power. As soon as a development project reaches a certain size it is subjected to a searching and often very complex investigation by the financial interests involved. Each party has, in proportion to the amount of finance contributed, a measure of control over carrying it out. For example, the tourist development of the 'Three Valleys' area of the Vanoise Alps is shared between two development companies affiliated to the Caisse des Dépôts, three local authorities and two chair-lift companies.

The semi-public companies (*sociétés d'économie mixte*) perfectly illustrate the intermixture of interests. Devised between 1955 and 1960, they allowed the local authorities to assume the initiative and responsibility for urban development projects 'from which any possibility of speculative gain would be excluded'. The controlling shareholding would be in public hands and the mayor would be chairman, although finance might come partly from private sources. The semi-public company would borrow, the banks would lend, and the local authority would guarantee the loan. These semi-public companies proliferated in the form of development and housing companies. The Territorial Equipment Companies

(Sociétés d'Equipement du Territoire), about a hundred of them, are semi-public companies in charge of carrying out important projects relating to infrastructure and large-scale housing schemes. To supervise them, in addition to the local authorities, the semi-public companies had either the powerful Caisse des Dépôts, acting through its subsidiary, the Central Company for Territorial Equipment (Société Centrale pour l'Equipement du Territoire), or private banking groups.

The achievement of these companies has been considerable. Between 1950 and 1975 the 300 semi-public companies were responsible for the construction of more than 300,000 dwellings, for 18,000 ha of urban development projects, 3,700 ha of industrial estates and 780 ha of urban renewal. However, the period before 1981 saw a shift of power to the detriment of the local authorities and in favour of the private or semi-public partners. The private sector gained more and more initiative and freedom of manoeuvre, both in the preparation of projects and commercially. The semi-public companies have been accused of 'privatizing the profits and socializing the losses', and of allowing technical and financial considerations to dominate the political side of things. Financial aspects have been allowed to dominate all other considerations, leading to the tight packing of dwellings so as to produce high residential densities, a shift in the range of dwellings produced towards the higher priced types, reliance on commercial developments because of the higher return, and a failure to provide adequate social amenities in residential projects.

After twenty years of euphoric development the semi-public companies fell into serious difficulties with the deterioration of the economic climate from 1975 onwards. By the beginning of 1979, these difficulties and shifts of power brought about a policy for recovery which gave renewed pre-eminence to the elected representatives within the National Federation of Semi-Public Companies, a policy which has been reinforced since 1981. Legislation in 1983 required, for example, that local authorities should have a capital participation of more than 50 per cent.

In the tangled networks of resources and interests, competition and rivalry between agents are inevitable. Conflicts arise not only between public and private interests but within each group, between various local authorities, between government agencies and local or regional institutions, and between the various specialist services of central government. The French administrative style of rigid sectorization both of management and finance at government level also increases the occasions for conflict. This multiplicity of powers and conflicts encourages intervention by pressure groups or by forceful personalities, such as mayors or the heads of major public departments.

Analysis of geographical change in France cannot overlook the impact of individuals, technocrats or politicians, where considerations of electoral advantage may be just as important as the influence of the *grands commis*, the top-ranking civil servants. The overlapping of the public and private sectors is found even at a personal level. Before taking a position in a private firm, nearly 45 per cent of the directors of companies having a stock-exchange quotation had worked in the public sector and more than half had been a member of one of the elite *Grands Corps de l'Etat*, the senior branches of the civil service. The role of *pantouflage* (leaving the state sector for the private sector) is thus considerable, and reveals the strength of the personal links between the two sectors.

6.2 Geographical consequences

The existence of various powers at local or regional level is reflected in geographical structures. In places, a single organization, be it commercial, industrial, educational or social, has stamped its imprint on a whole countryside. Such an ascendancy is particularly characteristic in industrial regions. Coal-mining areas were first developed by various private companies, subsequently by the nationalized Charbonnages de France which succeeded them. There is no doubt that in such circumstances the power of the commune was of little weight by comparison with the power of the mining concern, which was the sole employer and often the sole owner of property.

The situation most frequently produced at communal level is that of a multiplicity of powers, explaining, for example, the way in which various items of social equipment in a housing project are managed separately even where the smooth functioning and profitability of the scheme would demand their integration.

The essential characteristic of power in France is its concentration in one place: the Paris region. This is true of administrative or para-administrative bodies, where the Paris region accounted for 89 per cent of the positions occupied by graduates of the elite National School of Administration (Ecole Nationale d'Administration: ENA) between its foundation and 1976 or of the financial world (in the 1970s 70 per cent of company directors lived in Paris). As for the 126 firms which in 1975 had a turnover of 800 million francs or more, Paris accounted for 85 per cent of their registered head offices and 91 per cent of their turnover. In recent years, more and more head offices have been transferred from the provinces to Paris.

A table classifying European towns according to the total business turnover of firms having their head offices there places Paris in second place (527) between London (911) and Düsseldorf (121). Paris is the only French town in the first 28, compared with 11 German towns, 3 Dutch and 3 Swiss. Paris is thus the almost unique location of decision-making in France. The spatial coexistence of public and private centres of power mirrors their functional interdependence. This concentration of decision-making, taken together with the increasing size of the units of social equipment and improvement schemes, is reflected in increasing investment in the Paris region.

Since the 1960s, France has had a policy of industrial, and subsequent tertiary, decentralization, but the results, either in spatial or in qualitative terms, have not been commensurate with intentions or expectations. The entire spatial organization of France is marked by the focusing of powers and financial resources in Paris. Political centralization and the concentration of the levers of power in Paris have long since reduced the remainder of the country to a state of dependence or even, according to some commentators, to the status of a colony.

The state has not yet fully appreciated the geographical consequences of its economic and financial policies; the relationship between geographical facts and financial mechanisms is only just beginning to be grasped. It is not often recalled that geographical factors are involved in the mechanism of inflation. On the one hand, the extensive area of France, with the necessity of maintaining infrastructures for a population living at low density in widely dispersed settlements, necessarily gives rise to a high per head expenditure. On the other hand, urban concentration, particularly in the Paris region, produces excessively high levels of salaries, property prices and expenditure on social equipment. The inflationary role of the 'Paris phenomenon' has only recently become apparent, and is only dimly perceived.

IV

Resources, economic activity and economic enterprises

The activities by which resources are exploited and wealth produced are traditionally grouped into three sectors: primary (agriculture, forestry, fishing, mining, quarrying), secondary (manufacturing) and tertiary (business, administration, public services and transport). Convenient and attractive as this classification may be, it is of diminishing relevance to the modern French economy, where economic activities are increasingly linked across the conventional sector boundaries.

Information on economic activity is in the first instance provided by financial data such as turnover, or value added by production, but the assessment of such data is difficult and subject to differences of opinion. This explains why data of a social nature such as employment figures are often substituted. Recourse to such demographic data also distorts reality and gives no direct indication of output. Data of these two kinds tend also to be of a global nature, relating to units of the order of the economic sector or the agglomeration, concealing the fact that economic activities are fundamentally the result of the activities of individual firms in production or service provision. The French economy is made up of approximtely 2,475,000 individual enterprises of which the principal components are 1,200,000 agricultural holdings (1978), 45,000 industrial enterprises, 450,000 commercial enterprises, 755,000 craft enterprises and 25,000 enterprises in the field of transport.

This grouping together of enterprises having very different economic roles is not an artificial one, since all have a spatial location, and these locations reflect managerial decision and choice. All these locations, whether determined by existing or past economic conditions, act as poles which generate flows and around which the land of France is differentiated and structured. All locations have their own history, their own dynamics. The totals given for the different sorts of enterprises are the end product of numerous creations and of disappearances by closure or merger.

The picture is one of extraordinary diversity; enterprises may be old or new, traditional or ultra-modern, small or gigantic, ossified or dynamic, individual or part of a multinational firm, limited to one establishment or multi-plant in nature. Whether in agriculture, manufacturing or the service sectors, traditional activities and enterprises often stand in contrast with modern ones. Traditional enterprises can often be distinguished from modern ones by the degree of their recourse to paid labour. The latter is characteristic of relatively large-scale units of capitalist type: large farm, factory, department store, or major legal or architectural practice. The absence of paid workers, on the other hand, characterizes traditional activities and enterprises on the scale of the individual, the household or the family.

A map showing the distribution of wage-earners and salaried employees would contrast west and southwest France with the north, east and southeast; agriculture plays a large part in this contrast.

All enterprises exist in the same political context and in the same general economic situation. All benefit from, or are victims of, policies decided by the management of multinational firms, the European Economic Community and the French government. Since the Second World War, French firms have been subjected to influence by the state concerning their future plans or their location.

17

⚜ Agriculture and its transformation since 1950

1 General characteristics of agriculture

1.1 Agriculture's peculiar status

Agriculture and forestry have unique characteristics. In the first place they are unique in the degree of their dependence on a single factor of production, land. Unlike the extractive industries, agricultural land use does not, at least in theory, result in the exhaustion of resources; in order to survive, agriculture has to return to the soil the nutrients consumed in the course of production.

In respect of agriculture, France is clearly the most favoured country in western Europe, with in the 1980s about 32 million ha of agricultural land and 14 million ha of forest. Unused agricultural land covers only 5 per cent of total surface area, and non-agricultural land only 10 per cent. France has as much as 34 per cent of the total arable land of the European Community (the Nine), 37 per cent of its grassland and 46 per cent of its forest (Table 7.2). In addition, the variety of French natural environments has repercussions on agricultural activity, where the wealth of contrasts, whether in land use or production, is greater than in other European countries.

A second distinctive characteristic is that in two respects it is not on an equal footing with other economic activities. In the first place, it cannot match the bids for land made by other economic branches which need land as a resource. The price of agricultural land has certainly increased by a factor of 20, rising from 1,100 francs per hectare in 1950 to 21,300 francs per hectare in 1980, which

Table 17.1 *Land use, 1948–80*

Category	Thousand hectares		
	1948	1970	1980
Arable	18,368	17,047	17,259
Permanent grassland	12,302	13,934	12,905
Vines	1,550	1,324	1,173
Fruit	214	265	203
Market gardens and private gardens	560	348	307
Flower-growing and nurseries	34	22	27
Chestnut, olive and nut growing	243	92	56
Other agricultural use	6	2	1
Total agriculturally used land	33,277	33,034	31,931
Woodland	11,010	13,764	14,289
Poplar plantations	89	249	245
Fishponds	104	111	138
Unused agricultural land[a]	6,036	3,031	2,825
Land not used for agriculture or forestry	4,586	4,719	5,483

[a] Heathland not grazed or otherwise unproductive, fallows, uncultivated agricultural land and abandoned holdings.
Source: SCEES.

corresponds to an annual average increase of 10 per cent at present prices. Nevertheless, these prices are much lower than those that can be obtained for non-agricultural land, whether for open spaces, recreational purposes, for means of communication, for industry and, it goes without saying, are well below the prices of urban land, whether built-up or ripe for development. The price of agricultural land approaches the lowest price for non-agricultural land only in exceptional and local examples, such as famous vineyards or land for cut-flower production.

The total area of agricultural and forest land remains relatively static, losses being recouped by advances into marginal land such as heathland, abandoned farmland or even areas of scrub. Because agricultural land is more abundant in France than in other European countries it is also cheaper.

A second way in which agriculture is not on an equal footing with other economic activities is revealed by the continual drain of workers out of the industry and by the constant decline in its profits as compared with those of industry. A decline in the numbers employed in agriculture and in the contribution made by agriculture to gross national product is of course common to all countries of the European Community. In France, the gross value of agricultural production has increased constantly since the Second World War (18,000 million francs at current prices in 1956, and 112,000 million in 1978), but this represents a constantly diminishing proportion of gross internal product. Whereas in 1956 this share was 10.7 per cent, it was down to 8.4 per cent by

1967, and stood at 4.7 per cent in 1980. However, if returns from forestry, fishing and the agricultural processing industries are added to those of agriculture the proportion is raised to more than 10.0 per cent.

Agricultural mechanization and the substitution of capital inputs for labour inputs in agricultural production have greatly reduced the amount of time needed to produce a given quantity of agricultural produce, and this has brought about a reduction in the numbers occupied in agriculture. There has been an accelerating decline since 1954; those most affected have been paid agricultural workers and family members employed on the farm, and the rate of decline has been greater for women than for men. Agriculture shed a million workers between 1968 and 1975, at which point the agricultural work force of 2 million people made up only 9 per cent of the total working population, which is nevertheless a high figure when compared with other countries of the European Community. Parallel with this reduction in the numbers of actual producers in agriculture, there has been an increase in the number of people working in agriculturally related activities, in 'agro-business'. Such activities have continued to increase with the growth of services to agricultural enterprises, with the 'upstream' development of industries supplying materials and equipment to agriculture, and with the 'downstream' development of the processing and marketing of agricultural produce.

1.2 French agriculture in the European context

It is no longer possible to define the special characteristics of French agriculture without placing it in the framework of the European Community. Since the Treaty of Rome (1957) French agriculture has been involved in a slow process of integration, which is carried out through an organization of markets established on a competitive basis but closely protected from outside and tightly controlled at Community level. Since 1959, in spite of the necessary imports of agricultural products such as coffee, cocoa, citrus fruits, vegetable oils and fats, France has continued to improve its balance of trade in agricultural produce, achieving a balance between imports and exports in 1969–70 and becoming a net exporter thereafter.

The degree of self-sufficiency is higher than 100 per cent for most of the products that France is able to produce. Various tendencies can be discerned: there has been a marked increase in the exportable balance of cereals (soft wheat, barley, maize) as well as beet-sugar and milk products (concentrated, condensed and powdered milk, butter, cheese) and on balance a sufficiency in the supply of vegetables and fruit (citrus excluded) and poultry. On the other hand there is a growing trade deficit in meat, notably pork, lamb and horsemeat, although the balance with regard to beef is generally positive. Similarly, in spite of the increase in the forested area, there is not enough home-produced timber to supply the home market. Thus, notwithstanding the rapid growth of exports, to the EEC

Table 17.2 Land use in the countries of the European Community (the Nine), 1977

Country	Total of agriculturally used land Thousand ha	Arable Thousand ha	Arable %	Permanent grassland Thousand ha	Permanent grassland %	Permanent crops Thousand ha	Permanent crops %
France	32,193.2	17,314.8	53.8	13,073.6	40.6	1,547.4	4.8
United Kingdom	18,389.5	6,914.5	37.6	11,402.8	62.0	69.8	0.4
Italy	17,500.5	9,286.5	53.1	5,165.8	29.5	2,987.4	17.1
German Federal Republic	13,217.6	7,492.3	56.7	5,205.0	38.4	202.5	1.5
Ireland (1975)	5,716.0	1,000.4	17.5	4,712.5	82.4	2.5	. . .[a]
Denmark	2,927.5	2,634.3	90.0	279.3	9.5	13.9	0.5
Netherlands	2,068.6	827.0	40.0	1,196.4	57.8	37.9	1.8
Belgium	1,458.8	751.5	51.5	690.0	47.3	16.0	1.1
Luxemburg	132.4	58.9	44.5	71.7	54.2	1.5	1.1

[a] . . . Nil or negligible.
Source: Eurostat.

countries in particular, but also to other industrialized countries, French agriculture is increasingly placed in a situation of overproduction, leading to the piling up of stocks which are difficult to dispose of. Several pillars of French agricultural production, notably cereals (40 per cent of Community production in 1978), beet-sugar (32 per cent), wine (46 per cent) and milk products (26 per cent) are among the European Community's surplus products: an even greater quantity of surplus produce is predicted for the future.

1.3 The second agricultural revolution

French agriculture has been transformed as a result of a rapid expansion in production, yields and productivity of labour. From 1910 until 1946 French agriculture hardly changed. After 1946 it was subjected to a series of such radical transformations that they have become known as the 'second agricultural revolution'. All aspects of agriculture have been affected: biological, technical, managerial and educational.

The biological revolution was concerned with the improvement of existing varieties and with plant-protection procedures, with the introduction of new plant species and the creation of more productive and resistant varieties. There was also a reduction in the number of cultivations required by any particular crop. For example, the introduction of hybrid maize doubled the yields and allowed the expansion of this crop into northern France, where it replaced the cultivation of beet destined for distilling into alcohol. The revolution in forage crops has introduced a rational exploitation of grassland. It involves the introduction of temporary grass leys into the arable rotation and the substitution of high-yield grass types suited to the climate. It also involves rational pasture management, such as the clearing out of ditches and the partitioning of large fields to allow controlled grazing. A further innovation is the alternation of grass-harvesting by machine with grazing by cattle.

Biological progress has affected livestock also. Highly productive breeds such as the Holstein have been introduced, but it has above all been by improvements in scientific husbandry (selection of breeds, scientific breeding, careful feeding and the prevention of disease) that it has been possible to double the yields, for example the yield of milk per cow. The number of cattle, sheep and goats that can be pastured per hectare has continued to increase as a result of these various improvements. Whereas extensive grazing supports one ewe per hectare, natural grassland can support between four and six, and grass leys ten, thanks to the increased yield of modern forage plants.

It is difficult to separate this biological revolution from the technological revolution which accompanied it, since similar progress affected many branches of agronomy (agricultural zoology, plant pathology, plant pharmacology) whilst industry was developing ways of using these discoveries in new products such as selective weedkillers, fungicides, insecticides and balanced cattle foods. At the same time motorization and mechanization reached every farm, gradually replacing muscular energy. It is not necessary to list the innovations, from the tractor to the combine harvester, which have marked the stages of this technical progress. Irrigated lands which thirty years ago existed only on a small scale had increased to over 1 million ha by 1980, at which time almost 3 million ha of land had also been subjected to improvement and drainage.

The motorization of French farms began after the Second World War. The tractor, at first imported from America with the help of Marshall Aid, and subsequently manufactured in reconstructed factories in France, became the symbol of national recovery; few farmers resisted the temptation to own one, in order to be the first in the commune to do so, to gratify a son, or in order not to seem old-fashioned. The number of tractors, only 35,000 in 1938, rose to 44,000 in 1946, 120,000 in 1950, 1,230,000 in 1970 and 1,485,000 in 1979. Today we can no longer use the number of tractors as an indicator of agricultural progress, since nearly every farm possesses one. Of greater significance are the power of tractors and the growing capability of agricultural machinery, for example precision seeders.

The consumption of fertilizers has also been an important factor in the increase of gross output. Initially France lagged behind other countries: in 1938 the consumption of nitrogenous fertilizers was only 6.6 kg per hectare as compared with 23.6 in Germany. Since that date the utilization of nitrogen has continued to increase, reaching 126 kg in 1967 and 178 kg in 1978, but with a tendency for the increase to level out in recent years.

But technical progress has been chiefly evident in the form of combinations of techniques leading to new ways of organizing agricultural work. The spread of battery units is a good example. These enterprises, conforming to industrial standards and characterized by a growing rationalization of work methods, have benefited from the introduction of subsidies for the provision and equipping of buildings. A sign of technical progress is that the proportion of milk refrigerated on the farm rose from 41 per cent in 1974 to 62 per cent in 1980.

At the same time, information about the latest agricultural techniques and developments has reached growing numbers of farmers. Information has been propagated by way of public bodies (agricultural colleges and advisers of the Ministry of Agriculture), and by way of professional organizations such as *chambres d'agriculture* and local farmers' groups. The diffusion of information is increasingly provided by the 'upstream' and 'downstream' sectors, whether industrial or co-operative. This necessary advance in the technical standards of farmers is illustrated by the trebling of the number of farms inspected by the organization concerned with milk production.

The results of this second agricultural revolution are reflected in the rapid development of production yields and labour productivity. The value of agricultural production rose from 25,000 million francs in 1954 to 178,000 million at constant prices in 1980. In terms of volume, this increase represented an average

Table 17.3 *Changing output of selected agricultural products*

Mean annual output	Wheat (million quintals)	Maize (corn) (million quintals)	Beef (thousand tonnes)	Milk (thousand tonnes)	Dessert apples (million quintals)
1930–8	80.4	5.1	605	12.9	1.8
1955–9	96.4	15.4	974	19.4	4.3
1965–9	137.8	45.9	1,558	28.3	15.6
1975–8	169.0	79.5	1,833	30.1	16.3

Source: P. Viau, *L'Essentiel sur l'agriculture française* (Editions Ouvrières, Paris, 1978).

Table 17.4 *Changing yields of selected crops (quintals per hectare)*

Crop	Mean 1934–8	Mean 1961–3	Mean 1976–8
Wheat	15.6	27	44
Barley	14.5	26.9	35
Maize (corn) grain	15.8	28.7	48
Potatoes	111	156[a]	239
Sugar beet	276	328[a]	425
Fodder beet	360	416[a]	494

[a] 1962.
Source: Ministry of Agriculture, statistical data.

annual growth rate of 3 per cent, in spite of the stability of the last two years of the period. The principal animal and vegetable products all follow this tendency (Table 17.3). Compared with pre-war years, the basic products have generally doubled (wheat, milk) or trebled (beef) their output: in certain cases the production figures for the 1930s must be multiplied by 9 (dessert apples), by 17 (maize) or even by 36 (rape-seed oil or colza).

Increases in production are the consequence of a very rapid rise in yields. In 25 years the average yields of wheat and maize increased from 16 quintals to more than 40 quintals per hectare (a metric quintal equals 100 kg or one-tenth of a tonne). Milk yields have also risen greatly (Table 17.5).

The productivity of the agricultural labour force has greatly increased with the decline of the agricultural working population; the increase in productivity has been more rapid than in all other branches of the economy. This increase in the productivity of labour has only been made possible by a record increase in capital investment in agriculture which, however, has tended to stabilize since 1974, reflecting the first consequences of the oil crisis (chapter 15).

In spite of recent hesitancy, it is undeniable that French agriculture has made a considerable leap forward, to some extent narrowing the gap between France and

Table 17.5 *Changing milk yields*

Annual yield per cow, litres	2,175	2,710	2,860	2,900
French black & white Friesian	2,649	3,220	3,400	
Norman	2,562	2,980	3,080	
Holstein			3,980	

	1974	1975	1976	1977	1979
Annual yield of cows submitted for inspection	3,815	3,908	3,997	4,100	4,455

Source: Ministry of Agriculture, statistical data.

the more technically advanced countries of the European Community. France has secured a major place in the world market for agricultural produce, coming close to the level of the United States.

1.4 Problems of French agriculture

A phenomenal change such as this is not without its problems. A first problem, noticeable at the level of the producers themselves, is that the increase in yields and productivity has not led to an equivalent rise in the returns either to agriculture overall, or to the incomes of individual farmers. In 1959 gross agricultural income contributed 60 per cent of the total receipts of producers – if farm subsidies are included – whereas in 1976 it was only 38 per cent. Total gross agricultural revenue at constant prices was in 1976 no more than in 1966, reflecting the oil crisis, price inflation (an extremely sharp rise in the cost of industrial products required by agriculture) and the 1976 drought, which led to a drop in output. Income per head, on the other hand, rose more rapidly, due to the reduction in the number of farmers. However, the annual rate of increase of 2.5–3.0 per cent between 1950 and 1970 was below that of wage-earners, incomes in other sectors and the rate of inflation. Whereas returns to agriculture have gone down during recent years, the cost of serving loans has continued to grow. Regional disparities in income as well as disparities in income between holdings of differing size have not been narrowed. Undoubtedly the worst-paid workers are found in agriculture.

There is another contradiction which has already been pointed out: the growth in productive capacity has resulted in the accumulation of surplus stocks, so-called 'mountains', particularly of milk products. The problem of excess wheat is a different matter, as it is a sufficiently powerful strategic weapon to justify overproduction. The internal European market of the Nine is not large enough to solve these problems of over-supply, especially as the stocks of the German Federal Republic continue to increase. The enlargement of the Community to include Spain and Greece, even though it involves the exchange of some complementary agricultural produce, will cause extremely serious regional problems by introducing very keen competition in the majority of agricultural products of Mediterranean origin, especially wine, fruit and vegetables. The tendency for agriculture to decline in importance in relation to the economy as a whole leads to considerations other than agricultural ones being given priority in negotiations regarding the entry of southern European states into the Community.

Finally, and this is the most serious aspect, there is now a challenge to the very idea of agricultural progress, which is now considered to be a dangerous myth, not least by René Dumont, who once sang its praises. Others are still waiting for better results: 'The greatest increases of yield in European agriculture are still to come: annual yields of 8,000 kg of cereal per hectare or 8,000 litres of milk per cow will one day become a reality for the great majority of European farmers.'[1] Whereas the latter group of commentators stress anticipated biological and technical progress and support the setting up of 'development plans' which are to erect the final barriers between competitive farmers and the rest, the doubters in contrast emphasize the limits on growth and development. Some arguments are technical: the increase in production costs, in particular of energy, leads to absurdities such as selling wheat to buy fuel to work machines for harvesting wheat. Similarly, the rise of specialist enterprises leads to soil deterioration, through straw burning in areas of cereal monoculture, or through saturation of the soil with liquid effluent at industrialized pig units. Organic farming, a technique introduced into France a little more than ten years ago, is particularly characteristic of city dwellers returning to nature, who are beginning to set up joint marketing organizations (Syndicat Agri-Nature, for example), but some modernized holdings also make use of these techniques.

The strongest body of critical opinion, however, comes from the ecological movements, which denounce technical progress as an absurdity, link economic growth with the exhaustion of natural resources, and advocate the use of renewable energy resources and the autonomy of the family unit.

[1] G. Thiede, 'Capacité de l'agriculture européenne et son avenir', *Economie Rurale*, no. 116, 1977, pp. 47–52.

18

✦ Agricultural holdings

The location of economic activity in the agricultural sector is of a different order from that in the industrial and tertiary sectors. Industrial activity is discontinuous, distributed at scattered points, the number of establishments being sufficiently limited for deductions about the factors governing individual locations to be rendered possible. Agricultural activity, on the other hand, is widespread and continuous. It still depends on a very large number of units of production, an atomized structure which has scarcely been modified by developments since the Second World War. In 1980 there were still 1.26 million agricultural holdings.

This multiplicity of enterprises and their geographical heterogeneity complicate the search for links between location and economic scale. It is essential that holdings are classified in a way that makes it possible to analyse their uneven distribution in space and their development in time. This process leads inevitably to involvement in controversy over the most appropriate socio-economic classification of agricultural holdings, which in turn is linked with the controversy over theories of agricultural development.

1 Types of holding
1.1 Classification according to size

Holdings are commonly classified according to surface area; very small holdings having fewer than 5 ha, small 5 to 20 ha, medium-sized 20 to 50 ha, large from 50 to 100 ha and the very large over 100 ha.

Table 18.1 *Agricultural holdings and areas worked, by size-categories*

Size-categories of holdings (agriculturally used area in ha)	Holdings				Agriculturally used area			
	1970		1979		1970		1979	
	Thousands	%	Thousands	%	Thousand ha	%	Thousand ha	%
Below 5	492.4	31.0	356.8	28.3	952.7	3.2	676.8	2.3
5–20	605.3	38.1	409.9	32.5	7,010.2	23.4	4,778.4	16.2
20–50	369.6	23.3	347.3	27.5	11,345.2	37.9	10,962.2	37.2
50–100	93.2	5.9	114.1	9.0	6,240.9	20.9	7,683.4	26.0
100 and above	27.1	1.7	34.5	2.7	4,355.3	14.6	5,395.8	18.3
Total	1,587.6	100.0	1,262.6	100.0	29,904.3	100.0	29,496.6	100.0

Sources: Revue de Géographie Alpine, 1970 and 1979–80.

Table 18.1 shows the distribution of holdings by size-categories and by the proportion of the agriculturally used area taken up by each category in 1970 and 1979. In spite of the disappearance of a million holdings since 1955 (a yearly average of 40,000) and the great reduction in the smallest categories, France is still a country of small holdings. Numerically, holdings of fewer than 20 ha predominate, comprising nearly 60 per cent of the total, although occupying only a fifth of the total agriculturally used area. In terms of area, the 20–50 ha class predominates, taking up 37 per cent of the total. The continued existence of small and middle-sized holdings is confirmed by the very modest average size of agriculturally used area per holding, in 1980 only 23.4 ha. Yet by comparison with other countries of the European Community, France stands out as a country of relatively large holdings! Whereas the average size of holding in the European Community (the Nine) in 1975 was approximately 16 ha, the French average was exceeded only by that of Great Britain (64 ha) and equalled those of Denmark and Luxemburg.

With the widening range of new techniques and products, a classification based on the criterion of surface area can have only a very limited value. The category of holdings of fewer than 5 ha certainly includes highly labour-intensive specialized agricultural enterprises such as market gardening, the cultivation of trees and shrubs, the production of cut flowers, tobacco-growing and viticulture, as well as industrialized farming activities such as the battery rearing of chickens and pigs. Only a minority of very small holdings fall into this intensive category, however (only 1.4 per cent of holdings of fewer than 5 ha have a gross income higher than 100,000 francs, which according to the Farm Accountancy Data Network (Réseau d'Informations Comptables Agricoles – RICA) is the appropriate income for a specialized enterprise of this type). The overwhelming majority of holdings of this size are the property of retired farmers with or without an agricultural retirement pension (Indemnité Viagère de Départ – IVD). They may also be held by retired people from outside agriculture, or may be of a purely subsistence nature; or they may be holdings whose owner has another economic activity which is often his main occupation. When considering large holdings the same caution is necessary, since a holding of 50 ha on the Causses is the equivalent of only a small holding in a region of good soil elsewhere.

1.2 Alternative classifications

In spite of numerous attempts to produce agricultural typologies, it is difficult to escape from the use of variations in the size of holding as the basis of agricultural classification. However, the censuses of 1970 and 1980, in particular, have provided the opportunity for research into classification on an income basis. In fact, the distribution of holdings classified according to gross income is not very far removed from that based on size, as Table 18.2 shows. It confirms the image of a country of economically inadequate farms run by families receiving gross incomes lower than those of non-agricultural working-class families.

1.3 A proposed socio-economic classification

In spite of these difficulties, it is possible to work out a compromise between the demands of a theoretically satisfactory classification of holdings, and the limited possibilities offered by the available statistics (Table 18.3). One can first pick out a group of holdings which are outside the mainstream of agriculture, only partially subject to normal farming procedures and the laws of the market. The group includes holdings where the owner is over 65 and those where he has a principal occupation outside agriculture. These are sometimes classed as part-time holdings, but this leads to confusion since this term is meant to cover both the idea of under-employment (the farmer not working full-time, namely 2,400 hours a year) and that of multiple activity (a farmer having an outside job apart from the farm). Holdings in this group, which make up a third of the national total, are on the margin of the agricultural economy. This group of marginal holdings can be subdivided into two distinct categories.

1.3.1 Retirement or subsistence holdings

Three-quarters of the holdings in this category are in the possession of farmers who have no other employment and yet are under-employed on their own farms. They are over 65 years old, and they have cut down their activity to the bare minimum in order to live modestly on their retirement pension, and on the supplementary agricultural pension (IVD) they received when they handed over most of their land to their children or to supplement the holding of another farmer. Some of these holdings are also run by people who have retired from non-agricultural occupations, whether rural or urban, who try to supplement their resources by small-scale farming. The average size of holding of this type is 6.7 ha. The remainder of the category is made up of above-average holdings

Table 18.2 *Agricultural holdings, by gross income*

Gross income (in European Units of Account)	All holdings		Full-time holdings[a]		Part-time holdings	
	Thousands	%	Thousands	%	Thousands	%
Less than 2,000	335	26.5	48	5.5	287	72.1
2,000 to below 4,000	168	13.3	99	11.4	69	17.3
4,000 to below 8,000	238	18.9	209	24.2	29	7.3
8,000 to below 16,000	292	23.1	282	32.6	9	2.3
16,000 to below 40,000	191	15.1	188	21.7	2	0.5
40,000 and above	39	3.1	39	4.5	2	0.5
Total	1,263	100.0	865	100.0	398	100.0

[a] Holdings requiring the input of 1 annual work unit (that is, the equivalent of one full-time agricultural worker).
Source: Revue de Géographie Alpine, 1980.

Table 18.3 *An alternative classification of agricultural holdings, 1979*

Type of holding	Number	%
All holdings of ancillary type	416,852	33.0
Retirement holdings[a]	209,047	16.6
Part-time	207,805	16.5
Normal holdings[b], of which	845,820	67.0
having 1 permanent paid worker	79,718	6.3
having 3 permanent paid workers or more	17,514	1.4
Total	1,262,672	100.0

[a] Farmer over 65 years of age.
[b] Derived by deduction of all holdings of ancillary nature (retirement and part-time).
Source: Ministry of Agriculture, statistical data.

(14.2 ha) run by farmers who are over 65 and who work full-time, doubtless to improve their standard of living. Of all identifiable types of holding, these have the lowest agricultural output per holding and per hectare.

1.3.2 Supplementary or secondary holdings

These are holdings where in addition to income from agriculture the farmer or economically active members of the household earn income from outside activities. For statistical purposes, holdings of this type are defined as those where the farmer has another job, other family members being excluded. Holdings of this type make up 16.2 per cent, with an average size of 6.7 ha. They are mostly held by members of the working class, poorly qualified on the whole (two out of five farmers with an additional occupation are workers). Others are held by small shopkeepers and craftsmen (25 per cent) or agricultural workers (11 per cent). Holdings of this type have a more restricted range of activities than full-time holdings; the simplification of the system of production reflects the reduced labour available and makes the organization of the work easier. Output per hectare is higher than that of the previous group, reflecting the need to supplement the low incomes derived from activities off the farm. Occasionally the outside income is essential in order to pay the property tax and thus to preserve the inheritance which will perhaps one day enable the farm to be worked full-time. Holdings of more than 20 ha where the occupier has a supplementary occupation are either in the hands of farmers who have another holding or of industrialists, engineers and professional people who invest their capital in specialized holdings (orchards, for example), or who are hobby farmers. These 'rich man's holdings' are very much in a minority.

It is even more difficult to establish satisfactory criteria for the classification of full-time or 'professional' holdings which are subject to the logic of agricultural economics. The most favoured criterion is that of total labour input; the unit used is the labour input of one worker employed full-time for a whole year; when first established in 1970 this unit was assessed at 2,400 hours.

A first exceptional category is made up of the holdings of large farmers or company farms; these are relatively few in number, and even their share in the total agricultural economy is quite small (12.5 per cent of the final agricultural product), less than the return accruing to the category of ancillary holdings outside the full-time professional sector. These large holdings normally fall into the category receiving the equivalent of the labour input of four full-time workers per year, which usually means that the farmer employs three paid workers. Although it is difficult to find a common characteristic of holdings in this group, their earnings exceed the value of labour inputs employed and they achieve a rate of profit which justifies the investment of capital. They are characterized by a wide range of agricultural systems, from standard arable cultivation to horti-culture, large-scale viticulture or the production of quality wine. A core of rather more than 10,000 holdings may be regarded as representing this type, charac-terized by particularly high returns per hectare and per holding (a gross revenue per holding of 450,000 francs in 1975). Those who run holdings of this scale no longer participate in the day-to-day agricultural work but act only in a managerial capacity, directing the work of others, taking decisions on purchases and sales, and controlling the employment of capital.

The remainder of the group (about 15,000 holdings) has been named 'employers' holdings' or 'holdings of the agricultural middle class'. Here the person running the holding also participates in the day-to-day agricultural work. The gross income per full-time annual labour input of family members (which is an indirect indicator of the surplus of income over the cost of labour inputs) is distinctly lower than that of the preceding category (123,000 francs in 1975). The whole group is clearly distinguished from the remainder of professional holdings by much higher productivity per hectare and per holding, the latter averaging 100 ha, a size that would normally be associated with more extensive operations. Of course, their economic significance in terms of labour inputs and turnover does not allow them to be equated with non-farm capitalist enterprises, but their capital-intensive nature and their very high gross income per active family member (that is to say, per employer) reveal an effective pursuit of a rate of return on capital equal to that which might be obtained in other sectors, making it possible to apply the term 'agrarian capitalism' to this group.

These 'capitalist' holdings being excluded, the remaining full-time enterprises make up the great majority of family holdings (64.8 per cent by number and 77.9 per cent according to the area occupied). The unsophisticated nature of this type of farming is revealed in the low labour inputs derived from members of the family, often including women, and from an economic return to labour which is so low as to exclude any possibility of profit or of capital accumulation. In spite of having an average area markedly smaller than the previous category, these holdings have a much lower productivity per hectare. Apart from the common characteristic of unsophisticated organization, however, it is clear that this very large group is far from being homogeneous.

The distinction which remains, still according to labour inputs, is a very rough one. Nevertheless it allows us to identify two types of holding very different in average size and income, occupying approximately equal portions of the agriculturally used area.

Firstly there are the micro-holdings, producing little for the market, where to judge from their low farm incomes, poverty is doubtless common. Such holdings merely allow those who cultivate them to eke out an existence, but they cannot provide a living for grown-up children, who are forced to leave. The objective of the farmer, even if he is not forced to abandon the industry, can only be to reach retirement without falling into debt, applying minimum inputs to a mixed farming enterprise, probably dairy farming.

The other group consists of holdings of average size where the family still provides the labour force, but which since 1950 have modernized their activities with a view to increasing and intensifying their production, borrowing capital in order to maintain their growth, but securing on average only a mediocre return for their labours. In the category of average-sized holdings, some doubtless reach the 'capitalist' level, if only by restricting the work force to a few family members and by fully exploiting techniques producing high labour productivities. On the other hand, however, a large number tend to drift downwards, debt and the difficulty of expansion tending to form a new class of poor peasants. These two types of family holding provide the greater part of agricultural production in France.

2 The geographical distribution of holdings

Consideration of regional differences in the type and size of holding is an essential element of geographical analysis, for it provides an answer to questions relating to the preferred location of particular types of holding, to the degree of heterogeneity of agricultural activities in a given space, and the way in which various types of holding are combined regionally. Maps have been produced to illustrate these distributions, but they are limited by the nature of the available statistics.

2.1 Location of particular types of holding

Available statistics allow us to gain at least an approximate idea of the distribution of the two ancillary types of holding (retirement holdings and part-time holdings), as well as full-time holdings employing workers or using exclusively family labour (Fig. 18.1).

Ancillary holdings are particularly characteristic of the Mediterranean coastlands, the high mountain regions, eastern France (Alsace, Vosges, Lorraine) and the Gironde. The distribution of retirement holdings, however, shows a very clear distinction between north and south, percentages increasing with proximity to the Mediterranean coast and the Spanish frontier. To the north, only Alsace and the Vosges stand out, both regions of small-scale ownership, likewise the

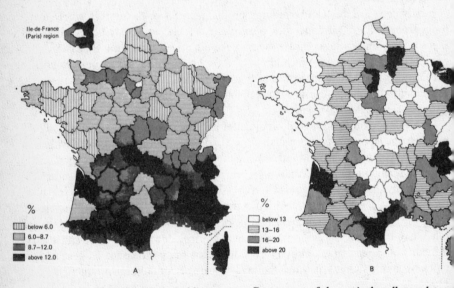

Figure 18.1 Marginal farm holdings, 1970. Percentage of the agriculturally used area occupied by: A. Holdings of retired persons (average for France 8.7 per cent) B. Holdings of part-time farmers (average for France 13.9 per cent). Source: Census, 1970.

departments southwest of the Paris agglomeration, and the plains of Normandy, where retirement holdings appear to be linked with a peri-urban situation.

The distribution of part-time holdings presents a more diffuse picture. Part-time farming is predominant in eastern France, where factory work is the chief additional employment. Other activities (office-workers and small shopkeepers) are little represented; if the term 'worker–peasant' does not apply to all farmers having more than one occupation, it applies to the majority. Numerous studies describe the way of life of these worker–peasants, whose problems are increased by the crisis in industry. In the Alps (Departments of Savoie and Haute-Savoie, also Isère, Hautes-Alpes and Jura) industrial workers predominate, but there is a growing development of seasonal activities linked with Alpine tourism: unskilled work on cable-cars, as perchmen on ski-lifts, in hotels and in the public services, or more skilled employment as ski instructors is carried out by farmers who use their newly earned money to pay off the annual instalments on their debts to the Crédit Agricole. By contrast, in the Mediterranean basin, the Gironde and the Landes, those concerned are mostly agricultural workers and artisans, rarely industrial workers; the part-time vine-grower is a very specific phenomenon. Ancillary holdings are particularly concentrated in the urban fringe, notably on the fringe of the Paris agglomeration. In peri-urban cantons of more than 50,000 inhabitants, part-time holdings are above the French average.

Capitalist holdings are distributed over a very limited area (Fig. 18.2), including the plains and plateaus of middle Loire, of the Paris basin (Plaine de

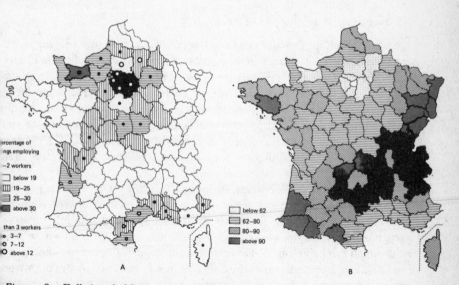

Figure 18.2 Full-time holdings, 1970. A. Percentage of full-time holdings employing farm workers, by department B. Family farms as a percentage of full-time farms, by department. Source: Census, 1970.

France, Brie, Soissonnais, Picardy) and of the Gironde, where holdings of more than three paid workers predominate, and when added to holdings employing one or two paid workers amount to 40–60 per cent of full-time holdings. Among areas of capitalist holdings can also be included Champagne and its vineyards, Normandy (Pays de Caux, Norman plains and *bocages*), the Nivernais and the Champagne *berrichonne*, where holdings employing between one and two paid workers are in a clear majority. Also to be included are the Mediterranean departments, where holdings of more than three paid workers, though certainly less numerous than in the Paris basin, have made an impact. Holdings with paid workers are also characteristic of departments in Languedoc specializing in viticulture.

The distribution of family holdings is evidently the converse of that of the capitalist type. In spite of the difficulties of distinguishing standard professional holdings from the small holdings of poor peasants, it is interesting to note that full-time family farming is practically the only form of production (more than 90 per cent of full-time holdings) in a zone of departments from Alsace to the Basque country, including the Vosges, Jura, northern Alps, almost the whole of the Central massif and the Pyrenees, and interrupted only by the Departments of Rhône, Cantal and a group in central Aquitaine. A second group of family farms is in the west, in Brittany, with the greatest number in Morbihan and in part of its fringes (Maine and Vendée). The Nord region also has a concentration of family holdings.

2.2 Combinations of types of holding

Each type of holding thus has a characteristic distribution. Figure 18.3 highlights certain fundamental contrasts in the distribution of agricultural activity in France by indicating particular regional groupings which stand out because of the predominance of one particular type of holding. Yet the great majority of agricultural regions have a size-distribution of holdings which does not greatly depart from the mean. At the level of the commune, of the agricultural region and even more of the composite space represented by the department, there is a coexistence of holdings of all types: large, medium, small, marginal, professional, family and capitalist.

Certain of these combinations are quite distinctive. The western type, in Brittany and the southern and western fringes of the Armorican massif, is almost totally dominated by family farms. Marginal holdings, whether of retirement or part-time type, are rare, as are capitalist holdings. In the Mediterranean type (with which can be grouped the Gironde area), capitalist, retirement and part-time holdings leave little room for full-time family holdings. An eastern type groups Alsace, the Vosges and Lorraine (where retirement holdings are also significant); the Landes and the high mountain regions may be added to this group, which is characterized by the reciprocal existence of family farms and marginal holdings. The Central massif type groups family farms and retirement

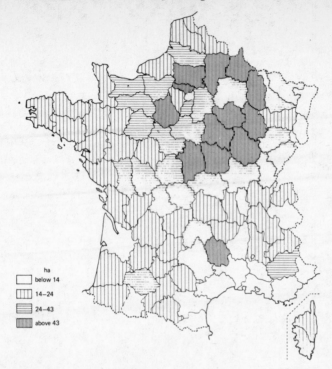

ha
below 14
14–24
24–43
above 43

Figure 18.3 Average size of agricultural holdings, 1975, by department. Average for France 22 ha. Source: Echantillon Permanent d'Exploitations Agricoles (Ministry of Agriculture).

holdings; the Paris region type is dominated by large capitalist holdings, intermixed with part-time holdings, unlike the Norman type where holdings of capitalist type coexist with retirement and part-time holdings.

3 The changing structure of agricultural holdings
3.1 Reduced numbers and increased size

Excluding holdings of less than a hectare (which have hitherto been difficult to assess because of problems of definition and deficiencies in statistical information), the number of holdings has decreased steadily from 3.5 million in 1892, 3.0 in 1929, 2.1 in 1955, to 1.4 in 1979. The annual rate of decline, which was 0.4 per cent between 1892 and 1929, then 2.1 per cent between 1929 and 1942, accelerated between 1955 and 1970, coinciding with the new impetus given at this time to the efforts to intensify production, which had made a first tentative appearance in the 1920s. Between 1975 and 1979, the rate of decline was reduced, due to fewer employment opportunities outside agriculture.

The interpretation of the available statistics presents difficulties (Table 18.4).

Table 18.4 Changes in the distribution of agricultural holdings according to the size-category, 1892–1979

Size category of holdings by agriculturally used area (ha)[a]	1892	1929	Number of holdings (thousands) 1955	1963	1970	1975	1979
Below 1	2,235.4	1,014.7	173.0	111.2	166.5	128.9	119.5
1–5	1,829.3	1,146.3	648.8	454.3	325.7	248.8	237.1
5–20	1,217.7	1,310.8	1,012.7	849.1	605.3	455.9	409.9
20–50	335.0	380.4	377.4	393.9	369.6	358.8	347.3
50–100	52.0	81.7	75.1	85.0	93.2	106.6	114.1
Over 100	33.3	32.5	20.0	23.5	27.1	32.2	34.5
Total	5,702.7	3,966.4	2,307.0	1,917.0	1,587.6	1,331.2	1,262.4
of which over 1	3,467.3	2,966.4	2,307.0	1,805.8	1,420.9	1,202.3	1,142.9
over 20	420.3	494.6	472.5	502.4	489.9	497.6	495.9
over 50	85.3	114.2	95.1	108.5	120.3	138.8	148.6

[a] Agriculturally utilizable area until 1970; agriculturally used area in 1970, 1975 and 1979.
Source: Recensement général de l'agriculture.

Undoubtedly there is a tendency towards the amalgamation of holdings and an increase in their size. The average size of holding was 8.74 ha in 1892, 11.6 in 1929, 14.1 in 1955, 18.8 in 1970 and 23.4 in 1980. But the distribution around the mean of those which survive is not radically different from that which prevailed after the Second World War, and holdings of below average size still account for the same overwhelming two-thirds of the total.

Concentration of holdings has differentially affected the various size-categories at different periods of development. Naturally the very small holdings of fewer than 5 ha have always been the most vulnerable, declining from 4 million in 1892 to 800,000 in 1955 and to fewer than 356,600 in 1979. But in the long term two periods of development can be discerned. Until the Second World War it was still the phase of the 'triumph of the family holding'. Of course, the interwar period saw the disappearance of thousands of dwarf holdings held by day labourers and paid agricultural workers, which were only viable through the existence of other sources of income and which were linked to a social organization still relying on a pool of locally available labour. However, holdings in the 10–50 ha category were increasing in number, whilst the age-old tendency towards the break-up of the large holdings continued, to the benefit of the medium-sized holdings, where the peasant family might be assisted by one or two paid agricultural workers. By contrast, after 1955 this tendency changed, and the phase of the one-person enterprise began. The 10–20 ha category began to decline, whilst the category over 50 ha increased; the greater the surface area, the faster the speed of growth. Since 1955 there has been an increasing annual rate of decline in the number of holdings of more than 1 ha, and a parallel increase in the number of holdings of more than 50 ha. Over the whole period, the number of holdings over 20 ha has remained remarkably stable.

3.2 Changing types of holding

In fact, the growth process of a holding shows infinite subtle variations, and the variety of cases makes all generalization difficult. The disappearance of a holding is not necessarily followed by amalgamation. Depopulation and the abandonment of a particular holding may result in its sale as a whole or in part or divided into parcels. The concentration of holdings proceeds more rapidly in regions dominated by the more readily mobile tenant farmers than in regions of owner–occupiers, who are more rooted in the soil. It also proceeds more rapidly in areas of openfield with grouped villages than in regions of *bocage* with scattered farms, and also more rapidly in plains than in areas of variegated terrain.

3.2.1 *The unequal survival of the family holding*

The development of mechanization and the introduction of new techniques have by increasing capital investment in the family holding brought about the decline of self-sufficiency and the increase of production for the market, but without establishing an exclusively capitalist type of agriculture. On the contrary, the small family holding has persisted, reflecting the greater relative share of labour inputs by family members. The decline in the number of paid agricultural workers is on the whole greater than that of other categories (excluding the very marked drop in assistance from members of farmers' families between 1968 and 1975) and is proceeding at an accelerating rate. In 1975 there were only about 250,000 paid workers, representing no more than 18.5 per cent of the agricultural work force. Whether measured in terms of persons occupied in agriculture or in the volume of work (full-time labour input per year), paid workers are diminishing but their relative share in the total work force remains stable. Farmers and members of their families make up 92 per cent of the agricultural work force, and are responsible for 85 per cent of agricultural work carried out. The introduction of new techniques, mechanization in particular, by reducing necessary work inputs per hectare for the same quantity of product, has reduced many holdings to an exclusive reliance on the labour of the farmer and members of his family.

The reduction of paid agricultural labour stems largely from the elimination of the paid workers who, 15–20 years ago, were needed to compensate for the diminishing amount of labour available from farmers' children. Mechanization has enabled farmers to eliminate these paid posts which they are unable to finance, even at the expense of over-equipment with tractors and combine-harvesters.

Figure 18.4 shows the departments in which family agriculture has survived; they are most often regions in which this type was predominant in 1955: the west (excluding the Departments of Côtes-du-Nord and Loire-Atlantique), the Nord region, the cattle-rearing departments of eastern France, and a few isolated departments in southern France. But contrary to the interwar period, it was not a question of the triumph of family holdings with several generations living under the same roof, but of holdings surviving with only limited numbers of family members. From 2.67 workers per holding in 1954, the figure dropped to 2.31 in 1962 and 1.77 in 1975. The work force appears even smaller if only full-time workers are considered: these dropped from an average of 1.03 per holding in 1963 to 0.86 in 1980. The reduction of the average work team on the farm is not only the result of the decline in paid workers. It also reflects the reduction in the number of family members active on the farm. In 1954 the number of family helpers exceeded that of farmers, but by 1975 they represented no more than 30 per cent of all family workers on farms.

Thus the work force of the family farm tends to be reduced to the farmer alone, with help from his wife, whilst the number of holdings able to employ two male work units has been reduced to the point of becoming the exception in some regions (Fig. 18.5). In addition to this decline in the number of workers per holding, which implies the departure of thousands of family members from

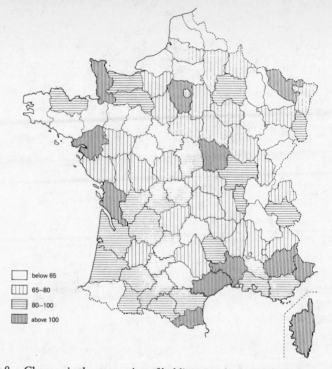

below 65
65–80
80–100
above 100

Figure 18.4 Changes in the proportion of holdings employing paid workers, 1955–70, by department. Calculation based on: (percentage of holdings employing paid workers 1970/percentage of holdings employing paid workers 1955) × 100. Source: Censuses, 1955 and 1970.

griculture, there are numerous other indications of the degeneration of family arming. There is a continuing reduction in the number of young people entering arming, and family holdings are declining in absolute numbers; the apparent tability of this category is only relative.

Statistics provide us with hardly any reliable clues as to the categories which an best withstand decline. Activities formerly carried out on the farm are ransferred to specialist undertakings, either upstream or downstream. These nclude the compounding of foodstuffs, vinification, the manufacture of dairy roducts, cattle insemination, repairs to equipment, the construction of build-ngs, and sales. At the same time there is a tendency for the number of stages needed in the production of any particular agricultural commodity to increase, with the need for the careful preparation of the product for marketing, packaging, he provision of special buildings, and the need for strict supervision with regard o health, financial and fiscal aspects. Full-time family holdings are gradually alling under the dominance of the agricultural and food industries, in whose

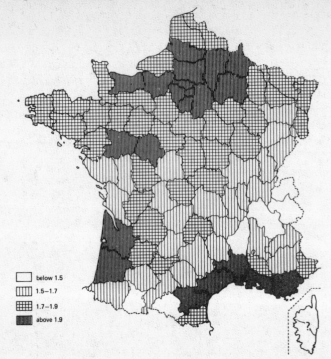

Figure 18.5 Average number of persons engaged in agriculture by holding, 1975, by department. Calculation based on: total number of persons engaged in agriculture/ number of farmers. Source: INSEE.

plans they are increasingly incorporated. Even if the farmers have some control over these new para-agricultural organizations through the development of co-operation and mutual assistance, the organizations have to act according to commercial considerations, being obliged to compete in the market with private firms, and the family farms are more and more reduced to a state of dependency. The development of contract growing is the clearest evidence of this penetration of outside capital, which tends progressively to change the nature of the family holding and to reorganize it for its own purposes. The impact of these developments on the survival of the family holding is difficult to assess; recent studies tend to show that many farmers who have borrowed heavily in order to modernize are on the verge of bankruptcy.

3.2.2 Contrasts in the evolution of marginal holdings

Retirement holdings where the farmer is over 65 fell sharply between 1955 and 1975 (432,000 in 1955, 274,200 in 1970, 209,047 in 1979), a phenomenon which is in line with the statistics showing a rapid decline in very small holdings.

Of all age groups engaged in agriculture, the 60–70 age group has shown the most rapid decline. The traditional poor peasant class continues to contract rapidly, although many elderly farmers go on producing in order to supplement their pensions, so that proportionately this category is only slightly in decline (18.9 per cent of total holdings in 1955, 17.3 per cent in 1979). In spite of massive losses, holdings of this kind survive because in terms of size and available capital they are unable to attract even one of the farmer's children to take over the farm. Such succession has been increasingly difficult since the war, as the Crédit Agricole (Agricultural Bank) will make loans only to farmers having holdings of at least the size deemed economically viable. The consolidation of holdings (*remembrement*) has not favoured these little family holdings either, and the government policy of giving special pensions to retiring farmers and transferring their land to others (Indemnité Viagère de Départ – IVD) has increased the disappearance of this important category of peasants who, without the possibility of modernization and without apparent heirs, have grown old on their farms, their only aim being to hang on to a little piece of land until their retirement, and to survive.

The pattern of development of part-time holdings is by no means comparable. It is true that the total of this type of holding declined between 1963 and 1975, but less rapidly than that of other categories of holding. Moreover, involvement in an additional occupation outside agriculture is even more common than engagement in two agricultural activities, where for example an agricultural worker also has a holding, or where a farmer has more than one holding. It seems that a new, somewhat poor peasant class is emerging from two main sources. One consists of existing farmers and members of farm families who try to escape the complete proletarianization epitomized by work in a factory or a petty clerical occupation by continuing to run a holding that is too small to offer employment to a full-time farmer. The second consists of persons born into farming families, who had outside paid employment before inheriting the family farm, and who try to preserve the family inheritance intact. The significance of these two types of part-time holding varies in time and space, increasing in importance where there are nearby opportunities of industrial, and above all tertiary, employment, while declining in traditional agricultural regions.

Certain regional characteristics are reinforced by these developments, notably the increase in the numbers of farmers in Alsace and Lorraine who are also workers, farmers occupying middle-management and clerical jobs in the Mediterranean south, and workers in craft occupations who are also farmers in Limousin and Poitou–Charentes.

3.2.3 *Regional development of holdings of capitalist type*

It must not be assumed, however, that capitalist forms of agriculture develop only by the elimination of marginal and family holdings. Capitalist agriculture develops also according to its own logic, which can be observed in regional, even local, aspects. The economic significance of the largest holdings has increased; the upper 10 per cent of holdings accounted for 33 per cent of agricultural production in 1963 and 44 per cent in 1970. Moreover, although the number of agricultural enterprises with paid workers is decreasing, the proportion of those employing more than five paid workers, which had declined until as late as 1963, has been increasing since that time. The average number of paid workers in holdings employing more than 10 paid workers has increased from 17.9 in 1946 to 20 in 1970. The significance and regional distribution of capitalist holdings are difficult to grasp by reference to census statistics, because of their spatial dispersion and the way in which holdings under a single ownership may be divided between a number of departments, and thus separately recorded. It is apparent, however, that there is increased geographical concentration of large holdings in the Paris basin, especially on its eastern fringes, a concentration which had its origin as early as the eighteenth century. Since 1963 there has also been an increase in the number of paid agricultural workers in departments near Paris, also in the Marne (Champagne vineyards), the Manche Department, the Landes (where large irrigated cereal holdings have been created out of former forest land) and in a number of departments in the Midi, in particular in Bouches-du-Rhône (Camargue). This development of capitalist holdings is therefore sometimes regional, when linked to a particularly favourable overall structure of agriculture, but sometimes reflects purely local opportunities of new agricultural developments, as in the Landes, the Champagne pouilleuse and the Camargue.

Thus the development of holdings, whether of family or capitalist type, accentuates rather than blurs a geographical division established for the most part in the nineteenth century between regions of high agricultural income dominated by capitalist agriculture and the vast majority of French departments where family production survives.

19

✧ Agricultural and forest production

A study of the process of localization and the causative factors involved necessarily leads to an understanding of three interrelated aspects of the production process: the natural environment, the agricultural system (an amalgam of land utilization, methods of cultivation and the final products involved) and overall economic conditions, which are ever more restrictive in nature. Agricultural geography is essentially about the relationships between these three forces, which do not necessarily pull in the same direction. The system of agriculture acts in many ways like a filter, in which family, personal and structural considerations lead progressively to a compromise between what it is possible to produce in a given natural environment and what the market demands.

1 Trends in agricultural output

Agricultural output has continuously increased since the Second World War, rising by about 3 per cent per year (Table 19.1). Obviously the upward curve is not an entirely smooth one, since it is affected by climatic fluctuations (for example the extremely dry summer of 1976) and by the well-known production cycles in commodities such as pork. Only a few commodities, such as veal and minor cereals, stand out against the upward trend.

Table 19.1 *Changing output of agricultural products, by value*

Current prices

	1959		1971		1981	
	Million	%	Million	%	Million	%
Crop production	13,591	42.4	31,384	44.2	88,236	44.8
Cereals	3,489	10.9	11,307	15.9	32,834	16.7
Potatoes and other vegetables	4,308	13.4	5,600	7.9	13,905	7.1
Fruit	1,237	3.9	2,866	4.0	7,511	3.8
Table wine	1,843	5.7	3,987	5.6	7,816	3.9
Quality wine	1,126	3.5	2,676	3.8	10,292	5.2
Beets	565	1.8	1,761	2.5	6,046	3.1
Other crops	1,023	3.2	3,187	4.5	9,832	5.0
Livestock production	18,494	57.6	39,580	55.8	108,706	55.2
Beef	3,124	9.7	8,908	12.6	25,364	12.9
Veal	1,703	5.3	4,101	5.8	8,950	4.5
Pigmeat and derived products	3,641	11.3	5,760	8.1	14,541	7.4
Poultry	1,716	5.3	2,921	4.1	10,705	5.4
Eggs	1,288	4.0	2,066	2.9	5,647	2.9
Milk	5,191	16.2	12,372	17.4	35,260	17.9
Other livestock products	1,831	5.7	3,452	4.9	8,239	4.2
Total production	32,085	100.0	70,964	100.0	196,942	100.0

Source: INSEE, *Comptes de l'agriculture.*

1.1 Crop production

The most spectacular progress has been in cereal production, which has practically trebled in volume by comparison with the pre-war years. For other crops the pattern is more variable. Crops requiring hoe cultivation have declined sharply, because of their heavy demand on labour. The exception is sugar beet; at first both the output of this crop and the area devoted to its cultivation had been held stable, a ceiling on output having been imposed in return for a European Community price guarantee, but the upsurge in world prices from 1972 onwards was reflected in a great increase both in the area devoted to sugar beet and the volume of output, a development made possible by improved methods of cultivation.

The production of fruit, vegetables and wine, together making up 23 per cent of the total agricultural production by value, raises difficult problems. The output of vegetables has been declining since 1961, leading to an increase in imports, which have trebled in 15 years. Vegetables grown as field crops are highly dependent on climatic conditions. Striking a balance between supply and demand is always difficult, so that annual price fluctuations are considerable. A substantial fall in prices will lead to a withdrawal of produce from the market and in some years to the destruction of crops by producers. The problem is still more serious in fruit production, which has been steadily increasing since the 1960s.

Until 1964–5 the growth of the industry kept pace with the sharp increase in home demand for the main types of fruit. In the 1960s, however, a too-rapid expansion in apple and peach orchards and the characteristic inflexibility of supply of such crops (derived from the long life-span of the trees) led to prolonged market disequilibrium. In spite of the practice of withdrawing produce from the market, given official backing from 1965 onwards, of a campaign of grubbing up orchards in the framework of the European Community, and of some spectacular instances of crop destruction by angry growers, seasonal surpluses have not always been eliminated.

French wine production poses a continual problem, which the entry of Spain into the European Community will aggravate. Wine accounts for 9–10 per cent of French agricultural output by value. France, like Italy, is responsible for a quarter of world wine output and nearly one-half of European Community production. In spite of a continuing slight decline in the area under vines, there has been a tendency towards a steady if slight increase in output, reflecting improved yields. As home consumption is declining year by year, reflecting a decreasing demand for table wines, market problems are serious. Sharp annual fluctuations in output (66.5 million hectolitres in 1968, 51.3 in 1969) complicate the operation of the market, masking structural imbalance and chronic overproduction. French wines vary greatly in quality, of course, ranging from the low-grade mass production of Languedoc to the finest-quality vintages of Burgundy or Bordeaux, and not all are equally affected by the market crisis. In spite of the policy adopted, especially since 1964, to transform wine production by eliminating mediocre vines and by encouraging the production of the higher quality Appellation Contrôlée wines (VAOC) or Vins Délimités de Qualité Supérieure (VDQS), the output of ordinary table wines is declining only slowly. The opening of the French market to unrestricted imports from other European Community countries after 1970 aggravated the problems of the producers of table wines, who were exposed to direct competition from Italian producers. The rise in the prices of quality wines, on the other hand, led to localized extensions of fine-quality vineyards. The tendency towards an increase in the total volume of wine produced in France means that the output of even a poor year (that is to say, a good year from the producers' point of view) is sufficient to satisfy national needs. Unless the quantity of wine diverted each year to distilling is increased, it seems inevitable that the area under vines and the number of vine-growers must be reduced. The fact that with state assistance quantities of vegetables, fruit and wine must regularly be withdrawn from the market or destroyed is an indication of the chronic problems of this part of the agricultural industry.

1.2 Livestock production

The rapid expansion of livestock production has been almost as spectacular as that of crop production. Beef and pork output has doubled, milk more than doubled, and modern poultry production created as an entirely new branch of the industry.

France has about 24 million cattle, the number fluctuating from year to year in response to climatic and market conditions. This is the largest herd of all the European Community countries. Of this total more than 10 million are cows, three-quarters of them in dairy herds. Cows in rearing herds, producing beef cattle for fattening, numbered 2.8 million in 1980. However, the production of meat and milk is closely linked, since animals derived from dairy herds account for about 65 per cent of beef production. This is the origin of the meat–milk contradiction whereby a commodity for which there is an expanding demand (beef) is jointly produced with a commodity in chronically surplus supply (milk). This makes it difficult to work out a rational overall policy with regard to cattle: any attempt to stimulate the production of meat is necessarily followed by an increase in the milk surplus. The situation is made worse by the tendency to replace dual purpose breeds by high-yielding dairy breeds such as Friesians and Holsteins.

Unlike beef, and especially milk, the production of pigs, sheep and horses fails to meet demand, despite a relative increase in numbers. French pig production has since 1976 been particularly affected by abnormally low prices. The proportion of home demand covered by imports, which at the beginning of the 1970s had been stabilized at about 200,000 tonnes a year, continued to increase thereafter, much to the disquiet of French pig farmers. Membership of the European Community has not helped pig producers, who in the absence of a guaranteed price for pigmeat or any system of permanent subsidies have been exposed to increased competition. France was also put at a disadvantage by the former system of Monetary Compensation Amounts given to producers in countries having strong currencies (the German Federal Republic in particular) to protect them from the adverse impact of fluctuations in Community currencies.

Poultry production has much in common with pork production in its reliance on battery farming, the large-scale use of factory-produced foodstuffs, and increasing standardization of production techniques, yet it has expanded rapidly and has succeeded in satisfying the needs of the home market and even in producing a surplus for the export market.

1.3 The changing nature of agricultural production

The entry of France into the European Community in 1957 introduced a period during which the share of livestock products in total agricultural output declined. The French share in Community production of cereals rose from 35.9 per cent in 1970 to 40.7 per cent in 1980, whereas that of beef and veal fell (28.1 per cent in 1970, 26.7 per cent in 1980). This indicates a real reversal of the long-term trend in French agriculture, which, having been based on cereal cultivation until about the end of the nineteenth century, had thereafter been characterized by a regular increase in areas devoted to fodder and in the share of livestock in the end product. Between 1950 and 1960 this trend was accelerated by advancements in techniques but it slowed down after 1964, except for milk and poultry. In the face of the considerable French potential for fodder-growing and livestock production, this relative decline is a first sign of a division of labour between the various European countries. France, with a lower density of agricultural labour and a still comparatively strong primary sector, tends towards the less intensive arable enterprises and perhaps towards the more extensive beef production. French competitiveness is enhanced by favourable natural conditions (adequate precipitation and lack of long periods of freezing), by its fairly large holdings, and by the fixing of relatively high prices within the European Community due to pressure from German producers.On the other hand, the importing of reasonably priced animal feedstuffs favours producers from the more industrialized Community countries which have a high density of labour to the hectare, especially those with strong currencies. They are able to specialize in the export of livestock products, pork in particular. This specialization on a European scale poses serious problems for some categories of French producers and even for entire regions.

2 The trend towards greater regional specialization

2.1 The more productive regions increase their dominance

Agricultural production is unevenly distributed; in 1975 a third of the departments were responsible for half the total production (Fig. 19.1). There are two main regions of high production: northern France (central and western parts of the Paris basin, the Flanders plain and the Artois plateau), and western France (Normandy, Brittany, the fringe of the Armorican massif, and northern Aquitaine). The only department of high production in eastern France is Saône-et-Loire. Fairly high levels of production are characteristic of the wine and fruit-growing regions of southern and southwest France, as well as of a few departments in the east of the Paris basin and in Aquitaine.

This remarkable geographical concentration of agricultural production goes hand in hand with a no less remarkable territorial division between regions of livestock production and those where crop production predominates. Half the crop production comes from the grain-growing Paris basin, the Nord region, the wine-producing Mediterranean departments, the Department of Maine-et-Loire and the Department of Charente-Maritime. Half the output of livestock products is derived from western France (the Armorican massif and its fringes), the Nord region and a few isolated departments (Saône-et-Loire, Aveyron and Pyrénées-Atlantiques). Departments with a high production of both livestock and cereals are rare, but include Nord, the Somme, Pas-de-Calais and Maine-et-Loire.

These differences in output and type of product have become more marked

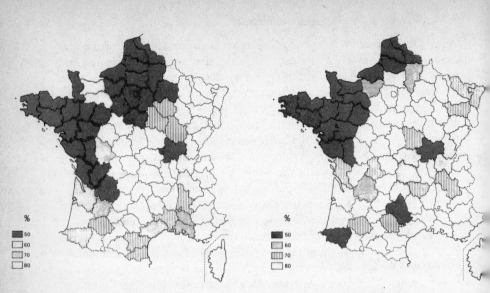

A. Total agricultural produce

B. Animal produce

%
50
60
70
80

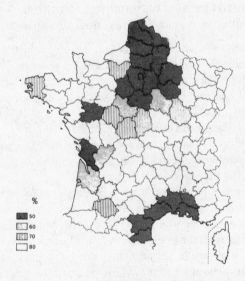

%
50
60
70
80

C. Vegetable produce

Figure 19.1 Spatial concentration of agricultural production, 1975. Calculation: For each of the three maps, departments are ranked in descending order according to the percentage of national output for which each is responsible. Beginning with the department producing the highest percentage, successive departments in decreasing order of output are added until the group of departments emerges which produces half the national

since 1955. A large part of the increase in the final agricultural production is contributed by Brittany and the Pays de la Loire regions, where livestock production has continued to increase in quantity and value. Regions which are making similar but less vigorous progress on the basis of crop production are Champagne (development of vineyards), the Paris basin, Centre, Poitou–Charentes and Provence–Côte d'Azur. By contrast, the share of mountain regions such as Limousin, Auvergne and Rhône–Alpes has declined.

2.2 Areas of increasing specialization

Certain regional specializations, already apparent in the mid-twentieth century, have become even more marked. This has partly come about by a reinforcement of the existing specialization, partly by the elimination or reduction of subsidiary products. The clearest example of this twofold development is provided by the increasingly distinct separation between the areas of cereal and milk production. Before the Second World War, cereal production was concentrated in the Paris basin, but there were secondary centres of production, particularly in Brittany. Today the Paris basin is unquestionably the chief producer, both in terms of the area under cereal crops and total output; within the region as a whole, there has been accentuated specialization in Beauce and Brie, and to a lesser extent in the departments fringing these areas to the south and east. At the same time they have dispensed with their livestock; the great farms of Brie and Beauce have seen the gradual disappearance first of draught animals, then sheep, then cattle (first the dairy herds and subsequently the beef cattle). Only the rearing of young cattle occasionally persists, with milk production confined to the smallest farms. It is in these regions of large-scale arable farming in the Paris basin that the cattle numbers are diminishing most rapidly. A similar decline is to be observed also in the traditional livestock region of Poitou–Charentes, where there is now a tendency towards arable enterprises, as well as in other areas of crop specialization such as Alsace and the Midi (where the climate is unfavourable to livestock farming).

Conversely, the map showing changes in the numbers of cows (Fig. 19.2) indicates the leap forward in milk production made by the departments of western France (Brittany, Lower Normandy and Pays de la Loire regions), which provided 46 per cent of the country's output in 1980 as against 26.4 per cent in 1950. This growth was achieved by an increase in the *cheptel de souche* (the milk cows which on any one holding also provide young stock for the continuation of the herd). It was accompanied by a reduction in the area devoted to cereals and

---

output, represented by the 50 per cent value in the key. The subsequent values in the key indicate the departments that must be added to account successively for 60 per cent, 70 per cent and 80 per cent of national output. Source: Comptes départementaux de l'agriculture.

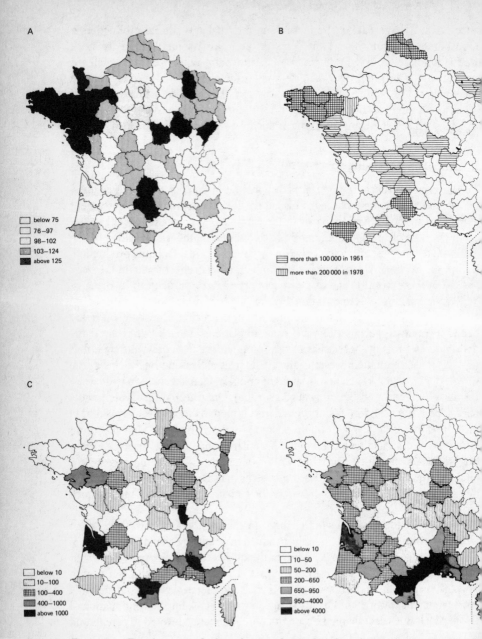

Figure 19.2 Development of selected types of agricultural production, by department. A. Changes in the number of cows, 1963–78 (1963 = 100) B. Spatial variation in pig production, 1951–68 (Calculation as for Fig. 19.1) C. Production of quality wine, in thousand hectolitres, 1978 D. Production of table wine, in thousand hectolitres, 1978. Source: Ministère de l'Agriculture.

sometimes, as in the *bocage* of Normandy, by a great expansion of the area permanently under grass. A similar increase in the number of breeding cows has been characteristic of other regions with a tradition of dairy farming, notably Lorraine, Franche-Comté and Nord, which nevertheless has not led to the great increase in the output of milk and dairy products characteristic of western France.

This reinforced regional specialization can plausibly be explained as an adaptation to natural conditions. Livestock production seems to have been concentrated in regions of oceanic climate. Cereal production has been preferred on level plains and plateaus where soil moisture conditions are good, where winter frosts are not severe, where there is no excess of rain in spring or summer nor of high temperature in late spring. Paradoxically, however, this apparent increase in environmental determinism has taken place in a period when technical progress has brought about a considerable relaxation of ecological constraints on crop production and a replacement of local breeds of cows by dairy strains developed in greatly differing environments. Maize (corn), which was originally introduced in the south of Aquitaine and which according to Arthur Young did not grow north of the Bordeaux–Strasbourg line, is now a major crop in the Paris basin. The French black and white Friesian cow, which originated in the Nord region, where dairy production is declining, is today the most numerically important breed in France, appearing in nearly every region, especially Brittany and Pays de la Loire; it competes with the Norman breed on its home ground.

In reality this development is essentially explained by the fact that the profitability of a particular product or a particular means of production is closely linked to the structure of the holdings. Cereal production, when compared with dairy production at a common level of technology, yields a lower return per unit of area but a higher return per unit of labour. Large holdings are accordingly directed almost exclusively towards cereal production, which allows the optimum relationship between their limited paid work force and the available area. By contrast small holdings, with a plentiful supply of family labour, have to use their limited area more intensively by means of dairy production and therefore allocate a higher proportion of their surface area to fodder production. The sharp division between the areas of cereal and dairy production thus reflects inequalities in the size and type of holdings which have already been pointed out. The distinction is also sharpened, however, by spatial variations in prices and availability of markets. There is a marked tendency for the industries processing food and agricultural products to coincide in their distribution with regions of the highest agricultural output. For example, it is in western France that we find the largest industrial milk-processing enterprises and where amalgamation into ever larger units has taken place most quickly in both the private and the co-operative sectors. This accentuation of the spatial division of labour is not without its problems; by physically separating cattle from cropping and dung from straw, it has serious effects on soil fertility, leading sometimes to a deficiency of humus (accentuated by stubble-burning) and threatening the maintenance of soil productivity in the long term.

Vineyards provide another example of increasing specialization. In 1980, vines occupied 1,139,000 ha; as many as 69 departments recorded more than 50 ha. The vine-growing area extends from the Mediterranean zone, where the plant originated, to a northern limit which has effectively not varied for a century. In the majority of the departments, only very limited areas are devoted to vine cultivation, which is concentrated into a limited number of regions within which there are areas characterized by a predominant specialization in wine production, areas whose boundaries have for many years varied only slightly. The sequence of events which resulted in the present distribution of vineyards in France was initiated by an increase in areas sown with vines, which reached its maximum between 1860 and 1870. The phylloxera crisis led to a massive decline followed by the reconstitution of the vineyards on a smaller scale and the transfer of some areas of production (the Languedoc vineyards were moved down to the coastal plain). A crisis of overproduction at the beginning of the twentieth century, a fall in prices, a new and more serious outbreak of mildew and an increase in production costs brought about the abandonment of many vineyards producing ordinary table wines, as well as many vineyards of the urban fringes, which proved to be commercially unattractive because of inadequacies of situation and quality. The wine map of France was then fixed by legislation in 1934, giving a monopoly of wine production to existing producers; the planting of new vineyards was forbidden unless an equivalent area was uprooted. In addition, there is a formal system of control and protection of the various grades of quality wines by the Institut National d'Appellation d'Origine des Vins et des Eaux de Vie (INAO), founded in 1935. Regions producing quality wines are strictly demarcated on the basis of soil quality, exposure, type of grape and maximum permitted yield per hectare (Fig. 19.2).

The production of quality or vintage wine is thus in principle strictly localized, for example the vineyards of Bordeaux, Burgundy, Champagne, Cognac, Touraine, Anjou, Alsace and the small vineyards of the southeastern Paris basin. While naturally varying according to the year, output of the great vintage wines tends to be stable in the long term. The output of other quality wines (VAOC, VDQS) tends to increase, in spite of strict control and the use of types of grape giving a limited yield. Indeed, in addition to the spatial extension of certain vineyards, notably Champagne, the increase in the output of wines of controlled quality is the result of the replacement of common grape varieties by superior varieties within the delimited areas wherever the terrain allows. Thus the small vineyards of the Paris basin (Chablis, Sancerre and Pouilly) have booming wine industries which benefit from their recognition as areas of quality wine production (Appellation Contrôlée).

Vineyards engaged in the quantity production of ordinary wine occupy extensive areas in the departments fringing the Mediterranean; they are responsible for more than half the national wine output in terms of quantity. Within the general Mediterranean area several quality wines can be distinguished, but the greater part of the output comes from high-yielding vines such as Aramon and Carignon whose output is further increased by irrigation.

In spite of state encouragement of the grubbing up of vines during 1953 and 1954, reduction in surface area has been negligible. The years since 1964 have even seen the addition of a quantity-wine area of 14,000 ha in the eastern plain of Corsica, developed by the Corsican Development Company (Société de Mise en Valeur de la Corse – SOMIVAC). Many residents of former overseas territories, particularly residents repatriated from North Africa, settled there. This development was not entirely in accord with the 1934 legislation and moreover it allowed *chaptalisation* (the adding of sugar to the must before fermentation).

The local and regional specialization of French wine production has thus been accentuated. Few plants are more responsive than the vine to minute variations in the natural environment. The reorganization of vineyards and their present distribution have therefore involved a selection of the most favourable sites in order to produce wines which are differentiated not only by their delicacy, body and bouquet but also by the different ways in which they are made. Market conditions have become paramount, increasingly dividing quality wines which can be exported from ordinary table wines, which not only suffer from a reduction in demand on the home market but from the competition of wine from other countries of the European Community, such as Italy and Greece. The development of local specialization in quality wine production is thus a positive feature, but the persistence of the Mediterranean specialization in the bulk production of ordinary wine points to a regional crisis.

2.3 Areas of relative stability

Parallel with the enhanced regional specialization in milk, cereals and wine, other regions have maintained their pre-existing forms of production. For example, the area of beef production from specifically beef breeds has remained stable in extent and relative importance. This type of beef production coincides with the areas of distribution of two major breeds of beef cattle. The Charolais originated in the area around Nevers, north of the Central massif, from which the breed spread into neighbouring departments. The Limousin breed coincides in its distribution with the region of the same name, in the western part of the Central massif. The area of beef specialization, especially at its core and in its eastern and northern extensions, coincides with an area dominated by large and medium holdings (averaging 50 ha for full-time holdings). They derive from tenant farms and holdings of share-croppers which were part of vast landed estates that had largely escaped being broken up. In this system of farming, the area of land necessary to keep a man in full employment is distinctly larger than in dairy farming. Of the two breeds concerned, the Charolais is most important, and has continued to increase in numbers since 1963. The relative stability of this type of beef production, which can be related to the size of holdings, the high reputation of the product and the natural environment, does not, however, exclude a much more spectacular development of beef production in regions where it is a by-product of dairy farming, that is to say, in western France.

Mountain areas provide another example of the relative stability of a regional specialization, while showing a strong tendency towards declining output. Since 1961, communes dependent on mountain agriculture have been officially designated on the basis of criteria such as altitude and slope. In 1980 they contained 171,330 holdings. The characteristic bias of mountain regions towards fodder production has been maintained; 83 per cent of the agriculturally used area of these mountain holdings was devoted to fodder crops and permanent grassland in 1967, and 86 per cent in 1980. Between 1970 and 1980 the share of the predominant livestock production in final agricultural production increased slightly from 59.1 per cent to 59.6 per cent, at the expense of fruit and wine; other crops maintained a stable proportion of the whole. The livestock category conceals, however, a great diversity of both products and farming systems: beef cattle, dairy cattle, sheep, cattle–sheep combinations and even industrial farming. In the mountain zone of Mediterranean France, where dependence on tree crops is traditional, fruit production has become prominent. This specialization in livestock and in tree crops, however different the systems of farming involved, can be related to climatic conditions: the availability of grazing increases with altitude, thanks to adequate rainfall and a reduced risk of summer drought. It can also be related to relief, notably to the existence of slopes of over 15 per cent. These environmental conditions, in addition to the smaller average size of mountain holdings, explain the expansion of fodder crops and permanent grass at the expense of cereal crops and often an overall reduction in the agriculturally used area. In mountain areas, contrary to the general tendency, an improvement in yield is not accompanied by an increase in the quantity produced. This stagnation is a sign of a crisis which the policy for mountain areas – now considered to be a problem related to the European Community as a whole – has not always solved.

2.4 Areas of rapidly changing specialization

In the spatial distribution of agricultural production some new areas of specialized production have emerged, occasionally ousting the old branches by a remarkable increase in their relative share in national production. Spectacular shifts have taken place in the location of poultry farming and certain fruit and vegetable crops; the most striking example, however, is that of pig production (Fig. 19.2B). During the 1950s, pig production was spread over nearly all regions, most holdings having a few pigs which were fed on the farm's by-products. Low pig populations were characteristic of Mediterranean France (with the exception of the Department of Bouches-du-Rhône, which had large pig farms supplying Marseille); the gap between the 15 departments with the highest pig population (195,000 head on average) and the 15 with the lowest population (20,000 head on average) was, however, relatively wide. The collection of milk from the farm, introduced from the 1960s onwards, meant that whey was no longer available for feeding pigs and led to the establishment as early as 1964 of groups of pig producers and financial encouragement for the setting up of factory farming. The marked progress which occurred after 1967 featured a certain number of regions which were among the leaders in 1950: Brittany, and especially the Departments of Côtes-du-Nord and Finistère (which far outstripped Ille-et-Vilaine, the leading department in 1951), the Nord region and the Department of Pyrénées-Atlantiques. The departments of the Centre region are still among the highest producers, but have not greatly changed in overall output. Everywhere else the trend is towards stagnation or slow decline; the gap is widening very rapidly between the regions in the process of specialization in pig production and the others. The Breton departments continued to maintain their supremacy after 1971, the four of them in 1980 accounting for 42.8 per cent of total pig numbers (14.4 per cent in 1951). By contrast the Nord region has entered a period of absolute and relative decline in pig numbers (5.1 per cent of the pig population in 1951, 12.1 per cent in 1971 and only 4.3 per cent in 1978). This is explained by the insignificant development of producer groups and by the spread of the Belgian method in which the pigs are housed singly. All the other regions of substantial pig production are declining in importance.

The remarkable spatial concentration of pig production in Brittany and the rapid expansion of output there stems from an increase in the numbers of intensive pig units. These use factory-made feedstuffs only, and increasingly operate on an industrial scale. They are organized on a contractual basis by groups of producers. Some are co-operatives, which may rear more than 400,000 pigs a year each, others are directly linked to animal feedstuff firms. To some extent this marked localization can be related to the predominance in Brittany of small farmers determined to stay in farming even at the cost of going into debt to modernize their meagre holdings. It can be related also to the willingness to join together in co-operatives which have become increasingly detached from any base in the soil. Undoubtedly the thrustful policies of animal feedstuff firms have been of importance, while government agricultural policy has strongly supported the vertical integration of the agricultural and food industries in western France. All these factors doubtless played a part, but the result has been that this area of specialization, in which poor farmers coexist with their more affluent neighbours who have modernized their holdings by the introduction of special pig units, and with large-scale agro-industrial battery producers, bears the brunt of the crisis in French pig production.

2.5 Regional specialization and the specialization of holdings

New agricultural regions of varying size have thus been created. They may owe their distinctive characteristics to the predominance of natural factors or to the structure of holdings (for example, the availability of family labour on small and medium-sized holdings, encouraging dairy production), or to the market organized by firms with government backing (industrialized pig production).

There is no doubt that agricultural holdings have tended during the past thirty years to become more specialized. Despite a rise in production costs, reflecting in particular increased energy consumption, there has been a decline in mixed farming (under which many inputs were produced on the farm itself) and an increase in simpler and more specialized systems. This is shown in Table 19.2, which compares, in terms of number and the area occupied, agricultural holdings classed according to their specialization in particular agricultural enterprises. There has been an above-average decline in holdings where no single specialization can be detected, holdings which defy classification. By contrast, above-average increases are shown by simple or specialized systems such as general arable specializations or glasshouse production; the latter has expanded with particular rapidity. Industrialized systems have either declined less rapidly than average (poultry) or have shown a slight increase (pigs). Holdings which combine two types of enterprise, notably crop–livestock combinations, are declining in varying degrees.

This tendency towards the simplification and specialization of farming systems by a reduction in the number of enterprises on each holding indicates that each system tends towards an optimum scale, with a minimum threshold size of land or stock, depending on the techniques used. The process has been accelerated by the tendency to remove activities from the holding to specialist concerns, both in upstream and downstream directions, through professional movements such as the Centres d'Etudes Techniques Agricoles (CETA), group farming and farm education programmes. Other influences have been a market switch from natural to synthetic products, and increased competition from produce of tropical origin. The process can also be regarded as a continuation of the trend, already a century old, towards the decline of traditional mixed farming (*polyculture*), which had reached its peak in the middle of the nineteenth century.

The progress of these simplified, specialized systems varies between regions which, as they emerge from traditional *polyculture* and define their specializations, become more and more distinct from each other. In some regions a pre-existing tendency towards monoculture or special crops has been accentuated. In the Ile-de-France region, for example, the system classified as 'general arable specializations' (which in this context corresponds to the large cereal and beet holdings of the central Paris basin) continued to increase its relative share of the number of holdings until in 1975 it reached 48.3 per cent of the total numbers

Table 19.2 *Selected agricultural specializations: changes in the number of holdings and the proportion of agriculturally used area involved*

	Number of holdings (thousands)		Annual change	Agriculturally used area (thousand ha)		Annual change
	1970	1975	%	1970	1975	%
General arable specifications	104.5	110.6	1.1	4,290.4	5,236.8	4.1
Arable specifications with horticulture	4.5	4.9	1.7	92.1	98.1	1.3
Glasshouse production	1.5	2.2	7.9	5.1	8.5	10.7
Pig production	15.6	16.2	0.7	186.7	289.9	9.2
Quality wine (Appellation Contrôlée)	52.9	49.6	−1.3	356.1	393.7	2.0
Arable–cattle	80.4	59.7	−5.8	2,704.7	2,251.1	−3.6
Cattle–arable	215.2	187.8	−8.5	5,408.1	4,069.4	−5.5
Cattle with pigs–poultry	84.7	46.5	−11.2	1,306.2	746.2	−10.6
Pigs–poultry with cattle	22.3	16.0	−6.4	409.2	328.8	−4.3
All holdings	1,587.6	1,331.1	−3.5	29,904.8	29,469.6	−0.3

Source: Recensement général de l'agriculture.

and 80.4 per cent of the agriculturally used area. Brittany has a comparable specialization in the beef–dairy system, which in 1975 was used by 46.6 per cent of all holdings. In other regions, however, specializations have gradually evolved out of initially more varied systems of production. Such is the case in Centre region, where the general arable system is spreading vigorously, partly under the impulse given by migrants (for example in Cher Department). The spectacular development of industrialized pig production in Brittany is a similar case. Another example is the progress of table-wine production in Corsica. By contrast, old-established cattle specializations have remained stable, such as cattle–beef in Lower Normandy, Limousin and Franche-Comté, similarly the wine-growing specialization in Languedoc.

The trend towards specialized systems must not, however, be taken as heralding monoproduction on every holding in every region. Several regions are still characterized by modified versions of *polyculture* or by the juxtaposition of a range of specialized and non-specialized systems, none of them achieving predominance. In the Nord–Pas-de-Calais area, no highly specialized system is making real progress. Intensive mixed farming (*polyculture*) is still the rule, the system being more or less specialized and more or less intensive according to the local significance of the grassland or fodder crops, the latter for example becoming important in the Pays de Caux and parts of Picardy. Other regions, such as Poitou–Charentes, Aquitaine or Alsace, appear to be moving towards relative diversification: vines, fruit crops, veal and cereals are the essential elements in this *polyculture*. In conclusion, while traditional *polyculture* is to be found in most regions, it contributes little to the total output from agriculture, for it is most frequently practised on retirement holdings and by the poorest small farmers who, lacking capital and sufficient land, cannot convert their holdings into profitable concerns.

20

✣ Types of agriculture and
agricultural policy

It is impossible to differentiate between regional systems of cultivation in the
same way as twenty or thirty years ago, to attribute a particular system of culture
or production to a particular region, in the way that it was once possible to speak
of the agriculture of the Pays de Caux for example, or of Santerre. It is similarly
no longer possible to allocate a region as a whole to a particular stage of
development, whether traditional *polyculture*, specialized systems or monoculture. These concepts no longer suffice to express the complexity of the
phenomena which have emerged in relation to agricultural localization. It is of
course true that a degree of regional uniformity is provided by the quantitative
predominance of particular products, and that increased specialization has led to
a sharpening of contrasts between regions. Yet the processes which have
produced these changes at a regional scale have failed to narrow the technical and
social gulf between farms and farmers within the region. The gulf has sometimes
even been widened in response to varying levels of the means of production and
invested capital, the chosen product, the intensity of labour used, and the
presence or otherwise of advantages of situation. It is therefore preferable to
concentrate research on identifying regional types of agriculture or regional
agricultural systems, by reference to a wider range of factors than those usually
associated with the notion of a system of cultivation. It is thus necessary to
proceed in two stages, first introducing a classification of French agriculture
according to a range of alternative criteria and objectives and then, by a process of

synthesis, attempting to produce an overall classification of French agriculture as a whole.

1 Alternative agricultural classifications
1.1 Classification according to tenure

One of the oldest and most deeply rooted contrasts in French agriculture is that which expresses the precise legal bond between the cultivator and the land that he occupies. In France a threefold classification of tenurial relationships is customary. *Faire-valoir direct* implies that the person cultivating a holding is also its owner. In *faire-valoir indirect* the person cultivating a holding is a tenant or share-cropper holding land from one or more landlords. In *mode mixte* the cultivator owns some land, but has the remainder in tenancy. The tenurial relationship, when taken in association with the size of holding, is an indication of marked regional and local contrasts. Thus in spite of the long and complex history of property transfers, it is possible to see for 1970, even more clearly than for 1892, the line from La Rochelle to Nancy by way of Nevers and Lyon which separates the owner-farming south and east from the tenant-farming north and west.

Small peasant properties have existed for centuries past in the area of old Roman law that coincides with the distribution of the *langue d'oc* (See chapter 12, 1.1), as well as in Alsace, Lorraine and Franche-Comté. In these regions there are only occasional islands of tenant farming or share-cropping, as in the Departments of Haut-Doubs, Landes or Ariège. Within the areas where tenant farming predominates, it is still possible to distinguish a range of types of farms and estates dependent on large landowners, such as the *bocage* regions of western France, the regions of medium and large tenant or share-cropping farms which still belong to large and often aristocratic property-owners (Pays Fort (Cher Department), the Limousin Marche, the Bourbonnais and Nivernais) and the large farms renting land from multiple proprietors in the Paris basin.

Recent developments, however, tend more in the direction of a relative equalization of regional property relationships. Wherever tenant farming was prevalent, farmers have tended to buy all or part of their holdings from the owners in order to safeguard their future: this is particularly characteristic of western France. On the other hand, owners of share-cropping holdings or tenant farms have often repossessed the land in their ownership in order to farm it themselves. In areas of owner farming, the large number of farmers' sons who have left very small properties have maintained ownership and often rented them out. Whereas traditional tenant farming is on the decline, the renting of land from members of the same family or between neighbours continues to spread. The overall result is a clear increase in mixed types of tenure, where the farmer owns part of his holding but holds the rest in various types of tenure.

1.2 Classification according to the level of intensification and the degree of integration into the market economy

By level of intensification is to be understood the level of input of capital and labour in a given system of cultivation; intensive systems are distinguished from extensive systems either by massive inputs of capital, or by equally massive inputs of labour, or both. As for the extent of integration into the market economy, it can be defined in relation to the stage reached in the substitution of capital for labour and thus by the level of labour productivity, but, more significant, it also reflects the degree of dependence on the food and agriculture industries. The available data do not permit a direct identification of regional levels of intensification and integration for all systems of production. We must be content with indirect indicators such as the number of male agricultural workers for every 1,000 ha of agricultural land, the gross value added per hectare of agriculturally used land and the amount of borrowed capital per hectare. Figures 20.1–3 tell, on the whole, a similar story. They emphasize the regions of intensive agriculture (whether in terms of capital or labour) in western France (in particular in the Departments of Finistère and Côtes-du-Nord) and in all the departments concentrating on special crops, such as the vineyards, market gardens and fruit of the Mediterranean coastlands, the Bordeaux region and Charentes, the Lyon region, Champagne and Alsace. The Nord region, still characterized by high labour productivity and a high value added per hectare, seems to have invested

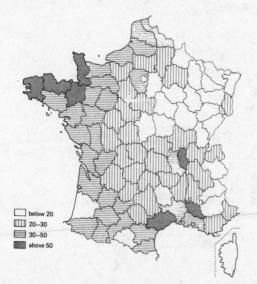

below 20
20–30
30–50
above 50

Figure 20.1 Density of active male population occupied in agriculture, 1975, by department. Males per thousand ha agricultural land. Source: INSEE and statistique agricole annuelle.

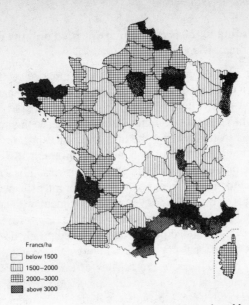

Figure 20.2 Gross value added per hectare of agricultural land, 1975. Source: Ministère de l'Agriculture (SCEES).

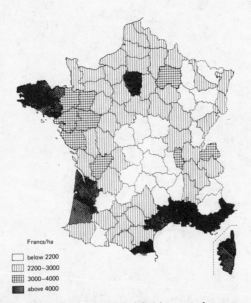

Figure 20.3 Average agricultural indebtedness per hectare, 1977. Source: Caisse Nationale de Crédit Agricole.

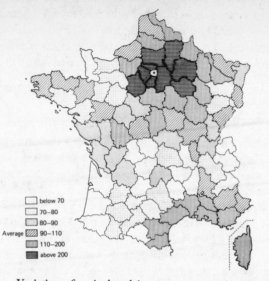

Figure 20.4 Variation of agricultural income per agriculturally active family member, 1975–6–7. Calculation based on: Gross revenue per holding/Work by family member (person/year). Source: SCEES.

less than the regions mentioned earlier. Extensive agriculture is characteristic of the regions of large-scale arable cultivation, of the departments of dairy-farming in the east of the Paris basin, in all departments where cattle are bred predominantly for beef, and in mountain regions. Exceptionally, however, value added is also high in the areas of large-scale arable farming on the plateaus near Paris, but extensification seems to increase in the peripheral departments of the Paris basin (Indre, Cher and Yonne). Geographical disparities in the levels of intensity have changed little in the postwar years; technical progress has allowed the further intensification of systems wherever they were already intensive, and has led to a more extensive agriculture by the reduction of labour requirements per hectare wherever the size of the holdings has allowed.

It is clear that in relation to the energy crisis, attitudes to intensive systems and regions of intensification are no longer quite the same. It is no longer sufficient just to observe that apart from the high-energy horticultural holding the average consumption of energy per hectare increases as the size of holding increases, and thus to deduce that regions orientated towards systems of 'general arable specialization' and 'arable–cattle combinations' have the highest average consumption of energy per holding. It is essential that the efficiency of systems of production be measured not in terms of labour productivity or profitability but in terms of the relationship between the output measured in calories and the calories consumed in the productive process. It is extremely important to realize that much more energy is needed to produce meat and milk than cereals, and that the figures become ever more unfavourable as the systems are intensified and specialized, with industrialized farming having the most unfavourable figures. From this point of view, cereal regions using the extensive system thus seem less vulnerable than regions where intensification has been carried out on the basis of battery units and industrial feedstuffs.

1.3 Classification according to financial results

Farm profitability and the return to labour inputs are clearly the most apt criteria for showing regional disparities in agriculture. The most satisfactory yardstick of a farmer's average income is provided not so much by the gross return per holding as by the gross return per family worker. Figure 20.4 shows that the regions of highest income in agriculture measured in this way are Ile-de-France, Picardy, Champagne, Nord–Pas-de-Calais, as well as the Departments of Eure-et-Loir, Loiret, Côte d'Or and, to a lesser degree, most of the Mediterranean departments. Average incomes per full-time family worker vary between the five poorest departments (Savoie, Ardèche, Ariège, Lot and Lozère), the majority of which are mountain regions, and the five richest (Marne, Seine-et-Marne, Val d'Oise, Essonne and Oise) in the proportion 1 : 6. The southern half of France, except for the Mediterranean departments, is characterized by below-average incomes, all the more pronounced because they are also mountain regions. An intermediate zone, stretching from Brittany to Alsace, is characterized by average incomes. These disparities do not seem to have varied significantly since 1950, either by efforts to modernize and intensify holdings in regions which were initially at a disadvantage or by the great reduction in family labour that has taken place.

The average figures by department tend to smooth out marked internal contrasts. The greater precision afforded by the map of gross income per full-time family worker calculated on the basis of groups of small agricultural regions (Fig. 20.5) makes it possible clearly to distinguish zones of high and low income, bringing out the contrasts between the Mediterranean coast and its hinterland, or between the plateaus and the valleys which cut through them. The peri-urban zones of intensive cultivation also stand out. The average figures have least meaning and it is particularly difficult to talk of a 'rich' or 'poor' region where holdings of great diversity exist side by side, for example retirement or part-time holdings with highly profitable holdings of full-time farmers. But where full-time farming and high incomes per family member are combined, as in the Paris basin, it is certainly possible to speak of an agriculture that gives an adequate return both to the family members and on capital invested.

1.4 Towards an overall agricultural classification

Attempts at defining and mapping agricultural systems are few. Klatzmann (1978)[1] and Bonnamour, Guermond and Gillette (1971)[2] used a combination of criteria, but at different levels of analysis and following different principles. Klatzmann established his classification on the scale of the large agricultural regions, some of them larger than the French administrative regions. He used the three criteria of density of active agricultural population, value added per hectare and value added per worker to produce a ranking in terms of potential, which appeared to reflect the economic results obtained regionally. The second group of researchers, on the contrary, based their interpretation on the finest possible spatial grid (small agricultural regions or groupings of such regions). The criteria selected were those which best revealed the functioning of the agricultural holding, even if this meant the assimilation of each small region to a single 'ideal type' of holding. Many criteria were used (as many as 14), grouped by dominant characteristics (land use, techniques employed, relative significance of livestock enterprises, economic results). The end result was an agricultural regionalization which clearly brought out the spatial diversity of French agriculture, but which also grouped in the same category regions of greatly differing agricultural orientation. Nevertheless some major agricultural realms stand out (Fig. 20.5), for example in northern France the rich, limon-covered plains of the central Paris basin, the crescent shape of the limestone plains which succeed this core area to the east and south from Lorraine to Champagne *berrichonne*, and similarly the plains to the north and in Upper Normandy. In other words, three types of agriculture emerge clearly: the highly productive farms of the limon-covered plains, which have the advantage of an excellent structure and which use the most profitable agricultural systems; the less productive farming of the limestone plains which nevertheless use similar systems, and the painstaking farming of regions such as the Pays de Caux and Flanders, where structures of medium-sized farms facilitate intensive agriculture.

Western France is characterized entirely by systems of low productivity per holding, per head and per hectare, in spite of a very clear trend towards intensification, while eastern France, from Roussillon to Alsace, is characterized by contrasts in systems and productivity.

In all approaches to agricultural regionalization the end result has a character that is closely determined by the method of analysis used. A completely different procedure is used by Gervais, Servolin and Weil (1965),[3] in an approach followed by Lipietz (1977)[4] to which the work of the geographer R. Livet[5] also

[1] J. Klatzmann, *L'Agriculture française* (Seuil, Paris, 1978).
[2] J. Bonnamour, Y. Guermond and C. Gillette, 'Les systèmes régionaux d'exploitation agricole en France. Méthode d'analyse typologique', *Etudes Rurales*, no. 43–44, 1971, pp. 78–169.
[3] M. Gervais *et al.*, *Une France sans paysans* (Seuil, Paris, 1965).
[4] A. Lipietz, *Le Capital et son espace* (Maspero, Paris, 1977).
[5] R. Livet, *Les Nouveaux Visages de l'agriculture française* (Editions Ouvrières, Paris, 1980).

has considerable similarity. A system of 'three agricultures' corresponding to a spatial division into three types of 'agricultural region' is built on a theoretical position which permits the definition of systems of agriculture 'in relation to the place assigned to them in the interregional segregation corresponding to the

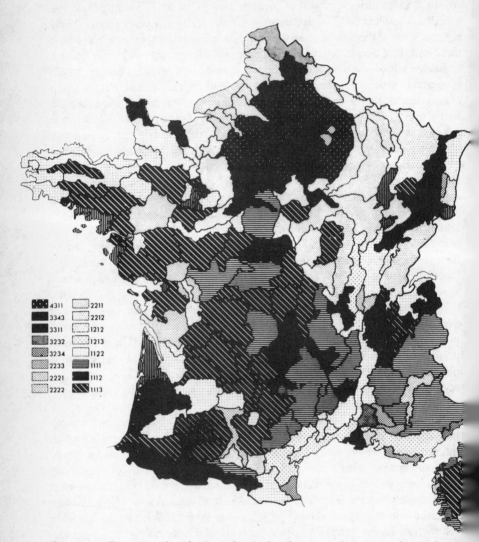

Figure 20.5 Economic classification of agricultural systems, by groups of agricultural regions, 1962. Each group of four digits indicates, reading from left to right: Digit 1: End production by holding on a scale 1–5. Digit 2: End production by man-years on a scale 1–5. Digit 3: End production per hectare on a scale 1–5. Digit 4: Estimated investment on a scale 1–4 (1 = extremely extensive system, 4 = extremely intensive system). Source: *Etudes Rurales*, no. 43–4, 1971, pp. 78–169.

monopolistic stage in the development of classic capitalism'.[6] The 'regions of classic capitalist agriculture' in which agricultural workers are eliminated as the substitution of capital for labour increases are situated mainly in the Paris basin. A second type consists of 'regions of intense transformation of small-scale market production characterized by pressure of a growing population which tends no longer to find an outlet in rural areas'. It is characteristic of Brittany, the Nord region, Upper Normandy and Alsace. A third type is that of 'declining regions, in which subsistence agriculture has not been transformed. Reduced to poverty, but not "proletarianized", an increasingly sparse population of ageing peasant farmers has already witnessed the departure of the young.' The Central Massif, the Pyrenees, the Alps and the eastern fringe of the Paris basin fall into this category.

These divisions, although based on different methodologies, agree in the identification of a number of major agricultural regions, which are unevenly integrated into the general economic system. The profound changes which have taken place in French agriculture from the 1950s onwards have defined ever more sharply these major agricultural regions with their totally different levels of economic integration. We must now examine the extent to which these changes are the result of the agricultural policy carried out since that date by the state and by farmers' organizations.

Agricultural policy since the Second World War

It is difficult to unravel the real agents of agricultural policy, to discover who made the decisions and who carried out the changes, what part can be attributed to successive governments, to particular laws and decrees, to particular ministers or to the European Community. Consideration has also to be given to the influence of farmers' organizations, to the policies of the food and agricultural industry, and to the role of international trade considerations. Agricultural policy, even when it is defined in the strict sense, is far from being a homogeneous and coherent whole. It has many evident contradictions, for example between social objectives and the policy of integration into the economic system, between policies for increasing production and policies for maintaining prices. These contradictions make it difficult to discover the effects of any given measure. As a final complication, the policies set up often have several objectives, or conceal other and more subtle aims under talk of a more obvious goal. This is the case, for example, with policies relating to land ownership and to certain localized policies (for example for mountain areas) which naturally are the concern of farmers but which also reflect the aims of developing and conserving the countryside, a subject of concern to non-farmers also. It is nevertheless possible to single out characteristic periods in the development of agricultural policies and to define turning points when new trends were introduced.

[6] Lipietz, *Le Capital et son espace*.

2.1 Agricultural policy until the 1960s

During the Fourth Republic (1946–58), several policy trends coexisted, reflect
ing contradictions between the paternalistic and protectionist policy inherite
from the pre-war Third Republic, and a modernizing and socially orientate
policy. During this period, which saw a transition of France from poverty to
prosperous, even over-prosperous economy, there was sometimes a discrepanc
between the announced political directions of French government policy and th
measures actually adopted. It was under a socialist government that large-farn
agriculture, that is to say the wheat and sugar-beet producers of the Paris basin
who were predominant in the Fédération Nationale des Syndicats d'Exploitant
Agricoles (FNSEA), won their greatest victory, the indexing of agricultural price
to the prices of industrial products necessary to agriculture. This was, in short,
period of transition, when policies wavered, not only according to the whims o
governments, but also in reflection of the power struggle between the trends o
reformism and protectionist conservation.

One of the main policy objectives involved the encouragement of the purchas
of land by the farmer, the protection of the integrity of the tenant holding b
limiting the power of the landlord, and the strengthening of the peasant holdin
both in the general interest and as a guarantee of liberty for the producer. Thi
strengthening was to be achieved by the modernization of agriculture, th
development of co-operatives and an improved organization of markets. Thes
policies took shape in several measures which did not, however, cover all th
objectives:

(1) The 1946 law on tenancy and share-cropping limited the right of th
lessor to reclaim his property, gave pre-emptive right of purchase to the tenan
made rents compulsorily payable in money and indexed to the price of agri
cultural products.

(2) The First Plan of Modernization and Equipment encouraged the expan
sion of mechanization but also of education in agricultural science and tech
niques, and the restructuring of holdings by the process of consolidation.

(3) The Laniel decrees of 1953 created the first organizations charged wit
the task of maintaining prices by a policy of buying in produce offered below
target price, of stockpiling such produce and selling it back to the market at price
above the target. For wine, the Institut des Vins de Consommation Courante
founded in 1953, is responsible for improving quality.

The second objective of policy consisted of finding solutions to the nev
problems raised by the disposal of surplus produce (especially dairy produce) an
affirming that the setting up of a common market between various Europea
states would make it possible in the long term to solve the question of outlets an
national prices. The negotiations came to a conclusion in 1957 with the signing c
the Treaty of Rome, instituting the European Community.

A third policy objective can be reduced to a simple unconditional option i
favour of price support; it implies a single concept of agriculture which it assume

that every category of farmer is willing to support. The directors of the FNSEA and many Chambers of Agriculture put pressure to bear so that this policy objective should be chosen, requiring high prices and guaranteed markets. In response to this pressure, the automatic indexing of agricultural prices was introduced in September 1957.

During this period, agricultural policy continued to have contradictory elements. One can understand why the 1950–60 decade was characterized by the resumption of an intensive agricultural exodus, by the beginning of mechanization and technical progress, by an expansion in production, and above all by the increasing dominance of the social category of the largest farmers, who gained the greatest advantage from the policy of price support.

2.2 Policy from 1960 to 1970–2

French agricultural policy is almost completely dominated by the concepts embodied in the agricultural orientation laws of 1960–2 and the growth of state intervention, which operates with the support of the farmers' organizations: these have become channels for the transmission of government decisions. The central objective of this policy is 'the integration of agriculture into the national economy' by giving the greatest possible help to family holdings and to the class of middle-sized peasant farmers. The principles of the orientation laws to some extent go back to the very beginning of postwar agricultural policy, but were also inspired by the Federal German system of 'Green plans' for agriculture. The orientation laws called for a complete and coherent agricultural policy, which was to be the instrument of a system of deliberate agricultural planning implemented in a completely different way from policies of the previous period. Moreover, the first decree proclaimed by de Gaulle when he came to power in 1944 was the abolition of the indexing of agricultural prices. This agricultural charter of the Fifth Republic was established by legislation in 1960 and 1962, concerned with agricultural policy directions, equipment, farm structure and tenure, agricultural education, and health insurance for farmers. It was completed by a supplementary law of 1962, the 1966 law on the livestock industry, the 1964 law on contractual organization and organizations of specialist farmers (Interprofession), and in 1966 the redefinition of the policy for agricultural development and popular education. The agricultural policy also included an important and successful component represented by the creation of a system of social insurance (Mutualité Sociale Agricole). We must now consider the principal objectives of these laws, the means of implementing them and the results obtained.

2.2.1 *The restructuring of holdings*

According to the doctrines of the National Centre for Young Farmers (Centre National des Jeunes Agriculteurs – CNJA), the integration of agriculture into a modernized economy was to be secured not by maintaining prices at an artificially high level but by giving dynamic farming families the means of transforming their holdings into efficient, productive enterprises, in particular by increasing the amount of land available. That is why the law defined a 'model' family holding, a viable unit, which must be encouraged to modernize. It is 'a holding in family ownership, occupying two full-time male workers in conditions which allow a rational application of capital and techniques, and capable of providing an adequate return to labour and to capital invested in the land and to working capital'. Such a model holding would accordingly ensure the full employment of those engaged in it and allow them parity of income with other sectors.

Commissions were created in each department to define for each small-scale agricultural region, and in relation to the system of production, the maximum and minimum area of holding considered likely to support the model type of holding as outlined above. Holdings above the upper limit were considered to involve an excessive concentration of land in single control, holdings below the lower limit were considered not to be viable, that is to say, not to qualify for the subsidies to young farmers setting up in farming for the first time, or for loans at special rates of interest from the Crédit Agricole (agricultural bank), or for the Indemnité Viagère de Départ, the special pension for the elderly farmer who gives up his holding. Restructuring thus aims to discourage the proliferation of holdings which are either too small or too large. The second of these two objectives, which aimed to prevent the setting up of large capitalist farms, the expansion of big farmers at the expense of small ones, and the purchase of holdings by people from outside agriculture, has not really been attained.

A policy of increasing the surface area of submarginal farms cannot, however, be achieved unless additional land becomes available and unless there is a proper policy for its allocation. One way of increasing the size of holdings is by the use of abandoned farm land. Since August 1962 any parcel of a maximum area fixed by decree which has not been cultivated for five years may be automatically rented out on request to a neighbouring farmer, the only condition being that the size of his holding should be below the permitted regional minimum.

The general effect of these efforts has been to enlarge the category of medium-sized holdings while helping to eliminate the smallest ones, which had no hope of expansion since it was not financially worth while to hand over land to them. It also had the effect of bringing new young blood into farming. The chief instrument of this land policy was the Société d'Aménagement Foncier et d'Etablissement Rural (SAFER) (see chapter 15, 3.2.1).

The desire to reconcile economic restructuring (requiring units of adequate size) with the preservation of the family farm and with the customary scale of the working team led to the encouragement of a type of agrarian concentration similar to a producer co-operative. The law of 8 August 1962 encouraged the setting up of groupings of farms (Groupements Agricoles d'Exploitation en Commun (GAEC)). These were associations which made possible 'the carrying out of farm work in common under conditions comparable to those which exist in family-type holdings'. Groups of farms have continued to increase and on 31 December 1979 numbered 16,150, working on 1 million ha. Contrary to the intention of the legislation, however, most groups unite only fathers and sons. They have doubtless played their part in the continued existence of the type of family holding described earlier, but have not had much success in 'restructuring' the work team and in preventing an increase in the number of holdings run by the farmer without assistance.

2.2.2 *Agricultural education as a means of modernizing agriculture*

It was the opinion of the legislators that restructuring in favour of the family farm could not succeed without a change in the traditionally conservative mentality of farmers and without a system for disseminating new ideas. The peasant had to be transformed into a businessman, able to master the techniques relating to his special type of farming and to assimilate the results of research. He had also to be able to manage his holding and, by keeping accounts, find a means of making a profit and then know how to reinvest it. Very few farmers had any technical training in agriculture. Admittedly the National Institute for Agronomical Research (Institut National de la Recherche Agronomique – INRA) had been founded in 1946 and had many field stations, laboratories and experimental farms. Other experiments encouraging modernization had proliferated in previous years, among them the mutual education groups known as Centres d'Etudes Techniques Agricoles (CETA), initiated in 1944 in the Paris region. These bring together about 15 farmers who pool their knowledge and share among themselves the task of study and information, with the help of experts from outside as appropriate. The problem was, however, to draw together the various ventures so as to provide a coherent system of agricultural education and the further training of adults capable of disseminating the results of the latest research to the farm population.

Accordingly, the 1960 orientation law provided for a complete reorganization of agricultural education. Agricultural High Schools (*lycées agricoles*) were introduced, while Agricultural Secondary Schools offered shorter courses giving a basic training to future farmers. The number of pupils in public agricultural education increased from 24,000 in 1960 to 47,800 in 1978, without any corresponding decline in the larger numbers in the private sector, most of whom were engaged on shorter courses. At the same time, an organized and hierarchical structure was provided for the dissemination of agricultural information, which was firmly put in the wider context of the drive towards agricultural modernization and development under the charge of farmers' organizations recognized by the government. These measures have contributed to the emergence of a recognizable category of informed and active farmers in the medium size-category.

2.2.3 Market organization and producers' groups

Restructuring and modernization might have resulted in a considerable increase in production with a consequent imbalance between supply and demand and an eventual drop in prices. This could have defeated the whole object of the programme, ruining farmers who had gone into debt in order to modernize. Legislative measures taken in 1958 at the beginning of the Fifth Republic attempted to deal with this problem, while at the same time abandoning the policy of price support. The approach was twofold. There was first of all the creation in 1960 of an organization for directing and regulating the market, the Fonds d'Orientation et de Régularisation des Marchés Agricoles (FORMA). It was responsible for intervening to check the excessive rise or fall of prices and for encouraging some types of production and discouraging others. The other approach was by encouraging the setting up of producers' groups under the supplementary law of 1962. The groups consisted of producers of a particular product in a defined geographical area. They committed themselves to respect a certain number of regulations regarding quantity and quality with the aim of stabilizing prices and providing a better response to the needs of the market. In return they received subsidies and special loans from the Crédit Agricole for storage, processing and marketing.

The initially rapid growth of producers' groups in 1964 and 1965 largely took the form of the recognition of already existing groups such as agricultural co-operatives and similar farmers' organizations, and subsequent progress has been much slower. Between 1970 and 1979 the fastest-growing groups were associations of wine producers, followed by groups in the livestock sector, whereas in the beginning the fruit, vegetable and wine sectors were the most affected (Table 20.1). The plan as a whole contributed to a regularization of prices. It also contributed to a cleaning up of certain sectors of the marketing system, for example cattle merchants and butchers doing their own slaughtering. However, the problems of supply, surplus and deficits are far from having been resolved.

2.3 1972–81

During these years, French agricultural policy again entered a period of uncertainty, reflecting internal contradictions and its failure to overcome some of the problems with which it had been faced. It became increasingly difficult to distinguish between agricultural policy carried out within the national framework and policies relating to the Common Agricultural Policy of the European Community, which affected not only prices but also the structure of holdings and the legal framework. The turning point was reached between the political unrest of May 1968 (which had repercussions on the position of agricultural workers) and the beginning of the energy and monetary crisis that began in 1974. The 1980 agricultural framework-law (*loi-cadre*) marks a break with the principles

Table 20.1 *Development of agricultural producers' groups*

Sector	1964	1968	1970	1975	1979
Fruit and vegetables	65	286	358	397	372
Poultry	27	111	125	159	158
Livestock	15	134	327	502	519
Wine		61	77	101	136
Specialized products		27	36	64	83
Total	109	619	923	1,223	1,268

Source: SCEES.

and objectives that had previously been established. Recognizing certain failures in the attempt to produce a coherently planned agriculture, it moved somewhat in the direction of the free market, regarded by the legislators of the period as the only possible way of allowing French agriculture to respond to the challenges offered by developments in the international context. The principal objectives of the amended agricultural policy are outlined below.

2.3.1 *More selective restructuring of holdings and a greater professionalism*

From 1968 onwards, with the publication of the Mansholt plan, it became apparent that the policy of changing agricultural structures conceived in the 1960s had run into difficulties and was being blamed for the increase in agricultural surpluses. Mansholt attacked the dual error of applying a misguided price policy to structures of production and marketing which were themselves defective. He proposed a programme which combined new policies for prices and marketing with a transformation of farm structures and markets. The size of holdings was to be increased by the creation of 650,000 viable new agricultural units in the European Community (the Six), a reduction by half in the number of farmers, and the creation of a corresponding number of new jobs outside agriculture. At the same time 5 million ha of agricultural land were to be taken out of production and devoted to forest or tourist use, and 3 million dairy cows slaughtered. It is easy to guess the reaction provoked by such an explicitly frank presentation of these radical measures.

The Vedel Report and later the reports of Gunther Thiede were on the same lines and called into question the financial aid which had contributed to the existence of a great number of small 'surplus' producers. They advocated, on the contrary, a policy which welcomed fully competitive holdings only, and which envisaged the disappearance of most of the small producers who cannot be brought under control and whose plight could be alleviated by social measures of a transitory nature.

One measure reflecting the new direction of policy was the introduction in 1974 of agricultural development plans. Special encouragement was given to farmers who planned, over a maximum period of six years, to develop to regionally established standards of scale, capital investment and return to labour inputs. In return, they then have the right to selective financial assistance, to contributions towards projects of capital investment as well as priority in the allocation of any land becoming available for redistribution. These plans for development make it possible to raise the lower threshold of holdings to be restructured. By 31 December 1978, 8,345 development plans had been approved. Holdings with predominantly livestock specialization accounted for 80 per cent of approved schemes. Progress, however, fell considerably short of the achievements of some other Community countries (35,000 plans approved in the German Federal Republic and 18,000 in the United Kingdom).

At the same time, much stricter conditions were attached to grants for the improvement of holdings, for example loans at reduced rates of interest and special modernization loans. Assistance to young people setting up in farming for the first time had been available under the orientation laws, but from 1973 there was a particular concern with the demographic renewal of the farm population. The principle of financial help to young farmers, initially established in mountain areas, was applied over the whole country in 1976 (in 1975 help was given to 3,300 young farmers, in 1978 to 7,300). This effort was reinforced by additional legislation concerned with the status of potential heirs on parental holdings and with providing heirs with the possibility of accommodation outside the parental home. The general objective was the creation of a new category of young farmers capable of entering the competitive arena.

2.3.2 *The opening up of agriculture to external capital, especially in relation to landed property*

The increase in the cost of land has become a handicap even for the new-style holdings which it initially favoured. It acts as a brake on those trying to enter farming for the first time. The activities of the departmental Land Authorities (SAFER) have been criticized not only because they contributed to this rise in prices but also because their intervention has been exclusively directed to the expansion of existing holdings rather than the establishment of new ones. Any economic crisis aggravates this phenomenon because it accentuates the role of agricultural land as a hedge against inflation. Even if the price of land cannot be brought down, the objective is at least to curb its upward tendency by adopting a policy radically different from that followed since 1946.

Measures reflecting this change of direction include the creation of farmers' groups (Groupements Fonciers Agricoles – GFA), as described in chapter 15, 3.2.1. The 1975 remodelling of the law regarding tenant farming increased the security of the tenant farmer and therefore his inclination to invest and buy equipment, while at the same time removing the control on rents.

2.3.3 *Market regulation left to the Common Agricultural Policy and to international competition*

Despite its attachment to planning, Gaullist agricultural policy failed to give a new direction to agricultural production. There has been a succession of policies, farmers being encouraged at different times to produce milk, meat, poultry and fruit. Producers chose their products in a random manner from incomplete information, from the views of agricultural advisers or propaganda from food-processing firms.

The direction taken by the agricultural industry is now effectively decided by the European Community and its Common Agricultural Policy (CAP), requiring the free circulation of products and capital, the negotiation of common guaranteed prices and a common customs tariff for non-Community imports ensuring a certain degree of protection. Import levies maintain the price of imported products at the level of those on the internal market, while export subsidies allow Community producers to receive the European guaranteed price when exporting to world markets. Agricultural production was until the mid-1980s also influenced by a system of Monetary Compensation Amounts set up to smooth out differences of currency between the EEC countries. The CAP is especially favourable to large-scale producers of cereals and requires the French budget to be responsible for a large share of the financing of surpluses and export payments. Similarly, it is the European Community which accentuates regional and national specialization by favouring countries with strong currencies: Federal German agriculture, for example, has expanded rapidly and continually increased its share of surplus production.

The government has tried hard to establish a policy for animal husbandry in order to stimulate the production of meat, which is unable to satisfy French demand. In 1973 an official organization entitled Office National Interprofessionnel du Bétail et des Viandes (ONIBEV) was established to co-ordinate the activities of producers and distributors.

This policy reveals a tendency towards market freedom: the government was unable to retain control over prices since these were considered to be the exclusive concern of the European Community. Furthermore, agricultural prices depend on negotiations in which agriculture represents only part of the issue: for example, agreements with other Mediterranean countries have consequences for the French wine industry; and relations with Great Britain involve the problem of the imports of lamb. The government therefore encourages the growth of competition by providing it with a positive role in regulating markets within the framework of agricultural producers' groups.

These thirty years of an agricultural policy characterized by changing directions are reflected in the geography of agricultural activity. The growing importance of the European Community's Common Agricultural Policy is reflected in the increased regional specialization that has been highlighted above in the analysis of the development of the localization of particular agricultural products. The results, but also the limitations, of the restructuring policies under the orientation laws are shown in the continued existence of regional disparities despite progress in technology. Regions dominated by medium-sized family holdings still predominate, but there has been an infusion of young blood into the farming community.

21

⚜ Non-energy mineral resources

Geology provides France with a range of mineral resources such as few other countries possess. The combination of ancient massifs with sedimentary basins, together with metamorphism and volcanicity, have increased the range of minerals, in both the ancient massifs and the younger fold mountains, although it should be noted that the Pyrenees are much richer in minerals than the Alps. Each region has its endowment of mineral resources, admittedly of unequal value, but which at some period in history contributed to economic activity, attracted industry, stimulated the development of infrastructures and encouraged people to settle there.

1 Products of quarrying

One has to look at the construction materials used before the era of concrete and prefabrication to realize how rich France is in building stones. These include granite, sandstone, lava and the burrstone (*meulières*) of Brie and Beauce. Freestone is drawn from the Jurassic limestones of Lorraine, Burgundy (notably the comblanchien stone of the Côte d'Or), Poitou, Charentes and Caen, also from the Tertiary rocks of the Paris region, such as the *Calcaire grossier*. Slates come in particular from the Department of Maine-et-Loire (France with an annual output of 120,000 tonnes is the leading world producer). There are numerous marble quarries in the Pyrenees (the chief region of extraction), Provence, the Alps, Burgundy, the Boulonnais and the Armorican massif.

Quarries are also the source of lime and plaster, the latter derived from the gypsum of the Paris region and from the Departments of Vaucluse and Bouches-du-Rhône, in southeast France. Quarrying also provides chalk and calcareous clays for cement manufacture; important sources include chalk from the rim of the Boulonnais and from the Oise valley, and calcareous clay from the Vivarais (Le Teil) in the southeastern part of the Central massif. Other quarry products are clays and limons for brick, tile and pottery manufacture, also refractory clays, moulding sands and limestone for use as flux in the iron and steel industries. Alluvial tracts provide sand and gravel, required in large quantities by the construction industries. Sands, according to their variable composition, can be used for a range of purposes; types include building sand and moulding sand. France also exports chalk for use as a filler in the manufacture of paint and in the plastics, rubber and mastic industries.

Most of these resources are dispersed over the whole country. Understandably the chief regions producing building materials are the sedimentary basins: the Paris basin, Alsace, the Aquitaine basin, the Rhône valley, Languedoc and Provence. The extraction of clays for refractory products is more concentrated, occurring in the Paris basin, the Nord region, the Rhône–Saône valley and the Aquitaine basin. Nevertheless France has to import special clays and dolomite, also black granite from South Africa and Scandinavia, mostly for making funerary monuments.

2 Metallic and non-metallic minerals

A complete list of the mineral resources would be of inordinate length. Minerals used in energy production will be referred to later; otherwise mineral production divides conveniently into metallic and non-metallic groups. Iron ore and bauxite are the two most important French mineral resources. Iron-ore reserves are estimated at more than 8,000 million tonnes; most is found in Lorraine and in the Armorican massif, and a small amount in the Pyrenees.

The Lorraine iron-ore field is one of the largest in the world. The Lorraine *minette* is an oolitic mineral situated at the top of the Lias, at the base of the Bajocian limestone. It outcrops for a distance of more than 120 km along the escarpment of the Côtes de Moselle. Its iron content ranges from 27 to 35 per cent, and it is characterized by its phosphorus content. Reserves are estimated at about 6,000 million tonnes of ore, with an iron content of 1,950 million tonnes.

The iron deposits of the Armorican massif by contrast are found in two sedimentary structures: one to the south, in Anjou and Brittany, the other to the north, in Normandy. The ore deposits are folded and fractured, resulting in mining conditions very different from those of Lorraine. On the other hand, the ore has a higher iron content (45 to 50 per cent) and contains no phosphorus. The reserves are also considerable, estimated at about 730 million tonnes of iron content. The iron-ore deposits of western France have, however, suffered from their location, which exposes them to competition from imported ores. They have also suffered from the absence of a local iron and steel industry of any importance, and from an inadequate system of transportation.

Until the 1970s the quantity of iron ore mined in France was low, and it came from many dispersed locations; in 1871 2.2 million tonnes were produced from as many as 64 departments. From 1878 onwards, the possibility of using the Gilchrist–Thomas steel-making process to remove phosphorus from iron ore allowed extraction to be concentrated on the orefields of Lorraine and western France. Peak annual production was 66.9 million tonnes in 1960. Since then output has steadily declined (1982 output 19.4 million tonnes), as a result of competition from extremely rich ores mined in Africa, America and Australia.

Bauxite, the result of the weathering of limestone raised above sea level in the Cretaceous period, is mostly extracted in the Provence–Côte d'Azur region. Probable reserves have been estimated as sufficient for about sixty years of mining at the present rate.

France has about forty deposits of lead and zinc which have been or are capable of being exploited. Their distribution coincides with that of the metamorphic rocks of the ancient massifs, particularly with lightly metamorphosed shales and limestones of the Armorican massif (two deposits), the Central massif, the axial zone of the Pyrenees, the central massifs of the Alps (La Plagne), the Maures (on the Mediterranean coast) and Corsica.

Tungsten ores are extracted in Auvergne, supplying 40 per cent of the country's needs; copper ores are derived from the Rhône Department, gold from Languedoc–Roussillon region and pyrites from the Rhône–Saône.

Potash, formed by the concentration of potassium salts in former lagoon deposits, is mined in a large field in Alsace, between Mulhouse and Guebwiller. Deposits of sodium chloride (common salt), which has important industrial uses, are found in lake deposits of the Triassic period. Salt is mined in Lorraine, Franche-Comté (Poligny and Salins), the Landes, the western Pyrenees and in the Midi–Pyrénées region. The output of these mines is far greater than that of the coastal evaporation pans.

Other minor minerals may produce some degree of local industrial activity, productive of present, potential or past wealth, at least leaving an industrial tradition behind their working. These substances are of unequal value but occasionally of great importance, even though the deposit is isolated or small. Examples include tin, which used to be mined at Saint-Renan, near Brest; sulphur at Marseille and in the Manosque area; and fluorspar used in the chemical and steel industries.

Kaolin, the product of the decomposition of felspar, used in the manufacture of porcelain, is found over a wide area in the Departments of Morbihan, Côtes-du-Nord, Allier, Indre-et-Loire and Dordogne. The talc deposit of Luzenac (Ariège) represents one-fifth of world production.

Exploitation of some mineral resources may have virtually ceased, but their former periods of intensive extraction have enlivened the regions concerned. This was true of the mining of sulphur in Provence, condemned to extinction by the extraction of sulphur from the natural gas of Lacq, and also of the deposits of phosphatic limestone, which have not been worked since the opening of deposits in North Africa.

This catalogue of non-energy-producing minerals found in mainland France must not obscure the fact that French industry is heavily dependent on foreign imports, particularly of antimony, copper, manganese, molybdenum, tungsten, asbestos, phosphates, titanium, vanadium, cobalt, diamonds and platinum. The mineral production of metropolitan France and of its overseas territories meets 15 per cent of national requirements by weight; recycling provides another 30 per cent, leaving 55 per cent to be imported.

Recent difficulties in the balance of payments have led government bodies to accelerate the search for minerals in metropolitan France, and to reopen known deposits. For example, a deposit of copper, lead and zinc was discovered in 1974 at Bodennec, 20 km south of Morlaix in Brittany. The Armorican massif is emerging as a 'mineral province' of some significance, containing, among other minerals, large reserves of titanium.

3 Mineral water

France is extraordinarily rich in mineral waters; there are some 2,000 springs of medicinal waters, of which 1,200 are used in 106 spas. Mineral waters are derived either from deep waters of great age (*eaux juvéniles*) or from water that has infiltrated from the surface, which emerges naturally or by pumping, often after a long journey through faults and fissures. Mineralized waters are particularly associated with ancient massifs affected by volcanic phenomena (Auvergne) or caught up in recent folding (Pyrenees). However, they are also found in the Alps and the Paris basin, where Triassic and Liassic sediments outcrop or are near the surface (Vittel, Forges-les-Eaux). The various mineral waters are very different in chemical composition and alleged beneficial effects.

Mineral deposits and mineral springs have in the past had important geographical consequences, and often still have today. Where they opened up new centres in difficult terrain, such as mountain areas, or in rural areas, they led to the creation of centres of activity which owed nothing to agriculture. Small mining settlements and spas sprang up at random as sites were found or discoveries made. The exploitation of some resources, notably iron, gave rise to the establishment of mines and industrial towns which were discordantly imposed upon the pre-existing rural spatial organization, creating isolated points of industrial tradition in the heart of the countryside.

22

⚜ Energy resources

1 Energy provision and the French energy balance

Energy supply is crucial to economic development, to industrial and urban activities, and to the everyday life of the entire population. Emergencies such as the Suez crisis of 1956, the Arab–Israeli war of 1974 (when the price of oil quadrupled in three months) or even strikes by gas and electricity workers show how dependent our civilization is on energy. The increase in energy production and consumption is the best available measure of a country's economic growth.

The presence or absence of energy resources, their nature and their location condition economy and geography; the energy situation is a determining factor in spatial organization and planning. Until the mid-nineteenth century, not so very long ago in fact, wood, water and wind were the only available sources of energy to supplement human or animal muscles. They were soon to be reinforced by coal, symbol of the industrial revolution. From the beginning of the twentieth century the monopoly position of coal, symbolized by the steam engine and the gasworks, was gradually eroded by hydroelectric power and the electric motor.

The second half of the twentieth century has seen an increase in the overall demand for energy and changes in sources of supply. Table 22.1 shows the changes that have taken place over half a century in the energy balance of France. The near monopoly of coal, which lasted until just after the Second World War, was succeeded by a phase of dual dominance by coal and oil (1960–70), with hydroelectric power accounting for about 10 per cent of the total. Beginning in

Table 22.1 *The changing energy balance*

Percentage of total consumption

	1929	1938	1955	1972	1982	1990[a]		
						A	B	C[b]
Solid fuel	92.1	83	65.2	19.1	18.0	14	11.5	11.0
Oil	5.2	8	25.0	64.9	47.3	28	33.0	33.1
Natural gas	0	0	0.5	8.3	11.3	17	15.5	13.0
Hydroelectricity	2.7	9	9.3	7.7	8.7	6	6.0	7.6
Nuclear power	0	0	0	0	12.7	30	30.0	31.0
Other sources (including new types of energy)	0	0	0	0	2.0	5	4.0	4.3
Total	100.0	100	100.0	100.0	100.0	100	100.0	100.0

[a] 1980 prediction. A: oil 'high' assumption. B: oil 'low' assumption.
[b] 1983 prediction (Ninth plan).
Source: Ministry of Industry, statistical data.

the 1960s, natural gas arrived on the scene, although it was never one of the major sources of energy supply. Much more significant was the reversal of positions within the coal/oil duopoly. During the 1970s oil was becoming the predominant energy source, but this tendency was halted by the oil crisis of 1974. The third important phase in energy supply began in 1975 with the search for an energy policy which would reduce the part played by oil, mostly by an increase in nuclear energy.

These changes in the composition of the energy balance of France took place at the very moment when energy needs and consumption were increasing rapidly. During the first half of the twentieth century, French energy consumption had doubled, rising from 45 million tonnes of coal equivalent in 1900 to 90 million tonnes in 1950. Between 1950 and 1972 energy consumption was increased by a factor of 2.7, approaching 250 million tonnes of coal equivalent. Gas production between 1959 and 1977 increased from 23,000 million to 212,300 million therms. The consumption of electricity has doubled every ten years: in 1930 it was 17,200 million kWh, in 1949 31,000 million kWh, in 1966 107,300 million kWh and in 1979 235,500 million kWh.[1] The result of this growth of consumption and the consequent development of new energy sources was an increased French dependence on external supplies.

In the 1970s France imported between 75 and 80 per cent of her primary

[1] One Watt (W) is defined as the capacity of a machine producing one unit of energy (one joule) per second. 1 kilowatt (kW) = 1,000 W; 1 megawatt (MW) = 1,000 kW; 1 gigawatt (GW) = 1,000 MW; 1 terawatt (TW) = 1,000 GW. A kilowatt-hour (kWh) is a measure of the output of a machine with a capacity of 1 kW; similarly MWh, GWh and TWh are employed. 1 tonne is to be understood as the metric ton of 1,000 kg or 2,204.62 lb. 1 tce = 1 tonne coal equivalent at 7,000 calories per gram. 1 toe = 1 tonne oil equivalent at 10,000 calories per gram.

energy requirements. The bill for oil imports was 21,000 million francs in 1973 and 59,000 million in 1974; by 1982 it had risen to 140,000 million, because of the rise of the price of oil in 1979 and gas in 1980. This dependence on external sources of energy made it necessary to evolve and apply a national energy policy, which, because it involved state supervision of the various producers, became one of the main elements of state intervention in the economy. Energy policy has a variety of basic principles:

1) The discovery of less costly sources of energy.
2) The search for security of supply, involving a diversification in the number of energy suppliers.
3) The development of new forms of energy, in particular solar energy.
4) The reduction of the proportion of imported energy in the total energy supply.
5) The introduction of methods of energy saving and conservation.
6) Development of the re-use of energy used for steam-raising, for example in district heating schemes.
7) Social implications to be considered in the development of all the above options.

The 1974 crisis accelerated the building of nuclear power stations, and their entry into service reduced dependence on imported energy (66 per cent in 1981).

2 Coal

2.1 The location of production

Coal mining in France has a long history; extraction at Decazeville (southern part of the Central massif) began as early as the fifteenth century. Development of the Nord field began in 1734, although its extension into the Pas-de-Calais Department dates only from the nineteenth century. Exploitation of the Le Creusot (Blanzy) field (northeast Central massif) began in 1769, and of La Grand-Combe (southern Central massif) in 1809. The Moselle (Lorraine) field arrived on the scene much later, at the end of the nineteenth century, when the Gilchrist–Thomas basic steel-making process made it possible to use the phosphoric iron ore of Lorraine. Its major growth dates from the years following the Second World War. In 1948 a new field was discovered at Lons-le-Saunier on the edge of the Jura, containing an estimated 250 million tonnes of coal, but it has not been worked.

Coal is derived from sources varying in location, size and quality of output. Table 22.2 indicates the changing output of the fields. Until just after the Second World War France, unlike other important coal-producing countries, had only one really large coalfield, the Nord field.

In most of the fields mining conditions are difficult. The coal seams are deep

Table 22.2 *Changing coal production by field*

Field	1929		1960		1967		1981	
	million tonnes	%	million tonnes	%	million tonnes	%	million tonnes	%
Nord–Pas-de-Calais	34.9	65.0	28.9	50.6	23.4	47.7	3.9	19.6
Lorraine	6.1	11.3	14.7	25.8	15.0	30.6	16.9	54.0
Blanzy	2.8	5.1	2.6	4.6	2.1	4.3	1.5	7.3
Loire	3.8	7.0	3.0	5.3	2.0	4.1	0.2	1.2
Cévennes	2.2	4.0	2.6	4.6	1.7	3.5	0.4	2.2
Aquitaine	1.9	3.5	2.1	3.7	1.6	3.3	0.9	4.7
Provence	0.9	1.6	1.3	2.3	1.7	3.5	1.6	7.9
Auvergne	1.1	2.0	1.1	1.9	0.8	1.6	0.2	1.3
Dauphiné	0.3	0.5	0.7	1.2	0.7	1.4	0.3	1.8
Total	54.0	100.0	57.0	100.0	47.6	100.0	20.2	100.0

Source: Annales des Mines.

(average 480 m), thin (Nord 1.06 m, Lorraine 2 m, Central massif and south 2.2(m, national average 1.59 m), are split by dirt partings and affected by the folding and faulting of the Hercynian orogeny.

Since 17 May 1946 nearly all mines have been nationalized and taken over by Charbonnages de France (French Coal Board). From 1946 to 1968 this organization successfully carried out the gigantic task of dealing with the heavy burdens derived from inadequate pre-war investment, antiquated machinery and war damage. During the 1950s and 1960s modernization produced great changes. The average daily output per man-shift at the coal face rose from 1,226 kg in 1938 to stabilize at about 2,140 by 1966. These figures are proof of the successful effort made by Charbonnages de France to modernize the industry. This success was in large measure due to the concentration of production; in the Nord–Pas-de-Calais field the number of active mines fell from 125 before the war to 59 at the end of 1960 and 41 at the end of 1966. This concentration was facilitated by the rationalization of production made possible by the abolition of divisions between mining concessions formerly owned by different companies. The modern pits typically have an output of more than 2,000 tonnes per day. Productivity was also improved by the electrification of underground operations and by the increasing mechanization of the mining process.

2.2 The crisis in coal

In spite of these efforts, however, the industry has remained vulnerable. Coal, a source of energy which has the advantage that it can be transported and stock-piled, has suffered in comparison with other sources from its slowness in adjusting output to changing demand, and from high transport costs. It also suffers from a poor public image, being associated with unpleasant working conditions, pollution, 'Black Country' development and nineteenth-century industrialization. Another problem is that the types of coal produced in France do not equate with demand. French coalfields do not produce enough anthracite, low-volatile and coking coals, while producing a surplus of coal suitable for general heating purposes, and low-grade coal.

It is therefore necessary for France to import anthracite and coke or coking coal. Even before 1940, imports were considerable, 29 million tonnes in 1913, 35 million in 1930 and 22 million in 1938. Postwar imports were 16 million tonnes in 1960 and 30 million in 1981.

By 1962 it seemed as though the case for coal had been lost:

The price of coal measured in calories tends inexorably to rise. This reflects the steady exhaustion of the deposits, which increases the cost of extraction. It also reflects the employment of a large body of workers whose wages rise in line with the general improvement in the standard of living and in social provision, without a corresponding rise in productivity. Coal cannot achieve the output per head of other sources of energy. Operating costs, moreover, suffer by comparison with the greater flexibility of oil and gas, where the need for storage can sometimes be completely eliminated, where operations can be automated and be interrupted or instantly restarted at need, with consequent reduction in operating costs. Such energy sources also have a psychological appeal, in that they are clean and need not be handled.[2]

French coal production reached its peak in 1958; only two years later a policy was emerging to organize an orderly reduction in output, making possible a redeployment of manpower and the creation of new economic activities in the regions concerned. Between 1960 and 1968, several plans proposed increasingly large reductions in production; in 1968, the objective was 26 million tonnes by 1975 and 10 million tonnes by 1983. The discovery and development of deposits of natural gas in Europe (section 4.1) reinforced this tendency. The 1975 target was in fact achieved by 1973. Between 1947 and 1974 the number of miners fell from 330,000 to 68,000.

The 1974 world energy crisis put coal in a new light. In September 1974, in order to reduce oil imports, the government requested the French coal industry to aim for the highest possible output, concentrating efforts on Lorraine. Revised targets were 20 million tonnes for 1980 and between 15 and 17 million for 1985. However, because of rising wages and declining productivity, the cost of producing coal rose by 20 per cent in two years whereas coal prices on the international market fell. In 1978 it was announced that all production in the Nord coalfield would cease in 1985.

The change of government in 1981 initially resulted in a decision to abandon previous plans; an annual production figure as high as 30 million tonnes was even envisaged. Production of coal was to be subsidized at 40 per cent of cost price. But the reality of the situation gradually made itself felt; target production was

[2] A. Delion, 'Le plan d'adaptation des charbonnages français', *Revue Française de l'Energie*, January 1962, p. 234.

reduced from 18.5 million tonnes in 1982 to 15 million in 1990, to be derived from the Lorraine and Provence fields and from a few pits in the Nord field.

It is clearly difficult for those who must decide on a policy for coal to steer a course between short-term and long-term considerations, between economic rationality and the national need for security of supply, between a purely economic approach and the consideration of social and regional factors. Yet it is an inescapable fact that imported coal costs on average 60 per cent less than coal mined in France. If France is to need coal in the future, it will have to be imported. France is the second world importer of coal after Japan; the principal suppliers are the German Federal Republic, South Africa, Poland, Australia and the United States.

Planning for the future of French coal mining is complicated by disagreement over the true extent of resources of underground coal in France and the absence of any relevant research programme. The Lons-le-Saulnier field remains undeveloped, while Charbonnages de France and the oil companies purchase mines in the United States and Australia. There is also a failure to agree on the underground gasification of coal.

The French mining areas – one would never have called them 'the Black Country' as in England – have played an essential part in the industrialization and development of the country. Large areas have been completely transformed by the mining of coal. The centuries-old rural landscape has been replaced by pithead gear, spoil heaps, open pits and rows of miners' houses. A new landscape has been created, a different society, a different geographical space. Finding a new vocation for these regions and their inhabitants once coal mining has ceased will be a major problem.

3 Oil
3.1 Home oil production

The only French source of oil until after the Second World War was Pechelbronn in northern Alsace; it produced 75,000 tonnes in 1929 and 70,000 in 1948. Operations ceased in 1963. The French and international oil companies were initially concerned only with oil refining, and showed no interest in prospecting for indigenous oil resources. However in June 1947 the Esso-Standard Company registered a claim in the Parentis (Landes) region; the first core impregnated with oil was brought to the surface on 25 March 1954.

In addition to the Parentis fields, about sixty bores were sunk, some of which proved productive; the Burosse-Vialer field in Béarn (foothills of the Pyrénées), discovered in 1979, is said to be capable of an output of 1 million tonnes per year. The total production of the Landes deposits was 2.3 million tonnes in 1962 and 1.4 million tonnes in 1981. Between 1958 and 1959 oil was discovered in Brie (Paris basin) between Gien and Meaux, but production is relatively small: 57,000 tonnes in 1964, 22,000 tonnes in 1979. At the present time prospecting licences cover almost all the sedimentary basins of France. Home oil production has grown rapidly, from 151,000 tonnes in 1950 to 885,000 tonnes in 1955, 1.9 million tonnes in 1960 and 2.9 million tonnes in 1965, but it is far from meeting national demand. After 1967 production declined sharply (236,000 tonnes in 1981).

France is almost totally dependent on oil as a source of energy; imports amounted to 134 million tonnes in 1973 and 76 million tonnes in 1982. French sources of overseas oil reflect both fluctuations of French foreign policy and the sequence in which new fields have been opened up throughout the world. Particularly favoured sources are the former French colonies, clinging to the advantage of membership of the franc currency zone. Of significance also have been favoured relationships with various North African states (the French oil companies in Algeria were expropriated in 1971), with Middle Eastern countries and subsequently with Mexico and Venezuela.

This dependence also explains the early formulation and originality of French policy with regard to oil. The organization of the petroleum market dates from the law of 30 March 1928, giving the French state a monopoly of petroleum imports; the state then granted import licences to the various oil companies. During and after the Second World War the French government set up companies for oil exploration and production. In addition to operations in mainland France, French companies opened up the Sahara field in pre-independence Algeria, and subsequently took an active part in the search for oil in many foreign countries. France has shared in the development of North Sea oil, which began in 1964 and where the first oil was produced in 1975; French companies were first engaged in the Ekofisk field in the Norwegian sector, and later in the British sector.

3.2 Oil refining

Until 1928 France had only five small oil refineries. Under the oil legislation of that year, French oil refining was given customs protection against imports of refined petroleum products, and by 1938 capacity had reached 8 million tonnes a year. All the refineries were destroyed in the war. Postwar development of the industry was given impetus by the Monet reconstruction plan, and, in response to rising demand, capacity increased rapidly from 13 million tonnes in 1950 to 43.6 at the end of 1961, 96.8 at the end of 1968 and 171.2 at the beginning of 1978, derived from 24 refineries.

After 1963, refinery location changed considerably in response to the anti-cipated increase in demand and the formation of the European Community. Earlier locations had all been coastal, but the new refineries were built in the heart of the continent, linked by pipeline to the oil ports. Typical of the new locations are Feyzin near Lyon, and the refineries at Herrlisheim and Reichstett, near Strasbourg, which not only supply eastern France but export to Switzerland

and to the German Federal Republic. A second generation of inland refineries came into operation with the opening of Vern-sur-Sèche near Rennes (1965), Grandpuits near Paris (1967), Gargenville in Vexin (1968), Valenciennes (1969), Haucencourt between Metz and Thionville (1970), and Vernon (1970).

Conditions of oil supply in France were drastically changed after the 1974 energy crisis. The development of oil refining in the overseas oil-producing countries, the rise in imports of refined products, often at favourable prices, and the decline in home demand led to the closure of four refineries in the period 1978–82. Oil-refining capacity was reduced to 141 million tonnes by the beginning of 1983.

4 Gas
4.1 From manufactured gas to liquefied natural gas

Gas was initially a by-product of blast furnaces, coking plants and oil refineries. Much of the gas produced in this way is used on the spot by industry and does not appear in the statistics of gas extracted, manufactured or sold. Gaz de France (French Gas Board), created as part of the nationalization measures of 1946, was the successor to countless companies formed for the manufacture and distribution of town gas. In the following twenty years the gas industry underwent profound changes. Previously the unsightly, inevitably ill-sited gas holder was a common sight in even the smallest town; the gasworks, fed by coal, was one of the earliest of the amenities of modern urban life! There were 546 gasworks in 1946, rarely distributing over a radius of more than 30 km. The immediate aims of the policy of Gaz de France were the closure of the oldest gas-making plant, the construction of modern works, the development of distribution networks radiating from large central gasworks and the installation of plants to make town gas from propane.

This policy was overtaken by the arrival of natural gas, which brought about the closure of almost all coking plants and plants making town gas from coal. In a few years natural gas took an almost exclusive share of the market; output of refined natural gas was 246 million cu m in 1950, 2,984 in 1960 and 7,871 in 1978.[3]

Natural gas in France is found in two neighbouring fields of unequal size at the foot of the Pyrenees: the Saint-Marcet and Charlas field, opened in 1942, and the Lacq field. There in 1951 drilling to a depth of 3,500 m discovered the vast reserve of gas known as 'Lacq profond' (the Lacq deep reservoir). Recoverable reserves were estimated at 200,000 million cu m, the equivalent of about thirty years of production. The utilization of the Lacq gas presented considerable technical difficulties, because of the depth of the deposit (3,000–5,000 m), its high temperature (140 °C), its pressure (670 kg to the sq cm) and the composition

[3] Data relating to quantities of gas are increasingly expressed in kWh (1 kWh = 0.86 therm; 1 therm = 1 million calories).

of the gas, which has a high content of carbonic acid gas and especially of sulphuretted hydrogen (15 per cent).

Lacq by itself was not, however, a sufficiently exceptional discovery to change the whole energy structure of France for decades to come; it was left to other deposits at home and abroad to provide a relatively long-term security of natural-gas supply. Since 1965 discoveries in the neighbourhood of Lacq at Meillon, Saint-Faust, Pont d'As and Rousse have added 110,000 million cu m of probable reserves to those of Lacq. The running down of Lacq is planned to begin in 1982–3 and to continue for about twenty years.

In spite of discoveries within France, the bulk of natural-gas supplies must come from abroad. In the space of two decades a variety of deposits have been discovered.

(i) Algeria. Enormous reserves were discovered at the same time as oil; at Hassi R'Mel reserves were more than 800,000 million cu m, and total resources far exceeded possible North African demand. There were two possible solutions to the problems of transporting the gas to the European market. One possibility was by pipeline; there were experiments in the laying of pipelines in the Mediterranean at a depth of 2,500 m. The other possibility was transport by gas tanker, in liquid form at low temperature. In 1962 the Compagnie Algérienne de Méthane Liquide (Algerian Company for Liquid Methane – CAMEL) built a liquefaction plant and since March 1965 the liquid gas tanker *Jules Verne*, with a total capacity of 25,000 cu m, has been in operation between the Algerian port of Arzew and Le Havre, where installations for methane storage have been built. A second methane terminal at Fos-sur-Mer (Marseille) receives Saharan gas from the port of Skidda (1972). A third terminal at Montoir-de-Bretagne, near Saint-Nazaire, entered service in 1981.

(ii) The Netherlands. In 1963 the discovery and rapid development of a major deposit of 2,000,000 million cu m at Groningen, in the north of the country, led to modification in the reliance on the Sahara deposits. Southern France being already satisfactorily covered, it was now the turn of northern France to be supplied either by way of the natural-gas terminal at Le Havre or by pipeline from the Netherlands. Since October 1967, 5,000 million cu m of gas have been supplied annually from the Netherlands; by 1967 the figure had risen to 7,000 million cu m, under an agreement to provide 185,000 million cu m over a period of twenty years. The Groningen deposit will be exhausted in the course of the 1980s.

(iii) North Sea. In 1975 the Ekofisk field in the Norwegian sector began production, with reserves of 20,000 million cu m, supplying 35,000 million kWh to France, followed by the Frigg field in 1977, with reserves estimated at 200,000

million cu m, resulting in an annual production of 15,000 cu m. The life of the field is estimated at twenty years.

(iv) The USSR. In theory France should have received 2,500 million cu m of gas annually from the USSR since 1976. In reality France has received an equivalent quantity of gas from the Netherlands, which had been earmarked for Italy. In compensation Italy receives an equivalent quantity of Soviet gas. From 1980, however, Soviet gas has been arriving in France by way of Czechoslovakia and the German Federal Republic at the rate of 4,000 million cu m annually. From 1984 onwards France was destined to receive 8,000 million cu m annually from western Siberia. Signing of the contract for this supply in 1982 had to overcome political hesitations about the wisdom of becoming dependent on an eastern bloc source for such a large portion of energy requirements.

In 1982, out of a total natural-gas supply equivalent to 281,000 million kWh, home production accounted for 25 per cent, imports for 75 per cent (Algeria 25.9 per cent, the Netherlands 20.5 per cent, and the Norwegian North Sea 9.9 per cent). By 1990 the share of the USSR will probably be more than a third.

5 Thermal and hydroelectric power generation
5.1 Production

Electricity occupies a special place among sources of energy because of its extraordinary rate of growth and the way that the extent and variety of its possible uses make it a universal source. The unique characteristic of the supply of electricity is that it cannot be stored; it requires a system of distribution making it instantaneously available in every part of France. Because of its widespread availability and the variety and flexibility of its use, the demand for electricity is characterized by marked variations between off-peak and peak periods. These may be daily, with peak demand between about 0800 and 1700, weekly or seasonal.

Until the advent of nuclear power France relied on both thermal generation and hydroelectric generation. After 1955 thermal power became the more important of the two, because good sites for hydroelectric plants were becoming hard to find, and because of the increasing length of time required to bring such plants into operation. It also seemed desirable that northern France (where hydroelectric possibilities are few) should to some extent be provided with its own sources of electric power. Other motives included the provision of an outlet for low-grade coal, and the use of energy sources other than coal in thermal power stations, such as blast-furnace gas, natural gas and heavy fuel oil.

Although electricity production was nationalized in 1946, Electricité de France (French Electricity Board) is not the sole producer. Thermal power is also generated at coal mines, oil refineries, and at large iron and steel, paper and textile plants. Similarly, hydroelectric power is generated by the Compagnie

Nationale du Rhône (responsible for the improvement of navigation and power generation on the river) and by large plants in the electro-chemical and electro-metallurgical industries. French Railways also own plants, traditionally concentrated in the Pyrenees. However, the proportion of total power output derived from Electricité de France has steadily increased.

5.2 Types of power stations
5.2.1 Thermal plants

Thermal power stations are located either at energy sources (coal or lignite mines, coal-importing ports, oil refineries, iron and steel plants) or on navigable waterways near centres of consumption. Plants are invariably located in relation to supplies of water, required in great quantities for cooling purposes. Most thermal generating capacity is located in the Nord and Paris regions. However, western and southwestern France have an increasing role in thermal power generation, because of the location of plants in relation to oil refineries and the Lacq gas field. New thermal plants have also been constructed on the northwest coast adjacent to oil refineries and the Dunkerque steel plant. The decisions to build new thermal stations at Cordemais (Loire-Atlantique Department) and at Gardanne, on the Provence coalfield, were in response to the policy to make greater use of coal in electricity generation.

Thanks to technical progress (a thermal plant is usually outdated and in need of replacement within 15 years) thermal plants now have an installed capacity greater than that of the biggest water-power plants. New technology plus economic considerations have brought about an escalation in the size of generating sets. Between 1951 and 1960, 125 MW generating units were standard, but by 1978 1,300 MW units were normal.

5.2.2 Hydroelectric plants

Hydroelectric output increased from 16.2 TWh in 1950 to 63.4 in 1978 and 67.9 in 1982. The main producing regions are the Jura and northern Alps, the Central massif, the Pyrenees, the southern Alps and the Rhône and Rhine valleys.

Hydroelectricity is particularly relied on for the provision of power at periods of peak demand; accordingly there is a tendency to build plants with an installed capacity out of all proportion to what they could sustain were they to be operated continuously.

Hydroelectric plants can be classified according to the following characteristics:

(i) Height of fall. Alpine high-fall plants are fed by pressure pipelines having falls of 200 m and more. Medium-fall plants have drops of 20–200 m. Low-fall plants, with drops of under 20 m, are built on rivers with a large volume of flow.

(ii) Type of structure producing the fall. This may be a simple diversion, a lateral canal beside a river, the capture by a leat of a series of streams descending from the mountainside above the plant, or a dam creating an artificial reservoir.

(iii) The nature of the power generated. This may be continuous base-load power (Donzère-Mondragon on the lower Rhône), power generated only at certain seasons of the year, power at peak periods (Serre-Ponçon on the upper Durance), or a mixture of types (Génissiat and Seyssel on the upper Rhône). The classification of plants by the type of power generated is further explained below:

(i) Base-load, run-of-stream plants. These involve the creation of an artificial difference of level, generally of only a few metres (26 m at Bollène on the lower Rhône). The necessary fall is created either by a barrage raising the level of the whole stream, or by diverting water upstream into a lateral canal or leat, which, having maintained a higher level than that of the main stream, ultimately rejoins it by passing through the turbines of a power-station. The storage capacity of run-of-stream plants is virtually non-existent, filling in under two hours, so that effectively whatever flow is available from the stream must be used immediately. Such plants are used for base-load generation, since otherwise the available energy would be wasted. The greater part of run-of-stream power comes from the Rhine and Rhône rivers.

On the Rhône below Lyon, improved sections of the original course plus periodic canal loops regularize the river, making it navigable while at the same time raising its level above the turbines of the power-station.

(ii) (a) Intermittent power generation: seasonal storage. The reservoirs of these works accumulate water in periods of high stream flow, having a capacity of at least 400 hours of turbining. The water so stored can be used for electricity generation at periods of low flow, thus regularizing output on a seasonal basis. Typical of this category are the strings of plants along the Alpine valleys, the plants of the Central massif and, to a lesser degree, of the Pyrenees. The autumn rains of the Central massif and the summer rains of the northern Alps are stored for use in the winter period of peak demand. In the Mediterranean area, as at Serre-Ponçon, spring rainfall is stored to generate power and to provide water for irrigation in the dry summer months.

Hydroelectric developments of this type have changed greatly in recent years. The isolated dam built at a spot where natural conditions are particularly favourable has been replaced by the comprehensive development of the whole of a basin. The downstream valley dam is increasingly giving way to the innovative exploitation of the mountains and headwaters. Here water may be brought through tunnels either to reservoirs or directly to the power-stations from the catchment areas of other river systems, from glaciers, lakes or mountain streams. Small power-stations are being replaced by collectors which concentrate the available water into a few particularly well-sited plants. This system makes it possible to reduce the number of dams constructed in the main valleys downstream, thus avoiding the difficult financial and social problems raised by the compulsory purchase of land and the drowning of whole villages (Tigues, Serre-Ponçon).

(ii) (b) Intermittent power generation: daily storage. These stations have a lower storage capacity (between 2 and 400 hours); they store water at night in order to generate power for daytime use. They are mostly situated in the mountains, but in downstream locations, and are important because of the large volume of water that passes through their turbines. Genissiat on the upper Rhône is an example of the type of plant which can accumulate enough water to keep its turbines going for five hours a day. The mountain basins with their high precipitation in the form of both rain and snow have a major role in this type of power generation.

New techniques have widened the range of possibilities for hydraulic power generation. For example, pumped storage plants use water almost in a closed circuit, utilizing cheap off-peak power to pump water to a high-level reservoir, which is then used to produce electricity at times of peak demand. The Coche plant in Savoie, opened in 1978, is an example of this type. New developments such as this could produce drastic changes in the future map of hydroelectric power production. From 1985 onwards it is anticipated that nuclear power plants will produce a summer surplus of power of 5–6 million kWh, which will be available for use in pumped storage plants.

6 Nuclear power
6.1 Uranium production

Uranium can be derived from a great variety of ores found in a wide scatter of mineral deposits; prospecting for uranium in France is still far from complete. The deposits are dispersed throughout the Central massif, the Vendée massif (Armorica), the Vosges, Lower Languedoc, Morbihan (Armorica) and eastern Provence. The map of uranium mining is constantly changing; proved reserves amount to 65,000 tonnes of uranium content, and possible reserves to 100,000 tonnes. Estimated consumption up to the year 2010 is put at 250,000 tonnes, necessitating imports of between 100,000 and 150,000 tonnes. Current imports come mainly from Niger (1,400 tonnes per year) and Gabon (700 tonnes per year).

6.2 Nuclear power generation

The development of nuclear power generation involves the mastery of a whole new technology, raising many problems with regard to choice of reactor type and the location of production. Problems are not only technological; every discussion and decision is overshadowed by both a good deal of myth surrounding every question relating to the atom, and the historical reality of the bomb which fell on Hiroshima.

The technology of nuclear power does not only involve the construction of nuclear power stations. Prior to power generation, it is necessary to produce enriched uranium in plants which have to be on a very large scale in order to be economic, involving massive capital expenditure. At first France relied on supplies of enriched uranium from the United States and the USSR. Then, together with Spain, Italy, Belgium and pre-revolutionary Iran, France originated the Eurodif plan, setting up the Tricastin enrichment plant in the lower Rhône valley, which began production in 1979 and which was destined to reach full production in 1985. By then a second enrichment plant, Coredif, will probably be operational, perhaps located at Gravelines.

Subsequent to nuclear power generation, reprocessing plants are beginning to appear. Instead of storing the spent uranium derived from the generating process, it is reprocessed to recover uranium and plutonium, leaving the radioactive products of nuclear fission as a final waste material. France, together with the United Kingdom, is ahead of the United States in this downstream technology. There are two reprocessing plants in France, at La Hague (Cotentin peninsula) and Marcoule (lower Rhône valley). The La Hague plants reprocess spent uranium not only from French power-stations but from other countries, including Switzerland, Japan and the German Federal Republic.

The production of nuclear energy for purely peaceful purposes involves the paradox that at several stages in its technology (heavy-water plants, uranium enrichment plants, reprocessing plants and fast breeder reactors) plutonium is produced, which can be used as the raw material for the production of nuclear weapons.

Although nuclear electricity was first produced as early as 1956 on an experimental basis, the French nuclear programme got off to a slow start. The Ministry of Finance was alarmed to see Electricité de France about to launch into expenditure far greater than that required for conventional power-stations. In addition there was a long debate about the cost of electricity generation when using the various energy sources. It was estimated that, in the conditions prevailing in 1979, the cost of a kWh produced in a 1,300 MW nuclear plant would be 13.5 centimes, as compared with 23 centimes for a coal-fired plant and 35 centimes for a plant based on oil. The oil crisis of 1974 and the subsequent price increases, coupled with the desire to strengthen the country's independence in matters of energy supply, finally ended the debate. In 1982, 39 per cent of the output of Electricité de France was already nuclear, a proportion destined to rise to 75 per cent by the year 1990.

Between 1970 and 1983, 51 reactors were either completed or under construction; in 1980, reactors were being completed at the rate of six a year. The political changes of 1981 brought to power men who were very hostile to everything 'nuclear', but as in the case of coal, realism modified electoral promises and ecological sensitivities. It was decided to taper off the rate of building reactors, with three to be completed in 1982 and one in 1985. The foreseeable excess generating capacity (50,000 million kWh by 1990) will require great efforts to stimulate consumption, especially in industry and by export to neighbouring countries. It will also result in the closure of many thermal power-stations.

6.3 The location of nuclear power-stations

Figure 22.1 shows the number and distribution of nuclear power-stations, including those in existence, those definitely proposed, and possible sites. The siting of nuclear power plants poses different problems from those involved in other types of plant. In addition to common factors such as the very high water consumption, requiring either the use of sea water or access to a steady, abundant or adequately regularized river flow, there are factors specifically related to the atom and to the risks of atomic radiation consequent on a nuclear accident which have made public opinion extremely sensitive in this matter. Every proposal to construct a nuclear power-station arouses opposition from anti-nuclear and ecological organizations. Electricité de France was not prepared for this opposition, which was of a different order from that aroused by its plans for conventional plants. Its officials and engineers are becoming belatedly convinced of the importance of informing the public and of public consultation with regard to factors which are relevant to the quality of life.

The search for sites for nuclear power-stations takes into account many different factors, such as geological conditions, the possibility of earthquakes, the risk of floods, the proximity of built-up areas and establishments that might be put at risk, prevailing winds and their force, the impact on the local environment, the existence of outlets for the secondary use of steam produced, and proximity to markets.

By 1985, two-thirds of the new nuclear power-stations will be located on rivers and a third on the coast. Nuclear energy will not therefore depart from the existing unequal distribution of electricity production. In the more distant future technological developments may change the situation: for example, there could be 'dry' cooling towers which would not need water, or fast breeder reactors producing only a small amount of radioactive waste. Moreover, fast breeder reactors, like Phénix at Marcoule (lower Rhône), produce a lower degree of heating of both water and air, and are almost entirely 'clean' with regard to radiation. Super-Phénix, northeast of Lyon, was due for completion in 1983.

Nuclear power makes it possible for the first time to envisage the generation of electricity in remote areas which up to now had to import supplies. Apart from

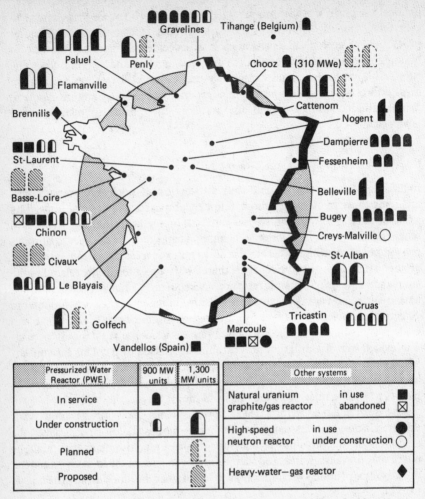

Pressurized Water Reactor (PWE)	900 MW units	1,300 MW units	Other systems		
In service	∎		Natural uranium graphite/gas reactor	in use ∎ abandoned ⊠	
Under construction	◗	∩	High-speed neutron reactor	in use ● under construction ○	
Planned		⬚	Heavy-water—gas reactor	◆	
Proposed		⬚			

Figure 22.1 Atomic power stations in France. Source: Francis Nallier, *Le Matin*.

questions of industrial location, the indirect repercussions of the presence of power-stations in terms of the availability of steam or hot water are only beginning to be perceived.

7 New types of energy

The problems created by the difficulty of ensuring a regular supply of oil, and by the rapid exhaustion of sources of energy such as natural gas, have drawn attention to the search for alternative sources of energy and to the re-evaluation of existing ones. Alternative sources include:

i) Bituminous shale. The new energy situation has again focused attention on the possibilities of the use of bituminous shale. France was the first country to establish the production of bituminous shale, but the industry did not survive competition from the abundant supply of cheap oil. The last active mine, near Autun, was closed as recently as 1957. In December 1973 the government formed a Groupe d'Etudes des Roches Bitumineuses to research the possibilities of bituminous shales.

ii) 'Green' energy. Wood is the oldest source of energy, provided through the centuries by the rational management of forest and by the use of coppice systems. Average annual production is of the order of 3 cu m of wood per hectare; total production is estimated at 8 million tonnes of oil equivalent (toe). It ws decided in 1979 to increase the annual output from French forests from 30 million to 40 million cu m.

Gas can also be produced by the fermentation of straw, vegetable refuse and dung. Potential annual production is estimated at 50 million tonnes of dry matter.

It is also possible to derive energy from cultivated plants, including sugar beet (alcohol), maize (methanol) or Provençal canes (reed). These 'green' energy sources do not, however, seem destined to play more than a marginal and highly localized role in energy supply.

iii) Tidal energy. After many years of research and hesitation, Electricité de France was persuaded in 1960 to undertake the construction of the tidal power-station at La Rance, on the north coast of Brittany, a modern version of the old tide mills. The Rance estuary was closed a few kilometres south of Dinard by a dam in which are fixed 24 turbines operating on both the rising and the falling tide. Since 1967 the plant has provided a capacity of 240,000 kW (540 million kWh annually) for the French power grid. This output is less than would be provided by a link between the Mont-Saint-Michel bay and the Chausey islands, which could provide 20–25 million kWh. Considerations of cost, however, and above all of the impact on the littoral and maritime environments, have repeatedly caused this plan to be shelved.

iv) Geothermic energy. This also has a long history; since the Middle Ages the inhabitants of Chaudes-Aigues (Central massif) have used the water from a thermal spring for heating purposes. Attempts to use geothermal energy are already in existence, for example in the Paris basin, the Central massif and Alsace.

v) New hydroelectric possibilities. Whereas since the 1960s and the era of cheap oil it had been accepted that France had no more hydroelectric sites worthy of development, we are now witnessing a rediscovery of hydroelectric power possibilities. Plans are being resurrected that had previously come up against

opposition on the grounds of ecology, economics or tourism. The accent
however, is put on a change of scale; several thousand small sites equipped with
micro power-stations could be installed and provided with turbines delivering
less than 2,000 kWh per year, which would provide 6,000 million kWh. It is no
difficult to imagine the effects that such plans would have on the environmen
and the opposition that they would arouse from ecologists, anglers and canoeists

(vi) Wind power. In 1980 Electricité de France installed a wind-powered
generator on the island of Ouessant (Ushant); unfortunately the Atlantic gale:
got the better of it after only a few months. There are plans to reintroduce wind
power into electricity production. It has been calculated that the power of the
1,800 hydroelectric plants existing in France today is 500 times greater than that
of the 80,000 windmills – on average two to a commune – recommended by
Vauban in 1694. Some 40 million windmills would therefore be necessary, more
in fact if they were not interconnected, in order to provide power equivalent to
that of the present stock of French hydroelectric power-stations, providing 7 per
cent of the total energy requirements of France in 1979.

(vii) Solar energy. This appears to be the most favoured type of new energy. It has
all the qualities needed to satisfy the ecologists; it is clean and 'free'. In 1979
however, the government estimated that it would satisfy at best 5 per cent of
French energy needs for the year 2000 (17 million toe). It is still impossible to
foresee the direction that might be taken by solar technology. It is just as possible
to envisage a proliferation of small plants either providing for all energy
requirements or supplementing existing sources, each supplying a single apartment block on a domestic scale, as it is to envisage the construction of large sola:
power plants in southern France, where two sites have been secured, Tergas
sonne in Cerdagne and Ajaccio in Corsica.

It is quite clear that energy from coal and oil is not easy to replace; the
substitution of one type of energy for another, especially in the case of new types
of energy or technological innovations, always poses problems of cost, capital
investment and time-scale, to say nothing of radical changes in our life-styles.

8 Energy and geography

Until the discovery of coal and the introduction of the steam engine, energy
sources were widely dispersed: wood and charcoal from the forests, wind power
and water power provided a multiplicity of points of industrial production. This
dispersed industrialization was destroyed by the use of coal in the industria
revolution. The difficulty and the cost of transporting coal encouraged the
concentration of economic activities and population. The arrival of electricity
scarcely changed the distribution map; all that happened was that a few new

dustrial users set up near hydroelectric plants. Western France appeared to be creasingly neglected.

As a result of the energy explosion of the 1960s, which provided cheap and oundant power from oil, natural gas and electricity, the cost of energy ceased to e an inhibiting factor in the choice of industrial location or the selection of a articular industrial process. This period is also characterized by an increase in rban growth, by increased automobile ownership, by the development of omestic air travel, by the growth of second homes and the expansion of tourism, l of which involved not only a high level of overall consumption but a high level energy use. Especially with regard to individual means of transport and cheap etrol, the spatial planning of society failed to take account of distance and the eds of public transport.

Since 1974 there has been a brutal reawakening. All previous values have been -examined, and with them all the principles of spatial planning; concentration stead of dispersion is now favoured, as is the use of public transport instead of dividual mobility. Building materials which provide efficient insulation are eferred to walls of glass. Losses sustained by transporting energy over great stances are to be avoided. It is still too early to know whether these changes are stined to have profound repercussions on the geography of France. It is, owever, important to reflect on these issues, owing to the long time-space and e uncertainties involved in geographical change. On the other hand, the energy ogrammes proposed by certain individuals, political organizations or trade nions question the present social and economic organization of society, and nce its geographical expression.

23

✤ The structure of industry

In 1975, 7.9 million workers were engaged in industrial occupations in France
figure which represented 39.5 per cent of the economically active population a
15 per cent of the total population. The corresponding figure for the Unit
Kingdom was 12 million persons in industrial employment, constituting 47.5 p
cent of the work force and 22 per cent of the total population, and for the Germ
Federal Republic 13.5 million people in industry, amounting to 50 per cent of t
active population and 23 per cent of the total population.

On 1 January 1980 France had 752,228 industrial establishments. Of thes
362,862 employed no paid workers (288,901 in 1966) and 297,404 between o
and ten workers; only 91,962 establishments employed more than ten worke
Three characteristics of French industry thus emerge: it occupies a relative
modest place in the French economy, industrialization is less intense than
neighbouring countries, and there is a high proportion of small or medium-siz
industrial establishments.

1 The branch structure of industry

The importance of an industry can be measured in various ways: by numbe
employed; by the volume of output, either by weight or value; by turnover; or
the area covered by industrial plants. These facts provide differing but com
lementary pictures of the branch structure of industry, which will here
investigated by using figures on employment, on the number of industr

establishments, and the relationship between the two. On 1 January 1980 the industrial branch with the largest number of establishments was baking and confectionery (53,680), following by the branch 'construction of automobiles and other forms of land transport' (35,001), which includes repairing garages, and then by printing and publishing (25,192). Building and construction occupied a very special place with 399,593 establishments under the heading 'building and civil and agricultural engineering industries'. At the other end of the scale the industries with the smallest number of establishments are armaments (43), tobacco processing (49), the manufacture of artificial and synthetic fibres (52) and iron-ore mining (87). Between these extremes the numbers of establishments differ greatly from branch to branch, in part because of the arbitrary nature of the industrial classification but above all because of the diverse forms taken by industry and whether the activity concerned occurs throughout the country or is highly distinctive and specialized.

2 The spatial distribution of economic activity

However surprising it may seem, information relating to the spatial distribution of economic activity in France is not easily accessible. Since 1966, the year of the

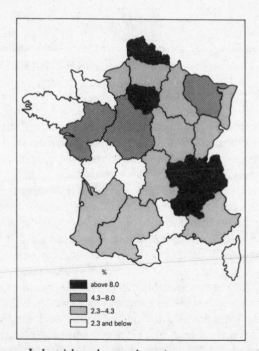

%
- ▮ above 8.0
- ▨ 4.3–8.0
- ▢ 2.3–4.3
- ▢ 2.3 and below

Figure 23.1 Industrial employment by region, as percentage of total national employment, 1983. Source: *Les Cahiers Français*, no. 211, 1983.

Table 23.1 *Industrial employment by region, 1981*

Region	Industrial employment[a]		Industrial employment (1981) as percentage of total employment (1982)
	Thousands	%	
Alsace	159	3.8	10.2
Aquitaine	136	3.2	5.2
Auvergne	105	2.5	7.9
Brittany	97	2.3	3.6
Burgundy	134	3.2	8.4
Centre	196	4.6	8.7
Champagne–Ardennes	128	3.0	9.5
Franche-Comté	133	3.1	12.3
Ile-de France (Paris)	932	22.1	9.3
Languedoc–Roussillon	59	1.4	3.0
Limousin	47	1.1	6.4
Lorraine	235	5.6	10.1
Midi–Pyrénées	117	2.8	5.1
Nord–Pas-de-Calais	381	9.0	9.7
Normandy, Lower	87	2.1	6.4
Normandy, Upper	172	4.1	10.4
Pays de la Loire	223	5.3	7.6
Picardy	166	3.9	9.5
Poitou–Charentes	88	2.1	5.6
Provence–Alpes– Côte d'Azur–Corsica	144	3.4	3.4
Rhône–Alpes	488	11.6	9.8
France	4,227	100.0	7.8

[a] In establishments with 20 employees or more, excluding agriculture and food, building, construction and defence industries.
For location of regions see Figure 13.3.

last non-computerized census of industrial establishments in France, INSEE has not released any statistical breakdown of industrial establishments by department. The only readily available information is on the regional scale, permitting only a very broad view of distributions.

Two impressions, more complementary than contradictory, emerge from any consideration of the industrial geography of France. One is the wide dispersion of industry, the other is the predominant role of about twenty departments as areas of concentration within this general dispersion. On the one hand, industry is to be found everywhere; the silhouettes of industrial buildings can be seen from most viewpoints in town or country. France seems to be a country which specializes in odd and apparently inexplicable industrial locations, whether the tyre plants of Clermont-Ferrand or the lock industry of Vimeu. On the other hand, the fact nevertheless remains that the bulk of French industry is concentrated in a quarter of French departments. In 1980, the Ile-de-France region alone contained 18.9 per cent of all industrial plants.

The spatial distribution of industry varies according to branch and size of plant. Some industries are ubiquitous; this may be because they are market-orientated, located at the point of consumption; it may be because their raw materials are widely available or easily transportable, or it may be that they are not affected by the process of industrial concentration. Such industries are represented in nearly all departments and regions, but nevertheless some degree of concentration can be perceived. This applies particularly to the wood, general machine construction and food and agricultural processing industries; in 1975 the latter had 3,856 firms; only one region (Limousin) had less than 2 per cent. The agricultural machinery industry is similar; each department has at least one plant, but three regions accounted for nearly 60 per cent of output (Champagne 24 per cent, Picardy 17 per cent and the Pays de la Loire 16 per cent). A second group consists of branches of industry with a widespread distribution, but where some regions are more important than others. An example is hosiery, where Champagne region (notably Troyes and Romilly) accounts for 25 per cent of output by value and more than a quarter of total employment in the branch.

Some extremely specific branches of industry are on the contrary highly concentrated and have either a predominant or exclusive role in a limited number of locations. For example, the production of railway locomotives is concentrated in 14 locations, and the manufacture of railway rolling stock in 15 locations, 5 of which are in the Nord region. Examples of predominant locations, where a town or region accounts for more than half of total output, include 80 per cent of spectacle manufacture located in the Jura, 77 per cent of lead smelting in Nord Department and 75 per cent of the production of bobbins for silk manufacture located in the three neighbouring Departments of Ardèche, Drôme and Loire, located astride the lower Rhône valley and the Central massif. In addition, Ardèche and Drôme have 80 per cent of the production of special spindles used in the manufacture of stretch nylon.

Above a certain figure (about 80 per cent of a branch) preponderant locations must be regarded as exclusive ones. Ninety per cent of woolcombing is located at Roubaix–Tourcoing in Nord region. The region has the same proportion of the woollen carpet industry (again mainly at Roubaix–Tourcoing) and 85 per cent of the linen industry. Eighty per cent of French production of stainless steel tubes comes from plants in northern France, in the Sambre and Ardennes Departments. Cutlery is almost exclusively derived from two regions: Thiers (Central massif) and Nogent-en-Bassigny (southeast of Paris basin). Eighty-nine per cent of the production of flour-paste products (pasta) comes from the Department of Bouches-du-Rhône (Marseille region).

The Ile-de-France (Paris) region is a special case of industrial preponderance, whether measured by the number of industrial branches and plants there, or by the large number of people employed in them. To take only two examples, in 1976 55 per cent of workers in the pharmaceutical industry were located in the region, which also accounted for 50 per cent of perfumery production.

Table 23.2 *Percentage intercensal employment change, by industrial branch*

Industrial branch	1954–62	1962–8	1968–75
Food and drink	+4.7	+4.2	0
Coal	−22.2	−21.9	−44.6
Gas	−26.0	−14.6	−27.5
Electricity	+12.1	+16.5	+9.6
Oil	+27.0	+10.8	+6.6
Building materials	−1.3	+12.1	+1.7
Steel	+9.4	−13.4	+6.7
Non-ferrous metals	+17.4	+5.4	+1.6
Metal products, excl. machinery	+14.1	+1.9	+11.5
Machine building	+41.0	+1.1	+19.5
Electrical machinery and electronics	+52.0	+18.8	+40.5
Vehicles	+31.2	+13.8	+37.8
Shipbuilding, aerospace and armaments	+19.3	0.0	+10.4
Chemicals	+29.5	+15.7	+15.0
Textiles	−16.8	−13.4	−16.7
Clothing	−18.8	−8.4	−6.0
Leather, boots and shoes	−16.2	−10.2	−14.5
Wood industry, furniture	−8.8	−0.3	+3.2
Paper and board	+16.5	+7.7	+12.7
Printing and publishing	+19.4	+30.3	−1.4
Plastics and miscellaneous industries	+12.2	+25.8	+16.0
Building and public works	+25.9	+23.2	−0.7
All industry	+11.6	+7.2	+5.7

Source: INSEE.

3 Industrial change

These notions of industrial structure and distribution in France must be placed in a dynamic perspective of industrial change, commonly and conveniently revealed by variations in employment; Table 23.2 shows the development of industrial employment between 1954 and 1975. Fluctuations in the work force are, however, an expression of the vigour of firms and industrial plants, in regard to which statistical information has been given above. Industrial life is made up of 'births' (the creation of new firms on new sites) and 'deaths' (the closure of plants and the disappearance of firms). Industrial deaths, like industrial births, have very varied causes and characteristics; they can for example occur as a result of a simple cessation of production, or through merger or absorption. Between creation and disappearance there are the intervening stages of expansion, crisis and conversion. All these changes in industrial life are reflected in spatial distributions.

24

⚜ Industrial location

A study of industrial development in France is for the most part a historical study extending over several centuries. We must untangle a web of causes of all kinds, of which the least logical are occasionally the most important. The geographical and structural distribution of French industry is a consequence of the early development of industrialization. We must therefore proceed chronologically and follow the changes in the location of industries, and their present-day survival.

1 Locations before the industrial revolution

The industrial geography of the *Ancien Régime* was very different from that of the present day. Motive power and energy were provided by wood, running water and wind; coal played only a minor part. (The first documentary reference to the mining of coal in the Creusot basin dates from 1510 and the Anzin Mining Company was founded in 1756.) Accordingly, industrial locations were extremely dispersed. Forests supplied wood and charcoal whilst the banks of rivers or streams provided sites for watermills, hammer-works or forges. For example, the swift, abundant waters of the transversal valleys emerging from the Pyrenees provided numerous water-power sites used by Catalan forges, spinning mills, jet-working mills and paper mills.

The iron industry, designed to supply local markets, also used local resources: surface deposits of iron ore (siderite concentrations from the Eocene deposits, ores contained in the Jurassic limestone and oolitic iron ore), timber from the forests, and river water to temper the metal, turn the water wheels and work the hammers.

Figure 24.1 shows the distribution about 1780 of six hundred recorded sites. The areas with fewest sites were the Mediterranean south, lacking forests, most of the Central massif, already deforested, and the Paris basin. The greatest

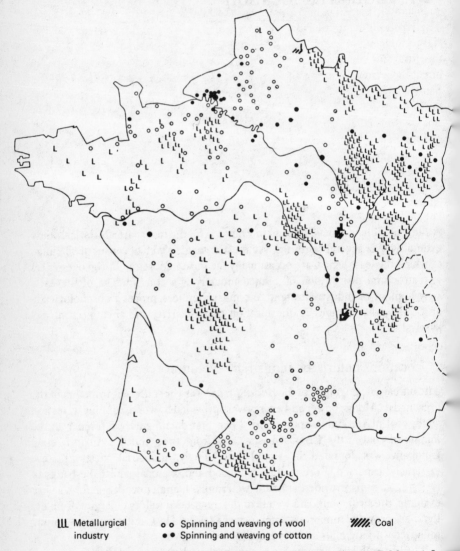

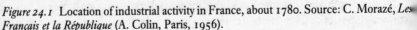

Figure 24.1 Location of industrial activity in France, about 1780. Source: C. Morazé, *Les Français et la République* (A. Colin, Paris, 1956).

concentration of sites was where iron ores in the Jurassic or Palaeozoic rocks coincided with extensive forests, or were in proximity to them, for example on the fringe of the Ardennes, in Alsace and Lorraine, the Dauphiné Alps, the eastern, northern and western fringes of the Central massif, the Pyrenees and the Norman *bocage*. In 1789 France had 1,000 iron-working establishments (smithies, blast furnaces, hammer-works and forges).

There were many regions of specialized domestic production, such as the lace and cloth of Livradois, the glassworks of Nivernais, the clothworking of Maine. The ribbon industry of Saint-Etienne and Saint-Chamond developed in the eighteenth century with the use of Swiss looms. The watch and clock industry of the Jura and the Arve valley was introduced in the eighteenth century by immigrants from Geneva and Neuchâtel. The cutting of precious stones in the Saint-Claude region of the Jura was linked with the clock and watch industry of the Pays de Gex, near Geneva. The wood-turning and *tabletterie* (assembling of small objects such as ornamental boxes from geometrical pieces of wood, ivory and mother-of-pearl) of the Saint-Claude and Oyonnax regions stem from the presence of boxwood on the limestone slopes.

The textile industry was already making the fame and fortune of many towns in the thirteenth century; domestic establishments of weavers, fullers, dyers and knitters, as well as merchants, ensured the prosperity and influence of Arras, Douai, Lille, Cambrai and Saint-Omer. In 1492 Amiens received from Tournai the manufacture of tapestry and of gold and silk cloth. In the sixteenth century, weavers of fine cloth migrated from Contrai, Ghent and Ypres to Valenciennes, Cambrai and Saint-Quentin. The establishment of the silk industry dates from 1536, when letters patent from Francis I accorded privileges to the town of Lyon on behalf of its silk workers.

These locations reveal even at an early stage one of the permanent features of French industrialization, the frequently decisive role of neighbouring foreign countries, by indirectly influencing the industrialization of frontier regions. For example, the art of silk-weaving was imported as an entity, complete with workers, looms and equipment for unwinding and reeling the silk, and for dyeing. Silk-throwing and doubling machines were set up towards the end of the seventeenth century at Virieux, Privas and Aubenas in the Rhône valley by an Italian mill-owner from Bologna. Industry on a larger scale began to emerge in the seventeenth and eighteenth centuries, but without the momentum or spontaneity which characterized growth in England. It is an established fact that before the profound upheaval of the industrial revolution France did not appear well suited to the growth of industry. The reasons for this could lie in the psychological characteristics already discussed in chapter 12 above, or in the politico-religious causes put forward by certain historians, who relate the lack of industrial progress to the weakness of Protestantism. From the very beginning, from Louis XIV's minister Colbert to Napoleon I, the establishment of manufacturing was the province of the state: as early as 1515 there was a national manufactory of arms at Saint-Etienne. In the seventeenth century the royal manufactories increased in number: weapons and military equipment at Tulle and in the Nivernais, tapestry at Aubusson, and woollen cloth at Sedan (1642), Carcassonne and Lodève. In 1664 the Van Robais family left the Netherlands and settled in Abbeville, and in 1692 the manufacture of mirrors began at Saint-Gobain. The eighteenth-century monarchy continued the process of innovation; in 1771 Turgot, when Governor of Limousin, founded the porcelain manufactory at Limoges. During the *Ancien Régime*, ports, stimulated by the growth of the colonial trade, became important industrial centres. Bordeaux, Nantes, Marseille, Le Havre and Rouen, which took part in the triangular trade (manufactured goods to Africa, slaves to the Americas, colonial produce to France), developed industries either in the port which received the raw materials (sugar-refining, soap manufacture) or nearby: for example Montauban, with its flour mills, cloth weaving and silk manufacture, was tributary to Bordeaux.

There are numerous examples of the continued industrial use of locations first established in the seventeenth and eighteenth centuries. However, their survival can variously be attributed to advantages of industrial infrastructure, labour, linkage in a complex of specialist production, or the efforts of a local or regional capitalism. For more than a century, through an unbroken succession of firms and activities adapted to current economic circumstances, the old industrial sites maintained their attractiveness, which explains the large number of early locations surviving on the present-day map.

Present-day industrial locations can often be traced back to the previous existence of a domestic textile tradition, the weaving of hemp or the spinning and weaving of flax and wool. The Basque linen-weaving mills in the Department of Pyrénées Atlantiques are the direct descendants of the Basque country farms which produced cloth from the sixteenth century onwards; the same is true of the manufacture of sandals and espadrilles. The workshops and the factory in Méru (Oise) producing buttons and small wooden objects (*tabletterie*), still active in the middle of the twentieth century, derive from workshops manufacturing trinkets – fans, brushes, frames for opera glasses – which flourished from the beginning of the eighteenth century, supplying Paris and the Court at Versailles. From the end of the sixteenth century, glove-makers were working in Grenoble: they were the precursors of today's glove industry. The port industries of the eighteenth century also influenced the industrial specializations of subsequent centuries: sugar-refining, food-processing and chemicals. This geographical momentum can also be seen in the impressive continuity of firms: in 1927, 62 out of 289 companies in the metal industries had their roots in businesses dating from before 1789.

2 The industrial revolution

The term 'industrial revolution' is convenient but vague, relating to a series of technical and economic changes which took place over more than a century.

2.1 The opening phase

In England, industrial transformation began in the eighteenth century, and even in France the first stirrings of industrial upheaval were already discernible before the Revolution of 1789 and the Napoleonic Wars isolated the country for nearly a quarter of a century from the model and inspiration provided by England.

English émigrés helped to establish the modern French cotton industry: John Kay, inventor of the flying shuttle, settled in France in 1747 and introduced the carding machine in 1771; in 1750 John Holker set up a cotton mill in Rouen. It was also an Englishman who installed blast furnaces in the cannon foundry at Indret. In 1779 the Milne family from Britain settled at Neuville-sur-Saône and introduced the first example of Arkwright's water frame, a spinning machine which used water power. In 1781 Marshal de Castries, Minister for the Navy, 'required Messieurs Wendel, Touffaire and Wilkinson to travel through various provinces in order to choose sites suitable for blast furnaces and forges in which iron ore could be processed by means of coal'. The site chosen was Montcenis (Le Creusot), where there was already a royal glassworks, and in 1782 the king authorized 'the establishment of blast furnaces for the smelting of iron according to the English method in order to supply the royal foundry at Indret'. The Vierzon forges were set up in 1791 by the Englishman Taylor.

History, however, was to delay the real beginnings of industrial change for twenty years, during which France was technically and financially handicapped by being deprived of maritime trade. The French industrial revolution was not only late by comparison with England, but eventually took place under less favourable conditions with 'a population deeply attached to the land despite agricultural changes, a commercial capitalism which was less well developed and attracted to other sources of profit, and an absence of competition which, from 1806 to 1860, sheltered manufacturers behind a veritable wall of customs protection and lulled them into a false sense of security'.[1]

Energy supply was also different. Coal in France was not rapidly adopted as a new source of energy, immediately transforming geographical locations. Its role was negligible until 1850, partly because of the conservatism of manufacturers who were not exposed to competition, partly because of a decline in demand for products of the metal industries, above all because of the inadequacy of transport. France is far from being built on coal: its deposits are peripheral or situated in hilly regions away from easily navigable rivers. What is more, the distribution of coal mining in France at the time bore only a faint resemblance to that of the present day. Towards the middle of the nineteenth century the Loire basin still provided a third of French coal production and the Nord field only 23 per cent. The entire reorganization of the French industrial economy was based on the Loire basins of central France, as illustrated by early French canal construction. The Blanzy and Loire coalfields were known as the French Ruhr. At first coal

[1] C. Fohlen: for current English version see 'The industrial revolution in France, 1700–1914' in C. M. Cipolla (ed.), *The Fontana Economic History of Europe* (London, 1973), vol. 4, pt. 1, ch. 1, pp. 7–75.

played only a secondary role, restricted to the coalfields themselves, their immediate surroundings and the towns and regions which could receive coal economically. Until about 1860 the railway network was fragmentary; the only continuous system radiated 200 km from Paris, linking the Nord and the lower Seine regions to the capital, which was beginning its industrial expansion.

Picardy, Champagne, Normandy and Paris, all near the northern coal basins, were favoured industrially; about 1815, Paris had 50 cotton mills. At about the same time the process of the development of industrial regions in coal basins began, with the changes in the iron and steel industry and the use of the steam engine. It was in 1815 at Saint-Etienne that Chaptal, in charge of industry in the Ministry of the Interior, decided to install a coke-fired steelworks run by the Englishman Jackson, and opened a School of Mines.

The first coke-fired blast furnaces were established in 1818 at Saint-Etienne and Pont l'Evêque, to the west of Vienne. They were based on ore from la Voulte (Ardèche) and coal from the Loire basin. The steam engine gradually gained ground; it appeared in 1817 in a cotton mill in Lille, in 1839 in a woollen mill in Fourmies, and in 1849 at Tarare, where a velvet factory was opened. In Picardy a flax mill powered by steam was established in 1838 by the Englishman Maberly; a second mill was opened by an Englishman at Pont-Rémy. In 1843 the Scottish Baxter brothers founded the first French steam-powered jute mill at Ailly-sur-Somme.

Steam engines were used only in regions where coal was easily accessible, in other words near coal basins; the result was a first stage of industrial concentration.

Yet French industry still remained broadly traditional in its structure and locations; side by side with its coke-based iron industries, which were narrowly localized in a very few areas, iron production continued in all the regions where it had existed for centuries. In 1815, for example, Haute-Marne in the southeast of the Paris basin was the largest iron-producing department. In 1819 the neighbouring department of Haute-Saône had 30 blast furnaces, 43 fining hearths, 23 tilt-hammers, 7 foundries and 4 wire mills. In 1826, whereas Great Britain had 2 wood-fired blast furnaces and 280 coke-fired furnaces, the figures for France were 379 and 4 respectively. Thus in the age of George Sand and Balzac, for want of coal and transport, it was water that drove the flour mills, the machines for tanning, the fulling mills, the forge hammers, the saw mills and the paper mills. Most rivers with any degree of gradient became veritable streets of industry. It was on the rivers that spinning mills concentrated from the beginning of the nineteenth century, except those in areas where coal was available. In 1862, in the neighbourhood of Evreux in the western Paris basin, there were 1,200 water-powered mills. For a hundred years or more their abandoned buildings were to house a range of successor enterprises.

In the first half of the nineteenth century the putting-out system (the 'factory system' in the original sense of the term) was the most widespread form of industrial organization in the textile industry. A 'factory' consisted of 'a group of merchants who bought the raw materials or intermediate products, such as spun warp or weft, and put them out to workers in small workshops or homes in town or country. What gave unity to the "factory" was its dependence on the town in which spinning was generally carried out and marketing concentrated'.[2] Towns on which factories were based included Reims, Roubaix, Sedan, Amiens and Cholet. In the 1850s Cholet was the site of a 'factory' which spread its influence over 120 communes and employed between 45,000 and 50,000 outworkers.

By this time new textile processes were appearing, which strengthened the hold of the industry in certain areas. In the west, from Cholet to Falaise, cotton replaced linen; in 1843 linen and hemp gave way to jute in Picardy. Elsewhere (the Departments of Calvados, Manche, Loir-et-Cher and Hérault) wool declined without being replaced by other textiles.

It was at this time that the Alsace textile industry grew up in the Vosges. Weaving started at the beginning of the nineteenth century, and spinning followed. Unlike other textile regions the rise of the Vosges industry was due entirely to the enterprise of individuals, owing nothing to inherited momentum from a pre-existing industry. The introduction of power looms dealt a death blow to many regions of rural handloom weavers: the industry was concentrated in Mulhouse, Rouen, Roubaix and Reims.

In the mid-nineteenth century the geography of the textile industry thus had two aspects which still exist today. On the one hand a dispersed industry persisted, drawing strength from local traditions, infrastructure, entrepreneurs and labour. On the other hand new industrial regions and centres were increasingly springing up. These were the nurseries from which emerged the industrialists of the second half of the century; the precursors of this new employer class were the owners in textile branches that had already been subjected to concentration, such as spinning and bleaching mills and dyeworks, cloth merchants and manufacturing merchants. The former 'factories' became nuclei of machine textile production, with the concentration of weaving round the existing spinning mills. Most of today's industrial centres were already marked on the map more than a century ago, with textile centres or other successor industries on the sites of previously existing textile enterprises. But in the organization of this new industry France was severely handicapped: the coalfields of the Nord region and Lorraine played no decisive role in the first decades. The entire industrial organization related to the coalfields of the Central massif.

2.2 The second phase

The second half of the nineteenth rather than the first deserves to be described as a time of industrial revolution. In the space of thirty years, from 1860 to 1890, the

[2] *Ibid.*, pp. 26–7 (see note 1, p. 363).

industrial face of France was to undergo profound and lasting changes. By that time the financial structures which were to open up France to the great capitalist companies and the banks had been established. It was a capitalism that was partly French and partly foreign. Without underestimating the part played by national initiatives, it is necessary once again to recognize the extent of foreign support and capital, and in addition the large numbers of foreign technicians and machines, brought in first clandestinely and later openly. It was neither fortuitous nor a reflection of geographical advantages that the industrialization of that time reinforced the peripheral nature of the distribution of French industry. The English invested in Calais and the northwest of the Paris basin and the Belgians in the Sambre valley, while Swiss bankers backed industrialists in Alsace and Franche-Comté. Industries developed in relation to financial centres, where family companies emerged and built factories in the same region. This new type of capitalism was to allow the diffusion and acceptance of all the changes brought about by progress and discovery. The combined power of coal, the steam engine, the railways and the canals ushered in a new phase in French industry.

Coal consumption rose from 7.5 million tonnes in 1851 to 21 million in 1869. The number of industrial establishments using steam engines rose from 6,543 in 1842 to 22,851 in 1870; the number of steam engines used in industry rose from 6,080 in 1852 to 27,088 in 1870 and 84,000 in 1900. The Nord coalfield was slow to arrive on the scene; in 1851 production was a mere million tonnes, exclusively from the Nord Department. The Pas-de-Calais field began to produce coal in 1854, but it was only in 1872 that production in the joint field rose to over 5 million tonnes and in 1886 that it reached the 10 million mark. It was not until 1900 that production reached 20 million tonnes, three-quarters of which was now produced by the Pas-de-Calais. During the first three-quarters of the nineteenth century the Nord coalfield played a purely regional role due to the fact that its peripheral situation was unfavourable to the easy transport of coal. The building of canals and railways made it economically possible to transport coal, while English coal could be shipped to the ports of western and southwestern France once tariff discrimination was removed.

The transport network established during this period accentuated regional imbalance within France. Wherever canals could easily transport coal and heavy goods, industries were developed and existing plants turned to the use of coal and converted to new activities. In western and southern France, away from ports, coal was expensive and access was difficult. Regions where coal was mined and which also had a dense network of rivers, canals and railways were particularly favoured. The prime example was the Nord region, whose slow-flowing rivers, unlike those of Alsace, Normandy and the Central massif, had not been useful for energy provision in the water-power stage (the first mechanical looms were turned by horses), but were much more useful for navigational purposes.

In all regions, however, the possibility of industrial development was decided by the railway. Towns which refused to have the railway deliberately placed themselves outside the industrial revolution. The tariff policies of railway companies played as decisive a role as decisions regarding their routes. By favouring the long-distance transportation of heavy goods, the rail tariff made it possible to establish industries far from sources of raw materials and energy. The

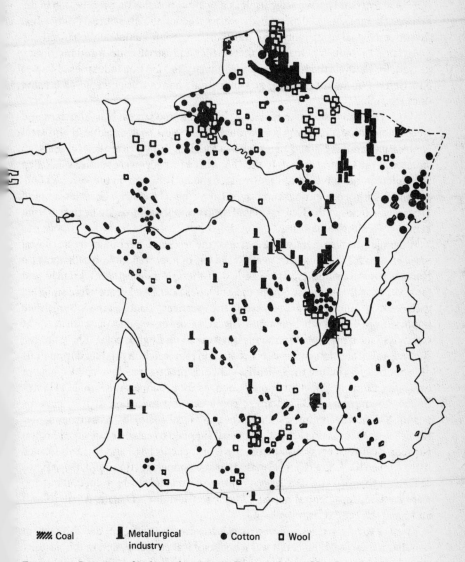

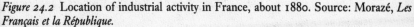

Figure 24.2 Location of industrial activity in France, about 1880. Source: Morazé, *Les Français et la République.*

development of heavy industries in the Paris region was to a large extent the result of the early decision by the rail companies to relate tariffs to the value of goods transported rather than to their weight or volume, thus favouring market-orientation of production. 'The railway was thus the tool which allowed the capitalist system to develop freely by extending its influence on all forms of human activity and by imposing itself as quickly as possible on every region in the country, demolishing all previously existing economic structures.'[3] The dual incentive of coal availability and transport provision completely changed the geography of industry; many of the smaller industrial concentrations disappeared, for example the Limoges textile industry and the iron industries of Poitou and Berry. On the other hand, new industrial centres were created or existing ones expanded.

From 1850 onwards coke replaced charcoal in the largest blast furnaces and steel began to oust cast iron and wrought iron. New coal-based iron and steel centres appeared at Saint-Etienne and in the Alès and Decazeville coalfields, all situated in the Central massif. In the 1860s blast furnaces were similarly installed at Pamiers in the foreland of the Pyrenees and at Tarascon on the lower Rhône, supplied with coal brought by rail from the Carmaux, Graissessac and Decazeville fields of the Central massif. Iron ore still continued to be drawn from extremely scattered deposits.

A parallel development was the rise of the iron and steel industry at coastal sites, chosen for the most part to allow the use of imported iron ore. Plants at Le Boucau near Bayonne (1881), Pauillac in the Gironde estuary, Trignac and Outreau near Boulogne-sur-Mer and at Dunes near Dunkerque were supplied with ore from Bilbao in Spain and from the Pyrenees. Plants on the lower Rhône imported ore from both Spain and Algeria. Conversely, the blast furnaces of Caen used local ore from Normandy but worked on English coke. These coastal sites appeared at a time when steel production required iron produced from non-phosphoric ores, before the Gilchrist–Thomas process was developed. Some of the older iron-producing regions, such as Bourbonnais–Nivernais, Haute-Saône, Champagne and Ardennes, continued in production at this stage by adapting to new techniques, either exploiting local coalfields, as at Commentry (Bourbonnais), or taking advantage of coal supplied by canal or railway. The first Bessemer converter was installed in the Dordogne in 1858 and by 1878 France had 24, 11 in the Loire (Central massif), 7 at Commentry (Bourbonnais) and two at Denain (Nord). The four largest centres of iron and steel production in 1870 were Le Creusot (Central massif), Hayange (Lorraine), Denain-Anzin (Nord) and Saint-Etienne (Central massif).

From 1860 onwards powered weaving spread rapidly at the expense of handloom weaving. The result was a geographical concentration in the 'factory' towns of Cholet, La Ferté-Macé, Flers, Condé, Rouen, Bolbec, Lillebonne,

[3] M. Wolkowitsch, *L'Economie régionale des transports dans le centre et le centre-ouest de la France* (Société d'Edition et de Diffusion de l'Enseignement Supérieur, Paris, 1960).

Roubaix and Sainte-Marie (Alsace). Fourmies, between Champagne and the Nord coalfield, became one of the most important woollen towns: in 1910 it supplied 47 per cent of France's production of worsted yarn and mills were sprouting up like mushrooms. In 1860 in the Pays de Caux rectangle (Dieppe–Yvetôt–Bolbec–Tôtes), 40,000 people worked in conjunction with the spinning mills and manufacturers of Rouen.

The process of concentration went hand in hand with the industrial revolution. The Anglo-French treaty of 1860 and the cotton famine at the time of the American Civil War accelerated this process by allowing only the most solidly established firms to survive or adapt. The cotton mills of the Seine-Maritime Department, which in 1859 numbered 233, had fallen to 185 in 1869. The 547 beet-sugar works of 1838 had dwindled to 288 twelve years later, while the Amiens worsted spinning mills fell from 43 in 1834 to 16 in 1864.

2.3 The third phase

Just before the end of the nineteenth century the industrial revolution entered its third phase with the arrival of hydroelectric power, the opening up of the Lorraine orefield, the use of new metals such as aluminium, and new industrial activities, for example branches of the chemical industry. Once again the industrial geography of France was modified, these new developments being responsible for determining present-day features, in particular the concentration of activity east of a line from Le Havre to Marseille.

The iron and steel industry of Lorraine was until 1848 merely a continuation of the industry that existed before the industrial revolution. The Lorraine ore was only belatedly exploited and used as a basis for an iron and steel industry. Between 1857 and 1881 French iron-ore production was stable at 3 million tonnes, whereas Great Britain was producing 14 million. The Gilchrist–Thomas basic steel process which made possible the use of ore from Lorraine dates from 1881. Between 1880 and 1913 basic steelworks using the Thomas process were constructed. Rapid expansion of iron-ore output followed: 5.4 million tonnes in 1900, 22 million tonnes in 1913 and 50 million tonnes in 1929.

The development of the Lorraine field dealt a severe blow to the traditional locations of the iron and steel industry; the coastal plants and plants based on the use of superficial deposits of ore had to give way to a field whose reserves were enormous. The low iron content of the ore made transportation expensive, so that smelting at the orefield was required, thus encouraging the geographical concentration of the industry. Blast furnaces increased in number on the Lorraine orefield, but it was only from 1900 that basic steel-making plant was added. In spite of this development Lorraine did not become a powerful industrial region devoted to the further processing of steel. The low-grade ore, the absence of waterways, and unfavourable rail tariffs relegated this field of potentially international significance to a purely regional role. It was in fact the older iron and steel regions which adapted to the new pattern of steel production by becoming the exclusive centres of the further processing of the metal. In southeast France, the discovery of the potentialities of aluminium led to the mining of bauxite; the four French alumina plants were situated in proximity to the bauxite mines and also to lignite deposits.

Last on the scene came hydroelectricity, providing a new source of energy. The first hydroelectric plant was built at Lancey, near Grenoble, by Aristide Bergès. The best sites were progressively equipped with dams and pressure pipelines. The rapid development of the sites by the manufacturers and the favourable cost of power in proximity to the power-stations encouraged the development of industry in the Alps. There was a particularly dense concentration of industries which were heavy consumers of electricity, such as chlorine production and the electro-chemical and electro-metallurgical industries. The same considerations explain the siting of aluminium plants in the valleys of the Alps and the Pyrenees.

Electricity, wherever available under favourable economic conditions, brought about a new wave of industrialization, at the same time allowing a return to a more dispersed spatial distribution. Thus the silk mills of the Lyon region passed directly from hand-operation to the use of machinery driven by electricity, without experiencing the concentration movement associated with the use of the steam engine. The Lyon region, which had 33,000 looms in 1866, had no more than 12,000 in 1888 and only 4,200 in 1914. In the Department of the Isère (northern Alps) the large establishments split up into small independent mills (62 in 1880, 357 in 1920).

The textile industry of the nineteenth century played a decisive role in stimulating the development of a certain number of linked industrial branches, which subsequently expanded and acquired an independent existence. In this way the demand for dyestuffs and textile dressings was at the origin of the modern chemical industries, and the building of textile machinery developed into a machine-building industry in the wider sense.

Each branch of industry has thus tended to produce a system of growth poles, reflecting horizontal linkages between particular branches and vertical relations between one stage of production branch and another. Linkages of coal, steel, glass and chemicals grew up on the coalfields. Often the existence of an unemployed female (or male) labour force was sufficient to call into existence new industries such as the clothing industry, which employed the wives and daughters of miners.

Wars or threats of war limited industrialization in frontier regions. On the other hand, changes in the eastern frontiers of France favoured other regions. After the war of 1870–1 thousands of people emigrated from Alsace to Belfort, where plants were created by major Mulhouse firms. Similarly the First World War saw a high concentration of refugee firms in Lyon. The shoe industry settled in Limoges during the First World War in place of the declining porcelain industry. The iron and steel and chemical industries of Rouen and the Seine-Maritime Department date from 1914, when the industry of the Nord Department had been taken over by the Germans.

The firm of Brissoneau and Lotz settled in La Rochelle because the Société des Entreprises Industrielles Charentaises was financially linked with the Standard Steel Car Company of Pittsburgh. During the First World War this firm supplied most of the wagons destined for the French railways and the American army. The equipment was unloaded at La Pallice and assembled in the workshops at La Rochelle. The company was bought by Pullman in 1931, passed under Rothschild control in 1947 and was taken over by Brissoneau in 1957.

These causes are not sufficient, however, to account for every industrial location. In a country of ancient settlement, with many industrial sites and increasingly diversified industrial activities, personal decisions are also very important. Of this type are the intervention of politicians in favour of their constituency or town, or the simple fact that a man of initiative and capital happens to live in a certain area. It is well known that the rubber industry was established in Clermont-Ferrand because an industrialist of the region married a niece of a Scottish Mackintosh. The reason why between 1860 and 1930 Mazamet was responsible for the removal of wool from three-quarters of the world's supply of sheepskins is because in 1851 this little wool centre had the idea of importing a few skins. This innovation, encouraged by the abundance and purity of the water supply, led to the development of an industrial centre 170 km from the coast for the treatment of imported skins!

Lastly in the industrial development of French towns, we must take into account psychological factors. Just as some towns refused to have railways, so others rejected industrial development because their ruling classes had well-established landed interests and were anxious to preserve political and social stability.

On the eve of the First World War, the industrial geography of France was clearly visible on the map: present-day industrial regions and industrial towns were established, with their managerial classes, their workers and their new landscapes.

But the industrial revolution of France did not have the same force as in England or Germany, which may be ascribed to the lack of plentiful supplies of coal and labour in the very early stages. More importantly, the fact that the industrial revolution had its principal impact in peripheral coalfields and orefields meant that earlier industrial centres in the interior of the country were not obliterated. They were strong in tradition and benefited from established infrastructures, and so were able to find means of adapting and surviving, adding a great number of isolated industrial centres to the industrial regions based on mining.

3 The interwar period

Between 1920 and 1945 French industry hardly changed; until 1939, because of the prevailing atmosphere of stagnation, there was little possibility of founding or extending industrial plants. Much of the backwardness of present-day French industry can be explained by this total lack of dynamism between the wars. The exceptions are all the more striking. After 1935 the aeronautical and armament industries of the Paris region were moved to the provinces for strategic reasons. Thanks to this policy, southwest and central France gained 62 plants. The creation of plants producing artificial textile fibres, mostly in the Lyon region, dates also from this period (Fig. 24.3). Between 1939 and 1945 France was outside the mainstream of industrial development, missing all the discoveries of industrial technology made in England and the United States in this period, a gap which was subsequently to prove difficult to close. For example, continuous steel strip mills had existed from 1923 in the United States and from 1938 in Great Britain, but were installed in France only after the Second World War.

4 Postwar industrialization

The France that emerged from the Second World War entered a new phase of industrial development. From 1949 to 1960 the average annual growth rate of industrial production, not including building and construction, was 6.9 per cent. This growth was accompanied by the creation of new industrial plants and the extension of existing ones. The choice of locations for new developments responded to factors which differed from those of earlier periods.

4.1 Changing location factors
4.1.1 Energy

Coal has ceased to be the main source of energy for industry; other sources of energy have been developed, which are often more competitive and attractive. While electricity is a major form of industrial energy, proximity to the actual point of generation is of diminished significance. The explanation is partly technical: the introduction of high-tension transmission lines for alternating current has greatly improved the economics of transferring power; the maximum range of economic transfer is estimated to be 200 km at 120,000 volts, 600 km at 220,000 volts but 1,000 km at 400,000 volts. Nationalization of electricity has also had an impact, by breaking the links of ownership between Alpine industrial plants and the hydroelectric plants built to supply them. Finally, the adoption of a uniform regional tariff policy removes most of the locational advantage of being near power-stations. One of the most important consequences has been the shift of the electro-chemical industry from Alpine locations towards the Rhône valley.

New chemical industries were grafted directly on to sources of energy: coal–

chemical plants adjacent to the coke ovens on the coalfields, and the petrochemical plants in relation to refineries and deposits of natural gas. The petrochemical industry did not develop in France until refineries were provided with installations capable of producing the hydrocarbons required for chemical synthesis.

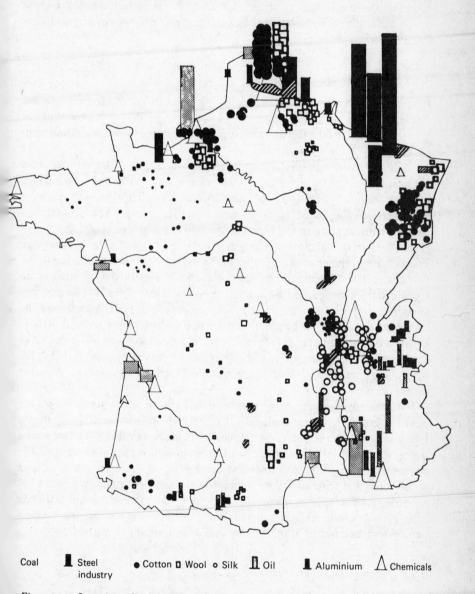

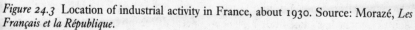

Figure 24.3 Location of industrial activity in France, about 1930. Source: Morazé, *Les Français et la République*.

The products of the petrochemical industry have a wide range of uses in detergents, solvents, synthetic tannin, resins, polyesters, nylon, Terylene, octile alcohols, carbon black, synthetic rubber and plastics.

Generally speaking, the advance along the chain of production from raw material to finished industrial product is marked by a reduction of energy costs as a proportion of total costs; however, the fact that energy costs vary regionally has some important consequences.

4.1.2 *Raw materials*

In many branches of industry the locational importance of raw material costs has declined, owing to the development of synthetic products, the recycling of industrial waste and the fact that industrial products tend to become lighter, thus reducing the cost of transport.

Some raw materials now come from different sources. The most obvious example is iron ore; the discovery of very rich deposits in Africa and the low cost of transportation by sea in 60,000–tonne bulk carriers led to a renewed emphasis on coastal sites for production, to the detriment of Lorraine. The first of the new coastal plants, at Dunkerque, began production in 1963. The choice of location is explained by the fact that it belonged to the Usinor group (based on northern France) and by the proximity of other plants in the Nord coalfield. Its construction necessitated large-scale building operations: part of the site had to be reclaimed from the sea, and the sand of the coastal dune belt had to be made firm enough to support the weight of blast furnaces and rolling mills. A dock had to be excavated in the port for handling iron ore and a water supply secured. Rivalry between Nantes and Marseille for a second coastal plant was settled in favour of the latter. The new plant at Fos was chosen in order to compensate Marseille for the loss of traffic and business activity suffered as a result of Algerian independence.

Industrial demand for water is constantly increasing; for plants which are heavy consumers, water availability has become an increasingly significant location factor. For example, the Dunlop and Goodyear rubber and tyre plants were established in Amiens because of the abundant supply of water available from the chalk aquifer and from the Somme. Rivers with an abundant and regular flow and sedimentary areas with copious aquifers provide a new kind of attraction for industrial development. The older industrial regions and coalfields are replaced by industrialized valleys offering ease of movement and water which can act both as a means of transport and as an industrial raw material.

4.1.3 *Transport and communications*

By comparison with conditions in the industrial revolution of the nineteenth century, there has since the 1960s been a great differentiation in available means of transport. Whereas at one time only railways and waterways were available, with road transport by motor vehicles arriving later on the scene, now there is also transport by air and pipeline, together with the varied forms of telecommunications.

Motorways undoubtedly attract industry. In the five years following the opening in 1967–72 of the Paris–Lille motorway (Autoroute du Nord), the number of persons in industrial employment rose by 40 per cent in the six cantons of the Somme Department through which, or close to which, it passed. There has been much industrial decentralization in the west of the Paris region because of the motorway to the west (Autoroute de Normandie) which allows rapid communication with the capital, where head offices have remained.

Similarly, air links and airports are now part of the industrial infrastructure, and this explains the choice of sites for some new plants. Location in proximity to an international airport is particularly attractive to managers of subsidiaries of foreign companies. As products become lighter and smaller, so the cost of transport is reduced.

4.1.4 Labour

In many industries, labour costs are such a small element of total production costs that the locational impact is small. In theory the twentieth-century labour force is more mobile than that of the last century, thanks to the availability of a variety of means of transport, both private and public, allowing great freedom of vocational choice. Political tendencies have also played a long-established role in determining plant location; a local labour force which is reputed – justifiably or not – to be militant and constantly claiming improvements in wages and other benefits inhibits the installation of new factories. This partly explains the difficulties which some towns have had in securing industrial expansion. During the recent phase of industrial expansion, firms have chosen to invest in places where they were able to find the cheapest available labour force, or potential labour force.

4.1.5 Industrial sites

Location factors have also changed as a result of developments in industrial technology. As factories increase in size, they require large surface areas. The large car factories of the Paris region moved away chiefly because they could no longer find enough space for expansion. Locations outside Paris, on the other hand, provide them with enough space for their needs as well as reserves for future expansion. The enterprises which were decentralized from the Paris region between 1954 and 1974 had occupied 3 million sq m of floorspace; in their new locations they occupied 16.5 million sq m.

New developments in technology had a lesser impact on the floorspace requirements of small and medium-sized firms for which the availability of vacant industrial buildings has been, even more than previously, a powerful attraction.

4.1.6 The environment

Environmental factors and amenities are becoming increasingly important. Today the choice of industrial location may depend on beauty of landscape, ease of communication with Paris or the nearest large town, university and cultural provision, a sunny climate, proximity to the sea, snow or lakes. They are not the only criteria, but in cases where economic considerations are equal, they sway the balance. In France, where the difference between location factors does not vary greatly from one town to another, these marginal factors are becoming decisive. Increasingly the presence of an attractive local environment plays an important role in determining industrial location.

4.1.7 Industrial linkage

Industrial plants are becoming less and less independent of each other, each plant being located in relation to all other plants above and below it in the chain of production. A vehicle assembly plant, for example, cannot be too widely separated from the sub-contracting firms which supply it with components and accessories.

25

Industrial policies

Since the end of the Second World War, French industry has been caught up in various political and economic currents. Faced with successive fluctuations in the economy, French governments have in the course of time favoured three more or less different economic policies.

1 Postwar policies

1.1 The policy of industrial decentralization

A policy of industrial decentralization emerged in the years of reconstruction between the 1950s and the 1970s. It sprang from the work of the Dessus Commission during the war and from J.-F. Gravier's book *Paris et le désert français* (*Paris and the desert of provincial France*).[1] The almost exclusive aim of this policy was to reduce the concentration of industry in the Paris region. The first of the so-called operations of industrial decentralization took place between 1950 and 1953 and included, for example, the establishment of a plant of the state-owned Renault car firm at Le Mans, the building of a Citroën plant at Rennes, and the transfer of Gillette to Annecy.

A great number of measures were then adopted in the context of strategic spatial planning (*aménagement du territoire*). In 1954 loans and reductions of interest were introduced to finance decentralization, also grants towards the costs of transferring members of the existing work force and training new ones.

[1] Published by Le Portulan, Paris, 1947.

In 1955 the development of any industrial building larger than 500 sq m was made conditional on government approval. From 1959 permission was also required for the construction of offices, or for the reconstruction of industrial plants in existing locations. This was followed in 1960 by the introduction of a grant (50–100 francs according to the zone) for every square metre of floorspace in factories or offices demolished, and of a tax (100–200 francs per square metre) on the construction of offices or factories in congested regions such as the Ile-de-France (Paris) region.

The golden age of industrial decentralization was between 1960 and 1968, reaching its maximum in 1961 with the movement of 289 establishments. During the two decades 1954–74, the departure of 3,200 enterprises from the Paris region involved the creation of 462,000 new jobs in the provinces. In relation to a total increase in employment in provincial France of 880,000, this is a substantial figure. Only 34,000 people, however, followed their firms into the provinces, which goes far to explain the continuance of industrial activity and employment in the Paris region. It was characteristic that head offices and research facilities remained in the Paris region, because they were unable to find transport facilities and environments in the rest of France attractive enough to compensate for the advantages of Paris.

The policy of industrial decentralization reveals the shortcomings of strategic spatial planning in France. Yet even when we take into consideration the limited effect of this policy, the results are incontestable; there have been important local multiplier effects as well as changes in attitudes. Figure 25.1 gives the result of the 14 most significant years of industrial decentralization. It shows the predominance of new locations immediately fringing the Paris (Ile-de-France) region: 44 per cent of new employment opportunities between 1954 and 1971 were in the Paris basin and 47 per cent between 1971 and 1975.

Mistakes were made: through narrow authoritarianism; through excessive simplification of the facts of the situation; through over-bidding by individual towns; through the ephemeral success of certain slogans such as 'Décentralisez-vous dans la chlorophylle' ('Move out into the countryside'); and because of the success of a few outstanding operations. The government for its part encouraged firms to move into regions which had no industrial tradition and were therefore incapable of understanding their problems and assimilating them. Local authorities and Chambers of Commerce viewed their arrival only from the viewpoint of financial advantage. Conversely, some firms saw in decentralization a good means of modernizing their factories at the state's expense and making the maximum profit out of the inducements offered; they have been called 'chasseurs de primes' ('subsidy-hunters').

The location of new industries reflects the dynamism and initiative of individuals, occasionally acting independently of existing structures and often in the face of opposition or apathy from local Chambers of Commerce and local authorities, who are more anxious to preserve their own interests and electoral

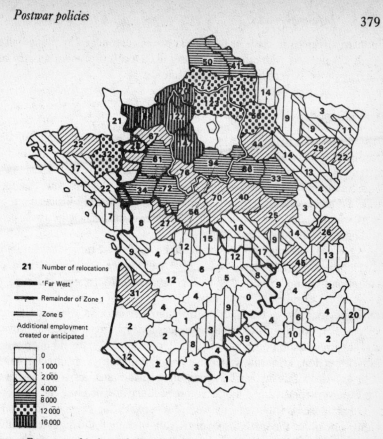

Figure 25.1 Progress of industrial decentralization 1954–67, and zones of differential assistance to industry. The assistance given to decentralized industry varied from zero in Zone 5 to a maximum in Zone 1, within which the 'Far West' received special subsidies. Source: DATAR.

majority than to ensure the future of their region or town. On the other hand, the presence of influential politicians has enabled some towns to attract high-quality industries in the space of a very short time. This goes far to explain the surprising spatial inequalities in the results of the policy of industrial decentralization.

In general, it can be said that the policy of industrial decentralization has produced a scattering of decentralized firms in too many small towns. Often, especially in the early days of the policy, moves to the provinces were determined by the availability of industrial buildings or by the delimitation of zones within which special assistance was available. In this way, many firms settled in towns affected by the textile crisis, such as Amiens or Reims.

Too many hopes have been pinned on industrial decentralization; it was a mistake to expect that it would bring about a new geographical balance in French industry. It was too liberal, too vague, not strong enough to reactivate existing industrial regions in crisis or to stimulate areas untouched by industrialization. Such was the case with industrial centres like Decazeville and industrial regions such as Berry, Nivernais and the Cévennes.

1.2 The policy of industrial development

After the period 1958–65 the policy of industrial decentralization gradually gave way to a policy of industrial development. This was necessitated by the internal demands of a baby boom, the need for housing and various forms of social equipment, and the arrival of the family car. Factors such as colonial independence, exposure to international competition and European integration increasingly revealed the structural weaknesses of the French industrial economy and necessitated its reorganization.

Since 1968 the emphasis has been on the need to create a policy for industrial development. The evidence was clear that France was indeed in a critical condition by comparison with the other great industrial states, and in particular those of the European Community.

There was also a tendency to question the attitude which preferred the spectacular, prestigious but unique project to slow, step-by-step improvements and the organization of sales networks. Unfortunately state aid operated in the same direction, favouring expensive prestige industries in direct competition with American industry, such as computers and aeronautics, to industries which were more 'plebeian' but doubtless more productive of revenue and employment.

Other more specific reasons were put forward for French industrial difficulties, including the small size of firms, rule-of-thumb and outdated methods of management, the low standards of management education, and a cost structure overweighted by an excessive tax burden.

At the same time, when the results of earlier policies were examined, their disadvantages became clearer; the systems of premiums and subsidies were too diverse, too incoherent and in the event less effective than a policy of easing credit facilities. Accordingly the various forms of aids and incentives to industry were modified. First of all, France was divided into zones, the amount of aid for industrial development or industrial adaptation diminishing from a maximum in Zone I (western and southern France) to Zone V (the Paris basin) which received no aid.

Aid to industrial development was also assimilated into the system of strategic spatial planning (*aménagement du territoire*). Two regions were accorded priority: western France and the coal and iron and steel areas. The objectives were to ensure the industrial revival of the towns and the older industrial regions, to encourage the development of a basic industrial structure in provincial France, and to assist in the growth of an appropriate urban structure in the regions of France. At the same time a more flexible attitude was adopted with regard to the Ile-de-France (Paris) region. It seemed dangerous and illusory to wish to halt the growth of the most important centre of industry in France, even though Paris appeared more industrialized than comparable capital cities. After 1968 the emphasis was therefore laid on the redistribution (*desserrement*) of industry within the Ile-de-France region itself, and on the creation of new industrial estates in relation to the proposed new towns.

From 1972, grants for regional development were given to assist in solving problems resulting from the closure of industrial plants or from a serious imbalance in industrial employment. The area to which they were applicable was more extensive and more variable and the conditions of application were more flexible. The maps showing areas in which aid to new industrial developments is available are subject to frequent revisions because of changes in economic or political circumstances. Between 1966 and 1976, DATAR (the official body concerned with strategic spatial planning) contributed a total amount of 3,329 million francs in aid, which assisted the creation of 404,067 jobs.

Together with these grants, there are tax concessions varying according to zones. In contrast to the system of grants and tax concessions, the requirements for development permission (1955) and of a development payment (1960) were introduced in regions considered sufficiently or excessively industrialized. Essentially these measures applied to the Paris region; the tax varied from 25 to 150 francs for every square metre constructed.

A policy of development contracts was introduced in 1977. They were signed between the state and the firm concerned, and made provision for a 50 per cent state investment participation over four years in return for a pledge to attain agreed objectives regarding the growth of the turnover, of exports and of employment. The list of aid to industry looks impressive, but quantitatively it is only relatively significant.

This policy of industrial incentives poses a fundamental problem as regards its aims and effectiveness. All these measures appear to be destined to direct firms towards locations which they would not have selected of their own accord, because of various disadvantages and restrictions. But monetary incentives do not cause these negative factors to disappear; they merely minimize them in the eyes of the industrialist by reducing their financial impact on the individual enterprise. All too rapidly, however, the problems reappear: inadequacy of infrastructure, cost of transport, distance from higher-level service centres. Some observers question whether financial support for industry might not be better employed in improving the overall quality of the reception area, in preparing an industrial seed-bed ready for future growth.

This industrialization was carried out under changed conditions. In the first place, access to foreign capital was made easier. After approaching foreign investment in industry with hesitation, even to the point of opposition, the government realized that this attitude was illogical since from 1 July 1968 manufactured products from other European Community countries could enter France free of import duties. Therefore since 1965 the path has been smoothed for foreign firms wishing to build new plants in France or to acquire interests in existing firms. In addition, the industrial structure and consequently the industrial geography of France were modified by a widespread process of concentration of ownership in French industry.

The process of concentration of financial power accelerated with the growing penetration of international capital and the creation of the European Community. Mergers, agreements between firms with regard to specialization, and financial participation by major firms in other companies have all increased, most spectacularly in steel and chemicals. The government has encouraged these mergers and partnerships, which increase productivity and international competitiveness. It signs agreements with the various branches of industry to provide considerable material assistance and to facilitate investment projects.

The process of concentration has significant repercussions on the location of industry. In the course of reorganization, plants are restructured or closed; some branches of industry are particularly suited to the dispersal of production into more or less autonomous plants, each manufacturing a specific product. Financial concentration and reorganization within the same firm have identical effects. It is not in a firm's interest to have plants scattered all over the country; on the contrary, they should be near head office or, failing that, in the same region or on the same traffic axis.

Concentration on technical grounds demands larger units and changes in the organization of production or plant mergers. Thus in the Nord Department the 3,000 breweries of 1914 had fallen to a mere 139 by 1957. Some plants were closed because they were below the optimum size of production required by modern technology, for example several arms plants at Châtellerault, posing difficult problems of industrial conversion and re-employment of labour.

Industrial concentration on economic grounds reflects the process of financial concentration described above. The industrial firms who are the beneficiaries carry more and more weight within their sector and on the market and increasingly tend to become monopoly producers.

This phase of industrialization developed in a general euphoria of expansion, progress and technical expertise, with the emphasis more on the quantity than the quality of industrial production.

1.3 New industrial policies: reconversion and redeployment

The transformation of French industry has taken place in an environment increasingly dominated by international developments and characterized by the speed of its structural transformation and by the suddenness and scale of the economic crises affecting it. In recent years this industrial environment has been affected by the new international division of labour, by the energy crisis, and by new attitudes relating to ideology, economics and ecology, notably the attack on the inevitability and desirability of continuing economic growth. From 1974 the general crisis in world economy, accelerated by the increase in oil prices, showed up inadequacies in the French industrialized economy. One industry after another was affected: iron and steel, textiles, shipbuilding, printing, pulp and paper, leather, fertilizers; in other words, the traditional industries. By contrast with young industries in full expansion, these older industries dating from the industrial revolution went through difficult times. Glass manufacture disappeared from Creil, and shoe manufacture from Amiens and the western part of the Nord coalfield. Many textile mills disappeared in the Nord region, in eastern France and in Normandy, which had been bastions of the industry. The number of workers in the cotton industry fell from 138,000 in 1955 to 72,000 in 1971. Between 1950 and 1960 2,800 plants were closed. Abandonment was most frequent in textiles and the metallurgical industry (old foundries in particular), but numerous plants were affected, for example flour mills, distilleries and silk mills. Faced with this situation, policies for industrial conversion were set in motion. In 1954 the cotton industry introduced a 15-year plan of reconversion and modernization. Two million spindles were scrapped and about 300 factories closed or converted. In all, between 1952 and 1964, the number of spinning mills fell from 320 to 238 and weaving mills from 977 to 705.

In order to facilitate the transformation of traditional industries, 'Commissioners for Conversion and Industrialization' were introduced in 1967 for Lorraine, the Nord region, the Centre–Midi coalfields, and then in 1970 for the Mediterranean and Atlantic coastal regions.

To the effects of the international economic climate were added from 1976 onwards the consequences of the government's move towards greater freedom of enterprise, shown by the reduction of direct state participation in industry, dismantling of price controls and an end to the practice of propping up loss-making firms. The result was an increase in plant closures and redundancies. The aim of this retreat from interventionist policies was to enable industry to adapt to the demands of international competition. However, the interministerial committee concerned with industrial restructuring, created in 1974 (Comité Interministériel pour l'Aménagement des Structures Industrielles), helped more than 500 firms in difficulty over a period of four years. A special fund (Fonds Spécial d'Adaptation Industrielle – CIASI) provided financial assistance to areas affected by serious industrial crisis, such as Nord–Pas-de-Calais, Lorraine and the Pays de la Loire.

After 1978 it was realized that in the light of developments in the world economy and of anticipated future trends it was essential to encourage French industry to develop in the direction of the sectors which were in world-wide expansion. This involved a concentration on high-technology products which combine high inputs of scientific and technological skill with the maximum value added in production, products which cannot in the short term be taken over by the technologically less advanced low-wage industries of the developing countries. In other words, French industry was to concentrate on nuclear energy, electronics, communications systems, information technology and office systems; also on fashion, machine tools, engineering design services and new types of energy.

In May 1980 the government formally recognized seven industrial sectors which will receive aid because they represent the industry of the future: office systems, general-access information systems, off-shore oil production, biotechnology, industrial robots and energy conservation. This reorientation of French industry is hindered, however, by its financial structures and by foreign penetration.

In French industry as a whole, branches of foreign and multinational companies are less prominently represented than in Germany and Great Britain, but they are established in the sectors which are the most promising in terms of growth and profitability. Foreign capital thus controls more than 50 per cent of subsectors such as agricultural tractors, computers, measuring equipment, and they have strengthened their position in electrical equipment, electronics, chemicals (especially fine chemicals and pharmaceuticals) and precision engineering . . . The search for the best way of restructuring our economy finds this a serious obstacle: the location strategy of the multinationals does not necessarily correspond to what would be best for France.[2]

With the arrival in power in 1981 of a socialist government, industrial policy took a new direction. The government's ability to intervene was increased through renewed nationalization measures, while a powerful Ministry for Industry and Research had a growing impact on the structure of French industry. At the same time, administrative decentralization has given local authorities increased possibilities of industrial assistance.

Even greater emphasis was placed on interventionist policies as the world economic crisis revealed the weaknesses of French industry, its archaic character and excessively high costs in all of the main industrial sectors. If mining, iron and steel and shipbuilding had been particularly affected, weaknesses also appeared in the automobile industry, telecommunications, building and construction.

In July 1982 an interministerial committee for industrial restructuring took the place of the CIASI. The Industrial Modernization Fund (Fonds Industriel de Modernisation), set up in 1983, introduced new forms of industrial assistance. In aiding the development of private firms it is able to draw upon the resources of the savings banks, while for nationalized industries reliance is placed on planning contracts drawn up with the government.

In February 1984 the government adopted a plan for transforming the structure of industry. It included social and economic measures destined to reduce unemployment and to encourage innovation and the creation of new businesses. In a spatial sense it defined 14 redevelopment poles (towns, employment regions or valleys) in which firms would benefit from particularly advantageous measures. Exceptional assistance was to be given to the two poles defined in Lorraine, because of the particularly critical state of the steel industry.

[2] C. Stoffaes and J. Vittori, *La Grande Menace industrielle* (Calmann Levy, Paris, 1978).

These policies were accompanied by a new wave of mergers, market-sharing agreements between firms and reduction and concentration of activities within firms.

The economic crisis and consequent policy changes have and will continue to have geographical consequences. Industrial dynamism has undoubtedly slackened and there will be fewer new plants, at least until the hoped-for arrival of new sectors. It is also anticipated that a tendency to enlarge or modernize existing factories will prevail over the building of new ones. Competition between regions and towns is intensified, with existing industrial regions in decline opposing the establishment of new plants in non-industrialized regions. New plants tend to be established either in regions with an existing industrial structure or in those already possessing a favourable provision of infrastructural facilities and amenities.

To these recent tendencies in the development of industry can be added the highly publicized intention to move towards 'factories on a human scale'. If the tendency continues it could have significant effects on location, allowing industrial development in towns and regions which could never accommodate the giant plants customary in the past.

The Paris region is the best example of the evolution of ideas and policies. There was initially no strong opposition to the policies of industrial decentralization and the industrialization of provincial France. A first difficulty emerged, however, in relation to industries wishing to settle in the new towns of the Paris region, which not only received no subsidies but, in common with all new developments in the region, were subjected to special payments, the *redevances*. Once the deteriorating economic situation began to result in plant closures, however, the locational policies for the Paris region were perceived as responsible for the 'deindustrialization' of the most powerful and dynamic industrial centre in France.

2 The balance sheet of French industrial development

French industry changed radically between 1950 and the present day, but this transformed structure had to be grafted on to a social and economic system which had known only stagnation during the previous thirty years. Imbalance and anomalies were therefore inevitable.

On the debit side, observers point to a continuing and excessive reliance on the kind of traditional industry that is the first to be taken up by developing cheap-labour countries. There is also too great a reliance on consumer-goods industries, as opposed to production goods and ultra-modern industries such as computers and associated equipment, electronics, electronic components, machine tools and industrial vehicles. The industrial labour force is not only inadequate in quantity but described by some as 'inferior' in quality, with an excessive reliance on migrant workers, women and casual workers, receiving low wages for work requiring only a low level of skill. Much industrial development took place in areas where it was necessary to resort to foreign labour, notably in the Paris region. Experts consider that the process of industrial concentration has still not gone far enough, while industrial exports suffer from an insufficient development of commercial houses specializing in international trade. All in all, France has far from completed the process of creating a modernized industrial structure. For example, in 1974, 10.82 man-hours were required to produce a ton of steel in France, as compared with 7.72 in the German Federal Republic, 7.24 in Belgium and 6.75 in Italy.

Nevertheless, the industrial map of France has been profoundly modified. The most important result was a change in the relative industrial significance of the Paris region and of the remainder of France. The process of decentralization and the additional costs of establishing new industrial plants have lost the Paris region some of its industrial weight and above all its dynamism, even though it still remains the country's most important industrial region. The share of the Paris region in new industrial building has greatly diminished. Of planning permissions issued for units of industrial floorspace over 500 sq m, the Paris region had 36.9 per cent in 1955, 19 per cent in 1960 and 9.8 per cent in 1965.

Decentralization of industry from Paris has particularly benefited the immediately surrounding regions, notably the lower Seine. Burgundy, although further from Paris, is favourably situated between the capital and the country's second major urban pole in the Lyon region. It is also well placed in relation to Germany and Switzerland. Within a few years this region, and Dijon in particular, received several electronic assembly plants, offering numerous opportunities for female labour. Châlon-sur-Saône has also become an important industrial centre, with metallurgical and machine-building industries.

The Alsace plain is without any doubt the most remarkable case of industrial development linked to a revolution in spatial relationships. Alsace was formerly very much a frontier region, exposed to invasion and destruction and therefore not industrialized, but the creation of the European Community transformed its geographical position, placing it at the very heart of a united and peaceful Rhineland Europe. As soon as the Treaty of Rome came into force Alsace received its first influx of industrial plants, mostly German firms from the Saar. Later many American firms chose sites there.

The Rhône corridor and the adjoining Alpine valleys also benefited greatly from industrial decentralization and expansion. To the purely economic attractions, such as location on the axial belt following the Rhône, were added other advantages such as proximity to major cities both in France and in neighbouring countries, and easy access to the mountains, with their recreational attractions in winter and summer. This explains the arrival of new industries in Annecy and in the valleys of the northern Pre-Alps.

In southern France, between the mouth of the Rhône and Marseille, the shores of the Etang de Berre have become the site of a vast zone of oil refineries, petrochemical plants and, later, iron and steel works. In southwest France a great chemical complex was created near Lacq. The Lacq natural gas is used in the manufacture of ammonia and acetylene, and the residual gas is transferred to an adjoining plant for the manufacture of methanol. Plants involved in the further processing of these chemicals have, however, not been attracted, so that Lacq has not evolved into a significant centre of varied manufacturing.

Western France benefited significantly from the decentralization of industrial plants, which followed the road and rail axes out of Paris. Labour-intensive production took over from industries in crisis such as textiles and footwear. Some notable successes, as at Lannion (telecommunications), cannot, however, mask the uneven and superficial character of this industrial development.

Industry is in a state of decline in regions where geographical isolation is made worse by poor communications, high transport charges and the lack of a supportive urban structure, and this in spite of all kinds of state assistance. Such is the case with the old metallurgical centres of the southern part of the Central massif and the industrial centres of the interior valleys of the Pyrenees and the Alps.

The older industrial regions have had fluctuating fortunes, often reflecting changing policies. The Nord is a typical example of an old, powerful industrial region in decline. Coal mining has gradually been abandoned, just like the heavy-textile industry, while inland iron and steel plants were endangered by the rise of coastal locations.

For many years the government showed no interest in the troubles of the region, giving priority to the non-industrialized regions in western, central and southwest France. It considered that the Nord, with its regional banks and great entrepreneurial families, was powerful enough on its own to carry through the necessary process of industrial adaptation. In the region itself, however, there was a division of opinions, the old traditional industries not favouring the installation of new enterprises; the coal mines themselves were reluctant to diversify their activities. There was a threat of a serious economic and social crisis, while each year the region showed a negative migratory balance.

Within two years the situation underwent a profound change; the authorities in Paris discovered the importance of a region which contained 10 per cent of the working population of France, and the region itself gradually acquired a sense of unity. Above all, industrialists and investors discovered the permanent attractions of the Nord, not least its privileged situation in the heart of the European Community and western Europe. This advantage had previously been concealed by the position of the region as a frontier post on the traditional invasion route across the northern lowland of Europe. This frontier situation inhibited the development of the further processing of the region's iron, steel and textiles. With the arrival of the European Community the natural advantages of the region asserted themselves. Another advantage was the reduction in the journey-time to Paris, thanks to new motorways and railway modernization. The region was very soon chosen as a location by important firms manufacturing television tubes and cosmetics in the Lille–Lesquin industrial zone and automotive products at Douvrin–La Bassée (with European Community assistance), in the Sambre valley, near Valenciennes and at Douai. At the same time, the textile industry reaped the benefits of a vigorous policy of mergers and modernization. Crises in the coal, steel and textile industries, however, demand industrial transformation and the establishment of new plants on quite a different scale.

The policy of industrial planning launched in the 1950s at a period of economic expansion had as its objectives industrial decentralization from the Paris region and the securing of a better balance of industrial location. Today, in a context of economic crisis, industrial planning has had to become defensive in nature, in an attempt to save entire industrial sectors and to protect as many jobs and plants in the old industrial regions as possible. It is, however, open to question whether the new industries of the year 2000 will find that these traditional industrial regions, these derelict landscapes of coal and steel, offer them acceptable locations.

26

⚜ Industrial environments

Industrial enterprises are found in a great variety of locations and contrasting environments, ranging from the small isolated village workshop to the vast plant in a regional industrial complex, which is in itself an environment with its own distinctive landscape.

1 Industry in a rural environment

It is well known that the definition of 'rural' presents considerable difficulties. Ideally, rural industrial locations should be further classified into peri-urban locations, mountain locations, rural industrial locations related to particular features of physical geography or to mineral deposits, and 'purely rural' locations. Rural industry is extremely heterogeneous, with a predominance of small-scale, old or inadequately modernized enterprises. Measured by workers employed, rural industry accounts for 28 per cent of food-processing, 15 per cent of textiles and clothing, 13 per cent of machine building, 11 per cent of chemicals, 39 per cent of timber and furniture, 25 per cent of leather and skins and 24 per cent of building and public works.

Industrialized rural regions are often the successors to earlier stages of industrial location dating from before and after the industrial revolution. In many regions, rural industry has developed from domestic industries associated with peasant farming, from craft enterprises linked with the growth of the royal manufactories in the seventeenth century, from specialized workshops linked to the putting-out factory system, or from small plants associated with the use of hydroelectricity.

After a long, slow process of rural deindustrialization which ruined manufacturing and the artisan class in some regions, a new wave of industrialization set in with the Second World War, linked initially with the evacuation of plants due to the war, and then after 1945 to the policies of strategic spatial planning and industrial decentralization. Rural areas benefited in particular from the special grants available from 1955 for zones in economic difficulties and from supplementation of wages. However, rural industrialism in this period mainly affected rural communes on the urban fringe (sub-contracting firms, firms attracted by existing buildings or by small industrial estates).

Without being able to give a precise date, a new stage of rural industrialization began about 1965, when a third generation of plants was born out of 'industrial redeployment'. These were plants requiring non-specialized labour for routine production, a labour force which would be cheap, predominantly female, and more docile than in the large towns. The automotive, machine-building, electrical equipment and agricultural processing branches were principally involved. This new industry was particularly attracted by the rural labour market of western France, with new plants located on the fringes of the Paris basin, of the Armorican massif, of the Aquitaine basin and in Limousin (for example, the domestic equipment firm of Moulinex at Caen and the 'rural' plants of the Legrand electrical equipment group in the Charentes). The establishment of plants in rural areas has also taken place sporadically and in a dispersed fashion.

The developments of the last few years have not greatly modified the characteristic structure of those branches of industry which seek privileged locations in rural areas. Although there are a few examples of the establishment of large isolated plants in rural areas, the general pattern is of the setting up of branch plants of between 100 and 200 workers, whether by large French industrial groups or by foreign firms, which has not led to any marked increase of scale. It must also be admitted that in spite of the establishment of new plants in recent years, the distribution of industry in rural areas remains very uneven. Most rural industry is still concentrated in the Lyon area and north of a line from Geneva to Le Havre. Nevertheless there is no doubt that the existence of industrial plants brings about profound changes in rural areas, giving rise to phenomena such as part-time farming, long-distance journeys to work, new building activity and the appearance of a new social class of 'rural workers'. These phenomena are to be found equally where an older industrialization occurs in industrialized valleys (Vosges, Alps), where there is an inheritance of an older, diffused industrial pattern (Choletais, Berry), where recent industrialization is found in large *bourgs* or small towns, or in simple rural communes.

2 The industrial town

The industrial town is the most widespread type of industrial location in France. The name of a town is often attached to a particular product, such as Amiens velvet, Calais lace, Thiers cutlery, Millau gloves or Dijon mustard. According to the degree of industrial development and the range of products, such towns may be mono-industrial or poly-industrial (see chapter 37.1).

There has been a major change in the relationship between urban space and industrial location. Traditionally, workshops and small factories were built in previously open areas in the interior of urban blocks, hidden from view by the rows of houses along the bordering streets. It is almost possible to speak of 'industries without factories', types of manufacturing which have no need of large areas of space and which owe their origin to scattered small workshops and to a diffusion of trades. An example of this type of location is provided by the Lyon silk industry, which has its own highly individual form of organization. There are several hundred 'manufacturers' with offices in the city. For the most part these firms pass on orders for manufacturing to the swarm of textile mills and workshops scattered throughout the Lyon region. The silk industry employs in all 55,000 people, 16,000 of them in the 57 communes that make up the Lyon 'urban community'. Hence the visitor is inevitably disappointed on his first contact with the silk industry of Lyon: he sees a hill called Croix Rousse, with winding streets, dirty forbidding apartment houses, but no factories. The characteristic industry of a town, therefore, is not necessarily reflected in buildings commensurate with its importance.

These locations within the town itself have long been the general rule for industrial buildings. This reflects the early date at which such buildings were established and their long-continued occupation. At a time when public transport was non-existent, factories were built in or immediately adjacent to towns, the source of their labour supply. Urban growth rapidly swallowed them up; this explains the extraordinary intermixture of residential and industrial uses. The availability of vacant industrial buildings has always been a powerful attraction to incoming firms; one industry has replaced another in the existing buildings, making it unnecessary to build a new plant. Much of French industry was therefore located in outmoded factories, unsuited to the particular technical needs of the occupiers, often with no proper storage space, and in slum workshops such as those in the city of Paris and its inner suburbs.

These traditional industrial locations, these 'invisible' factories, have declined in the face of the requirements of modern industry. The very inadequacy of the older industrial buildings has been a powerful incentive to industrial decentralization from the towns. Site requirements have become more and more restrictive with the need for vast floor spaces, the search for low-cost land, the problems of pollution and waste disposal, and the sheer weight of much modern machinery.

The industrial estate is a relatively recent innovation in France. Before the Second World War industrial estates were the exception, more often the result of chance than deliberate organization. The industrial zone of Saint-Fons (south of Lyon) had seven chemical factories on 136 ha of alluvial land. The industrial estate of Marquette-lès-Lille was built in the interwar period by a private builder of railway branch lines.

Since 1950, industrial estates have become classic tools of spatial planning. They sprang up all over France, due to the fact that many communes saw them as a means of attracting new industries, whether decentralized or not. Many were merely waste land or former pasture land which became industrial estates simply by putting up a notice at the corner of the street. Too many of these were merely pocket-handkerchief size and were incapable of providing the area required to meet the needs of large plants, far less of their future expansion: if a plant needs 10 ha for immediate occupation it will look for an industrial estate which can provide 40.

The nature of industrial estates has been considerably transformed as they have become the responsibility of organizations covering groups of communes and local authorities: by 1975, Chambers of Commerce and Industry had created 200 industrial estates covering 21,000 ha, and were associated with other bodies in a further 178 zones covering 27,000 ha. A modern industrial estate covers a vast area and is provided with all the necessary infrastructure such as high-tension power, water, road and rail links, public transport, security and maintenance services, and restaurants. Some industrial estates specialize in particular activities. For instance, the Bordeaux region has estates for light industry to the west at Pessac and Mérignac, estates for medium-sized industry near the Garonne at Bassens and Floirac, and an estate for major plants at Bec d'Ambès.

Since 1962, following the model of British trading estates, the Société Centrale d'Equipement du Territoire has provided prefabricated factory buildings which firms can occupy under hire-purchase arrangements.

Port industrial zones are a giant version of industrial estates; they cover 10,000 ha at Le Havre, 5,300 ha at Fos-Marseille, and 4,000 ha at Dunkerque. By their sheer size they reverse the usual relationship between the scale of the town and that of the attached industrial area.

3 The industrial region

Other forms of industrial distribution may be grouped in the general category of the industrial region, but there are, in fact, several distinct types.

3.1 Industrial–urban complexes

These complexes are extended versions of industrial towns. Some develop by the coalescence of neighbouring industrial towns having a wide range of activities such as the Lille–Roubaix–Tourcoing complex. Others develop by the expansion of a single large urban pole such as Lyon or Paris.

3.2 Mining industrial regions

The exploitation of mineral resources gave rise to a particular kind of industrialization, completely changing the pre-existing rural landscape by a juxtaposition of mines and plants based directly or indirectly on the use of coal or ore. The extent of such industrial regions is determined by the extent of the mineral deposit concerned, occasionally enlarged by tributary rural areas from which workers are drawn. The main mining industrial regions are the iron and steel region of northern Lorraine (218 communes), the Lorraine coalfield (152 communes), the coalfield of the western part of the Nord region (123 communes) and its extension into the lower Escaut field (119 communes), the Le Creusot region (20 communes), Saint-Etienne (59 communes) and Alès–La Grande-Combe (45 communes).

3.3 The industrial valleys

By combining a number of factors favourable to the location of factories, valleys have often influenced the formation of linear industrial region, bounded by the steep slopes of the valley sides. The density and continuity of industrial development are variable: there are veritable 'streets' of industrial plants (as in the Saint-Etienne depression and lower Seine valley), a string of factories as in the Oise valley, and intermittent industrial development as in the valleys of the Alps (Arve, Isère, Arc) of the Lorraine Vosges, or of Moselle upstream from Charmes. Further examples are the Sambre valley and the Risle valley in Normandy.

27

⚜ The tertiary sector

1 General characteristics

By 1975 the proportion of the working population engaged in the tertiary sector had exceeded 50 per cent (by 1978 it was 56 per cent), and the sector was responsible for about half of the country's gross domestic product. A high proportion of activity in the tertiary sector is generally considered to indicate a high level of economic development; in fact the figures for France are rather below the average for OECD countries, and below those for the United States, the United Kingdom or Scandinavia, although higher than in the German Federal Republic or Italy (Table 27.1).

1.1 The nature of tertiary activity

The adjective 'tertiary' has a certain ambiguity. In France the importance of tertiary activity may be measured by the number of persons exercising tertiary occupations: in 1975 they made up 46 per cent of the working population. Alternatively it may be measured according to the firms having their principal activity in the tertiary sector, which at the same period occupied a little more than 51 per cent of the working population (10,672,000 in all).

Tertiary occupations are defined generally speaking as non-manual occupations, or more precisely occupations which have no direct part in production ('white-collar' employment). The classification given by the socio-professional

Table 27.1 *The tertiary sector in selected industrialized countries*

Country	Persons employed in the tertiary sector (services and administration) as a percentage of total employed population	
	1955	1974
Italy	25.7	39.3
Austria	29.7	43.8
German Federal Republic	32.6	45.1
Switzerland	36.1	46.5
France	36.7	49.0
United Kingdom	45.1	54.8
Netherlands	42.4	57.9
Denmark	40.5	58.1
USA	45.2	62.4
Sweden	38.1	63.8

Source: The Economist, 29 November and 13 December 1975.

categories of INSEE combines status (wage-earning or self-employed) with qualifications. Among the wage-earning or salaried workers, the largest category is that of clerical workers (14.2 per cent of the working population). Middle management accounts for 9 per cent, service workers less than 6 per cent, higher management 4.7 per cent and shop assistants 3.4 per cent. The self-employed are chiefly small shopkeepers (4.2 per cent), owners of larger establishments in the distributive trades (0.9 per cent) and professional people (0.8 per cent) (Table 27.2).

The table illustrates the variety of status and occupation covered by the term 'tertiary'. It also shows that a certain number of workers in the tertiary sector are located within industrial firms. The proportion of tertiary employment in firms classified as having manufacturing as their principal activity is estimated at 20 per cent. This 'secondary tertiary' includes, for example, commercial services, transport, management, laboratories and research departments integral to industrial firms. It has also been estimated (1978) that 300,000 workers classified as belonging to the tertiary sector are in occupations directly linked to agriculture, working for example in agricultural co-operatives, credit provision or insurance services. On the other hand, about a third of workers in the tertiary sector have manual jobs, for example as warehousemen or in service occupations.

The tertiary sector is usually defined as a residual, containing activities which are neither agricultural nor industrial. The largest element is made up by service activities, whether provided in return for payment (17.7 per cent of the working population) or publicly provided (16 per cent). Commerce employs another 11.5 per cent of the working population, transport and communications 5.9 per cent (Table 27.3). If these activities are regrouped according to their final destination, 10 per cent of the working population is engaged in national government, local government and the defence services, another 10 per cent in personal services,

Table 27.2 *Changes in the socio-economic categories corresponding to tertiary occupations*

Category	Percentage of total occupied population			
	1954	1962	1968	1975
Owners and managers of large establishments in the distributive trades	0.9	0.9	1.0	0.9
Owners and managers of small establishments in the distributive trades	6.5	5.9	5.1	4.2
Professions	0.6	0.6	0.7	0.8
Teachers in secondary and higher education	0.4	0.7	1.1	1.7
Higher administration and management	1.5	2.0	2.2	3.0
Teachers in primary education	2.0	2.2	2.8	3.4
Medical and social services	. . .[a]	0.6	0.8	1.4
Middle administration and management	2.8	3.2	3.6	4.5
Office workers	8.5	9.8	11.6	14.2
Assistants in the distributive trades	2.3	2.7	3.1	3.4
Domestic servants	1.7	1.6	1.4	1.1
Female domestic help	1.2	1.1	1.1	0.7
Other service personnel	2.4	2.7	3.2	3.9
Others (artists, clergy, army, police, etc.)	2.7	2.9	2.6	2.4
Total	33.5	36.9	40.3	45.6

[a] Data not available.
Source: INSEE, *Economie et Statistique*, no. 91, 1977.

domestic services and entertainment, 20 per cent in distribution (transport, communications, wholesaling, retailing), and 30 per cent in banking and financial services.

A certain number of characteristics common to many of these activities help to give a clearer idea of the tertiary sector. Generally speaking, if we set aside transport, which caters for 'intermediate' needs, tertiary activities satisfy needs at a third level of priority and therefore develop after primary and secondary activities, which meet essential needs such as food, clothing and housing. Mobility, security, education, culture and credit are examples of needs which generate tertiary activities. In contrast with industry, which transforms raw materials into transportable goods, these activities have a non-material product, in the cost of which labour is the principal element. The rate of technical progress in the tertiary sector is generally low: between 1954 and 1974 the average annual improvement in productivity per worker was 3 per cent, as against 6 per cent in industry.

In any consideration of the economic structure of the sector it is necessary to exclude the public services, as well as members of the professions not operating on their own account. Among private businesses the degree of economic concentration varies considerably from one branch to another. The tertiary sector is characterized by a highly atomized economic structure. It includes a large proportion of small businesses: on average there are 7 paid workers per employer in consumer services, 11 in retailing and 27 in transport, as compared with 30 in industry. The 50 largest firms engaged in service provision account for

Table 27.3 *Changing composition of the tertiary sector*

Absolute numbers and as a percentage of total employed population

Branch	1962		1968		1972	
	Thousands	%	Thousands	%	Thousands	%
Transport	769	4.0	813	4.1	837	4.0
Telecommunications	290	1.5	348	1.7	402	1.9
Housing services	68	0.4	81	0.4	114	0.5
Other services	2,005	10.5	2,455	12.3	2,999	14.3
Distributive trades	1,942	10.2	2,223	11.1	2,396	11.5
Banking, insurance	253	1.3	332	1.7	496	2.4
Government service	1,005	5.3	1,269	6.4	1,686	8.1
Armed forces	372	2.0	318	1.6	314	1.5
Local government	276	1.4	345	1.7	452	2.2
Health and social security	108	0.6	149	0.7	214	1.0
Management in private sector	348	1.8	405	2.0	508	2.4
Domestic service	535	2.8	494	2.5	319	1.5
Total tertiary sector	7,971	41.8	9,232	46.2	10,737	51.3
of which wage-earning	...[a]	...	7,579	82.1	9,212	85.8
of which women	3,536	44.3	4,151	45.0	5,079	47.3

[a] Data not available.
Source: INSEE, censuses.

only 9.4 per cent of turnover in their particular sector, in distribution only 13.4 per cent, whereas they account for between 30 and 70 per cent in most of the major industrial sectors. A recent inquiry revealed that more than 84 per cent of enterprises in wholesale and retail distribution had fewer than 50 wage-earners and salaried employees, whereas in banking only 46 per cent of firms fell into this category, and in insurance 36 per cent. Firms with more than 1,000 workers represent 0.5 per cent of firms in wholesale and retail distribution, 5 per cent in banking and 8 per cent in insurance. The 250,000 workers in road haulage are spread over 25,445 firms, of which 20,000 have fewer than five workers.

Nevertheless the very great importance of the public sector must not be overlooked. Government employees make up 40 per cent of all workers in the tertiary sector; half of them are teachers in state schools and universities. Persons in government employment are, however, divided among a great many separate establishments and offices.

Because of the characteristic structure of the tertiary sector, wage-earners and salaried employees make up only 86 per cent of the total work force, as compared with 93 per cent for industry, but the proportion is increasing: it was 82 per cent in 1968.

The heterogeneous nature of the tertiary sector is again apparent in relation to efficiency and productivity. Because of difficulties relating to the classification of occupations, it is not easy to measure variations in productivity. Clearly, however, it is possible to distinguish types of tertiary activity with very greatly differing prospects. There is an 'artisan' type of tertiary (hairdressing, for example) where productivity is low and not likely to increase. By contrast, there is an 'industrialized' tertiary (for example, most of the non-personal services: transport, telecommunications and the everyday activities of high-street banking, insurance, commerce and the hotel trade), where productivity is increasing significantly. There is also a 'bureaucratic' tertiary concerned with both public administration and the private sector, where productivity is often held to be decreasing under the influence of bureaucratic proliferation (Parkinson's law). Other types of tertiary activity are concerned either with improving the quality of life (education, health, social security and leisure), or with improving the quality of organization (research, design and consultancy services). The latter is sometimes held to be the only part of the tertiary sector which has an economic multiplier effect, in that it makes it possible to increase productivity in agriculture and industry, whereas the development of tertiary activities is generally considered as induced by the growth of other activities or of the population. Several authors have suggested regrouping these multiplier activities in a new category of 'higher tertiary', 'decision-making tertiary' and even 'quaternary'.

The importance of female labour is another characteristic of the tertiary sector. Two out of three working women are found in this sector; in 1975, 47 per cent of the tertiary workers were women, twice the proportion in industry. The proportion of women employed has tended to increase (it was 45 per cent in 1968); in the secondary sector it remains stable at about 24 per cent, or is even tending to fall. The proportion of jobs occupied by women tends to vary in approximately inverse ratio to the level of qualifications required. There are great inequalities between the various branches; the proportion of women is high in the public services, low in consultancy and research. Inequalities are particularly marked in tertiary occupations; the proportion of female employment is low in senior executive posts (17 per cent) and the professions (20 per cent); it is average (between 40 and 50 per cent) for middle management, secondary-school teachers and small shopkeepers; and very high for primary-school teachers (63 per cent), office workers (65 per cent), and medical and social services (79 per cent).

1.2 Change in the tertiary sector
1.2.1 The reasons for growth

For a long period after 1850, tertiary employment expanded at the same rate as industrial employment, but after the Second World War it began to grow more rapidly. There was a significant increase in employment, with an average annual growth rate of more than 2 per cent, accounting for three-quarters of total employment expansion between 1962 and 1975 (Tables 27.2 and 27.3). Equally significant, however, were the proliferation and diffusion of a range of characteristic activities, from new bank branches to new universities. Their rise was a reflection of demand: between 1959 and 1973 the proportion of household expenditure devoted to services rose from 26 to 34 per cent, whereas that devoted to manufactured products rose only from 37 to 39 per cent. The consumption of services by private firms and the public sector rose even more rapidly, increasing fivefold in the same period. The business world has thus become the chief consumer of services in France, accounting for 48 per cent of consumption, compared with 44 per cent absorbed by households and 8 per cent devoted to export needs.

Faced with a growing demand, a sector of activity in which productivity is increasing very slowly can only develop by creating new jobs. The rise in the standard of living of the French people, allowing them to increase and diversify their consumption of services, is one of the important factors in the growth of tertiary activities. The increase reflects the growing role of the administrative and other services of the state, a process that has been described as revealing an increasing socialization of the French population. There were 845,000 civil servants in 1952 and 1,872,000 in 1975.

The development of the tertiary sector is also carried out by a progressive elaboration of the division of labour. Functions which were formerly regarded as an integral part of industrial enterprises and therefore classed as belonging to the secondary sector of the economy are increasingly breaking free to form independent service enterprises. Advertising, works catering, laundry services, company vehicles, security and the provision of temporary employment are all examples of services provided by specialist firms. The growth of the tertiary sector relates also to its progressive diversification, as shown, for example, by the appearance of new categories in the 1973 list of economic activities, in fields such as specialist repair services, leasing and research. The most spectacular tertiary growth rates can be observed in the most recently developed services to firms, in such fields as information technology and office systems.

An excellent example of rapid development in new directions is provided by the recent growth of technical and business consultancy, designed to provide a creative intellectual input into the process of investment optimization. Approximately 50,000 persons, one-third of them executives and one-third technicians, are employed in 800 independent firms in this field. To these we must add similar offices integrated within industrial firms and in the public sector. These activities take two main forms. About four-fifths of firms and persons employed are engaged in the provision of engineering and technical services in relation to projects of investment in building, construction and industry. A smaller, but rapidly growing, group of consultancy firms provides advice and know-how in relation to management, organization, training, market research, publicity, computers and data-processing. France takes second place in the world with respect to business turnover in this particular field. The scarcity of these services, their necessary proximity to the places where the vital decisions are made, and the importance of personal contacts explain their very great spatial concentration. The Paris region contains more than half of the firms in this field and accounts for four-fifths of employment and turnover; it is followed by the Rhône–Alpes region with below 10 per cent of firms and 6 per cent of employment.

Tourism has been one of the most important elements in the growth of tertiary activities and occupations, and, more generally speaking, in the increase of mobility and travel. The proportion of people taking holidays away from home rose from 43.6 per cent in 1964 to 54 per cent in 1976; 3,800,000 people took a winter-sports holiday of four days or more in 1978–9 as compared with 1,250,000 in 1968–9. In 1976 an inquiry at the frontier put at 25 million the number of foreigners coming on holiday to France, representing 234 million bed-nights. By comparison, French people on holiday accounted for 557 million bed-nights. In 1978 tourist expenditure in the widest sense amounted to 180,000 million francs, or 8 per cent of gross internal product. Foreign tourists spent 27,000 million francs in France, equivalent to 8 per cent of French foreign-currency earnings, more than the export earnings of automobiles or agricultural products.

1.2.2 *The special case of rural tourism*

The development and spread of tourist and recreational activities in rural areas show the extent of changes in French society. It is difficult to give a precise description of this development, partly because of changing definitions of what is 'rural', partly because of the difficulty of reconciling the categories used in specific inquiries into vacation patterns and tourism with those of the census. It is, however, certain that the recreational use of the countryside, itself no new phenomenon, has greatly extended since the Second World War. It has recently become even more attractive following the economic crisis and the move towards a 'return to nature'.

The countryside and the mountains attract more than half of holiday visits, amounting in all to more than 400 million days, of which 241 were in country areas. In 1975 the countryside alone had nearly half of the total tourist accommodation in France, with 4.9 million beds; the size of this figure is chiefly explained, however, by the great number of second homes, which account for 80 per cent of the 'tourist' beds available in the countryside. Caravan and campsites account for 12 per cent of the total, while the specifically rural forms of tourism such as *gîtes* (simple self-catering accommodation), guest rooms with families and camping holidays on farms represent barely 5 per cent of the total in spite of their recent rapid growth. In fact, rural areas offer all kinds of vacation provision: second homes, rural *gîtes*, farm holidays, camp sites and the characteristically French vacation colonies for children.

The spatial distribution and consequences of this diffused tourism are much more difficult to demonstrate. One basis of differentiation could be provided by an analysis of the social categories which locally characterize this 'green' tourism. The most basic type would be provided by those areas where people of modest means spend weekends or school holidays at relatively low cost because they can use their inherited family home. Of a similar nature are areas where low-income people prepare for their retirement by buying or building inexpensive pre-retirement second homes, or those where people return to their rural origins. In spite of municipal efforts to supply here and there an artificial lake or a swimming pool, this type of tourism is barely sufficient to support local shopkeepers in depopulated areas.

The level of development of rural tourism in any particular locality is closely connected not only with the qualities of the landscape but also with the social environment. Sometimes this is open to tourist penetration, but is elsewhere dominated by local notables who rely on state institutions like national parks, regional parks or forest administrations to direct and contain this diffused tourism so that it does not develop into mass tourism in the hands of property developers or in relation to tourist complexes.

1.2.3 Growth disparities in the tertiary sector

The overall development of the sector does not preclude great disparities in growth between the different branches. Banks, national administration and local authorities saw their numbers increase by more than two-thirds between 1962 and 1975, employment in services to the public increased by half, whilst growth was low in commerce and transport, and zero in domestic services and the army.

On the other hand the growing cost of some services, for which labour costs are mostly responsible, may lead to a contrary trend in employment, through the substitution of goods for services, for example the replacement of domestic servants by household equipment. Public transport is expanding less rapidly than the rest of the tertiary sector, whereas the consumption of private cars is increasing. Technical innovations such as cable television and mini-computers suggest the likelihood of similar substitution in other fields, for example education, information provision and culture. On the other hand these innovations are often accompanied by the creation of new tertiary occupations such as social workers, youth-club leaders and directors of cultural centres.

Even within a particular sphere of activity there may be conflicting developments; the distributive sector is a good example. Since the 1950s the general tendency is towards economic concentration, a process which in France has gone much less far than in the German Federal Republic or the United Kingdom. Between 1962 and 1975 the number of firms in the distributive sector fell by 1.8 per cent a year and of separate establishments by 1.2 per cent a year, whereas turnover increased annually by more than 10 per cent and employment by about 2 per cent. Nevertheless, businesses were affected unequally according to their structure, size, position in the distributive chain, and the type of goods sold. Thus firms which combined wholesale and retail distribution accounted for 28 per cent of retail trade in 1972 as against 15 per cent in 1960. In the retail trade, multiple trading increased its market share from 20 to 23 per cent, with the increase falling to the retail chains rather than to department stores or co-operatives. This concentration was carried out at the expense of independent retailers, whose share in sales fell from 88 per cent in 1950 to 55 per cent in 1972. The very smallest retailers, associated in voluntary chains, held out better, their share rising from 6 per cent in 1960 to 14 per cent in 1972. Wholesaling has generally been less affected by concentration than the retail trade.

Whereas the total number of sales outlets has fallen, there has been an increase in stores with a very large sales area: supermarkets (400–2,500 sq m) increased from 626 in 1963 to 2,842 in 1975, hypermarkets (over 2,500 sq m) from 1 to 298 in the same period. More than 140 giant shopping centres of over 10,000 sq m were opened in the largest urban agglomerations during 1970–5 alone. By contrast, large numbers of small village shops and neighbourhood shops in towns have disappeared, but there has been an increase in small luxury shops in town centres.

Within retailing, the food trade has declined in respect of both the number of shops and the market share, whereas non-food shops such as those selling leisure goods, cosmetics or pharmaceutical products are increasing.

Although the distributive branch offers a particularly clear example of the differential growth involved in a change from a traditional to a modern type of organization, similar contrasts are found in other branches of the tertiary sector. In general, however, the adaptation of the tertiary sector to modern conditions has probably taken place more slowly and certainly at a later date than the parallel development in manufacturing. It is nevertheless justifiable to speak of an explosion of tertiary firms and occupations during recent years. Between 1955 and 1978 the numbers engaged in the property sector rose by 392 per cent, in banking by 170 per cent, in specialist services to firms by 130 per cent, and in insurance by 124 per cent.

2 The location of tertiary activities

The first result of the explosion of tertiary activities was the proliferation of businesses and other units of service provision, with a consequent increase in the number of separate locations and in requirements for appropriate premises. This remarkable growth in the number of separate establishments was shown alike in retailing, the health services, education and leisure provision.

Unlike manufactured goods, services cannot be stored; the simultaneous nature of their production and consumption makes proximity of supply and demand the essential factor in their location. Their spatial distribution is thus for the most part less concentrated than that of manufacturing. While the density of services depends on the level of function provided and the spatial range that they cover, their presence or otherwise depends on the distribution of demand, and on the degree and immediacy of their reaction to this demand.

2.1 The provision of services to the population in general

The most widely distributed form of tertiary activity consists of the direct provision of personal services. This does not mean that such services are uniformly distributed over the country as a whole, but that their distribution corresponds to that of the population. This distribution is organized according to two principles, spatial and hierarchical. Spatially, a centre of service provision is related to the contiguous area that it supplies, whether urban neighbourhood or urban sphere of influence. It is also ranked in an ascending hierarchy of centres providing services of progressively increasing rarity and spatial range, from the simple neighbourhood shopping centre to the elaborate services and facilities of a regional capital. Evidence of the way in which service provision leads to a division of space into contiguous and hierarchical service areas, closely resembling those predicted by central-place theory, is to be found in the existence of tributary areas and retail centres at local level and of spheres of influence relating to the provision of high-level goods and services around the largest towns. This spatial organization is partly the result of a spontaneous commercial response to the demand for goods and personal services, and partly the reflection of the planned provision of public services, health and education in particular.

Certain ubiquitous tertiary activities are organized either spatially or hierarchically, but not both; for example, postal services tend to provide the most uniform service possible over the whole country, so that there is a much less obvious development of a hierarchical response to the density of demand.

Services to the individual have a spatial distribution which is very nearly proportionate to the distribution of the resident population; the various services also have a close association with one another in their spatial provision. Nevertheless the close relationship to the distribution of population applies only to the most common everyday services such as the retail food distribution. It has been calculated, for example, that the rural communes, although they contain 30 per cent of the French population, have only 25 per cent of all shops: in other words 53 food shops and 34 non-food shops per 10,000 inhabitants, as against 55 and 64 for France as a whole. This deficiency is to some extent compensated by the over-provision of such facilities in the small towns (between 2,000 and 10,000 inhabitants), which have 69 food shops and 85 non-food shops per 10,000 inhabitants.

The remaining service activities tend to be slightly over-represented in areas of greater population density. Their location quotient is greater in highly urbanized departments than in rural departments and in large towns rather than small towns

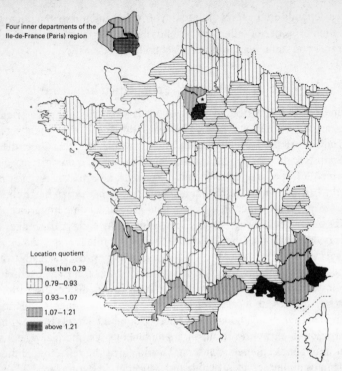

Four inner departments of the
Ile-de-France (Paris) region

Location quotient

	less than 0.79
	0.79–0.93
	0.93–1.07
	1.07–1.21
	above 1.21

Figure 27.1 Location quotients of tertiary employment, in relation to the total population of each department, 1975. Sources: INSEE; Census, 1975.

(Fig. 27.1). Tertiary activities are also over-represented wherever purchasing power is high, either as a result of high local economic activity and income levels or in consequence of a seasonal influx of population, as in tourist areas. Conversely, some tertiary activities are relatively over-provided in the less densely populated areas, particularly those with a strongly spatial relationship, such as educational and postal services.

If there is a correlation between the extent of tertiary activities in a given area and the size of the population, the relationship is certainly not one-way. If it is true that the location of a large part of the tertiary sector – the everyday tertiary of services to households – is dependent on the size of the resident population, it is also true that some tertiary activities seem capable in their turn of attracting additional activities and hence an increased population. This basic role of certain tertiary activities in regional development seems true not only of specific tertiary activities such as transport or tourism but also of service activities, and especially specialist services to firms, as demonstrated in the Rhône–Alpes region.

2.2 The location of specialized tertiary activities

The more specialized tertiary activities have a more concentrated, sporadic distribution, similar to the pattern of industrial activities. In particularly favoured locations there may be disproportionately large concentrations of tertiary activities, for example of transport services in major maritime or river ports such as Marseille and Le Havre, or tourist activities in resorts, notably on the Côte d'Azur.

Local concentrations of tertiary services are also to be found in association with areas of specialized agriculture producing wine, fruit or early vegetables. Such areas give rise to specialized local markets, contrasting in their sporadic occurrence with the more regular distribution of wholesalers, which seek to occupy positions of centrality with regard to their customers. Activities relating to national defence are also found in clusters that are sporadically distributed across the country. The degree of concentration appears to be even greater than for the previous category, either in ports, naval bases, dockyards and arsenals as at Toulon, Lorient and Brest, or in inland garrison towns such as Metz or Verdun.

In health and social services there are some establishments which lack close connections with a population base and are situated in the country. These include hospices, homes for the aged, convalescent homes and institutions for the education of handicapped children. Provision for these disadvantaged people is almost industrial in nature, with associations and charities running chains of health establishments of all kinds and residential homes for maladjusted children and adolescents, typically situated in areas of sparse population.

Nevertheless, in spite of their high degree of geographical concentration, these activities rarely generate related urban developments on the scale associated with some branches of industry. Cases of urban development dominated by a single type of specialist tertiary are rare; tertiary specialization usually involves several linked activities, such as distribution, tourism or transport.

2.3 Concentration or dispersal of tertiary activities?

Changes in the spatial distribution of tertiary activities are difficult to measure. Much depends on the scale of study: what appears as a specialist concentration at the local level may disappear when the scale of study is widened. Moreover existing statistical categories scarcely allow an appreciation of the changes which have the greatest significance for spatial planning, in particular those which differentiate levels of tertiary function within the same branch of activity.

Considered at the regional scale, there has been a recent tendency towards the diffusion of the majority of the branches of tertiary activity over the whole of France. This reflects a certain equalization of standards of living throughout the country, an evening out of the disparities in provision, particularly with regard to services to the individual. Thus during the past twenty years there has been a catching up in respect of tertiary provision of the industrial regions as opposed to France as a whole, and of medium-sized towns as opposed to large towns. The concern to give the whole population, wherever located, equal access to facilities, a concern inherent in the notion of a truly public service, requires a decentralized distribution of schools and hospitals which may involve a compromise with the ideal of locating such facilities in the most economic and rational locations.

The diffusion of everyday tertiary is therefore a reality, but a true equalization of economic activity throughout the country would require the decentralization of higher tertiary functions. But it is precisely these functions which show a marked tendency towards concentration; both in regions of low density and in the interstices of the urban framework, an increased facility of movement favours the development of central places at the expense of the periphery. In the sector of 'productive tertiary' (section 1.1), there is an increasing tendency for activities at the highest level (product development, research, decision-making) to be concentrated in the Paris region or in the Rhône–Alpes region, dissociated from executive activities like management and sales. The tendency towards the spatial concentration of higher tertiary activities may strengthen this movement by creating poles of tertiary attraction. In the very broadest sense, however, the distribution of tertiary activities in France is still uneven.

2.3.1 *Concentration in Paris*

The Paris agglomeration, in addition to its functions as the national capital, contains a high concentration of other administrative services. More importantly it groups the decision-making and administrative staffs of the majority of large French firms: 80 per cent of registered head offices are in Paris. Not only the higher tertiary but also the upper level of the productive tertiary are found there. In 1975 the Paris region had more than 35 per cent of all French office space; 4.0 million sq m of office floorspace have been built there since the 1950s, as compared with 7.5 million in the provinces. All the most recent developments in tertiary, such as computer advisory services, are also heavily concentrated in the capital.

2.3.2 *The deterioration of public services in rural areas*

The population decline in rural areas and the continuing lowering of density led as early as 1942–4 to a questioning of the viability of the rural commune as an elementary unit of social life. This questioning came first from the Church, and there was doubt, not only about the value of the small village as a unit for evangelization, but also as a meaningful social unit, which gave rise to the idea of concentrating activities on 'central' or 'key' villages. This was then taken up as one of the predominant concepts in rural planning.

As early as 1942 the state tried to reorganize the spatial pattern of rural organization by encouraging the merger of communes, or, failing that, the creation of multipurpose intercommunal associations (*syndicats intercommunaux à vocations multiples*, chapter 13). From 1959 onwards the state contributed to a growing underprovision of services in rural communes. Under the pretext of securing efficiency and providing a proper level of provision there has in fact been a withdrawal of rural services in nearly every field of social life: education, health, transport and communications. At the most basic level, public services such as primary schools or post offices, with which the public is most immediately in contact, have been subjected to widespread closure. Services at the next level, such as secondary schools and hospitals, were concentrated in the towns, with the exception of the very smallest towns, which were unable to attract the social equipment that depended on finance provided by the local authorities themselves.

Privately provided services, requiring a minimum number of clients to survive, have also disappeared; it is usual for inquiries into the fate of small rural communes to begin with the litany of shopkeepers and craftsmen who have disappeared: café-owners, bakers, hairdressers, grocers, garage proprietors and owners of small general stores. Similarly, the number of country doctors has declined more rapidly than the rural population as a whole; not enough young doctors have set up in country areas to compensate for the disappearance of their predecessors. In 1962 there were 49.6 doctors for every 100,000 people in country areas; by 1975 the figure had fallen to 46.4, in spite of the decline in rural population.

All these closures clearly involve a quantitative reduction in the availability of services to the population that remains. Services are much more thinly spread than in densely populated areas. This implies higher transport costs, which have repercussions either on the functioning of the service, through the long journeys necessary to reach the consumer (postal services, travelling salesmen or mobile clinics), or on the individuals and organizations which support them (families travelling long distances by car and children by school bus). Distances separating rural consumers from amenities and services have continued to increase, reaching their greatest extent in mountain regions of low population density and in areas of dispersed settlement. Figures 1.3C and D illustrate these specific difficulties of rural areas. They show that the problem of accessibility to amenities affects a greater number of rural areas than the problem of a low level of provision in proportion to population. The low density and the small size of communes are important factors in this uneven geographical distribution, but fundamental regional contrasts remain significant, doubtless because ingrained cultural attitudes are involved. A lower provision of educational facilities does not exclude higher proportions of children attending school in the south, while the higher proportion of doctors there mirrors the traditional north–south division of the country (see chapter 12).

3 Policies for the tertiary sector

The problems posed by the excessive concentration of tertiary activities in the Paris region and by their underprovision in some provincial regions were not at first perceived as interrelated and dealt with simultaneously. The first step was a policy of tertiary decentralization from Paris; only later was this followed by a policy for maintaining a more efficient spatial distribution of tertiary activities in the country as a whole.

3.1 Decentralization of tertiary activities from Paris

Concern with tertiary location manifested itself as early as 1955 with the formation of a special committee to arrange the transfer out of Paris of government offices and other organizations under government control. This committee proposed the first transfers to the provinces, for example the National Centre for Telecommunications Research (Centre National d'Etudes des Télé-communications – CNET) to Lannion and the *grande école* for training technologists for the aerospace industry (Ecole Supérieure d'Aéronautique) to Toulouse. The measures used, constantly increased and intensified, were the same varied collection that had been developed in relation to industrial decentralization: subsidies, tax concessions, restriction on office construction in the Paris region, a special office under DATAR (the spatial planning organization) to encourage office-building in the provinces, and location contracts between large firms or administrative services providing for the establishment of tertiary employment.

The government intervened directly in relation to the civil service and organizations over which it had influence, such as nationalized firms. In 1975 it decided that no additional floorspace would be allocated to the central administration in the Paris region, except in new towns. The Seventh national plan laid down that 85 per cent of new laboratories and research centres would be compulsorily located in the provinces. Financial and banking decentralization was encouraged by the creation of banking centres in the provinces, notably at Lyon.

In order to accommodate these decentralized tertiary activities and to provide for consequent growth, the authorities created a series of major provincial administrative and office centres, often associated with projects of urban renewal, for example Bordeaux–Mériadeck (150,000 sq m) or Lyon–La Part-Dieu (400,000 sq m).

3.1.1 *Sophia-Antipolis*

A symbolic and monumental expression of tertiary decentralization is provided by the Sophia-Antipolis science park, which extends over the territory of five communes at Valbonne near Nice. The project was conceived in 1969 by Pierre

Laffitte, director of the School of Mines in Paris. The plan was to create a 'science city' on an attractive site in an attractive region of provincial France, where scientists, engineers and technicians would work together. The concept of rapid development through the intellectual cross-fertilization involved in the close proximity of research laboratories and high-technology industries derives from the USA. The operation began in 1969, and by 1972 the original 47 ha of the scheme had been expanded to provide a government-recognized international science park of 2,400 ha, containing research, production and tertiary activities of the highest quality. In 1974 the scheme was recognized to be of national interest, and by 1979 1,500 jobs had been created. Of 20 establishments on the site, 5 belong to multinationals, the largest group being in the field of computer science, including the Digital Equipment Corporation. A second group centres on the development of solar energy. The French National Science Research Council (CNRS) and the School of Mines have laboratories on the site. Residential units (250 in 1980), a school complex and other social equipment complete the site.

3.1.2 Planning maps

In order to have control over the location of social equipment, the state developed the practice of drawing up planning maps relating to schools, universities, health services, sport provision and socio-cultural activities. The aim was to prevent the development through local or regional initiatives of investment which from the point of view of the government were judged to be excessively expensive or to involve unnecessary duplication. Just as industrial estates had been provided in excessive numbers, so swimming pools and sports centres figured in the plans of too many communes. At a higher level many councils in large towns began by financing institutes of higher education; later the state was forced to recognize their existence, transform them into universities and bear the resultant costs. The planning maps were designed to produce a rational spatial distribution of facilities, but because they were drawn up according to national norms, they did not take sufficient account of geographical diversities, or of the social and economic inequalities stemming from them.

In fact the maps drawn up by Ministers, whether relating to schools or health, reveal a hierarchy of provision which has a spatial expression. The non-specialized secondary schools (high schools) and the rural hospitals are low-level facilities reserved for the most rural departments. One-class schools, which are the product of the policy of abolishing undersized classes, do not provide the same quality of education as larger schools.

3.1.3 Public services in rural areas

It was only from 1974 that the government gave thought to the maintenance of services in rural areas. In 1975, grants were introduced to encourage the establishment of craftsmen in rural areas. Working parties were also set up in a number of departments (19 in 1978) and in 1979 at interministerial level to propose measures for rural service improvement. The measures proposed included the creation of intercommunal commercial and craft centres, and more especially the introduction of multipurpose offices uniting various local branches of the central administration. This last measure is an almost revolutionary innovation, since in the French administrative tradition the various branches of government have always been rigidly separated at all levels. Under this system one of the most commonly available public services, such as the Post Office, would in rural areas take over a number of other tasks previously reserved for separate offices, such as social security payments, the issue of vehicle log-books or identity cards. Where it proves impossible for one service to take over these additional functions, then at least all of these basic government services should be located in one place; for example by grouping the various local offices in the same building, probably the post office. It was similarly suggested that school buses could provide a wider range of services to the public.

3.1.4 Results

Government intervention in the provision of rural services is too recent to have provided any measurable results, but there are some significant pointers to a degree of success. Between 1970 and 1975, 73 operations of tertiary establishment, involving 45 companies, resulted in the creation of 15,000 jobs in the provinces, mainly in the sectors of banking, insurance and social provision. It was only after 1976 that new office floorspace authorized in the Paris region began to decline in favour of the provinces, but the disparity is nevertheless still overwhelming, with the Paris region absorbing 1.5 million sq m of the 2.5 million built each year.

The weight, dynamism and attraction of the Paris region are so strong and so unique, beyond any competition, that restoration of the spatial balance in the location of tertiary activities is difficult. Between 1962 and 1975 the Paris region's share of all wage-earners and salaried employees in the tertiary sector fell from 28.1 per cent to 27 per cent, and of workers in banking and insurance from 49.8 to 43.9 per cent. These were not insignificant reductions, but they made no real change in the relationship between tertiary employment in Paris and the provinces.

In 15 years (1963–77), 130 administrative departments were set up in the provinces, creating 21,800 jobs. Activities transferred or created from the beginning included the retirement pension services of various ministries, the registration services of the Ministry of Foreign Affairs, research and study centres, statistical offices, one or two *grandes écoles* (prestigious state-run schools in the higher education sector) and supply services for the central administration. Alongside these successes must be set the various failures and delays, such as the failure of the French national cartographic service (Institut Géographique National) to transfer to Bordeaux, as decreed in 1969.

It is not really possible to decentralize offices without decentralizing power and responsibility, and without moving towards a structure of regional governments having autonomy and adequate resources at their disposal. All too often the points at which new tertiary activities are installed, and the decision-making at government level regarding such installation, relate to the political influence of the individual mayors, reinforced during any period when, in the fashion of French politics, they simultaneously hold ministerial office. The difficulties facing such developments are formidable; all too often they remain as spectacular but isolated achievements. The position changed somewhat after the introduction of a more vigorous decentralization policy under the new 1981 administrative reforms, which gave local and regional authorities increased responsibilities with regard to the planned distribution of tertiary activities.

V

✢ The infrastructure of spatial
interaction

28

 General characteristics of transport and communications networks

1 Transportation networks and geography

All manufacturing industry, all service activities, almost all aspects of human life, whether personal or social, necessarily involve movement. No location or distribution of phenomena on the earth's surface is intelligible without introducing the notions of flow, migration and exchange. Farms, factories, villages, towns, power-stations and mines exist and function only in relation to an infrastructure of transport and communications such as roads, canals, railways, telephone lines and airlines.

These links are structured into networks; some are visible forms on the earth's surface, others are invisible, evidence of their existence appearing only sporadically, as in airports and telephone exchanges. Either way a service is provided, and the land is covered by networks of varying density, typically characterized by some degree of hierarchical structure. The characteristics of the networks determine the degree of accessibility of every area and point in the country.

The networks are thus the essential agents of geographical organization, and their nodes are particularly significant; these most commonly take the form of settlements, ranging in size from villages to large towns. However, not all nodes generate concentrations of population: electrical switching stations and railway marshalling yards are examples of nodes which commonly stand isolated and alone. Each network has a corresponding mode, or corresponding modes, of transport. But if such modes as cars, lorries, buses, boats or planes and their degree of use derive from individual initiative and enterprise, the same does not apply to the infrastructures, except for car parks and private roads belonging to farms. The networks are the expression and instrument of political power; their role is essentially to ensure or strengthen national cohesion as well as external relations, to allow the dissemination of decisions made by the various authorities, and to allow the maximum development of the country.

During the last hundred years there has been a remarkable expansion of the means of transport and their associated infrastructures and a parallel increase in mobility. Until the middle of the nineteenth century mobility was minimal and of limited radius. The available means of land transport, unlike existing waterways, did not allow the transportation of large, heavy loads. From the 1850s the railway began the process of establishing new networks. It was followed by the internal combustion engine and the tarred road, then the aeroplane, telecommunications and motorways; at the same time individual mobility increased and its range widened. Changes in means of transport and associated infrastructure have led to a relative shrinking of geographical space. The spheres of influence of urban centres were enlarged, spatial integration encouraged and regional specialization increased. But by their very existence the new networks also fixed and fossilized spatial organization, because of their resistance to change.

The actual pattern of networks upon the earth's surface reflects two requirements: firstly the attempt to provide the most complete spatial covering so as to optimize the opportunities for economic and social life, and secondly the need to adjust to the characteristics and limitations of physical geography.

The influence of physical environment on transport networks is obvious. Irrespective of the period at which networks were developed, we can discover repeatedly used routeways such as the Alpine passes, the Lauragais, Poitou and Burgundy gaps, the lowlands of the Rhône and Rhine, and the Saône corridor. By contrast, all the maps show regions which are hostile to the setting up of a dense network of communications, for example the southern Alps and the entire southern part of the Central massif.

With regard to relief and its advantages and limitations for transport infrastructures, France shows a marked east–west contrast. On the other hand, chapter 2 proposed a division of France into three morphological units, within each of which transport networks were differentially affected by physical geography. The Hercynian plains and plateaus of northern and western France are open to circulation; if obstacles exist, they are less attributable to relief than to soil and vegetation. The chalk and limestone plains are particularly open to the development of communications. Nowhere is movement inhibited; roads and railways radiate from every town and thus there is a great choice of alternative routes.

In the faulted and folded country of Hercynian and Alpine France, movement is overwhelmingly controlled by relief: the transport links are channelled along valleys or grouped on to the interfluves. Transverse communications across the grain of the country are limited and difficult. On the whole, routes in a southerly direction predominate, but must from time to time take up the transverse direction for short distances, giving them their characteristically zig-zag pattern, as in the Jura; the impact of local conditions of slope means that all these routes are afflicted with numerous curves. On the scale of France as a whole, the major transport links follow lowland corridors and the gaps that link them, notably the plain of Alsace, the Rhône–Saône corridor, the plain of Languedoc and the gaps of Belfort, Burgundy and Lauragais. Relief conditions severely limit the choice of routes, even if they do not entirely determine them; the influence of relief is reinforced by the way in which the towns and the areas of economic activity served by the routes are themselves concentrated in the valleys and lowlands. In the third region, the high folded chains of the interior Alps and Pyrenees, determination of routeways by relief becomes virtually total.

Climatic conditions in France do not inhibit movement on any significant scale. Snow periodically closes the passes of the Alps, Pyrenees and Central massif, but modern machinery enables the roads to be rapidly cleared. The greatest human problems are provided by the thinly scattered settlements of the Central massif. On main routes, traffic may be interrupted for short periods only, but on secondary roads the situation is more difficult. Villages and hamlets may be cut off for weeks in areas such as the plateaus of Velay and Vivarais, the Causses and the Margeride mountains. Modern roads engineered along hillsides or through cuttings are more easily blocked than the old *drailles*, trackways which ran along the ridges. Nevertheless an exceptionally harsh winter can still cause considerable frost damage to the road system, freeze the waterways and put the main axes of communication out of action for weeks. The economy is less and less able to adapt to interruptions of access and transport delays. This is the reason for the large investments that have been made to provide frost-free routes.

All networks are subject to restrictions of a climatic nature, but in varying degree. For example, according to the French electric power supply organization, fog, wet snow and frost in the Central massif cause greater problems with regard to electric power lines than in the more continental valleys of the Alps. Areas subject to violent winds such as the mistral experience periodic restrictions on all forms of transport.

Although some of the networks, such as motorways, are of recent origin and still incomplete, and others, such as airlines, are highly adaptable, the most important networks – roads and railways – have a long history; decisions regarding their design and density were taken in response to conditions that may date back a century or more. The great inertia of the transport systems and the difficulty of adapting them in response to modern conditions are a key factor in the geography of French transport and communications.

The spatial distribution of the French population poses particular problems in the development of a coherent network. The areas of dense population and high economic activity are widely separated. Links between them have to pass through areas of typically low and sparse population, which generate little traffic, a situation very different from that of neighbouring states such as Germany or England.

The essential characteristic of the French transport and communications networks, as any map shows, is the central role of Paris. The way in which routes radiate from the capital is far more important in shaping the networks than relief. The national system of trunk roads, the main railway lines, the principal motorways and domestic air routes all radiate from Paris.

2 Networks and the environment

Relatively little land is taken up by transport and communications links as such. Exactly how much land is so used is a matter of some uncertainty. A 1974 estimate, which included urban roads and airfields, put forward a figure of 1,034,000 ha, the size of an average French department. However, because networks have great spatial variations in density, their local and regional impact is highly unequal. It is also significant that it is in the course of movement along the transport lines that individuals perceive and evaluate the environment. Lastly, the structures associated with the various networks become themselves elements of the landscape and the environment. Their forms and how they are fitted into the environment are therefore of considerable importance.

Under laws dating from the beginning of the nineteenth century, frontagers were obliged to plant trees along the sides of public roads and field paths. Roads in France have traditionally been an important element in the landscape because of these rows of trees, which advertise their presence from afar and break the monotony of the plains. Road-widening schemes and concern for the safety of motorists have resulted in the destruction of the trees. At the same time, a new landscape is being shaped along the motorways. Their construction involves earth movement on a massive scale to create the necessary embankments and cuttings. In addition the surroundings of the roads are usually landscaped: hedges are planted to cut down sun dazzle, plantations of shrubs and trees laid out to avoid monotony, and rest areas and restaurants provided. The straightness of French roads is still as evident on the ground as it is on the map. It is not only to be attributed to the Gallo-Roman heritage; a decree of 1705 ordered the building of roads in straight sections without taking account of the pattern of land ownership.

As they grow and change, the transport and communications infrastructures are important factors both regionally and in their impact on the immediate environment. The building of high-voltage cables across fields, over mountains or through forests has an adverse effect on the environment only from the aesthetic or ecological point of view; at worst it inconveniences the occasional farmer on whose land the pylon is erected. Similarly, as long as a motorway runs through rural areas, its value nationally and internationally can be held to justify the inconvenience it imposes on the agricultural world in the form of consumption of land, the splitting up of holdings and a lengthening of travel distances. Perception of the adverse environmental impact of transport infrastructures is diminished by the fact that they are for the most part constructed in areas of low population. But as soon as the network links converge on nodes such as railway junctions, especially where more than one system is involved, problems of a quite different order arise. Regions of high urban density, especially the urban fringes, suffer most. Adverse environmental impact in the form of excessive noise and biological or chemical pollution may exceed the thresholds of tolerance. Less attention has naturally been paid to strictly geographical aspects, and yet the convergence of infrastructural links towards town centres, railways stations and power installations results in a fragmentation of the space into narrow strips and sharply pointed triangles. Space becomes saturated, balance is lost and geographical coherence is destroyed. The problems thus raised show the difficulty of achieving an orderly spatial integration of the structures associated with the various networks in a restricted geographical area.

29

 The networks of transport
and communications

---

1 Roads

The French road network is one of the most dense and most varied in the world. It includes 935,000 km of roads of all categories, 128 km per 100 sq km, compared with 50 in Germany and 30 in Italy. For every 1,000 inhabitants there are 16 km of roads to be maintained as against 6 in Great Britain, 5 in the German Federal Republic and 4.5 in Italy. This network is organized into a functional and administrative hierarchy.

1.1 Farm tracks

The first level in the hierarchy is provided by the network of farm tracks which give access to the vast area of agricultural land. For a long time they were considered inseparable from the cultivated land, and their maintenance was the responsibility of the frontagers. Under a decree of 7 January 1959 the farm tracks were incorporated into the highway system of the communes; the network has a total length of 750,000 km, of which 250,000 km are private farm roads. These tracks have not the durability and permanence of roads in other categories. Rural landscapes bear traces of dead, fossilized roads, only identifiable by the unusual length and straightness of hedgerows and parcel boundaries.

1.2 Roads

A hierarchy of roads other than farm tracks was established by a law of 1836. The present classification repeats the pattern of the administrative hierarchy; roads are communal, departmental or national, the latter group divided into primary and secondary categories.

The transfer of roads from one category to another is frequent, the result of political or budgetary decisions to move either towards or away from centralization. Thus in 1930, 40,000 km of local and municipal roads were integrated into the national system. After 1972 the reverse took place, and 55,000 km of secondary national roads were transferred to the departments.

The pattern of roads radiating from Paris is one of the most familiar factors in the spatial organization of France. This system is very old, dating back to the achievement of political unification. From as early as the reign of Louis XI the road network has been an instrument of centralization, the deliberate creation of the central power, whether monarchy, empire or republic.

This network, centred on Paris, took the place of the former Gallo-Roman and early medieval network, which was organized very differently: its axis ran through what is now eastern France, from Marseille to Trier, with a transverse branch from Langres towards Boulogne. Other branches left the main trunk at Narbonne, Lyon and Châlons, providing links towards Bordeaux, Nantes, Brest, Paris and Rouen to the west and towards Italy and the Rhine to the east. Lyon, the capital of Roman Gaul, was the main point of radiation of these roads. The emergence of Paris as the major route node distorted the pre-existing network, wrenching it away from the great south–north axis Rhône–Rhine–Netherlands, to the advantage of the northern half of France. The great axes of circulation gradually evolved from itineraries followed by the royal post. The road network benefited very early from the attention of the central power; its greatest creators and administrators were Sully, grand superintendent of roads at the beginning of the seventeenth century, and Colbert at the end of the century, who created Commissioners for roads and bridges and subsequently the elite Corps of Bridge and Highway Engineers (Corps des Ponts et Chaussées), which became autonomous in 1716. At the end of the eighteenth century, however, the map of the postal routes already showed a very unequal density of roads, favouring the north and east. The width of the roads was determined by the amount of traffic they carried, and they were classified according to their importance; the royal roads, the ancestors of modern national roads, had a total length of 40,000 km.

Until the 1950s the French road system remained remarkably stable, but in the space of the next twenty years was revealed as totally unsuitable for modern traffic conditions. There was an astonishing rise in the number of cars and lorries; the number of vehicles on the road, which had been 1.5 million in 1930 and 2.3 million in 1950, shot up to 7.3 million in 1960 and 15.5 million in 1975, to which must be added 2,300,000 utility vehicles and 1,300,000 agricultural tractors.

Pressure on the road system was increased by the continued growth of the road haulage of freight, the closure of railway branch lines, the wider dispersal of economic activities and the development of systems of collection and delivery in rural areas. Other influences, of a more social nature, included the increasing separation between residence and workplace, the development of the school bus system, the increase in second homes, and more generally speaking the phenomena relating to dispersed urbanization.

A master plan for the road system as a whole was drawn up in 1960; it was followed by the 1971 road structure plan. The latter involved a total of 27,500 km; it distinguished between first-class and second-class routes; the former were to link all urban agglomerations of more than 50,000 inhabitants, that is to say Paris, the regional centres of provincial France and major centres in neighbouring countries. Routes in the second category were to link towns of more than 40,000 inhabitants; they corresponded to roads which at that time had an average traffic flow of 2,000 vehicles a day over more than 75 km (Fig. 29.1). The plan included three north–south links (of particular interest to British drivers) and six interregional east–west links. All the new routes were intended to avoid the Paris region, thus breaking the traditional pattern of convergence on the urban bottleneck provided by the capital.

1.3 Motorways (*autoroutes*)

The French *autoroutes* provide a system of specially constructed highways, characterized by a minimum of two traffic lanes in each direction, limited access and grade-separated intersections; they are similar in nature to the British motorways or American expressways. The present motorway-building programme was initiated under legislation passed in 1955; the only previous motorway construction had been 25 km running westwards from Paris (now part of the Autoroute de Normandie), built between 1937 and 1942. A network length of 143 km in 1960 had been increased to 5,400 km by 1980; a ministerial programme in 1977 forecast the doubling of the network to reach 7,500 km by 1983.

In 1969 a distinction was made between inter-urban motorways, which would be subject to tolls, and urban motorways and motorways leading out through the urban fringes (in particular in regional metropolises and industrial regions) where, because of the heavy traffic of commercial vehicles and commuters, there would be no tolls. Two associated measures hastened the building of the motorways. The first was the introduction of the toll system for roads in open country and the second was the introduction from 1970 onwards of concessions to build sections of motorways and to operate them for 35 years. Of the ten companies receiving concessions, six were semi-public companies founded between 1956 and 1963, and four were private companies dating from 1970.

This system of concession has varying effects. The concessionary companies, anxious to maximize their returns, concentrated on the motorway stretches in open country between agglomerations, building the most 'promising' sections on the plains or following valleys, which required the least investment. They were more interested in links between major urban centres and powerful industrial regions than in building up a regional motorway network; they built fewer access points than on the motorways constructed by the state and sought to make 'their' motorways profitable by encouraging urbanization near these access points.

The motorway network, as it has been completed to date, together with

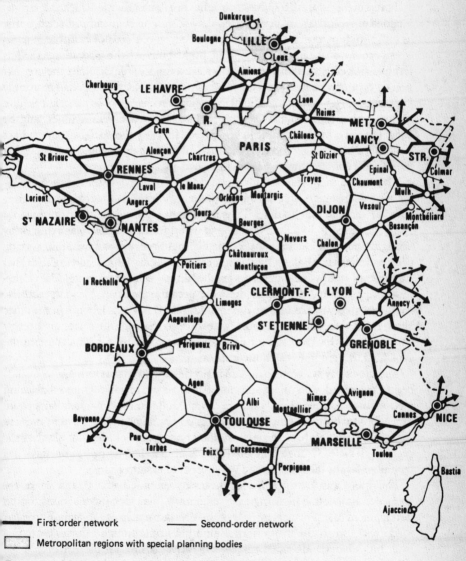

First-order network ————— Second-order network

☐ Metropolitan regions with special planning bodies

Figure 29.1 Master plan for roads, 1971. Source: Ministère des Transports.

sections contained in existing medium-term plans, is marked by a continuing centralization on Paris and a predominance of radial links over transverse or peripheral ones. The network was developed to accommodate existing traffic and not to anticipate it, still less to channel it into new directions in the interests of spatial planning.

Proposals for new motorways are developed by the government's road-planning services to cover a period of about ten years ahead. Proposals have to be approved by the Cabinet (Conseil des Ministres). It is at this level that authorities and pressure groups try to exert their influence. The order in which the various sections of motorway are constructed depends on present and projected traffic levels (a minimum of 15,000 vehicles per day is required to justify motorway construction) and on the anticipated profitability of the operation. Various formulas for construction and operation are available; for example, the concessionary company may be expected to take on an unprofitable stretch of motorway if it can be offset against a profitable section elsewhere. These procedures have not prevented some companies from falling into financial difficulties, and by 1984 only two private companies survived. In 1983 the socialist government established a public motorway authority (Autoroutes de France) to ensure that the mixed-economy concessionary firms had adequate resources.

The routes finally selected for motorways reflect the decisions of the government's road planners and the impact of the various pressure groups; objectives have varied from time to time. Thus the cost of constructing the Autoroute du Nord, designed to link the Nord region with the Paris region, was reduced by taking the most direct and most economic route between the two, thus serving neither Amiens nor Saint-Quentin nor even the industrialized valley of the Oise. Because of the same concern for the direct economic route, the Lille–Dunkerque link runs through the least urbanized part of Flanders and the southern motorway (Autoroute du Soleil) similarly neglects Dijon. On the other hand, the lengthening of the route originally proposed for the eastern motorway (Autoroute de l'Est) to serve Reims and other towns of Champagne is to be explained by their political influence.

The motorway system was not originally developed so that its major crossing-points coincided with the government-designated regional counterbalancing metropolises (*métropoles d'équilibre*); Lyon, Lille and of course Paris were exceptions to this rule. The few intersections to be found in provincial France are situated in the middle of the countryside or near small or medium-sized towns such as Beaune, Orange and Bourgoin. The development of motorways has tended to favour the lowland and valley areas of eastern France.

The motorway network has of necessity an international and therefore European function. The European Community in its recommendations for the development of a transport infrastructure drew up a map of the main European road axes. Two of the major north–south links run through France. One runs from the Netherlands and Brussels and, after picking up the Antwerp–Lille motorway, continues by way of Paris and western France to the border crossing into Spain at Hendaye. The second route links the Rhine–Ruhr agglomeration to the Mediterranean by way of Luxemburg, Nancy, Langres, Dijon and the Rhône valley. The recommended transverse routes are much less satisfactory from the French point of view; they comprise a Bordeaux–Toulouse–Marseille–Nice link, and a Le Havre–Paris–Saône valley diagonal. Two Alpine tunnels were also included in the recommendations. The Mont-Blanc road tunnel was agreed in 1949; tunnelling operations lasted from 1959 to 1962 and it was opened to traffic in 1965. The 12 km Fréjus road tunnel on the route Lyon–Chambéry–Turin was agreed by the French and Italian governments in 1968, the formal agreement signed in 1973 and the tunnel opened in 1980. However, the most important routes proposed for linking northwest Europe to Mediterranean Europe and Italy do not run through the French Alps but through Switzerland, where the Grand-Saint-Bernard road tunnel was opened to traffic in 1964.

Until as late as 1979–80, roads of a standard between ordinary roads and motorways were poorly provided; at the end of 1980 there were only 1,750 km of 'express roads' (dual carriageways with a central divide but without grade-separated junctions). Yet this type of road appears to be appropriate to a great number of stretches which do not reach the minimum flow of 15,000 vehicles a day required to justify motorway construction (a normal four-lane road reaches saturation point above 10,000 vehicles a day). The express road has been chosen only very locally, for example between Amiens and Roye, by reconstructing an existing two-lane road, and in the regional road plans for Brittany and the Central massif. Since the economic crisis of 1974, however, ideas have been changed, influenced by the cost of fuel, problems of finance, the generalization of speed limits, and greater sensitivity to the carnage on the roads. In 1979 a Ministry of Transport directive suggested that preference should in future be given to express roads, which were less difficult and cheaper to build than motorways, a policy which was reinforced in 1984. But as the motorway network has developed radially from Paris, this proposal risks producing a very uneven structure, with the towns and regions far from Paris, which have not yet been included in the motorway network, being given only express roads.

1.4 Road haulage

Road haulage has developed spectacularly since 1960, in 1975 accounting for more than 56 per cent of the transport of goods over more than 150 km. Since 1975 the share of road haulage in the total of overseas trade moving by land-transport systems has overtaken that of the railways: in 1976, 351,667 goods vehicles passed through the Mont-Blanc road tunnel and 214,000 through the port of Calais. In ten years (1968–78) the transported tonnage has doubled; in 1978 4,500,000 journeys were made, transporting 62.8 million tonnes, representing 24,300 million tonnes-kilometres.

It is difficult to obtain an overall view of road haulage because of its heterogeneous nature. From each town of any degree of importance, a star-shaped pattern of traffic radiates for varying distances, revealing the degree of influence that the central place exercises upon its hinterland. Until about the 1960s these locally radiating patterns dominated the road-traffic map of France. The absence of medium- or long-distance links between urban centres was remarkable, revealing the underdeveloped state of the road haulage industry at the time, and the incomplete spatial–economic integration of France. Within the space of 15 years a change took place; recent road maps show that goods-traffic flows have developed on a national scale, their development going hand in hand with the continuing expansion of the existing systems radiating from central places. The changes reflect the general increase in economic activity, the policy of decentralization from Paris, the boom in tourism and leisure activities, the building of the motorway network and the growth of international trade.

Nevertheless the changes have not produced an overall spatial uniformity of road-traffic density throughout France. The greatest intensity of movement is found in northern and eastern France, from Normandy to Provence. The northern regions of lower Seine, Paris, the Nord, Lorraine and Alsace are connected by an axis of heavy road and motorway traffic by way of the Rhône-Alpes region to the Mediterranean. Traffic flows reach spectacular peaks during the great holiday migrations (Fig. 29.2).

The growth of the road haulage of goods has brought about the creation of corresponding fixed installations in the form of freight depots, collection points and *marchés-gares* (combined markets and distribution centres).

2 Navigable waterways
2.1 The waterway network

The length of French waterways classified either as navigable or as suitable for timber rafting is as high as 15,228 km, revealing the favourable conditions provided by the natural environment, both in relation to relief and to climate and hydrology. Of the total length, however, the navigable length is 8,623 km, and only 7,192 km of rivers, lakes and canals are in fact used. Present-day conditions give scant indication of the essential role played by rivers throughout France before the arrival of modern roads and railways. The 'moving roads' were used to the full despite all limitations of excessive gradients and inadequate flow; for example, in the seventeenth and eighteenth centuries, the upper Dordogne, the Lot and the Tarn (rivers of no navigational importance today) channelled the wood, coal and minerals of the Central massif to Bordeaux.

France's navigable waterways have two characteristics: their extreme geographical concentration and the archaic nature of the network, which recent efforts are beginning to remedy. Most of them, and certainly the most important ones, are east of a line linking Le Havre, Orléans and the mouth of the Rhône. It

is only in northern and eastern France that there is a real network of navigable
waterways linking the basins of the Seine, Rhône, Rhine, the Flemish rivers and
the Meuse. South and west of the dividing line there are only occasional
waterways, such as the Canal du Midi and the canal from Nantes to Brest, and the
river basins are not linked with each other.

These marked contrasts are partly explained by natural conditions; the
morphology of the Paris basin, and the sills which lead from it to the north, east
and southeast, facilitated the making of links between basins, while in these areas

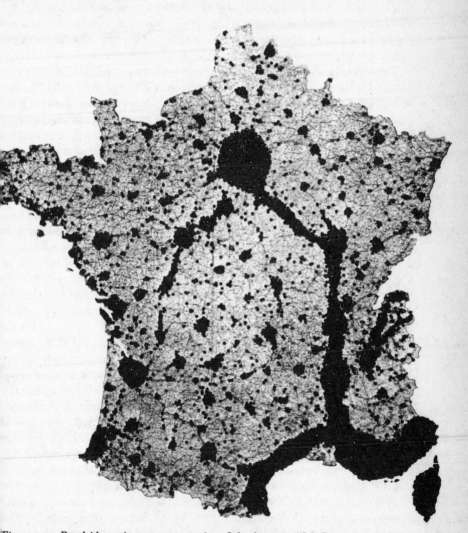

Figure 29.2 Roadside assistance to motorists, July–August 1980. Reproduction of a
coloured map showing service given by the 'Europ Assistance' organization.

of oceanic or modified oceanic rainfall regime a regular flow of water was relatively easy to obtain. In the Loire and Garonne basins, by contrast, the low river-flows of summer necessitated the costly construction of storage reservoirs. But it is chiefly to economic history and to political decisions that we must look for an explanation of the network.

Until the middle of the eighteenth century, rivers were used in their natural state, but a few canals were constructed. The Briare canal (1604–43), joining the Loire to the Seine by the Loing valley, was the first canal with locks to be built in France. The Canal du Midi, constructed between 1666 and 1681, linked the Garonne with the Mediterranean. Eighteenth-century developments consisted for the most part of short canals linking two navigable rivers. On the eve of the Revolution (1789) there were 1,000 km of canals in service.

The network expanded in the nineteenth century, particularly under the restored Bourbon monarchs (1815–30) and Louis-Philippe (1830–48). The aim was to serve the expanding industrial regions, to enable iron ore and coal to be brought together for smelting, and to provide the towns with coal and building materials. Between 1815 and 1830 the length of canals doubled, and doubled again between 1830 and 1848. Canals constructed in this period mainly served the industrial Nord and Lorraine, and the Paris region.

The canal network that had been established by the end of the nineteenth century showed the same convergence on the region of Paris that has already been noted in relation to other forms of transport. This development was encouraged by the natural convergence of the Seine and its major tributaries on or near Paris, even if not all the links reflected the availability of a substantial volume of traffic. For example, the Marne–Rhine canal (1854) was little used, as the Rhine could bring nothing to Paris, situated as it was on a great river flowing westwards into the Channel. The network of navigable waterways substantially reinforces the contrasts between a well-equipped northern and eastern France, and an under-equipped western and southern France.

Some decisions of the nineteenth-century canal builders appear at first glance to be difficult to explain. This particularly applies to links across the boundary between France and Belgium, which were poor or non-existent, in spite of the high volume of traffic potentially available in this industrialized region, and the lack of physical obstacles to construction. The poor quality of the link southwards from the Sambre to the Oise can be ascribed to the desire to keep Belgian coal out of the Paris market. Still more curious was the failure to link the Sambre westwards to the Escaut (Schelde), whereas as early as 1807 the Mons–Condé canal had provided such a link for the Belgian Borinage field. The difference is that the Borinage field was controlled by French capitalists, while it was felt desirable to protect the French Nord coalfield against competition from the Belgian coal of the Charleroi field, served by the Sambre. The inadequacy of links to the Belgian canals and thus to the mouth of the Rhine still remains a feature of the French canal system.

From the 1880s onwards French waterways were faced with competition from the phenomenal growth of the railways, which were capable, so it seemed, of taking over the transport of heavy goods. Accordingly, waterway construction virtually ceased in the first half of the twentieth century. This explains the considerable age and inadequate scale of most of the network. By far the greater part of the network in terms of length (4,150 km) is accessible only to barges of the size laid down by Freycinet in 1879, up to 600 tonnes and a maximum draught of 2.2 m. A further 2,030 km are restricted to even smaller vessels: the Canal du Midi, now a well-known tourist attraction, takes vessels below 250 tonnes only. Waterways capable of taking the standard 1,350 tonne 'European' barges and push tows total only 1,460 km, but include some of the important stretches: the Seine to Montereau above Paris, the Oise as far as Compiègne, the canalized Moselle, the Rhine and the Rhône upstream as far as Lyon on the lower Saône. Yet the waterways of neighbouring countries are predominantly of 'European' standard or better. In consequence the vessels normally used on the German, Belgian and Netherlands waterways cannot pass through most canals in France. Even French barges operating on the Seine, the Rhône or the Rhine have no access to the rest of the national network; conversely, the ordinary barges from the French system cannot venture on some of the more important waterways such as the Rhône or the Rhine, because their flow is too strong. It is also true to say that France provides an obstacle in Europe's waterway system. Neither the Rhône nor Europe's second most important navigable river, the Seine, connect adequately with Europe's most important waterway, the Rhine. Not only are most of the French waterways narrow and of shallow draught, but they have far too many locks which raise costs, lengthen transport times and slow down the turn-round of the barges.

2.2 Recent projects of modernization

For the first fifty years of the twentieth century France had no policy for improving its waterways; moreover it seemed that this method of transport could be considered outdated. Any proposals for modernization encountered the opposition of the railways, which had an effective monopoly in the transport of heavy goods.

By the end of the Second World War the modernization of the navigable waterways had become urgent, all the more so when the European Community denounced the French system for being archaic. A number of modernization proposals emerged.

(1) *Construction of the Canal du Nord (1965)*. This shortens the journey between Béthune and Paris by 45 km, with the abolition of 23 locks. But to shield French barge operators from foreign competition the canal was not built to 'European' dimensions, a typical example of the persistence of protectionist reflexes.

(2) *Moselle improvement*. Since 1964, barges of 1,350 tonnes have been able to navigate upstream from the Rhine as far as Metz.

(3) *Denain–Dunkerque*. To give the Nord industrial region an improved connection with the French port of Dunkerque, existing waterway links between Denain–Valenciennes and Dunkerque were improved (1968) to take vessels of up to 3,000 tonnes.

(4) *Seine*. Work continued on the improvement of the waterways of the Seine basin upstream and downstream from Paris.

(5) *Rhine*. France participated in the improvement of the upper Rhine to 'European' standard, in particular by the completion (1980) of the lateral Grand Canal d'Alsace.

(6) *Link to the Belgian system*. The French and Belgian systems were linked by the completion of the section Valenciennes–Denain.

From the 1960s onwards, the major preoccupation of waterway planners was the completion of a Rhine–Rhône link, which would provide a route from the Mediterranean to the North Sea. The first aspect of this great project was the improvement of navigation on the Rhône below Lyon. This was achieved by the construction by the Compagnie Nationale du Rhône of a series of dams and barrages, which also provided for electric-power generation. By 1980, push tows (*convois poussés*) of 4,000 tonnes could navigate the Rhône from its mouth to the Lyon region. The even more difficult project of crossing the watershed to link the Rhône basin with the basins of the Rhine and Meuse, draining to the North Sea, had been declared indispensable by the Chamber of Commerce of the Department of Saône-et-Loire as long ago as 1870! There was first of all a conflict about routes, the alternatives being a Saône–Meuse link (which would serve the Lorraine industrial region) or a Saône–Rhine link by way of the Doubs river in connection with the improvement of the upper Rhine; it was this solution which was finally adopted.

The Rhône–Rhine link was for long the only project of this magnitude, but came to be challenged by other projects; because of the scale of investments involved, not all could be pursued simultaneously and it became clear that difficult choices would be involved. The most important proposal was for a European-standard 'Seine–East' link between the Seine waterway system, the Meuse, the Lorraine industrial region and, by way of the improved Moselle, the Rhine. The idea was to 'recapture' for the ports of Dunkerque and the lower Seine (Le Havre) the waterway traffic of eastern France, which was 'escaping' to the Belgian and Netherlands ports at the mouth of the Rhine. The improvement of the Saint-Quentin canal up to European standard would avoid a situation in which the traffic generated by the new system would simply be drained away across the Belgian boundary for the benefit of Antwerp and Rotterdam. The competition from European waterway improvements outside France must not, however, be minimized; the final cross-watershed section of a Rhine–Main–

Danube link was, after some vicissitudes, under active construction in the mid-1980s.

Since the 1950s a great debate has been under way between supporters of the Rhône–Rhine project and those who support the Seine–East project. The former represents a gamble on the growth of traffic between industrial northern Europe and Mediterranean Europe. The second rests on a modernization of waterways linking regions already industrialized. Yet it can be argued that projects already started, such as the improvement of the Rhône and the Fos industrial complex, need the additional Rhône–Rhine link to realize their fullest potential.

The economic leaders in western France criticize both projects as likely to accentuate yet further the transport imbalance between east and west. Experts on regional economic planning have also raised questions about the likely return on the capital invested in the Rhône–Rhine project and the repercussions on the regions traversed. They emphasize that to achieve success it is not sufficient simply to build the canal, although even this involves formidable technical problems, notably of water supply. The Rhône–Rhine project was finally given government approval in principle in June 1978, but all indications are that finance will be made available only in reluctant instalments, and that progress will be very slow. It may even be that the crisis in the steel industry will lead to its postponement.

The results of recent projects of waterway improvements have been encouraging; for the Moselle and the Oise from Pontoise upstream to Compiègne they have frequently exceeded the forecast traffic. The only exception is the Dunkerque–Valenciennes link, the construction of which was so long deferred that its opening coincided with the transfer of the iron and steel industry to coastal sites and the decline of the coalfield. In addition, while the link was constructed to take large vessels of up to 3,000 tonnes, they were as late as 1980 unable to pass into the Belgian network or into the rest of the French network.

The advantages of navigable waterways cannot be disputed: they include low operating costs, low energy consumption, opportunities for multiple uses and the ability to blend into the landscape. These offset such disadvantages as slow speed or the cost of assembling and subsequently breaking up large bulk loads. On the other hand, the capital costs of waterway projects are high: an estimated 6,000 million francs for the Rhône–Rhine link, and 3,300 million francs for Seine–East. These vast sums must be contrasted with the actual annual budgetary allocations for all waterway projects, which in 1975 amounted to 410 million francs and in 1979 to only 228 million. In pushing their claims upon the national purse the inland waterway interests carry far less weight than the powerful pressure groups of the French Railways (SNCF) and the road haulage industry.

The inland-waterways fleet is also out of date: more than half the boats date from before 1940. It is also extremely heterogeneous: of 6,650 units, 3,560 belong to the same number of self-employed operators, the remainder belonging to larger firms. The greater part of the network inherited from the nineteenth century is accessible only to the standard barges, which are 38.5 m in length. There is also a fleet of 1,350 tonne self-propelled 'European' barges and push tugs for use in push tows, their use restricted to the major trunk waterways.

Traffic on navigable waterways has, with interruption by wars and economic crises, shown a generally upward trend. The figure of 32 million tonnes at the beginning of the century had increased to 53 million tonnes in 1930. After the Second World War, traffic increased again from 42 million tonnes in 1950 to 119 million in 1974: the 1978 figure was 91.5 million tonnes. The proportion of total inland freight traffic carried is, however, in marked decline. The waterways concentrate on the mass transport of heavy and bulky commodities, especially building materials, oil and grain.

If the canal is the poor relation in the world of transport, river ports are even more underrated. Compared with seaports they pass unnoticed, since they lack spectacular visual features and the attraction and mystery of the gateway to the open sea. Yet the river port of Denain handles as great a tonnage of goods as Boulogne, and more than such well-known seaports as Dieppe or Lorient.

3 Railways

In 1978 the nationally owned French Railways (SNCF) had a total of 34,597 km of lines and 4,140 stations.

3.1 The rail network

The first railways were built in two separate regions. The oldest lines were built to open up the coalfields of the Central massif, which at that time was the 'French Ruhr'. In 1827 a single line using animal traction was opened to link Saint-Etienne with Andrézieux on the Loire. In 1830 steam traction replaced animal traction on the Lyon–Givors line; in 1833 the Andrézieux–Roanne line was constructed in parallel with the shallow and dangerous Loire waterway.

Soon, however, railway construction developed in a second region, centred on Paris, where the famous Paris–Saint-Germain line was opened in 1837. It was economically insignificant but psychologically important as marking the advent of the new era. Yet at the end of 1841 France had only 573 km of railways in service, whereas Great Britain had 3,800 km.

The railway age began with the law of 1842 which made provision for 3,600 km of track. That year saw the beginning of construction on the pattern of lines radiating from Paris, mirroring the network of the royal roads. The lines Paris–Orléans and Paris–Rouen were opened in 1843, but in 1847 France still had only 1,900 km of lines, compared with 5,900 km in England and 5,000 km in the German states.

The real establishment of the French national rail system dates from the Second Empire. Paris–Strasbourg was opened in 1852, Paris–Belfort in 1858, and 1859 saw the establishment of the six big companies which were to run the railways until they were merged under the single French Railways (Société Nationale des Chemins de Fer Français – SNCF) in 1938. The network patterns and associated transport operations had a profound influence on the economy of France. The 3,554 km of lines in place at the end of 1851 had become 8,681 in 1858 and 17,440 by 1870. Railway development continued to be vigorously pursued in the time of the Third Republic under the guidance of the Freycinet plan of 1879, which filled all the remaining gaps in the network, in particular ensuring that each sub-prefecture was linked with Paris. The network length was 19,600 km in 1875 and 43,731 by 1910, by which time the railway had reached the most distant and inaccessible towns of the Central massif and the Alps. After 1918 about 900 km of lines were added, including some important interconnecting sections, notably the Vosges tunnels and the two international lines through the Pyrenees, where the Somport tunnel was opened in 1928.

Thanks to this national policy of extending the railway to all parts of France, there are no glaring disparities in provision between the various regions. This even distribution of lines is a special characteristic of France in comparison with other countries.

The main network is supplemented by local lines serving rural areas and towns not on the main lines; in 1878 about a hundred small companies were responsible for 5,650 km of track. In 1914 the network of local lines covered 22,000 km, of which 17,500 were in use. A large part of this secondary network was built to lower standards, with narrow gauge, sharp curves and steep gradients. Defects, becoming ever more apparent with time, included slow speeds which could not be improved, the need for transhipment between systems, and rolling stock incompatible with the requirements of the main system. Understandably, this secondary network was the first to be affected by competition from road transport and to be subjected to line closures.

In 1933 a process of network reduction was initiated, reflecting competition from the roads and road haulage, changes in the distribution of the population, and pressure from powerful interest groups. Lines were either closed completely, or were deprived of passenger services, since goods traffic can tolerate lower standards of track maintenance and safety. The process of closure continued after the Second World War; lines operated by the SNCF fell from 41,200 km in 1951 to 34,597 km in 1978. Lines were closed first in areas where relief posed no problems for the running of substitute bus services throughout the year, without imposing excessively long journeys on passengers.

At the same time, however, French Railways began the construction of new lines. The majority were in the Paris region: lines serving the new town of Evry and Roissy airport; the underground link through central Paris between the Invalides and Orsay stations (1979); and the interconnection between the SNCF network and the Paris urban transport system (RATP) by means of an underground link between the Gare du Nord and the Gare de Lyon via an interchange at Châtelet–Les Halles (1981) associated with the redevelopment of the former Les Halles central-market site.

In the provinces, the improvement of the line linking Paris through Lyon to southern and southeast France for the high-speed train (Train à Grande Vitesse – TGV) symbolizes the transformation of the French railway system. From Combes-la-Ville, 23 km southeast of Paris, to Sathonay, 8 km north of Lyon, an entirely new line 390 km long is used by electric trains travelling at up to 260 km (*c.* 160 miles) per hour. The improvements result in a considerable saving of time not only between Paris and Lyon but on all journeys from Paris to the south and southeast of France. By October 1983 the journey time from Paris to Lyon had been reduced to less than 2 hours, to Chambéry 3 hours, and to Marseille 4½ hours. The high-speed train provoked debates similar to those relating to the Rhône–Rhine canal link, with economists, technologists, ecologists and farmers all advancing their particular views. A government decision has already been taken in favour of an 'Atlantic' high-speed train serving west and southwest France, while regional pressure groups are expounding the advantages of a 'northern' high-speed train (possibly in relation to a future Channel tunnel) and an 'eastern' high-speed train, possibly connecting with cities of the German Rhineland.

Since the end of the Second World War, the SNCF has carried through a major modernization both of infrastructures and rolling stock. Electrified lines, which in 1938 amounted only to 3,340 km, had reached 9,862 km by 1979. A major advance was introduced from the 1950s onwards through the discovery that it was possible to run engines not only on the direct current of 1,500 volts but also on alternating current at the normal industrial frequency. This reduced the cost of equipping lines for electric traction by about a third. The profitability of electric traction was thus increased, and the reduction in cost increased the number of lines where electrification was economically possible. Electrified rail transport is particularly advantageous because the production of electricity is becoming less and less dependent on imported oil, while night movements use off-peak electricity for which there would otherwise be no demand.

On lines where electrification is either impossible or not economically justified, diesel trains have replaced steam traction. Since 1970, turbo-trains (powered by gas turbines) have been introduced to provide fast services on lines which are not electrified. The introduction of continuously welded track has brought a similar technical progress to the permanent way. This modernization has enabled considerable increases in speed.

Two consequences for French spatial organization have emerged from these measures. Firstly, there has been a considerable but unequal space–time shrinkage to the advantage of eastern and southeastern France and the detriment of western France (the 'consolation prize' of an 'Atlantic' high-speed train was decided on in 1981 on the initiative of the President of the Republic). Secondly, there was a growing disparity in the frequency and speed of service between main lines and other lines (Fig. 29.3).

3.2 Rail traffic

Passenger traffic (Table 29.1) reached its absolute maximum in 1925, when 802 million passengers were carried. Measured in passenger-kilometres, however, traffic has increased year by year. This development proves that rail passenger transport is rather more than holding its own, despite the considerable increase in road transport.

Rail passenger movements fall into two completely distinct geographical categories: suburban commuting and long-distance passenger movements. Commuter lines have benefited from progressive suburbanization, from their ability to offer improved services through electrification, and from the increasing congestion of urban road traffic. Traffic on the main lines has benefited from the increase in business journeys, with special 'business trains' radiating from Paris, and the Trans-Europ express services (TEE) linking the major European cities. The survival and even the increase of a railway clientele has also been assisted by the growth of tourist travel. The increasing popularity of winter sports, the introduction of car–sleeper services and special tourist itineraries have all played

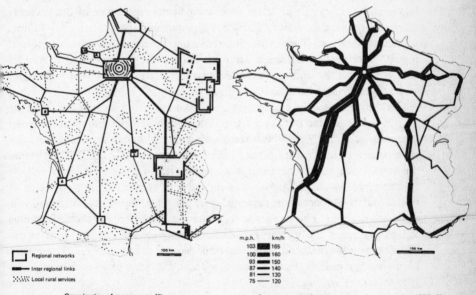

m.p.h.	km/h
103	165
100	160
93	150
87	140
81	130
75	120

Regional networks
Inter-regional links
Local rural services

Organization of passenger traffic

Average speeds of passenger trains (winter service, 1976–7)

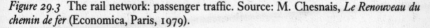

Figure 29.3 The rail network: passenger traffic. Source: M. Chesnais, *Le Renouveau du chemin de fer* (Economica, Paris, 1979).

Table 29.1 *Rail traffic (SNCF system)*

Year	Passengers carried (millions)		Passengers carried (thousand million passenger–km)		Freight traffic (million tonnes)
	Total	Paris suburban traffic	Total	Paris suburban traffic	
1929	765	356	28.2	5.0	223
1938	540	250	22.1	3.7	132
1960	570	318	32.0	4.5	227
1966	628	374	38.4	5.8	233
1976	675	436	51.5	7.6	227
1983	734	...[a]	58.4	...	176

[a] Data not available.
Source: SNCF.

their part, while contributing to an increasingly wide seasonal variation in traffic. The most characteristic feature of French rail passenger transport is its intense concentration in the Paris region, which accounts for 64 per cent of all movements.

Until recently, only in the Paris region had it been necessary to provide for regular suburban commuter traffic, but a change of policy in this respect has followed the sharp rise in urban development, the emergence of the counter-balancing regional capitals (*métropoles d'équilibre*) and the phenomena of linear urbanization. Rapid inter-urban links have been created, providing services at regular intervals, among them Metrolor (Thionville–Nancy–Metz–Lunéville) opened in 1970, the summer-season Metrazur (Cannes–Nice–Menton) in 1970, and Stelyrail (Saint-Etienne–Lyon) in 1976.

Goods traffic reached a record 72,000 million tonnes-kilometres in 1974, the year of the beginning of the oil crisis. The railway remains the chief means of long-distance transport of bulk and heavy goods, although in recent years the composition of internal traffic has undergone considerable changes, reflecting the transformation of the French economy. Rail freight traffic is markedly concentrated: in 1976, 8 per cent of the network accounted for 46 per cent of traffic, and 33 per cent of the network for 92 per cent. Spatially the distribution is extremely uneven. The dominant radial pattern based on Paris which characterizes passenger traffic emerges almost as strongly for freight, but with the addition of a pronounced transverse link Nord–Lorraine–Dijon. The Paris–Lyon–Mediterranean trunk which dominates the map of French roads also appears on the rail map (Fig. 29.4).

Goods traffic is organized by means of a system of marshalling yards and central goods stations. The most important marshalling centres are those of Sotteville (Rouen), Hourcade (Bordeaux), Sibelin (Lyon), Woipy (Metz),

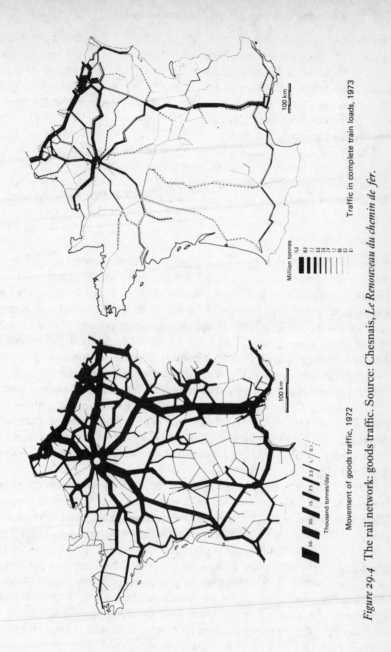

Million tonnes

15,0

Traffic in complete train loads, 1973

Thousand tonnes/day

50. 30. 15. 7.5 2.5 1. 0.1

Movement of goods traffic, 1972

100 km

Figure 29.4 The rail network: goods traffic. Source: Chesnais, *Le Renouveau du chemin de fer.*

Hausbergen (Strasbourg), Gevrey (Dijon), and Villeneuve–Saint-Georges (Paris). The first five are accepted to be major nodes of the system and are automated. Further down in the hierarchy there are goods stations and goods yards. The system is characterized by the multiplicity of access points; more than half of rail transport operates between the 11,000 sidings belonging to particular industrial plants or other installations, and 90 per cent of all traffic either originates or terminates at such a siding.

The SNCF tries to minimize as much as possible the technical deficiencies of its rolling stock. Efforts have chiefly been directed to the improvement of loading and unloading, notably by the increased use of containers and the introduction of the 'kangaroo' system for the long-distance transportation of road trailers.

4 Seaports

It has been asserted that there is no spontaneous feeling for the sea in France. It cannot, of course, be denied that maritime trade has played its part in the economic development of France from the earliest times, but this development has to some degree been imposed by history, by the creation of a colonial empire, and because of the length of the sea coast. France has never been a maritime nation to the same extent as England or the Netherlands. From early in the nineteenth century, inward-looking protectionist policies relegated port activity to the margin of economic life, a situation which was masked by relations with colonial possessions. Ports were required only to balance out the minor variations between internal industrial and agricultural production and internal consumption. They also provided for the importation of luxury and exotic products, highly dependent on changes in fashion. Of the raw materials essential to economic life, non-ferrous metals, cotton and wool were almost the only ones to be derived wholly or mostly from imports.

The opening of the French market to the international economy after the Second World War, the abolition of protectionism and the growth of international maritime commerce created a new situation. This phase of expansion in maritime links again revealed that France had distinct advantages of geographical situation, with favourably situated ports in close proximity to deep waters, giving them superiority over ports located deeper within the European land mass or ports in seas with only a shallow draught of water, impeded by shoals. At the same time, over a period of two decades, maritime transport was subjected to a series of significant technical changes, which had profound consequences for port organization. These included a marked increase in the size of ships (the capacity of the largest tankers rose from 100,000 tonnes in 1965 to more than 500,000 tonnes in 1976), the increased use of specialized carriers (oil tankers, liquefied-gas tankers and ore-carrier), the development of container traffic, which increased from 800,000 tonnes in 1968 to 1,990,000 tonnes in 1972 (6.9 per cent of all general cargo traffic), and the introduction of roll-on–roll-off carriers. The first container ports handled 300 units in 1967; at the present time the figure is between 2,000 and 3,000.

These changes, combined with the attraction of coastal industrial sites, have brought about a parallel transformation of the French port system. Traditionally this was characterized by the great number of ports. In all, 71 could be recognized, and in 1983 as many as 21 had an overseas traffic of 500,000 tonnes or more. But these ports were handicapped by their very number, by geographical situation and by sites, typically in rias or estuaries, which permitted them neither to expand nor to receive the larger modern vessels. Port administration was also archaic and over-centralized.

The first elements of a policy for ports date only from 1965. The six main ports were made administratively autonomous and benefited from a concentration on them of government investment designed to adapt them to new conditions. The port of Marseille expanded westwards into the gulf of Fos; Le Havre increased the area of its docks and in 1975 opened the outlying tanker terminal of Antifer on the coast of the Pays de Caux, the only north European port capable of receiving 500,000 tonne tankers. Dunkerque also developed towards the west, attracted by a natural channel allowing access to ships of 275,000 tonnes. There was similar expansion at Bordeaux, with its outport at Le Verdon. These port extensions took place in conjunction with the building of vast industrial zones and the siting of large steel and petrochemical plants.

Traffic passing through the ports of metropolitan France reached its maximum of 313 million tonnes in 1974 (compared with 171 million tonnes in 1967); traffic has since declined (266.6 million in 1983). Table 29.2 shows the changing traffic of the principal ports. The three main groups of ports are Marseille–Fos, Le Havre–Rouen, and Dunkerque–Calais: they have the best motorway, rail and waterway links with the interior and benefit from vast areas of associated industry. Between them they accounted in 1977 for 83 per cent of imports and 72 per cent of exports.

Port traffic is characterized by the dominance of petroleum and petroleum products (167.6 million tonnes out of a total for all imports of 335 million tonnes in 1979) and of other heavy goods.

Coastal traffic is also mainly concerned with heavy commodities such as petroleum products, coal and cement, but is relatively unimportant, amounting to only 10 per cent of total port traffic.

Passenger movements through French ports are substantial, reflecting the geographical situation of the country in relation to the British Isles and North Africa, the fact that the territory of metropolitan France includes the important island of Corsica, and traditional relationships with former colonial possessions. The pattern of passenger traffic today is dominated by the short sea links with the British Isles and Corsica.

The ferries between the British Isles and French ports from Dunkerque to Roscoff are used not only by private cars and buses but by an important freight

Table 29.2 *Freight traffic of sea ports*

Million tonnes

Seaport	1966	1978	1983 Total	Non fuel
Marseille and satellites	62.4	93.6	86.6	22.4
Le Havre	29.6	76.7	53.5	16.6
Dunkerque	12.0	35.6	30.1	20.8
Rouen and satellites	6.8	18.3	20.1	15.0
Nantes–St-Nazaire	8.6	16.1	20.1	4.0
Bordeaux and satellites	4.5	12.4	9.4	4.1
Sète	3.1	7.0		
Calais	0.9	6.2		
La Rochelle	1.7	3.9		
Boulogne	0.8	3.3		
Bayonne	0.6	2.6		
Brest	0.7	2.2		
Lorient	0.7	1.9		
Caen	1.5	1.8		
Dieppe	0.6	1.8		
Saint Malo	0.6	1.3		

Source: INSEE, statistical yearbooks.

trade carried on roll-on–roll-off services, and also for the delivery of new cars. These freight services are significant not only for France but for exchanges between the British Isles and more distant continental countries, especially Spain.

Traffic movement through French ports is low when compared with other European neighbours. In 1977 Le Havre held fifth place among European ports for container traffic (370,000 units, compared with Rotterdam's 1,318,709), and Marseille–Fos was in eleventh place. French ports do not cater for the country's entire maritime trade: Antwerp, Genoa and even Rotterdam and Hamburg benefit from the diversion of traffic. In 1978, 40 per cent of non-containerized general cargo imports passed through foreign ports. In 1979 Antwerp handled as much traffic destined for France as all the French autonomous port authorities put together. This weakness is matched by a corresponding under-representation of the French shipping fleet in handling French trade. In 1977 French vessels handled 75 per cent of fuel movements, 46 per cent of general cargo, and 24 per cent of dry bulk cargo. In 1979 the French merchant fleet, with 450 vessels totalling 11.6 million gross registered tonnes, was the ninth largest in the world.

Within the small space of western Europe, the European Community policy of equal access to ports, the well-developed transport networks and freedom from competition mean that the struggle between the various European ports and between French ports themselves is severe. This calls for the replacement of such individualistic behaviour by the planned development of the European coast as a unity.

5 Airways

With the exception of some postal services, the first air links to be developed were external services, created to serve the French colonies, remnants of which survive in the form of the French overseas departments and territories. The development of ever more advanced aircraft is both the cause and the consequence of the astonishing development of international air transport. Proximity to an international airport has become an important element in the location of many manufacturing and tertiary activities.

With regard to international traffic, France benefits from its central position in relation to the land hemisphere (see chapter 1, 2.1) and from the length of experience of its airlines. International traffic is in the hands of Air France, the national company formed in 1945 from a merger of three existing companies, and by the private-enterprise UTA, founded in 1963 by the merger of two former companies. International traffic is shared in greatly varying degree by the French international airports: Paris–Orly, Paris–Charles de Gaulle (Roissy), Nice–Côte d'Azur, Marseille–Marignane, Lyon–Satolas, Lille, Bordeaux, Toulouse and Strasbourg. The airports on the Channel coast (notably Le Touquet) have a specialized role in handling cross-channel traffic.

Pressure from the three big national airlines (Air France, Air Inter and UTA) and the restrictionist attitude of the government explain why French airports play a relatively small part in charter traffic flights. Much of this traffic is diverted to nearby foreign airports such as London, Brussels, Frankfurt, Luxemburg, Basle and Zurich. Only since 1980 has the situation shown some signs of change.

Since 1960 France has had a network of domestic air services, some operating on a permanent basis, others seasonally. The state-owned airline Air Inter has developed a network serving Paris and large towns in the provinces: from the 91,251 passengers carried in 1961, the total had reached 6 million by 1978. The development of these domestic lines was considered to be a contribution to the spatial planning and development of France. The result was a veritable airline mania: every town of any claim to importance wanted to have its own air links so that it would not be isolated and so that it would be in a position to attract the industrial tertiary developments which would create employment. The setting up of these lines and the responsibility for their deficits were the province of the town councils and the Chambers of Commerce, assisted from 1972 by subsidies from DATAR, the government organization for strategic spatial planning. Services to towns not served by Air Inter were provided by regional companies, the so-called third-level carriers. The network developed in a random manner, without any serious study of the market.

The map of domestic airlines once again shows the dominance of Paris: centralization is even greater than that of the rail network. However, a structure plan for air transport was drawn up in 1970 and adopted in 1973. By 1985 each town of more than 50,000 inhabitants was to have an airport, giving a total of 168 access points to the network. But it arrived too late, and was the expression of an optimistic vision which the 1974 oil shortage and the economic crisis that followed were to destroy. From 1976 onwards the proliferating lines and their excessive subsidies were pruned. Companies disappeared, others have been merged. Lines were closed down or transferred to small companies. Air France and Air Inter sub-contracted some of their passenger operations. By the end of 1979 there were ten regional companies, which in that year had carried 1,330,000 passengers. Fifty towns were served by this regular regional network, of which 16 were also served by Air Inter.

Because of the centralization of the international and domestic networks, most French air traffic is monopolized by the two Paris international airports, Orly and the newer Charles de Gaulle (Roissy), opened in 1974, which are run by the public Paris Airport Authority (Aéroport de Paris). In 1983 the Paris airports handled 28.8 million passengers and 662,000 tonnes of freight; the Paris airports handle 4.5 per cent of French exports by value. The geographical position of Paris enables its airports to have a very important transit function. The most important provincial airports were Marseille (3.8 million passengers in 1982), Nice (3.5 million) and Lyon (2.6 million).

6 Specialized transport networks

The forms of transport described above are not the only means of providing movement and spatial interrelationship. An increasing role is being played by a variety of specialized networks.

6.1 Oil and gas pipelines

Oil pipelines are a vital part of the oil economy; they are used for transporting both crude oil and refined products. Until 1962 there were few pipelines: of a total length of 223 km, 115 km were used to transport oil derived from the deposits of Aquitaine and the Paris basin; other lengths transported oil from the port of Le Havre to the refineries of the lower Seine and from Lavéra (west of Marseille) to the refineries of the Etang de Berre. The pipelines carrying refined products were located exclusively in the lower Seine area. A 243 km product line dating from 1953 and subsequently duplicated, links Le Havre and Paris.

In 1963, the 36 cm South European pipeline was opened for the transport of crude oil by way of the Rhône and Rhine valleys to the refineries of Feyzin near Lyon, Strasbourg and Karlsruhe; it has a length of 782 km. The Grandpuits refinery southeast of Paris is supplied with crude oil from Le Havre through a

250 km pipeline. At the beginning of 1969 a pipeline was opened which by way of Feyzin and Grenoble transports refined products to 27 depots spread out between Berne and Geneva in Switzerland. The introduction of this distribution network is explained by the resultant economies: the transport cost per tonne-kilometre is 30 to 40 times less than by road (although three times more expensive than by sea). As for gas pipelines, apart from a few local interconnections, chiefly in the Paris region and the Nord, there was in 1946 no national network for the transport of manufactured gas. The first element of a national network, completed in 1956, was a 300 km pipeline making it possible to transport about 1 million cu m a day from the coking plants of the Saar and Lorraine to Paris.

The discovery of natural gas deposits at Lacq gave rise to great hopes that this source of energy would make possible a high degree of industrialization in southwest France, one of the least developed regions of the country. These hopes were soon dashed: on economic grounds it was necessary to have regular, assured, mass outlets; it was more advantageous, moreover, to sell the gas to a small number of large consumers reached by pipelines of the largest possible capacity over the shortest possible distance rather than to supply a host of small, scattered industrial consumers. By 1956 it was clear that the entire gas production of Lacq could not be absorbed in southwest France alone. A distribution network directed towards regions of heavy consumption was rapidly constructed: 3,800 km of gas pipelines leave from the underground purified gas reservoir at Lussagnet in the Landes. One branch was built to serve the Atlantic coast as far north as Lorient, allowing imports of American coal to be reduced and feeding the power-station at Nantes-Cheviré. A second branch was built to serve the Lyon region, le Creusot and the Saône valley. The main pipeline was aimed at the Paris region, where gas was supplied to individual consumers but above all to thermal power-stations.

The third stage in the development of the gas network reflected the importation of gas from abroad. From Le Havre a network supplies Algerian gas to Normandy and the Paris region. Netherlands gas arrives by way of Maubeuge, whence major pipelines lead to Artois, to eastern France and Switzerland and to the Paris region. A large-diameter pipeline channels Algerian gas from Fos-sur-mer (near Marseille) into the Lacq network.

Soviet gas comes via the European pipeline network. This was built by a company in which the nationalized French gas company (Gaz de France) has a 43 per cent participation, together with Germany, Austria and the Netherlands.

This national gas network is linked to an increasing number of underground natural reservoirs. As early as 1958 the underground reservoir at Beynes, 40 km west of Paris, was storing gas brought from the Lorraine coke ovens. The capacity of the reservoir is 340 million cu m, the equivalent of the capacity of 550 of the largest overground gas holders of the normal type. Since then there has been a systematic search for geological structures suitable for the construction of these giant natural reservoirs, which can be used to even out daily and seasonal variations in consumption. Among the reservoirs are Saint-Illiers, near Mantes (1965: 800 million cu m) and Chémery between Blois and Tours (2,500 million cu m). Gas from the Netherlands is stored in reservoirs near Compiègne and Nancy. The contorted geology of southeast France offers no suitable structures, and consequently caverns for gas storage have been created by dissolving out underground salt deposits. The caverns are at depths of between 400 and 1,500 m and are interconnected.

6.2 Electric power networks

The consumption and supply of electicity are normally in a state of imbalance at regional level, not only because consumers are unevenly distributed but because the opportunities for production vary markedly both in space and time. For example the Alpine region, a major producer of power during the period of spring and summer snow melt, produces little electricity during the winter freeze, and must then import current from other regions. Complex energy accounting between the various regions results from situations such as this.

The inter-regional exchanges of power are provided by a network of high-tension lines which form an interconnected system able at any time to supply current available in one region to consumers in another. Despite appearances, the transport of electricity is costly, amounting on average to 12 or 13 per cent of the final price. The quantity of power supplied has constantly increased; the high-tension networks at 63 kV, 90 kV, 220 kV and 400 kV had a total length of more than 73,000 km in 1978. The 400 kV system alone accounted for 36,000 km. The arrival of nuclear power-stations will undoubtedly require appreciable changes in the structure of the electric power network.

6.3 Telecommunications networks

Telecommunications occupy an increasingly important role in the relations between private individuals and between organizations. Not very long ago they were limited to the telegraph and the telephone; now they have increased to include not only the ordinary telex but the interconnection of computers, the transmission of data and the visual presentation of information of all kinds. There is every certainty that the future will see a considerable increase in communications systems of these types. The repercussions on spatial organization, on the distribution of people and on new locations of economic and administrative activities have yet to become clear; an increase in local autonomy in decision-making is just as possible as an increase in supervision from the centre. It may be possible for economic and administrative activities to disperse from the traditional centres of information, diffusion and control.

The telecommunications network is a state monopoly offering a common service to all users. For years the inadequacies of the system were condemned by private users, industrialists and the public services alike; the difficulties of securing adequate telecommunications links have even played a major role in reducing the choice of locations available for economic or administrative developments. However, the mid-1970s saw the beginning of a major effort of modernization, one of the priorities of the Seventh national plan of 1976. There were 4 million telephone subscribers in 1969, 12 million in 1978, and 21 million in 1983. The transmission of information for instantaneous visible presentation is a growing element in the telecommunications system.

30

☙ Transport policies

The networks and the means of transport which use them compete in the same market for the same pool of travellers and goods. A particular method of transport is chosen in relation to its cost and characteristics such as speed or safety. Table 30.1 gives a breakdown of the changing division of traffic between the four principal modes of land transport.

The possibility of choice between alternatives promotes price competition and sensitive adjustment to changing conditions, both of which may be beneficial to users, but may also lead to anarchy, and hence, as an indirect consequence, public intervention and control. Transport is a basic element in the organization of space and therefore an object of concern to governments. Various considerations govern the formulation of public policy for transport; it is impossible to leave the layout of networks, the frequency of services and tariffs to the free play of market forces alone. For most means of transport, infrastructural provision is a public responsibility; this is often ill-defined, but in principle the responsible organizations can expect to have their investment costs met by the state.

1 Tariff policies

Changes in rail tariffs may be used to illustrate the development of government policies. For the long period between its creation and the 1930s, the railway system benefited from an effective monopoly, since the roads were not able to compete for goods traffic as they do today. The railway was considered as the

Table 30.1 Changing structure of inland freight traffic, by means of transport employed

Thousand million tonnes-kilometres

Year	Road		Rail SNCF		Waterway		Oil pipeline		Total	
	t-km	%	t-km	%	t-km	%	t-km	%	t-km	%
1972	74.6	39.9	68.8	36.6	14.2	7.6	29.7	15.9	187.1	100
1974	87.4	41.4	77.1	36.5	13.7	6.5	33.1	15.6	211.3	100
1976	83.9	43.0	68.5	35.1	12.0	6.1	30.8	15.8	195.2	100
1982	85.3	...[a]	57.4	...	10.1	...	...	...	...	...

[a] Data not available.
Source: Loi des Finances pour 1978, etc.

great instrument for opening up the countryside to a modern economy and for the creation of a national market. The instrument used was a simple uniform tariff which took no account of the actual costs of operating the various lines. There was a double adjustment of tariffs between the 'rich' lines in the plains and industrial regions and the 'poor' lines, and also between light goods which were charged at high rates and heavy commodities which travelled more cheaply. Mountain regions in particular benefited from these favourable tariffs which made it possible to bring in essential products such as fertilizers, agricultural machinery and raw materials for industry, and to dispatch agricultural and industrial products.

In 1951, and then more decisively in 1962, the SNCF responded to road competition by introducing differential tariffs, which tapered with distance, reflecting the actual cost of movement, as well as involving variations according to the type of traffic. The reform markedly changed spatial relations, some towns being effectively brought closer together, others thrust further apart. The new rates underlined the advantages of the railway for long-distance movements of freight, and discouraged short-distance movements. The new solution favoured the concentration of traffic into major axes connecting regions which were the origin or destination of substantial volumes of traffic. It can well be imagined that this favouring of high-volume and long-distance traffic had marked conse-quences on industrial location, on the operating costs of firms, and on inter-urban relations. There were immediate protests from the disfavoured regions such as Brittany and the Central massif, which resulted in some modifications to the new tariff structure.

The existence of alternative means of transport by rail, road, waterway or air results in a fierce and generally unregulated competition, each trying to increase its share of traffic at the expense of the others. Many plans for co-ordination have been made but no satisfactory solution has ever been found; there is too much at stake, not only on the part of the transport interests themselves but of their suppliers of fuel and equipment. This competition, particularly between road and rail, hindered the development of a rational transport system.

Road transport, developing later than rail transport and operated by numerous owners, has always had to struggle to free itself from restrictions imposed to protect the powerful interests of the state-owned railway system. Road transport operators are obliged to hold licences which restrict vehicles to a particular part of the country, and which allocate a quota of freight which may be carried. Licences may be issued for long-distance use (in fact for the whole of France), for short-distance (a department and bordering departments within a radius of 200 km), or for use within a single department. Tonnage quotas were abolished in 1963 for haulage within a single department and in 1973 for the short-distance zone. This relaxation explains the marked increase in the use of firms' own vehicles, which in 1976 carried twice the weight of goods carried by the 3,300 independent operators who provide a public service available to all individuals and companies.

In 1978 a report to the government by Pierre Guillaumat was marked by a desire, characteristic of the period, to remove restrictions on enterprise. The report recommended the expansion of road transport, arguing that the rise in the number of motor vehicles had to be accepted as an irreversible trend of the times. The problem in fact reduced itself to the proper sharing of functions and traffic between the railways and the roads. The most extreme solution would have restricted rail to an inter-urban passenger service and a freight service in full train loads only, on a drastically reduced network. A less extreme solution would have involved a reduction of the network by between 15,000 and 20,000 km, with 1,000 stations remaining open for goods traffic (in 1978 the figure was 4,200).

The Guillaumat Report proposed that both rail and road transport should be submitted to the free play of market forces, but that users of both systems should bear the total costs of providing and maintaining the necessary infrastructures, both rail tracks and road system. The report also recommended that the current system of fixing tariffs should be replaced by tariffs that would fully cover costs. The subsidies granted to the SNCF in respect of its public service obligations would be replaced by direct aid to the person or organization concerned.

This report gave rise to a very frank debate. Some denounced its excessive bias towards road transport and its favouring of individual transport and realistic pricing. Many commentators felt that the report had underestimated the cost of road transport in terms of energy and human lives. The human sacrifice paid to road transport is high: 13,000 dead and 350,000 injured each year, at an annual cost to the community that was estimated in 1977 at 35,500 million francs, to which must be added the problems of safety and adverse impact on the environment. Because transport networks are essential agents in the spatial organization of the country, they necessarily involve an element of public service. The fixing of tariffs to cover actual costs, particularly on the railways, is likely to be disadvantageous to the more remote and deprived areas. On the other hand, the adverse social costs involved in road transport should not be allowed to conceal the advantages of individual movement provided by the motor car. In the postwar years the use of the private car has freed the urban population from dependence on the rail lines and allowed a widespread dispersion of settlement. For the scattered populations of rural areas also, the private car provides a valuable service.

Tariff policies have in fact been radically changed. Since 1979 the SNCF has benefited from much greater freedom to fix tariffs; it has almost complete freedom in the fixing of goods tariffs, and can vary passenger tariffs according to the time of travel and the itinerary selected. Road haulage tariffs were freed in the same year. The system of varying tariffs according to day and season, which was applied from 1978 for domestic airlines and from 1979 for rail passenger traffic, introduced a new spatial variation into transport provision.

In 1982 the socialist government passed an orientation law for internal transport, establishing general principles to guide the organization and development of the public transport of people and goods. These included the right of access to transport facilities, the idea of transport as a public service, and the notion that the various forms of transport should be complementary rather than competitive. Decision-making was to be decentralized, with priority given to public transport (especially in towns).

2 Network policies

Tariffs can easily be modified, but the same cannot be said for networks, which have a physical existence on the ground, have for the most part been inherited from the past, and are resistant to change.

2.1 Network patterns

The spatial organization and differentiation of France are the result of the superimposing of different networks and the coexistence of several means of transport. The structural characteristics of the network considered as a whole create unequal spaces in terms of accessibility and cost.

The most obvious structural characteristic is the dominance of Paris, from which road, rail, motorway and air routes radiate to the whole of the rest of the country. Their superimposition one by one strengthened the predominance of Paris, a natural expression of the concentration there of the controlling powers of the country.

A second structural characteristic is the contrast between western and eastern France. Western France is 'organized' by rail and road radials diverging from Paris to Rouen and Le Havre, Caen, Rennes and Brittany, Bordeaux and Toulouse. But none of these radials operates so as to have any great impact on the spatial structure of the regions through which they pass, and transverse links are weak or absent. The radials operate independently, at broadly similar levels of activity.

In eastern France, by contrast, relief conditions have led to the development of a system of major axes which act in combination with the pattern of radial divergence from Paris. Hydrological and relief conditions accentuate spatial contrasts in density of occupation, accessibility and service provision.

On a country-wide scale, the introduction of air transport and motorways and the improved efficiency of the railways have produced an effective shrinkage of the French space, but not equally in all directions. On the contrary, there is a persistent, one might say historic, tendency for the radials from Paris to be favoured at the expense of transverse links. There has also been a process of selection and concentration on the most favoured nodes and axes, modernized rail stations, major seaports, motorways, motorway interchanges and new stretches of canal, accentuating space–time contrasts. Increasingly, two contrasting types of space coexist. There is a France of high-speed and high-volume movements, of maximum accessibility and minimum unit costs; there is also a France of restricted speeds and high costs of movement. It is easy for these variations to become self-perpetuating, circular in nature; no motorway is built in the Central massif since no existing or expected traffic justifies it, but no firm likely to generate such traffic will settle in an isolated region where existing road speeds hardly exceed 60 km (*c.* 35 miles per hour).

In regional terms, French space is becoming more and more sharply differentiated in terms of accessibility, transport speeds and costs of movement. The motorways in particular introduce breaks and discontinuity: they are even physically isolated by being fenced off, connecting with the rest of the road network only by rare interchanges. For long stretches they have no connection with the regions through which they pass. The same applies to the modernized rail network, with the closure of many lines and stations and the opening of specially constructed stretches of track for the new high-speed train.

2.2 The impact of network change

Changes in the networks taken individually have already been mentioned. Taken together, these changes have radically transformed the spatial organization of France.

Until 1981 the policy of rail closures had a relatively minor impact on traffic (since 90 per cent of traffic was in any case handled by 50 per cent of the network) but accentuated regional imbalance within France. Rail closures appear to have been approached in too simplistic a fashion: the axed lines may have carried little traffic, but they were the outermost tributaries feeding the network as a whole; their amputation could not but have serious consequences. Rural areas which have lost their rail services have not found the replacement road services to be of similar quality, especially in upland areas where the roads are liable to icing for several months of the year. The problems of energy costs and the security of oil supply must also not be forgotten, now that many industrial plants are situated in rural areas. Even if many parts of rural France are suffering from continuing depopulation, they nevertheless receive a seasonal invasion of vacation residents. The ageing of the French population and the increase in the number of retired people will surely increase the future numbers of people dependent on rail transport, although the places at which this increased demand will be located cannot at present be predicted.

The increasing variation in the quality and cost of transport between different sections of the networks accentuates the differences between towns and regions which have a satisfactory level of services and those which are isolated and forgotten. Moreover, such network improvements as are introduced relate almost invariably to links with Paris, and rarely to intra-regional links. Transport is an economic enterprise; its managers are concerned with profitability or at very least with breaking even. Such objectives may produce policies which are quite contrary to the attempts of planners to build up coherence and integration at regional level. From the 1970s there was growing appreciation both at regional and national level and on the part of rail users of these spatial consequences of decisions regarding transport, a concern expressed in the emergence of regional transport policies.

Regional transport plans appeared in 1975 for five pilot regions (Lorraine, Pays de la Loire, Franche-Comté, Limousin and Nord–Pas-de-Calais). From 1977 onwards the government encouraged the regions to work out co-ordinated policies for public transport, based on surveys of existing road and rail services and on traffic flows to and from schools and places of work. The regions are allowed to finance research, make agreements with passenger transport firms for the provision of services, contribute to the cost of new road and rail vehicles and even since 1979 (in the case of Brittany) to finance a modernization programme for goods traffic. The Nord–Pas-de-Calais region led the way by aiding and encouraging the SNCF to renew its equipment and to improve the Lille–Valenciennes link, and also by co-ordinating road and rail services.

These achievements and the principle of regional plans are positive signs, but they presuppose that the transfer of responsibility to regional level is accompanied by a corresponding transfer of financial resources. Regional plans must also not become merely another way of closing down local rail links. It was also essential that decisions regarding the rail elements in these plans should not continue to be made exclusively by the SNCF. Nevertheless some local authorities envisage the reopening to passengers of lines which are currently closed. With regard to Corsica, which is further from the mainland than is customarily shown on maps of France, the government has proclaimed the principle of disregarding the sea distance in the calculation of transport rates.

The integration of national territories within a wider European space brings into question plans for transport networks which have been conceived on a purely national basis; France has been particularly affected. The establishment of the European Community has led to a shift in the flows of goods and people to the benefit of the Rhône–Rhine axis, attracted towards the vast hive of people and activities in northwest Europe. Year by year interchanges across the land frontiers to European Community neighbours have increased.

Philippe Lamour aptly described the consequences of this situation:

At the present time [the 1960s] the greater part of French territory is not directly linked to Europe; indeed vast tracts of the country turn their backs on Europe, looking towards the empty spaces of the Atlantic or the Iberian peninsula. Even the regions which are situated along the natural axes of the European economy are cut off from the main mass of the country by barrier regions, as between the valleys of the Rhine and the Rhône, which bring isolation rather than improved accessibility.[1]

Progressively these barriers, and even the major mountain ranges, are being overcome by the construction of a motorway network on a European, rather than purely national, scale.

[1] Unpublished report.

VI

✤ Landscape and environment in rural France

There is hardly a feature of the rural landscape of present-day France which cannot be explained by an evolution rooted in the mists of time.

Marc Bloch

Before embarking on a description of the French countryside and its recent transformation, it might be helpful to start with the apparently banal observation that in recent years the term 'countryside' has tended to be replaced by the term 'rural space'. This expression, introduced in the 1960s by writers on planning themes, has obtained general acceptance. The change in terminology expressed the desire to indicate the extent of the new phenomena which occurred from about 1965, notably the appearance of new functions, bringing about new conflicts, and the change from a countryside which was a 'reservoir of labour' to one which is a 'reserve of space'. Thus 'space' replaced 'environment' and 'rural' replaced 'agricultural'.

In this context, the controversies with regard to the definition of rural space and the relations between town and country are understandable. In the 1950s, relations between town and country were still thought of as contradictory, the town being the artificial environment and home of the bourgeoisie, the country the natural environment and home of the peasants. From the 1960s onwards, the relationship of town and country was redefined in terms of the concept of urbanization; emphasis was placed on the interpenetration of the two environments by the progressive diffusion of the material and moral values of urban society, although at the same time a 'geographical' trend of thought persisted in emphasizing the morphological and functional distinctiveness of this 'rural space' when compared to the urban system. After 1972, town–country relationships came to be seen in terms of the domination and integration of rural space. The contradiction is no longer between two types of space but between the capitalist mode of production and the local social systems that are dominated and integrated, although the way in which this process develops will differ according to whether urban or rural space is concerned.

Thus the concept of countryside or rural space has changed, both with regard to its significance in France as a whole and with regard to urban–rural relations. A precise definition of what is 'truly rural' presents considerable difficulties: certainly it has to be accepted that rural space is decreasingly to be defined in terms of its agricultural function. But there is at least a degree of consensus regarding its empirical identification with a distinctive form of land utilization, and at least so far as France is concerned, a characteristic form of socio-spatial organization. Rural land use is (by comparison with industrial–urban use) extensive, mainly devoted to arable, pasture and forest, with a corresponding discontinuity of the built environment. Population density is low, settlement takes the form of small units, with a predominance of single-family houses. The network of social provision is extremely sparse and of a generally elementary character, even when the lowest-order central places are taken into consideration.

That there is no consensus on a single definition of rural France is understandable, reflecting as it does the reality of the diffusion, penetration and interrelation of the urban, industrial and rural environments. There are in fact conflicting interests attempting to produce wider or narrower definitions of rural France which have little to do with objective reality. There have been conflicts of territorial jurisdiction between the Ministry of Agriculture and the Ministry for Town Planning (Ministère de l'Urbanisme, at times known as the 'Ministère de l'Equipement'), and spatial competition between financial interests, notably marked by the enlargement of the area of competence of the Crédit Agricole (Agricultural Bank) in 1978. There is much criticism of the definition of 'rural' adopted by INSEE (National Statistical and Economic Research Institute), which appears to accept the existing relationship of dominance and dependence by treating 'rural' as a residual category for whatever is left over from the occupation of space for industrial and urban purposes. Despite these criticisms, the area it defines as rural has contracted in each succeeding census: by the census of 1975 it was basing its projections of future rural population only on those communes which were outside what it defined as zones of industrial and urban population (zones de peuplement industriel et urbain – ZPIU), a very restricted and fragmented area indeed, which excluded all points with some intensity of economic activity, even where this was directly linked with the rural environment.

For want of a better definition, however, the attempt to analyse the quantitative changes affecting rural France has to fall back on the simple statistical definition that a commune is deemed to be rural if its largest agglomeration has fewer than 2,000 inhabitants. According to this definition, French rural space in 1975 covered 4.6 million sq km (86 per cent of the area of metropolitan France) and had 14.3 million inhabitants (27 per cent of the French population). It comprised not only a great variety of landscapes and environments, reflecting a physical geography which is itself extremely varied, but also highly differentiated economic structures, very varied levels of integration into the national system and a wide range of social structures.

It is open to question whether the general trends which affect rural space are operating in the direction of maintaining the characteristic variety of the rural landscape and of French rural society, or are tending towards a general uniformity.

31

⚜ Old and new uses of rural space

Since the end of the Second World War in 1945 there has been a diversification of activities and functions within rural space, or at least a recognition of aspects such as the cultural heritage which were formerly not clearly appreciated. Formerly, rural space was essentially devoted to agriculture, with a predominantly agricultural population; but as the number of farmers declined and as the agricultural sector underwent a radical transformation, an increasingly empty space was revealed, open for multiple alternative claims upon its usage.

The new types of rural environments stem from a combination between the traditional forms of agricultural and industrial utilization and the appearance of new functions related to residential and tourist activities, which result in the emergence of new land-use values. It is difficult exactly to define these new types of environment, because there is a considerable difference between one sector and another. However, before venturing on a classification, certain general tendencies can be outlined.

1 Diversification of activities

The economic base of rural space has undergone a profound change since 1945 (Table 31.1). Is it possible to speak of a 'diversification of economic activities' following a long period of purely agricultural occupation of rural communes? It is in fact difficult to attribute such a complex change to a single explanation. There has obviously been a transformation in the nature of agricultural activity which

Table 31.1 *Changing occupational distribution of the working population in rural communes*

As defined in the census concerned

By workplace	1962		1975		Employment per sq km	
	Thousands	%	Thousands	%	1962	1975
Primary sector	3,487.6	56.4	1,704.7	40.4	7.02	3.65
Secondary sector	1,418.8	22.9	1,286.2	30.5	2.85	2.75
of which building and construction	422.2	6.8	418.2	9.9	0.85	0.89
Tertiary sector	1,278.5	20.7	1,225.7	29.1	2.56	2.62
Non-farm employed population	2,697.3	43.6	2,511.9	59.6	5.41	5.37
Total employed population	6,184.9	100.0	4,216.6	100.0	12.44	9.02

By place of residence	1954		1975	
	Thousands	%	Number	%
Primary sector	4,726.7	57.2	1,708.9	32.3
Secondary sector	1,991.7	24.1	1,835.8	34.7
Tertiary sector	1,492.4	18.1	1,746.7	33.0
Non-farm employed population	3,484.0	42.2	3,582.5	67.7
Total employed population	8,210.8	100.0	5,291.3	100.0

Source: SEGESA, after INSEE.

has led to a sharp decline in the number of agricultural workers; conversely, this decline could itself be the cause of agricultural change. But it is quite clear that non-agricultural activities have retained their employment potential, thanks to a growth in the tertiary sector which makes up for the marked decline in the industrial sector. The tertiary sector and building are net creators of employment and thus participate in a positive diversification of the rural economy, whereas industries processing agricultural products barely manage to survive in spite of their direct links with the rural economy. These various changes meant that whereas in 1954 just over half of the economically occupied persons were employers or self-employed, by 1975 the proportion of wage-earners and salaried employees had risen to 64 per cent.

But the fact that there are possibilities of employment outside agriculture does not mean that there is an end to employment problems. The vulnerability of productive structures in rural areas means that any economic crisis has an even greater impact on employment. If unemployment appears lower than in urban areas this is because it is so frequently hidden by the practice of having more than one occupation, by odd-jobbing and subsistence agriculture. Certainly female activity rates are low: 46 per cent of women between the ages of 20 and 64 who live in rural communes are in registered employment, as against 54 per cent in towns. The increase in non-agricultural activities has not been sufficient to make up for the loss of employment in agriculture. Between 1962 and 1975 overall employment in rural areas actually fell, so that rather than speaking of a modest diversification of the rural economy, it would be more appropriate to speak of a decline in its productive functions. This decline is in reality all the more evident since the marked increase in non-agricultural workers in rural areas must be linked to the growth of rural–urban commuters, and thus reflects the residential rather than the productive function of rural space.

These general trends in the economic change of rural space differ regionally (Fig. 31.1). The classification of rural departments according to the predominant economic sector (primary, secondary or tertiary) in 1954 and 1975 shows that the number of departments dominated by one or at most two sectors has fallen sharply, from 38 to 9; three very specialized types (primary alone, primary–secondary and secondary–primary) have disappeared and have been transformed into diversified types (primary–tertiary–secondary, primary–secondary–tertiary and secondary–primary–tertiary). Four new types appeared: two diversified (tertiary–primary–secondary and tertiary–secondary–primary), emerging chiefly from the primary–secondary–tertiary type of 1956, and two relatively specialized (secondary–tertiary and tertiary–secondary), revealing an increased degree of specialization of departments which were diversified in 1954. But the trend towards diversification and the various stages by which this is achieved do not exclude the presence, even the strengthening, of regional contrasts. The specialization of rural economies in the widest sense is accepted so far as the development of agriculture is concerned; it is underestimated and even ignored with regard to the other sectors of activity.

Some rural areas therefore remain predominantly agricultural, despite a diversification of activities and the rapid decline in the number of those occupied in farming. These areas are situated almost entirely in western France and form two distinct centres of agricultural resistance, one in Brittany and Normandy, the other more to the southwest, with Limousin and the southern part of the Central massif as cores. The first area is made up of the departments which are the biggest producers of agricultural products, and the second is an area where farmers are distinctly less productive yet form a dominant element in rural society. This highly agricultural western France is divided in two by a corridor of departments (Loire-Atlantique, Vendée, Maine-et-Loire, Sarthe) in which industrialization has spread out from the western periphery of the Paris basin, displacing the agricultural predominance in favour of the dominance of a secondary economy. In contrast with these western departments, whose agricultural specialization is being relatively reinforced, there are departments in eastern and northeastern France where the secondary sector was already predominant in 1954. All (except for the former Department of Seine-et-Oise) remained industrial in 1975, in spite of the sharp decline in the rural non-farm

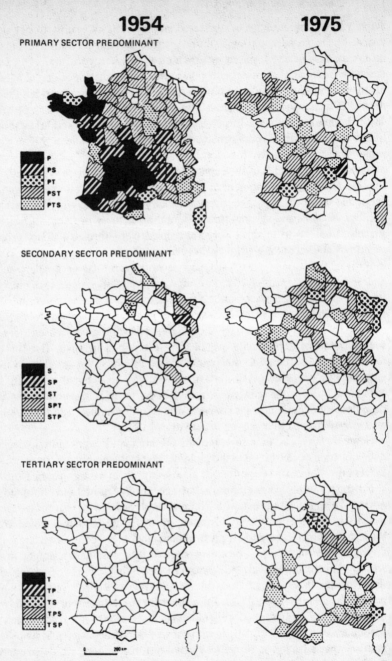

Figure 31.1 Diversification of employment in rural areas, 1954–75. P = Primary sector. S = Secondary sector (manufacturing). T = Tertiary sector. The combinations of letters indicate the degree of dominance and the hierarchy of the various sectors. Source: Census.

active population, which was a clear sign of the crisis in these rural areas. By contrast the regions already specializing in industry in 1954 did not decline, but so to speak conquered their fringing departments in the Nord, the eastern Paris basin and Franche-Comté, which permanently lost their agricultural character in favour of a rural–industrial combination. Between the two types of stable regional specialization of the rural economy two directions of evolution are emerging, one, as already described, in the direction of industry, the other towards a dominance of tertiary activities. Yet once again these developments show a markedly regionalized distribution. A widespread change to a predominance of tertiary activities in the rural economy occurs only in the Alpine and Mediterranean departments and to the southeast of the Paris region; elsewhere this change is limited to departments which are dominated by a large town.

This division of the country into specialized economic regions, despite a general trend towards diversification, may be regarded as a spatial manifestation of the social phenomenon of the division of labour.

2 Changing values in rural land use

The excessive concentration of population in urban areas and the sense of an 'urban crisis', whether springing from economic factors such as the cost of land, the cost of housing and high rents, or from ideological factors such as the desire for a return to nature, the rediscovery of the countryside or the triumph of the individual house and garden, have given rise to a new perception of the advantages of rural living. There has been a reversal of the values connected with the rural world, an ideological about-turn, a rehabilitation of the countryside. Rural space is increasingly consumed for purposes of housing and recreation, both because it is less expensive than urban land and because the countryside satisfies new perceptions of need. There are very few villages and hamlets which do not in one way or another reflect these changes in use values or the mechanisms by which the use of space is being changed. At the same time the increasing awareness that this spatial reserve was in fact limited and was not subject to reproduction led to the emergence in the 1970s of a new attitude to rural space, the conservation ('green') movement.

Rural France, because of its low population, provides ample opportunity for the operation of such basic processes as the hydrological cycle, the purification of the atmosphere, the regeneration of the soil and the 'reproduction' of floral and faunal regions. Public opinion has also become convinced of the necessity of preserving the quality of rural landscapes, and of preventing the loss of their visual attractiveness and variety in the face of an increasingly standardized agriculture. In particular, the preservation of the surviving rural landscapes that lie within generally urbanized areas has become a major preoccupation of spatial planning. Similarly, in continuation of this new myth of the rural world as 'the guardian of nature' and the last bastion against the excesses of urbanization, there has been an obvious renewal of interest in everything connected with the cultural heritage of the countryside: rural house styles, dialects, popular traditions, festivals and village life. The more this natural and cultural inheritance is destroyed or absorbed into new ways of life acquired from abroad, the higher the value that is placed upon it.

There is still no geography of these new values attached to the countryside and still less any systematic regional inventories of the rural heritage: forests, mountain regions, particularly attractive rural landscapes or cultural traditions. In principle, these areas of particular significance are supposed to be protected by their designation as national and regional parks, nature reserves, listed sites of special cultural or scientific interest, or village conservation schemes. But how can such areas be effectively protected when these increasingly rare spaces are ever more frequently visited, and are the object of more and more schemes for change and development? Should they be left to the farmers, 'nature's gardeners', guardians of traditional values, or to the new rurals who opt out to practise organic farming or set up as artists–craftsmen, or left to the civil servants of the state to try to strike some sort of balance between the protection of nature and the rights of the public? It is easy to understand how the efforts of the latter result in conflicts in heavily protected areas such as the Cévennes, the fringes of national parks, the high mountains or the wetlands.

3 Land-use change and social change

The radical social change which has been going on for nearly half a century has without doubt affected the whole of France, but the most radical and rapid change has been in rural areas (Table 31.1). Whereas agricultural population as a whole continues to decrease, the influence of the farmers of modernized but medium-sized holdings has been strengthened, particularly with regard to claims on such additional land as becomes available, thus erecting obstacles against new forms of land utilization and consumption. The explanation of these new contradictions is to be found in the social composition of rural France, which has greatly changed since the 1950s. Table 31.2 shows that the two groups that have most increased their significance in the social structure of rural areas are at opposite ends of the social spectrum: high-income categories, attracted by the natural environment and the village life-style, and low-income groups, driven out of urban areas by the high cost of living, especially the high cost of housing. Between the two, the very social groups which are responsible for the maintenance of rural space are in marked decline. They include, above all, the farmers, who by owning and working the land are solely responsible for the upkeep of the rural landscape, and the artisans and small shopkeepers without whom the farming population would have to travel long distances for the services that they require. Whereas the price of agricultural land and of areas of high landscape value is constantly rising, the sharply declining economic groups which have created them and which have hitherto held local political power are fiercely

Table 31.2 *Changing socio-economic composition of the population of rural communes*

Socio-economic category	1962		1975	
	Total	%	Total	%
Owners and directors in industry and large concerns in the distributive trades	49,647	0.7	49,485	0.9
Professions and higher administrative categories	66,731	0.9	137,545	2.5
Sub-total		1.6		3.4
Farmers	2,790,450	39.6	1,408,575	25.9
Middle management	243,857	3.5	405,535	7.5
Craftsmen, small shopkeepers and owners of fishing concerns	644,540	9.2	441,110	8.1
Sub-total		52.3		41.5
Manual workers	1,879,209	26.7	1,895,640	34.8
Non-manual workers	315,208	4.5	513,230	9.4
Service sector	212,478	3.0	221,220	4.1
Agricultural workers	700,592	9.9	270,070	5.0
Sub-total		44.1		53.3
Other categories	141,676	2.0	98,040	1.8
All workers	7,044,388	100.0	5,440,450	100.0
Retired:				
Farmers and business	795,437		1,219,900	
Public and private sector employees	700,157		944,195	
Others over 65 years	766,313		601,645	
Total population	17,098,347		14,211,385	

Source: INSEE.

resisting their political elimination. Conflicts abound: between permanent residents and those with second homes, foresters and farmers, old and young farmers, holidaymakers and farmers, property developers and local conservationist groups, clubs preserving areas for hunting and fishing, and new groups wishing to walk in the countryside and enjoy the beauties of nature.

All these conflicts reveal the changes in social relationships in rural areas. Moreover the government also creates conflicts by large-scale requirements of space for purposes such as airports, motorways, power dams, military training grounds and nuclear power-stations. The 'battles' of the Larzac military training area and of the Bugey nuclear plant are examples of conflicts in which farmers play a very important role, supported and encouraged by members of the ecological ('green') movements: ecologists, organic farmers, new groups such as urban people returning to live off the land, and second-home owners. The state in its turn tries to arbitrate between all these interest groups by relying on old or new public figures and institutions. In all rural areas the 'public interest' can be maintained by means of the rural development plans (*plans d'aménagement rural* – PAR), the land-use plans (*plans d'occupation des sols* – POS), local development plans (*contrats de pays*), the prefects, government officials at regional level concerned with construction and agriculture, farmers' organizations, and a range of semi-public companies.

32

⚜ The built environment in rural France

The rural landscapes of France are the geographical expression of the many factors analysed in preceding pages, but they also reflect social concepts relating to the organization of agricultural and rural space. The changes which have characterized the last forty years have been reflected by major changes in economic activities and life-styles.

1 Rural settlement

The French rural landscape is profoundly humanized, and this characteristic can be linked to the high density of the rural settlements which are the points from which the countryside is organized and adapted. There are, however, many different rural-settlement types. There are farmsteads, but there are also buildings in which the non-agricultural population lives and works. Almost everywhere the countryside is dotted with manors, châteaux, residences of the nobility or the upper bourgeoisie, all bearing witness to the continuing privilege of the great landowners in rural society. Built at different periods in a range of historical styles, they frequently occupy superb sites, either for strategic reasons or to command widespread panoramas. Others simply stand in the middle of their estates, but all of them give the countryside an undeniable distinction with their architectural beauty, their ancient trees and wide vistas. There are some tens of thousands of them in France as a whole, including 700 in Vendée and 1,200 in Périgord. Most of them have one or more adjacent farms.

There are also areas empty of habitation. These are first of all the uplands, where the altitudinal limit of permanent rural settlement is very high, situated between 1,000 and 2,000 m; Saint-Véran in Queyras (southern Alps), at an altitude of 2,000 m, is the highest village in France. In the young fold mountains, generally, as well as in the Central massif, the upper limit of permanent settlement is situated between 1,100 and 1,200 m, with a few local exceptions. In the Central massif, however, there are considerable regional variations. The upper limit is at no more than 750 m in the Morvan, and above 900 m the long upland spine of Limousin is left to moorland and forest, but farms are to be found at 1,000 m around the sources of the Allier and the Loire, and reach 1,500 m in the volcanic Mézenc in the southeast of the massif.

The great forests and heaths constitute the lowland areas devoid of rural settlement. Yet such rural deserts are rare, for the rejuvenation of erosion by breaking through old surfaces has created slopes and fresh soils, and has thus opened the way to agricultural settlement. Broadly speaking, the existence of extensive forests with a lack of rural settlement can in northern France be attributed to soil conditions, to which in southern France must be added the effect of altitude and rugged relief.

The rural house, whether isolated or grouped with others, is an integral part of the complex of parcels, field ways, trees and crops whose long history and gradual change have created intensely humanized and harmonious landscapes. The dwelling is fundamental; everything revolves round it, and it is the feature most easily grasped. It is the house, rather than the field system, that has so long attracted the attention of geographers, hitherto providing an apparently inexhaustible source of material for study and research.

Rural settlement even more than field systems is deeply rooted in the past; even though explanations in terms of ethnic origin are today no longer acceptable and though it no longer seems necessary to link contrasts in settlement to very ancient civilizations, it is nevertheless true that its foundations were laid in very ancient times.

To put the case in its simplest terms, we may assume that present-day rural settlement in France evolved in the course of two main periods. The first phase, from the widespread destruction of the second half of the third century to the close of the barbarian invasions, that is to say until the second half of the tenth century, had a closed economy as its keynote. The second phase developed with the resumption of trade and the growth of towns from the eleventh century onwards and lasted until the arrival of the railways.[1]

A third period began at the end of the 1960s with the expansion of the rural–urban fringe and housing developments in rural areas unrelated to agricultural settlement.

The distribution of settlement over the whole country is extremely varied.

---

[1] R. Dion, *La Part de la géographie et celle de l'histoire dans l'explication de l'habitat rural du Bassin Parisien* (Publications de la Société de Géographie de Lille, 1946).

There are two main types: grouped settlement and dispersed settlement, but they are more often intermixed than clearly distinct. There are very few regions in which rural settlement consists entirely either of isolated farms and hamlets or grouped villages; in most cases the pure types have to give way to combinations which are difficult to analyse and interpret. Definitions themselves present problems, as it is not easy to determine exactly where concentration ends and dispersion begins. On the other hand there is no possible comparison between the dispersion of a very dense human occupance in Brittany and the sparse dispersion of human occupance in the Causses. The term *village* itself covers settlements as different as the small nucleations of the Central massif and the large grouped settlements of Beauce, Picardy or Champagne. In Brittany, *village* contrasts with *bourg* (the lowest level of central place); it consists of a group of farmsteads having neither the church nor the cemetery that would be associated with the term *village* elsewhere.

1.1 The origins of rural settlement

It is often claimed that the original settlement forms were grouped settlements, and that, for example, the villages of Alsace are the descendants of those which existed in Celtic times; the Gallo-Roman *vici* were either agricultural villages or settlements of artisans. But as far back as it is possible to go in attempting to analyse the landscape of Gaul, it is clear that rural settlement was complex, combining concentrated and dispersed forms. Above all, concentrated settlement corresponded to a communal form of agrarian organization with a precise system of legal obligations which stamped itself on the soil.

The village as a unit was often separated from the cultivated land by a visible feature such as a wall, hedge or back lane, and was immediately surrounded by an inner ring of land where crops requiring heavy manuring and intensive cultivation were grown. The formation of villages in the modern period is rare. There are instances of manor farms or medieval granges being transformed into new agglomerations of small farms and cottages huddled within their former courtyards. In the seventeenth and eighteenth centuries, some new villages were founded in Provence or reconstructed in Lorraine following wartime destruction.

1.1.1 Stages of settlement dispersal

It has hitherto been accepted that before the tenth and eleventh centuries primary rural settlement in dispersed form was rare, being discouraged by natural, political, legal and economic conditions. As might be expected, the more marginal areas had dispersed individual settlements of foresters, swineherds, hunters and hermits. But both in the heights of the Auvergne and on the plains of Brie, examples are reported of isolated farms surviving on the sites of Gallo-

Roman villas, to which the great feudal estates appear to have been direct successors. These conclusions have been confirmed by recent progress in air photography, which has revealed the enormous density and overwhelming spatial predominance of the Gallo-Roman villa in the great limon and limestone plains.

From the tenth and eleventh centuries onwards, dispersed settlement increased in connection with the progressive clearance of the forest or the outward expansion of existing areas of occupance. From the tenth to the thirteenth centuries, the large southern-type unitary farmhouse (*mas*) spread in the eastern and southern parts of the Central massif. Further north, the Bourbonnais and the Morvan were colonized about the year 1000. In the tenth century, Bresse was still an almost unbroken forest; its settlement in hamlets under the supervision of the local aristocracy dates from the end of the century. In the late eleventh and twelfth centuries, there was an increase in the number of monastic granges built outside the existing villages.

There was a further increase in dispersed settlement in the thirteenth century, especially after 1225, in connection with the clearance of the forest for the establishment of new settlers under the direction of the manorial lords. In Brie, dispersed settlement followed the creation of *villeneuves* (fortified new towns) as part of the colonization of the last areas remaining unoccupied. The new farms, hamlets and small villages that were characteristic of the period often have names evocative of the site: Beaulieu, Clairefontaine, Chantecoq, Grange-au-Bois. Also characteristic are place-names preceded by the definite article (which came into general use only from the eleventh century onwards), settlements called after the names of saints, and also place-names indicating 'new' or 'free' settlements (La Villeneuve or Neuville, Francheville or les Franchises).

This movement towards the establishment of isolated farms on the edge of existing village lands and in previously unpopulated regions began in the thirteenth century and gathered pace in the fourteenth, the dispersal of population helping to reduce social tensions in existing settlements. The new developments took the form of substantial farms, each situated on its own area of enclosed land. From the middle of the fifteenth century onwards, there was an increasing tendency to establish dispersed farms on land bought by members of the urban bourgeoisie, the estates typically having names with suffixes in *ière* or *erie* added to the name of the founder. Between the fourteenth and seventeenth centuries, monastic granges and mountain chalets were built on the higher chains of the Jura.

The eighteenth century was marked by an increase in rural population (30 per cent between 1715 and 1789), with a consequent expansion of cultivation and settlement at the expense of heathland, common land, areas of poor soil and flood plains. The isolated farms and, more rarely, hamlets of the period often bear names recalling the French colonial experience of the period, such as Les Loges (after the American Indian lodge), Canada, le Nouveau Monde (New World),

Mississippi or Cayenne. The last stages in the agricultural occupation of the land date from the nineteenth century. Large isolated farms were built in areas of marginal land: on the chalk plateaus of 'dry' Champagne, in the woods and clay-with-flints soils of Upper Artois and Upper Boulonnais, on the heathlands of Berry, Poitou and the Sologne, on the plateaus of Touraine and in the Landes of southwest France. Once again the period when the farms were established is often revealed by names recalling historical events: Moscow, Algiers, Sebastopol or Solferino.

1.1.2 Factors favouring the emergence of dispersed settlement

Over the centuries, settlement dispersion has been influenced by the following factors:

(i) The importance of cultivation systems. Duby[2] relates settlement dispersal to assarting (the creation of additional fields out of the 'waste' beyond the existing area of cleared land). A day came when, in order not to have to return to the village each evening at periods when the work of the fields was particularly heavy, settlers built improvised shelters in the most distant fields, which subsequently became permanent homes. Distance may not have been the only factor, however; it is also probable that from the thirteenth century onwards families began to own agricultural equipment on an individual basis, and so were able to extricate themselves from the older communal systems of mutual aid. Soil conditions may also have been relevant; it is possible that these later stages of agricultural colonization took place in areas which required different and more individualistic combinations of cereal and livestock, particularly the latter. It seems reasonable that dispersed settlement is better adapted to livestock enterprises, where proper care of the animals is facilitated by short distances between farmyard and pasture. Early dispersion often reflects the predominance of a pastoral economy. In areas specializing in market gardening or the growth of crops under irrigation, the system of culture was itself a cause of settlement dispersion because of the need for constant care and supervision.

(ii) Tenurial influences. Generally speaking, the isolated farmstead reflects a particular structure of property relationships, having frequently developed on estates owned by the aristocracy or the urban bourgeoisie, or in relation to sharecropping. In parts of the Central massif, and on the southern fringe of the Paris basin, isolated farmsteads relate to estates held by the aristocracy or the urban bourgeoisie, or else to the inalienable possession of religious bodies or corporations, while the villages and hamlets are associated with the field complexes of peasant proprietors. In the open, cleared areas (*campagnes*) of the

[2] G. Duby, *L'Economie rurale et la vie des campagnes dans l'Occident médiéval* (2 vols., Aubier, Paris, 1962), vol. 1, pp. 166-7.

Nantes region, for example, there was a contrast between the fragmented land systems of the villages and hamlets and the more orderly apportionment of land on the large estates belonging to the châteaux. In every region where land ownership was dominated by a well-established urban bourgeoisie, large isolated farmsteads were built and large estates formed in the sixteenth century, which continued to increase in the seventeenth and eighteenth centuries.

(iii) The influence of physical geography. At one time the prevalence of concentration and dispersion was habitually related to conditions of physical geography, with concentrated village settlement being held to be characteristic of the limestone plateaus, and dispersed settlement characteristic of the clays or of regions of crystalline rocks. In limestone regions, the water-table is accessible only at great depth by means of deep wells that are difficult to construct and to maintain. It therefore appeared logical that in order to share the cost of obtaining access to water, settlements in such areas would be grouped together; on the other hand, in areas of impermeable soil the abundance of streams and springs would favour the dispersal of settlement. Critics of 'geographical determinism', however, have not failed to find exceptions to this 'law of determinism by water-availability'. For example, the clay lowland of the Woëvre in the east of the Paris basin (Fig. 2.5) has village settlement, whereas the limestone Causses are settled with hamlets and isolated farms.

(iv) Relief. A varied relief also involves a fragmentation of cultivable soils and a restriction of possible farm sites. It is clear that in the ancient massifs the distribution of the basic unit of agricultural settlement – the farm or the hamlet – relates to the degree of dissection of relief. In the traditional agrarian landscape of the Vosges, agronomists have recently restored relief to its place, the isolated farms corresponding to a small island of a few steeply sloping hectares. In the Terrefort of southwest France 'the agricultural unit is the ridge between two valleys, when its size matches the labour inputs likely to be available from a single family. On wider ridges, two, three or even four holdings each centre their fields on a single farmhouse, the holding slanting obliquely down the ridge slope from top to bottom.'[3]

(v) The extent of land available for settlement. Fragmentation of the agricultural land in areas of varied relief also has an effect on the size of settlement.

All physical features which tend to break the continuity of agricultural land and to divide it into fragments too small to provide an economic base for the population of a village, and which put obstacles between these fragments, are unfavourable to the growth of village communities. Disadvantages are not only derived from relief features; they may also result

[3] D. Faucher, *La Vie rurale vue par un géographe* (Institut de Géographie de la Faculté des Lettres et Sciences Humaines, Toulouse, 1962), p.270.

from a combination of geology and climate, and may appear in the most varied environments.[4]

For example, the dispersal of settlement on the karst plateaus of southern France is clearly linked to the restriction of arable land to scattered areas in valley bottoms and dolinas; it is difficult to imagine how it would be possible to establish villages in such conditions.

In regions of poor clay or siliceous soils, where the cultivable area is broken up by the relief variations, infield–outfield systems are characteristic. Each area of cultivated land (infield) has associated with it

an uncultivated piece of land at least as extensive, usually heath (*garrigue*), which functions as a reservoir of fertility. This may be provided either in the form of the soil itself, which is stripped off after burning the covering vegetation, or in the form of farmyard manure derived from the animals which graze the heath and use it for litter. This system makes it necessary to mix uncultivated land and cultivated fields, and thus prevents the formation of extensive uniform areas of arable land ... Villages with open fields and associated rotation systems in their fully developed form could not therefore be established on the sheets of granitic sand surrounding the Central massif or on decalcified clay soils.[5]

(vi) Soils and types of terrain. Late settlement often took place in areas where soils were developed on clays, sandy clays or marl, previously considered unattractive because they were harder to work and made movement more difficult. Such areas were more frequently left under grass than used for arable cultivation. Everything therefore led to the restriction of the area of land available to any settlement, the fragmentation of the population, and the concentration, so far as possible, of farm land around the individual farmsteads:

it is rare, in a region of clay soil, that we can walk two kilometres without having to cross several watercourses. The abundance of shallow streams and the speed with which the smallest erosional incision expands, cause the low-lying marshy ground to spread, making it difficult to cross, even in summer, if there is no proper provision of roads. The farmer would encounter more than one of these obstacles on the way to his fields if his farmhouse were not in close proximity. Impermeability or decalcification of the soil – defects generally associated in those regions of France which long remained uncultivated and covered with forest – imposed restrictions on agriculture incompatible with the existence of long distances between the farmstead and its dependent fields.[6]

Strictly speaking, it cannot be claimed that the natural environment in any way determines the settlement pattern: in the end, decisions have to be taken by individuals or groups according to their evaluation of available alternatives. It must also be remembered that dispersion may be a secondary form of settlement,

[4] Dion, *La Part de la géographie et celle de l'histoire*, p. 48.
[5] *Ibid.*, p. 57.
[6] *Ibid.*, p. 33.

replacing or modifying a quite different form which previously existed in the same environment.

1.2 Changes in rural settlement forms up to the mid-twentieth century

The analysis and interpretation of rural settlement forms is made all the more difficult because of the profound changes they have undergone over the centuries, changes which are unconnected with the expansion of the inhabited land or the late colonization of some areas. Modification of the pattern of settlement has taken place through both changes in density and changes in settlement form. Increased density of settlement frequently occurs by means of the intercalation of hamlets or isolated farms into an existing pattern of villages. Farms were established in the waste on the fringes of the communes, or on other unfavourable sites such as abandoned land and windswept heights. Place-names often reflect these locations: Heurtebise (windblown) or Bellevue.

This intercalated settlement is found in parts of Lorraine; in the Metz region, the establishment of numerous farms between the villages took place over a period of two thousand years. The first were the descendants of the Gallo-Roman villas, the last were built in the nineteenth century. In the Pyrenees, the intercalation of dispersed settlement was encouraged by the continued existence of common forest and pasture land which were only belatedly appropriated by settlers. Field barns for storing hay and sheltering stock were established on common land in the valleys, parts of which could be cleared and enclosed. From the eighteenth century onwards, pressure from a mounting population caused the temporary enclosures to be made permanent and pass into private hands. The process of intercalation could also take place in areas of dispersed settlement. In the Comtat-Venaissin (present Vaucluse Department, east of the lower Rhône) at the end of the nineteenth century, additional *mas* (southern-type farmhouses) and smaller rural houses were added to the existing pattern of dispersed settlements which had been established in the eighteenth century and earlier. At the end of the Middle Ages and in the subsequent modern period, a swarm of new farms with at least some element of unauthorized squatting crept in among the established settlements. Not surprisingly, they had difficulty in withstanding crises such as wars, economic pressure and demographic change.

Much more important than these additions of new rural settlements has been the disappearance of existing ones. From the fourteenth century onwards, wars, epidemics and climatic disasters led to the abandonment of numerous farms and whole villages. In some areas, rural depopulation brought about a contraction of the cultivated space, with the abandonment of the areas which had been most recently acquired, where human occupance was the least well established. In Brie and Provence, hamlets disappeared in the second half of the fourteenth century. In Artois, Picardy and Lorraine, hundreds of villages disappeared as a result of destruction by the wars which took place between the fifteenth and eighteenth centuries, changing not the nature of settlement but its intensity. The lost villages left the way clear for a later intercalation of dispersed settlement.

In the fifteenth, sixteenth and seventeenth centuries, a hamlet destroyed by war was frequently replaced only by a single isolated farm. Changes in land ownership, depopulation and the concentration of holdings played a decisive part in changing the pattern of settlement. In the Gâtine area of Poitou, from the sixteenth century onwards, the amalgamation of land holdings led to the replacement of dispersion in small hamlets by dispersion in isolated *métairies* (farms occupied by share-croppers). In the nineteenth century, a new wave of isolated *métairies* occupied the interfluves which had previously been left as uninhabited heathland (*brande*). This agrarian colonization was the result of the introduction after 1850 of the sowing of grass leys.

A rural settlement can even change its site, without necessarily changing other characteristics. Thus hilltop villages often migrate downhill in search of a better water supply, to be nearer to the arable land or to have a more convenient access to communications.

1.3 Settlement forms
1.3.1 Grouped settlement forms

Village forms are extremely varied. Demangeon[7] suggested a classification which differentiates between linear, clustered and radial villages.

(i) Linear villages occur very frequently, spreading along a single street which may be straight or curved. There is little development in depth to either side of the street. There is sometimes a clear relationship to the natural environment, the village being aligned along a valley, a narrow interfluve or a river dyke. Linear forms also occur, however, where there is no obvious relationship to environmental features, so that any explanation of the occurrence of the form must be sought elsewhere.

(ii) Clustered villages are particularly characteristic of southern France, located in the middle of their cultivated land. They were often deliberately founded by lay or ecclesiastical landlords. They also take the form of hilltop villages such as those in Provence, perched high like eagles' nests, their houses huddled together on a defensive site. Today these are often abandoned, or their houses converted into second homes.

(iii) Radial villages. In this type, instead of remaining in a compact group, the farms are spread out along the roads and lanes which diverge from the centre of the village.

[7] A. Demangeon, 'Types du peuplement rural en France', *Annales de Géographie*, no. 271, 1939, p. 121.

1.3.2 Dispersed settlement forms

The nature of settlement dispersal varies considerably from one region to another and even from one commune to another. Even in regions of extreme dispersion a certain variety of form is introduced by the presence of the *bourg* (the lowest-order central place), or by *villages* in the Breton sense, that is hamlets where the population is not solely employed in agriculture.

(i) Dispersal in isolated farmsteads. Many regions are dotted with farmsteads completely isolated from each other, as in the Vosges mountains, maritime Flanders, or the molassic hills of the Aquitaine basin. In some cases of extreme dispersal, even the public buildings are completely split up, church, town hall and school being situated some distance from each other, sometimes on different hilltops.

(ii) Dispersal in hamlets. Settlement exclusively in hamlets is relatively rare, as this kind of structure is very sensitive to demographic and economic change. Examples can be found in Champsaur (upper Drac valley in the Alps) and the southern Jura.

In the Central massif, Lower Provence and many other regions, hamlets were often originally of the familial type, occupied by an isolated, extended family which has given its name to the settlement (patronymic hamlets). The sub-sequent division and break-up of the family then led, generation by generation, to an increased dispersal of settlement through the creation of new farms, often leaving the old centre reduced to a single isolated farmstead.

An unusual form of hamlet is associated with the openfield areas contained within the *bocage* of western France. From three to six farms are built in a row, side by side under a single roof; sometimes several rows are arranged parallel to each other. Similar forms known as *barriades* are found in the Monts Dore (Central massif); they probably correspond to hamlets which were originally occupied by a single extended family.

Hamlets provide a rather ambiguous settlement form, sometimes having the characteristics of grouped settlements, sometimes of dispersed: Breton farm-steads, only a few score metres apart, turn their backs on each other. The hamlets of upland Beaujolais (eastern Central massif) have the same aspect: the farmsteads carefully avoid any communal arrangements, each having its own well or spring, its own farmyard, and completely separate access. Each farmstead opens out directly on to its own land, which often lies all on one side of the hamlet. These hamlets, despite the apparent closeness of the buildings, are simply collections of farms having very little relationship with each other . . . in Lower Provence, the hamlet retains some of the characteristics of grouped settlement.

(iii) Intermingled hamlets and farms. This is the most common type, resulting from

the factors already mentioned. It predominates in Armorica, the Pays de Caux and the plateau of Millevaches in Limousin.

1.3.3 Intermediate and mixed types

(i) Loosely grouped villages. Sometimes it is not possible to use the term 'dispersed' because there is a clear contrast between the rural space devoted exclusively to cultivation, and the rural space devoted to settlement. It is equally impossible to speak of concentration, for the farms, far from clustering together, seem to avoid contact with each other. They are strung out along roads and tracks, producing a rather nebulous association. This type is found in Vimeu (Picardy), in certain Breton coastal 'villages' and in southern Lorraine. Towards the east of Lorraine, around Sarrebourg, there are villages in clearings, with houses strung out along the road for several kilometres.

(ii) Intercalated dispersal. Mention has already been made of the creation of isolated farms or hamlets in connection with late clearances on the fringe of the fields of existing villages. This type of dispersed settlement is typically of high density because it took the form of small farms worked by a single family, perhaps supplemented by a little hired labour at times of particular pressure. After the destructive impact of the Hundred Years War, there was a great shortage of labour, which was hardly conducive to the formation of large estates. Between the thirteenth and sixteenth centuries, there was thus established the swarm of isolated farms which was to a very large extent to determine the pattern of rural settlement to this day.

(iii) Linear settlements. There are many examples of settlements being strung out for some kilometres along a road. Farms are rarely contiguous, being more usually separated by a paddock. These linear settlements are neither true villages nor examples of characteristic dispersion. This settlement form is found in polder regions, where farms and roads follow the lines of the dykes for protection against flooding. It is also the settlement type of many clearings dating from the twelfth and thirteenth centuries, as in the Forest of Lillebonne (lower Seine) or in the Aliermont (east of Dieppe), where 'villages' stretch without interruption for 17 km.

1.4 Recent changes in rural settlement

Both concentrated and dispersed settlements have been subjected to recent modification. Villages can no longer be regarded as exclusively inhabited by farmers, farm workers and related craft workers, nor can hamlets be assumed to be essentially small groupings of farmsteads. An insight into the changing nature of rural settlement is seen in the examination of changes in rural population and in the growing proportion of rural non-farm population. Rural settlement is now occupied by a range of non-farm persons who predominate over the farm population almost everywhere. This group includes retired people, second-home owners, industrial workers and managers, owners and workers in distribution, and other members of the tertiary sector. Settlements where rural depopulation has not been compensated by an influx of commuters, retired people or second-home owners, whether the linear villages of eastern France or the clustered hilltop villages of southern France, appear to have gone into hibernation, but few in fact have been spared from change. Shops, houses and, even more markedly, agricultural buildings have been abandoned without new occupants or uses being found for them. The decline of the rural population has not necessarily had an equal impact on all constituents of mixed settlement patterns. Occasionally the villages have been hard hit by the loss of their small farmers and small landowners, while their outlying farmsteads, whose land was conveniently grouped around them, have maintained their original function. On the other hand, there are examples of outlying hamlets being reduced to a few dwellings for retirement people, second homes or a single farm.

Most of the villages, in fact, have been gradually taken over by new functions and uses, which have affected their very form. Fundamental to the change are, on the one hand, tourism and second homes, and, on the other, the implantation of new industrial and tertiary activities, and the growth of the daily journey to work. Occasionally new isolated settlements are created when a farmer builds a house away from his farmyard, or when new houses or second homes are built. But above all, new houses and industrial buildings are strung out along the roads. Housing estates (subdivisions) or small blocks of flats appear in a way which accentuates linear dispersion or changes the shape of the initial settlement according to the ownership pattern of parcels; new nuclei thus emerge at varying distances from the original centre. This erosion of the countryside and the chaos of recent building are the recurrent themes of those seeking to preserve the rural landscape.

Tourism and the popularity of country life have been responsible for new settlement sites such as holiday villages, seaside or winter-sports resorts, and retirement villages. A feature of the last twenty years has been the establishment of so-called commuter settlements of single-family houses near large towns. In the same way, American-style housing estates in Sologne, on the fringe of the forest of Fontainebleau or in the great forest of Chantilly are providing a new sort of dispersed settlement, appropriate to the considerable financial resources of those who purchase the houses either as permanent residences or second homes (chapter 35.2.5).

2 Rural house-types

In 1975 there were 4.6 million dwellings in rural communes, but of this total only 1.1 million dwellings (23 per cent) belonged to farmers. Dwellings in blocks of flats, although very much in the minority, had by that date risen to 6 per cent of the total rural housing stock. These figures indicate the extent of recent changes in rural residence, and the pointlessness of grouping together agricultural and non-agricultural dwellings as a uniform 'rural' type. Even before 1939, village housing had become differentiated in function, having to provide for agricultural workers, shopkeepers, craftsmen, prominent members of village society and retired people with or without private incomes. Moreover, while it is true that many farm buildings which have lost their initial function through economic and demographic changes are occupied by non-farm people, they have often been extensively modified in the course of renovation and there has also been much new construction. Traditional classifications of rural housing forms are therefore increasingly difficult to apply, and not particularly fruitful; their principal remaining interest lies in the portrayal of styles of rural building as expressing the reaction of a variety of rural cultural traditions to local and regional conditions.

2.1 The traditional classification of farmsteads

It is to Albert Demangeon that we owe a definition and classification of the different rural building types. He stresses the distinctive character of buildings in rural areas; it was not a matter of classifying an individual building but a complex of buildings, each designed to perform specific agricultural functions. A farmstead combines on one site not only residential accommodation, but also accommodation for crop storage, livestock, poultry, agricultural machinery and stocks of fertilizers and seeds. Every attempt at classifying rural building types must be in terms of materials used, the arrangement on the site, and adjustment to environmental conditions, the most important of which is climate.

If we follow the broad outlines of Demangeon's classification, there is an initial distinction to be made between single-unit farmsteads and farmsteads with multiple buildings.[8]

2.1.1 *The single-unit farmstead*

This is the simplest kind of farmstead, with everything under the same roof: people, animals, crops and implements. There are many sub-types.

(i) Horizontal single-unit farmsteads. All the buildings of this type of farm are under one roof. The absence of an upper floor or the existence of only one upper floor means that the surface area is relatively large. It is to be found in every region in France, with the exception of the Mediterranean south (but it exists in Corsica), the central Paris basin and the sedimentary areas of Normandy (Fig. 32.1). Once again there are sub-types:

[8] A. Demangeon, *Géographie universelle* (A. Colin, Paris, 1946), vol. 6, pt. II (1), ch. 8, p. 166; and *Annales de Géographie*, no. 161, 1920, pp. 352–75.

(a) The horizontal single-unit farmsteads of elementary type. The typical example is
the *bourine* of the Poitou marshes, a low building consisting of one or two rooms,
with earth walls covered with rushes, and a small extension for poultry. This type
is relatively rare in France, however.

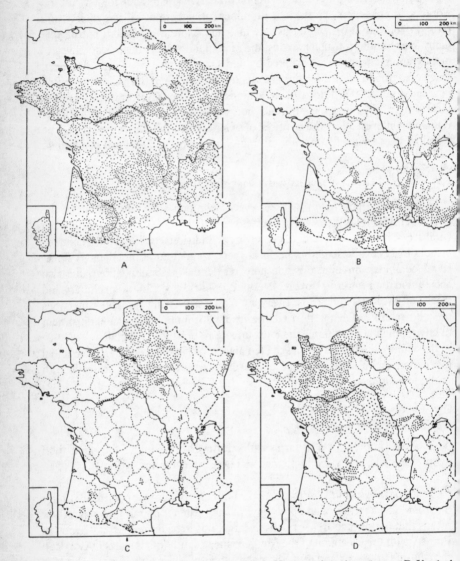

Figure 32.1 Distribution of types of farmstead. A. Horizontal single-unit type B. Vertical
single-unit type C. Closed courtyard farmstead D. Open courtyard farmstead. Source:
A. Demangeon, *Géographie universelle* (A. Colin, Paris, 1946), vol. 6, part II (1), Figs. 61,
66, 70, 73.

(b) The horizontal single-unit farmstead with transverse elements. The house and the farm buildings – the stable and cowshed – are in the case of small farms built in a row under the same roof. Large farms are made up of a sequence of juxtaposed units having roofs of differing heights. The traditional Breton farmstead is of this type, as are the farmsteads of Berry, the Toulouse region and the Central massif, and the *mas* of the Rhône valley in Provence. This type is probably derived from the rudimentary house, or occasionally from a hut to which additions have been made over a period of time.

(c) The horizontal single-unit farmstead with development in depth. This type is represented by the farms of Lorraine. All units are grouped under one roof in a rectangular block: on the right is the residential accommodation, with usually the 'room' looking out on to the street. A passage in the middle separates the cowsheds and barns to the left; the stable may be behind the house. The Lorraine-type plan is linked to a very rigid system of parcels consisting of strips, between 6 and 12 m wide, arranged perpendicularly to the main street. As there is no farmyard, its functions are taken over by a space in front of the farm, called the *usoir* (or *barge* or *aisance*), of varying depth. The house fronts rarely follow a single building line, while the remainder of the deep plot is occupied by garden and orchards.

(ii) The massive single-unit farmstead. This type is found in the Basque country, Auvergne, Limousin, the Alps of Savoie, and the Jura. Its plan is characteristic of cattle-rearing areas, where the barn and cowshed must be large. Climatic conditions (long winters and snow) have made it necessary to put all the buildings under the same roof. The cowsheds and living quarters occupy the ground floor, while hay is often stored in the roof space above, which has direct access from the hillside behind the farmhouse

(iii) The vertical single-unit farmstead. In this type, each floor has a special function. The ground floor houses the animals, and has storage for agricultural implements and heavy or bulky produce such as wood and wine. The living quarters are on the floor above, and above them the loft, to which grain, fruit and even hay are hoisted by means of a pulley. This type is characteristic of southern France – Roussillon, Languedoc, Provence and Corsica – but it extends over large parts of the southern Central massif and of the Aquitaine basin (Causses du Quercy). The type has also extended up the Rhône–Saône valley and even infiltrated the Alpine valleys of the Maurienne (Arc river) and Tarentaise (upper Isère river). This is above all the farmstead of the wine-grower or sheep farmer, essentially a village house, often a village with a distinctive site on a hilltop or clinging to a valley side. It is also today a highly inconvenient form, as any extension or alteration is extremely difficult.

2.1.2   *The farmstead with multiple buildings*

In regions where farms are bigger and there is a wider range of cultivation, where crops are as important as cattle-rearing, the grouping of all farm buildings under a single roof is no longer possible. Particular buildings acquire functionally distinct usages: dwelling, stable, sheepfold, cowshed, pigsty, poultryhouse, barn, dairy and sheds are spatially distinct one from another.

(i) The closed courtyard farmstead. This classic type, in which the various buildings are grouped around a courtyard, is found in many regions, in isolated farms as well as villages. Normally, all four sides of the courtyard are occupied by buildings, with the barn on the street side. A wide gateway gives access to the courtyard, but there are also other openings so that the crops can be stored away without the carts having to go into the yard. The living quarters are usually at the rear of the court, with perhaps a small stable; a narrow passage gives access to a small garden behind the farmhouse, and then to a paddock. On either side of the courtyard are cowsheds, pigsty, dairy and various sheds for implements. Sometimes only three or even two sides are built up, the other sides having only a wall, one perhaps broken by the principal entrance.

This type is restricted to a few clearly defined areas: the plateaus of the Tertiary Paris basin, Picardy, Champagne, Artois and certain parts of the Nord region such as Cambrésis and Walloon-speaking Flanders. Outside this main area of distribution it is found in other areas of arable specialization such as the plains of Caen, the Forez and Lower Alsace. It is a type that can be adapted to both large and small farms.

In some cases it has been possible to show how this type has evolved. Many large farms seem to have had this form from the beginning, because the arrangement of the buildings on four sides of a courtyard was functionally desirable, but the same does not apply to all closed courtyard farmsteads. Smaller farmsteads had at first only two buildings: the street front had the barn and implement store, while the parallel range behind contained the living quarters, stable and the cowshed. The two main buildings were not linked, so as to limit the risk of fire. If the holding grew in area, and with changes in the farming system such as an increase in livestock, additional buildings were added, completing the enclosure of the courtyard.

(ii) The open courtyard farmstead. Here the buildings are more spaced out, while still roughly arranged in the shape of a courtyard. This is the characteristic form of the large farms of western France, Sologne, Berry, Bresse, the *hofstede* of Flanders and, more generally speaking, of all recently established farms. It requires an extensive site and is often associated with dispersed settlement in regions of livestock specialization where ease of access from the pastures to the farm buildings is desirable.

(iii) The farmstead with scattered buildings. This is a random enlargement of the open-courtyard plan. The courtyard shape is no longer visible; the buildings appear to have been established haphazardly in response to successive changes in the agricultural system employed, changes in the area of the farm, and changes in the field pattern. In the Pays de Caux, farm buildings are widely scattered over an area of pasture (*masure*) enclosed by a massive bank crowned with beech trees.

(iv) Mountain chalets. These stand apart from the general classification of farm buildings, being temporary residences used by men from the valleys who in summer tend the flocks and herds in the mountains and if need be make butter and cheese. In the Alps they are termed *chalets* and in the Central massif *burons*.

2.1.3 Farmstead design and construction materials

This diversity of farmstead plan is paralleled by an astonishing variety of building styles and materials employed. The particular combination of gallery, balcony, porch, staircase and roof gives each farm a degree of individuality, expressing detailed social and cultural differences even if it is derived from a single regional type.

Local resources clearly determine the materials used for walls and roofs, but cultural and even ethnic factors are equally important. Stone houses are obviously found in regions where stone outcrops, varying in appearance according to the local geology: basalt in the Aubrac (Auvergne), pink or grey granite in Brittany, dry-stone walling in the Midi, limestone blocks in Franche-Comté or Burgundy. The half-timbered house, consisting of a timber framework with cob infilling, accounted for one-fifth of all farmsteads at the end of the nineteenth century. This type is typical of the Basque country, Normandy and Alsace, the *paillebart* houses of the Toulouse and Marmande regions of the Aquitaine basin, the *pisé* (cob) houses of northern France and the Lyon region, and the *torchis* of Picardy. All farmsteads of this type show marked regional variations. It has already been noted that the division between northern roofs (flat tiles) and southern roofs (round or Roman tiles) is one of the main contrasts within France (Fig. 12.1).

Differences in design and materials also reflect social differences; in southwest France, for example, there is a contrast between the manor houses, with steep roofs covered with small tiles, and the peasant farm buildings with their low-pitched roofs covered with Roman tiles. Moreover there is never a single regional type, whether in respect of layout, style or materials. Closed-courtyard farmsteads generally correspond to holdings of 100–200 ha, whereas in the same region single unit farmsteads are associated with very small farms.

2.2 The transformation of the built environment in rural areas

It is important to distinguish between the transformation of existing buildings and the addition of new ones.

2.2.1 Changes in the existing structures

In 1975 there were still 1.8 million principal residences (that is to say, not second homes or abandoned dwellings) built before 1871, comprising 40 per cent of the stock of principal residences of rural areas, as opposed to 12 per cent in urban communes. Given that new construction is heavily concentrated in the rural fringes of towns, it must be accepted that there has been very little addition to the housing stock in 'truly rural' areas in the last thirty years. There is clearly a close connection between age and the level of sanitary and other equipment; rural houses are only half as well provided as urban ones.

The conversion of the older rural buildings reflected changes in their function and utilization. In part the changes relate to the transformation of rural life itself; traditional buildings are often unsuited to new agricultural systems. Long before 1950, changes in methods of production forced farmers to change the uses of some buildings and especially to extend them. Thus in Lower Languedoc the introduction of vine monoculture forced the peasant to set up his wine cellar in a former cart-shed or in the yard. In the Valence plain, the introduction of lucerne before the First World War made it necessary to build storage sheds, just as other specialist cultivators had to build drying sheds for tobacco or walnuts.

The 'agricultural revolution' that has taken place since the 1950s has involved the spread of new life-styles, reflecting the reduced labour force and the desire to break away from the extended family to withdraw into the nuclear family. This economic and social transformation has been reflected in striking changes in the farmstead. New agricultural techniques have increasingly necessitated the separation of the living quarters from the agricultural buildings. Wherever possible, farm buildings and dwellings have been converted to meet the new requirements, but in many cases, particularly in eastern France, the layout of the farmstead does not allow this. As the size of herds has increased, and with it the quantity of hay and straw to be stored, cowsheds, barns and lofts in the farmstead itself have been abandoned and replaced (with considerable government assistance) by prefabricated agricultural buildings along the roads or on outlying parcels. There has thus been a breaking up of the traditional pattern of rural housing.

Rural exodus has also resulted in the abandonment of houses, in part isolated farmsteads but more especially hamlets and villages, and even occasionally *bourgs* (lowest-order central places). To the extent that these properties remain in the ownership of farmers, possibilities of continuing use are limited to transformation into rented holiday homes (*gîtes*), to their use by children remaining on the farm, or by family members returning from the towns for the summer vacation.

The condition of older buildings belonging to farmers is extremely varied. Some lie abandoned with caved-in roofs, increasingly overrun by weeds and brambles. Others have been converted to new uses either in relation to production or consumer provision. Some old buildings remain as the over-crowded dwellings of large rural families; others have been restored, sometimes in a deliberately rustic, 'olde worlde' style. Because older buildings have largely remained in the hands of farmers, they hold the record for lack of modern facilities; in 1975 only 16 per cent of farmers' houses had the full range of sanitary and other provisions considered desirable, whereas the national average was 48 per cent.

The older rural housing stock has also been affected by influences from outside, in particular by the vogue for rural living. Farmhouses, barns and even ruins are converted into second homes or even permanent residences. The rapid rate of abandonment of farms in the 1960s facilitated this transformation by making low-priced properties available; today the acquisition of second homes is more difficult, owing to the spectacular rise in the price of older rural properties. The number of second homes in rural areas has more than trebled in twenty years, reaching the million mark (Table 32.1). Some, of course, still belong to the original inhabitants, who left the countryside in search of work and still use them for family holidays, but most belong to town dwellers or foreigners. Their greatest concentrations are found within a radius of 150 km of Paris and Lyon, on the Breton and Mediterranean coasts, and above all in the Alps, where second homes are as numerous as principal residences. Today, when farms are sold, the agricultural land is disposed of separately from the various buildings, as the latter will raise a higher price as second homes. As the final stage of this process, some old houses revert to being permanent homes either because their occupants have retired, or because they are situated near a centre of employment.

The change of use and renovation of old farmsteads cause appreciable changes in the interior and exterior appearance. The conversion of a small farm into a second home, or a large farmstead into a tourist complex, calls for a complete remodelling. From the exterior it is sometimes possible to guess the identity of the new occupier by observing the types of fencing, the extent to which gardens are of purely decorative nature, the change made to windows and balconies, and the type of materials used. The aesthetic effects are not always agreeable to the eye, and the difficulty of finding old materials creates a certain uniformity in the style of renovation and occasional incongruous effects, such as the use of thatched roofs in areas where they have traditionally never existed. These changes certainly relate to social and cultural differences which are, of course, new, but no less striking than in earlier rural society.

2.2.2 *New construction*

It is not true to say that there has been no new building in rural areas since the end of the nineteenth century, because in 1975 32 per cent of permanent residences

Table 32.1 *Second homes*

Thousands

	1954	1975
Total for France	447	1,685
of which in rural areas	329	998
Second homes in rural areas by sq km	0.65	2.14

Source: INSEE, census.

in rural communes were built between 1871 and 1948, a percentage quite close to that in urban areas. Since the 1960s there has been a marked increase in building in rural areas. The growth in second homes has been particularly related to new construction in mountain regions, the coastal regions and their hinterland, and on the rural fringes of towns.

New housing construction in rural areas reflects the establishment of new residents, whether retired persons returning to their area of origin, or other retired persons. It also reflects the establishment of daily commuters or of workers in an industry newly implanted in a rural region. Loans from the Crédit Agricole (Agricultural Bank) to persons building houses in rural communes have certainly contributed to new housing development. Farmers have also played an active part in the transformation of the built form of the countryside, not only by the erection of prefabricated agricultural buildings but by the replacement of the old farmhouses by new dwellings, also of standardized type.

The effects of these changes have been mentioned earlier in relation to changes in the rural settlement pattern. There is an overall standardization and uniformity, reflecting the frequent use of a limited range of house types supplied by large firms, and also reflecting the minimum building standards which must be met in order to obtain a building permit (*permis de construire*). Contrasts in building style relate principally to social and cultural differences. Persons of higher income tend to prefer to roof their houses with weathered tiles rather than with the standard factory-made product, while small farmers and low-income retired people have no hesitation in choosing a roof of corrugated fibro-cement sheeting made in mock-antique style. It would be interesting to draw up a classification of new houses according to their dates of construction and the socio-professional origin of their inhabitants.

Rural housing has been greatly improved by renovation and new building, as well as by improvements in public services such as the bringing of electricity to the smallest hamlets and isolated farms, the widespread provision of piped water, and sewerage schemes. There are still, however, great variations in the level of provision between one region and another, and also between the various socio-economic categories of the population.

33

⚜ Rural landscapes

The great variety of French rural landscapes reflects the various agrarian cultures which, through their agricultural techniques and forms of social organization, have fashioned them. Because of this wide range of influences, the identification and classification of French rural landscape types present a task of considerable difficulty.

It is certainly possible (Fig. 33.5) to map rural settlement forms in France following the classification proposed by A. Meynier,[1] which is based on:

(1) the intensity of human occupance of the soil, as revealed by the densities of rural population and settlement;
(2) field patterns, the form and dimensions of parcels in relation to patterns of ownership;
(3) the lines of contact between fields or parcels; the presence or absence of a visible barrier; visible signs of 'mental or social structures'.

But such a classification is purely descriptive and formal, whereas rural landscapes are constantly changing. Classification can only seize one moment in a long process of evolution, in which lengthy periods of relative stability were broken by bursts of rapid change due to technical revolutions or transformations of the socio-political system.

Progress in our knowledge of French rural landscapes has been achieved by means of two distinct approaches, neither of which has hitherto been the subject

[1] A. Meynier, *Les Paysages agraires*, 4th edn (A. Colin, Paris, 1967).

of a coherent publication. The first approach is essentially genetic and is represented in the work of geographers such as A. Meynier, X. de Planhol, J. Peltre and P. Flatrès, continuing to some extent the tradition of Marc Bloc. Their starting point is the traditional rural landscape in what is considered to be its 'climax' or 'mature' form. Sometimes this can be directly observed today, but more frequently use has to be made of archive material such as terriers (lists of tenants and their holdings) and cadastral surveys (detailed plans of parcels drawn up mainly for taxation purposes), supplemented by aerial photographs. There has been an attempt to discover the origin of particular landscape types and to evolve methods of dating them. Research has also been directed towards finding ways of determining boundaries between the main types at the various stages of their evolution, and towards exploring possible links with ethnic characteristics, method of social organization or the natural environment. This research has confirmed, with some modifications and refinements, the familiar broad divisions of the French rural landscape into *bocage*, openfield, Mediterranean and Aquitaine types. Progress has also been made in the analysis of long-term landscape changes, for example the transition from the Gallo-Roman period to the Middle Ages. In summary, this first approach is characterized by a preference for a distinctly 'archaeological' reading of the rural landscape.

The second approach reflects the interests of spatial planners; the focus is on the landscape as perceived, experienced and evaluated, whether in aesthetic or economic terms. The basic landscape elements may be the same – forms of enclosure, land use, settlement, roads and tracks, parcel – but they are not observed from the same viewpoint. A number of significant conclusions relating to postwar upheavals emerge from a careful study of recent changes in agricultural landscapes and rural space, which may be regarded as the expression left by the forces of economic activity, or as the end result of the competing strategies of different claimants to the use of land. The object of this approach is thus not to discover the historical origins of a landscape, but to see in it the impact of competing functions and a demonstration of the consumption of rural space. Moreover, the problem of the relationship between humanized landscape and natural environment is approached differently; notions of ecosystems, equilibrium and flux are distinguished from explanatory concepts relating to the adaptation of man to nature.

These two approaches are usually followed independently, with little serious attempt to relate them, except perhaps in a few regional monographs. It would be of considerable interest to demonstrate the interaction between the forces producing an overall transformation of the rural landscape and the inherited forms. In the absence of a general work of this kind, it will be necessary in the following pages first to describe the types of agrarian landscape as they appeared in their prime at the end of the nineteenth century, and then to outline the principal changes that have occurred since the 1950s.

1 Principal rural landscape types

The agrarian landscape is fundamentally determined by the pattern of parcels and by the presence or absence of enclosure. A third element is provided by the field ways, which up to now have tended to be ignored. The fundamental rural landscape division of France is between openfield (*champagne*) with grouped villages situated to the north and east of a line linking the mouth of the Seine with Geneva, and the enclosed *bocage* with dispersed settlement to the west and south. Scholars have long been fascinated by the completeness of this contrast and all it seems to imply in terms of explanation. This initial twofold division is, however, subject to numerous modifications and exceptions.

1.1 Openfield landscapes

In openfield areas there are no hedges or fences to break the view, and generally no trees, although in southern France these appear sporadically. The division of the field into parcels is indicated only by the stone landmarks at ground level and by the contrasting patterns of crops.

1.1.1 *The classic openfield*

The best examples of openfield are to be found in Lorraine, Alsace and on the limestone plateaus of Franche-Comté. The right of the inhabitants to pasture their animals over the whole of the arable land once freed of crops, and the use of a common pattern of crop rotation necessitated a division of the agriculturally used land (*finage agricole*) into separate fields (*soles*), fields into furlongs (*quartiers*) and the furlongs into parcels. Because of the communal nature of agriculture there were no physical obstacles between parcels, only the field tracks, and this is still a characteristic feature. The village typically occupies the centre of the commune and of the agriculturally used land. The great number of parcels into which the ploughed land is divided usually take the form of strips, that is to say they are at least five times as long as they are broad. More extreme examples can be found, however, with the length up to 15 times the breadth, resulting in long cultivated ribbons a few metres wide and several score metres long. The dimensions of the fields are not arbitrary; research has increasingly revealed characteristic lengths corresponding to old measures of land, which in turn were related to very ancient cultivation techniques. The explanation of parcel dimensions is often to be sought in the equipment used (swing plough, heavy plough) and the method of traction. The elongation of the fields is explained by the desire to avoid excessive turning by the yoked animals on reaching the end of the ploughed furrow, while the minimum width of 4 or 5 m was determined by the span over which the peasant could conveniently broadcast seed. In Alsace, however, there are some remains of the Roman centuriated field pattern. The edge of the cultivated land is frequently marked by communal woodland.

The strip parcel is also found in large parts of the Paris basin, the plains of Poitou and Charente, the Rhône valley, and the great valleys of Aquitaine. Isolated groups of parcels also interrupt the *bocage* along the coasts of the bays of Mont-Saint-Michel and Saint-Brieuc, on the southwest coast of Brittany and in the whole of southern Finistère. The origin of strip parcels is not clear. The strip is better suited to cereal-based economy with a strong element of communal organization than to the more individualistic system of stock-rearing. In most cases it seems that the strips emerged through the subdivision of larger parcels (normally in the process of inheritance). This method of division gives fair shares where there are varied soil conditions within the original parcel and avoids the need for new access roads.

The openfield parcels are often extremely small. An investigation of 1882 revealed a group of departments with very small parcels in eastern France, and in the eastern and central parts of the Paris basin, extending into the Jura. Over limited areas, extraordinary concentrations of dwarf parcels are to be observed. Alsace provides a veritable caricature of agricultural structure, the Department of Bas-Rhin holding the record for miniature parcels (departmental average of 17 ares (0.17 ha) per parcel).

The causes of this fragmentation of parcels in France are multiple and of long standing. One of the most important is undoubtedly the adjustment of the surface area to the technical conditions of working the land, an adjustment of very early date. Many parcels have a surface area corresponding to the day-work, the *journal*, the area which a man and his team could cultivate in one day. The size of the *journal* varied from 34 to 39 ares (0.34–0.39 ha), according to local conditions. Communal systems of cultivation, by dispersing the parcels of each holding over the various fields, accentuated the degree of fragmentation. Small parcels are also associated with particular systems of cultivation, for example hillside vines, market gardens and other forms of specialized cropping.

Fragmentation has been considerably accentuated by the inheritance process. In regions where the holding was not grouped round the farmstead but distributed throughout the common fields under systems of common rotation, it was essential that each parcel in each field should be divided into as many strips as there were inheritors. Continued subdivision at each stage of succession ultimately resulted in the creation of miniature parcels which were virtually useless. In a still more general sense, fragmentation is linked to the tenurial system and the type of exploitation of the soil; small parcels have survived longest in areas where small peasant proprietors work their own land; the island of Ouessant (Ushant), a mere 1,960 ha in extent, had 43,000 parcels in 1850 and 75,000 in 1963.

The Lorraine type of openfield therefore corresponds to a collective agrarian organization combining cereal cultivation with a substantial livestock element in a region where meadowland is rare. Its communal practices were rooted in a firmly based social organization, concentrated settlement and the division of the parcels belonging to the individual holding between each of the common fields.

Openfield within regions of bocage. Small openfield islands have been recognized in the very heart of the *bocage* country of western France and of the Central massif. They have their distinctive names: *méjou* in Breton-speaking Brittany, *champagne*, *campagne*, *plaine* or *quartier* in northern Brittany; *bandes*, *gaigneries* and *domaines* in southern Brittany; *versenne*, *champs* and *chaumes* in Vendée, and *coutures* in Limousin.

These islands of openfields are very often associated with farmsteads built side by side in rows (chapter 32, 1.3.2). In the southeast of Vendée, the *gaignerie* is essentially the best ploughland. It appears in the rural landscape as an extensive and distinctive openfield of always more than 3 ha in extent, which cannot be confused with the individual block fields of the isolated farms (*métairies*) of share-croppers. The *gaignerie* is surrounded by a substantial bank crowned with hawthorn, gorse and brushwood, and is divided into strips, each several metres wide, which sometimes all run parallel to one of the axes of the field or are sometimes grouped into furlongs (*quartiers*). Within the *gaignerie* there are no interruptions from hedges or ditches. The boundaries between the strips are indicated by a simple furrow or by landmarks planted on a substratum of tiles.

Some examples of the Breton *méjou* undoubtedly derived from the subdivision into strips of an ecclesiastical estate which had been sold. In the Vendée *bocage* the open and subdivided *gaignerie* resulted from collective clearing by small peasant proprietors. In conclusion, it is only possible to reiterate the conclusion reached by A. Meynier that 'the openfield divided into strips of western France, the date and origin of which are uncertain, is generally to be associated with the activities of small farmers who at certain periods in history and occasionally even up to the present day have practised a partially collective economy'.[2]

1.1.2 *Unenclosed landscapes in southern France*

Southern France has an open, unenclosed landscape, but of a completely individual type. The Mediterranean and Aquitaine regions are entirely distinctive, with areas of pasture quite independent of their cultivated lands. The problem has been clearly stated by R. Livet:

It is impossible to demonstrate, as in northern France, any link whatsoever between unenclosed fields and collective forms of social organization. In particular the idea of a common openfield (*sole*), so characteristic and widespread in other regions, is completely foreign to Provence, where a patchwork of crops has always been the rule. It is therefore

[2] *Ibid.*, p. 167.

difficult to speak of a Provençal openfield if by this is implied not merely a particular form of agricultural organization but a complex and coherent set of traditions, restrictions and customs that are reflected in the creation of an individual landscape.[3]

The author suggests the use of the more modest and more exact term 'open landscape' instead of the term 'openfield'.

The field system is composed of small rectangular blocks, the typical structure of the Middle Ages. The block fields vary in length from 35 to 100 m, and their width is not less than half their length. It is possible that this type of parcel dates from very ancient times, and that it was perpetuated by the use of the swing plough and the practice of cross-ploughing. The block pattern is still perceptible in recently created parcels, which are often merely regroupings of old ones. Parcels of this type are also characteristic of vineyards.

Although the block parcel is standard for Mediterranean France, there is a great deal of detailed variation reflecting differences in soil and microrelief. Enclosure is rare, and even if there are small stone walls or piles of stones at the corners of fields, they are easily surmountable and do not indicate a desire to provide an effective barrier.

In both Aquitaine and Provence there is a greater variety of rural landscape than in northern France. The more irregular pattern of parcels is in part a reflection of the more varied physical geography, but also relates to more varied systems of cultivation and tenurial structures. Openfield complexes of narrow strips are frequently interrupted by larger enclosed block parcels on wetlands or following even the smallest streams. In the Mediterranean south, the irregular fields of the hillsides and *garrigue* (Mediterranean 'rock heath') contrast with the narrower and more regular parcels of the plains. There can also be a variation of field patterns according to exposure: in the dissected Terrefort plateau of southwest France, the large arable parcels of the sunny south-facing slopes contrast with the small enclosed pastures of the shady slopes.

As the density of human occupance or land use increases, however, 'the social factor takes precedence over the geographical factor'.[4] The most usual contrast of a social nature occurs between the vast parcels of the great estates, farming their land either directly or through share-cropping agreements, and the small parcels of the small farmers.

1.2 Enclosed landscapes

Enclosed landscapes are not exclusively of the hedged *bocage* type, even if the latter is the most characteristic form. Enclosure can also be by walls, whether of masonry or of dry stone. In some rocky areas, such as Béarn (western Pyrenees), the Causses du Quercy, certain Alpine valley slopes and in Provence, parcels are

---

[3] *Habitat rural et structures agraires en Basse Provence* (n.p., Gap, 1962).

[4] J. Sion, 'Géographie et ethnologie', *Annales de Géographie*, no. 263, 1937, pp. 449–64.

defined by piles of field-stones, which, however, scarcely constitute an impenetrable enclosure. In slate country, as near Allassac in Corrèze (Central massif) and Redon (Armorica), parcels were bounded by sheets of slate set vertically.

1.2.1 Types of bocage

True *bocage* can be divided into a number of sub-types according to the particular element in the assemblage of the *bocage* features which is predominant. It will be recalled that *bocage* areas are on the whole areas of dispersed settlement. The most common classification of *bocage* is morphological. It is customary to distinguish *bocage* with large parcels from fine-grained *bocage*, between regular and irregular enclosures, and above all to take into account the characteristics of the barrier separating the parcels: *bocage* where live hedges constitute the enclosure, and *bocage* where the separation is by means of earth banks.

An eastern type with hedges but without field banks is found in some areas of the northern, western and southern fringes of the Paris basin (Thierache, Bray, Perche, Maine, Nivernais), the western and northern parts of the Central massif, parts of Aquitaine and parts of the Pyrenees. The hedges usually consist of a mixture of trees and bushes, with the branches of the bushes interlaced so as to make them impenetrable, and they usually enclose pasture land. The western or 'Armorican' type of *bocage*, with hedges set on earth banks, is found in Brittany: the earth bank is built up with soil from the parallel ditch which provides for drainage from the plot, which may be arable as well as grass.

There are numerous variations; some combine enclosures with incompletely fenced parcels, as on the fringes of the Armorican massif, the northern fringe of the Central massif (Bourbonnais) and Bresse. Others involve the combination within the same commune of areas of *bocage* and fragments of openfield, as in southern Brittany, or enclosed pasture with groups of arable parcels surrounded by a peripheral hedge, as in the western parts of the Central massif. An original type of *bocage* in Mediterranean France is found between Avignon and Carpentras (lower Rhône valley) where the division between parcels of meadowland is provided by willows and screens of reed.

A kind of *pseudo-bocage* is produced where the hedges, although present, are not continuous; they do not enclose, but follow the edges of cultivation terraces, line the roads, pick out the long sides of elongated parcels, grow on the heaps of fieldstones bordering parcels or follow stream courses. In other regions, the appearance of a *bocage* or *semi-bocage* landscape is due solely to the hedges and trees which surround the farmhouse and its outbuildings; for example the Pays de Caux, without the majestic trees screening its widely scattered farmyards, would be revealed as a purely openfield landscape. The so-called 'Flemish *bocage*' is similarly made up of hedges surrounding the farmstead and its contiguous paddock.

An alternative system of classification was proposed in 1975 by M. Palierne, on the basis of the *bocage* of the Nantes region. It distinguishes between 'organic' *bocage*, so called because it constitutes a kind of organism of the landscape parallel to the spontaneous forms of the biosphere (soils and natural vegetation), to which it is remarkably well integrated, and an 'imitation' *bocage* which repeats the features of true *bocage* only by a superficial coincidence of forms. This may be of recent, even present-day, origin. It can be described as 'primary or intercalated' where it has developed on land that was once fallow, and 'secondary or replacement' when it has taken over or replaced the non-enclosed parcels of *gaigneries*. This classification comes close to being a genetic one, which would make it possible by establishing clear dating of the different periods of formation to arrive at a genuine *bocage* classification.

In the meantime we must fall back on the regional classification of P. Flatrès that has already been referred to above and which contains an element of historical explanation. The regular, wide-meshed eastern *bocage* is historically of recent origin, associated with the rise of livestock-based agriculture. For the most part it replaced pre-existing agrarian structures of a different type, the process beginning at the end of the Middle Ages and continuing with greater intensity during the modern period. The fine-meshed, irregular western *bocage*, on the contrary, with its hedge-crowned banks, although only achieving its final form quite late, occasionally in the nineteenth century, inherits at least some of its constituent elements from the Middle Ages and in some cases from prehistoric times.

A functional classification is proposed by A. Fel in his study of the uplands of the Central massif.[5] He distinguishes 'field *bocage*' where the enclosure is cultivated and has to be protected against grazing livestock from 'meadow *bocage*'. Hedges have, in fact, very variable connections with fields and methods of land use. In Brittany every parcel is enclosed, whatever its type and use; in Limousin, on the other hand, only meadow parcels are enclosed (meadow *bocages*); the same applies to the Basque country and the central Pyrenees, where only mowing grass is fenced. An enclosure may surround a single parcel or a group of parcels, creating a *bocage* of multiple-parcel units as opposed to a *bocage* of individual parcels. In extreme cases a closed boundary is only used to separate a group of parcels from the road which runs alongside them or from another group of parcels, or simply encloses an isolated individual parcel. Figure 33.1 shows that when examined in detail the Armorican *bocage* reveals a great variety of field patterns.

1.2.2 The history of the bocage

Bocage is not an original feature. It is true that as early as the ninth century the Redon cartulary describes ditches and enclosures, and that coins of the tenth and

---

[5] A. Fel, *Les Hautes Terres du Massif Central* (Publications Faculté des Lettres, Clermont-Ferrand, 1962).

eleventh centuries have been found in an embankment in Finistère, but it does not follow that the whole of the Armorican west was *bocage*. From the beginning of the Middle Ages onwards, the erection of temporary enclosures was authorized, but enclosed parcels and openfield existed side by side. Enclosure took place over a long period of time and at varying speed; in some regions *bocage* gradually invaded the openfields and heathlands, which elsewhere remained unenclosed. But most of the enclosures date from after the thirteenth century, corresponding either to areas of late settlement by an agrarian society more individualistic than that of earlier centuries, or to the transformation of a pre-existing openfield system.

The first mention of the *bocage* in the Central massif goes back to the fifteenth century. In the sixteenth century, enclosure was permitted under the established rural customary rights of Marche, Bourbonnais and Nivernais. Much more often the enclosures on land already occupied date from the eighteenth century, and from the nineteenth century on cleared heathlands. Between 1771 and 1777, the Intendants (representatives of the king) in most provinces issued edicts for the enclosure of common fields and common pasture, following in the footsteps of England. Thus in Thiérache (northern Paris basin) the *bocage* dates from the eighteenth century. In the waterlogged valleys of Lorraine, many meadows enclosed by hedges were carved out of the common pastures in the reign of Louis XVI.

Administrative attachment to a region where agricultural individualism and *bocage* were already customary was often a cause of the rapid spread of the system; the attachment of the Revermont in the eighteenth century to the *bocage* region of Bresse led to a marked increase in the number of enclosures.

In Finistère the last heathland enclosures date from the beginning of the twentieth century. The dispersed settlement and *bocage* landscape of Cotentin are recent features, replacing an earlier landscape of grouped settlement with openfield. In Thiérache (northern Paris basin) the late development of much of the *bocage* can be observed: in the fifteenth century, 50 per cent of the agricultural land was enclosed and under grass; about the year 1700 it was 70 per cent, and by 1950 almost 100 per cent. While simple, monogenetic *bocage* exists, formation usually took place at several stages. The *bocage* in the Gatine first appeared with the share-cropping (*métairie*) system, created by the nobility in the aftermath of the Hundred Years War as a consequence of a vast process of consolidation of holdings carried out at the expense of the previous structure of openfield with hamlets. After 1850 the heathlands, hitherto abandoned, were in their turn colonized and transformed into *bocage*.

1.2.3 *The objectives of* bocage *formation*

Bocage regarded as an improvement in agricultural technique is a complex system which serves a variety of ends. The ditch, which is almost always found next to the planted field bank, plays an important role in drainage in areas of heavy rainfall

Figure 33.1 Types of field pattern in Brittany. *Top left.* The most widespread type: rectangular parcels with slightly curved sides and little evidence of a systematic plan. Roads and the long sides of parcels tend to have a similar alignment. Parcels are of unequal size. Some field tracks may not be represented. Source: Air photograph (northern Brittany, to the west of Dinard). *Top right.* Type found where heathland areas have been

and impermeable soil. This presupposes regular and general maintenance of the system of ditches; the bank may indeed be nothing more than the by-product of this process. The hedge, whether planted on a bank or not, plays an important part in providing protection from the wind, drizzle and frost; the hedges prevent the meadows from drying out and promote drainage; in the past, the hedgerows used to provide useful timber, stakes and leaves, used both for litter and as food for the animals in winter. The density of the trees in *bocage* country often makes us forget the absence of any true woodland cover in west and central France. By the eighteenth and nineteenth centuries excessive clearances had deprived the peasants of their normal sources of wood. This deficiency was then made up by resorting to the hedgerow trees of the newly enclosed heathlands (it is often noticed that the parcels belonging to farms near woods have fewer hedges); the *bocage* was 'the forest of those who have none'. But these are secondary advantages stemming from the very existence of the *bocage*; a fundamental examination must go further, probing into the reasons for the creation of *bocage*, and analyse the part played by both natural and human factors in its development.

(i) Bocage *in relation to the system of cultivation*. The first explanation that comes to mind is that of protection; a fence or a hedge is erected so as to isolate a parcel, a group of parcels or a larger part of the agriculturally used area. In every system of cultivation which puts crops and animals on different parts of the land, the former must clearly be protected from destruction. Either the cultivated land or the grazing land may be enclosed, according to which type of agriculture predominates, to the surface area affected, to the precedence in time of one or other of the types of use, and to natural conditions. Enclosure can thus offer a double protection, against intrusion from the exterior and against the escape of animals pastured on the inside.

According to the extremely ancient Breton custom, the cultivated lands were enclosed: otherwise their owners would have had to renounce their claim to common pasture. Elsewhere, enclosures were established on areas where there was a right of establishment within the common lands. In the Pyrenees, for example, the inhabitants could settle in the middle of common pastures; they began by putting up temporary habitations such as barns (*bordes*) which later became permanent homes. These *bordiers*, scattered over the common land, enclosed their fields to protect them from the village herd and to affirm their

---

subdivided since the nineteenth century; parcels are set out with straight boundaries, with no dominant orientation; many parcels of approximately equal size. Source: Air photograph (the north of the Department of Loire-Atlantique). *Bottom left. Méjou* type: core of unenclosed strips with surrounding block fields. The broken lines represent boundaries not visible in the terrain. Linear hamlet of Kerringuy. Source: P. Flatrès, 'Le pays nord-bigouden', *Annales de Bretagne*, 1944. *Bottom right.* Pattern resembling openfield with elongated and slightly curved parcels. Source: Flatrès, *ibid.*, 1944, and A. Meynier, *Annales de Géographie*, no. 309, 1949, p. 9.

property rights. The formation of this Pyrenean *bocage* dates from the seventeenth century and more especially the eighteenth century, and continued until the nineteenth century. The process was similar in Brittany and Auvergne; arable occupance of the heathland was accompanied by enclosures protecting all the cultivated land against the animals which grazed freely there.

Formerly, forests were also enclosed to prevent wild animals from invading the cultivated land or, more rarely, to prevent domestic animals from grazing in the forest. In some regions, such as Artois, these forest boundaries remained as residual features even after the forest itself had been cleared, enabling the former forest land to be claimed as 'ancient enclosures', not subject to the communal rights which were otherwise rigorously maintained.

The connection which is always made between the development of stock-rearing and the growth of *bocage* is sufficient proof of the function of hedges. In a more general way these enclosures serve as protection against any encroachment of communal agricultural society; they are the geographical expression of agrarian individualism. This movement developed out of progress in agricultural techniques which permitted autonomy from communal endeavour, allowing farmers to keep for themselves the benefit of improvements derived from manuring or irrigation, and affording them protection from the practice of communal grazing over land not bearing standing crops. '*Bocage* developed particularly in the less densely populated regions, where the village communities were more widely distributed, where their hold on the soil was less tenacious, and where the most recent forms of clearing were more distinctly orientated towards individual agriculture and stock-rearing.'[6]

The forces ranged against agrarian individualism were still powerful, justifiably so when the occupiers defended the communal land and access to the forest without which they could not survive, more debatable in the case of nobles defending free access to their hunting forests.

In openfield regions, only rarely could *bocage* spread over the whole area; there was a conflict of interest between small farmers tied to the age-old community practices and the big landowners anxious to be free of all restriction. In general, the result was a compromise, a landscape half openfield, half *bocage*, the ancient rights of pasture being maintained only after lengthy litigation.

The protective nature of *bocage* has not been universally accepted. A. Meynier advances several adverse arguments. He alleges that hedges are ineffective: 'cattle and horses can get through hedges even when they are on embankments'.[7] But perhaps this relates to hedges which are not expected to be animal-proof, but which are required as a legal boundary.

(ii) Bocage *and the property structure. Bocage* may be seen as the visible expression of the individual appropriation of land. Documentary evidence shows that

[6] G. Duby, *L'Economie rurale et la vie des campagnes dans l'occident médiéval* (2 vols., Aubier, Paris, 1962), p. 269.
[7] Meynier, *Les Paysages agraires*, ch. 11.

ecclesiastical and seigneurial estates were enclosed, whereas peasant holdings were not; the lord of the manor could appropriate open land and enclose it. If the occupant was unable to produce title deeds, enclosure was the means of affirming possession. The sale of communal land contributed to the creation of a regular *bocage*, a further affirmation of rights of ownership. Elsewhere, as on the Margeride area of the Central massif, the hedge by its mere presence legalized encroachment on the heathland; in the Mediterranean *garrigue* enclosure was a means of affirming that possession was the better part of the law. Only in second degree did the enclosure serve to protect the parcel from damage by invasive sheep (and more especially goats), for the walls were low and the goats daring.

(iii) Bocage *and the natural environment.* The natural environment is clearly not in itself a determinant in the origin and spread of the *bocage*. However, given that the *bocage* is composed of live hedges and as it is linked to a pastoral economy, it would be paradoxical to deny its connection with the conditions of soil, water and climate which are favourable to the growth of trees, shrubs, bushes and grass. *Bocage* prospers fully only in humid regions with clay soils and an abundance of streams. In the Central massif there is an undeniable link between high rainfall and the spread of *bocage* over all the north and west borders, from the Morvan to the Montagne Noire. Occurrences of *bocage* in exceptional locations must be examined with great care, and as much attention must be paid to natural conditions as to the socio-economic conditions of the past.

1.3 Rural roads

Considerable effort has been devoted to research into rural settlement and field systems, but the third element in the rural landscape, roads and farm tracks, has been relatively neglected. Its importance, however, should not be underestimated. Within the mesh of the inter-regional and inter-urban road network, rural roads serve villages, hamlets and farms, and allow access to the agricultural land. These roads and tracks, through their distribution, density, networks and development, are a basic element for the analysis of the rural landscapes. In 1958 this road network of agricultural France totalled 650,000 km, including 280,000 km of publicly maintained rural roads and 160,000 km of farm tracks.

The rural road network is heterogeneous in nature. In addition to roads and tracks which have been constructed specifically to give access to the various parts of the agriculturally used land, there are ancient routeways, formerly important but now in decay, such as pilgrim roads or saltways. Often the presence of a crossroads in open country is the only surviving visible sign of a place which was once inhabited, a village or hamlet destroyed by war or simply abandoned, a former mill or an ancient shrine.

M. Gautier has singled out the main features of this network of rural roads:

The sparse, radial patterns of the openfield tracks are often contrasted with the dense, intricate maze in the *bocage*, but this view is too generalized and very superficial. The basic pattern of the rural networks is everywhere the same: routes radiate from the principal settlement of the commune, situated in the centre of the first area to be cleared. From these routes run short branches, which peter out among the crops. Longer routes link one *bourg* to another. To crown all are the very long roads which are probably the ancestors of all the others, cutting diagonally across the network, ancient trackways which were only occasionally used to give access to the fields ... In the bocage, however, a secondary network has grafted itself as adequately as possible on to the primary network, developing contemporaneously with the intercalation of dispersed settlements.[8]

These roads and tracks are themselves features of the landscape. In limestone or chalk areas, or where the underlying rock is resistant, they run at ground level. On slopes they run as hollow ways, perhaps several metres below the surface of the fields, their formation due to the carts that 'grind away at the edges, crushing the earth, which falls as dust. Running water carries this debris away and the road sinks down.'[9] In the *bocage* the roads run between earth banks, crowned by hedges. This type probably results from the digging of a ditch by the landowners to either side, the excavated soil being used to build the embankments. These sunken and winding roads are a serious obstacle to the modernization of agriculture, as they prevent the passage of modern machinery.

Until the middle of the nineteenth century most parishes, and subsequently the rural communes, led an isolated existence far from the main traffic routes; the roads linked the farms and hamlets to the village, and served the various parts of the agricultural land; links between the communes and with the town were possible only with difficulty. Insecurity, tolls and the collection of customs duties aggravated this situation, which was only tolerable in a largely self-sufficient rural economy with a low degree of urbanization.

After the first improvements under Napoleon I, legislation in 1836 established a regular system of rural byroads, maintained by the taxes or direct labour of the inhabitants, supplemented by aid from the department and the state. In a few years the existing roads were straightened, metalled and linked up with the systems of adjoining communes. In 1866 there were 122,000 km of local roads, by 1898 275,000 km. In 1881 the rural roads were declared by law to be public property, thus securing them from encroachment by farmers and avoiding disputes between landowners.

Since the 1960s many rural roads have been tarred, often in association with the consolidation of holdings (*remembrement*); this has led to many modifications of the detailed alignment of roads without, however, making significant changes in the network as such. The maintenance of rural roads poses a problem for the communes, a problem aggravated by population decline, and particularly severe in areas of dispersed settlement. In some areas of high depopulation, such as Creuze (Central massif), many rural roads have been completely overgrown; in

[8] M. Gautier, 'Un chapitre négligé de la géographie agraire: les enseignements des chemins ruraux', *L'Information Géographique*, no. 3, 1954, p. 95.
[9] *Ibid.*, p. 96.

other areas maintenance leaves much to be desired. Well-maintained rural byways are today the sign either of a local community of prosperous farmers, or of an effort to encourage tourism. A recent development has been the restoration of ancient trackways through field and forest to form long-distance paths (*sentiers de grande randonnée*).

2 Recent changes in the rural landscape

In order to realize the extent of recent changes in the landscape it is necessary to distinguish between different levels of analysis, which correspond to the different levels of decision-making and hence of spatial organization.

2.1 The first level: the farm and the parcel

The lowest level of territorial organization is represented by the parcel, which is the smallest unit of land in respect of which it is possible to see the results of decisions taken by the occupier and to follow one type of recent change in the rural landscape.

The main factor in the spatial organization of farm holdings continues to be the estate, the unit of land ownership. Several types of spatial relationships between the unit of land ownership and the holding can exist. First of all, correspondence between the unit of ownership and the holding may be total; this is often the case with the large isolated farms, intercalated between the villages in the plains of the Paris basin. It is also often characteristic of farms held under share-cropping agreements (*métairies, bordes*) in west and southwest France, and in some regions of Provence. A holding may, however, take up only a portion of the unit of ownership if this is particularly extensive. In western France the large estate continues to exist, divided into medium-sized holdings, a legacy of the days when the land belonging to the nobility or bourgeoisie was divided into rented holdings of a size which could be worked by a single family. Alternatively the holding may be made up of a union of two or more units of ownership; in extreme cases the holding may consist of a jigsaw of parcels belonging to different owners, one of whom may be the farmer himself; some of the vast farms in regions such as Beauce are of this nature.

The spatial organization of holdings is influenced not only by the structure of ownership but by the type of rural settlement. In regions of grouped settlement, it is common to find that parcels from the same farm are scattered over the whole commune and even beyond. This dispersal is explained by the constraints of traditional communal forms of agriculture, which distributed parcels according to the varying quality of the various parts of the agriculturally used area. Parcels may be completely dispersed, each unit of cultivation corresponding to a unit of ownership, or they may have been partially consolidated so as to make up 'islands of cultivation' reflecting the 'islands of ownership'. The degree of fragmentation varies with the size of the enterprise. Whereas the large holding tends to group its land round the buildings, the small farmer often has a highly fragmented pattern of cultivation, with some parcels as much as several kilometres away.

In areas of dispersed settlement, there is in theory less dispersal of parcels, as the land tends to be contiguous with the farm buildings; there are, however, many exceptions, which can be explained by the recent addition of parcels at some distance from the original block of land adjacent to the farmstead.

Physical conditions come into play to the extent that not all parts of the agriculturally used area are equally suited to agricultural use. When the system of cultivation involves a range of activities and the parcels of crops, meadows, woods and heathland cannot be adjacent, then the holding has to involve dispersed parcels. Conversely, extensive plains of homogeneous soil types, as well as impermeable regions with a close drainage network, lend themselves to the creation of holdings consisting of parcels in a single contiguous block. In areas of sedimentary plateaus incised by broad valleys, the small farms in the valley bottoms with their fields climbing the slopes contrast with the big farms of the interfluves.

In regions of highly dissected relief, both in the ancient massifs and in the sedimentary basins (Terrefort plateaus of Aquitaine), one cannot fail to notice a relationship between the site afforded by the geomorphological pattern and the size of the holding. Sometimes the natural environment is an obstacle to the extension of the holdings; if they are situated in the bottom of steep-sided valleys, or on the contrary clinging to narrow interfluves, they cannot easily appropriate additional land from which they are separated by excessively steep slopes or uncultivable areas.

The situation of parcels affects their attractiveness to purchasers wishing to extend their holdings. In areas of dispersed settlement, where parcels are grouped round the farmstead, only the immediate neighbours would be tempted to buy any parcel becoming available; there is in any event reluctance to sell off land, a process which is likely to destroy the farm as a viable unit. Only holdings that are too small and unprofitable disappear and are incorporated into one or more neighbouring holdings, which alone can benefit from their incorporation. In areas of grouped settlement and openfields, holdings may be sold off as a whole or the individual parcels may be sold separately; either way the position is similar: because all holdings already consist of scattered parcels, all farmers are equally placed with regard to acquiring the land.

In practice, the sale of any particular parcel is only of interest to a small number of farmers, not only for financial reasons, but also for reasons related to the size of parcel and to its situation in relation to the farmsteads of potential purchasers. Demand is liveliest for small and medium-sized parcels, which are more appropriate to the financial and technical means of the greatest number of farmers; very large parcels are of interest only to the big farmers. When expansion adjacent to the holding is impossible, some farmers set up a separate centre of activities at some distance from their original base. Some even migrate totally to areas where land is cheaper and easier to find.

It is at the level of the agricultural holding and the parcel that the different changes influencing the rural landscape can be clearly seen. For example, it is possible to understand the role of technical progress and new systems of production in bringing about an increase in the size of parcels, secured by the removal of superfluous hedges, by friendly exchanges of lands or by the formal consolidation of holdings (*remembrement*). Big capitalist farmers and average farmers alike contribute to the standardization of the rural landscape. Each simplifies his farming system by concentrating on the most profitable enterprises and replacing hedges by barbed wire.

2.2 The second level: the commune

The 'communal' division of agriculturally used land was in the past the most formative influence on the French rural landscape. There still exists today the skeletal framework of the ancient organization of the agriculturally used area, as seen in the pattern of roads and field ways, the sites of villages and numerous farms, the ruins of former field systems which have been abandoned or given over to specialized crops. Today, this traditional scheme for the communal organization of the agriculturally used area is outdated in so far as power to make major decisions is no longer in the hands of the lord of the manor or a council of the villagers themselves but is distributed among a number of impersonal authorities dependent on the state and surrounded by innumerable regulations and controls. And yet the study of the recent changes in the rural landscape is meaningful at the level of the commune in so far as it is the theatre in which competing strategies of land use and land appropriation work themselves out, the actors being both individuals and groups, both private enterprise and public bodies.

The pattern of agricultural change is clearly revealed in the rural landscape of the commune, particularly when the consolidation of holdings (*remembrement*) has taken place (Fig. 33.2). Here parcels are bigger and they are more geometrically shaped; the triangular and H-shaped parcels of the old system disappear. No parcel is hemmed in by others; all are served by a road or field way. The road network is completely restructured, straightened, extended or reduced according to need; a rectangular system tends to replace the original pattern radiating from the village. Newly organized parcels gradually take the place of the archaic system inherited from the past. Nevertheless the consolidation of holdings does not necessarily eliminate contrasts in the shapes of parcels within a commune, since the whole of the commune is not included in the process; inhabited areas and their surroundings as well as meadow land are excluded. The process is also affected by tenurial patterns as well as by physical condition; markedly smaller parcels are found along the valleys, on hillsides, in highly dissected terrain and in the vicinity of villages.

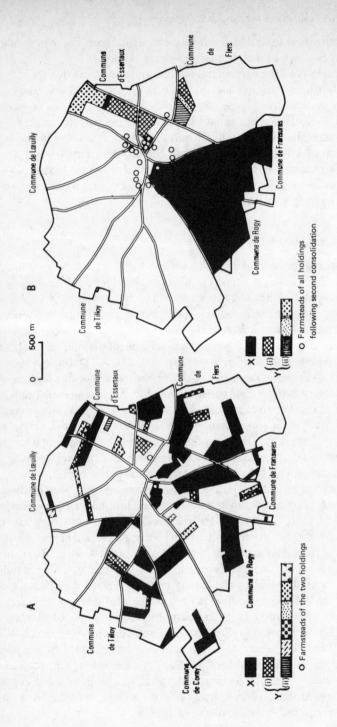

Commune de Lœuilly   Commune d'Essertaux   Commune de Flers

Commune de Tilloy

Commune de Rogy   Commune de Fransures

B

0   500 m

X   ■

(i)   ▩

Y (ii)   ▨

○   Farmsteads of all holdings following second consolidation

Commune de Lœuilly   Commune d'Essertaux   Commune de Flers

Commune de Tilloy

Commune de Conty

Commune de Rogy   Commune de Fransures

A

X   ■

(i)   ▩

Y (ii)   ▨

○   Farmsteads of the two holdings

But even where there has been no large-scale consolidation of holdings, the observant eye can pick out evidence of the strategies used by the different social categories of farmers and of the farming systems utilized. The nature of political leadership and the dominant social group at communal level also play a part. According to whether or not the farmers are prosperous and dynamic, the commune will behave as 'strong' or 'weak' in relation to farmers in other communes or regions.

It is also at the level of the commune that one can appreciate the extent of non-agricultural changes; it is not only the evolution of the agrarian landscape which changes the rural landscape. Camping sites or other recreational facilities and natural or artificial lakes equipped for leisure pursuits reveal the importance of tourism. The communal territory may also bear the marks of such major consumers of space as electric power installations, motorways, airports and military bases.

2.3 The regional level

If we confine ourselves to pinpointing the internal changes in agriculture, it must be accepted that there is simultaneously a persistence of regional contrasts in land use and a trend towards the production of a uniform landscape, according to the predominant type of agriculture. Figure 33.3 shows the regional differences in the agricultural landscape according to the statistical data of land use available in 1967. It can be said that the regional pattern revealed is not markedly different from that provided by J. Klatzmann on the basis of crop and animal production

---

Figure 33.2 Consolidation of holdings as part of the rural planning process: the Commune of Le Bosquel (Somme Department). A first consolidation, of classic type, took place in 1934. It was exclusively concerned with agricultural land, reducing the number of parcels so that each holding consisted of parcels of an economically viable size. The total destruction of the village in 1940 offered the opportunity for a more radical transformation. A second consolidation was able to go beyond the normal legal framework for such operations, reflecting instead the requirements of agricultural organization. Parcels of land cultivated by a single farmer but belonging to different owners were grouped into one or more continuous operational units; the number of owners per holding worked had in any case declined since 1934, as a result of land transfers. The farmhouses and associated economic buildings, rebuilt on strikingly original plans, were repositioned on the fringe of the village, each with direct access to its consolidated holding. The village, also rebuilt, made provision for services and for housing agricultural workers and retired persons. A. *First consolidation, 1934*. The parcels allocated to holding X are shown in black; the entire holding was cultivated by its owner. Holding Y was composite with respect to tenure, consisting of land in the ownership of the farmer (i) and of land rented from six other proprietors (ii). B. *Second consolidation, 1944*. Parcels worked by holding X are shown in black. Holding Y consisted partly of land owned by farmer (i) and partly of land rented from three other proprietors (ii).

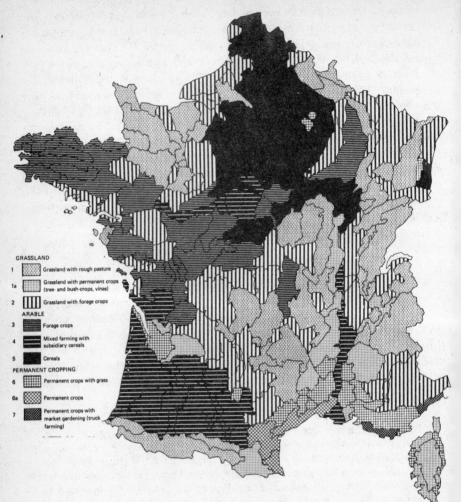

GRASSLAND

1		Grassland with rough pasture
1a		Grassland with permanent crops (tree- and bush-crops, vines)
2		Grassland with forage crops

ARABLE

3		Forage crops
4		Mixed farming with subsidiary cereals
5		Cereals

PERMANENT CROPPING

6		Permanent crops with grass
6a		Permanent crops
7		Permanent crops with market gardening (truck farming)

Figure 33.3 Agricultural land use, 1967. The map is based on a statistical method of classification developed by Y. Guermond and A. Leduc. For the determination of the classes to which the numbers in the key refer, see their original article in *L'Espace Géographique*, no. 1, 1975, pp. 45–52.

portrayed in the 1942 census.[10] The great grassland areas (Normandy, Lorraine, Ardennes and the plateaus of Burgundy) as well as the mountain pastures are clearly visible. We are here dealing with grassland established on volcanic soil rich in lime and phosphorus, on calcareous clay soils developed from the Lias and

[10] J. Klatzmann, *La Localisation des cultures et des productions animales en France* (INSEE, Paris, 1955).

on the rich alluvium of the valleys. The importance of hay meadows also increases in upland areas with higher rainfall and in particular less risk of drought in summer.

This grassland predominance began to make itself felt in the second half of the nineteenth century, affecting more particularly those cool, wet regions where grain was difficult to grow and the harvest was late, but also regions badly affected by a shortage of labour resulting from rural depopulation, such as the plateaus of Burgundy or regions of large estates. It remains true that around the concentrations of grazing land are peripheral zones where grassland is combined with fodder crops as in Brittany, Maine, Vendée, the western Central massif and the Saint-Dié basin west of the Vosges. In central France, arable land predominantly produces feed crops for livestock. The Paris basin is distinguished by the predominance of wheat, whereas the Mediterranean south is characterized by its vines, flowers, fruit and market-garden crops.

Yet this relative permanence of the types of cultivated landscape does, in fact, mask a transformation of the agricultural space involving two opposing tendencies. One is the shrinking of the agriculturally used area, particularly in mountain and hill areas, where it is common parlance that deserts are being created. Agricultural land in these areas is being abandoned either because of a difficult relief or because of difficulty of access. The degree of abandonment can vary; there can be total abandonment of a former arable field, vineyard or parcel of mulberry trees, or it can be that formerly cultivated land tumbles down more or less naturally into grass, which may sometimes serve as pasture for a few cattle or sheep. A stage intermediate between pasture and woodland emerges. Grasses, scrub, bracken and reeds gradually invade the abandoned plots; the hedges, left to themselves, run riot, paradoxically heightening the impression of *bocage*. 'It is the spread of grass and scrub over so much of the French landscape which draws our attention to the progressive or, rather, regressive development of the land of France during a single life span.'[11]

The interrelationship between abandoned land, steeply sloping land, poor soils, small holdings and agricultural depopulation is well enough known. Shortage of labour, but also of capital, leads to a failure to clean out ditches, allowing moss and reeds to overrun waterlogged valley bottoms and depressions within the higher plateaus, transforming once-cultivated areas into swamps.

In upland areas generally there has been a progressive destruction of the former equilibrium of ploughland, grassland and forest, associated with depopulation. The 'alps' (mountain pastures) have been abandoned and have turned into heathland with rhododendron and green alder. Such developments are particularly characteristic of the lower mountain areas, such as the Maurienne Alps, the intermediate mountains of the Central massif, characterized by sporadic reafforestation, and the plateaus of Limousin. The retreat of

[11] L. Gachon, 'Population et friches', *L'Information Géographique*, no. 5, 1948, pp. 175–9, and no. 2, 1949, pp. 56–9.

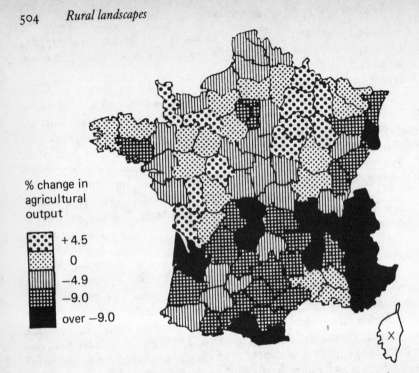

% change in
agricultural
output

+ 4.5
0
−4.9
−9.0
over −9.0

Figure 33.4 Changes in the agriculturally used area of holdings 1955–70, by department.
×: Data not available. Source: Censuses, 1955 and 1970.

agriculture in mountain areas is illustrated by the map of changes in the
agriculturally used area (Fig. 33.4). The process is illustrated by a study carried
out in the communes of Languedoc. The decline of the agriculturally used area
was concentrated in the *garrigue* (Mediterranean rock-heath) areas of the interior
plateaus of Gard and Hérault, and on the limestone *causses* yet further inland.
This decline of the hinterland is irreparable, since the disadvantages of isolation
and a harsh mountain climate are added to unfavourable conditions of slope.

In all other regions, the change in the agricultural landscape reveals increasing
output from each unit of land, the adaptation of the system of parcels to
mechanization and even, despite differences in climate, a standardization of
landscapes which are distinguished only by their differing product specializations. P. Brunet has shown how changes in the same direction can have varying
regional expressions: the decline and disintegration of *bocage* in the Atlantic
regions, the growing simplification of the agricultural landscape in the Paris
basin, the woodland clearances to increase the arable area in Champagne, and
the invasion of the Landes of southeast France by orchards are all analogous
movements.[12]

[12] P. Brunet, 'L'évolution récente des paysages ruraux français', *Géographie Polonica*, no. 29, 1974,
pp. 13–30.

Two vast categories of landscape, an agricultural landscape in decline and an agricultural landscape which maintains its position, reflect in fact the same agricultural process: the rapid development of productive techniques, mechanization, the mastery of biological processes and specialization. These developments explain the hunger for suitable land and the eradication of the banks and hedgerows of the *bocage* to produce an open landscape of vast fields.

The transformation of the *bocage* reflects technical processes, but can occur in a variety of ways. It can be produced by the contraction of the cultivated land, by the consolidation of holdings and by changes in the systems of cultivation in areas of progressive depopulation. Hedges are no longer maintained and are left full of holes, making it easy for cattle to get through. Gates are not replaced, and the *bocage* becomes a redundant feature. In other regions, the hedge is no longer the provider of wood and is no longer repaired; when holes appear, the farmer closes them with barbed wire. Frequently the hedge becomes a nuisance and the farmer decides to cut it down, replacing it (if at all) by an almost invisible electric fence. Progressive farmers resent the hedge because it occupies an area of ground which could otherwise be cultivated and because it harbours weeds and vermin. They believe that it keeps the fields damp, slows down the thawing of snow and cuts down the amount of sunshine received. Moreover, the sunken roads of the *bocage* are ill-adapted to modern agricultural machinery.

The first stage in the transformation of the *bocage* began with the destruction of hedges and banks, often independently of any movement towards the consolidation of holdings. The process began at the end of the nineteenth century and developed between the two wars. Since 1945 and particularly since 1958 removal has accelerated, helped by subsidies. The removal of field banks and hedges allows a significant addition to be made to the area cultivated.

It is above all the consolidation of parcels (*remembrement*) which is chiefly responsible for the transformation of the *bocage*. For a long time the *bocage* regions, with their banks and hedges, were resistant to consolidation, but the process is now well advanced. Regrouping involves the removal of hedges, the levelling of their supporting embankments, and the filling in of ditches by earth-moving machinery. Large, regular parcels are created, served by a network of newly built roads and widened existing ones.

The necessary exchanges of land during the consolidation process provide more delicate problems than in openfield areas, because relief conditions usually result in a greater variety of soils, slopes and exposure. However, conditions in the *bocage* are not entirely unfavourable to the consolidation process. Because more farmers own their land than in the openfield areas, negotiations are simplified. Parcels are frequently grouped close to the farmstead already, with hedges used only to surround the entire farm and a few pastures. In the process of consolidation a new landscape takes shape, creating unexpected broad clearings in the old *bocage*. The process has its critics: there is a danger that in meeting the more obvious disadvantages that *bocage* presents to agricultural operations its advantages will be overlooked, because they are less easily recognized. Hedges

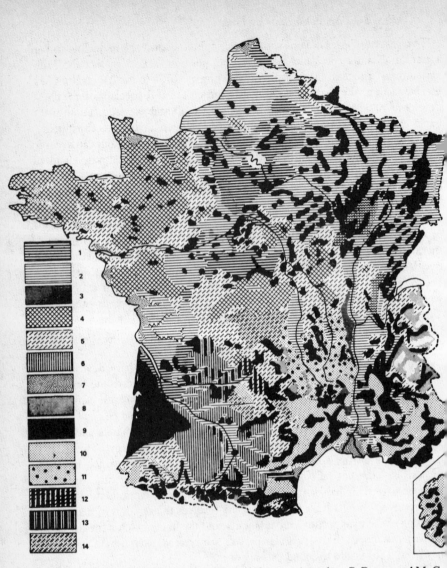

Figure 33.5 Types of rural landscape. Acknowledgement is made to P. Brunet and M. C. Dionnet, who provided the above simplified map. 1. Openfield with block parcels 2. Openfield with bundles of strips 3. Irregular small open fields 4. Enclosed fields (*bocage*) 5. *Semi-bocage* 6. Aquitaine type 7. Marshes and polders 8. Mountain pastures 9. Forest 10. Heathland and *garrigues* 11. Isolated openfield areas in heathland 12. *Bocage* intermixed with forest 13. Aquitaine type with woodland 14. Intermixed *bocage* and heathland.

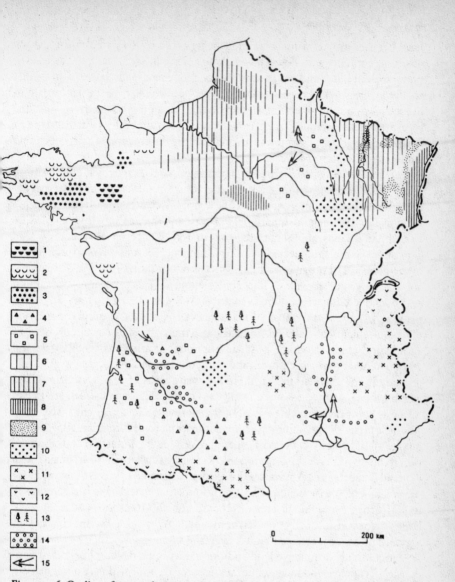

Figure 33.6 Outline of recent changes in the rural landscape. 1. Hedges removed from the field banks of the *bocage* 2. Partial removal of field banks 3. Total removal of field banks 4. Total removal of Toulouse-type landscape 5. Major clearance of vegetation 6. Consolidation of openfield producing parcels of 7–10 ha 7. Consolidation of openfield producing complexes of parcels of 2–3 ha 8. Consolidation of openfield producing complexes of parcels of 1 ha 9. Widespread social fallow (abandonment) 10. Fallows and coppices of the limestone plateaus 11. Major decline in mountain regions 12. Minor decline in mountain regions 13. Major areas of reafforestation 14. Expansion of orchards 15. Direction of advance of certain structural innovations. Source: P. Brunet, *Geographica Polonica*, no. 29, 1974, p. 17.

have been destroyed without account being taken of their role in the natural environment. On steep slopes they help to anchor the soil, stabilize the level of underground water and act as windbreaks, reducing evaporation and providing shelter for livestock. There is an obvious necessity to improve the jigsaw pattern of the *bocage*, but the operation should be carried out more selectively, with due regard to local variations of environment. The creation of an English type of *bocage* with large parcels would seem preferable to the creation of a new openfield landscape in western France.

The two main regional types of agricultural landscape which emerge from recent changes are thus grafted on to older structures. It is not, however, easy to describe the subtle differences that these origins create, or to understand the relationships between the inherited landscape and the new one (Fig. 33.6). The French rural landscape is not changing merely as a result of changes within agriculture; it is also subjected to external influences. Land is being lost because of the demands of urban growth, new means of transport, industry, recreational areas and leisure activities. The consumption of space for non-agricultural purposes (including recreation) is conservatively estimated at 75,000–80,000 ha per year. In 1972 and 1973, of the net balance of 63,000 ha consumed in meeting the requirements of building, industry and transport, 25,000 ha consisted of agricultural land, 15,000 of heathland or rough grazing, 6,000 of forest and 17,000 of other non-agricultural land. Agricultural space is thus being gradually eroded, all the more so in that there are many areas of non-agricultural land which cannot easily be assigned to any particular category but which are in fact formerly cultivated areas in process of transformation into residential space.

These losses of agricultural land are not spaced evenly throughout the country but are found chiefly in areas of expanding residential, industrial and transport requirements. There is also appreciable loss in areas where there is considerable demand for recreational purposes (for example, attached to second homes) or for the creation of tourist facilities. This transformation changes the rural landscape in peri-urban zones, along axes of urbanization and transport, and in areas of large-scale tourism, such as coastal or mountain resorts. Lastly, this conquest of agricultural space is realized indirectly by the superimposing of new use-values on agriculturally productive land and unproductive land alike. In areas of low-density occupance and in agricultural areas, the transformation is often masked by a stage during which a range of uses coexists; the natural agrarian landscape, the houses and villages, sites and monuments survive, but have new use-values attached to them. Tourism is also an indirect consumer of space through 'the consumption of the landscape' in protected zones, as in regional nature parks or national parks such as the Cévennes.

In this way a new regional typology of rural landscapes is taking shape which no longer bears any relationship to the typology of the agrarian landscape. Regions of the new type include peri-urban rural landscapes, coastal and valley landscapes, where there is keen rivalry between different types of use, but they also include rural landscapes altered by tourism. It is easy to understand the difficulty involved in drawing up a new classification and interpretation of rural landscapes at the regional level, as will be shown in the following chapter.

34

 Rural environments and rural planning

The analysis of rural environments and the way in which they are changing reveals landscapes at their most beautiful – the expression of the way in which rural societies have over the centuries adapted to their environment – and at their most degraded and neglected. Observation of the gradual erosion and degeneration of the rural landscape leads to an understanding of changes in the legal, economic and social structures of which these transformations are a reflection. The recent upheaval has been so great, however, that this approach alone is not a sufficient guide to the definition of rural environments.

1 Types of rural space

An examination of both the old and the new functions of French rural space, as well as the principal problems encountered there, must begin with the acceptance of spatial diversity. There is not one rural space but several, involving different combinations of functions and uses, social categories, amenities and ways of life. It would be interesting to be able to identify and label these various environments, some of which are the product of the gradual adaptation of declining rural regions, some of the introduction of new functions and an abrupt integration into a new economy. The establishment of a typology of rural space, however, poses problems of methodology; the existing classifications waver between several empirical and theoretical procedures. There are also problems of data availability, both with regard to the areal units and the classificatory frameworks employed by the various statistical offices concerned.

1.1 Empirical classifications

These proceed either from the observed morphology or from descriptions of functions; frequently both are used conjointly. Sometimes the morphological aspect is the main one, producing categories such as 'low-density rural space' or 'peri-urban rural space'. Sometimes the functional aspect is preferred, in which case categories such as 'industrialized rural space' or 'rural space devoted to tourist activities' might emerge. Frequently, however, function and spatial form are difficult to distinguish; the *bourg* or small town can here serve as an example.

1.1.1 Rural space classified according to population density and the level of urban organization

(i) Peri-urban regions of diffused urbanization. This type of rural space can easily be identified; it consists of agricultural or forest land situated within a radius from a town which will be proportional to the town's size. This type of space is characterized by the diffusion of urban population, producing some of the highest densities of 'rural' France. Visually, the most immediately obvious effect of this urban diffusion is seen in the construction of new housing. This usually consists of detached single-family houses, 'new villages' and *lotissements* (land subdivided to produce building plots) in communes which are still characterized by a rudimentary settlement organization and where the way of life is still based on agriculture or forestry. The new inhabitants are essentially of urban origin, people of modest means attracted by the low cost of building land, or well-to-do people searching for their ideal way of life. The new population is characterized by a relative over-representation of young married couples and young children, as well as by low female activity rates. The incomers work in the parent town or in suburban employment nodes; the existence of adequate road and rail links is thus a vital element in diffusion. The detailed aspect of this new urbanization is greatly dependent on the pattern of land ownership, the strategies of developers and the policies of local administrations; the outcome may be modest housing estates strung along the main roads, or landscaped parks appealing to higher-income groups. The social and political conflicts specific to this type of rural space often involve the opposition of new and old residents. Farmers play a different role according to whether they are trying to create modernized farm enterprises, are ready to speculate on the increase in the price of land, or are engaged in agriculture only on a part-time basis. There is a basic problem of establishing public control over the use of land, preventing sporadic and unplanned development, protecting an environment already penetrated by the speculators and providing adequate reserves of open space. Seen on the map (Fig. 34.1), this type of space takes the form of concentric rings with linear extensions around the larger towns. Clearly these new patterns extend over areas of greatly differing environmental characteristics; equally clearly they have little or no relationship to the inherited pattern of local administrative units.

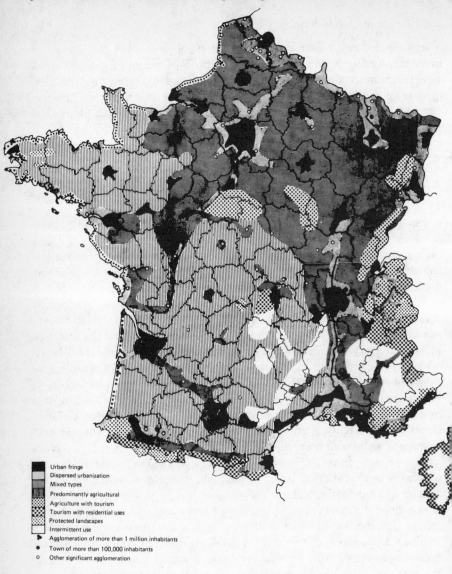

Figure 34.1 Types of rural space. Source: SEGESA.

(ii) Low-density rural space. This type is characterized not only by low population densities but by a feeble degree of urbanization and extremely extensive forms of land utilization, both in relation to productive uses (forests, livestock enterprises, cereal-growing, space-demanding industries and other economic activities) and to non-productive uses (housing, defence establishments, parks and nature reserves). The definition of low-density space (Fig. 34.2) is based on the

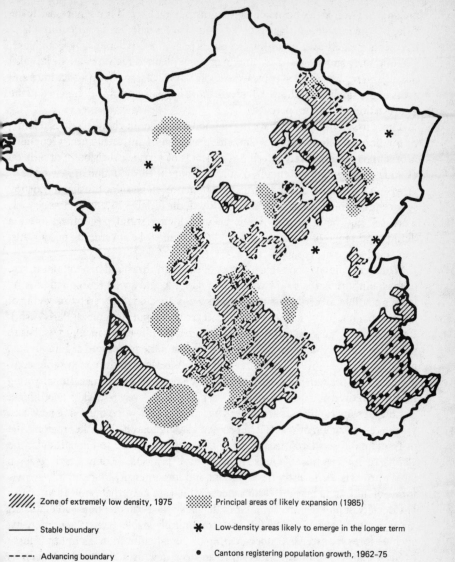

/////, Zone of extremely low density, 1975   ::::::: Principal areas of likely expansion (1985)

——— Stable boundary   ✱ Low-density areas likely to emerge in the longer term

- - - - Advancing boundary   • Cantons registering population growth, 1962-75

Figure 34.2 Areas of low population density, with the density thresholds separating them from neighbouring regions. Cantons are included if rural population density is below 20 inhabitants to the sq km, and total population density is below 25 inhabitants to the sq km. Source: SEGESA.

observation of marked breaks in the geographical distribution of population. Within these areas it is possible to recognize common problems and characteristic life-styles. It had always been assumed that the problem associated with low density was the abandonment of agricultural lands, the expansion of rough grazing and the extensification of agriculture. In reality this is not necessarily the case, for the low-density type is also found in areas where new agricultural land has been created as a result of clearance operations (Champagne pouilleuse, Châtillonnais and the Landes), and in areas of planned reafforestation. It is also possible to recognize great contrasts between areas of large-farm agriculture and areas of the smallest holdings, which are more open to land abandonment and the afforestation of random parcels.

These low-density areas have in common a number of characteristics relating to public and private services and the provision of infrastructure. Generally, provision is quantitatively inferior at all levels of service provision. Not only do existing services find it difficult to function, but the introduction of new types of provision tends to be belated; indeed there may even be some erosion of existing service provision. Primary schools are closed, the number of single-class schools increases, journeys by school bus become longer, rural post offices offer a diminished range of services, increasing areas must be covered by postal vans, and small shops are disappearing.

Whether or not it is possible to speak of a density threshold or a minimum size of local authority area below which demographic and social reproduction is no longer possible, nevertheless low-density areas are characterized by an ageing of the population. In the Departments of Nièvre and Yonne (southeast Paris basin), Corrèze and Creuse (Central massif), Landes (southwest France), as well as in all of the eastern Pyrenees, the southern Alps and the hinterland of Languedoc, one person out of three is of retirement age. In regions of dispersed settlement, hamlets lose their population and the only survivors are an occasional young farmer or retired people who for the most part live in poverty-stricken conditions.

Low-density rural areas are above all characterized by the finding of new uses for the re-utilization of space. After some delay compared with other regions, the price of land rose sharply as a result of changes in land use and in particular the claims of military installations, hydroelectric projects, national and regional parks, projects for forestry development and low-intensity tourism. These new forms of utilization take different aspects, which are nevertheless all adapted to a low density of population. Sometimes they take the form of a renewed emphasis on agricultural structures which are economically viable even at low intensity, such as forestry, extensive stock-rearing or cereal cultivation, as in the Causse Méjean and the southern Morvan. Elsewhere new uses are involved, such as military bases, installations related to social provision or tourist developments. Alternatively, land may be devoted to the preservation of the natural or cultural heritage. These developments will be reflected in a diversity of social environments, depending on the level of integration of the old and new functions. Some areas are only weakly stratified, with low-income groups predominating. These are often the refuge of those who seek to escape more demanding conditions elsewhere, such as young people trying to live from farming or craft occupations and retired people with modest incomes. Other areas are dominated by a well-to-do social class which controls their future while the poorer people – small farmers, old people, shopkeepers – live in increasingly difficult conditions due to the deterioration in services.

One last type of rural space that may be identified from morphological criteria is the rural space of highly urbanized regions such as Alsace and Nord. This is not a type of space into which urban diffusion is taking place, as in peri-urban rural space, but it is distinguished by a good level of provision in retailing and in public and private services, which it acquires as a result of the high density of its small, medium and large towns.

1.1.2 Rural space classified according to predominant function

These spatial types coincide with or complement those just described.

(i) Types with predominantly agricultural function are found in western and southwestern France, in rural areas of medium or very low density. The classification of these areas rests, however, on an uncertain basis and there is a tendency to introduce as a criterion the degree of agricultural modernization, that is, to fall back on the typology of agricultural regions. It is nevertheless essential to remember that these types have other equally characteristic functional aspects, even if they are not the dominant element in determining land use or total population.

(ii) Types with residential, tourist or mixed agricultural–tourist function are found on the coasts, in the high mountains, occasionally in hill country or in areas of wooded lowland such as the Sologne (south of Orléans). This tourist and residential specialization takes different forms according to whether the region is of high or very low density. The contrast is, however, not in itself sufficient to account for the characteristics of the different levels of tourist function in rural space; the social–spatial segregation characteristic of the postwar development of tourism reserves some areas for high-income categories, whereas the majority of rural areas tend to receive lower-income groups, unable to guarantee the profitability needed to sustain investment in large-scale tourist projects, especially in times of crisis. The most remote and unspoiled areas have been appropriated by the 'new' middle class with cultural and ecological aspirations; in this group middle and upper management, students and teachers in schools and universities are disproportionately represented.

The growing demand for tourist and leisure facilities led first to a period of massive investment in tourism which resulted in the building of new ski resorts and the tourist complexes of coastal Languedoc–Roussillon and Aquitaine. The prospect of profit encouraged financial concerns to take an interest in 'white gold' (tourism) and, helped by state subsidies, to build 'integrated resorts'. New systems were developed to maximize returns from the residential developments that accompanied the tourist amenities, for example the time-sharing of apartments. This type of recreational function has radically changed rural space in certain mountain areas, and has created a new rural environment, where the inhabitants live according to a marked seasonal rhythm. These areas have their characteristic conflicts, between local councils and speculators, between full-time farmers, landowners and tourists. They have also acquired a certain capacity for population growth, based on incomes generated by retailing and the seasonal employment of part-time farmers as ski instructors or perchmen on the ski-lifts.

(iii) Types with multiple functions with no dominant specialization are orientated towards the secondary sector in eastern France and the tertiary sector in the southeast and along the Rhône valley. But the mere classification of an area as predominantly agricultural with industrial specialization or even with diversified characteristics does not provide an understanding of functional relationships or enable it to be located with regard to the overall system. Each activity or function which has a specific spatial expression has its particular scale and system of organization and can be assigned to a particular stage of development. Function is not entirely independent of the level of integration into the wider socio-economic system, to the extent that, for example, large state-financed projects in fields such as transport or power generation imply a very advanced level of integration.

At another level, the *key villages, bourgs and small towns* cannot be dissociated from their surrounding rural environment. Although these may be very small, sometimes with populations as low as 500–1,500 inhabitants, they serve as locations for public and private services. Rural centres stand out from their surroundings by a greater density of population and of tertiary employment (40–80 heads of household active in the tertiary sector in the key villages, 80–200 in the *bourgs* and 200–400 in small towns). Their former close links with the surrounding countryside as local market centres are today still maintained under other arrangements for supply and sale, notably the establishment of small supermarkets and co-operatives. In addition, and generally because they are administrative centres for cantons, they have benefited from the establishment of activities and services such as secondary schools, rural hospitals, police stations and banks. Sometimes these small towns have attracted some industrial establishments, offering low-wage, unskilled employment. Essentially, however, the *bourgs* and small towns are economically dominated by the tertiary sector, perhaps excessively so; they are dependent on the population levels and the disposable income in their surrounding countryside. This explains the financial difficulties of their town councils. In these small towns a local bourgeoisie of doctors, lawyers, tradespeople and bank managers rubs shoulders with groups having decidedly lower incomes, notably retired people who, attracted by the low cost of living, make up a substantial part of their population.

1.2 Statistical classifications

These are clearly distinguished from the previous ones by the terminology used and by the techniques of identification and classification.

(i) Rural spaces classified according to their structures. The basic units used are the administrative divisions for which statistical information is available: communes, cantons or departments (usually the latter). Quantitative techniques are then used to produce groups having similar characteristics.

Thus according to R. Calmès and others[1] the assignment of French rural communes into five groups produces:

(1) the coherent mass of the departments of western France, with high rural and agricultural densities, an adequate level of public and private service provision and a reasonably good urban system;

(2) rural spaces, equally dominated by agriculture, but with agricultural densities distinctly lower than the first group, showing many signs of deteriorating conditions (central and southwest France, the Central massif and the northern Alps);

(3) the rural spaces of the outer eastern and western parts of the Paris basin, characterized by numerous small communes with much non-agricultural employment; the distances that must be travelled to reach towns and schools are about average for France;

(4) the rural spaces of the Mediterranean south, characterized by viticulture and considerable tourist activity;

(5) the rural spaces of highly urbanized and industrialized regions, such as the departments near Paris, the Nord, Rhône, Alsace and Lorraine.

(ii) Rural spaces classified according to their level of modernization, according to their degree of participation in a developing urbanization. According to L. M. Coyaud and R. Chapuis,[2] there are three types, each divided into two variants:

(1) A pre-industrial type has as the first of its variants sparsely populated areas with very little urbanization, where agriculture is outmoded and industry and tourism are marginal. The other variant consists of non-integrated space; rural areas which are still agricultural but where the influence of the industrial world has not resulted in any significant economic or social progress.

(2) Integrated rural space has as its first variant spaces where industrialization and urbanization have sterilized the countryside, which plays no part in

---

[1] R. Calmès, A. Delamarre, F. Durand Dastès, J. Gras and J. P. Peyon, *L'Espace rural français* (Masson, Paris, 1978).

[2] L. M. Coyaud, *Essai de typologie des espaces ruraux français* (Comité Nationale de Géographie, Paris, 1977); R. Chapuis, *Les espaces ruraux du Doubs* (n.p., Besançon, 1979).

economic progress. In such areas agricultural land has been widely abandoned or turned to non-agricultural uses. In the second variant, urban influences have stimulated the development of a type of agriculture which guarantees high returns together with a general range of diversified activities. Farms are highly mechanized; the agricultural scientist replaces the peasant.

(3) The final type is marked by the coexistence to the widest degree of the characteristics of the pre-industrial economy and those of the industrial–urban generation. Its first variant consists of rural space in the process of integration into the modernized economy; agricultural production continues to develop towards the level of the previous type, while at the same time often retaining family-type agriculture and a pre-industrial type of urban distribution. With this variant can be associated the areas of large-scale tourist development in the mountains and on the coasts, which cannot be assigned to any more specific type. The second variant of this type comprises rural spaces defined as marginal, where evolution is made difficult by the fragmentation of holdings, the absence of innovators and leaders, and in general the absence of support for diversification of activity.

These attempts have brought a new vigour to the geographical analysis of micro-regions.

2 Spatial planning policies for rural France

Understanding planning policy for rural space, its agents and its effects, is for various reasons less easy than attempting to understand agricultural policies. The concept and practice of state involvement in the improvement of rural areas has a long history, going back at least to the draining of marshland in the eighteenth and nineteenth centuries and the nineteenth-century afforestation of the Landes with pines. Only very recently, however, and only after the formation of the concept of strategic spatial planning had emerged was a policy for the planning of rural space conceived as having its own coherent complex of objectives and its own specific methods of attaining them. Spatial planning for rural areas really came into existence only with the 1967 legislation concerning urban and rural planning (*Loi d'orientation foncière*).

It is in fact difficult to pin down ultimate responsibility for rural planning, in so far as the territorial spheres of activity of various government departments are overlapping and even contradictory, and in so far as the official doctrine of rural planning is of necessity distorted by the fragmentation of the different administrative arms of the government which are supposed to apply it. The place of rural planning in the overall policy for strategic spatial planning has always been much debated; there are 'ruralist' and 'urbanophile' factions which contest their right to have the major voice in deciding on policies. The discrepancy between official policy and reality is therefore not due merely to the practices of private individuals and companies who plan rural space spontaneously and for their own ends, but also to the simultaneous application of a wide range of sectoral policies by different branches of the administration, for example in respect of education, health, agriculture and rural industry. All too often these separately conceived policies are contradictory. Lastly, the decisions relating to rural planning, as to spatial planning in general, are subject to the political choices of mayors of communes, members of departmental councils and still more of the new regional authorities.

In spite of all these difficulties of analysis, it is possible to distinguish a number of stages in the evolution of rural planning policy.

2.1 Origins and directions of postwar agricultural policies

The first stage, from the 1940s until the beginning of the 1960s, was characterized by a decline in the global and territorial conception of rural planning in favour of a sectoral approach. The origins of rural planning can be traced back to the Vichy period (1940-4), which saw a proliferation of theoretical analyses and proposals for action and experiments, demonstrating a distinctly global concern for rural space, its functions, its future and its planning. At the same time, and throughout the period up to 1952-3, discussion on rural planning took place in parallel with the debate on the industrialization of rural areas. A report, entitled *Matériaux pour une géographie volontaire de l'espace rural*, published in 1949, examined the capacity of the rural environment to respond to the industrial decentralization from urban areas that was then considered desirable. This can be regarded as the first attempt to formulate a policy for rural planning incorporating the general principles of strategic spatial planning.

Yet shortly after the Liberation in 1945 this concern for global planning grew less keen; even before earlier attempts could show any results, the policy followed became essentially sectoral. The main concern was to secure an increase in agricultural production. In the development of policies for rural planning, a predominant role was reserved for the Ministry of Agriculture, which was primarily concerned with agricultural development and the provision of the necessary supporting structure. The government at this period intervened in rural areas to secure the rebuilding of villages and farms, the consolidation of holdings (*remembrement*), land drainage, the clearance of waste areas, rural electrification and water supply. All these activities had the implicit aim of making possible an increase in the agricultural population.

Yet it was at this time that the first integrated spatial policies were launched: the policy for mountain regions initiated in 1946 at the instigation of the Commissariat Général du Plan, and in particular the initiation of projects of large-scale spatial reorganization (*grandes compagnies d'aménagement régional*, see chapter 14, 2.2.2). Some of these projects have been successful, for example the Canal de Provence scheme for water provision in the region of Aix, Marseille and Toulon.

The majority of these projects, and policies for the transformation of rural

France in general, were in this period restricted to the objective of producing a modernized agriculture. Some associated improvement in rural living conditions went hand in hand with depopulation, the abandonment of houses and even of whole villages, thus eroding an organization of space whose roots went back to the Middle Ages.

2.2 The institutionalization of rural planning

Just as with agricultural policy, 1960 marks a turning point in the development of policies for rural planning. In this year new directions were to some extent established by an important circular issued jointly by the Ministries of Equipment, the Interior and Agriculture, and in framework legislation (*Loi d'orientation*) envisaging the setting up of 'special zones of rural action' which were to some extent the prototype of the whole policy for rural planning. These new proposals contained many of the theories and objectives of the preceding period, but under pressure from admittedly conflicting currents of opinion there was evolved a genuine planning doctrine for rural space (the term appeared only about 1965). A global concept of spatial planning emerged; new policies were forged which would allow equality of opportunity between town and country at economic, demographic, social and cultural levels. At last there appeared to be a means of combating the processes that were turning rural France into the 'French desert'.

The Ministry of Agriculture, DATAR (Delegation for Strategic Spatial Planning and Regional Development) and the Plan Commission (Commissariat Général du Plan) were all involved. First in the field was the Ministry of Agriculture. One of its more important proposals envisaged the study of 'pilot' or 'demonstration' sectors (*secteurs pilotes*) which were defined as small rural areas dependent on a central 'key village'. After due investigation they were to be the subject of proposals for the creation of infrastructures and amenities, which would take account of likely future population levels and endeavour to create living conditions equivalent to those of town dwellers. A second approach to the problem was the setting up of rural special-action zones (*zones spéciales d'action rurale* – ZSAR), from 1967 renamed zones of rural renewal. These benefit from co-ordinated improvement measures and have priority for public investment in road schemes, the generation of industrial employment opportunities, the provision of social equipment and professional training. Among the criteria used for the definition of zones were agricultural overpopulation and substantial out-migration, as in Brittany, Manche Department (Cotentin Peninsula). Other criteria were an inadequate urban system and a lack of non-agricultural employment, as in Limousin or Auvergne.

In 1970 27 per cent of French rural space was covered by zones of rural renewal, which included 13 per cent of rural population and a little more than one-third of all holdings. Operations in each zone are under the control of a commissioner, who is able to use combinations of existing sectoral policies, such as the special agricultural policy for mountain areas, industrial development subsidies and low-interest loans in some of the zones. All the zones benefited from additional government assistance channelled through the Intervention Fund for Strategic Spatial Planning (Fonds d'Intervention pour l'Aménagement du Territoire – FIAT) on the basis of special programmes for the improvement of agricultural structure, roads, the processing of agricultural produce, tourism and rural craft industries.

The results achieved during this particular period of the development of rural policies were rather disappointing. The application of these policies was perhaps rather hasty, and their impact was dissipated by being dispersed over scattered micro-regions, with the result that the economic and demographic imbalance actually worsened. Several ministries applied a policy with regard to the provision of public services which intensified rural depopulation and exodus. Similarly, despite the 'ruralist' pronouncements of DATAR, this period was marked by the policy of building up counterbalancing regional capitals (*métropoles d'équilibre*), the building of large ski resorts, and the tourist developments of the Languedoc–Roussillon coast. All these were measures which destroyed local rural society, set off a process of decline in their hinterland, initiated the phenomenon of peri-urbanization and accentuated the abandonment of precisely those regions included in the Zones of Rural Renewal or mountain economy.

On the positive side, credit must be given to the setting up of the necessary legal and administrative framework to permit research into the problems and to allow effective action. In particular it was accepted that the Ministry of Agriculture should take the lead in the formulation and implementation of a coherent policy for rural space, a policy which would combine both agricultural and non-agricultural aspects. In the period 1960–70 rural planning acquired the status of a full department (Direction) within the Ministry, which was represented at national, regional and local (departmental) level by organizations for research and implementation (Ateliers d'Etude et d'Aménagement Rural). It was during this period that the Ministry of Agriculture, following experimental applications in a limited number of localities, introduced the system of rural development plans (*plans d'aménagement rural* – PAR) as provided for in the 1967 urban and rural planning legislation (*Loi d'orientation foncière*). The creation of these plans marked the summit of the achievement of the Ministry of Agriculture in a battle for control of rural planning, in which the problem was to decide which was the best government organization to provide an integrated policy for rural space.

2.3 From the policies of the European Community to the policy of development by *pays*

The period from 1970 to 1980 was a turning point, with the creation of the Interministerial Fund for Rural Development and Planning (Fonds Interministériel de Développement et d'Aménagement Rural – FIDAR). A growing awareness of the need for a planned approach to rural problems was fostered by a consciousness of the discrepancy caused by the desertion of rural areas at a time of massive urban growth. The rise of regional and ecological movements also served to alert public opinion. It was felt that spatial planning as hitherto practised had not prevented the running down of rural public services, the piecemeal destruction of the countryside, and large-scale changes of land use in some regions. As a consequence, rural planning became one of the government's chief concerns. Opinions in both the Ministry of Agriculture and in DATAR converged on the desirability of focusing efforts on the *pays*, as a space comprising one or more small towns and the surrounding rural area. This convergence of views found expression in the use of the rural development plans (PAR) and the creation in 1975 of the special planning procedure for small rural regions known as *contrat de pays*.

The PAR is essentially a programme for change, for the development of all aspects of rural regions, drawn up with the maximum participation of the people and the political and socio-professional organizations representing them. The legal standing of the PAR is similar to that of the structure plan (*schéma directeur d'aménagement et d'urbanisme* – SDAU) of which they may be considered an extension or for which they may be substituted (chapter 38). Between 1971 and 1983, 260 PARs were launched. To some extent the PARs operated as envelopes within which could be gathered a number of the familiar projects of rural improvement, such as land drainage, road improvements or the creation of small industrial estates. But in the spirit of the PAR system a number of new measures of co-ordinated rural planning emerged, such as the development of tourism, the encouragement of cultural activities or the improvement of service provision.

The PARs represent the comparative success of rural planning policy as it was envisaged by the Ministry of Agriculture, which has nevertheless had to watch its power in this area slip away to other bodies. The activities of the Ministry of Agriculture have appeared as sporadic and dispersed when faced with the work of other ministries who have also had their local instruments, and above all compared with DATAR and the system of *contrats de pays*. The Ministry of the Environment (Ministère de l'Environnement) has also continued to extend its grip on rural projects. The Ministry of Agriculture has proved unable to benefit from the trend of opinion favourable to the rural environment. The dismantling in 1979 of the Centre for Rural Research and Planning (Atelier Central d'Etudes et d'Aménagement Rural – ACEAR) clearly reveals the tendency for the Ministry of Agriculture to lose its grip on overall rural planning and to retreat into an exclusive concern with agricultural production and the needs of farmers.

The *contrat de pays* procedure for the co-ordinated planning of small homogeneous rural regions was inaugurated by DATAR (chapter 14, 2.2.2).The objectives and procedures are reasonably close to those of the PARs, but there are some specific features, notably the requirement that not only a homogeneous rural area should be included but also the small town that functions as its 'central place'. Designation results in the receipt of increased financial support for technical assistance, the provision of organizers (*animation*), employment provision and the improvement of public services.

Although in theory the PAR and *contrat de pays* procedures were complementary and connected (a *contrat de pays* following the establishment of a PAR), the overlapping powers of the various ministries and other government organizations have led to frequent conflicts. Both procedures have the same defect: they involve the sporadic application of many kinds of projects at scattered points, perhaps a cultural centre in one place, a housing programme in another.

Because of this diffusion of objectives and resources it is very difficult to determine the success of these two policies. Yet one ruling trend can be discerned, which is to develop these *pays* to the level at which they can be integrated into the global economy, while slipping in a few schemes such as nuclear power-stations, dams and tourist projects, which go far beyond the local scale and which cast doubt on the reality of local autonomy. Considerations of electoral advantage are frequently of significance in allocating priorities.

At national level, predominance is given either to sectoral policies (the agricultural policy, for example), or to the large-scale 'spatial policies' which relate to concepts of strategic spatial planning developed at the European rather than the regional scale, such as policies for disfavoured agricultural areas and the mountains. Nevertheless co-ordinated programmes for regional development retain their importance; the financing of regional development companies (chapter 14, 2.2.2) has allowed the undertaking of many schemes for water control, afforestation, livestock husbandry, wine production and tourism.

2.4 The protection of rural landscapes

Policies for the protection of the natural environment, whose aim is to save or restore the ecological balance, and the policies for rural planning, the development of which has been outlined above, are not the only forms of planned intervention in rural areas. In parallel with the movement for ecological preservation there has developed a growing concern with the quality of landscapes in a wider sense. These are no longer viewed exclusively as natural environments, nor simply as spaces devoted to increasingly varied activities whose locations have to be planned and organized; they are perceived as an essential part of the cultural and historic heritage of France. They are seen both as geographical structures created and integrated over the centuries, and as humanized landscapes, the creation of rural societies, which appear remarkable and worthy of preservation.

These landscapes of the present, moreover, enfold important legacies of the past. The archaeological heritage ranges from prehistory to the industrial establishments of the seventeenth, eighteenth and nineteenth centuries. The architectural heritage includes not only a host of humble vernacular buildings but also thousands of châteaux and manor houses, which throughout French history have been the initial points of radiation of the polarization and organization of the territory.

Since the 1960s there has been legislation to protect and conserve landscapes in this wider sense. These processes have been reinforced by two additional concepts. The 'sensitive zone' (*zone sensible*) was directed primarily at the preservation of areas of high quality from unsuitable building activity, while the 'sensitive perimeter' (*perimètre sensible*) was intended to encourage the acquisition of open space by the departments. The relevant regulations were re-issued in 1978, then a further category was introduced that came to be known as 'zones of landscape protection' (*zones de protection des paysages*). In these zones, whether or not they were covered by a legally established communal land-use plan (*plan d'occupation des sols* – POS), special requirements to assure development of a sufficiently high quality can be applied to building permits.

All these efforts were, however, of limited effect, and, in particular, rural landscapes of high quality were less well protected than urban conservation areas. More ambitious legislation in 1976 created Protected environmental zones (*zones d'environnement protégé* – ZEP) with the announced objective of 'the protection of rural space, agricultural activity and landscapes'. The ZEP procedure was particularly applicable to low-density regions where the drawing up of a full-scale communal land-use plan (POS) is not necessary. It provides for such areas a simple, easily comprehensible zoning system accompanied by simple, easily understandable regulations. The ZEP procedure permits a 'rule of thumb' planning, better suited to the needs of small rural communities than the elaborate national legislation.

It is indeed difficult to find a middle way between total preservation which would transform the countryside into a museum or reservation, draining it of all vitality by turning it into a fossil, or alternatively a free-for-all resulting from the removal of planning restrictions, the operations of speculators and almost irresistible financial pressures, which could destroy the landscape heritage of France.

2.5 Trends and policies since 1981

Since June 1981 the two policies of rural planning and the protection of the rural landscape and environment have undergone significant changes, less in respect of ideas and objectives than of the legal and institutional frameworks within which they are applied. The policy of decentralization at the departmental and regional scale (chapter 13, 2 and 3) has transferred many of the powers of decision and responsibility for finance to the regional and departmental councils. The rural development plans (PAR) are reappearing in the form of intercommunal agreements for planning and development (*chartes intercommunales de développement et d'aménagement*). The agreements (*contrats du pays*) between the state and the smaller rural regions again include a number of planning and protection measures, with particular emphasis on planning laws relating to mountain and coastal areas. The Interministerial Fund for Rural Development and Planning (FIDAR) co-ordinates the activities of local and regional government in this field.

VII

❧ The urban environment

35

⚜ The urban system and its development

The urban phenomenon is difficult to define; a town is at the same time a landscape, a centre of economic activities, a concentration of population and a place in which to live and work. More fundamentally, perhaps, towns are given individuality by their particular atmosphere and character. The geographer is primarily concerned with the distribution and spatial organization of towns, but these aspects cannot be properly understood without reference to the various factors – physical, human and economic – which, interacting in time and space, have led to the astonishing variety of French towns.[1]

1 Characteristics of the contemporary urban structure

Table 35.1 shows two characteristics of French urbanization. The first is its relative weakness: 67.5 per cent of the population lives in urban units of more than 5,000 inhabitants, as against 75–80 per cent in other European countries of comparable size. The second is the high concentration of urban population in the largest agglomerations; of the population of urban units of more than 5,000 inhabitants, two-thirds live in agglomerations of more than 100,000 inhabitants, half in agglomerations of more than 200,000, and a quarter in the Paris agglomeration. The degree of primacy of Paris in the French urban system is well known. It is the result of a cumulative process of concentration over several

[1] For the statistical definition of the urban population, see chapter 9. The problem of defining and demarcating urban areas is dealt with in chapter 36.

Table 35.1 *Size-distribution of towns in France and other European countries*

Size-category (no. of inhabitants)	France (1975) (1)	France (1975) (3)	Italy (1971) (2)	Italy (1971) (3)	German Federal Republic (1977) (2)	German Federal Republic (1977) (3)	Great Britain (1971) (1)	Great Britain (1971) (3)
5,000–10,000	381	7	1,123	17	899	12	368	⎫
10,000–20,000	181	7	518	16	598	16	240	⎬ 27
20,000–50,000	117	10	279	19	324	19	200	⎭
50,000–100,000	53	10	74	11	84	11	93	
100,000–500,000	52	29	41	17	56	21	58	19
Over 500,000	6	36	6	19	12	21	7	54
Total urban population	38,403,000		44,634,000		49,298,000		42,702,000	
Population of urban settlements of 5,000 and above, as a percentage of total population	67.5		79.7		80.0		80.0	
Population of the largest town divided by the population of the second largest town	7.3		1.6		1.2		3.1	

(1) Number of urban settlements.
(2) Number of urban communes.
(3) Percentage of total population of urban settlements of 5,000 and above.
Source: UN demographic yearbook.

centuries, and has, as one of its consequences, the relative weakness of large regional capitals. In 1975 France had 58 agglomerations of 100,000 population and above, a comparable total to those of major European neighbours (Italy 47, German Federal Republic 68, United Kingdom 65), but only 6 of 500,000 and above. While this figure equalled that for Italy, the United Kingdom had 7 and the Federal Republic 12. France also stood out as having few small towns, but the medium-sized towns in the 50,000–100,000 category were relatively strongly represented. The spatial distribution of agglomerations is extremely irregular (Fig. 35.1); the larger the size-category of agglomeration concerned, the greater this irregularity becomes. Agglomerations of 200,000 inhabitants and above are peripherally located and are not found in the central area of the country. Only towns of between 50,000 and 100,000 inhabitants have a more even distribution than their size would lead one to expect. At a lower level there are on average about 15 towns of fewer than 20,000 inhabitants in each department. These towns – administrative centres of the cantons, sub-prefectures, *bourgs* and small industrial centres – provide the lowest level in the urban structure of France.

The uneven distribution of towns is reflected in the differing degrees of urbanization in the various departments. The percentage of the population living in urban settlements of 2,000 inhabitants and above ranges from 22 per cent in Creuse to 100 per cent in the four inner departments of the Paris (Ile-de-France) region (average for all French departments 73). The nature of the urban hierarchy also differs; the manner in which population is distributed between urban centres of differing size varies markedly from one department to another.

French towns are mostly situated in areas of plain, plateau and low mountains. Above the altitude of 500 m there is only one town of more than 100,000 inhabitants (Saint-Etienne, owing its development to coal mining), and four towns of between 20,000 and 45,000 inhabitants (Aurillac, Rodez, Le Puy and Gap). The 'highest' towns in France are Pontarlier (837 m, 19,000 inhabitants) and Briançon (1,250 m, 13,000 inhabitants). The detailed examination of urban sites also reveals the surprisingly low elevations of the large Alpine centres; Grenoble, capital of the Alps, is situated at only 212 m. In fact, towns are much more 'mountainous' in the southern part of the Central massif which, unlike the Alps, is not endowed with structural depressions and river valleys, filled in and levelled by glacial and fluviatile deposits. On the contrary, the Central massif is highly fragmented; the narrow, deeply incised valleys hinder rather than help communications and rarely provide favourable sites for urban development. In 1954, the quarter of France lying below 100 m had 52 per cent of the population of towns with 20,000–30,000 inhabitants, 49 per cent of those between 30,000 and 50,000, 65 per cent of those between 50,000 and 100,000, 37 per cent of those between 100,000 and 200,000, and 85 per cent of those with more than 200,000 inhabitants.

Most towns are sited on rivers or on the coast, having been established at a time when water was the main source of transport and energy. Water was also of defensive significance: when not available naturally in the form of river, lakes or the sea, it could be provided artificially by the construction of moats. Nearly two-thirds of French towns and four-fifths of all departmental capitals are on rivers. In 1954, out of 165 towns of more than 20,000 inhabitants, only eight had no direct connection with a river or canal. Of these, two (one of them Versailles) were in the Paris (Ile-de-France) region, three were industrial towns (Henin-Liétard, Forbach and Hayange), two were in the Mediterranean region (Aix-en-

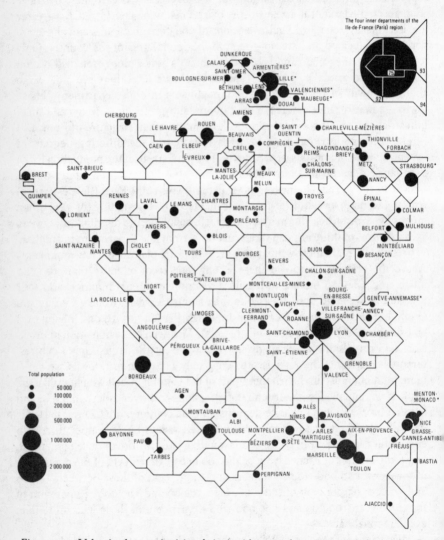

Figure 35.1 Urbanized areas (*unités urbaines*) with more than 50,000 inhabitants, 1982. * denotes 'cross-frontier agglomerations'. Source: INSEE.

Provence and Nîmes), and one was the classic hilltop town of Laon. Limoges and Clermont-Ferrand are the only French towns of more than 100,000 inhabitants which are situated neither on the coast nor on a navigable waterway.

The spatial diversity of France, by juxtaposing regions of complementary agricultural or industrial character, encouraged the growth of towns at points of contact and interchange, between uplands and lowlands, ancient massifs and sedimentary basins, productive and poor regions or forests and cleared areas. Geographical values are not, however, unchanging; any analysis of the stages of urban development will show how the physical environment has been constantly re-evaluated in the course of the process that has led to the creation of the present urban system.

2 Stages of urban development

The origins of the urban network of France lie buried deep in past history. Most of the present towns had some sort of proto-urban existence, whether as stopover or transfer points, military camps, small ports, religious centres, pilgrimage sites or periodic markets. The early origins of the human occupance of the land of France, the many routes crossing it, the proximity of Mediterranean urban civilization, not to speak of the numerous potential sites, combine to explain the early development of towns. Since the Gallo-Roman period successive generations of towns have sprung up, reflecting the changing military, commercial, administrative or industrial conditions.

2.1 Gallo-Roman towns

France's oldest urban network was that of the Gallo-Roman towns, a relatively dense network with a well-developed urban hierarchy of *civitates*, *pagi* and *vici*. Some towns were of exclusively Celtic origin, former *oppida* (fortresses), places of refuge, tribal capitals or route centres such as Paris, Bourges, Vannes, Arras and Amiens. Other towns were developed by the Romans on the Rhône–Rhine axis and in the Mediterranean coastlands; they included Lyon, Autun and Narbonne, but there were many such towns in southern France. At the end of the Gallo-Roman period, additional towns were created by the concentration into places of refuge of villagers and townspeople fleeing from the barbarian invaders. An example is Chauny, on marshy land in the Oise valley.

2.2 Medieval towns

A second generation of towns dates from the Middle Ages, chiefly from the eleventh and fourteenth centuries. A first group of medieval towns had no pre-urban nucleus but grew in particularly favourable situations at crossroads, bridging points, near a mill (Mulhouse), at places where periodic markets or fairs were held, or at staging points for travellers. A second group of towns grew up around pre-urban nuclei provided by the presence of a religious house or a castle. Cluny, Moissac, Saint-Omer, Fécamp and Saint Denis are well-known examples of the many French towns associated with religious houses. Most of them have remained small, as the site chosen for monastic purposes was frequently unsuitable for large-scale urban development. Some, although today only sleepy little *bourgs*, have buildings of high artistic value, which bear witness to a previous importance. Occasionally *bourgs* grew up in association with religious houses situated outside towns, which ultimately absorbed them (Bourg Saint-Martin at Tours, Saint-Martial at Limoges). Towns associated with castles are even more numerous, whether or not their place-names reflect their origin: Amboise, Chinon, Châteauroux, Château-Thierry or Bar-le-Duc are but a few examples.

The whole history of France is reflected in its towns. Protected by its castle, the town was the capital of the little political, economic and administrative entity over which the feudal lord had sovereign power. Other fortress towns guarded the frontiers of each feudal state. They were usually situated on rivers or set back behind forest marches, like Saint-Jean-de-Losne and Auxonne, strongholds on the old frontier between Burgundy and Champagne. Many of the peculiarities of the French urban network have their origins in frontiers which no longer exist; such an example is provided by the twin towns of Tarascon and Beaucaire on either side of the Rhône. Medieval towns established for strategic reasons have had varying fates. Site characteristics which were valuable under medieval conditions have not necessarily continued to be relevant to the needs of later periods; the steep-sided fortified site, for example, has not proved favourable to subsequent urban expansion.

Entirely new towns were created by the will of members of the nobility as a means of increasing their dependent populations and their incomes. For example, the lords of Beaujeu built Villebranche-sur-Saône, Saint Louis created Aigues-Mortes in 1246, and Alphonse de Poitiers founded Villefranche-de-Rouergue in 1256. Montferrand and Barcelonnette originated in the same way. Medieval new towns were particularly concentrated between the Pyrenees and the Central massif, reflecting the rivalry between the counts of Toulouse and the kings of France, and between the French and the English. Between 1250 and 1350 many *bastides* and *villeneuves* were created on either side of the frontier between the kingdom of France and the English in Aquitaine; among others were Mirande (1282), Villeneuve-sur-Lot (1264) and Revel (1280). Very few of these new foundations grew to any significance; exceptions included Carcassonne and Montauban (1144) and Libourne (1269).

Thus medieval France already had its own network of towns. The regional capitals had populations that were large for the time; in the thirteenth century Toulouse and Arras had between 30,000 and 40,000 inhabitants, and Paris undoubtedly had more than 100,000.

2.3 The sixteenth and seventeenth centuries

During this period of royal dominance, colonial expansion, wars and centralization, there was a rapid urban growth, encouraged by the surpluses exacted from the countryside and the colonies.

Among the many new towns of this period, some were created as fortresses. Sixteenth-century foundations were Rocroi, Villefranche-sur-Meuse (near Stenay) and Vitry-le-François (1545), the latter built to replace Vitry-en-Perthois, burned down by Charles V's troops. Henrichemont (Cher), founded by Sully in 1608 as a Protestant stronghold following the Edict of Nantes, was never finished. In the seventeenth century Vauban built many fortified towns: Huningue, Sarrelouis and Longwy in 1678, Montlouis in 1681, Montdauphin in 1692–3, and Neuf-Brisach in 1698.

Towns were also founded or reconstructed as royal or princely residences, including the 'new town' of Nancy (1587–8), Charleville (1608), Richelieu, built at the gates of the Cardinal's château (1635–40), and Versailles (1671).

A third category consists of towns founded for economic reasons. These were mostly ports like Le Havre (1517–43) and Colbert's creations: Rochefort in 1657, Brest, Lorient and Sète in 1666. Colbert, the forerunner of industrial decentralization, favoured the establishment of royal factories outside towns, a policy which if successful could have resulted in the creation of new industrial towns. Attempts were made with a cloth factory at Villeneuve (Hérault), and with a glassworks at La Glacerie near Cherbourg, but these towns did not develop.

An important phase in the urban development of France ended with the seventeenth century. The preceding centuries had established a relatively dense urban network, within which the newly founded towns occupied a privileged place. From this time onwards urban growth was to take place by the expansion of existing towns rather than by the addition of new ones. Rare exceptions to the rule are provided by the towns of Pontivy and La Roche-sur-Yon, built by Napoleon I.

Urban development in the eighteenth century was somewhat different from that of the previous century. It reflected a significant increase in the population, which brought about the expansion of many towns. Thanks to the removal of encircling walls, most large towns were able to expand easily.

2.4 The nineteenth and early twentieth centuries

From the middle of the nineteenth century, urban growth in France responded to the new stimulus provided by the development of heavy industry, new sources of energy and a new technology.

It might be expected that the nineteenth and early twentieth centuries, which experienced such great upheavals in economic activity and in the distribution of population, would have seen the foundation of many new towns. If the census is to be believed, this was true; many new names appeared on the list of urban places, but most of these were in fact communes which had been rural at the time of the preceding census, but which had been reclassified as urban communes because their population had risen above the ceiling of 2,000 inhabitants grouped in the central place. Many of the new urban communes were situated in the suburbs of large and expanding towns; of the 31 towns of more than 20,000 inhabitants which in 1851 were not yet urban communes, 28 were in the Paris agglomeration, and were really villages absorbed by the expansion of the city.

The concept of a new town must be reserved for an autonomous urban unit established on a site previously vacant or only occupied by a village. In the last two centuries, new towns of this type sprang up in the coal and iron-ore fields in association with pits or with iron and steel plants, surrounding and occasionally engulfing existing villages. The nineteenth century also saw the launching of numerous seaside resorts and spas, such as Aix-les-Bains, Trouville, Deauville and Vichy. Lourdes is something of a special case, as it already had a population of 4,000 at the time of the visions of Saint Bernadette. The railway town was another new element, growing up around marshalling yards (Tergnier, between Paris and Belgium, or La Roche-Migenne, half way between Paris and Dijon).

2.5 Developments since 1945

From 1945 onwards, demographic and economic growth gave rise to a new phase of urban development in France. Many new towns grew out of industrial or tertiary activities. In Lorraine, Saint Nicolas-en-Forêt was entirely dependent on the Sollac steel plant, and at Behren, a settlement of 2,700 dwellings, built to house 13,000 people, was added to the old village of only 500 inhabitants. In the same way a string of industrial towns has grown up around the Etang de Berre, with a combined population of nearly 100,000.

The tourist industry has been responsible for much new development; since 1950, numerous small settlements of an urban nature have grown up on the coasts or on sites suitable for winter sports. Earlier developments were attracted to places where tourism and leisure activities had already been developed. Until the publication of the *Plan Neige* (the government's plan for winter-sports development) no one could conceive of the establishment of a winter-sports resort in the middle of nowhere, however inconveniently situated the old villages were in relation to the ski slopes. The development of centres of this new type has been sporadic and uncoordinated, depending on the availability of private capital, but progress was nevertheless made. Courchevel and Tignes are particularly successful examples of completely new creations exclusively devoted to leisure activities, and Megève really falls into the same category, having had only 1,746 inhabitants in 1911.

Between 1960 and 1970, further towns sprang up in the wake of the great tourist developments in coastal and mountain areas. La Grande-Motte, Leucate-

Bacarès and le Grau-du-Roi were established on the Languedoc coast, and Flaine, Avoriaz, Corbier, Saint-Martin-de-Belleville and Isola 2000 in the Alps. In Savoie alone, the number of beds in winter-sports resorts rose from 42,000 at the end of 1964 to 165,000 at the end of 1977.

Side by side with these new developments, an official policy for the creation of new towns gradually evolved. The origins of the new policy may be seen in some of the larger *grands ensembles* (public housing projects) of the Paris region, such as Massy-Antony, Stains, Sarcelles and Vitry-sur-Seine. At their conception they were heralded as 'new towns and cities'. A new dimension was introduced in 1965 with the publication of the *Schéma Directeur*, the urban structure plan for the Paris region. This envisaged nine new towns with target populations of up to 700,000, disposed on two axes running tangentially to the existing Paris agglomeration. The targets for this new-town programme have been progressively reduced; only five new towns have been completed or are approaching completion.

Outside the Paris region, Villeneuve d'Ascq can perhaps be regarded as an urban link between Lille and Tourcoing, dressed up as a new town. Near Rouen, Le Vaudreuil was ambitiously conceived as an experimental town. The Lyon region received a new town at L'Isle-d'Abeau, near the airport of Satolas. Urban developments associated with the industrial complex of Fos–Etang de Berre also have some new-town characteristics.

By comparison with the officially supported new towns, the projects of private developers are usually on a more modest scale. Mostly they are commuter settlements on the urban fringe, often described as 'new villages', but some projects are of greater interest. The town planner Gaston Bardet carried out an interesting experiment in the neighbourhood of Rennes, involving the creation of satellite *villettes* (townlets) on the basis of rural communes such as Le Rheu. At the other end of the scale, Créteil is effectively a private-enterprise new town embedded in the Paris suburbs, the product of the will and determination of a prominent politician who was mayor of the commune. Créteil has benefited economically by being selected as the site of the Prefecture of Val-de-Marne (one of the new developments of the Paris region) and of a new university.

Recent decades have seen the growth of a hitherto unknown type of urban phenomenon, taking the form not of towns but of a loose, sprawling development on the urban fringe. The terms 'exurban', 'peri-urban' and 'rurban' have been applied to this development, which is clearly a response to new characteristics of French society and to the greater geographical mobility relating to the widespread use of the individual motor car. A first manifestation of change was the phenomenon of second homes. This secondary exurbanization, seasonal and temporary in character, took the form of the repossession either of abandoned agricultural buildings, such as farmhouses, barns or labourers' cottages, or of non-agricultural buildings in the countryside: manor houses, priests' houses or artisans' cottages. There is also new construction to meet the demand of the second-home market. At first, second-home development was limited to the fringes of large urban regions such as Paris, Lyon and Marseille, but now it has spread over nearly the whole of France, with the highest densities being found either near large urban centres or in regions which are highly attractive by reason of their natural beauty, climate or opportunities for leisure.

A second type of exurbanization affects rural communes within commuting range of urban centres of employment. Thanks to new means of transport, and to the rise in living standards which brings the motor car within reach, people who thirty years ago would have had to migrate to find work can continue to live in their native commune, enjoying a way of life which has elements of both rural and urban character.

A third type of exurbanization is provided by households which leave the town where the principal salary earner continues to be employed, in search of what are perceived as the advantages of rural living.

36

✤ Urban development since 1851

The growth of the urban population of France has already been described in chapter 9. While urban growth affected towns unequally at different periods, it scarcely affected the nature of the urban hierarchy. Figure 36.1 shows that at the beginning of the nineteenth century the size-distribution of French towns was already strongly marked by the primacy of Paris, which in relative terms has not increased since. The general stability of rank-size distribution over this long period is not, however, incompatible with significant changes in the relative positions of towns in the urban size-hierarchy.

1 Variations in urban development between 1851 and 1954

The urban growth that has characterized the years since the middle of the nineteenth century scarcely affected the smallest towns, the *bourgades* of fewer than 10,000 inhabitants. In 1954 the group of towns of 3,000–5,000 inhabitants had a total population that was within 160,000 of the 1851 figure.

Table 36.1 makes it possible to follow the variations in urban growth according to size-categories. One obvious characteristic is the scale of urban growth, the trebling within a century of towns of over 20,000 inhabitants, and the sizeable increase in towns of over 100,000 inhabitants. A second characteristic is the relative stability in the distribution of the urban population between the different size-categories: if the percentages calculated in relation to the French population as a whole emphasize urban growth, those calculated in relation to the total urban

Table 36.1 *Urbanized areas (unités urbaines), 1851–1975*

Urbanized areas by size-category	1851	1901	1954	1962	1968	1975
20,000–50,000						
Number	40 (75.4%)	87 (70.1%)	117 (67.2%)	127 (61.65%)	119 (55%)	117 (51%)
Population	1,234,562	2,531,586	3,586,265	3,955,081	3,775,432	3,625,883
Percentage of population in urbanized areas over 20,000	35.7	27.0	22.1	18.3	13.7	11.9
Percentage of French population	3.4	6.2	8.3	8.55	7.6	6.9
Percentage of French urban population	13.5	15.8	14.9	13.4	10.8	9.4
50,000–100,000						
Number	8 (15%)	22 (17.7%)	29 (16.6%)	38 (18.44%)	46 (21.4%)	53 (23%)
Population	557,941	1,484,889	1,932,448	2,451,532	3,193,283	3,547,732
Percentage of population in urbanized areas over 20,000	16.2	15.8	11.9	11.3	11.6	11.6
Percentage of French population	1.5	3.6	4.5	5.3	6.4	6.7
Percentage of French urban population	6.1	9.3	8.0	8.3	9.2	9.2
100,000–200,000						
Number	4 (7.5%)	10 (8%)	17 (9.7%)	24 (11.65%)	28 (13%)	32 (14%)
Population	603,639	1,217,922	2,220,882	3,066,018	4,044,209	4,434,068
Percentage of population in urbanized areas over 20,000	17.5	13.0	13.7	14.1	14.7	14.5
Percentage of French population	1.6	2.9	5.1	6.63	8.1	8.4
Percentage of French urban population	6.6	7.6	9.2	10.4	11.6	11.6
Over 200,000						
Number	0	4 (3.2%)	10 (5.7%)	16 (7.76%)	20 (9%)	25 (11%)
Population	0	1,417,594	3,593,563	5,717,680	8,289,887	10,316,655
Percentage of population in urbanized areas over 20,000	0	15.1	22.2	26.4	30.1	33.9
Percentage of French population	0	3.4	8.4	12.26	16.7	19.6
Percentage of French urban population	0	8.8	15.0	19.3	23.8	26.9
Paris agglomeration[a]						
Population	1,053,262	2,714,068	4,823,252	6,454,345	8,196,746	8,549,898
Percentage of population in urbanized areas over 20,000	30.5	28.9	29.8	29.9	29.8	28.0
Percentage of French population	2.9	6.6	11.2	13.95	16.5	16.24
Percentage of French urban population	11.5	17.0	20.1	21.8	23.5	22.3

	53 (100%)	124 (100%)	174 (100%)	206 (100%)	214 (100%)	228 (100%)
Urbanized areas over 20,000						
Number	53 (100%)	124 (100%)	174 (100%)	206 (100%)	214 (100%)	228 (100%)
Population	3,449,404	9,366,059	16,156,410	21,644,656	27,499,557	30,474,236
Percentage of French population	9.63	23.0	37.5	46.8	55.2	57.9
Percentage of French urban population	37.75	58.6	67.0	73.2	79.0	79.4
Urbanized areas below 20,000						
Number	1,030		1,387	2,333	1,305	1,413
Population	5,686,055	6,591,131	7,790,261	7,906,331	7,327,745	7,929,208
Percentage of French urban population	62.2	41.4	32.6	26.8	21.0	20.6

[a] Agglomeration in the restricted sense, as defined by INSEE.
Source: INSEE.

population reveal smaller variations. Exceptions to this rule are provided by the largest towns, those with more than 200,000 inhabitants, including the Paris agglomeration, and towns of fewer than 20,000 inhabitants. This dual nature of urban change can be illustrated by reference to Paris. In absolute terms there was a substantial increase in the population of the city of Paris, from 1.2 million in 1851 to 4.1 million in 1931, but the share of Paris in the urban population of France remained relatively stable. The population of the former Departments of Seine and Seine-et-Oise (approximating to the Paris region) was 21 per cent of the urban population of France in 1872 and 26 per cent in 1962.

Obviously, the rate of urban growth did not remain constant in the century since 1851, being most striking in the period of industrialization. From 1901 onwards urban growth was both weaker and more restricted spatially, with industrial towns and towns of the Paris suburbs standing out most strongly. There were also marked contrasts between towns. Some, such as Toulouse,

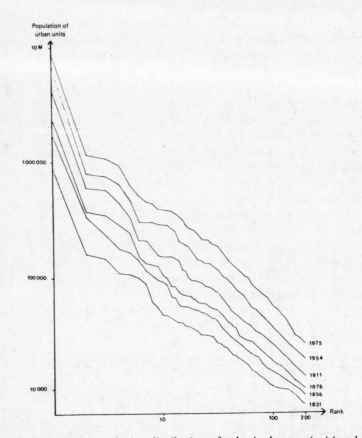

Figure 36.1 Changes in rank-size distribution of urbanized areas (*unités urbaines*), 1831–1975.

Bordeaux, Lille and Rennes, experienced strong and uninterrupted growth after 1851. Other towns grew less regularly; some, mainly industrial towns, even slipped back for a time, before renewing their advance.

Another category consisted of towns which were in the forefront of urban growth until the beginning of the twentieth century, then stagnated until just after the Second World War. Included in this group are the textile towns of the north (Roubaix), of Alsace (Mulhouse) and of the Paris basin (Saint-Quentin, Reims and Troyes).

A final group consists of stagnant or declining towns, sleepy little towns still untouched by industrialization on the eve of the Second World War: examples are Blois, Laval, Lunéville and Rochefort.

2 Changes in the urban system

This growth of towns had important repercussions on the urban network and on the size-distribution of towns in France (Fig. 36.2). In 1851 the pattern was still very loose, based on only 58 towns of more than 20,000 inhabitants. Urban life essentially depended on relatively small towns of fewer than 50,000 inhabitants (24 between 20,000 and 30,000 and 17 between 30,000 and 50,000). There were only 6 towns of more than 100,000 inhabitants, spaced very far apart. They were also unevenly distributed; large towns were absent from whole regions such as Normandy, Maine, Brittany, the southeast and east of the Paris basin, southwest France and the Alps. The urbanized regions (other than Paris) were the Nord region north of the Somme, Languedoc, the lower Rhône, the Loire valley from Orléans to Nantes, and the Lyon–Saint-Etienne region.

A comparison of the maps of 1851 and 1881 shows clearly the extent of the urban revolution experienced by France within the space of thirty years. The number of towns of 20,000 inhabitants and above rose to 96 by the creation of 40 new ones. The broad outline of the 1954 urban system was already laid down by this stage, although the pattern of the distribution of towns had some curious features. North of a line from Besançon to Nantes – as well as east of the Rhône–Saône axis – the predominant pattern was made up of large towns of more than 50,000 inhabitants; towns of between 20,000 and 30,000 inhabitants were very rare, apart from those of the Nord region, which was expanding rapidly as a coal and iron and steel region.

In northeast France in particular, towns of more than 50,000 inhabitants appeared to be isolated within their own regions, not linked to other towns in a regular urban system. The towns of the Loire valley, with Le Mans and Rennes, formed a network, unique in France, of towns of 50,000 inhabitants with a maximum distance of 150 km between them. South of the line Besançon–Nantes, on the contrary, there appear to have been many more small towns irregularly spaced between the major poles provided by the towns of over 100,000 inhabitants and the seven towns of between 50,000 and 100,000

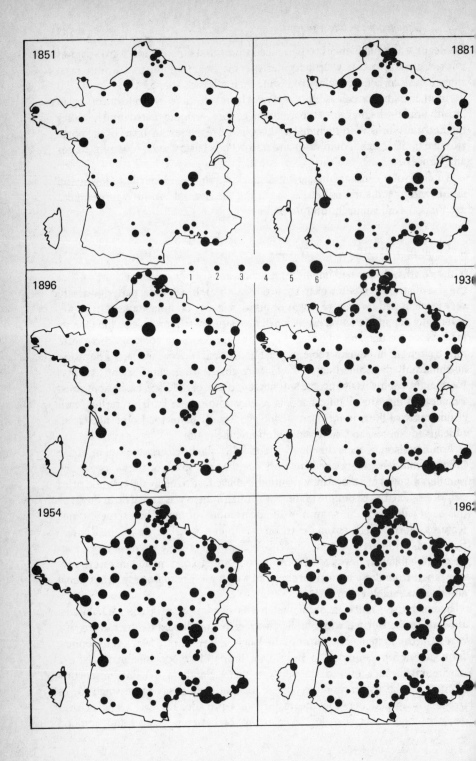

1851   1881

1 2 3 4 5 6

1896   1936

1954   1962

inhabitants. Small towns were particularly numerous in Languedoc and in the triangle formed by Châteauroux, Chalon-sur-Saône and Valence.

Fifteen years later, in 1896, the urban system had scarcely changed; the 106 towns of 1881 had increased to 111 in 1896, and only 7 passed the 20,000 mark for the first time. Changes during these 15 years were related to urban growth rather than to the recruitment of new towns into the system, in particular by the increase in the number of towns in the 30,000–50,000 category, which rose from 18 to 30. This change is clearly visible on the map, although the contrast to either side of the Nantes–Besançon line noted in 1881 is still apparent. The distribution of the largest towns was still mainly peripheral; five were ports and three others situated on land or river frontiers. The only large inland towns were Reims, Nancy, Lyon, Saint-Etienne and Toulouse.

The urban network was scarcely modified in the thirty years to 1926, the number of towns over 20,000 inhabitants increasing only from 111 to 128. Most of the newcomers were rising industrial centres, but a few reached the required population in consequence of a long continuance of slow urban growth (Auxerre, Bourg-en-Bresse, Dole and Annemasse).

In 1954 the urban network still showed no striking transformations. In the 28 years since 1926, only two important changes had emerged. One was the appearance of a considerable number of small towns of 20,000–30,000 inhabitants; in particular they were to be found filling in the space between Paris and the nearest towns of 100,000 inhabitants. Secondly, there was an increase in the number of towns of more than 100,000 inhabitants, from 19 to 27. To towns of this category, which are the backbone of the urban system of France, were added Limoges, Dijon, Metz, Brest, Rennes, Le Mans, Angers and Tours.

This analysis confirms the early origin of the urban system of France. In the course of time the population contained in the system has increased, and it has been augmented by the addition of small and medium-sized towns, but the overall pattern was already in place by the end of the nineteenth century.

3 The nature of urban growth since 1954

Urban growth after the Second World War was vastly different in scale from what had gone before, with annual increases of 1–2 per cent, and it was much more varied in nature. The very great disparities in urban growth which now appeared related in part to the size of the agglomerations concerned, in part to the regions in which they were situated, and in part reflected their economic activities. However, the nature and intensity of these contrasts have varied over the past thirty years.

Figure 36.2 The French urban system, 1851–1962. Town sizes: 1. 20,000–30,000 2. 30,000–50,000 3. 50,000–100,000 4. 100,000–200,000 5. 200,000–500,000 6. Above 500,000.

3.1 Size and urban growth

Recent urban growth has differentially affected towns according to their size. By the increased concentration of the urban population in units of more than 50,000 inhabitants it has modified the form of the urban hierarchy (Table 36.1). Between 1954 and 1968 urban growth was particularly strong (1.9 per cent per year between 1954 and 1962, and 1.8 per cent between 1962 and 1968). Up to a threshold of 200,000 inhabitants, the larger the size-category of town involved, the greater the growth rate (0.9 per cent for towns of 2,000–5,000 inhabitants, ranging upwards to 2.5 per cent for those of between 100,000 and 200,000 inhabitants). The reason for this was mainly that net migration gain increased as the size of town increased, and was augmented by a parallel if very slight upward movement in rates of natural variation. In absolute terms these large agglomerations absorbed a very large share of urban growth: nearly a quarter of new urbanites in the period 1954–62 came to the Paris agglomeration alone.

In comparison with the 1954–62 period, 1962–8 showed a very marked tendency towards the lessening of the disparities between categories of towns so far as migration gain and growth rates were concerned.

The continuation of these trends in 1968–75 led to the appearance of new aspects of urban growth. The reduction in the average rate of urban growth to not more than 1.1 per cent per year (10.1 per cent for the intercensal period) was the result of a general decline in net migration gains (the only exceptions were the smaller towns of between 2,000 and 5,000 inhabitants, where, however, the gains were largely offset by a weakening in their rates of natural increase). The overall decline in migratory gain was mainly related to the end of the massive rural exodus of the postwar years. This tendency had already been perceptible in the preceding period, but was then masked by an influx of people repatriated from Algeria. In the 1968–75 period, the different levels of the hierarchy developed in a much more uniform manner than formerly, with annual growth rates in the range 1.1–1.6 per cent. The exception was the Paris agglomeration, where growth fell sharply to 0.5 per cent annually, the equivalent of only 9 per cent of total urban growth. This new pattern of growth was also shown by a marked slowing down of the process of concentration of urban population in units of more than 50,000 people.

In the period 1975–82 urban growth slowed down. Just under 1.5 million people were added to the urban population, equivalent to an intercensal growth rate of 3.8 per cent, similar to that for France as a whole (3.3 per cent). The dominant features of this period were a marked urban deconcentration and a transfer of urban growth into a deep urban–rural fringe, reflecting the increasing degree of individual motorization.

These population changes have given rise to two errors of interpretation. The first is that towns are believed to be declining, whereas it is merely a question of a decrease in the population of the overcrowded core communes of urbanized areas. The second is the belief that there has been a demographic revival of rural areas, whereas the apparent population growth is merely a factor of the peripheral expansion of urban centres.

3.2 Migration and urban growth

Migratory movements had their greatest impact on the intensity of urban growth and on the amplitude of disparities between size-categories of towns during the period 1954–75. Until 1968, migration contributed more than half of intercensal urban growth; for agglomerations of more than 50,000 inhabitants the contribution was 60 per cent in 1954–62, 54 per cent in 1962, but only 32 per cent in 1968–75. The variations in net migratory gain from one agglomeration to another were always much greater than natural variations. These movements also resulted in a very considerable changeover in population; in the average agglomeration, 40 per cent of the 1954 population had either left or moved by 1975.

The impact of this migratory changeover on population composition affected towns very unequally according to their size, the proportion of inhabitants involved in migratory movements tending to decrease as the size of the agglomeration increased. After an interval of six to eight years, immigrants in an agglomeration of fewer than 10,000 inhabitants would on average correspond to more than 20 per cent of the final population, whereas in agglomerations of over 200,000 the proportion would be not much more than 10 per cent. This would seem to contradict the popular image of the small town as having a stable, inward-looking society. It would seem that large agglomerations have a greater capacity for retaining their inhabitants. Evidence for this is provided by their relatively low emigration rates in the period under discussion, which may be explained by their ability to offer employment opportunities matching a very wide range of demands.

Migration from rural areas was the prime component of the growth of large agglomerations until the 1960s, since which time it has tended to decline, irrespective of the size-category of the urban destination. This development corresponds not only to a decline in the rural exodus, through exhaustion of the reserves of population available to move, but also to a progressive increase in the number of people leaving the larger towns to reside in rural communes. A specific characteristic of the larger agglomerations has been the tendency for migration to take place over ever greater distances: between 1954 and 1962, nearly 50 per cent on average of the immigrants in each large agglomeration came from the department in which it was situated; between 1962 and 1968, the proportion was little more than 40 per cent, and between 1968 and 1978 fell to only 30 per cent.

The importance of migratory flows in urban growth is not measured only in quantitative terms, or in relation to the degree of turnover of the population. A study of the composition of migrant flows according to age, activity rates, occupations or socio-economic categories reveals great variations, according to the agglomeration of destination. This qualitative impact made by migration upon the character of urban population is doubtless as important for the future of towns as the quantitative contribution.

The analysis of the composition of migration flows throws light on the declining growth rate of the Paris agglomeration. This has been much more marked than in other agglomerations of 20,000 population and above. In 1954–62, the Paris agglomeration grew by 1.9 per cent annually, as against 2.1 per cent for the other towns of 20,000 and above. In 1962–5 the figure was reduced to 1.3 per cent (as against 2 per cent), and in 1968–75 to 0.5 per cent (as against 1.3 per cent). The marked slowing down of growth reflects the decline in the net migratory balance (1.16 per cent in 1954–62, 0.5 per cent in 1962–8, and −0.26 per cent in 1968–75). The fall was mainly due to an increase in the rate of emigration, from 5 per cent in 1954–62 to 11 per cent in 1968–75. This explains why the net migration balance became negative although the rate of immigration remained relatively stable.

3.3 Regional aspects of urban change

Between 1954 and 1975, towns in the same region tended to exhibit similar growth characteristics (Fig. 36.3). Since these postwar regional growth rates have been independent of the previous level of urbanization, they have sometimes operated so as to produce a better balance of urban development between regions, but have partly accentuated regional disparities. The towns of the Nord region, the Central massif and southwest France lost ground relatively. In contrast, there was very rapid growth in the towns of already highly urbanized southern France as well as in two regions which at the beginning of the 1950s had still been essentially rural: western France (especially Brittany) and the southern fringe of the Paris basin.

Fluctuations in the intercensal growth rates of towns are closely related to their net migration figures. On the whole, these showed a marked decline in northern and eastern France, whereas towns in southern France continued to have a strong attraction.

3.4 Urban functions and urban change

The growth of a town is primarily linked to the growth of its working population, which in turn relates to the increase of employment opportunities. Until the 1950s this growth of the active urban population mainly reflected developments in the manufacturing sector. Towns grew in so far as they were able to attract new and successful industries. More recently, the 'tertiary revolution' has taken over from the 'industrial revolution' as the main motor of urban growth. Between

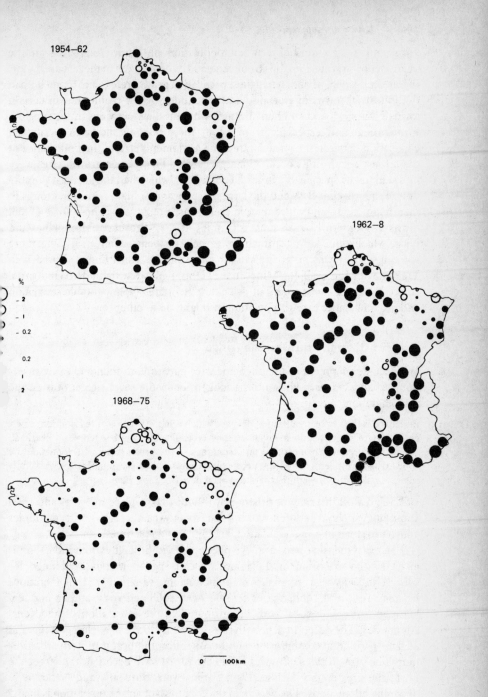

1954—62

1962—8

1968—75

%
— 2
— 1
— 0.2

0.2
1
2

0   100 km

Figure 36.3 Percentage net migration balance of agglomerations. Source: INSEE.

1954 and 1962, the active urban population of France employed in the manufacturing sector rose by 16 per cent, and by 20 per cent in the tertiary sector. In this transitional period, the highest population growth rates were found both in the industrial towns of Lorraine and the Rhône–Alpes region and in certain towns of western and southern France, where tertiary activities predominated. From 1962, and especially from 1968, there was an increasingly marked correlation between the growth rate of an agglomeration and the importance of the tertiary sector in its occupational structure. The highest growth rates were found in towns specializing in tertiary activities, which had the smallest proportion of the working class and the largest proportion of higher-income groups in their populations, and which were in every sense prosperous. These are above all towns in southern France, such as Cannes, Aix-en-Provence, Montpellier and Nice, which offer strong attractions to new residents. Conversely, the more working-class towns such as Lens or Douai in the Nord region, Forbach in Lorraine or Montceau-les-Mines in the Central massif, with outdated industrial structures and a low standard of living, are in a state of demographic stagnation and are on balance losing population by migration to other towns.

3.5 Growth in the rural–urban fringe

With the development of the phenomena of peri-urbanization and exurbanization, urban expansion is also to be looked for in the rural fringe, outside the agglomeration.

Perhaps it is the whole organization of space which is in the process of redefinition, a new geography of social relations which is being created ... In the last ten years nearly all demographic growth has centred on communes of the urban fringe, often outside the zones that have been created for urban planning and thus escaping from the skilfully perfected planning procedures that have been developed for them.[1]

The greatest intensity of urban growth today takes place in *bourgs* and rural communes situated between 5 and 15 km from towns, that is to say in communes which are small in area, population, amenities and resources.

The exact measurement of these phenomena is difficult. A first indication is given by the extension of the boundaries of agglomerations as defined for successive censuses: 40 per cent of population variation in agglomerations between 1962 and 1968, 23 per cent between 1968 and 1975, and 42 per cent between 1975 and 1982 is to be attributed to the integration of additional communes. The differential growth rate of the core towns of agglomerations and of their peripheral communes is another significant indicator of peri-urbanization. The growth rates of most of the core towns have declined; the larger the town, the greater the decline. Even Paris, Lyon, Bordeaux and Nancy have declining populations. The growth of the core town of an agglomeration is nearly always markedly lower than that of the peripheral communes (Table 36.2).

[1] J. Mayoux, *Demain l'espace, l'habitat individuel périurbain* (Documentation Française, Paris, 1979).

Table 36.2 *Average annual percentage change in the*
populations of urban cores and fringes, by size of
agglomeration, 1968–75

Size of agglomeration	Urban core	Urban fringe
Paris	−1.69	1.46
Above 500,000 inhabitants	−0.74	2.99
200,000–500,000	0.46	2.20
100,000–200,000	1.12	2.36
50,000–100,000	1.06	2.74
20,000–50,000	1.00	2.21
10,000–20,000	1.48	1.02

Source: M. Goze and B. Leymarie, *Revue d'Economie Régionale et Urbaine,*
1977, p. 65.

In addition to the peripheral communes contained within the agglomeration as
statistically defined, rural communes fringing agglomerations are showing ever
greater increases in population. Whereas between 1954 and 1975 the 24,000
rural communes outside the zones of industrial and urban population (*zones de
peuplement industriel et urbain* – ZPIU) sustained an annual loss of on average 0.8
per cent of their population, rural communes contained within the ZPIUs
increased their populations by 0.3 per cent annually between 1954 and 1962, 0.6
per cent between 1962 and 1968, 1.3 per cent between 1968 and 1975 and 1.9
per cent between 1975 and 1982.

The extension of the residential function of rural communes, particularly near
areas of employment, was made easier by the increase in private means of
transport and by the extension of public transport networks. But above all it was
stimulated by the speculative increase in the cost of building land in urban areas
and by the increasingly felt need to escape from the excesses of urbanization and
to find a way of life close to nature.

It is not easy to estimate the number of people living in rural areas and working
in urban communes. At each census the transfer to urban agglomerations of a
great many communes with fewer than 2,000 inhabitants has led to a continual
shrinking of rural space, removing from the rural category precisely those
communes which have acquired a residential function. Yet in spite of this
statistical annexation, the percentage of people living in the country and working
in towns has continued to increase (Table 36.3). This phenomenon is mainly
concentrated in certain frontier and industrial regions, in the outer departments
of the Paris (Ile-de-France) region, and in a few other departments which
contain a major regional capital.

There is insufficient information to give a precise picture of the social
categories involved in this move to rural-fringe residence. But statistical cross-
checks and monographs on rural-fringe communities show that the two groups
which have grown most strongly since 1962 were situated at the two extremes of
the social scale. High-income groups (the professions and senior executives)

Table 36.3 *Changes in the economically active population resident in rural areas*[a]

	1962		1968		1975	
	Total	%	Total	%	Total	%
Resident active population	7,003,530	100.0	5,954,692	100.0	5,291,340	100.0
Active population recorded at place of work	6,184,993	88.3	5,127,800	86.1	4,216,620	79.7
Rural residents employed outside rural areas	818,537	11.7	826,892	13.9	1,074,720	20.3

[a] As defined at the date of census concerned.
Source: INSEE.

have more than doubled in percentage despite the shrinkage of rural space, attracted by the natural environment and by the 'village way of life'. They have been joined by less affluent groups such as unskilled workers, clerks and workers in service trades, driven out of the towns by the cost of property and by the operation of official housing policy. Some observers have even spoken of a 'proletarianization of the rural space', these industrial workers being resident in rural areas because it is the only place where they can afford to live.

There is a parallel migration of persons of retirement age. Since 1962 there has been a continuous increase in the number of retired people and those over 65 residing in rural communes, despite the losses in the numbers of residential communes through statistical transfer to the agglomerations at successive censuses. The traditional phenomenon of generations of former rural people returning to their native villages after spending their working life in the towns can still be observed. Its main impact has been on the regions strongly affected by rural–urban migration after 1945, such as the Central massif, Morvan, Nivernais and Limousin. It continues to swell the ageing population in many rural departments which are otherwise not numbered among the most attractive to migrants. Increasingly, however, this retirement movement is being joined by people who have always been town dwellers but who buy or build a retirement home in a rural commune.

4 Planning policies for the urban system

Official attempts to modify the pattern of urban distribution in France have not been limited to the creation of new towns; from the 1960s onwards there were policies designed to modify the urban system and the urban hierarchy. The first studies of the urban system were undertaken on the initiative of the Plan Commission (Commissariat au Plan) in 1963–4.

The first significant result on a national scale was the 1963 policy of 'counterbalancing regional metropolises' (*métropoles régionales d'équilibre*). Its aim was to encourage the emergence in provincial France of a small number of large agglomerations whose attractiveness would be increased by investment in additional social equipment and where appropriate functions would be concentrated. The aim was to provide a more balanced distribution over the country as a whole of the urban development which hitherto had been too exclusively centred on Paris. Policies for the decentralization from Paris of manufacturing and tertiary activities and proposals to curb the growth of the Paris region were a necessary complement to the attempts to develop the *métropoles d'équilibre*.

Following research into the French urban hierarchy, eight *métropoles d'équilibre* were selected; the aim from the start was to build up the gravitational pull of a substantial mass of population and activities. The metropolises selected were Lille–Roubaix–Tourcoing, Nancy–Metz–Thionville, Nantes–Saint-Nazaire, Bordeaux, Toulouse, Marseille–Aix-en-Provence and Lyon–Saint-Etienne–Grenoble. Strasbourg also appeared on the list, with special reference to its European role, and later Dijon was granted the same status; this decision was political in origin, but the town in fact usefully filled a major gap in the system. Other gaps nevertheless continue to exist in the whole of the centre of France. The fact that certain *métropoles* involved the association of towns that could be anything up to 80 km apart gave rise to great problems of co-ordination.

The special policy for medium-sized towns dates from 1973. It was implemented by means of 'planning contracts' between the central government and individual towns, which had economic, social and town-planning objectives. The effects of these contracts may have been to strengthen the towns concerned in relation to their regions and spheres of influence, but they did not add up to a policy for urbanization on a national scale.

Nevertheless, as the major problem was caused by the sheer size of the Paris region, it is clear that the primary policies affecting the urban structure of France were those for industrial and tertiary decentralization (see chapters 25 and 27).

In 1962, 29 per cent of the urban population of France lived in the Paris region, a figure never before attained; by 1982 it had fallen to 21.8 per cent. Does this reduction indicate the success of government policies? At best it is only a partial explanation; it is impossible to say whether the Paris region would have continued to expand had these policies not existed. It is true to say that the decline in the population of the Paris region was contrary to the predictions of the experts, who had anticipated a population increase. In any event, the percentage points gained can have had little impact on the enormous influence of Paris in the urban system of France.

5 Types of towns and urban agglomerations

This unevenly distributed urban development with its spatially varying growth rates, further complicated by the impact of spatial planning, is imposed upon a network of communes characterized by its intricacy and high density. In 1982,

4,888 communes, 13.4 per cent of the French total, were classified as urban. These communes are unevenly distributed. There is also a range of possible relationships between the framework offered by the communal structure and the nature of the urbanization imposed upon it.

5.1 Single-commune towns

Before the recent wave of urban expansion, town and commune were identical: the boundary of the commune marked the limits of the town. There are still many examples today of towns contained within the territory of a single commune: in all, 952 in 1982. To this group could be added communes where the principal concentration of population does not reach the minimum 2,000 population necessary to be classified as urban but where this concentration is effectively of urban nature, whether in appearance or function.

5.2 Urban agglomerations with a single core town

Because of the fine mesh of the network of communes in France (chapter 13, 1), urban expansion rapidly spilled over the communal boundary surrounding the town into the territory of neighbouring communes. These were thus drawn into a single area of continuous urban development, thereby constituting an agglomeration. Such urban expansion does not even stop at national boundaries: in 1968, INSEE (the French national statistical office) listed 20 'international agglomerations' where the core town was either situated in France (Valenciennes, Lille) or in a foreign country (Geneva, Basle).

The concept of an agglomeration is very easy to describe but very difficult to define precisely. Since 1954, the agglomeration definition has changed, as at each census INSEE has used more and more refined methods. Multiple criteria are employed in the definition, including the size, density and growth rate of population, the proportion of the active population still engaged in agriculture, and the physical continuity of the built-up area.

These criteria have the disadvantage of being static in nature; they do not make clear the functional linkages which might justify the inclusion of a commune in a particular agglomeration. The criteria indicate adequately enough whether a commune can be regarded as urban or not, but the system breaks down in heavily urbanized regions, such as the Nord coalfield, where the agglomerations run together and there is uncertainty over the core town to which a particular commune may belong.

5.3 Conurbations

As has been seen, the statistical method of defining the agglomeration as a group of urbanized communes round a central pole does not adequately cover all possible conditions. If there are several core towns in a contiguous extent of urbanized communes, it is preferable to use the concept of 'conurbation'. For example, the Lille conurbation includes the two agglomerations of Lille and Roubaix–Tourcoing. The agglomerations of Biarritz, Bayonne and Le Boucau also form a conurbation.

5.4 Urbanized tracts with multiple nuclei

Industrial regions, especially coalfields, are characterized by a widespread urbanization emanating from numerous separate points, such as mines, factories and their service infrastructures. Villages, small towns and above all extensive areas of rural land have been incorporated into this urban development without any particular centre rising to dominance. Pre-existing urban nuclei have most often been enveloped by mining villages and workers' settlements, without any adjustment of their functions or social provision to the new environment surrounding them. The tract of urbanized communes is neither organized into a hierarchy nor functionally linked to an urban pole.

5.5 Chains of towns in rural areas

The long history of urban development in France and the succession of contrasting influences which have determined that development have frequently resulted in the juxtaposition of several towns which are quite close to each other but which do not form a true agglomeration or conurbation. There are many examples: La Fère, Tergnier and Chauny in the Oise valley are spread out over a distance of 15 km, with between them more inhabitants than a town such as Laon or Soissons. At a higher level, the same applies to Creil, Senlis and Chantilly north of Paris, to Saint-Raphael and Fréjus on the Mediterranean coast, and to Moirans and Voreppe (near Grenoble). This type is often found where twin towns are situated on either side of a river, for example Beaucaire and Tarascon on the Rhône, or where towns are situated on a bay of the sea or on an estuary.

5.6 The urbanized region

In the final stage, urban development may extend over an entire region, any agricultural use being reduced to occasional enclaves which are yet to be filled with houses, factories or means of communication. In such regions the texture of urban development may be very variable, depending on the size of the towns involved and the nature of the process of urbanization that has been involved. Urban development of this type is rare in France, where great metropolitan regions are relatively few, but examples are provided by the Paris region, the Nord region and the coast of the Côte d'Azur.

37

❧ Urban functions
___

1 Change and composition of the economically active urban population

1.1 Composition of the economically active population

Table 37.1 provides an overall view of the occupational structure of the working population of France in 1975. There are appreciable differences between the occupational structures of agglomerations of 50,000 inhabitants and above (and even more of the Paris agglomeration) and France as a whole. Well over half of the employed population in these larger agglomerations are in the tertiary sector. Paris is at the head, alone accounting for 27 per cent of tertiary employment in France.

1.2 Activity profiles of towns

It is possible to distinguish three types of agglomeration. A first type specializes in one or more activities, markedly over-represented in relation to the average for all French towns, to the point that they may be regarded as constituting a distinctive urban function. The remaining towns, with more diverse activities, may be divided into two fairly distinct groups according to whether their main orientation is towards a production or a service function.

Table 37.1 *Active population by economic category, 1975*

Economic category	Percentage of economically active population		
	France	Paris agglomeration	Towns 50,000 and above
Primary sector	10.1	0.1	0.2
Secondary sector	38.5	35.0	39.9
Extractive industries	1.4	1.2	1.4
Building and construction	9.1	7.7	9.2
Metal products, machinery, electrical equipment	13.4	14.6	15.6
Chemicals	4.2	3.6	3.9
Food and drink	2.9	1.7	2.2
Textiles, clothing	3.3	1.8	4.0
Miscellaneous manufacturing	4.2	4.4	3.6
Tertiary sector	51.4	64.4	58.0
Transport	4.2	5.6	4.7
Business, banking, insurance	13.9	17.8	19.8
Administration and services	33.3	41.0	33.5

Source: INSEE, census.

1.2.1 Agglomerations with highly specific functions

Among the largest French agglomerations, about thirty stand out clearly from all the others by the extreme nature of their specialization (Fig. 37.1). They have one or at most two industrial activities, showing a very high degree of localization. Towns specializing in the extractive industries are thus located in the coalfields of the Nord or the Pas-de-Calais (Lens, Douai, Bruay-en-Artois), Lorraine (Forbach), or the eastern edge of the Central massif (Montceau-les-Mines, La Grand-Combe). Frequently associated with the extractive industry is a marked specialization in chemicals (Alès in the Central massif, Béthune and Denain in the Nord region), or in the smelting and working of metals (Saint-Etienne in the Central massif, Valenciennes in the Nord and Mulhouse in eastern France).

The smelting and working of metals are responsible for a high degree of specialization in eastern France, at Longwy and Thionville in Lorraine, Montbéliard at the northern end of the Jura, and Le Creusot in the Central massif. Towns with a high degree of specialization in textiles are mainly in northern France (Armentières, Calais, Cambrai, Lille, Saint-Quentin), but there are two in the Lyon area (Roanne, Villefranche-sur-Saône) and two isolated centres (Castres in southwest France and Troyes in Champagne). The chemical industry gives rise to less intense specialization in agglomerations that are not quite so completely dominated by industry, having less than 50 per cent of their population employed in manufacturing as compared with about 60 per cent in the very specialized agglomerations: examples are Compiègne north of Paris, Montargis south of Paris, and Clermont-Ferrand.

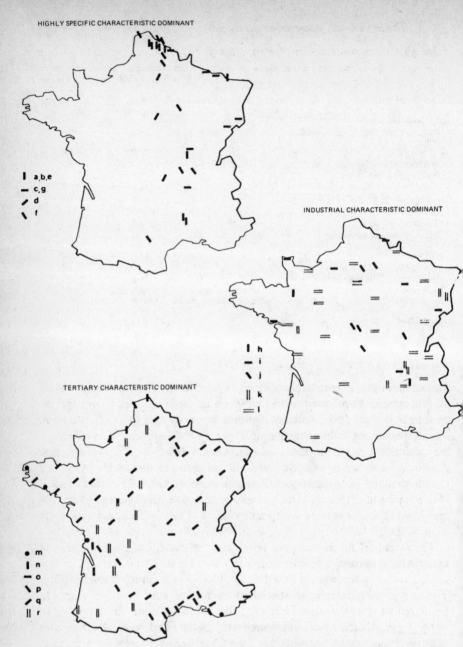

Figure 37.1 Functional distinctiveness of agglomerations, 1968. a, b, e: extractive industries; c, g: processing of metals; d: chemicals; f: textiles; h: miscellaneous industries; i: processing of metals; j: chemicals, processing of metals; k: textiles and miscellaneous industries; l: weak development of metal processing; m: defence; n: transport; o: hotel trade; p: personal services; q: food and drink industries, transport; r: administration. Source: D. Pumain and T. Saint Julien, *Les Dimensions du changement urbain* (Centre National de la Recherche Scientifique, Paris, 1978).

A high degree of specialization in mining or manufacturing does not necessarily have an adverse effect on the remaining urban activities. Only single-industry towns with perhaps 60 per cent of their active population employed in these branches are markedly deficient in most tertiary activities. Agglomerations which are so highly dominated by industry as these tend to have a very restricted role in the provision of goods and services to their surrounding regions. The low disposable incomes in such agglomerations, derived almost exclusively from the wages of the working class, are often reflected in a marked local underprovision of services. The originality of this group of agglomerations lies more in the existence of a very high degree of specialization than in the precise nature of that specialization; in such cases, evolution towards possession of a full range of urban characteristics is generally retarded. On the other hand, agglomerations specializing in the chemical or textile industries, or even a few large towns specializing in the extractive and metal industries, such as Saint-Etienne, Valenciennes and Mulhouse, are not marked by such deficiencies in the tertiary sector.

Fishing ports also come into the category of highly specialized towns, but this time there is no question of one activity dominating all others. Fishing as an activity is everywhere in decline: it occupies only between 2 and 5 per cent of the total work force of ports such as Lorient, Sète, Boulogne or Douarnenez, but it still gives a certain individual character to these agglomerations.

Specialization of comparable intensity is only seen nowadays in small urban units of between 2,000 and 10,000 inhabitants which are expanding rapidly. The localized resource most usually exploited today is suitability for tourist development, usually on the coast (La Grande Motte) but sometimes in ski resorts. Sometimes the concentration of a certain type of activity in one place is deliberately planned, so as to improve the effectiveness of developments where a multiplicity of contacts is of prime importance. This is seen in the establishment of the 'science city' near Valbonne, in the hinterland of Nice (chapter 27, 3.1.1).

1.2.2 Agglomerations with predominantly industrial function

Despite the existence of 30 large agglomerations with a high degree of specialization, France is surprisingly deficient in the number and size of industrial towns. The industrial revolution had only a local and partial impact on French towns; there was a scanty development of great industrial cities on the scale of Manchester or Birmingham in England or Düsseldorf in Germany. Those that exist in France are highly concentrated in regions of the north and east (Fig. 37.1).

In only about 15 of the 40 agglomerations that can be classified as industrial is industry occupationally predominant, engaging more than half of the working population. They are characterized by three types of industrial specialization: varied industries (Romans, Fougères), metal industries (Saint-Nazaire, Saint-Dizier) and metals with chemicals (Bourges). It is not possible to describe the remaining 25 agglomerations in this group as being industry-dominated, as their employment structure does not depart from the national average to a very significant extent. In all of them, however, the proportion of industrial workers is rather higher than the urban average of 45 per cent. Some owe this characteristic to textiles and assorted industries (Lyon), but in most of them a branch of metal processing predominates (Alençon, Caen, Grenoble).

These two levels of intensity in industrial activity are, moreover, clearly revealed in the social structure of these towns. The great majority are classed as essentially working-class towns, but in those of the first, more highly specialized group, the working-class characteristic is dominant (unskilled workers at Romans, Fougères and Elbeuf, skilled workers at Saint-Nazaire and Cherbourg), whereas the industrial towns in the second group are for the most part characterized by a large proportion of workers in the supervisory and white-collar grades (Beauvais, Nevers and Le Mans).

1.2.3 Agglomerations with predominantly tertiary functions

Tertiary functions are predominant in most provincial towns in France. This is not surprising, since typical urban central-place functions such as commerce, public and private services, administration and transport fall within this sector. As compared with industrial towns, towns where tertiary activities predominate are much more widely dispersed over the whole of France (Fig. 37.1) and do not normally reach a very high degree of specialization. The most extreme examples of specialization are provided by two types of activity which result in relatively unique functional characteristics in the agglomerations in which they are concentrated. They are defence (Toulon, Brest and Rochefort) and transport (Le Havre, Dunkerque and Saintes). These towns are slightly more industrialized than the others in this category, which all have more than two-thirds of their working population in the tertiary sector.

Towns in this category are characterized by a complex of related tertiary activities, including also ubiquitous industries. They include the hotel trade, building and construction (Vichy, Cannes and Nice) and the transport and food industries (Marseille, Avignon, Cognac and Epernay). The most frequently occurring case combines over-representation of administration and of certain service activities with a proportion of industrial activity (notably in metal processing and textiles) well below the urban average; Auxerre is an example of this type. Nearly all these towns are seats of prefectures, and their essential role is the administration of the surrounding department. Most prefectures which are not the largest towns in their department belong to this type (Quimper, Arras, Aix-en-Provence).

With regard to social structure, agglomerations which specialize in transport, whether associated with other activities or not, resemble industrial towns, with a strong working-class element in their population: examples are Dunkerque, Sète and Dole. Otherwise, the social structure of towns dominated by tertiary activities is characterized by an under-representation of the working class. Such towns may be divided into two distinct groups: towns dominated by commerce and craft industries, particularly numerous in the southern part of France, and towns in which administrative occupations are more important: these are typically located in a central band running from the Pays de la Loire region to Burgundy, and in eastern France; examples are Poitiers, Auxerre, Chaumont and Metz.

On the whole, towns dominated by tertiary activities are more attractive residentially than industrial towns. They tend to have a positive migration balance as compared with other towns, and in consequence their growth rates are generally higher. Their average standard of living is most often superior to that of industrial towns, a reflection above all of the income levels of the element of the population that is not wage-earning. Some towns stand out not because of the characteristics of their working population but because of the size of their non-working population; these are the towns with large numbers of inhabitants relying on private incomes or who are retired. Not all are situated on the Côte d'Azur; Brive, for example, is favoured by retired railway people. It is indeed difficult to explain how some towns survive at all, since they appear to be lacking in industrial resources, with no commercial or service functions of any significance. They may perhaps be classified as 'landlord towns', living off property rents drained from their surrounding regions.

This study of functions underlines one of the urban characteristics of France; the presence, in the majority of regions, of towns with very varied occupational structures. The long history of urbanization, the juxtaposition of towns of different ages and the random impact of industrial development have led to a heterogeneity of regional urban structures.

2 Changes in urban functions since 1954

In the last thirty years, in spite of the rapidity of urban and economic growth, there has been a remarkable stability in the overall functional characteristics of French towns. This can be related to the geographical inertia of economic activities. Thus for any one town the main direction of the urban economy, whether towards manufacturing or service activities, is reflected in other urban characteristics such as the socio-economic composition of the population, the standard of living, the growth rate or residential attractiveness. The principal activity of a town was still as important in differentiating between agglomerations in 1975 as in 1954.

Recent urban growth, which brought about such drastic changes in the appearance and life of so many agglomerations, hardly changed their relative socio-economic ranking, for it affected all agglomerations at the same time and to the same extent. The main features in the transformation of activity structures were a process of tertiarization (the percentage of tertiary employment in urban areas rose from 55 per cent in 1954 to 59 per cent in 1975) and a process of substitution by which activities where employment was declining (textile and food industries, retailing) were replaced by growth sectors such as electronics and certain service industries. At the same time paid workers were replacing the self-employed, and semi-skilled or unskilled workers in manufacturing were increasing at the expense of the skilled employees in nearly all agglomerations.

2.1 The process of change

This general socio-economic transformation, the most significant change affecting French towns since the Second World War, has nevertheless not affected every agglomeration with the same intensity nor with the same speed. Differences in development have been reflected in two main processes of evolution in the functional structure of the French urban system.

The first has been a growing similarity of economic activity and of socio-economic structures, together with a diminution of income differentials; these changes have tended to lessen inequalities between agglomerations. Thus about thirty agglomerations, in which employment is dominated by one or two branches of industrial activity, have lessened the degree of their specialization and at the same time made good their deficiencies in the tertiary sector. The result is a relative weakening of their monolithic social structures. Most of the steel and mining towns of northern France and the eastern Central massif come into this category (Fig. 37.2). Conversely, about 30 agglomerations which initially were among those most completely dominated by the tertiary sector were able to make good their deficiencies in industry and to increase their share of secondary employment; among such towns are Poitiers and La Roche-sur-Yon. Elsewhere, towns with an average socio-economic structure, such as Alençon, Caen, Bourg-en-Bresse, have been able to acquire a modest industrial specialization. This industrial expansion has been reflected in an increase of population growth rates radiating concentrically from the Paris region (Fig. 37.2), and is the only change to have affected such a large number of towns. It mainly corresponded to a process of geographical diffusion of expanding activities, which took place in relation to a dispersion of growth away from the Paris region.

Conversely, a second process tended to widen the gap between the two types of agglomerations. The first type consisted of towns such as Lyon, Annecy or Dunkerque, where new forms of industrial development predominate, where service activities are well represented, and where the average wage level is high; these towns also have a positive migratory balance with regard to other towns. By contrast, towns such as Périgueux, Perpignan, Cherbourg and Toulon are characterized by antiquated structures, with a predominance of self-employed workers, low salaries and low demographic growth rates.

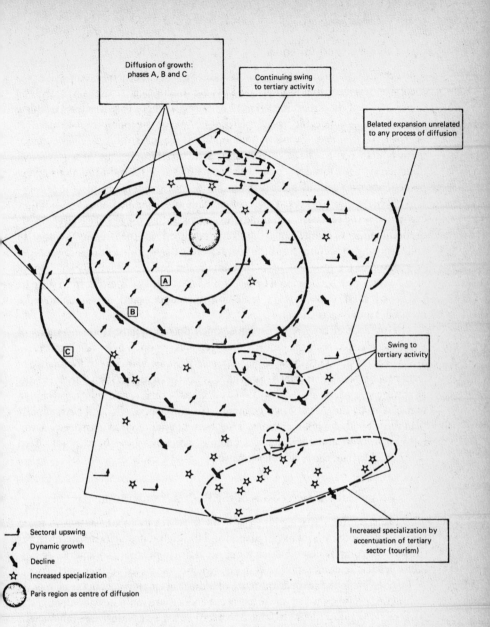

Diffusion of growth:
phases A, B and C

Continuing swing
to tertiary activity

Belated expansion unrelated
to any process of diffusion

Swing to
tertiary activity

Increased specialization by
accentuation of tertiary
sector (tourism)

↳ Sectoral upswing

↗ Dynamic growth

↘ Decline

☆ Increased specialization

◯ Paris region as centre of diffusion

Figure 37.2 System of socio-economic change in agglomerations of more than 20,000 inhabitants, 1954–75. Source: Pumain et Saint Julien, *Les Dimensions du changement urbain*.

2.2 Town size and function

The activity structure of towns, just like their growth, bears little relationship to their size. It is nevertheless interesting to note some special features typical of the upper levels of the urban hierarchy. For example, there has over the last thirty years been a noticeable convergence of the socio-economic structures of *métropoles d'équilibre* towards a common metropolitan type. These major metropolitan centres have an economic structure close to the urban average, dominated by the tertiary sector, with production and transport functions taking precedence over central-place activities. With the exception of Lille, the proportion of blue-collar workers in the economically active population is low, but they can in no way be regarded as middle-class towns; rather they have a characteristic predominance of white-collar workers occupied in the tertiary sector. In endeavouring to account for these characteristics, it is difficult to distinguish the part played by the programmes of investment and development from which these agglomerations have benefited in their roles as *métropoles d'équilibre* from the part played by their sheer size in lessening fluctuations and in stimulating the diversification of activities.

The other twelve regional capitals, which do not benefit from the status of *métropoles d'équilibre*, form a more heterogeneous group. Their social structures are in general similar to those of the *métropoles d'équilibre*, with a predominance of tertiary activities. Their growth rates have always been higher than those of towns of similar size which do not function as regional capitals, and this gap widened between 1954 and 1975. Their economic structures have changed more rapidly than those of other agglomerations. They have all undergone at least one phase of industrialization and their socio-economic structures have been modernized more quickly than those of other towns.

2.3 The special characteristics of the Paris agglomeration

The place of the Paris agglomeration in the French urban system is more remarkable for the size of its population and the high status of its urban functions than for the composition of its economically active population; its superiority over other French agglomerations has in any case not increased further since 1950.

The decline in the relative influence of industrial employment in the economically active population had an earlier onset and a more rapid development in the Paris agglomeration than elsewhere. Nevertheless, with industrial employment accounting for 37.5 per cent of the active population in 1975, as against an average of 41 per cent in large towns, the Paris agglomeration holds approximately the median position with regard to the degree of industrialization in agglomerations of over 50,000 inhabitants (46 out of 100 towns have a lower proportion employed in industry). In spite of the more rapid swing towards the tertiary sector in Paris, the activity profile of the agglomeration in 1975 remained quite close to that of all other towns. The Paris region lost 121,000 jobs in industry between 1962 and 1975, which may be regarded as proof of a certain degree of success in decentralization policies, although some 'deindustrialization' would certainly have occurred in any case. In the same period, the rise in tertiary employment was 30.9 per cent, only slightly lower than the 34.7 per cent of other French towns.

The Paris agglomeration stands out from most other large towns in France not by the profile of its economic activities, which does not greatly depart from the average, but by the social and occupational composition of its active population. As compared with other French agglomerations, Paris in 1975 had a much smaller proportion of self-employed and unskilled workers, twice as many senior executives and 50 per cent more middle managers, clerical workers and supervisory grades. Without being in an extreme position, the Paris agglomeration belongs to the group of towns characterized by their high proportion of the upper social and occupational classes. Only Aix-en-Provence, Montpellier, Poitiers and Rennes have a higher proportion, but when it is considered that the position of these towns reflects their almost exclusive reliance on tertiary activities (none has more than 25 per cent of employment in industry), the distinctive nature of society in the Paris agglomeration can be better appreciated.

3 The hierarchy of urban functions

It is difficult to determine precisely the exact place of each town in the urban hierarchy. Each town exercises a regional influence commensurate with its population, the facilities it has to offer and its means of transport and communication. France is thus divided into urban spheres of influence of unequal size, which in turn are grouped within the spheres of influence of the provincial metropolises. Figure 37.3A is based on criteria such as telephone calls, railway journeys and internal migration. It confirms the importance of Paris as a provincial metropolis, and conversely the limited spheres of influence of some large centres which are in competition with each other, such as Strasbourg and Nancy, or Montpellier and Marseille.

Research into the communal attractiveness of towns (Fig. 37.3B) shows spheres of 'general attraction' of metropolitan and regional capitals which are smaller than those in the first map. Above all they are not contiguous, being perceptible only within a radius of 50 km. The attraction exercised by very large centres is almost completely non-existent beyond 100 km.

Not all French towns can be fitted into a regular hierarchy of urban regions as described above. In some regions two competing centres arose, the product of the demographic history of France, the long history of urban development and the element of chance in urban growth and economic development. In the same way some metropolitan centres have been prevented from reaching their full development. Towns such as Roubaix, Saint-Etienne and Vichy are to some extent

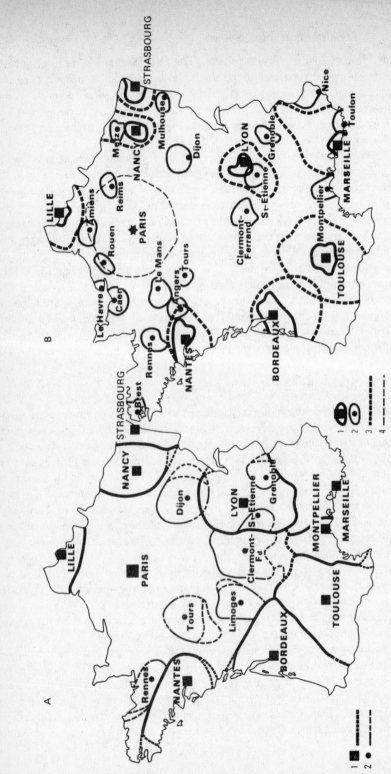

A

1
2

B

STRASBOURG

LILLE
Le Havre
Caen
Rouen
Amiens
Reims
PARIS
Le Mans
Angers
Tours
Metz
NANCY
Mulhouse
Dijon
Rennes
Brest
NANTES
Clermont-
Ferrand
St-Etienne
LYON
Grenoble
Nice
BORDEAUX
TOULOUSE
Montpellier
MARSEILLE
Toulon

1
2
3
4

STRASBOURG

NANCY
Brest
Rennes
NANTES
PARIS
LILLE
Dijon
Tours
Limoges
Clermont-
Fd
St-Etienne
LYON
Grenoble
BORDEAUX
TOULOUSE
MONTPELLIER
MARSEILLE

outside the urban hierarchy, superimposed on the urban network, resulting in a costly and regrettable rivalry.

All French urban centres, from Paris to the smallest *bourg* of between 1,800 and 2,000 inhabitants, have as the result of the functions that they fulfil a specific rank in the urban hierarchy and a particular sphere of influence.

3.1 *Bourgs*

These little urban centres of perhaps 1,000–5,000 inhabitants form the lowest level of the French urban hierarchy. They are spread out every 15–20 km at intervals between the larger towns. Their functions are mainly commercial; at one time, every square in these little centres bustled with activity on market day. Although the markets have declined in importance, often becoming merely an excuse for a day out, the *bourg* has retained a distinct role as a retailing and service centre. It may even have increased its importance in this respect with the disappearance from the villages of shopkeepers and artisans who, with the arrival of the motor vehicle, have settled in these smaller urban centres.

In the *bourg* it is possible to find shops providing for daily needs, such as foodstuffs, as well as items such as shoes and ready-made clothes. Here too is the secondary school, the police station, the pharmacy, as well as the medical practitioner, the lawyer and other professions connected with the agricultural population served by the little town. In many cases the economic life of the *bourg* is enriched by some form of minor industrial activity. In the majority of cases the *bourg* is also the administrative centre of a canton (a group of communes); exceptions to this rule occur where the rail and road services or advantages of situation have favoured another commune.

3.2 Small towns

These small towns of between 5,000 and 30,000 inhabitants are part of the heritage of France, with their reputation for clinging to past ways, for sleepiness. They have been described as conglomerations of landowners, administrators of various rural organizations, civil servants whose careers have landed them in positions in provincial France, shopkeepers and craftsmen, with occasionally a

Figure 37.3 Urban spheres of influence. A. Principal urban centres and their spheres of influence. 1. Major centres and the boundaries of their spheres of influence 2. Centres of secondary importance and their spheres of influence. Broken lines have been used either where the extent of the sphere of influence is uncertain, or where two centres are in competition. Source: J. Hautreux, *Urbanisme*, 1963. B. Zones of general urban attraction (non-food goods). 1. Metropolitan centre (*métropole d'équilibre*), with sphere of both strong restricted influence 2. Regional centre, with sphere of both strong and restricted influence 3. Extreme limit of metropolitan influence 4. Limit of restricted influence of Paris. Source: Survey by A. Piater.

factory or two and a few workshops. Yet they fulfil important functions in the fields of administration, law and education in relation to the regions that surround them. There is normally a secondary school or *lycée*, a number of medical practitioners, occasionally a dispensary or clinic, and various other services such as lawyers. There is above all a concentration of retailing and other commercial and technical functions. These towns come alive on market days and at the time of periodic fairs and agricultural shows.

As the years go by, however, they experience increasing difficulty in preserving their role, partly because their dependent rural populations are declining in numbers and are increasingly dominated by the older age groups, and partly because with motorization the larger towns are able to make a direct impact on rural areas without the intermediary of the small market towns. Towns of this size are extremely vulnerable; economically they can be thrown out of balance by events such as the building of a bypass, meaning that motorists are no longer tempted to stop, by the closure of a railway line, the transfer of a government office or court of law, or the closure of an industrial plant. On the other hand, adverse trends may be reversed by the arrival of one or two industries, the discovery of a tourist attraction or by improvements in schools, health services and hotel facilities.

3.3 Sub-regional (departmental) capitals

In most cases this type of town is also the administrative centre (prefecture) of a department. Its sphere of influence extends over a radius of about 45 to 50 km, usually covering an entire department, but rarely going beyond it. Especially where population densities are relatively high, two and even three towns of similar size may coexist in the same department, dividing it between their respective spheres of influence. This sometimes arises where the department is naturally divided by features of physical geography but may also relate to human factors, as when one or more industrial towns arise alongside the traditional departmental capital.

These towns are essentially characterized by tertiary activities. Leaving aside any industrial activities that they may have acquired, they are administrative centres at departmental level and economic centres, with Chambers of Commerce, wholesale and retail distribution, and appropriate transport facilities. The variations in the size of towns included in this category may at first seem surprising. Yet excluding any industrial function that they may have, and taking account of population size, whether one of these towns has like Beauvais a population of 30,000 or like Valenciennes one of 170,000, all fulfil the same functions.

3.4 The metropolitan centres of provincial France

Leaving aside Paris, which is in a class apart, the metropolitan centres occupy the highest level of the urban hierarchy. They are set apart by their large size and by the importance of their provincial functions, which are of a higher order than those of the departmental capitals. They normally have the offices of the regional administration, at least one university and a Court of Appeal. Newspapers published in the metropolitan centre, and professional associations located there, serve the surrounding region. High-level tertiary functions include specialist medical services, theatres and all sorts of professions relating to the law, from barristers to valuers. The large population to be served permits the development of specialized wholesale and retail outlets, including department stores and luxury shops.

These urban functions are provided by metropolitan centres which vary greatly in size. A few stand out clearly above the rest, Lyon and Marseille with more than 800,000 inhabitants, Bordeaux and Lille with more than 400,000 and Toulouse and Nantes with more than 300,000. These six towns together with Paris do not include the whole of France in their respective spheres of influence. Identification of provincial *métropoles* below this level is, however, not easy, because of the large number of competing centres of between 100,000 and 250,000 inhabitants. With no tradition, until very recently, of regional government, France is understandably short of really large cities, which are lacking over wide areas of the country. This is why Rennes could not in the present circumstances be considered as the effective capital of Brittany. The obvious desirability from the spatial planning point of view of endowing each of the new administrative regions of France with a single strong capital runs into difficulties where there are competing claimants, as Rouen and Le Havre in Upper Normandy, or Metz and Nancy in Lorraine; these pose formidable problems from the point of view of territorial planning.

Dijon is a good example of a provincial metropolis. It is the only large town in the centre of the Paris–Strasbourg–Lyon triangle, surrounded by a cluster of departments with little urban development or with only medium-sized towns. Its growth is assured by its administrative, commercial and service functions. Under the new system of regional government in France it has become the capital of Burgundy region. It has a university, an administrative centre for the girocheque (postal bank) system, a regional telecommunications administration, it is the headquarters of a military region and has an air force base. All these activities strengthen its influence. So far as distributive activities are concerned, Dijon has the advantage of its position at a crossroads in the heart of Burgundy, storing and redistributing agricultural produce and machinery. It is also an important railway, hotel and tourist centre, and it has acquired a range of industrial activities. Table 37.2 puts forward a possible two-stage hierarchy of metropolitan centres, which are identified according to the significance of their tertiary populations.

Table 37.2 *Hierarchy of the metropolitan centres of provincial France*

Upper level:	(a) Lyon, Marseille.
	(b) Bordeaux, Lille, Strasbourg, Toulouse, Nantes, Nancy.
Lower level:	(a) Grenoble, Nice, Clermont-Ferrand, Saint-Etienne, Dijon.
	(b) Rouen, Rennes, Metz, Limoges, Tours, Montpellier, Reims.

Sources: J. Hautreux, J. Lecourt and M. Rochefort, *Le Niveau supérieur de l'armature urbaine française* (Ministère de la Construction, Paris, 1963) (report).

3.5 Paris

Paris has a threefold importance in the urban hierarchy. It is a national capital, it is one of the great world capitals, with functions and influence extending far beyond national frontiers, and it also takes its place among the provincial metropolises of France. This triple role goes far to explain its important concentration of activities.

The sphere of influence of Paris as a regional capital is extremely wide, both because it exerts a powerful attraction and because there is no neighbouring metropolitan centre to counterbalance its influence. The gravitational attraction of the mass of population and services concentrated in Paris is so great that theoretical studies have suggested that it extends to three-quarters of France. Other centres of metropolitan size have been able to grow up only in peripheral locations far from the capital, more particularly in southern France, where distance from Paris is maximized. The predominance and influence of Paris are a permanent part of French civilization. As early as the thirteenth century Paris was already considered to be a city of gigantic proportions, with five or six times the number of inhabitants of any other large town. But the problem of the disproportionate role of Paris within the urban network is less related to the mass of its population than to its economic power and to the excessive concentration there of the powers of government, of business decision-making and financial control.

38

⚜ Urban landscapes

In 1968 the total built-up area of France was estimated to be about 650,000 ha, the equivalent in size of two average departments. This relatively modest area is, however, characterized by a considerable degree of diversity, the product of the long period during which urban landscapes have evolved, and the geographical inertia which has preserved built forms from the past long after their original functions have been lost. Other sources of diversity have been referred to earlier, notably the openness of French territory to a wide range of cultural influences (chapter 12). These varied influences contribute to the astonishing variety of French towns, from the Mediterranean type, with their tall, close-packed houses roofed with the characteristic Roman tiles, and their shady, tree-lined avenues, to the grey towns of the industrial north.

1 The urban heritage

The urban landscape of France, at least as it existed at the outbreak of the Second World War, can only be understood by reference to history. Elements derived from the Gallo-Roman, medieval and modern periods of history are found juxtaposed, even superimposed one on another.

1.1 Prior to the eighteenth century

The oldest contribution to the urban fabric is provided by the ruins and surviving monuments which give to so many towns their visible pedigree, witnessing to a prosperity and importance which may have disappeared for ever. There are frequent remains of Gallo-Roman temples, baths and theatres, even whole districts, as well as the gates, towers and defensive walls which enclosed them. In some towns Gallo-Roman spatial organization is much more evident in the present-day town plan than in monuments, which inevitably survive only sporadically; at Boulogne, for example, the upper town still reflects the plan of Caligula's camp. In many towns a first circuit of walls, often built at the onset of the Middle Ages as a protection against barbarian invasions, still clearly shows the boundary of the first urban nucleus; inside, the regular Gallo-Roman street pattern still survives. This first town wall also played an important if indirect role in later urban extensions; it marked the first contrast between the urban nucleus (*cité*), inward-looking behind its ramparts, and the early suburbs (*faubourgs*) spreading freely outside. Sometimes one of these *faubourgs* became more important than the Gallo-Roman *cité* and as a result of a transfer of the urban centre of gravity became, as at Arras, the central nucleus of the medieval town.

Throughout the Middle Ages and the modern period up to the mid-nineteenth century, urban expansion took place by the construction of successive circuits of walls. The first wall often links the Gallo-Roman *cité* with the first medieval nucleus, whether *faubourg* or castle (for example Strasbourg's eighth-century wall or the eleventh-century wall of Philippe Auguste at Paris). Successive walled extensions of towns date chiefly from the twelfth, thirteenth and fourteenth centuries. Each extension incorporated into the town a portion of rural space with its farms, abbeys and noblemen's houses hitherto situated 'without the walls' (*hors les murs*) or in the fields (*dans les prés*). While there were some examples, as at Lille, of new extensions being supplied with a regular street plan, more usually the pre-existing network of rural roads and the layout of parcels provided the basis of urban development. While the streets in these new extensions became progressively built up, the interiors of the blocks often remained in agricultural use or as the private gardens and parks of religious houses and of great houses belonging to the nobility and the wealthier bourgeoisie, hidden from the eyes of passers-by. As time went on and population grew, these residual areas of open space were gradually built up.

French towns have preserved from the medieval and early modern periods their irregular town plans, their narrow winding streets without pavements (sidewalks) or with excessively narrow ones added later, and their irregular but charming little squares. They have also retained some beautiful facades of Renaissance houses, a few medieval houses, and historic monuments ranging from cathedrals to street fountains. In towns which had little subsequent development, the walls themselves have often remained wholly or partially intact. Elsewhere, except in fortified towns along the frontiers, the walls were demolished from the eighteenth century onwards and replaced by circular boulevards, interior boulevards following the line of the oldest circuit of walls, and exterior boulevards following the most recent ones.

The foundation charters of medieval new towns often specified the dimensions of the building plots allocated (7 m × 14 m at Montauban). Although these new towns did not all have a uniform plan, there was a clear tendency towards 'rectilinear' street patterns. In the new towns of southern France the municipal square occupied a prominent place in the plan. In fortress towns or royal and princely court-towns built from the sixteenth century onwards, the checkerboard plan was supplanted by radial–concentric patterns.

1.2 The eighteenth century

Most provincial towns bear the imprint of the eighteenth century, more particularly the later eighteenth century. This was a period when the desire for beauty was combined with rational planning, particularly for improved hygiene and adequate provision for traffic flow in towns that were undergoing rapid expansion. These concerns were expressed in formal plans which were drawn up to guide the improvement and extension of towns.

Nantes, Bordeaux, Rouen, Tours, Lille, Lyon and Marseille are examples of towns which acquired either new, well-ordered quarters or at least imposing new streets. This was the great age of the creation of the formal square, typically named in honour of the monarchy (Place Royale), although often renamed in more democratic times since, such as the Place de la Liberté (Dijon), Place de la Bourse (Bordeaux) or Place Stanislas (Nancy). Typical of the period also were public open spaces of all kinds: parks, gardens, promenades, formal avenues and boulevards. Many towns to this day owe their only public open spaces (all too many, alas, used for parking) to the 'town planners' of two hundred years ago!

The *hôtels particuliers*, those elegant town houses belonging to the nobility and the bourgeoisie, also date from the seventeenth and eighteenth centuries. Their characteristic horseshoe shape round an inner courtyard, isolated from the street, combined all the techniques then available for entertainment and comfort. With its double orientation, with rooms on one side looking on to the courtyard, on the other to the garden, this town house was the model for all urban architecture until the nineteenth century. Many of these old *hôtels* are to be found in the Marais quarter of Paris. In the provinces most towns of any importance have some examples, whether as isolated buildings or comprising entire streets or districts. In particular they distinguish the eighteenth-century quarters of towns in Provence and Languedoc, concealing behind their richly ornamented facades a wealth of architectural detail which reflects the prosperity enjoyed by the nobility and upper bourgeoisie of the time.

1.3 The nineteenth century

The essential feature of nineteenth-century urban development is the change of scale. Towns were able to spread out freely, without the military or geographical restrictions of earlier times, sending out long tentacles along the roads leading to the surrounding countryside, with particular concentrations around the railway stations. Indeed the *quartier de la gare* (the railway station district with its approach road, forecourt and associated buildings such as cafés and hotels) and the factory can be regarded as the characteristic offspring of nineteenth-century urban development. It was a general trend of the urban growth of this period to develop around, or to be a product of, new buildings containing facilities or providing services which were previously non-existent or scarcely developed. In addition to factories and railway stations, these included grammar schools (*lycées*), teachers' training colleges, barracks, hospitals, offices for the local administration, slaughterhouses and gasworks. Many of these facilities needed large amounts of space and so were often constructed on the edge of the densely built-up area, thus creating new poles of urban development.

The urban growth of the industrial revolution took place when the climate of opinion was dominated by *laissez-faire* ideology, with housing provision regarded as no different from any other business. Towns surged beyond their ramparts, or the boulevards that had replaced them, in a totally unplanned fashion. The location of the new quarters, the alignment of the roads serving them, and the division of land into building plots were regarded as matters of purely private decision by entrepreneurs, guided by the free play of the market and by the necessity of housing thousands of new citizens. The result was a chaotic and disorganized land-use pattern mingling blocks of rented apartments, private houses, factories, gasworks and tangles of rail lines.

This soulless landscape was a reflection of the new economic and social structures that had been established in France. Nineteenth-century urban structure revealed the growth and opposition of the two largest social classes: the working class and the bourgeoisie (upper middle class). The organization of space differed according to the social category living in it. The healthiest and most pleasant areas were reserved exclusively for the development of neighbourhoods inhabited by the rising commercial middle class. Their great town houses, noted for their austere facades provided with entrances for carriages, and concealing large gardens, were built along wide avenues or in newly built squares: the Chartrons at Bordeaux, the Boulevard Vauban and the Boulevard de la Liberté at Lille, the Cours Pierre Puget and the Cours du Chapitre at Marseille, and the neighbourhood of the Place Bellecour and the Parc de la Tête d'Or at Lyon. In Paris, the most widespread type of building in the upper middle-class business quarters dates from 1880–1910. This is the apartment house, built of freestone derived from the Calcaire Grossier limestone, the seven-storey facade provided with balconies and containing about twenty dwellings.

The rising lower middle class lived in neighbourhoods of small individual houses or in rented apartments. These building conditions resulted in a characteristic organization of urban space; in order to achieve maximum economy of land, apartment blocks were packed tightly together on each plot of land, reducing the inner courtyards to mere ventilation shafts. In this way the entire interior of a block could be occupied by apartment buildings built one behind the other or by other buildings served by private entries, dead-end streets and passages (Fig. 38.1).

Working-class housing was relegated to less favourably situated areas further from the centre. Their joyless streets, uniformly lined with workers' houses or shabby-looking apartment blocks, constructed from the middle of the nineteenth century onwards, absorbed thousands of migrants from the countryside. Such housing still exists in working-class quarters of industrial towns such as Lyon or Lille and makes up most of Saint-Etienne and Le Creusot. Before the era of mass urban transport, workers had to be housed as close as possible to their place of work. In order to pack the maximum number of people into the smallest possible area, all possible gaps in built-up areas were filled up, eliminating courtyards and gardens. In some towns, particularly in the textile regions of the north, working-class housing was provided in the form of *courées* (simple row-housing built in internal courtyards). In the coal and iron regions, by contrast, employers often provided housing in the form of industrial villages (*cités ouvrières*) or rows of single-family houses with gardens (*corons*).

Attempts to provide some measure of town-planning control were not unknown in this period, but were few in number and extent. Where they existed, they were restricted to controls over building lines along streets and over the height and volume of buildings. The Paris town-planning act of 1884 fixed the minimum size of interior courtyards at between 100 and 150 sq m, irrespective of the area of the parcel involved. This explains how it was possible to achieve such extraordinary building densities. Nineteenth-century town planning is famous above all for the work of Haussmann, Prefect of the Department of the Seine, 1853-70. His projects were concerned essentially with the improvement of the existing built-up area of the city of Paris. Whole neighbourhoods of narrow streets and slum houses were razed to the ground, to be replaced by a new network of broad, straight streets defining a new structure of urban blocks. Priority was given to facilitating the movement of traffic, which was already becoming a major problem. The great width of Haussmann's avenues and boulevards constructed at this period is certainly evidence of forward-looking planning, although it must be accepted that they were also designed with the political purpose of physically eliminating areas of poverty and possible insurrection, and with the strategic purpose of providing ample opportunities for the employment of repressive military force. But this was only a partial town planning, concerned with grand facades only. The upper middle-class apartments and business premises along Haussmann's boulevards backed on to and concealed the surviving old quarters with their narrow, winding streets and ancient houses.

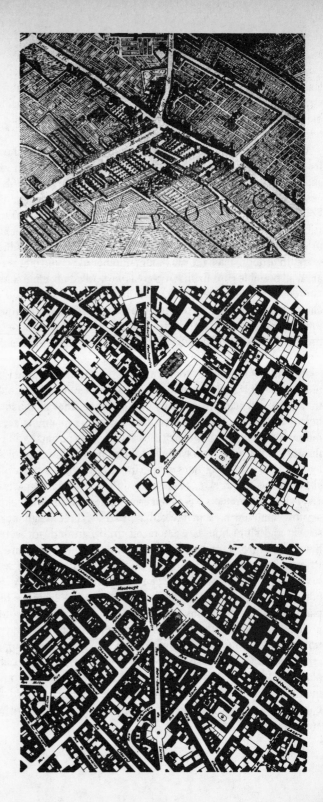

1739

1836

1936

1.4 1900–40

Nineteenth-century trends continued in accentuated form into the twentieth century. The developing means of mass urban transport – trams, buses, suburban trains – and, in Paris, the Métro (underground railway, subway), together with the individual motor vehicle, allowed suburban development to spread ever further into the surrounding rural communes. Particularly around Paris, the period 1910–30 was characterized by the process of *lotissement*, under which large areas of agricultural land were bought by speculators who marked out networks of streets and subdivided the land into the smallest possible plots. These were sold at a high profit as sites for what the French call *pavillons*, detached single-family houses, generally of the most rudimentary standards of construction. Frequently the roads of the *lotissements* remained seas of mud for years, and the houses were not provided with basic amenities such as piped water and main drainage. The trend towards single-family houses was stimulated by the Ribot and Loucheur laws of 1928, favouring accession to the ownership of property.

Yet this large-scale change in the suburbs of Paris should not draw attention away from the general state of stagnation into which French urban development had fallen. During the interwar period the majority of towns continued to lack suburbs. Only 1,500,000 new dwellings were built in the whole country, a figure equivalent to 13 per cent of the housing stock that existed in 1914. Corresponding figures for neighbouring countries were Germany 22 per cent, the United Kingdom 30 per cent and the Netherlands 60 per cent. The relative rarity of urban developments that date from the first half of the twentieth century is to be related to the economic and demographic stagnation of the time, but in retrospect is perhaps something to be welcomed, in view of the indescribable ugliness of such suburban landscapes as were created in this period.

The degree of urban anarchy that prevailed, for example in the Paris suburbs, could not fail to provoke reactions. From the end of the nineteenth century, the idea of social housing began to emerge. Attempts were made to provide decent housing at reasonable rents by forming workers' co-operative housing associations, by philanthropic housing projects and through the formation by towns and departments of housing associations to provide Habitations à Bon Marché (HBM), a form of low-cost housing, which in the Paris suburbs of the former Department of the Seine were sometimes grouped to form *cités-jardins* (garden-suburbs, or working-class housing estates).

The first attempt to introduce national town-planning legislation dates from 1919. Every town of more than 10,000 inhabitants and all communes in the then

Figure 38.1 Development of the Quartier Saint-Georges, Paris. Photo: Service technique d'urbanisme de la ville de Paris. Source: Y. Salun, *Raisons d'être de l'urbanisme* (Vincent, Fréal, Paris, 1948).

Department of the Seine (in effect the Paris suburbs) were required to draw up a town plan, known as a *plan d'extension et d'aménagement*. By 1940, however, only one plan had progressed as far as receiving the government approval necessary to give it legal force! Other legislation included the 1924 Cornudet law, requiring plans for the subdivision of land into building plots to be submitted in advance to the local administration; the 1919 and 1924 laws introduced measures to protect buildings in towns considered to be of visual, historic or artistic importance.

1.5 The Second World War and postwar reconstruction

Nearly 5 per cent of the French building stock was destroyed between 1940 and 1945. From 1940 onwards the rebuilding of towns, especially those which had suffered the greatest war damage, gave town planners the opportunity to create new street patterns, to rearrange land holdings so as to produce more rational plots for building, in short, to work in unusually favourable conditions. The most extensive changes were naturally made in the rebuilding of the towns which had been most severely damaged, such as Maubeuge, Le Havre, Amiens, Orléans, Boulogne or Caen. Their systematic reconstruction proceeded along very different lines from those of pre-war urban planning. In central districts apartment blocks replaced the former one-family housing. At the same time more specific town-planning legislation was introduced. Legislation passed in 1943 introduced the requirement that a building permit (*permis de construire*) be obtained from the communal administration before the commencement of building operations. Although many town plans were drawn up, the majority had no effect whatsoever and made no provision for the postwar increase in urban population, which was already making itself felt.

2 1950–80

Between 1954 and 1978 the number of new dwellings in France increased by 7,853,000, a figure equivalent to 56 per cent of the 1954 housing stock. While some building took place in rural communes, it is clear that the great majority of these new dwellings were associated with urban growth of all types, including urban development in rural areas.

2.1 The scale of building

The fundamental renewal of the stock of dwellings that took place in the period 1950–80 (Table 38.1) was urgently necessary. There was an immediate need to replace dwellings destroyed in the war, but apart from this the situation with regard to housing supply was critical. The years before 1940 had seen the near-stagnation of the building industry. Rent control, introduced in 1918, had discouraged private investment in the housing sector: demand was in any event

Table 38.1 *Changes in the stock of dwellings*

Thousands

Dwellings	1954	1962	1968	1975	1978
Principal residences	13,042	14,565	15,763	17,745	18,641
Vacant dwellings	534	854	1,233	1,633	1,751
Second homes	447	973	1,267	1,696	1,844
Total	14,023	16,392	18,263	21,074	22,236

Source: INSEE.

low because of the lack of population growth in this period. The dwellings that existed were for the most part old, lacking modern sanitary facilities. Most of the dwellings existing in 1945 were more than fifty years old. Some industrial towns had scarcely changed since their period of nineteenth-century growth; their populations were stationary, generation following generation in the same houses. The situation was exacerbated by the population explosion of the postwar years, manifested in the marked increase in the number of households, the rise in the birth rate, and finally by the emergence of the new post-1968 generation, demanding housing away from the parental home and insisting on separate housing for single persons.

An annual construction figure of 300,000 dwellings, considered as the minimum which could satisfy the enormous demand, was not achieved until 1959, 15 years after the end of the war. By comparison with other countries, the production of housing in France was for a long time inadequate. Between 1945 and 1960, 2,265,000 dwellings were built in France, but the German Federal Republic built more than 6,000,000 and the United Kingdom about 3,700,000. The French annual total exceeded 400,000 by 1965, and had reached 500,000 in 1972; after 1976 the figure was initially stable, then fell to about 350,000 by 1982.

Although housing dominates the urban scene quantitatively and visually, the mainspring of urban growth is provided by the basic functions of production, administration and service provision. The growth of these activities and functions has resulted in great demands on space. The single *lycée* (grammar school, high school) of the end of the nineteenth century is today represented by a complex of schools on an educational campus. Parallel space-consuming developments have overtaken the university, the hospital and the administrative offices of the prefecture. Shopping centres and recreational facilities also make much greater demands on space than they did thirty years ago.

The Sixth national plan estimated that urban growth would consume 12,000–15,000 ha per year. The Seventh plan put consumption at 32,000 ha annually, divided between housing (23,000 ha), retailing (300), offices (120), industry (1,350), public services (3,300), roads (2,000) and public open space (1,900).

2.2 The organization of building and construction

In order to satisfy the enormous demand for housing after the Second World War, a policy of state intervention in the building industry was essential. It was necessary to find ways of financing a vastly increased housing provision and to modernize a building industry which until the postwar years had been almost exclusively based on the efforts of the individual craftsman.

2.2.1 *Aid to the building industry*

The first and perhaps most important postwar development was a reform of the rent structure with the aim of restoring some degree of profitability to investment in housing. The 1948 rent law laid down the basis of this policy by requiring that rents should be calculated in a uniform manner according to the size and equipment of the dwelling; rents would be increased in a series of stages up to 1961. The progressive removal of rent control once more made investment attractive to private capital, which took over the high-quality end of the housing market. A government Minister likened the housing industry, booming after years of neglect, to the 'Wild West', fought over by developers large and small, by builders of social housing and by speculators alike.

Under legislation passed in 1950 and subsequent years, finance was channelled into housing from the public sector by means of subsidies and loans at favourable rates of interest provided by the Crédit Foncier (the public-sector bank specializing in housing finance). A key position in housing finance and management is occupied by the *Société Centrale Immobilière de la Caisse des Dépôts* (SCIC), which is able to draw upon the massive financial resources of the Caisse des Dépôts et des Consignations (see chapter 16, 3.1). Financial assistance is not limited to rented housing; home ownership was opened to those on modest incomes, the transfer to buying rather than renting being encouraged by loans and subsidies from the Crédit Foncier.

Government assistance to housing can take two very different forms; it can be given to builders to encourage the construction of housing (*aide à la pierre*) or it can be given directly to the families in housing need (*aide à la personne*). In March 1962 conditions in the housing market were radically transformed by an apparently innocent change in the tax structure, benefiting the big companies building housing for renting, while withdrawing some tax advantages from small companies. Housing aid given directly to the individual (*aide à la personne*) can be varied according to circumstances. Of the two policies it has been said that the first subsidizes housing supply while the second brings decent housing within the reach of the less affluent and so stimulates demand; both systems have their advantages and disadvantages.

The channelling of aid through the builder offers definite advantages. There is no doubt that it encouraged the emergence of a modernized building industry using techniques of industrialized building and prefabrication. The system also enabled the government to influence the location of housing developments. On the other hand it undoubtedly contributed to the mediocre quality of much postwar building, for in order to keep within the financial yardsticks laid down by the government, developers had to give preference to low-cost (i.e. inconvenient) sites, reduce the size of dwellings and skimp on materials and domestic fittings.

Direct aid to the individual (*aide à la personne*) initially existed only in the modest form of social security payments (*allocation-logement* and *allocation-loyer,* 1961). From 1966 onwards the system was gradually extended to give assistance to individuals wishing to purchase their own dwellings (*plans d'épargne-logement,* 1969). The years 1970–3 saw a boom in non-subsidized building, which reflected a switch to reliance on the private sector for housing construction and the setting up of a whole system to make it easier for individuals to invest their savings in order to provide a home of their own.

In 1975 the Barre Report recommended a return to realistic prices in the housing market. It proposed a much greater reliance on private finance, and the encouragement of competition between the private sector of the building industry and the publicly sponsored HLM (Habitations à Loyer Modéré – officially backed bodies for the provision of low-rent housing) sector. These ideas were embodied in the housing reform law of 1977, which continued direct aid to housebuilding but reduced its amount by half and similarly reduced the provision of subsidized housing. Instead, aid was to be channelled directly to the family according to its size and financial need (*aide personnalisée au logement*). Encouragement to individuals to own their own dwelling has been a consistent thread running through all the detailed government housing support. In 1954, 36.5 per cent of French families owned their dwelling; by 1975 the figure was 46.6 per cent.

The various forms of personalized housing aid have proved a heavy burden on the state budget, especially after the change of government in 1981; by 1984, government assistance for housing amounted to 85 billion francs. For this reason it is probable that there will have to be some return to the direct support of housing construction, with aid to individuals based more closely on actual needs, with particular emphasis on assisting tenants (especially in the subsidised HLM schemes) to buy their own properties.

2.2.2 *The builders*

Housing construction involves numerous organizations: private or semi-public companies, housing associations, co-operatives and other groups, as well as individuals. In the public sector a fundamental role is provided by public or semi-public bodies set up to acquire land, provide it with the necessary infrastructure and resell it for building purposes (chapter 16, 3.1).

Public-sector housing developers include the CIL (Caisse Interprofessionnelle du Logement), the SCIC (mentioned above), with its 380 subsidiary companies, and the building and administrative organizations of the HLM.

These bodies of the public sector naturally operated over areas of greatly differing extent. In 1976 there were 3,200,000 dwellings in the HLM sector, of which 2,200,000 were rented, housing 10 million people, or 20 per cent of the French population.

Private developers and builders may be individual entrepreneurs, subsidiaries of banking groups, or public companies investing in construction. The massive intervention of the banks in the housing sector has already been described (chapter 16, 5.1). According to a 1977 inquiry, 1,100 firms had each built in the preceding years more than 20 single-family houses (a total of 92,000 in 1976 alone). In addition, small artisan–builders had built 93,000 houses. At the same time, the builders of *villages* (the French expression for urban-fringe housing estates or subdivisions where developers offer finished single-family houses for sale) provided 66,000 homes. Of the 1,100 builders, only 38 built more than 250 houses a year. It must of course be accepted that the distinction between the public and private sector made here must be qualified, since the characteristically French semi-public companies (*sociétés d'économie mixte*) straddle the borderline between the two (chapter 16, 6.1).

Specialization among builders has brought about a spatial differentiation according to their financial resources. Because of the high cost of urban land, social housing has had to be located on the periphery of towns, often poorly served by public transport; the travelling distances involved have resulted in fatigue and wasted time for the inhabitants concerned. Moreover the very large scale of programmes of social housing resulted in a high degree of social segregation. The HLM White Paper of 1975 stated the situation in clear terms: 'As regards housing, France is divided into as many categories as there are levels of income. Thus a dozen different categories of housing have been created, each destined for a small section of the people . . . In no other country is society so socially segregated as ours'. Persons applying for housing in the public sector are immediately directed to the category appropriate to their income. It has been argued that this is a system which 'inscribes social inequality on the land'.

2.3 The nature of the housing stock

The housing stock which resulted from this building activity undoubtedly produced a higher quality of housing and, as the standard of living rose, a higher standard of domestic equipment (Table 38.2). Yet despite this growth and modernization, housing in France is still far from reaching a satisfactory standard. The average size of dwelling and number of rooms have increased (1968: 3.29 rooms per dwelling; 1978: 77 sq m per dwelling and 3.7 rooms). However, the average number of rooms per dwelling is below the averages for the German Federal Republic (4.4) and Belgium (5.1).

Dwellings of five or more rooms account for 21 per cent of the total housing stock, as compared with 33 per cent in the German Federal Republic, 60 per cent in the United Kingdom and 64 per cent in the United States. The French figure

Table 38.2 *Changes in the domestic equipment of dwellings*

Percentage of dwellings owning	1954	1962	1968	1978	1982
Running water within dwelling	58.0	71.0	91.0	98.7	...
Internal WC	...[a]	40.0	55.0	79.1	...
Bath or shower	...	29.0	47.0	77.1	84.7
Central heating	...	19.0	35.0	60.3	67.5
Telephone	7.0	15.0	15.0	44.6	74.4

[a] Data not available.
Source: INSEE.

reflects the proportion of single-family houses, still relatively low, and the large number of tiny one-room ('studio') and two-room flats.

Modern sanitary facilities are less widely available than might be expected. Certain categories of housing, especially social housing in some towns, notably Paris, have a particularly poor level of provision. According to a 1973 survey carried out by INSEE, 41.7 per cent of HLM dwellings had only very basic sanitary installations. In 1977, an estimated 600,000 HLM dwellings were deemed to be in need of modernization on the grounds of noise and lack of sanitary facilities.

In 1978, 84 per cent of all dwellings were being used as main residences, 8 per cent as second homes, and 8 per cent were empty. The figures show the simultaneous existence of over- and under-used dwellings. In 1977, 13 million people in France were living in dwellings that were officially recorded as overcrowded. On the other hand large apartments are often inhabited by elderly couples, while substantial town houses, once filled with large families, may be inhabited by one grandparent living alone. Dwellings with the lowest level of sanitary provision and other facilities are typically the most overcrowded, especially in agglomerations of over 100,000 inhabitants and in the Paris region.

3 Town-planning policy
3.1 The development of policy to 1965

The background against which town-planning policy evolved was one of demographic and economic growth, affecting mainly towns and manifesting itself in a considerable demand for building land, housing, social facilities and infrastructure. Town planning fell into place as part of a wider movement towards a more rigorous overall development of planning.

At this stage town-planning methods were still relatively undeveloped and experimental. Building was controlled by a collection of regulations and orders which together could be regarded as defining a town-planning policy, or more precisely a town-planning code. Year by year new laws and regulations appeared, introducing more explicit controls over the extension of urban development.

The government tried to mitigate the consequences of speculation by defining the areas to be developed. It introduced the concepts of priority planning zones (*zones à urbaniser par priorité* – ZUP) in 1958, and zones of deferred development (*zones d'aménagement différé* – ZAD) in 1962 (chapter 15, 3.2.2 and 3.2.3). In these zones the state and other public bodies have a right of pre-emption over sales, that is, where a sale of land has been arranged they can step in and take the land at the same price. The ZUPs made it possible to produce a systematic development over large areas by preventing the building of a great number of uncoordinated individual projects. The law on legal plot ratios also dates from 1962 (chapter 15, 3.2.3).

These policies had to be implemented by architects with no specific training in town planning, who had to learn on the job, and who had little experience of dealing with a great increase in population, of planning for thousands of dwellings and of building new towns. The forecasts and planning programmes envisaged a powerful increase in the urban development of France. Plans were accordingly drawn up in anticipation of annual urban growth rates of between 1.5 and 2 per cent.

All urban development during this period was carried out on the assumption that the private motor vehicle would be the chief method of transport. In other words, any location was possible, and there was no attempt to concentrate growth in urban nuclei round railway or bus stations. On the contrary, the presence of rail and bus stations resulted in increased land prices which inhibited building development.

Postwar town planning was also based on the idea of the separation of functions by zoning, a concept developed in the interwar years which was applied without regard to the changes of scale which had occurred since that period.

The massive high-rise housing projects were the physical expression of town planning by means of the ZUP and the ZAD. These *grands ensembles* were seen as the solution to the enormous housing shortage and rapidly spread to the whole of France. They consisted of high-rise blocks sometimes containing several thousand dwellings. Their creation was undoubtedly a reaction against the *lotissements*, the expanses of private, single-family houses (*pavillons*) built in the interwar years. It was felt that accommodation could be more economically provided in large apartment buildings than as single-family houses. Concentration of development into *grands ensembles* would also prevent the waste of agricultural land through urban sprawl. It was also intended that the *grands ensembles* would be carefully planned to incorporate all the necessary commercial, educational and cultural facilities. As has been noted above (chapter 35, 2.5), the largest of these *grands ensembles*– Massy-Antony (Paris), La Paillade (Montpellier), Le Mirail (Toulouse) and Sarcelles – were considered at the time to be effectively new towns, and indeed they were often conceived as twin towns, built in parallel with their parent settlement: the private-enterprise 'Parly 2' was originally to be called 'Paris 2'.

The location and size of the *grands ensembles* were nearly always dictated by local circumstances. They required extensive tracts of land which had not been built on, if possible divided into a minimum number of parcels, in order to reduce the cost of land acquisition. Sites were preferred that did not require extensive earth-moving operations or present excessive difficulties in the provision of necessary services. Two categories of site suited these conditions: sites on the extreme edge of the town, on the rural–urban fringe, and sites that had been left vacant between the ribbons of housing following the routes radiating through the suburbs. Both types of site were likely to present considerable difficulties of accessibility to future residents. Within the existing built-up areas, it was sometimes possible to make use of unbuilt land in the centre of large blocks, to use land where building had previously been forbidden for reasons of defence, or abandoned industrial land. The size of the *grands ensembles* was determined by the size of site available and the number of dwellings it could contain or be made to contain.

The design of the early *grands ensembles* was one of a degree of uniformity and monotony which indicates the extreme urgency of housing the homeless and the total lack of originality and research. In order to facilitate the use of tower cranes, running on rail tracks, the high-rise blocks were mostly aligned parallel to each other and made as long as possible: there are some examples more than 300 m long. The anonymous slabs of between four and twenty storeys were divided into cell-like compartments, all resembling each other. In the second generation of *grands ensembles*, aesthetic considerations led to the introduction of tower blocks in combination with low-rise slabs; these latter have the economic advantage that if limited to four or five storeys there is no need to provide expensive lifts.

The design concept of the *grand ensemble* combines high residential densities with a considerable amount of free space. The street, once characteristic of the urban scene, disappears and gives way to green spaces, sports grounds and unused land. The green space provided round the blocks is all too often more of a feeble apology than a coherent, well-thought-out attempt to create a pleasant environment. A few lawns and rows of poplars, a few sandpits, swings and benches are quite inadequate for the needs of the inhabitants.

The policy of building *grands ensembles* was the French solution to the urgent need for new housing; it profoundly changed the traditions of urban life and the whole of urban society. The policy was not without its merits. It favoured the industrialization of the building sector by encouraging prefabrication and standardization, permitting the mass production of housing. In this way it was possible to keep costs low enough to enable those with modest incomes to rent or buy apartments. The concentration of dwellings into apartment blocks also avoided excessive consumption of land while minimizing the cost of public investment in services such as access roads, water supply and sewage systems. The building of apartment blocks was also favoured by the development from 1954 of the system of co-ownership of residential buildings by their occupiers, almost non-existent before the war.

Even leaving aside consideration of the architecture and siting of *grands ensembles*, most criticism has been adverse. Because provision of amenities such as shops, health clinics, cultural centres and schools menaces the economic success of projects, they tend to be either inadequate or non-existent. The most severe criticism of all relates to the lack of local employment; there are usually no office blocks or industrial estates, thus forcing the inhabitants to make long daily journeys to work.

Apartment blocks all too often bear the imprint of the bodies financing them, which have multiplied since the end of the Second World War. Whether HLM project or development by the Caisse des Dépôts, the style is distinctive and instantly recognizable. Within the different complexes the apartment blocks are differentiated according to the size of the flats that they contain, with between them or around them rows or a scattering of single-family houses, reserved for large families or for higher-income groups.

The building of large housing projects composed of blocks, each consisting of apartments of uniform size, results in a segregation of the generations. An element of social segregation also develops from the way in which *grands ensembles* are often considered as transit dwellings, places to live in while waiting until it is possible to move to a more comfortable, more conveniently located dwelling.

The *grands ensembles* were often built in or near suburbs without an overall town plan which might have made it easier to incorporate and integrate them into the pre-existing urban fabric. Whatever their merits, however, they have profoundly changed the appearance of the French urban landscape. They were often the first buildings to break out of the traditional geographical frame by expanding beyond valley slopes on to the surrounding plateaus. Today the tall silhouettes of their apartment blocks break the line of the horizon, marking a new frontier in the advance of urban development.

A total of 3 million dwellings was built in the ZUPs, but the *grands ensembles* of which they largely consist have been completely rejected by the people, on the grounds that they lead to segregation, enforced conformity, confinement in barrack-type buildings, and too close a contact with neighbours.

3.2   1965–75

The policies for building and town planning that were evolved over the period 1963–8 were formalized in 1969. At this point the government moved in the direction of a free market in building land. 'The whole of the country . . . must be opened up to the building of single-family houses. Scarcity rent will thus be eliminated and prices will fall at the same time. If the whole country is considered to be available for building, the supply of land will be out of all proportion to the demand.'[1]

[1] A. Chalandon, newspaper reports.

3.2.1 The decision-makers

Changes also took place in the way that decisions about town planning were made. The drawing up and implementation of town plans have since 1966–7 been entrusted to multidisciplinary agencies covering different territorial areas. In each department the government set up a Research and Planning Group (Groupe d'Etudes et de Programmation – GEP) responsible for structure plans (*schémas directeurs d'aménagement et d'urbanisme* – SDAU). In many large urban areas and counterbalancing regional metropolises, special Structure Plan Organizations (Organismes d'Etudes et d'Aménagement des Aires Métropolitaines – OREAM), set up from February 1966, had a similar task. At government level, an interministerial central group for urban planning, set up in 1964, was responsible for developing policy and intervened directly with regard to planning and financing developments in the largest towns.

After 1965 the supervision of town planning was entrusted to the elite government Corps of Bridge and Highway Engineers (Ingénieurs des Ponts et Chaussées), at the expense of the town-planning architects of the previous period and in the absence of properly trained town planners. These engineers brought to the operation the qualities of their profession, their prime concern with transport, their sense of service to the state. But they were not necessarily trained in the practice of town planning. Their scientific training strengthened the importance given to statistical forecasts, to the planned provision of infrastructure, and to fixed and restrictive qualitative goals.

3.2.2 The instruments of town planning

The 1967 urban and regional planning law (*Loi d'orientation foncière*) had a widespread impact. One of its chief merits was to assert the principle that both the local authorities and the government should be associated in the town-planning process. The three essential policy instruments under this law were the ZAC, the SDAU and the POS.

The zone of joint public and private development (*zone d'aménagement concerté* – ZAC) was the successor to the ZUP. It is to be created when the local authorities or other public bodies decide to intervene in a particular area in order to produce properly planned and serviced building sites which can then be further developed by public or private users. The introduction of the ZAC was an important departure in town planning. The previous legislation had envisaged a tight control, channelling urban growth to precise locations. The results of this policy were, however, disappointing. While the permits (*permis de construire*) issued in respect of particular buildings were perceived as being overladen with petty restrictions, town-planning schemes in a wider sense were lacking in effectiveness. In particular the widespread practice of *dérogation* (allowing a dispensation from town-planning requirements) permitted a highly anarchic speculative development to emerge.

Thus, from the beginning of 1969, the accent was on the removal of restrictions on urban development (*urbanisme libéré*). This move can be seen as a reaction against excessively costly and ambitious projects, and against paralysing regulations. The new proposals aimed to integrate town planning into the market economy and, as exemplified in the ZAC system, to open up a wide range of contractual relations between public bodies and private developers.

A ZAC is divided into sections, each of which is provided with a detailed town plan. A section usually corresponds to the portion of the ZAC entrusted to one particular developer. The town plan must include details of proposed buildings and land use, but is in fact of limited value. In practice the establishment of a ZAC or other co-ordinated project, with an overall plan approved by the commune concerned, effectively bypasses any planning restrictions. The ZAC procedure thus openly institutionalizes what had previously only been possible by dispensation (*dérogation*).

A decree of 1969 also stipulates that towns of more than 10,000 inhabitants should have a structure plan. This is to include a communal land-use plan (*plan d'occupation des sols* – POS). Plot ratios (*coéfficients d'occupation du sol*) are required to establish the relationship between the permitted total floorspace and the area of the building site. The structure plans (SDAU) must conform with national directions of strategic spatial planning (*aménagement du territoire*).

The POS divides land into the following categories:

U: Urban zones; land which is already developed or which is sufficiently provided with the necessary services and is therefore ripe for development.
N: Natural zones, subdivided:
Na: Reserved for future expansion; development is prohibited as long as the necessary service provision is lacking.
Nb: Unprotected; building is permitted only at very low density (minimum plot 1,000 sq m per dwelling).
Nc: Zones of economic and natural significance; only buildings related to agriculture are allowed.
Nd: Zones of environmental protection; building is prohibited.

The drawing up of a land-use plan (POS) is obligatory for communes which are part of an agglomeration of more than 10,000 inhabitants and communes which are classified as being in environmentally sensitive areas.

3.2.3 *The return to single-family housing*

The period 1965–75 was characterized by a reversal of the tendency with regard to housing provision; there was a change from official favouring of the building of apartment blocks to favouring of the building of single-family housing. The

Table 38.3 *The changing balance of dwellings in apartment blocks and in single-family houses*

	Single-family houses authorized (thousands)	Apartments authorized (thousands)	Single-family houses as a percentage of total authorized
1960	109	264	29
1971	248	386	39
1976	315	260	55
1977	303	200	60
1979	309	153	67

Source: Statistiques de la construction.

policy went hand in hand with a relaxation of the idea that each agglomeration should be rigidly bounded. The developing techniques of prefabrication were applied to the production of groups of single-family houses, provided in increasingly large numbers both by housing associations in the public sector (HLM, CIL) and by private developers. Since 1969 restrictions on large apartment blocks have been progressively increased and single-family housing has been encouraged. In 1973, further circulars forbade the building of *grands ensembles* of more than 500 dwellings on the same site and designed by the same architect.

Table 38.3 illustrates the trend towards the provision of single-family houses. It was in 1976 that building permits given for single-family houses first exceeded those for dwellings in apartment blocks. The French proportion of single-family housing in relation to all new construction was, however, well behind the USA (78 per cent), Denmark (77 per cent) and the United Kingdom (73 per cent). Single-family houses may be located in the form of 'new villages' (exurban housing estates or subdivisions) in the luxury or middle-income class, as housing estates provided by the various public-sector housing associations, or as individual units either provided by private builders or bought 'off the peg' from the catalogues of manufacturers of prefabricated houses.

All kinds of ulterior motives have been attributed to this policy of encouraging single-family housing. There have been passionate debates between its advocates and those favouring housing provision in the form of apartment blocks. The latter criticize individual housing for being more expensive, for using much more land, for making journeys to work unnecessarily long, and for leading to urban sprawl. The defenders of the single-family house use the counter-arguments of its superiority as an environment for family life, with its larger and more numerous rooms, its possibility of developing outbuildings, its garden, so invaluable for children, and its independent access from the street. Their proposals contrast these advantages with the small, noisy and anonymous dwellings of the *grands ensembles*. The main criticism directed at single-family housing is its excessive consumption of land, but against this it appears that provision of a single-family house (and garden) is a disincentive to the acquisition of a second home. An INSEE survey of 1973 showed that 24 per cent of dwellers in urban apartments had second homes as against 9 per cent of owners of single-family homes on the urban fringe.

The style and layout of single-family housing varies from one region to another. In general the northern half of France, especially the Ile-de-France and Nord regions, is characterized by the grouping of single-family houses into 'new villages', exurban housing estates and subdivisions. In southern France, on the contrary, most single-family houses are built as individual units, not part of housing estates.

3.2.4 Developments in existing urban areas

In the central areas of the majority of French towns single-family houses have been swept away, to be replaced by multi-storey buildings intended either for residential use, as offices, or for other purposes. Such houses were not necessarily slums; the determining factor in the location of new blocks was the size of the building site, which has to be large enough to provide a plot ratio allowing a building of sufficient height and to guarantee the profitability of the operation. A second consideration was the width of the road, which under building regulations determines the maximum elevation of the proposed block. Developers were therefore particularly interested in securing possession of the sites of large private town houses bordering on wide avenues, also of workshops and factories, which often meant the interiors of blocks in which these uses were located. In consequence of these developments the appearance of a street or boulevard could be transformed in a few years, with resultant changes in its population, its activities and its density.

Other attempts at urban renewal occur on a larger scale, affecting one or more districts, whether old historic quarters or more modern districts. The historic urban centres, where land values are at their highest, are also occupied by the oldest housing. Year by year the conditions of urban life are rendered increasingly unfavourable by reason of the narrow streets and the difficulty of access both to residential and commercial premises. A policy of urban renewal took shape in the 1960s, under the influence of the Fourth national plan. Legislation in 1962 introduced for the first time the idea of a 'protected sector' wider than the protection previously accorded to individual historic monuments and sites. The owners of old apartment blocks were given the same financial advantages as the builders of new blocks.

This policy of attempting to retain the historic fabric of towns was impeded by the high cost of urban land, by economic considerations, including the high density of shops and workshops, by social considerations (the need for temporary or permanent rehousing) and by urban politics (after all, every inhabitant is also a voter).

There could be more than one approach to the problem. Where the areas concerned were old, insalubrious and of no aesthetic value, urban renewal took the form of complete clearance and rebuilding. But frequently the surveys undertaken prior to urban renewal, that is in anticipation of total destruction, have brought to light unknown or forgotten artistic treasures. Frequently, in fact, a change in the use made of old buildings, the accretion of extensions, changes of frontage at ground-floor level, and the accumulated grime of ages have been found to conceal not so much isolated monumental buildings but whole sections of artistically valuable urban environments. An example of this type of rediscovery is provided by the old part of Lyon (the Saint-Jean, Saint-Georges and Saint-Paul districts); its buildings, dating from the fifteenth to the eighteenth centuries, have courtyards which reveal elaborate vaulting, galleries, arcades, balconies and splendid towers and staircases. The stripping away of all ugly or useless sheds and workshops accumulated over the centuries has restored to the streets and courtyards their former attractive appearance. There is of course a considerable battle between traditionalists and modernists over whether these quarters should be restored or torn down and rebuilt.

In the peripheral quarters of towns, rebuilding takes precedence over renovation. A master plan is drawn up for the whole sector concerned, with planned provision for social equipment, residential densities and public open space. Public-sector housing associations, semi-public companies and private developers provide the necessary new housing.

3.3 1975–81

From 1975 onwards, the government was increasingly concerned with problems of urban development. The context within which government intervention took place was, however, markedly different from that of earlier years. The 1975 census had confirmed a slackening of urban population growth, while politically there was a wish to decentralize control and responsibility for town planning. There was also a growing concern with the quality rather than the quantity of development, in part a response to the growth of the ecological movement. Finally, there was a continuing tendency to look to private enterprise rather than to the public sector in promoting urban growth and change.

What some went as far as calling 'a new urban policy' could be subsumed under such headings as consistency, flexibility, adaptability and moderation. In 1975, legislative provisions finally provided local administrative authorities with the means for an effective land-use policy by giving them the right of pre-emption (the right to intervene and acquire for themselves land offered publicly for sale) and also the right to impose maximum plot ratios (1.5 for the city of Paris, 1.0 for the rest of the country). A developer wanting to build at higher densities was obliged to pay to the local authority a sum of money equal to the value of the land it would have been necessary to acquire in order to keep within the density limit laid down for the area concerned. The legal plot ratio (*plafond légal de densité* –

PLD) came into force in 1976 (chapter 15, 3.2.3). More coherent financial assistance by the government was provided by the introduction in 1976 of the Town Planning Fund (Fonds d'Aménagement Urbain), which replaced the previous multiplicity of specialized funds.

So far as the evolution of town-planning theory was concerned, there was certainly a reassessment of the notion that every urban settlement should be divided into zones, each containing only one form of activity. Town planning became more modest in its aims, rejecting grandiose schemes of development, avoiding projects which violate community consciousness, yet trying not to be relegated to mere trend-planning.

The laws relating to the ZAC and to housing estates placed great emphasis on the quality and coherence of urban provision. These measures also attempted to upgrade the quality of developments, by requiring that an architect be employed in relation to all important buildings. In 1978, departmental councils for architecture, environment and town planning were set up.

The new laws affected all types of urban development. Public opinion, but also the economic calculations of investors and speculators, led to an increasing concern with the preservation and rehabilitation of ancient buildings and with the maintenance of a varied urban scene of high architectural quality. The emphasis was placed on the restoration and rehabilitation of the 6 million old dwellings in poor condition. In 1975 the Nora Report on old housing proposed that financial assistance be given directly to the occupants. This form of urban renewal applied also to dwellings in industrial regions.

In 1977 the government banned apartment blocks of more than four storeys in towns of fewer than 30,000 inhabitants, and of more than seven storeys in towns of 30,00 inhabitants or more. In the same year a government circular warned of the dangers of *mitage* (the eating up of agricultural land by the unplanned dispersal of single-family houses), the subdivision of forests, the denial of access to the coast and incursions into the mountains. It was felt that there was a danger that the fringe of the city would be neither a fully urban nor a fully rural landscape, but rather a sprawling suburb.

There is in fact an appreciable difference between the environmental impact of the single-family house sited haphazardly according to the inclinations of its inhabitants or the chance availability of building land, and single-family houses grouped in estates or subdivisions. It is not easy to find the right balance between the complete dispersion of single-family houses and oversized *lotissements*, but by 1980 official opinion inclined to the grouping of single-family housing in housing estates or subdivisions.

3.4 New developments since 1981

The framework within which urban planning must operate has been profoundly modified by administrative decentralization, which has transferred responsibilities and resources to the local and regional authorities. Since April 1984, for example, the mayors of the 6,287 communes provided with a POS have been allowed to issue building permits on their own responsibility. It seems likely that there will be further changes in this direction. At the same time the government has set up a range of new central bodies to encourage projects with a view to improving the quality of urban living, which under the rubric 'Mieux vivre dans la ville' was one of the objectives of the Ninth plan.

4 Conclusion

It is difficult to evaluate the results of these successive policies. The impact of the most recent ones, as enshrined in the structure plans (SDAU) and land-use plans (POS) are not yet apparent. It is also true that, as so often in France, there is a gap between the intentions and content of the laws and regulations and what happens in practice. A further difficulty in assessing the results of recent policies springs from the evident contradiction between the express reliance on the suppression of controls and restrictions over free enterprise in urban development, and the existence of a body of laws and regulations (which are in fact flouted with increasing openness). Dominated by market forces, the town cannot be other than subject to segregation. The market calls into existence what can be marketed – dwellings, offices and shops – and sacrifices what is not marketable, such as social equipment and open spaces.

It cannot be said that the new urban landscapes that have emerged in France since the 1950s are very good advertisements for the merits of the town-planning policies carried out by successive governments. Even on the generous assumption that in recent years there has indeed been a political will to action in town planning, it has to be accepted that this action came too late, when the period of postwar demographic and economic growth was coming to an end. It was within this period that effective action in the sphere of town planning could have been taken, directing and channelling the migratory flows, natural increase and industrial expansion.

As it is, French urban landscapes are more the joint expression of finance capital and landed property than the result of town-planning policies. The features which objectively constitute the urban landscape, such as land use, the building programme, the area devoted to construction, or housing densities, are determined by land values and profit margins. Either one increases densities, perhaps to an excessive extent in order to reduce the price per square metre, making housing accessible to people of modest incomes, or else one provides some space around the dwellings, one shows concern for the environment. Land costs then become excessive and the resultant housing can be afforded only by the rich. One cannot have both.

The greatest reservations about the transformation of the built environment of France are more fundamental than this. It must seriously be asked whether or not there is really a policy for town planning. There are of course individual policies with regard to landed property, the allocation of the use of land, aid to the building industry and the provision of social equipment. But do they add up to an accurate forecast of the totality of urban change over the next decades? Just as in the past a number of policies operated in parallel to redistribute urban growth within France without ever really weakening the dominance of Paris, so too town-planning policy has failed to create new urban forms corresponding to the new functions and conditions of urban life.

During the periods 1950–60 and 1970–80 the 'planners' offered the high-density, under-equipped, aesthetically impoverished world of the *grands ensembles* to people whose standard of living was rising, who had perhaps two or more children and who were beginning to enjoy the freedom of movement offered by private motor transport in an era of cheap energy. At the same time the planners were failing to come to terms with the mass invasion by the motor car of the central districts of towns, which were often more than a hundred years old. Then from the end of the 1970s, just when the oil crisis was beginning, town-planning policies favoured the energy-consuming dispersed single-family house, at the same time advocating an increased reliance on public transport.

Politicians and planners considered it sufficient to have a degree of control over the allocation of land. The consequence has been jigsaw urban development, each piece left to the initiative of the owner, the investor and the builder, provided only that minimum town-planning regulations were respected. What was missing was the integration of each piece into the whole in order to ensure the coherence of the town as a whole, to guarantee the smooth functioning of the system, in fact to create a properly planned urban environment.

VIII

Conclusion

39

✣ The complexity of the
geography of France

Complexity is first of all due to the diversity of the factors which shaped the land; largely unrelated mosaics are superimposed one upon the other. They may consist of the thousands of valleys, large or small, which together with their interfluves and slopes make up the natural sites. They may equally be mosaics of soils, local climates, communes, human occupance, agricultural holdings, fields or agricultural utilization. Every chapter has given the same impression not only of the density, intensity and continuity of geographical phenomena in French space, but also of their fragmented, dispersed and overlapping nature. Complexity also relates to the long history of human intervention in the environment. No simple or recent explanation can account for all the varieties of relief, soil, population distribution, techniques of land utilization, town plan or industrial location.

No part of the French landscape can be attributed to a single origin; the network of land parcels, for example, is rarely appropriate to its content of crops, buildings and factories; the same is true of the network of administrative regions, and the transport networks; all have evolved from a variety of sources.

A final complexity relates to recent changes in the spatial organization of France. Until the period 1945–50 the landscapes of France were undoubtedly diverse in origin, but had become fossilized; there were few changes after 1910 and these were very localized (some consolidation of parcels, the rebuilding of farms and houses in areas affected by the First World War, and a few new factories).

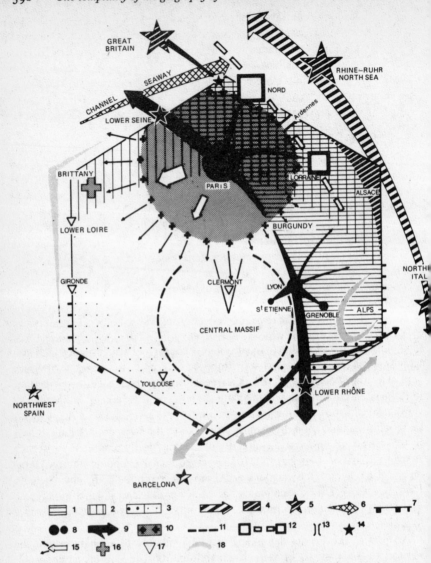

Figure 39.1 Major characteristics of French spatial organization. 1. High degree of urbanization and industrialization 2. High fertility, high proportion of young people in economically active population 3. 'Southern' type, more or less apparent 4. Rhine axis and its direct impact upon French territory 5. Major centres of economic activity, decision-making and investment in neighbouring countries 6. Major flows of international maritime traffic 7. Frontiers more or less closed 8. Major French development pole 9. Major French development axis, with branches 10. Expanding area of major attraction 11. Negative area 12. Axis of centres of first industrial revolution, in process of transformation 13. Tendency to interruption of this axis 14. Expanding areas of major

Since 1945, on the contrary, all the constituent elements of French space have been affected by forces which have transformed them, or are about to transform them. The geography of France has been reshaped; new administrative units have been created, slums have been razed, new factories and nuclear power-stations built and rail lines closed, to be replaced by new stretches of line and by new motorways.

After fifty years of stagnation there was an urgent need to meet the demands of a growing population and an increasingly strong international competition, yet there was frequently expressed apprehension that the inherited weight of opposition to change would result in growth that was too slow, too fragmented and insufficiently co-ordinated in nature. Present-day needs are numerous and all apparently of a similar degree of urgency, ideally requiring the determination of priorities both between sectors and between regions, priorities which always have serious consequences. Yet the modernization of French space has proceeded by the simultaneous implementation of numerous unrelated policies and decisions, whether public or private, in an entirely incoherent and disorganized fashion.

In defence of those responsible for decision-making, it must be said that co-ordination is not very easy in France. From the beginning of its political existence France has been in a state of tension between the opposing poles of central power and local interest, a theme which runs through nearly every chapter in this book. The political, administrative and legal organization, strongly monolithic and centralizing in character, stands in opposition to regional trends which are firmly rooted in areas of greatly differing landscapes, people and economy. Particularly noteworthy in this respect are the major contrasts between northern and southern France, between the France of the *langue d'oil* and the France of the *langue d'oc* (chapter 12, 1.1), between lowland France and upland France, and between maritime and continental France.

The general arrangement of French space reflects this duality: northern France centred on the Paris basin, lacking internal barriers, at the meeting point of major rivers, contrasts with southern France, where the isolated lowlands of Vendée, Aquitaine and the Rhône valley abut on the great barrier of the Central massif, which also cuts them off from easy access to the Loire valley.

A closer study of resources and regional structures has revealed the extent of the geographical inequalities between the different parts of France. The lengthy economic crisis that began in 1974 accentuated these contrasts and inequalities; the establishment of the European Community with its centre of gravity along the Rhine favoured the continental regions of France at the expense of the western

port activity 15. State-encouraged spatial decentralization of Paris region, impinging on 16 16. Potential surplus of labour consequent on changing rural structure 17. Peripheral or isolated urban centre functioning as local focus of attraction 18. Development of tourism. Source: R. Brunet, *L'Espace Géographique*, no. 4, 1973, p. 251.

regions. The latter open on to the Channel and the Atlantic, where the United Kingdom (which entered the Community only in 1973) and Spain provide no equivalent counterbalance. The north–south alignment of the original six member-countries of the Community was also unfavourable to the development of transverse links, except when these were already well established, as in the case of the Seine below Paris.

The complex differentiation and structuring of French space bear witness to the historical play of many forces. Three maps allow a first appreciation of these characteristics. The first map, published by Roger Brunet in 1973 (Fig. 39.1) brings out the main contrasts within France as well as the axes and poles of economic activity situated outside the country but influencing its spatial structure. Western and eastern France are separated by two great circular areas: one consists of the Paris region within the wider area of expansion constituted by the Paris basin, and the second is the area of repulsion created by the Central massif. The 'national growth axis' formed by the Seine–Saône–Rhône valleys runs across the country, although attenuated in its crossing of the uplands of Burgundy.

The map of the homogeneous regions of western Europe (Fig. 39.2) was drawn up in 1976 by a research team attached to the Regional Research Centre (Centre de Recherches Régionales) of the French Science Research Council (Centre National de la Recherche Scientifique – CNRS) led by E. Juillard and H. Nonn; it is based on the identification of three types of regional model:

(1) The 'Paris type' expresses the dominant presence of a very large core city which exclusively dominates a vast hinterland. The three stages of this type reflect the nature of the links between core city and hinterland. In stage I the impact of the city on the hinterland may be adverse, draining it of vitality, as with present-day Madrid or pre-war Paris. In stage II the hinterland may benefit from some degree of industrial dispersal from the core. Stage III represents a real demographic and industrial revitalization brought about by a major redeployment of metropolitan activities, as exemplified by southeast England.

(2) The 'Rhenish type' corresponds to a different organization. High rural densities are associated with a dispersed industrialization and a close network of towns, with no single predominant core city. There is a dense network of communications, the various lines frequently converging to run in parallel along the natural axes provided by the river valleys and lowland gaps through the hills.

(3) The 'peripheral type' is characteristic of regions which are sparsely populated, less industrialized and less urban. Development is structured round large urban centres, most of which are ports. Stage II of this type may be interpreted as a transition towards the Rhenish type.

The third map (Fig. 39.3), unlike the previous ones, is not an attempt to depict the regional structure of France but shows the price zones for petroleum products. These are fixed for each canton in relation to the actual cost of transport from the refineries. While there are some obvious differences of detail, the map usefully complements the picture given by the two previous maps. The

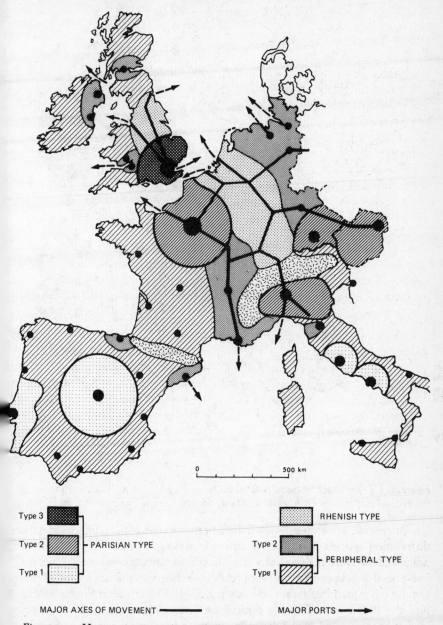

Type 3 — PARISIAN TYPE

Type 2

Type 1

RHENISH TYPE

Type 2 — PERIPHERAL TYPE

Type 1

MAJOR AXES OF MOVEMENT ——— MAJOR PORTS ——▶

Figure 39.2 Homogeneous regions of western Europe. Source: CNRS (Centre de recherches régionales), Strasbourg, 1976.

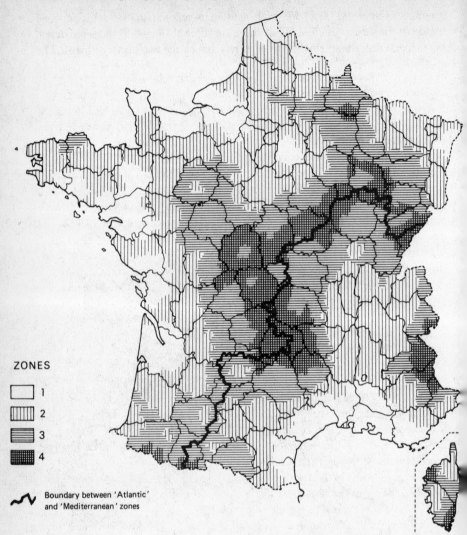

ZONES

☐ 1
▥ 2
▤ 3
▦ 4

⌇ Boundary between 'Atlantic'
and 'Mediterranean' zones

Figure 39.3 Price-zones for petroleum products, as at 17 May 1976. The eleven zones of the original map have been grouped into four. Source: Comité Professionnel du Pétrole.

low-price zones are obviously determined by the location of the refineries and the distribution systems. Areas of low prices in western France, Paris, the lower Seine and the Nord region clearly relate to coastal refining complexes, while the low-priced area in northeast France relates to refinery complexes on the Rhine. On the other maritime facade, the low prices of Mediterranean France extend into the Rhône valley, clearly centred on Lyon. These areas of low prices obviously correspond to the dynamic, urban and industrial regions of France.

This is also lowland France, the France of rivers and valleys, (with the significant exception of the middle and upper courses of the Loire and the Garonne), and also coastal, peripheral France.

These regions are separated from each other by a vast diagonal zone stretching from the Ardennes to the central Pyrenees. This zone of highest prices broadly corresponds to the uplands over 250 m in height, but it is also characterized by low population densities, an ageing population and a low degree of urban development. The map also includes a dividing line between Atlantic and Mediterranean France which recalls, although shifted somewhat towards the west, the fundamental physical divide of France (chapter 2, 1.1).

The geography of France clearly reflects the dual relationship that every society has to its environment: a relationship to the natural world and a relationship to a geographical space created by human occupance, by management of resources, by population distributions and by the various networks. The product of such disparate influences is an incoherent regional pattern juxtaposing physical regions of essentially geological origin, ancient historic regions, and an incomplete assemblage of polarized regions. Given this archaic, inherited regionalization, lacking any contemporary catalyst, it was hardly surprising that Paris was able to extend its dominance and supremacy over the whole of France.

After the Second World War, successive governments tried to develop a coherent regional structure, but they attacked the superficial aspects of the problem rather than the root causes, so that results did not always come up to expectations. Efforts could even be counter-productive: because the emphasis continued to be on 'vertical' sectoral policies, even when applied to provincial France, the decisional power of Paris over French space continued to be emphasized. Yet these first thirty years after the Second World War were ones when economic and demographic growth was producing migration flows and new economic activities which were thus potentially available for the planned strengthening of the French regional structure.

After the middle of the 1970s, economic and demographic crises considerably reduced the room to manoeuvre; there are no longer any surpluses to play with and even the developed regions have been experiencing grave difficulties. Accordingly, the geographical situation of France in the late 1980s is more critical than that described by J.-F. Gravier just after the Second World War;[1] the ageing of the population, low population densities and migration out of rural areas are more widespread than thirty years ago. Many areas are now even closer to the threshold of the 'desert of provincial France' that Gravier described. At the same time Paris is less and less willing to admit any weakening of its power and influence, and it will take years before the policies of regionalization and decentralization launched in 1981 have a noticeable effect.

This geographical situation will not be changed by movements which are exclusively ecological or environmentalist in their objectives: policies which aim

[1] *Paris et le désert français* (Le Portulan, Paris, 1947).

to change the nature of geographical space are just as important. Because such policies affect settlement, networks and infrastructures which are expressed on the landscape of France, they are persistent. Unlike interventions in the economy, which may have impermanent effects, interventions in the spatial pattern of a country are long-lasting, because of the inertia implied in any modification of the geographical landscape.

To succeed in the difficult operation of restructuring the regional pattern of France, it is essential to appreciate the spatial expression of the new social, cultural and economic trends affecting France. It is also essential to be aware of the geographical aspects of decision-making in sectors of economic and social life. It is important to evaluate, for example, the influence of geography on the building in of structural inflation (chapter 16, 6.2) or on the environments created by town-planning policies.

The future of France and its regions is linked to planning policies which are directed towards the creation of the spatial structures of the year 2000 and after. Ideally these developments should provide France with a genuinely human geography, reconciling the requirements of profitability with social progress, freedom and the rights of the individual with the interests of the community and the common good.

Bibliography

A complete bibliography of the geography of France would demand a very substantial volume in itself. The present bibliography is necessarily highly selective and is based on a substantial revision by the authors of the bibliography of the French edition of 1980. T. H. Elkins has helped with the selection and presentation of material for English-language readers, and has provided a number of English-language items. The revision has concentrated on the period since c. 1970 (somewhat longer for English-language items). For earlier literature reference should be made to the successive French editions from 1964 onwards. It should be noted that an increasing contribution to the understanding of the spatial organization of France is to be derived from a range of other disciplines in the natural and social sciences, to which only a partial reference can be made below.

Abbreviated titles of publishers, series and organizations

ACEAR	Atelier central d'études d'aménagement rural
BRGM	Bureau de recherches géologiques et minières (Orléans)
CAES	Comité d'action économique et sociale
CES	Conseil économique et social
CNASEA	Centre national d'aménagement des structures d'exploitation agricole
CNRS	Centre national de la recherche scientifique
CRDCG	Centre de recherche et de documentation cartographique et géographique (CNRS)
CRU	Centre de recherche d'urbanisme
CSU	Centre de sociologie urbaine
CTHS	Comité des travaux historiques et scientifiques
CUP	Cambridge University Press

DATAR	Délégation à l'aménagement du territoire et à l'action régionale
DF	La documentation française
EHESS	Ecole des hautes études en sciences sociales
ENSA	Ecole nationale supérieure agronomique
EPHE	Ecole pratique des hautes études (subsequently EHESS)
FNScP	Fondation nationale des sciences politiques
IAURIF	Institut d'aménagement et d'urbanisme de la région Ile-de-France (before 1976 known as IAURP)
IBG	Institute of British Geographers
IGN	Institut géographique national
INED	Institut national d'études démographiques
INQUA	International Association for Quaternary Research
INRA	Institut national de la recherche agronomique
INSEE	Institut national de la statistique et des études économiques
ISEA	(subsequently ISMEA) Institut de sciences mathématiques et économiques appliquées
LGF	Librairie générale française
LITEC	Librairies techniques
MIT	Massachusetts Institute of Technology (Boston, Mass.)
OUP	Oxford University Press
PUF	Presses Universitaires de France
PUG	Presses Universitaires de Grenoble
SCEES	Service central des enquêtes et études statistiques (Ministère de l'agriculture)
SECLAF	Société d'édition des coopératives La Fayette
SEDES	Société d'Edition et de diffusion de l'enseignement supérieur
SEGESA	Société d'études géographiques, économiques et sociales appliquées
SESAME	Système d'étude du schéma d'aménagement
TRP	Travaux et recherches de prospective (DATAR)

1. General works and background material

1.1 Bibliographies and indexes

The *Bibliographie géographique internationale* (*BGI*), published annually 1945–76 by the Association de géographes français, under the auspices of the International Geographical Union, contained a particularly detailed section devoted to France. The *BGI* became from 1977 a computerized quarterly publication produced by the Laboratoire d'information et de documentation en géographie (Intergéo) (Paris: CNRS).

From 1976 DATAR has published an annual *Bibliographie sélective: Aménagement du territoire, Environnement, Urbanisme* (Paris: DF). From 1979 Urbamet, in association with Micro-Urba, has issued *Référence–Urbanisme, Aménagement du territoire, Environnement, Transport* (Paris: IAURIF–DCID).

The Institut Franco-Allemand, Ludwigsburg, publishes the bibliographic and thematic guide *La France contemporaine*. Other useful guides are *Répertoire permanent de l'administration française* (Paris: DF) and *Répertoire des publications officielles (séries et périodiques)*; *Administrations centrales françaises* (Paris: DF). See also:
Westfal, G. 1980: *French official publications*. Oxford: Pergamon (Guide to official publications 6)
References to geographical books and contributions to books in English and lists of

numerous articles on France in the journals *Geography* and *Geographical Magazine* are to be found in:
Rogers, C. 1982: *France* (Bibliographic notes 16). Sheffield: the Geographical Association

1.2 Maps and atlases

A fundamental work, although inevitably dated in parts, is the *Atlas de France*, published by the Comité national de géographie in 1931, and reissued with new sheets 1951–8. More recent items include:
Grand atlas de la France, 1969. Paris: Sélection du Reader's Digest
Atlas économique et social pour l'aménagement du territoire, 1967–, 5v. Paris: DATAR
Atlas historique de la France contemporaine 1800–1965, 1966. Paris: Colin (Collection U)
Deffontaines, P. & Brunhes-Delamarre, M. J. 1955–64: *Atlas aérien*, 5v. Paris: Gallimard
Aydalot, P. & others 1982: *Atlas économique des régions françaises*. Paris: Economica
Savy, M. & Beckouche, P. 1985: *Atlas des Français*. Paris: Pluriel
See also:
Trancart, P. & Briend, A. M. 1983: La cartographie française; bibliographie commentée sur les atlas et cartes thématiques de la France publiés entre 1976 et 1983. *Intergéo Bulletin* 17 (72), 1–50
A new *Atlas de France* is under preparation by the Reclus Group (Montpellier). Most of the regions of France have a regional atlas. See also sections 3.1, 3.2.1, 6.3.1 and 17.2 below.

1.3 Statistical sources

Essential guidance is provided by two INSEE publications: *Répertoire des sources statistiques françaises* and *Répertoire du système statistique français*. INSEE publishes the *Annuaire statistique de France*, a publication richly provided with information on demographic and economic developments, illustrated by numerous maps and diagrams, and *Tableaux de l'économie française*. See also: *Les collections de l'Insee* (detailed statistical studies): Série C: *Comptes et planification* (national accounts, projections, economic policy). D: *Démographie et emploi* (structure and change of the population as a whole and of the economically active population). E: *Entreprises* (changes in the productive system with references to agriculture, industry and the tertiary sector). M: *Ménages* (social conditions, consumption and incomes of households). R: *Régions* (economic space, spatial planning; includes the invaluable annual *Statistiques et indicateurs des régions françaises*).

1.4 General surveys: geographical

Clout, H. D. 1972: *The geography of post-war France: a social and economic approach*. London: Pergamon
1982: A new France? *Geography* 67, 244–9
Estienne, P. 1978–9: *La France*, 4v. Paris: Masson (most of the first volume is devoted to a systematic approach, the remainder to regional geography)
Géographie universelle. Issued under the direction of P. Vidal de la Blache & L. Gallois. V. 6, *La France*. Pt. 1, 1947: *France physique*, by E. de Martonne. Pt. 2, 1946, 1948: *France économique et humaine*, 2v., by A. Demangeon. Paris: Colin
House, J. W. 1978: *France: an applied geography*. London: Methuen
Noin, D. N. & Brocard, M. 1984: *L'espace français*, 4th edn. Paris: Colin
Quant, T. (ed.) 1984: *Géoscopie de la France*. Paris: Paradigame/Minard (Terres et sociétés 4)

Thompson, I. B. 1970: *Modern France; a social and economic geography*. London: Butterworth

Vidal de la Blache, P.-M. 1903: *Tableau de la géographie de la France*. Originally issued as v.1, pt. 1 of 'Histoire de la France', ed. E. Lavisse. Facsimile edition 1979 with introduction by P. Claval, Paris: Tallandier. Translated in part 1928 as *The personality of France*, by H. C. Brentnall, London: Christopher (generally held to be a masterpiece of French geographical writing)

1.5 General surveys: politics, economics and society

Ardagh, J. 1968: *The new French revolution*. London: Secker & Warburg. Reprinted 3rd edn 1977 as *The new France*. London: Penguin
     1982: *France in the 1980s*. London: Penguin

Baleste, M. 1981: *L'économie française*. Paris: Masson (refers to population and urban development as well as economic sectors and industrial branches)

Coffey, P. 1973: *The social economy of France*. London: Macmillan

Coront-Ducluzeau, F. 1964: *La formation de l'espace économique national*. Paris: Colin
     La France en mai 1981; forces et faiblesses. Paris: DF

Gourbet, M. & Roucolle, J.-L. 1984: *Population et société françaises 1945–1984*, 2nd edn. Paris: Sirey

Hanley, D. L. 1984: *Contemporary France: politics and society since 1945*, 2nd edn. London: Routledge & Kegan Paul (a brief survey)

Holmes, G. M. & Fawcett, P. D. 1983: *The contemporary French economy*. London: Macmillan

Melitz, J. & Wyplosz, C. 1985: *The contemporary French economy*. Boulder, Colo.: Westview

Parodi, M. 1981: *L'économie et la société française depuis 1945*. Paris: Colin

Potel, J. Y. 1985: *L'état de la France et de ses habitants*. Paris: La découverte

Tuppen, J. N. 1983: *The economic geography of France*. London: Croom Helm & Totowa, NJ: Barnes & Noble

1.6. General surveys: by historians and historical geographers

Braudel, F. 1986: *L'identité de la France*, v. 1, *Espace et histoire*. Paris: Arthaud-Flammarion

Braudel, F. & Labrousse, E. (eds.) 1976–82: *Histoire économique et sociale de la France*, 4v. (in all 8 pts.). Paris: PUF

Chaunu, P. 1982: *Les Français et la France*. Paris: Laffont

Dupeux, G. 1976: *French society 1789–1970*. London: Methuen

Dyer, C. 1978: *Population and society in twentieth-century France*. Sevenoaks: Hodder & Stoughton

Fierro-Domenech, A. 1986: *Le pré carré; géographie historique de la France*. Paris: Laffont

Fox, E. W. 1971: *History in geographic perspective: the other France*. New York: Norton

Pitte, J. R. 1983: *Histoire du paysage français*, 2v. Paris: Tallendier

Price, R. 1981: *An economic history of modern France 1730–1914*, rev edn. London: Macmillan (first published 1975 as *The economic modernization of France*)

2 General characteristics

2.1 Territorial formation; political geography

Beer, W. R. 1980: *The unexpected rebellion: ethnic activism in contemporary France*. New York University Press

Demangeon, A. 1971a: Les provinces françaises et le problème d'une réorganisation régionale. *Acta Geographica*, 3rd series, 7, 151–208

    1971b: La formation de l'état français. *Acta Geographica*, 3rd series, 8, 217–38

Dion, R. 1947: *Les Frontières de la France*. Paris: Hachette

Jarry, E., 1942, 1950: *Provinces et pays de France; essai de géographie historique*, v. 1, *Formation de l'unité française*. Paris: Biggon

Loughlin, J. 1985: Regionalism and ethnic nationalism in France. In Y. Méry & V. Wright (eds.), *Centre–periphery relations in western Europe*. London: Allen & Unwin, ch. 8

Mirot, L. 1947, 1950: *Manuel de géographie historique de la France*, 2nd edn. Paris: Picard

Pernoud, R. 1966: *La formation de la France*. Paris: PUF (Que sais-je? 155)

2.2 Wealth, class and status

INSEE conducts regular surveys of households, savings, real estate and, every five years, incomes, based on income-tax returns (in France notoriously inaccurate for those whose incomes are derived from professional services, farm ownership or shopkeeping). The Centre d'études des revenus et des coûts (CERC) also publishes periodic reports on incomes and wealth.

Browaeys, X. & Chatelain, P. 1984: *Les France du travail*. Paris: PUF

Fourastié, J. & Bazil, B. 1980: *Le jardin du voisin: les inégalités en France*. Paris: LGF (Collection Pluriel)

Gaspard, M. 1985: *Revenus et consommation des Français: le grand tournant* (Notes et études documentaires 4800). Paris: DF

Madinier, P. & Malpot, J.-J. 1979: La répartition du patrimoine des particuliers. *Economie et Statistique* 114, 77–93

Marceau, J. 1977: Class and status in France: economic change and social mobility 1945–1975. Oxford: Clarendon

Morris, P. (ed.) 1984: *Equality and inequalities in France* (Association for the Study of Modern and Contemporary France, Annual Conference, Leeds, 1983). University of Nottingham

Regnier, J. & Sailly, J. C. 1980: *France: pays des inégalités: Position et propositions*. Toulouse: Privat

2.3 Growth

For growth in the first three postwar decades:

Carré, J. J., Dubois, P. & Malinvaud, E. 1972: *La croissance française; un essai d'analyse économique causale de l'après-guerre*. Paris: Seuil

Dalmasso, E. 1984: Le commerce extérieur français; situation et problèmes. *Annales de Géographie* 93, 350–68

Fourastié, J. 1979: *Les trente glorieuses, ou la révolution invisible de 1946 à 1975*. Paris: Fayard

Parodi, M. 1971: *L'économie et la société française de 1945 à 1970*. Paris: Colin

Sautter, C. 1975: L'efficacité et la rentabilité de l'économie française de 1954 à 1974. *Economie et Statistique* 68, 7–21

2.4 Regional disparities

The awakening of French public consciousness to the fact of regional disparity was the achievement of J.-F. Gravier:

Gravier, J.-F. 1947, 1958: *Paris et le désert français*. Paris: Flammarion
  1949: *Mise en valeur de la France*. Paris: Portulan
  1972: *Paris et le désert français en 1972*. Paris: Flammarion. See also:
Aydalot, P. 1984: Questions for regional economy. *Tijdschrift voor Economische en Sociale Geografie* 75, 4–13
Aydalot, P. & others 1982: *Atlas économique des régions françaises*. Paris: Economica
Beaujeu-Garnier, J. 1974: Towards a new equilibrium in France? *Annals of the Association of American Geographers* 64, 113–25
Brunet, R. 1973: Structure et dynamisme de l'espace français; schéma d'un système. *L'Espace Géographique* 2, 249–54
Chanut, T. M. & Tréca, L. 1975: Analyse régionale et indicateurs régionaux. *Les Collections de l'Insee R*, 16–17
Commissariat général du plan. 1984: *Disparités spatiales: rapport du Groupe de Travail*. Paris: DF
Dossier sur les disparités régionales, 1983. *Economie et Statistique* 153 (entire number)
Dunford, M. (forthcoming): *Social reproduction and spatial inequality; studies in French and Italian regional development*. London: Pion
Flockton, C. 1984: French regional inequalities and regional economic policy. In P. Morris, (ed.), *Equality and inequalities in France* (Association for the Study of Modern and Contemporary France, Annual Conference, Leeds, 1983). University of Nottingham, 107–29
Knox, P. L. & Scarth, A. 1977: The quality of life in France. *Geography* 62, 9–16
Le Bras, H. & Todd, E. 1981: *L'invention de la France: atlas anthropologique et politique*. Paris: LGF (Collection Pluriel)
Passeron, H. 1978: Les régions face à une croissance ralentie. *Economie et Statistique* 101, 33–47
Turpin, E. 1981: Disparités régionales; croissance et crise. *Economie et Statistique* 133, 77–9

3 Relief

3.1 Maps

The IGN *Carte générale de la France 1:100,000* gives an admirable overall impression of the relief of France. Use can also be made of three remarkable maps:

(1) The morphological map of France published by E. de Martonne in four sheets in the *Atlas de France*, and also contained as an unpaginated map in his *France physique* volume of the *Géographie universelle* (see 1.4 above).

(2) The map of France prepared by J. Bertin and published in various works and at various scales, usually as a basis for other detail. It is to be found, for example, in the *Atlas aérien* of P. Deffontaines and M. J. Brunhes-Delamarre.

(3) The mosaic at 1:1,000,000 and 1:2,000,000 *La France vue du satellite* (Orléans: BRGM).

3.2 Geology

3.2.1 Geological maps

Carte géologique de la France et de la marge continentale à 1:1,500,000, 1980. Produced under the direction of J. Goguel, with an explanation by O. Dottin & others. Orléans: BRGM

Geological maps are also produced by BRGM at scales of 1:1,000,000, 1:250,000 and 1:50,000.

3.2.2 *General geological works*

Ager, D. V. 1980: *The geology of Europe*. London: McGraw-Hill, esp. chs. 9, 13, 14

Anderson, J. G. C. 1978: *The structure of western Europe*. Oxford: Pergamon, esp. chs. 5, 7, 8, 9

Debelmas, J. (ed.) 1974: *Géologie de la France*, v. 1, *Vieux massifs et grands bassins sédimentaires*; v. 2. *Les chaînes plissées du cycle alpin et leur avant-pays*. Paris: Doin

Goguel, J. 1975: *Géologie de la France*. Paris: PUF (Que sais-je? 443)

3.2.3 *Quaternary studies*

This field has seen a notable expansion in recent years. Significant contributions relating to France are to be found in *Etudes françaises sur le Quaternaire*, published 1969, on the occasion of the INQUA congress, as a supplement to *Bulletin de l'Association française d'études sur le Quaternaire*. It is extended and updated in *Le Quaternaire; géodynamique, stratégraphie et environnement, travaux français récents* (1973: Comité national français de l'INQUA).

3.2.4 *Geological guides*

Pomerol, C. 1980: *Geology of France with twelve itineraries and a geological map at a scale of 1:250,000*, trans. A. Scarth. Paris: Masson. The same publisher issues a series of *Guides géologiques régionaux*, edited by C. Pomerol, which are of unequal value to the geographer, but sometimes contain material of great interest.

3.3 General geomorphological works

The fundamental contribution in this field is:

de Martonne, E. 1947: *France physique* (see section 1.4 above) The rapid advance of geomorphological research has inevitably overtaken much of the content of the work. For a substantial updating see:

Beaujeu-Garnier, J. 1972: *Le relief de la France*. Paris: SEDES. Information on recent research on all aspects of physical geography in France is to be found in *Annales de Géographie* 93, 1984, 129–275, ed. A. Godard. For an English-language survey see:

Embleton, C. (ed.) 1983: *Geomorphology of Europe*. London: Macmillan. In addition to material relating to France in chapters on Europe as a whole, major physical regions within France or overlapping its boundaries are covered by a range of contributors. There is an extensive bibliography.

3.4 Coastal forms

For a review of research see:

Guilcher, A. & Moign, A. 1977: Coastal conservation and research. *Geographical Journal* 143, 378–92. See also:

Ottmann, F. 1962: Sur la classification des côtes. *Bulletin de la Société Géologique de France*, 7th series, 4, 620–3

Verger, F. 1968: *Marais et wadden du littoral français; étude de géomorphologie*. Bordeaux: Biscaye

4 Climate, soils, vegetation and hydrology

4.1 Climate

Aléry, R. 1970: The climate of France, Belgium, the Netherlands and Luxembourg. In C. C. Wallen (ed.), *Climates of northern and western Europe*. Amsterdam: Elsevier, ch. 4

Atlas agroclimatique, 1980. Paris: Direction de la météorologie (140 maps)

Escourrou, G. 1982: *Le climat de la France*. Paris: PUF (Que sais-je? 1967)

A detailed climatic map at a scale of 1:250,000 has been in course of publication since 1971 under the direction of C. P. Péguy (Paris: Ophrys).

4.1.1 Regional climates

Balseinte, R. 1966: *Climats montagnards et stations climatiques d'altitude en France*. Paris: Fabre

Bénévent, E. 1926: *Le climat des Alpes françaises*. Paris: Chiron (Mémorial de l'office national météorologique de France)

Dauphiné, A. 1976: *Les précipitations dans les midis français; étude de climatologie inductive*. Université de Lille III & Paris: Champion

Escourrou, G. 1978: *Climats et types de temps en Normandie*, 2v. Paris: Champion

Estienne, P. 1956: *Recherches sur le climat du Massif Central français*. Paris: Météorologie nationale

Pédelaborde, P. 1957: *Le climat du Bassin parisien*. Paris: Génin

Simi, F. 1963: Le climat de la Corse. *Bulletin de la Comité des Travaux Historiques et Scientifiques, Section de Géographie*, 1–122

4.1.2 Climatic accidents and climatic problems

Chartier, M. 1962: Contribution à l'étude de la sécheresse, 1959–60. *Bulletin de l'Association de Géographes Français* 307–8, 209–22

Kaiser, B. 1974: Faciès locaux et provinciaux du temps en France; les 17 et 28 mars 1972. *L'Information Géographique* 38, 108–24

Lejeune, C. & Saintignon, M.-F. 1970: Les précipitations anormales de février à avril 1970 dans le Nord des Alpes françaises. *Revue de Géographie de Lyon* 45, 215–42

Péguy, C. P. 1976: Une nouvelle expression graphique de la variabilité interannuelle des climats; les 'calendriers de probabilités'. *Bulletin de l'Association de Géographes Français* 53 (431), 5–16

4.2 Vegetation

The Service de la carte de la végétation (CNRS) was founded in Toulouse by H. Gaussen after the Second World War. The coverage of France by vegetation maps at a scale of 1:200,000 is virtually complete.

Material on the vegetational pattern of France is to be found in a range of treatises and textbooks of biogeography. Useful guidance is also provided by:

Polunin, O. & Walters, M, 1985: *A guide to the vegetation of Britain and Europe*. OUP

Plaisance, G. 1959: *Les formations végétales et paysages ruraux; lexique et guide bibliographique*. Paris: Gauthier-Villars

4.2.1 Forests

Gadant, J. 1982: *La forêt et le bois en France* (Notes et études documentaires 4665–6). Paris: DF

Plaisance, G. 1961: *Guide des forêts de France*. Paris: La Nef de Paris (a mine of information of all kinds). See also the same author's:
1979: *Le forêt française*. Paris: Denoël
Le Ray, J. 1977: *La forêt française* (Notes et études documentaires 4441–2). Paris: DF

4.2.2 Particularly related to Mediterranean France

Douguédroit, A. 1976: *Les paysages forestiers de Haute Provence et des Alpes maritimes*, 2v. Aix-en-Provence: Edisud
Kunholtz-Lordat, G. 1952: *Le tapis végétal dans ses rapports avec les phénomènes actuels de surface en Basse-Provence*. Paris: Lechevalier (a most important contribution to the analysis of the vegetational pattern and its transformation under human impact)
Neboit, R. 1981: La forêt méditerranéenne française depuis 10,000 ans, d'après des travaux récents. *Annales de Géographie* 90, 445–50
For additional items on forests see 17.4.5

4.3 Soils

The Institut national de la Recherche Agronomique published in 1966 a soil map of France on a scale of 1:1,000,000, in two sheets. See also:
Dudal, R., Tavernier, R. & Osmond, D. 1966: *Soil map of Europe 1:2,500,000*. Rome: FAO, sheets 4–5, with accompanying 'Explanatory text'
Agafonov, V. 1936: *Les sols de France au point de vue pédologique*. Paris: Dunod (still of fundamental importance)
Boulaine, J. 1970: *Les sols de France*. Paris: PUF (Que sais-je? 352)

4.4 Hydrology, water supply

Bodelle, J. 1980: *L'eau souterraine en France*. Paris: Masson
Cheret, I. 1967: *L'eau*. Paris: Seuil
Colas, R. 1965: *Le problème de l'eau en France*. Paris: DF
Livre blanc de l'eau en France, 1973. Paris: DF

5 Environment and ecological movements

5.1 The environment

In recent years there has been an explosion of literature, often highly polemical in nature, on the environment and environmental protection:
Arnaud, B. 1975: *La neige empoisonnée*. Paris: Moreau
Aubert, M. J. 1978: *La mer assassinée*. Paris: Moreau
Barrière, M. & others 1984: *L'environnement, l'écologie*. Paris: Syros
Bériot, L. 1976: *Les pieds dans la mer*. Paris: Lattès
di Castri, F. 1984: *L'écologie, les défis de la science en temps de crise*. Paris: DF (Rapport au Ministre de l'industrie et de la recherche)
Garnier Expert, C. 1973: *L'environnement démystifié; le dossier français*. Paris: Mercure de France
Works on more closely defined aspects of the problem include:
Elkins. T. H. & Marstrand, P. K. 1975: Pollution of the Rhine and its tributaries. In *Regional management of the Rhine*. London: Chatham House/PEP (European Series 26)

Escourrou, G. 1981: La pollution atmosphérique en France. *Revue Géographique de l'Est* 21, 153–62

Frécaut, R. 1972: La pollution chimique et minérale des eaux fluviales dans le bassin de la Moselle. *Revue Géographique de l'Est* 12, 407–20

George, P. 1971: *L'environnement.* Paris: PUF

Margant, H. 1973: L'environnement, signification et portée du concept. *Aménagement du Territoire et Développement Régional* (Grenoble) 6, 121–46

Michaud, J.-L. 1983: *Le tourisme face à l'environnement.* Paris: PUF

Préau, P. 1972: De la protection de la nature à l'aménagement du territoire. *Aménagement du Territoire et Développement Régional* (Grenoble) 5, 119–72

Tarlet, J. 1977: Milieu naturel et aménagement; les méthodes de planification écologique. *Annales de Géographie* 86, 164–200

For the Rhine see also the annual *Rapport d'activité* and *Tableaux numériques* of the Commission internationale pour la protection du Rhin contre la pollution (Koblenz: The Commission). The 'Groupe interministériel d'évaluation de l'environnement' has published an annual report since 1974 (Paris: DF)

5.2 National and regional parks

Lachaux, C. 1980: *Les parcs nationaux.* Paris: PUF (Que sais-je? 1827)

Leynaud, E. 1985: Les parcs nationaux: territoire des autres. *L'Espace Géographique* 14, 127–38

Morineaux, Y. 1977: *Les parcs naturels régionaux.* (Notes et études documentaires 4439–40). Paris: DF

5.3 The coasts

Forget, J. P., Muret, J. P. & Prouzet, M. 1979: *Sauvegarde et aménagement du littoral.* Paris: CRU

Guilcher, A. & Moign. A. 1977: Coastal conservation and research. *Geographical Journal* 143, 378–92

Littoral français: perspectives pour l'aménagement, 1973. Paris: DF

Michaud, J. L. 1976: *Manifeste pour le littoral.* Paris: Berger-Levrault

Picon, B. 1978: Mécanismes sociaux de transformation d'un écosystème fragile: la Camargue. *Etudes Rurales* 71–2, 219–29

Renard, J. 1984: Le tourisme: agent conflictuel de l'utilisation de l'espace littoral. *Norois* 31, 45–61

5.4 The mountains

For a review of geographical research see:

Barbier, B. & Gabert, P. 1984: Equilibres et déséquilibres montagnards. In Comité national français de géographie (ed.), *La recherche géographique française.* Paris: The Committee, 133–41 (valuable bibliography)

For special numbers of periodicals devoted to mountain problems see La Montagne; espace délaissé, espace convoité, *Cahiers de l'Aménagement du Territoire* 3, 1979 (Grenoble), *Revue de Géographie Alpine* 72 (2–4), 1974, and *Etudes Rurales* 71–2, 1978. For the particular problems of 'la moyennne montagne' (mountain areas of intermediate elevation) see *Bulletin de l'Association de Géographes Français* 57, 1980, 157–85

A collection of papers which, although devoted to various aspects and problems of the

Alps as a whole contains much information relating to France, was issued on the occasion of the 25th International Geographical Congress (*Les Alpes*, Caen, 1985). See also:

Besson, L. 1983: *Politique de développement et de protection des zones de montagne; rapport au Premier ministre.* Paris DF

Brochard, J. 1975: *L'aménagement du territoire en montagne; pour que la montagne vive. Rapport au gouvernement.* Paris: DF

Mériaudeau, R. 1976: Contribution à une réflexion sur la politique d'aménagement de la montagne, à partir de l'évolution démographique de la zone de montagne française (Corse exclue) entre 1962 et 1975. *Revue de Géographie Alpine* 64, 449–82

6 Population

6.1 Sources and general statistics

The basic source of information on population is the census, the first of which took place in 1801. From 1821 to 1936, with very few exceptions, the census was held every five years. From 1946 the interval was more irregular: in recent decades the census has been held in 1962, 1968, 1975 and 1982. Since 1945 INSEE has been responsible for carrying out the census and processing the resultant data. The first results appear as a volume devoted to France as a whole, together with a separate publication for each department, giving the most important data for each commune. Subsequent publications are devoted to tables of sample data and to specialized volumes, for example towns and urbanized areas (*villes et agglomérations urbaines*).

6.2 General works

Three concise historical studies are offered by:

Armengaud, A. 1971: *La population française au XIXe siècle.* Paris: PUF

Armengaud, A. & Fine, A. 1983: *La population française au XXe siècle*, 6th edn. Paris: PUF

Dupâquier, J. 1979: *La population française au XVIIe et XVIIIe siècles.* Paris: PUF (Que sais-je? 1786)

See also:

Beaujeu-Garnier, J. 1976: *La population française (après le recensement de 1975).* Paris: Colin

Noin, D. 1973: *Géographie démographique de la France.* Paris: PUF

6.3 Population change

6.3.1 Maps and atlases

Carte de la répartition de la population de la France 1:1,000,000, 1962. Paris: CRDCG (CNRS)

Carte de la variation de population de la France par cantons, 1806–1962 1:1,000,000, 1967 & 1969. Paris: CRDCG (CNRS)

Cartes de l'évolution de la population 1962–68–75 par arrondissement, 1975. Paris: CAES (DATAR)

Cartographie statistique, v. 1, 1980: *La population française*; v. 2, 1981: *Activité et habitat.* Paris: INSEE & IGN

6.3.2 Population variation in general

The journal *Population*, published by INED, is an invaluable source of up-to-date information on population developments in France. It includes an annual 'Rapport sur la situation démographique en France', which in addition to a general review of developments gives special attention to a different subject each year. The monthly *Population et Société* of the same organization contains brief but authoritative items on French population, for example:

L'évolution démographique comparée de la France. *Population et Société* 200, 1986. See also:

Calot, G. 1981: The demographic situation in France. *Population Trends* 25, 15–20

Noin, D. 1984: La population de la France au début des années 1980. *Annales de Géographie* 93, 290–302

Ogden, P. E. 1981: French population trends in the 1970s. *Geography* 66, 312–15

6.3.3 Natural variation

Biraben, J. N. & Dupâquier, J. 1981: *Les berceaux vides de Marianne.* Paris: Seuil

Blanchet, D. 1981: Evolution de la fécondité des régions françaises depuis 1969. *Population* 36, 817–44

Courgeau, D. 1976: Mobilité géographique, nuptualité et fécondité. *Population* 31, 901–15

Le Bras, H. 1971: Géographie de la fécondité française depuis 1921. *Population* 26, 1093–125

Nizard, A. & Prioux, F. 1975: La mortalité départementale en France. *Population* 30, 781–824

Scargill, D. I. 1985: *The population of France.* University of Oxford, School of Geography (Research Papers 34)

6.3.4 International migration and migration from overseas departments

The journal *Population*, published by INED, contains an annual *Chronique de l'immigration*. In addition to a general survey of recent developments, this includes an investigation of a different special topic each year, for example birth rates (1980) or housing conditions (1982). See also:

Bailley, P. 1976: *Les rapatriés d'Algérie en France* (Notes et études documentaires 4275–6). Paris: DF

Cross, G. S. 1983: *Immigrant workers in industrial France; the making of a new labouring class.* Philadelphia: Temple University Press

Granotier, B. 1979: *Les travailleurs immigrés en France*, 5th edn. Paris: Maspero

6.3.5 Seasonal and trans-frontier migration

Aubry, B. 1984: 100,000 travailleurs frontaliers. *Economie et Statistique* 170, 13–23

Brahimi, M. 1980: Les travailleurs frontaliers. *Population* 35, 456–8

Les travailleurs saisonniers et frontaliers, 1979 (Notes et études documentaires 4519–20). Paris: DF

6.4 Spatial aspects of population change

6.4.1 Overall change

Boudoul, J. & Faur, J.-P. 1982: Renaisssance des communes rurales ou nouvelle forme d'urbanisation? *Economie et Statistique* 149 (supplément) I–XVI

Fielding, A. J. 1982: Counterurbanization in western Europe. *Progress in Planning* 17, 1–52

Ogden, P. E. 1985: Counterurbanization in France: the result of the 1982 population census. *Geography* 70, 24–35
Pumain, D. 1983: Déconcentration urbaine. *Population et société*, 166

6.4.2 Rural areas

Limouzin, P. 1980: Les facteurs de dynamisme des communes rurales françaises. *Annales de Géographie* 89, 549–87
Merlin, P. 1971: *L'exode rural*. Paris: PUF
Ogden, P. E. 1980: Migration, marriage and the collapse of traditional peasant society in France. In P. E. White & R. I. Woods (eds.), *The geographical impact of migration*. London: Longman, 152–79
Pitié, J. 1979: *L'exode rural*. Paris: PUF (Que sais-je? 1747)
White, P. E. 1980: Migration loss and the residual community: a study in rural France 1962–75. In White & Woods, *The geographical impact of migration*, ch. 11
See also 17.6

6.4.3 Urban areas

Bonvalet, C. & Tugault, Y. 1984; Les racines du dépeuplement de Paris. *Population* 39, 463–81 (longer-term development since 1801)
Jones, P. N. 1978: Urban population changes in France 1962–75. *Erdkunde* 32, 198–222
Lefèbvre, M. 1981: Evolution démographique des villes de plus de 500,000 habitants hormis Paris de 1954 à 1975. *Population* 36, 295–316
See also 18.5.

6.5 Internal migration

6.5.1 The general pattern

Aydalot, P. & de Gaudemar, J. P. 1972: *Les migrations*. Paris: Gauthier-Villars
Bastide, H. & Girard, A. 1974: Mobilité de la population et motivations des personnes; une enquête auprès du public. *Population* 29, 579–607
Boudoul, J. & Faur, J.-P. 1985: Depuis 1975, les migrations interrégionales sont moins nombreuses. *Economie et Statistique* 180, 11–21
Courgeau, D. 1978: Les migrations internes en France de 1954 à 1975, 1: vue d'ensemble. *Population* 23, 525–45
Tugault, Y. 1970: La mobilité géographique en France depuis un siècle; une étude par générations. *Population* 25, 1019–36
Winchester, H. P. M. 1977: *Changing patterns of French internal migration 1891–1968*. University of Oxford, School of Geography (Research Papers 17)

6.5.2 Vacation, leisure and retirement movements

Cribier, F. 1969: *La grande migration des citadins*. Paris: CRDCG (CNRS)
1973: *La migration de retraite*. Paris: CORDES
1975: Retirement migration in France. In L. A. Kosinski & R. M. Prothero (eds.), *People on the move: studies in internal migration*. London: Methuen, 361–73
Flament, F. 1984: Les vacances des Français. *Revue de Géographie de Lyon* 59, 7–14
Mirloup, J. 1984: Les loisirs des Français: approche géographique. *Revue de Géographie de Lyon* 59, 15–28

6.6 Structural–spatial differentiation

6.6.1 Age–sex structure; marital status

Durr, J.-M. & de Saboulin, M. 1985: L'âge des Français: contrastes régionaux et opposition ville–campagne. *Economie et Statistique* 173, 25–32

Guibourdenche, H. 1979: Croissance et Structures démographiques des régions françaises de programme depuis 1968; vers une nouvelle géographie des grands déséquilibres territoriaux. *Revue de Géographie Alpine* 67, 173–94

Jegouzo, G. 1979: Le célibat paysan en 1975. *Population* 34, 27–43

Paillat, P. 1983: Le vieillissement de la campagne française: phénomène démographique et social. *Espaces – populations – sociétés* 39–44

Paillat, P. & Parent, A. with others. 1980: *Le vieillissement de la campagne française.* Paris; PUF (INED Travaux et documents 88). See also *Population* 35, 1980, 167–71

Parant, A. 1978: Les personnes âgées en 1975 et le vieillissement démographique en France 1931–75. *Population* 35, 381–411

6.6.2 Active population

Fruit, J.-P. 1978: L'évolution récente de la population active rurale en France (1968–75). *L'Information Géographique* 42, 159–67

Mabile, S. & Jayet, H. 1985: La redistribution géographique des emplois entre 1975 et 1982. *Economie et Statistique* 182, 23–35

Marc, N, & Marchand, O, 1984: La population active de 1975 à 1982: les facteurs d'une forte croissance. *Economie et Statistique* 171–2, 5–23

Nizard, A. 1971: La population active selon les recensements depuis 1946, *Population* 26, 9–61

Rault, D. 1984: Secteurs d'activité: l'évolution des structures de la main d'oeuvre. *Economie et Statistique* 171–2, 35–47

Thevenot, L. 1978: Les catégories sociales en 1975; L'extension du salariat. *Economie et Statistique* 91, 3–31

6.6.3 Women and employment

Fagnani, J. 1983: Women's commuting patterns in the Paris region. *Tijdschrift voor Economische en Sociale Geografie* 74, 12–24

Sztokman, N. 1978: Les Françaises et le travail. *Annales de Géographie* 87, 673–95

7 Contrasting mentalities and civilizations

7.1 Mentalities

France, French civilization and the mentalities of French people have long attracted the attention of writers, particularly foreign ones:

Ariès, P. 1948: *Histoire des populations françaises et de leurs attitudes devant la vie depuis le XVIIIe siècle.* Paris: Self. Reprinted Paris: Seuil, 1971, 1976 etc. with a preliminary note

Combe, P. 1959: *Le drame français, du libre échange au Marché commun.* Paris: Plon (contains interesting preface by A. Siegfried)

de Madariaga, S. 1928: *Englishmen, Frenchmen, Spaniards: an essay in comparative psychology.* London: OUP

Morazé, C. 1956: *Les Français et la République.* Paris: Colin

Pitts, J. R. 1963: Continuité et changement au sein de la France bourgeoise. In S. Hoffman & others (eds.), *A la recherche de la France*. Paris: Seuil

Zeldin, T. 1983: *The French*. London: Collins. Also issued 1983 as Flamingo paperback (London: Fontana)

See also section 1.5, in particular the various works by J. Ardagh.

7.2. Influences on French civilization

Deléage, P. 1941 *La vie rurale en Bourgogne jusqu'au début du XIe siècle*. Mâcon (on the prehistoric origins of the north–south division)

Derruau, M. 1949: *La Grande Limagne auvergnate et bourbonnaise*. Clermont-Ferrand: Delaunay (part 4, 405–88, is entirely devoted to the 'north–south contrast')

Flatrès, P. 1957: *Géographie rurale de quatre contrées celtiques: Irlande, Galles, Cornwall et Man*. Rennes: Phinon (especially the Conclusion, 561–75)

1959: Les structures rurales de la frange atlantique de l'Europe. In *Géographie et histoire agraires*. Nancy (Annales de l'Est Mémoire 21)

Fox, E. W. 1971; *History in geographic perspective: the other France*. New York: Norton

Jeanton, G. 1937: Les limites respectives des influences septentrionales et méditerranéennes en France. *Société des Amis des Arts et des Sciences de Tournus* 38, 125–42 (contains map relating to France as a whole)

Lafont, R. (ed.) 1971: *Le sud et le nord; dialectique de la France*. Toulouse: Privat

Lebeau, R. 1948: Les contrastes du nord et du midi dans la géographie humaine du Jura français. *Études Rhodaniennes*, 23, 93–103

Specklin, R. 1978: Contrastes nord – sud en France. *Regio Basiliensis* 20, 16–63

8 Administrative geography

8.1 General works

Lagroye, J. & Wright, V. (eds.) 1979: *Local government in Britain and France; problems and prospects*. London: Allen & Unwin

Simonetti, J. O. 1977: L'administration de l'espace; l'exemple français, *Annales de Géographie* 86, 129–63

Vernet, M. 1970: Les circonscriptions administratives de la France métropolitaine. *Economie et Statistique* 10, 39–56

See also, 2.1

8.2. Communes and departments

A remarkable map of the communes of France by the 'Laboratoire de cartographie de l'école pratique des hautes études' under the direction of J. Bertin is available with accompanying commentaries:

Meynier, A., Perpillou, A., Juillard, E., Enjalbert, H., Barrère, P., Duby, G. & Piatier, A., 1958: *Annales: Économies, Sociétés, Civilisations* 13, 447–87

The first article to draw attention to the interest of studying the French communal network was:

Meynier, A. 1945: La commune rurale française. *Annales de Géographie* 53–4, 161–79. Also:

1967: Départements et communes de France: sont-ils trop petits? in J. Sporck & B. Schoumaker (eds.), *Mélanges Tulippe*, v. 2. Gembloux: Duculot, 442–51

Calmès, R., & others 1979: Le fait communal en France. *Espace 90*, 91
Givaudan, A. 1978: *La question communale.* Paris: Editions de la revue politique et parlementaire
See also the proceedings of the *Colloques organisés par l'Association pour l'étude de fait départemental*, for example Poitiers 1981, Rennes 1982.

8.3 Regions and the advocacy of regional government

Dayries, J. J. & M. 1978: *La régionalisation.* Paris: PUF
Flory, T. 1966: *Le mouvement régionaliste français; sources et développement.* Paris: PUF (Travaux et recherches de la Faculté de Droit et des Sciences Politiques de Paris, série 'Science politique' 6)
Gras, C. & Livet, G. 1977: *Régions et régionalisme en France du XVIIIe siècle à nos jours.* Paris: PUF
Two brilliant books by a Frenchman of Occitan origins, who became a fervent proponent of regionalism:
Lafont, R. 1967: *La révolution régionaliste.* Paris: Gallimard
    1968: *Sur la France.* Paris: Gallimard

8.4 Decentralization and administrative reform

Bélorgey, G. 1984: *La France décentralisée.* Paris: Berger-Levrault (detailed description of new administrative structures)
Bernard, P. 1983: *L'État et la décentralisation: du Préfet au Commissaire de la République* (Notes et études documentaires 4711–12). Paris: DF
Frears, J. R. 1983: The decentralization reforms in France. *Parliamentary Affairs* 36, 56–66
Meny, Y. 1983: Permanence and change: the relations between central government and local authorities in France. *Environment and Planning C: Government and Policy* 1, 17–28
Rondin, J. 1985: *Le sacre des notables: La France en décentralization.* Paris: Fayard (Espace et politique)
Schmidt, D. 1984: *La région à l'heure de la décentralisation* (Notes et études documentaires 4772). Paris: DF
See also 11.3.

9 Planning

9.1 General works

Most items relate to economic planning at national level:
Bauchet, P. 1971: *La planification française; du premier au sixième plan.* Paris: Seuil
Estrin, S. & Holmes, P. 1983: *French planning in theory and practice.* London: Allen & Unwin
Le Garrec, J. 1984: *Demain la France; les choix du IXe plan.* Paris: La découverte
Pascallon, P. 1974: *La planification de l'économie française.* Paris: Masson
    1979: *Quelle planification pour la France?* Paris: Ed. l'épargne
Treize, R. 1976: *La planification française en pratique.* Paris: Ed. ouvrières
Ulmo, Y. 1974; *La planification en France.* Paris: Dalloz
The text of each of the French national plans (*plans de modernisation et d'équipement*) is published in the *Journal Officiel* and also issued as a separate publication (DF). The reports

of Commissions established for the preparation of the plans are also published (DF) and provide a valuable source of information on spatial distributions and problems in France. The execution of each plan is the subject of annual reports (Paris: Imprimerie Nationale). Useful periodicals include:

Inter-régions; Revue du Conseil National des Économies Régionales et de la Productivité
La Lettre de la DATAR (1973–)

9.2 Regional and spatial planning

9.2.1 Works covering the two fields

Claval, P. 1975: Planification régionale at aménagement du territoire. *Revue Géographique de l'Est* 15, 169–216
de Lanversin, J. 1979: *La région et l'aménagement du territoire*, 3rd edn. Paris: LITEC
Lajugie, J., Delfaud, P. & Lacour, C. 1985: *Espace régional et aménagement du territoire*, 2nd edn. Paris: Dalloz

9.2.2 Regional planning

The regional action programmes (*programmes d'action régionale*, subsequently *plans régionaux de développement et d'aménagement*) were published in the *Journal Officiel* and also as separate documents. The relevance of the programme to the problems of one particular region was traced in a book of general interest:
Phlipponneau, M. 1957; *Le problème breton et le programme d'action régionale*. Paris: Colin (Centre d'études économiques 6)
The principles and practices of French regional planning have attracted the attention of many authors, particularly in the English-speaking lands:
Allen, K. & Maclennan, M. C. 1970: *Regional problems and policies in Italy and France*. London: Allen & Unwin (University of Glasgow, Department of Social and Economic Research, Social and Economic Studies)
Bruyelle, P. 1982: La réforme des aides de développement régional en France. *L'Information Géographique* 46, 133–7
Chapuy, P. M. B. 1984: France. In R. H. Williams (ed.), *Planning in Europe: urban and regional planning in the EEC*. London: Allen & Unwin, ch. 4
Clout, H. D. 1981: Regional development in practice: France. In H. D. Clout (ed.), *Regional development in Western Europe*, 2nd edn. Chichester: Wiley, ch. 8
Deves, C. 1977: *Les sociétés d'aménagement régional*. Clermont-Ferrand: Université I
Flockton, C. H. 1984: France; ambitious Gaullist designs and constrained socialist plans. *Built Environment* 10, 132–4
Hansen N. M. 1968: *French regional planning*. Edinburgh University Press
Perrin, J. C. 1975: *Le développement régional*. Paris: PUF
Prud'homme, R. 1974: Regional economic policy in France 1962–1972. In N. M. Hansen (ed.), *Public policy and regional economic development; the experience of nine western countries*. Cambridge, Mass.: Ballinger, ch. 2
Ross, G. W. & Cohen, S. S. 1975: The politics of French regional planning. In J. Friedman & W. Alonso (ed.), *Regional policy; readings in theory and applications*. Cambridge, Mass.: MIT Press, 727–50
Savy, M. 1984: Regional development issues in France. In M. Demko (ed.), *Regional development problems and policies in eastern and western Europe*. London: Croom Helm, 200–13

Growth-pole planning in relation to the Marseille–Fos project appears particularly to have attracted radical criticism:

Bleitrach, D. & Chenu, A. 1982: Regional planning – regulation or deepening of social contradictions? The example of Fos-sur-Mer and the Marseilles Metropolitan Area. In R. Hudson & J. R. Lewis (eds.), *Regional planning in Europe*, 148–78 with a footnote by the editors, 179–83

Durrieu, Y. 1973: *L'impossible régionalisation capitaliste; témoignages de Fos et de Languedoc.* Paris: Anthropos

Kinsey, J. 1978: The application of growth-pole theory in the Aire Métropolitaine Marseillaise. *Geoforum* 9, 245–67

9.2.3 Strategic spatial planning

Official acceptance of a policy of *Aménagement du territoire* was signalled in three 'green papers':

Ministère de la reconstruction et de l'urbanisme, Direction de l'Aménagement du territoire. 1950: *Pour un plan d'aménagement du territoire.* Paris

    1950: *L'aménagement du territoire, premier rapport.* Paris

    1962: *L'aménagement du territoire, deuxième rapport.* Paris

DATAR has since 1968 published a series 'Travaux et recherches de prospective' (TRP) devoted to all aspects of spatial planning. DATAR also published the periodical *2,000.* Other notable publications include:

DATAR 1979: *Nouvelles orientations pour l'aménagement du territoire; Conférence nationale d'aménagement du territoire 1978.* Paris: DF

DATAR (SESAME) 1971: *Une image de la France en l'an 2000, scénario de l'inacceptable,* Paris: DF (TRP 20) and *Le scénario de l'inacceptable, sept ans après.* Paris: DF (TRP 68)

Those responsible for the leadership of DATAR have published their personal views, either during their period of office or on leaving it.

Guichard, O. 1965: *Aménager la France.* Paris: Laffont

Monod, J. & de Castelbajac, P. 1971: *L'aménagement du territoire.* Paris: PUF

Monod, J. 1974: *Transformation d'un pays; pour une géographie de la liberté.* Paris: Fayard

Essig, F. 1979: *Datar; des régions et des hommes.* Paris: Stanke

Lamour, P. 1980: *Le cadran solaire.* Paris: Laffont

The Centre d'étude et de recherche sur l'administration économique et l'aménagement du territoire (Institut d'études politiques de l'Université de Grenoble) has published annually from 1968: *Aménagement du territoire et développement régional; les faits, les idées, les institutions.* Each annual volume comprises original articles, surveys, bibliographies, official documents and biographies relating to this field of activity. The same centre publishes *Cahiers de l'aménagement du territoire* (see for example n. 5, 1979: *Agonie ou relance de l'aménagement du territore*). Other contributions to the debate include:

Gravier, J.-F. 1964: *L'aménagement du territoire et l'avenir des régions françaises.* Paris: Flammarion

Audouin, J. 1977: *La France culbutée.* Paris: Moreau

Aydalot, P. 1978: L'aménagement du territoire en France; une tentative de bilan. *L'Espace Géographique* 7, 245–53

Frémont, A. 1978: L'aménagement régional en France; la pratique et les idées. *L'Espace Géographique* 7, 73–84

10 Property and tenure

See the quarterly revue *Etudes Foncières*.

10.1 General and social aspects

10.1.1 Rural land ownership and tenures

Bergmann, J. 1977: Le facteur terre; le problème foncier agricole. In *Politique agricole*, v. 2, *Structures*. Paris; INRA

de Farcy, H. & Gastaldi, J. 1978: *La propriété agricole*. Paris: PUF (Que sais-je? 1737)

Houillier, F. 1982: *Structure foncière et exploitations agricoles* (Notes et études documentaires 4655–6). Paris: DF

Vaillant, J. 1980: *La propriété foncière agricole, rentes et plus-values*. Paris: PUF (Travaux et rech. Univ. Paris II)

In the period 1948–68 geographers were actively engaged in research into rural land ownership and its spatial consequences. In addition to numerous articles there were two major works:

Dugrand, R. 1963: *Villes et campagnes dans le Bas-Languedoc*. Paris: PUF

Elhaï, H. 1965: *Recherches sur la propriété foncière des citadins en Haute-Normandie*. Paris: CNRS (Mém. et doc. 10, fasc. 3)

Thereafter work by geographers in this field diminished, without totally disappearing:

Chevalier, J. 1948: Les conflicts fonciers: nouvelles perspectives et géographie agraire. In *De la Géographie urbaine à la géographie sociale*, ed. Collectif français de géographie urbaine et sociale. Paris: CNRS

Dorel, G. L'étude de la propriété foncière. *Travaux de l'Institut de Géographie de Reims* 7, 57–70, & 8, 3–24

10.1.2 Urban land ownership and tenures

Guigou, J. L. 1978: L'espace public urbain. *Revue d'Economie Régionale et Urbaine* 2, 149–71.

In the course of 1973, the Centre de sociologie urbaine (CSU) published a series of works on urban property:

Combes, D. & Latapie, E. *L'intervention des groupes financiers français dans l'immobilier*

Propriété foncière et processus d'urbanisation (3 v., monographs on Paris quarters and suburban *lotissements*)

Topalov, C. *Capital et propriété foncière*

10.2 The property market

Barthélemy, D. & others 1976: *Propriété foncière et réorganisation sociale*. Dijon: ENSA (survey of literature)

Derycke, P. H. 1979: *Economie et planification urbaines*, v. 1, *L'espace urbain; l'espace urbain et son prix*. Paris: PUF, ch. 4 (important bibliography)

Postel Vinay, G. 1974: *La rente foncière dans le capitalisme agricole*. Paris: Maspero

Scott, A. J. 1976: Land and land rent; an interpretative review of the French literature. *Progress in Geography* 9, 101–45

10.3 Problems and policies with regard to land

Brun, A. 1979: Propriété foncière et exploitation agricole; contradictions et conflits. *Economie Rurale* 3, 19–33

Chassagne, M. E. 1977: Aspects fonciers de l'aménagement de l'espace rural. *Economie Rurale* 117, 35–47

Gilli, J. P. 1975: *Redéfinir le droit de propriété*. Paris: CRU

Lipietz, A. 1974: *Le tribut foncier urbain; circulation du capital et propriété foncière dans la production du cadre bâti*. Paris: Maspero

Marek, G. 1976: Les instruments d'une politique foncière des communes urbaines; les enseignements de l'analyse économique. *L'Espace Géographique* 5, 107–13

Marini, P. & Remont, B. 1976: *Spéculation et politique foncières*. Paris: Berger-Levrault (Collection 'L'administration nouvelle')

See also 13.3

11 Agents of geographical change

11.1 Powers and decisions

This is a topic on which published work has increased greatly in recent years:

Crozier, M. 1977: *L'acteur et le système; les contraintes de l'action collective*. Paris: Seuil

Grémion, C. 1979: *Profession: décideurs*. Paris: Gauthier-Villars

Grémion, P. 1976: *Le pouvoir périphérique; bureaucrates et notables dans le système politique français*. Paris: Seuil

Sfez, L. 1970: *L'administration prospective*. Paris: Colin

    1976: *Critique de la décision*. Paris: Colin

    1978: *L'enfer et le paradis*. Paris: PUF

    1979 (ed.): *Décision et pouvoir dans la société française*. Paris: Christian Bourgeois

For the geographical impact, see:

Reynaud, A. 1977: Centre de décision et localisations industrielles; l'exemple de l'Europe occidentale. *Travaux de l'Institut de Géographie de Reims* 31–2, 19–34

Thibault, A. 1976: La structure économique des espaces locaux en France; dépendance et domination. *L'Espace Géographique* 5, 239–49

11.2 Financial resources

Historical:

Bergeron, L. 1978: *Les capitalistes en France, 1780–1914*. Paris: Gallimard

Palmade, G. 1961: *Capitalisme et capitalistes français au XIXe siècle*. Paris: Colin

The first geographical treatment of the theme was by:

Labasse, J. 1955: *Les capitaux et la région*. Paris: Colin

    1974: *L'espace financier*. Paris: Colin. See also:

Bellon, B. 1980: *Le pouvoir financier et l'industrie en France*. Paris: Seuil

Beginning in 1969, the January number of *L'Usine Nouvelle* contains a survey of annual public and private investment projects of 10 million francs or more.

11.3 The state

Ménard, L. A. 1973: *Administrations centrales et aménagement du territoire; rapport au gouvernement*. Paris: DF

Thoenig, J. C. 1973: *L'ère des technocrates; le cas des Ponts et Chaussées*. Paris: Ed. d'Organisation

Traband, A. 1971: Dynamisme urbain et tutelle administrative. *Revue Géographique de l'Est* 11, 415–21

For impact of decentralization at local level see also 8.4.

11.4 Local government

Bouinot, J. 1977: *La nouvelle gestion municipale; comptabilité et management d'une commune.* Paris: Cujas

Bouinot, J. & Maarek, G. 1974: Les grandes agglomérations et leurs finances. *Economie et Statistique* 58, 15–31

Bouinot, J. & others 1976: *L'influence des finances municipales sur le processus de croissance urbaine.* Paris: CNRS (Collection des actions thématiques programmées)

Limouzin, P. 1973: Signification géographique de la fiscalité et des finances locales. *Annales de Géographie* 82, 732–42

Research on the relationship between the financial policies of local authorities and their political allegiance has hitherto been scanty:

Guemonprez, G. 1977: *Les finances départementales.* Paris: Berger-Levrault

Kobielski, J. 1978: Tendance politique des municipalités et comportements financiers locaux. *Rev. Éco. Rég. et Urb.* 479–510

11.5 Regions

Deneux, M. 1979: *L'évolution du rôle des établissements publics régionaux dans le domaine économique et social.* Paris: CES

Dulong, R. 1978: *Les régions, l'état et la société locale.* Paris: PUF

Gueslin, A. 1977: Le Crédit agricole et l'espace régional. *Economie Rurale* 118, 24–32

Lesourne, J. & Loué, R. 1979: *L'analyse des décisions d'aménagement régional.* Paris: Dunod

11.6 Foreign capital

Delapierre, M. & Michalet, C. A. 1976: *Les implantations étrangères en France.* Paris: DF *Firmes internationales et division internationale du travail.* TRP 55, 1975. Paris: DF

11.7 The private sector

Bakis, H. 1977: *IBM; une multinationale régionale.* Grenoble: PUG

Combes, D. 1974: *Les sociétés-supports de l'intervention immobilière des groupes financiers; essais de classement en fonction des combinaisons de capitaux.* Paris: CSU

12 Economic activities

12.1 General works

Books on the French economy in general are too numerous and are replaced at too fast a rate for individual mention here: some are to be found in section 1.5. See in addition:

DATAR 1977: *Sur l'emploi.* Paris: DF (TRP 73). This publication contains maps of economically active population by arrondissement for the years 1962, 1968 & 1975, which have also been separately published by DF

DATAR (SESAME) 1978: *Activités et régions; dynamique d'une transformation.* Paris: DF (TRP 75). This publication contains two studies, on regional employment and on regional aspects of tertiary development.

DATAR 1979 (and subsequent edns.): *Association bureaux province; aides au développement régional: industrie, tertiaire, recherche.* Paris
Economic survey: France. Paris: OECD (an annual publication covering somewhat different matter each year)

Noin, D. 1973: Essai d'établissement d'une carte économique de la France sur des bases comptables. *L'Espace Géographique* 2, 257-65. See also 14. 1

12.2 Mineral resources

The fundamental work remains:

Lacroix, A. 1962: *Minéralogie de la France et de ses anciens territoires d'outre-mer,* revised edn. Paris: Blanchard.

See also

Callot, F. 1962: Répartition géographique des productions minérales en France. *Annales des Mines,* 667–93 (ingeniously provides an index expressing mineral resources in relation to the area and the population of each department of France)

Laffitte, P. 1966: La métallogénie de la France. *Bulletin de la Société Géologique de France,* 52–72

Annales des Mines publishes an annual survey, 'L'énergie, les métaux et les minerais en France'. See also 'Les ressources minières françaises' (with a map at 1:1,500,000), *Annales des Mines* 186 (7–8), 1980

12.3 Energy

12.3.1 General works

Contributions in this field are liable to be rapidly overtaken by events, particularly in relation to the changing price of oil. Of continuing importance are the periodicals *La Revue de l'Energie* and *Annales des Mines.* See also:

Bilans de l'énergie 1970 à 1984, 1985. Paris: DF

Les chiffres clés de l'énergie (annual). Paris: Dunod

Other publications, all to some degree overtaken by events, include:

Chardonnet, J. 1973: *Les sources d'énergie.* Paris: Sirey

Oizon, R. 1973: *L'évolution récente de la production énergétique française.* Paris: Larousse

Seyer, C. 1980: L'évolution de la consommation et de la production des différentes sources d'énergie en France entre 1970 et 1980. *Revue Géographique de l'Est* 20, 43–64

12.3.2 Coal

The principal sources are the statistics and annual reports of Charbonnages de France. See also:

Lepidi, J. 1976; *Le charbon en France* (Notes et études documentaires 4280–82). Paris: DF

12.3.3 Oil and gas

The principal sources are the publications of the various oil companies and trades associations (Union des chambres syndicales de l'industrie du pétrole, Paris). 'Gaz de France' publishes statistics and an annual report.

Di Meo, G. 1982: *Pétrole et gaz naturel en France; un empire menacé,* 2v. Aix-en-Provence: Edisud

12.3.4 Electricity

Electricité de France publishes statistics and an annual report.

Electricité de France 1981: *Electricité de France: enterprise nationale, industrielle et commerciale* (Notes et études documentaires 4475–6). Paris: DF

Oizon, R. 1978: Géographie de la production d'énergie en France; les grandes vallées: le Rhône, le Rhin et la Durance *Revue de l'Énergie* 29, 269–74
Soumagne, J. 1973: Problèmes géographiques de l'énergie nucléaire en France. *L'Information géographique* 37, 43–51

13 Agriculture

In addition to the works of specialists on agriculture as such, geographers have written extensively on spatial aspects of agricultural activity. Major contributions have also been made by economists, sociologists, anthropologists and historians. For works on rural life and landscape in a wider sense see section 17. An essential periodical is *Economie Rurale*, which produces special numbers, for example 1982: *Inégalités et solidarités dans l'agriculture française*; 1983: *Où va l'agriculture française?*

13.1 General characteristics

13.1.1 Historical development

Clout, H. D. 1980: *Agriculture in France on the eve of the railway age.* London: Croom Helm
  1983: *The land of France 1815–1914.* London: Allen & Unwin (The London Research Series in Geography 1)
Duby, G. & Wallon, A. (ed.) 1973–6: *Histoire de la France rurale*, 4v. Paris: Seuil
Goldsmith, J. L. 1984: The agrarian history of pre-industrial France. *Journal of European Economic History* 13, 167–99 (useful review of literature and bibliography)
Grantham, W. 1980: The persistence of open-field farming in nineteenth-century France. *Journal of Economic History* 40, 515–31
Houssel, J.-P. (general editor) 1976: *L'histoire des paysans français.* Roanne: Horvath
Newell, W. H. 1973: The agricultural revolution in nineteenth-century France. *Journal of Economic History* 33, 697–731
See also 17.3.2

13.1.2 Basic literature

Dumont, R. 1956: *Voyages en France d'un agronome.* Paris: Médicis
Dumont, R. & de Ravignan, F. 1977: *Nouveaux voyages dans les campagnes françaises.* Paris: Seuil
Franklin, S. H. 1969: *The European peasantry: the final phase.* London: Methuen, ch. 3
Gervais, M. & others 1965: *Une France sans paysans.* Paris: Seuil
Houée, P. 1972: *Les étapes de développement rural*, v. 1: *Une longue évolution (1815–1950)*; v. 2: *La révolution contemporaine.* Paris: Ed. ouvrières
Klatzmann, J. 1972: *Géographie agricole de la France.* Paris: PUF (Que sais-je? 420)
  1978: *L'agriculture française.* Paris: Seuil
Livet, R. 1966: *L'avenir des régions agricoles.* Paris: Ed. ouvrières
  1980: *Les nouveaux visages de l'agriculture française.* Paris: Ed. ouvrières
Viau, P. 1978: *L'essentiel sur l'agriculture française.* Paris: Ed. ouvrières
Wright, G. 1964: *Rural revolution in France; the peasantry in the twentieth century.* Stanford University Press

13.1.3 Capital and agriculture

Bentolila, M. 1974: *Le capital en agriculture.* Paris: Connaissance de l'agriculture

Brangeon, J. L. 1972: La place des capitaux dans l'explication des évolutions de l'agriculture des régions françaises 1953–64. *Annales d'Economie et de Sociologie Rurales* 1, 47–67

13.1.4 Disparities

Bentolila, M. 1977: L'évolution récente des disparités. Cahiers du Bureau Agricole Commun 1, 45–81
Pautard, J. 1965: *Les disparités régionales dans la croissance de l'agriculture française.* Paris: Gauthier-Villars
Quaden, G. 1973: *Parité pour l'agriculture et disparité entre agriculteurs; essai critique sur la politique des revenus agricoles.* The Hague: Nijhoff
Rainelli, P. 1980: Essai d'explication des disparités départementales de l'agriculture française. *Economie Rurale* 137, 10–19

13.1.5 Modernization and transformation

Bodiguel, M. 1975: *Les paysans face au progrès.* Paris: Presses FNScP (Travaux et recherches de science politique 37)
Fel, A. 1984: L'agriculture française en mouvement. *Annales de Géographie* 93, 303–25
Jollivet, M. (ed.) 1971: *Structures agraires et diffusion de l'économie contractuelle en agriculture.* Paris: CNRS
Mendras, J. 1970: *The vanishing peasant: innovation and change in French agriculture.* Cambridge, Mass.: MIT Press
Reboul, C. 1978: *Déterminants économiques de la mécanisation de l'agriculture; l'accroissement du parc des tracteurs de grande puissance.* Paris: INRA
Verrière, J. 1977: Le progrès agricole est-il devenu un mythe dangereux? *Norois* 95 ter (special no.), 247–56
Vert, E. 1984: Agriculture: l'émergence de nouveaux comportements. *Economie et Statistique* 171–2, 59–66

13.2 Agricultural statistics

Basic statistics are provided by general agricultural censuses (for example 1955, 1970) which are the subject of special publications. Sample censuses (1963, the 1967 EEC census, and the 1975 census carried out by EPEXA) are normally published in the SCEES series, *Etudes de la statistique agricole.*

Among INSEE publications, commentaries on agricultural accounts as derived from the national accounts appear in *Economie et Statistique.* A particularly important item is:
Girard, J.-P., Gombert, M. & Pétry, M. 1977: Les agriculteurs, v. 1, Clés pour une comparaison sociale. *Les Collections de l'Insee E*, 46–7. See also:
Données sociales annuelles. *Les Collections de l'Insee M.*
Réseau d'information comptable agricole. *Les collections de l'Insee E*, 1975 and subsequent years

The Ministry of Agriculture publishes *Statistique Agricole Annuelle, Collections de Statistique Agricole* and *Cahiers de Statistique Agricole*, as well as a range of special publications.
Reference can also be made to statistical publications of professional associations such as the Bureau agricole commun, the Chambres d'agriculture and the Caisse nationale de crédit agricole.

In the publications of the *Journal Officiel* reports from the CES are often of great interest, for example 'Les mutations structurelles de l'agriculture' (16 March 1973) or 'Le secteur agro-alimentaire dans la balance commerciale française' (26 & 27 June 1979).

13.3 Holdings

13.3.1 Types of holdings

Approche géographique des exploitations agricoles, 1976. Université de Paris I & Ecole Normale Supérieure, Fontenay-aux-Roses (extensive bibliography)

Bonnamour, J. 1977: Bilan de l'approche géographique des exploitations agricoles. *Cahiers de Fontenay* 7, 5–65

Deffontaines, J.-P. & Osty, P.-L. 1977: Des systèmes de production agricole aux systèmes agraires; présentation d'une recherche. *L'Espace Géographique* 6, 195–9

Faudry, D. 1974; Les différences de productivité dans l'agriculture; éléments d'une typologie des exploitations agricoles. *Economie Rurale* 101, 25–31

Houillier, F. 1982: *Structures foncières et exploitations agricoles* (Notes et études documentaires 4655– 6). Paris: DF

Mainié, P. 1971: *Les exploitations agricoles en France*. Paris: PUF (Que sais-je? 354)

Rey, V. 1980: *L'aggrandissement spatial des exploitations agricoles*. Paris: Economica

13.3.2 Holdings and social structure

Blanc, M. 1977: *Les paysanneries françaises*. Paris: Delarge

Calmès, R. 1974: L'avenir des exploitants familiaux. *L'Information géographique* 38, 83–91

Cavaillhès, J. 1976: L'analyse léniniste de la décomposition de la paysannerie. *Critiques de l'Economie Politique* 1

Mathieu, M. 1974: Quelques aspects principaux des transformations récentes de la structure sociale dans les campagnes françaises. *Geographica Polonica* 29, 169–80

Mollard, A. 1977: *Paysans exploités*. Grenoble: PUG

13.3.3 Part-time farming

de Farcy, H. 1979: *Un million d'agriculteurs à temps partiel?* Paris: Le centurion

La double activité en milieu rural; avis et rapports du CES. *Journal Officiel* 18 March 1977

Laurent, C. & others 1979: Les agriculteurs à temps partiel; dynamique et évolution entre 1963 et 1970. *Statistique Agricole* 174

Regnier, E. 1985: La pluriactivité en agriculture. *Economie et Statistique* 173, 17–24

13.3.4 Structural reform

Bowler, I. 1979: *Government and agriculture: a spatial perspective*. London: Longman, ch. 3

Butterwick, M. & Rolfe, E. N. 1965: Structural reform in French agriculture – the work of the SAFERs. *Journal of Agricultural Economics* 16, 548–54

Martin, J. 1971: Les GAEC en France. *L'Information Géographique* 35, 163–70

Perry, P. J. 1969: The structural revolution in French agriculture. *Revue de Géographie de Montréal* 23, 137–51

Rambaud, P. 1974: *Les coopératives de travail agraire en France*. Paris: EPHE (substantial bibliography)

Reboul, C. 1977: Les groupements agricoles d'exploitation en commun 10 ans après. *Economie Rurale* 4, 49–61

13.4 Agricultural production

13.4.1 Agricultural systems

Bonnamour, J. 1974: Régions agricoles et modernisation de l'agriculture française. *Geographia Polonica* 29, 295–306

Bonnamour, J. & Gillette, C. 1970: *Types d'agriculture en France: essai méthodologique.* Paris: CNRS

Bonnamour, J., Guermond, Y. & Gillette, C. 1971: Les systèmes régionaux d'exploitation agricole en France; méthode d'analyse typologique. *Etudes Rurales* 43-4, 78–169

Guermond, Y. 1979: *Le système de différenciation spatiale en agriculture; la France de l'ouest de 1950 à 1975.* Paris: Champion

13.4.2 Spatial aspects of production

Altmann, G.-C. & others 1973: *La spécialisation des productions céréalières et bovines et ses conséquences économiques; une étude de la structure de la production agricole en France.* Paris: INRA (Série économie et sociologie rurales)

Carles, R. 1979: *L'efficacité des exploitations agricoles françaises produisant des céréales, du lait ou des porcins.* Grignon: INRA

Klatzmann, J. 1955: *La localisation des cultures et des productions animales en France.* Paris: INSEE

Reboul, C. 1977: Déterminants sociaux de la fertilité des sols. *Actes de la Recherche en Science Sociale* 17–18, 85–112

13.4.3 Specialized enterprises

Aubert, D. & Debailleul, G. 1979: Les groupements de producteurs; le cas de l'élevage porcin. *Recherches Économiques et Sociales* 15, 47–93

Frémont, A. 1967: *L'élevage en Normandie; étude géographique,* 2v. Caen: Publ. Fac. Let. Sci. hum.

Huetz de Lemps, A. (ed.) 1979: *Vignobles français.* Paris: CNRS

Lamarch, H. 1977: Les paysans face au marché: l'élevage hors-sol en Bretagne. *Sociologie du Travail* 19, 138–56

Leroux, D. 1976: *La production fruitière en France* (Notes et études documentaires 4321–2). Paris: DF

Les productions végétales en France: la vigne et le vin. 1973 (Notes et études documentaires 3956–7). Paris: DF

Les productions végétales en France: les céréales. 1972 (Notes et études documentaires 3901–2). Paris: DF

Spindler, F. 1976: *L'élevage en France* (Notes et études documentaires 4341–2). Paris: DF

13.5 Agricultural policies

The first resource must be to the texts of the various plans. The Mansholt and Vedel plans were issued in a single volume in 1969 (Paris: DF) and in the same format by SECLAF. See also the periodic plans issued by the Ministry of Agriculture and its various official series, such as *Bulletin d'Information du Ministère de l'Agriculture* and the *Bulletin de l'AIEAR. Economie Rurale* is a valuable guide to the sequence of events.

Augé Laribé, M. 1950: *La politique agricole de la France de 1886 à 1940.* Paris: PUF

Barral, P. 1968: *Les agrariens français de Méline à Pisani.* Paris: Colin

Chombart de Lauwe, J. 1979: *L'aventure agricole de la France de 1945 à nos jours*. Paris: PUF

Cloarec, J. 1978: Un exemple de l'intervention de l'Etat; le financement public de l'agriculture. *Etudes Rurales* 69, 15–25

Coulomb, P., Nallet, H. & Servolini, C. 1979: La politique agricole et son élaboration. *Recherches Economiques et Sociales* 15, 129–55

de Farcy, H. & Groussard, R. 1980: *Contribution à une nouvelle politique de l'exploitation agricole*. CNASEA

Klatzmann, J. 1972: *Les politiques agricoles; idées fausses et illusion*. Paris: PUF

Mahé, L. & Roudet, M. 1980: La politique agricole française et l'Europe verte; impasse ou révision. *Economie Rurale* 135, 12–27 (excellent bibliography)

14 Manufacturing industry

14.1 General works

Geographical studies of the spatial distribution of industry most frequently make use of statistics of the employed or the active population (6.6.2). Information on industrial firms and plants is more difficult to use, in spite of a multiplicity of sources and classifications. INSEE published statistics of industrial establishments for the last time in respect of 1971 (3v., Paris, 1974), since which date the information has been computerized. See, however:

Battiau, M. 1977: Esquisse d'une classification des industries selon l'importance de la valeur ajoutée. *L'Information Géographique* 41, 73–9

The Ministry for Industry publishes *Les chiffres clés de l'industrie française* (Paris: DF). Also of interest is *Géographie et Industrie*, published monthly by a group of professional organizations grouped within the Conseil national du patronat français. Other works of a general nature include:

Bellon, B. & others 1983: *L'industrie en France*. Paris: Flammarion (a treatment of industry branch by branch)

Chardonnet, J. 1965: *Géographie industrielle*. Paris: Sirey 1970–4: *L'économie française*, 4v. Paris: Dalloz (see 1.5)

Cotta, A. 1977: *Le redéploiement industriel; études de politique industrielle*. Paris: DF

Dezert, B. & Verlacque, C. 1978: *L'espace industriel*. Paris: Masson

Di Meo, G. 1984: La crise de système industriel en France, au début des années 1980. *Annales de Géographie* 93, 326–49

Fruit, J. P. 1981: Spécificités industrielles régionales en France. *L'Information Géographique* 45, 120–1

Gachelin, C. 1977: *La localisation des industries*. Paris: PUF

Guibert, B. & others 1975: *La mutation industrielle de la France: du traité de Rome à la crise pétrolière*. Paris: INSEE (Collections de l'Insee E31-2)

Stoffaes, C. 1978: *La grande menace industrielle*. Paris: Calmann-Lévy

Stoleru, L. 1969: *L'impératif industriel*. Paris: Seuil

Tuppen, J. N. 1980: *France*. Folkestone: Dawson & Boulder, Colo.: Westview (Studies in Industrial Geography)

14.2 Stages of industrial development

See the references on general economic development in 1.5 and 2.3, also:

Dunham, A. L. 1955: *The industrial revolution in France, 1815–1848*. New York: Exposition Press

Fohlen, C. 1973: The industrial revolution in France, 1700–1914. In C. M. Cipolla (ed.),

The Fontana economic history of Europe, 4.1: *The emergence of industrial societies*. London: Collins, ch. 1. What appears to be essentially the same paper is also to be found in R. Cameron (ed.), *Essays in French economic history*, 1970. Homewood, Ill.: Irwin, 201–25

Henderson, W. O. 1972: *Britain and industrial Europe*, 3rd edn. Leicester University Press, ch. 2

Lévy-Leboyer, C. 1968: Les processus d'industrialisation; le cas de l'Angleterre et de la France. *Revue Historique* 239, 281–98

Markovitch, T.-J. 1966: *L'industrie française de 1789 à 1964*. Paris: Cahiers de l'ISEA
    1974: la révolution industrielle; le cas de la France. *Revue d'Histoire Économique et Sociale* 52, 115–25

14.3 Industrial decentralization and redevelopment

Bastié, J. 1973: La décentralization industrielle en France de 1954 à 1971. *Bulletin de l'Association de Géographes Français* 408–9, 561–8
    1980: La décentralisation industrielle en France, 1954– 80 *Analyse de l'Espace* 2

Battiau, M. 1978: Quelques remarques sur l'évolution de la répartition géographique des emplois industriels en France entre 1954 et 1975. *L'Information Géographique* 42, 170–88

Bilans régionaux ou départementaux de la décentralisation industrielle. *Analyse de l'Espace* 4, 1981

Durand, P. 1974: *Industrie et régions; l'aménagement industriel du territoire*. Paris: DF

Grelet, J.-L. & Thélot, C. 1977: La prime de développement; un rôle incitatif discutable. *Economie et Statistique* 89, 21–37

Saint Julien, T. 1973: Signification géographique des implantations industrielles décentralisées en province. *Annales de Géographie* 82, 557–75
    1982: *Croissance industrielle et système urbain*. Paris: Economica

Seyer, C. 1976: La décentralisation industrielle en Lorraine. *Revue Géographique de l'Est* 16, 63–74

Le tissu industriel. *Les Cahiers Français*, May-June 1983 (Paris: DF)

14.4 Industrial branches

The literature is extensive but has the disadvantage that items rapidly become dated The 'Notes et études documentaires' published by La documentation française contain periodic monographs on the various industrial branches; some of the more recent examples are included in the following list:

Battiau, M. 1976: *Les industries textiles de la région Nord–Pas-de-Calais*. Paris: Champion

Fontaine, P. 1980: *L'industrie automobile en France* (Notes et études documentaires 4583–4). Paris: DF

Freyssenet, M. 1979: *La sidérurgie française 1945–1979*. Paris: Savielli

Jalabert, G. 1974: *Les industries aéronautiques et spatiales en France*. Toulouse: Privat

Marthey, L. 1978: *L'industrie chimique en France* (Notes et études documentaires 4454). Paris: DF

Mazataud, P. 1978: *Les constructeurs de matériel informatique en France*. Paris: CTHS

Thouvenin, M. 1981: De WENDEL-SIDELOR à SACILOR- SOLLAC 1968–1980: 13 années de mutations difficiles en Lorraine. *Revue Géographique de l'Est* 21, 37– 63

14.5 Patterns of industrial distribution

14.5.1 Industry in rural areas

Beteille, R. 1978: L'industrie en milieu rural en France. *L'Information Géographique* 42, 28–43

Bontron, J.-C. & others 1979: Effets de l'industrialisation en milieu rural. *Recherche Sociale* 69

Chavannes, G. 1975: *Usines à la campagne.* Paris: DF

14.5.2 Industrial towns

Aydalot, P. 1979: L'entreprise dans l'espace urbain. Paris: Economica

Bonneville, M. 1975: La désindustrialisation urbaine; le cas de Villeurbanne. *Revue de Géographie de Lyon* 50, 97–105

Noel. M. 1974: Mobilité spatiale des industries; croissance et urbanisation. *L'Espace Géographique* 3, 47–56

14.5.3 Industrial regions

Battiau, M. 1981: Un essai d'analyse des difficultés du Nord–Pas-de-Calais. *L'Information Géographique* 45, 97–102

Bonnefont, J. C. 1984: *La Lorraine.* Paris: PUF

Burtonshaw, D. 1976: *Saar–Lorraine.* Oxford: OUP

Clout, H. D. 1975: *The Franco–Belgian border region.* Oxford: OUP

Dezert, B. 1969: *La croissance industrielle et urbaine de la porte d'Alsace.* Paris: SEDES

Schnetzler, J. 1973: *Les industries et les hommes dans la région de Saint-Etienne; étude de géographie humaine.* Saint-Etienne: Impr. 'Le feuillet blanc'

14.5.4 Industrial estates

Masson, J.-L. 1984: Situation et devenir des zones industrielles. *Revue de Géographie de Lyon* 59, 261–75

15 The tertiary sector

15.1 Nature and development

Braibant, M. 1982: Le tertiaire insaisissable? *Economie et Statistique* 146, 3–18

Lengellé, M. 1966: *La révolution tertiaire.* Paris: Genin

Lipietz, A. 1980: Polarisation interrégionale et tertiarisation de la société. *L'Espace Géographique* 9, 37–42

Saint Julien, T. 1975: Le tertiaire industriel, une réalité peu connue et mal nommée. *Analyse de l'Espace* 2, 31–46

Tauveron, A. 1974: Le tertiaire supérieur; moteur du développement régional. *L'Espace Géographique* 3, 169–78

Trogan, P. 1984: L'emploi dans les services; une croissance quelque peu ambiguë. *Economie et Statistique* 171–2, 49–58

15.2 Tertiary activities

15.2.1 Distribution

Coquery, M. 1972: *Atlas urbain des commerces de grande surface.* Paris: Comité de la recherche commerciale

1981: *Mutations et structures du commerce de détail en France,* 2v. Paris: Signe

Metton, A. 1982: L'expansion du commerce périphérique en France. *Annales de Géographie* 91, 463–79

15.2.2 Banking and finance

Battiau, M. 1977: Evolution récente de la répartition géographique de l'activité bancaire en France. *Hommes et Terres du Nord* 1, 81–8
Labasse, J. 1974: *L'espace financier, analyse géographique.* Paris: Colin

15.2.3 Health services

Labasse, J. 1980: *L'hôpital et la ville.* Paris: Hermann

15.2.4 Education and research

Brocard, M. 1979: *Recherche scientifique et développement régional en France.* Paris: Université de Paris I
    1981: Aménagement du territoire et développement régional; le cas de la recherche scientifique. *L'Espace Géographique* 10, 61–73
Pinchemel, Ph. 1969: La ville et l'université. *Projet* 822–35
Pinchemel, Ph. & others 1971: Groupes universitaires en France et à l'étranger. *Cahiers de l'IAURP* 23

15.2.5 Office development

Bateman, M. & Burtenshaw, D. 1983: Commercial pressures in central Paris. In R. L. Davies & A. G. Champion (eds.), *The future for the city centre.* London: Academic Press (IBG Special Publications 14), ch. 11. See also 18.5.5
Bonnet, J. 1976: L'essor du tertiaire supérieur à Lyon; le centre régional de La Part–Dieu. *Revue de Géographie de Lyon* 51, 5–33

15.2.6 Information technology

Paré, S. 1979: *L'informatisation des régions françaises; approche géographique.* Paris: DF (Informatisation et société 4)

15.2.7 Leisure activities and tourism

Barbier, B. 1984: Capacité d'hébergement et régions touristiques en France. *Revue de Géographie de Lyon* 59, 41–9
Cazes, G. 1984: *Le tourisme en France.* Paris: PUF (Que sais-je? 2147)
Mirloup, J. 1984: Les loisirs des Français; approche géographique. *Revue de Géographie de Lyon* 59, 15–28
Robinson, H. 1976: *A geography of tourism.* London: Macdonald & Evans, 263–81

15.3 Policies for the tertiary sector

Bastié, J. 1978: La décentralisation des activités tertiaires en France. *Analyse de l'espace* 4
Brocard, M. 1976: Recherche scientifique et développement régional en France. *Cahiers de Géographie de Rouen* 5
La décentralisation des activités tertiaires, 1972. Paris: DF
Delion, A. G. 1974: *Institutions sociales et aménagement du territoire; rapport au gouvernement.* Paris: DF

Duchêne-Marcillaz, M. 1976: *L'aménagement des services publiques dans les zones à faible densité de population.* Paris: DF
Lisle, E. 1973: *Recherche scientifique et aménagement du territoire.* Paris: DF
Menard, L. A. 1973: *Administrations centrales et aménagement du territoire.* Paris: DF
See also the publications of the Association Bureaux-Province

16 Transport and communications

16.1 General works

Bernadet, M. & Jolly, G. 1977: *Le secteur des transports.* Paris: Economica
Chesnais, M. 1980: *Transports et espace français.* Paris: Masson
Clout, H. D. 1977: Industrial development in the eighteenth and nineteenth centuries. In H. D. Clout (ed.), *Themes in the historical geography of France.* New York & London: Academic Press, 447–82
Derycke, H. & Pland, A. 1977: *Transports et aménagement du territoire; réflexions sur le rééquilibrage Est–Ouest.* Paris: DF
Guillaumat, P. 1978: *Orientation pour les transports terrestres.* Paris: DF
Quinet, E. (ed.) 1982: *Les transports en France: situation au début des années 80 et politique nouvelle* (Notes et études documentaires 4684–6). Paris: DF
Renouard, D. 1950: *Les transports de marchandises par fer, route et eau depuis 1750.* Paris: Colin
Wolkowitsch, M. 1973: *Géographie des transports.* Paris: Colin

16.2 Roads

Cavaillès, H. 1946: *La route française, son histoire, sa fonction.* Paris: Colin
Duval, P.-M., Jean, H., Livet, G., Trenard, L. & Coquand, R. 1959: *Les routes de France, depuis les origines jusqu'à nos jours.* Paris: Fabre
Fabre, J. 1982: *Les liaisons autoroutières et routières à fort débit.* Paris: CES
Fayard, A. 1980: *Les autoroutes et leur financement* (Notes et études documentaires 4597–8). Paris: DF
Labasse, J. 1971: Le réseau autoroutier français. *Revue Géographique de Montréal* 25, 235–44
Plassard, F. 1977: *Les autoroutes et le développement régional.* Paris: Economica & Lyon: Presses Universitaires de Lyon (Collection économie publique de l'aménagement et des transports)

16.3 Rail

Auphan, E. 1975: Les noeuds ferroviaires. *L'Espace Géographique* 4, 127–40
Chesnais, M. 1979: *Le renouveau du chemin de fer.* Paris: Economica
Tuppen, J. N. 1982: France's train à grande vitesse: its development and implications. *Geography* 67, 343–4
See also the annual *Activité et productivité de la SNCF.*

16.4 Inland water transport

The Office national de la navigation publique publishes annual statistics. The *Revue de la Navigation Fluviale Européenne* also publishes annually *Le trafic sur les voies navigables françaises.*

See also:
Jeffries, J. 1982: The Rhône–Rhine link in perspective. *Geography* 67, 56–9
La liaison Rhin–Rhône (Notes et études documentaires 4547–8, 1979). Paris: DF
Schéma directeur et organisation du transport fluvial; rapport de la commission Grégoire, 1983.
Paris: DF (Coll. des rapports officiels)

16.5 Seaports

Charlier, J. 1983: Ports et régions françaises, une analyse macrogéographique. *Acta
Geographica Lovaniensis* 24
Hoyle, B. S. & Pinder. D. A. (eds.) 1981: *Cityport industrialization and regional development.*
Oxford: Pergamon (includes case studies of Bordeaux, Dunkerque, Le Havre and
Marseille), 115–19 & 122–6
Soumagne, J. 1975: Les conteneurs et la mutation des ports français. *Acta Geographica*
3rd series, 21, 41–59
Vigarié, A. 1983: Les ports de commerce français de 1965 à 1983. *Norois* 31, 15–29
Villes et ports: actes du second colloque franco-japonais de géographie 1978, 1979. Paris: CNRS
(contains a general presentation by A. Vigarié: 'Diversité et évolution des ports
français métropolitains; présentation générale villes et ports' and items on the
individual French ports)

16.6 Air transport

Spill, C. 1973: Le transport aérien et la région. *Annales de Géographie* 82, 316–30
Spill, J. M. 1977: Réflexion sur l'évolution des transports aériens intérieurs en France.
L'Information Géographique 41, 225–36

16.7 Telecommunications

Bakis, H. 1984: *Géographie des communications.* Paris: PUF (Que sais-je? 2152)
See also the publications bulletins and reports of colloquia); of the Institut pour le
développement et l'aménagement des télécommunications et de l'économie (Montpellier).

17 The countryside

17.1 Bibliographies

Chiva, I. (ed.) 1972: *Les études rurales en France; tendances et organisation de la recherche.*
Paris: Mouton
Desroches, H. & Rambaud, P. 1971: Le village français; bibliographie méthodique. In
Village en développement. Paris: Mouton
Flatrès, P. 1972: La géographie rurale en France. In *Recherches géographiques en France.*
Paris: Comité national français de géographie, 189–94
Juillard, E. 1964: Géographie rurale française; travaux récents (1957–63) et tendances
nouvelles. *Etudes Rurales* 13–14, 46–70

17.2 Atlases and maps

Brunet, P. & Dionnet, M. 1984: Présentation d'un essai de carte des paysages ruraux de la
France. *Bulletin de l'Association de Géographes Français,* 98–103
Brunet, P. & others 1984: *Carte des mutations de l'espace rural français 1950–1980* (map on

scale of 1:1,000,000 and accompanying commentaries). Caen: Centre de recherches sur la vie rurale, Université de Caen

Duplex, J. (ed.) 1984: *Atlas de la France rurale*. Paris: DF (Cahiers FNScP)

140 cartes sur la France rurale, 1984. Paris: Géomedia

17.3 Rural space

17.3.1 General works

See also section 13, Agriculture (13.1, General characteristics of French agriculture, and 13.1.1, Historical development). The journal *Etudes Rurales* regularly publishes special numbers, for example: 1973: *L'urbanisation des campagnes*, 49–59; 1977: *Le pouvoir au village*, 63–4 & 65; 1978: *Campagnes disputées, campagnes marginalisées*, 71–2; 1978:*Avec nos sabots; la campagne rêvée et convoitée, autrement*, 78

Berger, A. 1975: *La nouvelle économie de l'espace rural*. Paris: Cujas

Bontron, J. C. 1975: Le fait rural en France; propos critiques sur sa définition. In *Réflexions sur l'espace rural français*. Paris: ENS Fontenay-aux-Roses

Boudeweel-Lefebvre, M. A. 1969: *La mutation de la campagne française*. Gap: Ophrys

Calmès, R. 1978: *L'espace rural français*. Paris: Masson

de Farcy, H. 1975: *L'espace rural*. Paris: PUF (Que sais-je? 1585)

Gachon, L. 1970: *La vie rurale en France*. Paris: PUF (Que sais-je? 242)

Mathieu, N. 1982: Questions sur les types d'espaces ruraux en France. *L'Espace Géographique* 11, 95–110

Piatier, A. & Madec, J. 1977: Comment et pourquoi définir un espace rural. *Economie Rurale* 118, 3–13

17.3.2 Contributions of historians and historical geographers

Bloch, M. 1931, 6th edn, 1976: *Les caractères originaux de l'histoire rurale française*. Paris: Colin. Also *Supplément établi d'après les travaux de l'auteur, 1931–44*, ed. R. Dauvergne, 4th edn, Paris

Clout, H. D. (ed.) 1977: *Themes in the historical geography of France*. London & New York: Academic Press (eight out of thirteen contributions are on rural themes)

Dion, R. 1959: *L'histoire de la vigne et du vin en France des origines au XIXe siècle*. Paris: published by the author

1943, 1981: *Essai sur la formation du paysage rural français*. Reprinted Neuilly-sur-Seine: Duvier

Pesez, J.-M. & Le Roy-Ladurie, E. 1972: The deserted villages of France; an overview. In O. Forester & O. Ranum (eds.), *Rural Society in France: selections from Annales: économies, sociétés, civilisations*. Baltimore and London: John Hopkins University Press, ch. 5

Pitte, J.-R. 1983: *Histoire du paysage français*, 2v. Paris: Tallandier (covers urban as well as rural landscapes)

Price, R. 1983: *The modernisation of rural France; communications networks and agricultural market structures in nineteenth-century France*. London: Hutchinson

Weber, E. 1976, 1977: *Peasants into Frenchmen: the modernization of rural France 1870–1914*. Stanford University Press & London: Chatto & Windus

Works of rural regional history are often of the greatest importance:

Agulhon, M. 1970: *La république au village*. Paris: Plon

Bercé, Y. M. 1974: *Croquants et nus pieds; les soulèvements paysans en France du XVIe au XIXe*. Paris: Gallimard

Le Roy-Ladurie, E. 1969: *Les paysans du Languedoc*. Paris: Flammarion

17.4 Rural landscapes

17.4.1 General works

Works covering the entire field are rare. Reference can still be made to the remarkable synthesis:

Juillard, E. & Meynier, A. 1955: Die Agrarlandschaft in Frankreich; Forschungsergebnisse der letzten zwanzig Jahre. Münchner Geographische Hefte 9. The text was reprinted in French in the volume of the colloquium 'Structures agrares et paysages ruraux', Nancy, 1957. *Annales de l'Est* 17, 1957 (substantial bibliography). Other works of synthesis include:

Meynier, A. 1968: *Les paysages agraires*, 4th edn. Paris: Colin

See also:

Bonnamour, J. (ed.) 1972: Colloque sur l'organisation spatiale des exploitations agricoles. *Bulletin de l'Association de Géographes Français* 397–8, 79–143

Deffontaines, J.-P. & Denis, J.-B. 1975: Des unités de paysage aux unités de développement en milieu rural. *L'Espace Géographique* 4, 259–71

Dufournet, P. 1978: *Pour une archéologie du paysage*. Paris: Picard

Massonie, J.-P., Mathieu, D. & Wieber, J.-C. 1971: Premiers résultats d'une application de l'analyse factorielle à l'étude de l'équilibre des paysages. *Bulletin de l'Association de Géographes Français* 387–8, 203–7

17.4.2 Rural landscape change

Brun, A. & others 1978: *Pays, paysans, paysages dans les Vosges du Sud; les pratiques agricoles et la transformation de l'espace*. Paris: INRA

Brunet, P. 1974: L'évolution récente des paysages ruraux français. *Geographia Polonica* 29, 13–30. See also 17.2

Le Thun, P. Y. 1977: Destruction d'un paysage: protestations paysannes et réflexions théoriques. *Hérodote* 7, 52–70

17.4.3 Land use

Two attempts at the land-use mapping of France have used greatly differing methods and scales. J. Klatzmann's work has been recorded in section 13.1.2. A. Perpillou produced maps at a scale of 1:400,000 relating to the early nineteenth century and to two periods in the twentieth century. See:

Solle, H. 1981: L'utilisation agricole du sol en France: les cartes Aimé Perpillou. *Acta Geographica* 45, 1–25

Among numerous other comments on the facts and techniques of depiction are:

Brunet, P. (ed.) 1974: Cartographie de l'utilisation du sol. *Bulletin de l'Association de Géographes Français* 420–1, 275–322

Flatrès, P. 1976: Les cartes de l'utilisation du sol en Europe occidentale; l'exemple de la France, *Geographia Helvetica* 31, 7–12

17.4.4 Forests and the rural environment

Revue Forestière Française publishes special numbers, for example 1978: B. de Jouvenel, *Vers la forêt du XXIe siècle*. The Ministry of Agriculture published an *Atlas forestier* in 1966.

Association des ruralistes français. 1979: *La forêt et la ville; essai sur la forêt dans l'environnement urbain et industriel*. Paris: INRA

Dewailly, J. M. & Dubois, J.-J. 1977: Nécessité et ambiguité récréative de la forêt; le cas du Nord – Pas-de-Calais. *Hommes et Terres du Nord* 1, 5–30

Kalaora, B. & Pelosse, V. 1977: La forêt-loisir; un équipement de pouvoir. *Hérodote* 7, 92–128

Le Ray, J. 1977: *La forêt française* (Notes et études documentaires 4441–2). Paris: DF
Poupardin, D. 1976: Les forêts péri-urbaines dans le système social; le cas du département des Yvelines. *Etudes Rurales* 61, 93–101
Viney, R. 1972: *L'économie forestière*. Paris: PUF (Que sais-je? 149)

17.4.5 Parcels and their boundaries

Colloque de géographie agraire de Rennes 1963, 1963 Rennes.
Caumier, J.-M. & Gillardot, P. 1974: L'évolution du paysage rural de la grande Sologne. *Norois* 21, 393–410
de Planhol, X. 1965: L'openfield à noyers dans le sud-est du Bassin parisien. *Revue Géographique de l'Est* 5, 473–82
Flatrès, P. 1967: Les structures agraires du nord de la France. *Mélanges de géographie offerts à M. Omer Tulippe* 2. Gembloux: Duculot. 309–21
Meynier, A. 1966: La genèse du parcellaire breton. *Norois* 13, 595–612
Peltre, J. 1975: *Recherches métrologiques sur les finages lorrains*. Paris: Champion

17.4.6 Rural settlement

Shortly after the Second World War an interdisciplinary study produced some hundreds of plans of traditional farmsteads. They were published only from 1980 onwards: *L'architecture rurale française; corpus des genres, des types et des variantes*. Paris: Berger Levreault. For a bibliography see:
Meirion-Jones, G. I. 1977: *La maison traditionnelle; bibliographie de l'architecture vernaculaire*. Paris: CNRS (CDSH)
Among recent items of an extensive literature are:
Actes du colloque sur la maison rurale, Poitiers 1967, 1969. Poitiers: Impr. M. Texier
Actes du colloque sur les transformations de la maison agricole, 1974. *Hommes et Terres du Nord* 1 (special issue)
Bonnier, J. & Coste, M. 1978: Consommation d'espace et habitat individuel. *Revue Géographique de Lyon* 53, 313–37
Delamarre, A. 1976: Les bâtiments d'élevage en France. *Revue Géographique des Pyrénées et du Sud-ouest* 47, 139–58
de Planhol, X. 1971: Aux origines de l'habitat rural lorrain, in 'L'habitat et les paysages ruraux d'Europe'. *Les congrès et colloques de l'Université de Liège* 58, 69–91
Duboscq, P. 1976: Les paysans et leur logement dans le sud-ouest aquitain. *Revue Géographique des Pyrénées et du Sud-ouest* 47, 121–38
Flatrès-Mury, H. 1970: Matériaux et techniques de construction rurale dans l'ouest de la France; l'exemple des confins normands, bretons et manceaux. *Norois* 17, 547–65
Gaillard-Bans, F. 1976: Maison longue et famille étendue en Bretagne. *Etudes Rurales* 62, 73–87
Gerard, C. & Peltre, J. 1978: *Les villages lorrains*. Nancy: Service des publications de l'Université de Nancy
Meirion-Jones, G. I. 1977: *Vernacular architecture and the peasant house*. In Clout, *Themes in the historical geography of France*, ch. 10 (see section 17.3.2)

17.5 Rural people and rural communities

17.5.1 French-language studies

Chapuis, R. & Brossard, T. 1986: *Les ruraux français*. Paris: Masson
Forsé, M. 1981: les réseaux de sociabilité dans un village. *Population* 36, 1141–62

Friedman, G. 1970: *Villes et campagnes; civilisation urbaine et civilisation rurale en France*, 2nd edn. Paris: Colin

Jollivet, M. 1974: *Sociétés paysannes ou lutte de classe au village*. Paris: Colin (Les collectivités rurales françaises 2)

Mendras, H. 1959: *Sociologie de la campagne française*. Paris: PUF (Que sais-je? 842)

17.5.2 Some studies available in English

Helias, P. J. 1978: *The horse of pride: life in a Breton village*. Translated by J. Guicharnaud. New Haven: Yale University Press (first published as *Le cheval d'orgueil: mémoires d'un Breton du pays bigouden*. Paris: Plon)

Lévi-Strauss, L. & Mendras, H. 1973–4: Rural studies in France. *Journal of Peasant Studies* 1, 363–78 (important bibliography)

Morin, E. 1971: *Plodémet: report from a French village*. London: Allen Lane (first published in 1967 as *Commune en France*. Paris: Fayard)

Wylie, L. 1957, 1961, 1974: *Village in the Vaucluse*. Cambridge, Mass: Harvard University Press. The later editions give brief accounts of later visits to a village that has changed greatly under the impact of rural modernization, second homes and tourism.

Wylie, L. (ed.) 1966: *Chanzeaux: village in Anjou*. Cambridge, Mass.: Harvard University Press

17.6 New functions and new uses of rural space

17.6.1 General surveys

Bontron, J.-C. & Mathieu, N. 1973: Les transformations de l'espace rural, problèmes de méthode. *Etudes Rurales* 49–50, 137–59

Canevet, C. 1980: Les mutations de l'espace rural. *Norois* 27, 5–17

Mathieu, N. 1980: Réflexion sur l'analyse de la diversification des activités dans l'espace rural. *Actes du Ve colloque franco-polonais*. Caen: Centre de recherche sur l'évolution de la vie rurale (bibliography)

17.6.2 Urbanization and modernization

Bodiguel, M. 1968: Trois sociétés rurales; trois processus de changement. *Revue Française de Sociologie* 9, 497–511

Chamboredon, J.-C. 1980: Les usages urbains de l'espace rural; du moyen de production au lieu de récréation. *Revue Française de Sociologie* 21, 97–119

Cohou, M. 1977: La population non-agricole au village: differentiation et prolétarisation de la société rurale. *Etudes Rurales* 67, 47–60

Coyaud, L.-M. 1973: *L'urbanisation des campagnes*. Paris: CRU

Mendras, H. 1970: *The vanishing peasant: innovation and change in French agriculture*. Cambridge, Mass.: MIT Press

Reiter, R. A. 1972: Modernization in the south of France: the village and beyond. *Anthropological Quarterly* 45, 35–53

Renard, J. 1984: Changement social et sociétés rurales. In *De la géographie urbaine à la géographie sociale*, ed. Collectif français de géographie. Paris: CNRS

17.6.3. Rural abandonment

La désertification de l'espace montagnard, 1977. Grenoble: INERM (Etude 111)

Faudry, D. 1973: La désertification de l'espace rural; sa logique sociale et ses conséquences. *Aménagement du Territoire et Développement Régional (Grenoble)* 6, 149–64

Faudry, D. & Tauveron, A. 1975: *Désertification ou réutilisation de l'espace rural.* Grenoble: Institut de recherche d'économie politique

Larrère, G. R. 1978: Desertification or annexation of rural space? The case of the Millevaches Highlands. *Etudes Rurales* 71–2, 9–48

Morvan, J.-C. 1981: Pour une géographie de l'abandon: l'exemple des Monts de l'Espinouse. *Bulletin de la Société Languedocienne de Géographie* 15, 215–29

17.6.4 New occupants of rural space

Belliard, J.-C. & Boyer, J.-C. 1983: Les 'nouveaux ruraux' en Ile-de-France. *Annales de Géographie* 92, 433–51

Chevalier, M. 1981: Les néo-ruraux. *L'Espace Géographique* 10, 33–47

Collomb, G. 1977: Les agriculteurs: jardiniers de la nature? Le cas du Beaufortin. *Etudes Rurales* 66, 36–42

Guerin, J.-P. 1983: L'exode urbain: nouvelles valeurs, nouvelles élites. *Revue de Géographie Alpine* 71, 267–77

Kayser, B. 1980: Le changement social dans les campagnes françaises. *Etudes Rurales* 135, 3–11

Leger, D. & Hervieu, B. 1979: *Le retour à la nature.* Paris: Seuil

17.6.5 Tourism

Beteille, R. 1976: Le tourisme en milieu rural français. *L'Information Géographique* 40, 174–89

Colloque sur le tourisme dans l'espace rural. *Bulletin de l'Association de Géographes Français* 417–18, 1974

de Farcy, H. & de Gunzbourg, P. 1967: *Tourisme et milieu rural.* Paris: Flammarion

Guignand, A.-J. & Singer, J. 1980: *Villages – vacances – familles.* Paris: PUF (Que sais-je? 1825)

Mallet, M. 1978: Agriculture and tourism in a mountain environment; the case of the Briançonnais (Hautes-Alpes). *Etudes Rurales* 71–2, 111–54

Mirloup, J. 1984: Tourisme et loisirs en milieu urbain et péri-urbain en France. *Annales de Géographie* 93, 704–18

17.6.6 Second homes

Clout, H. D. 1969: Second homes in France. *Journal of the Town Planning Institute:* 55, 440–3

Renucci, J. 1984: Les résidences secondaires en France. *Revue de Géographie de Lyon* 59, 29–40

Sarramea, J. 1980: Les résidences secondaires dans les départements français (1962–1975). *L'Information Géographique* 44, 39–41

17.7 Types of rural space

Béteille, R. 1981: *La France du vide.* Paris: LITEC

Bonnamour, J. 1976: *A propos de typologie des espaces ruraux.* Odessa: International Geographical Union

CERAT 1979: *La montagne; espace délaissé, espace convoité.* Grenoble: PUG

1978: La question des types d'espaces ruraux; les apports d'une équipe de recherche. *IRU Environnement*, 11–16

Mathieu, N. & Dubosq, P. (eds.) 1985: *Voyage en France par les pays de faible densité.* Toulouse: CNRS

SEGESA 1977: *La France des faibles densités; délimitation, problèmes, typologie.* Paris: Ministère de l'agriculture

17.8 Rural planning

17.8.1 The plans

Commissariat Général du Plan 1976: *Développement des zones rurales et de leur armature urbaine.* Paris: DF

Daunay, M. 1978: La rénovation rurale; élément de la politique d'aménagement du territoire. *Journal Officiel (Avis et rapport du CES)* 2 June
Politique des contrats de pays; bilan et directives, 1977. Paris: DF

17.8.2 Contributions to the debate

Badouin, R. 1979: *Economie et aménagement de l'espace rural.* Paris: PUF

Houssel, J.-P. 1978: Aménagement officiel et devenir du milieu rural en France. *Revue de Géographie de Lyon* 53, 283–93

Jung, J. 1971: *L'aménagement de l'espace rural: une illusion économique.* Paris: Calmann–Lévy

Kayser, B. 1979: *Petites villes et pays dans l'aménagement rural.* Toulouse: CNRS

18 Urban France

18.1 General works

Significant periodicals include *Urbanisme* and *Les Annales de la Recherche urbaine.* For surveys of work in the field of urban geography by French geographers see:

Dalmasso, E. 1976: La géographie urbaine en France. In *Human geography in France and Britain.* London: Social Science Research Council, 73–7

1980: La géographie urbaine en France; évolutions récentes. In *Recherches géographiques en France.* Paris: Comité national français de géographie, 139–44

18.1.1 Historical evolution

Beresford, M. 1967: *New towns of the Middle Ages.* London: Lutterworth

Clout, H. D. 1977: Urban growth 1500–1900. In H. D. Clout (ed.) *Themes in the historical geography of France.* New York & London: Academic Press, 483–540

Dickinson, R. E. 1951: *The West European city.* London: Routledge & Kegan Paul, esp. chs. 3, 7

Dollinger, P. & Wolff, P. 1967: *Bibliographie d'histoire des villes de France.* Paris: Klincksieck

Duby, G. (ed.) 1980–5: *Histoire de la France urbaine,* 5v. Paris: Seuil (of fundamental importance)

Ganshof, E.-L. 1943: *Etude sur le développement des villes entre Loire et Rhin au moyen age.* Paris: PUF

Gutkind, E. A. 1970: *Urban development in western Europe: France and Belgium.* New York: The Free Press (International History of City Development 5)

18.1.2 General works

Borde, J., Barrère, P. & Cassou-Mounat, M. 1980: *Les villes françaises*. Paris: Masson
Carrère, F. & Pinchemel, Ph. 1963: *Le fait urbain en France*. Paris: Colin
Scargill, I. 1983: *Urban France*. New York: St Martin's Press & London: Croom Helm

18.1.3 Individual towns

Beaujeu-Garnier, J. (ed.) 1978–80: *La France des villes*, 5v. Paris: DF (accounts of most French towns of importance)
Issues devoted to individual towns or agglomerations appear regularly in Notes et études documentaires (Paris: DF).
See also 18.5

18.2 Urban Agglomerations

The definition and delimitation of urban units and agglomerations create considerable difficulties:
Le Fillâtre, J. 1961: Nouvelle délimitation des agglomérations urbaines utilisées par l'INSEE. *Etudes Statistiques* 1, 3–55
Le Fillâtre, J. & Gérard, M. 1968: Révision de la délimitation des agglomérations urbaines utilisées par l'INSEE. *Etudes et Conjoncture* 23, 49–112
INSEE 1975: *Villes et agglomérations urbaines; délimitation 1975*. Paris
Pailhé, P. 1973: L'urbanisation en France à travers les données statistiques. *Bulletin de l'Association de Géographes Français* 406–7, 461–72
For the more comprehensive Zones de peuplement industriel et urbain (ZPIU) see the appropriate census volumes of INSEE and:
Thibault, A. 1974: Espaces géographiques en construction; une source documentaire, les ZPIU. *Analyse de l'Espace* 3 & 4

18.3 Urban growth

Dalmasso, E. 1978: Le thème de la croissance urbaine dans les recherches françaises. In *Urban growth in Japan and France; premier colloque franco-japonais de géographie 1976*, Tokyo, 9–27
Derycke, P.-H. 1973: Les coûts de la croissance urbaine. *Revue d'Economie Politique* 83, 121–70
Fontanel, C. & Peseux, C. 1976: Potentiel de population et réseau urbain en France. *L'Espace Géographique* 5, 251–4 (includes eight particularly significant maps)
Juillard, E. 1972: Croissance urbaine et accessibilité des villes. *Revue Géographique de l'Est* 12, 257–69
Pinchemel, Ph., Balley, C., Pumain, D. & Robic, M.-C. 1972: Croissance urbaine et apports migratoires. In *L'analyse interdisciplinaire de la croissance urbaine*. Paris: CNRS, 23–65
Saint Julien, T. 1982: *Croissance industrielle et système urbain*. Paris: Economica

18.4 Urban functions

Carrière, P. & Pinchemel, Ph. 1973 *Le fait urbain en France*. Paris: Colin

Chatelain, A. 1956: Géographie sociale des villes françaises en 1946. *Revue de Géographie de Lyon* 31. 119–28 (the article that marked the beginning of thirty years of French geographical interest in this theme)
Noin, D. 1974: Les activités spécifiques des villes françaises. *Annales de Géographie* 83, 531–44
Pumain, D. 1976: La composition socio-professionnelle des villes françaises; essai de typologie par analyse des correspondances et classification automatique. *L'Espace Géographique* 76, 227–38
Pumain, D. & Saint Julien, T. 1976: Fonction et hiérarchie des villes françaises. *Annales de Géographie* 85, 385–440
    1978: *Les dimensions du changement urbain*. Paris: CNRS

18.5 Urban system and urban hierarchy

18.5.1 Urban system

Coppolani, J. 1959: *Le réseau urbain de la France: sa structure et son aménagement*. Paris: 1959
Dalmasso, E. 1984: The French national settlement system. In L. S. Bourne (ed.), *Urbanization and settlement systems: international perspectives*. London: OUP, ch. 7
Hautreux, J. & Rochefort, M. 1965: Physionomie générale de l'armature urbaine française. *Annales de Géographie* 74, 660–77
Pumain, D. 1982: *La dynamique des villes*. Paris: Economica
Pumain, D. & Saint Julien, T. 1978: *Les dimensions du changement urbain; évolution des structures socio-économiques du système urbain français de 1954 à 1975*. Paris: CNRS

18.5.2 Bourgs and small towns

Bontron, J. C. 1970: Armature urbaine en milieu rural. *Urbanisme* 118, 31–6
Coyaud, L.-M. 1978: Les bourgs. *Revue Géographique de l'Est* 17, 1–9
Kayser, E. 1979: *Petites villes et pays dans l'aménagement régional*. Paris: CNRS
Laborie, J. P. 1980: *Les petites villes dans le processus d'urbanisation*. Paris: CNRS
Mathieu, N. 1972: Rôle des petites villes en milieu rural. *Bulletin de l'Association de Géographes Français* 400–1, 287–94

18.5.3 Les villes moyennes

Les villes moyennes. *Urbanisme*, 1973, 136
DATAR 1974: *Scénarios pour les villes moyennes*. Paris: DF (TRP 48)
Michel, M. 1977: Ville moyenne, ville-moyen. *Annales de Géographie* 86, 641–85
Scargill, D. I. 1983: The ville moyenne: a French strategy for town expansion. In J. Patten (ed.), *The expanding city*. New York & London: Academic Press

18.5.4. Major cities

For the notion of *métropoles d'équilibre* see:
Hansen, N. M. 1968: *French regional planning*. Edinburgh University Press, ch. 10
The structure plans for the various *aires métropolitaines* were published in numbers of Notes et études documentaires in 1967–8. Individual cities and metropolitan regions are also covered from time to time in this series, for example:
Coppolani, J., Jalabert, G. & Levy, J. P. 1984: *Toulouse et son agglomération* (Notes et études documentaires 4762). Paris: DF
Joly, J. 1985: *Grenoble et son agglomération* (Notes et études documentaires 4769). Paris: DF

Nonn, H. 1982: *Strasbourg et sa communauté urbaine* (Notes et études documentaires 4657–8). Paris: DF
See also section 19 (Regional geography).

18.5.5 Paris and its region

A wide range of research studies on the Ile-de-France region is to be found in *Cahiers de l'IAURIF (formerly Cahiers de l'IAURP)* (Paris: Institut d'aménagement et d'urbanisme de la région Ile-de-France). Useful material is also to be found in *Bulletin d'Information de la Région Ile-de-France* and (for the city of Paris) *Paris-Projet* (Paris: Atelier parisien d'urbanisme).
Bastié, J. 1984: *Géographie du grand Paris*. Paris: Masson
Beaujeu-Garnier, J. 1977: Paris et la région d'Ile-de-France, 2v. Paris: Flammarion (Atlas et géographie de la France moderne)
Beaujeu-Garnier, J. & Bastié, J. 1967: *Atlas de Paris et de la région parisienne*, 2v. Paris: Berger-Levrault
Bentham, G. & Moseley, M. J. 1980: Socio-economic change and disparities within the Paris agglomeration. *Regional Studies* 14, 55–70
Brunet, J.-P. 1985: Constitution d'un espace urbain. Paris et sa banlieue de la fin du XIXe siècle à 1940. *Annales: Economies, Sociétés, Civilisations* 40, 641–59
Dagnaud, M. 1983: A history of planning in the Paris region: from growth to crisis. *International Journal of Urban and Regional Research* 7, 219–36
Evenson, N. 1979: *Paris: a century of change*. New Haven & London: Yale University Press
   1984: Paris, 1890–1940. In A. Sutcliffe (ed.), *Metropolis 1890–1940*. London: Mansell, ch. 10
Hall, P. 1984: *The world cities*, 3rd edn. London: Weidenfeld & Nicolson, ch. 3
Lavedan, P. 1975: *Histoire de l'urbanisme à Paris*. Paris: Hachette
Lojkine, J. 1972: *La politique urbaine dans la région parisienne, 1945–1972*. Paris: Mouton
Merlin, P. 1982: *L'aménagement de la région parisienne et les villes nouvelles* (Notes et études documentaires 4677–8). Paris: DF
Moseley, M. J. 1980: Strategic planning and the Paris agglomeration in the 1960s and 1970s; the quest for balance and structure. *Geoforum* 8, 199–223
Pinchemel, Ph. 1979: *La région parisienne*. Paris: PUF (Que sais-je? 1790)

18.6 Urban spheres of influence

The first synthetic view was provided by:
Chabot, G. 1971: Cartes des zones d'influence des grandes villes françaises. *CNRS Mémoires et Documents* 8, 141–3
The results of the first of two national surveys under the direction of A. Piatier were issued on a local or regional basis by chambers of commerce and the like. The second survey resulted in: *Radioscopie des communes de France: ruralité et relations villes – campagnes, une recherche pour l'action*, 1979. Paris: Economica. See also:
Terrier, C. 1980: Réalité des régions françaises. *Economie et Statistique* 118, 53–9 (a new calculation of urban spheres of influence)

18.7 Housing and housing policies

18.7.1 General surveys

Butler, R. & Noisette, P. 1983: *Le logement social en France, 1815–1981; de la cité ouvrière au grand ensemble*. Paris: La découverte

Duclaud–Williams, R. H. 1978: *The politics of housing in Britain and France.* London: Heinemann

France: Ministère de l'Environnement et du Cadre de Vie 1980: *La ville à livre ouvert: regards sur cinquante ans d'habitat.* Paris: DF

18.7.2 Housing finance and management

Housing provision has been the subject of a sequence of reports. The year 1975 saw both the *Rapport Barre* on the reform of housing finance (Paris: DF) and an important white paper from the Union nationale des HLM entitled *Propositions pour l'habitat.* These were followed in 1976 by the *Rapport Nora* on the improvement of the older housing stock (Paris: DF). See also:

Duclos, D. 1978: *La maîtrise du procès de production du cadre bâti.* Paris: CSU

Heugas-Darraspen, H. 1985: *Le logement en France et son financement* (Notes et études documentaires 4719). Paris: DF

18.8 Urban planning

18.8.1 Planning history

Gaudin, J. P. 1985: *L'avenir en plan; technique et politique dans la prévision urbaine (1900–1930).* Seyssel: Champ Vallon

Sutcliffe, A. 1981: *Towards the planned city.* Oxford: Blackwell, ch. 5

18.8.2 Planning and planning policies

Chaline, C. 1981: Urbanization and urban policy in France. *Built Environment* 7, 233–42 (survey of policies *c.* 1970–81)

Flockton, C. 1982: Stragetic planning in the Paris region and French urban policy. *Geoforum* 13, 193–208

1983: French local government reform and urban planning. *Local Government Studies* Sept./Oct., 65–77

Goze, M. 1982: De la politique urbaine centralisée à la décentralisation de l'urbanisme. *Revue Eco. Rég. et Urbaine* 3, 333–62

Lefebvre, A. 1973: *Villes et planification.* Paris: Berger-Levrault

Loinger, G. 1981: Esquisse d'analyse de l'évolution de la politique urbaine en France depuis la libération. *Espaces et Sociétés* 36–7, 91–109

18.8.3 Specific planning procedures

Chaperon-Davidovitch, E. 1976: *Les instruments de la planification urbaine.* Paris: DF

Danan, Y. M. & Forget, J. P. 1986: *Processus et procédures d'aménagement et d'urbanisme,* v. 1. Paris: Dalloz

Hutter, R. 1978: Les enseignements à tirer des expériences de villes nouvelles, de création de quartier et de rénovation urbaine. Avis et rapports du CES. *Journal Officiel* 5 July, 13, 683–730

Jamois, J. 1968: *Les Zones à urbaniser par priorité.* Paris

Kinsey, D. N. 1969: The French ZUP technique of urban development. *Journal of the American Institute of Planners* 35, 369–75

Lacaze, J.-P. 1979: *Introduction à la planification urbaine.* Paris: Ed. du Moniteur

Prats, Y. & others 1979: *La dérogation d'urbanisme; le droit et la pratique.* Paris: Ed. champ urbain

Veltz, P. 1978: *Histoire d'une réforme ambiguë, les POS.* Paris: CRU
Wilson, I. B. 1983: The preparation of local plans in France. *Town Planning Review* 54, 155–73
Les ZAC. *Urbanisme* 161, 1977

18.9 Urban spaces

18.9.1 Urban structure

Beyer, M.-C. 1971: Essai d'étude comparée des formes et tendances de l'organisation de l'espace d'une vingtaine de moyennes et petites villes françaises. *Revue Géographique de l'Est* 11, 399–414
Castex, J. & others 1977: *Formes urbaines; de l'îlot à la barre.* Paris: Dunod
Debonneuil, X. & Gollac, M. 1978: Structure sociale des villes. *Economie et Statistique* 98, 51–65
Pumain, D., Saint Julien, T., Saunders, L. 1984: Dynamics of spatial structure in French agglomerations. *Papers of the Regional Science Association* 55, 71–82
Tilmont, M. & others 1978: *Les IGH dans la ville; dossier sur la cas français.* Paris: CRU (refers to tower-blocks)
Vigouroux, M. & Volle, J.-P. 1982: L'espace social des centres et quartiers traditionnels à Nîmes, Montpellier, Perpignan – un essai d'écologie factorielle. *Bulletin de la Société Languedocienne de Géographie* 16, 287–319

18.9.2 Social space, community, neighbourhood

Bertrand, M. J. 1978: *Pratique de la ville.* Paris: Masson
Coing, H. 1966: *Rénovation urbaine et changement social.* Paris: Ed. ouvrières
Lefebvre, H. 1970: Quartier et vie de quartier. In H. Lefebvre (ed.), *Du rural à l'urbain.* Paris: Anthropos, 207–15
Verret, M. & Creusen, J. 1979: *L'espace ouvrier.* Paris: Colin

18.9.3 Urban renewal; urban conservation

Appleyard, D. (ed.) 1979: *The conservation of European cities.* Cambridge, Mass.: MIT Press
Castells, M. 1978: *City, class and power.* London: Macmillan, ch. 5 (urban renewal and social conflict)
Devavry, J. 1977: Les rues piétonnes en France. *Hommes et Terres du Nord* 1, 45–61
Les ensembles historiques dans la reconquête urbaine, 1973. Paris: DF
Kain, R. J. P. 1975: Urban conservation in France. *Town & Country Planning* 43, 428–32
    1981: Conservation planning in France. in R. J. P. Kain (ed.), *Planning for conservation: an international perspective.* London: Mansell, ch. 12
    1982: Europe's model an exemplar still? The French approach to urban conservation 1962–1981. *Town Planning Review* 53, 403–22

18.9.4 Types of housing

Bertrand, M.-J. *Architecture de l'habitat urbain.* Paris: Dunod
Clerc, P. 1967: *Grands ensembles: banlieues nouvelles.* Paris: PUF (INED travaux et documents 49)
Guinchat, B. & others 1981: *Il était une fois l'habitat, chronique du logement social en France.* Paris: Ed. du moniteur

Lacoste, Y. 1963: Un problème complexe et débattu; les grands ensembles. *Bulletin de l'Association de Géographes Français* 318–19, 37–46

Lefebvre, H. 1960: Les nouveaux ensembles urbains. *Revue Française de Sociologie* 1, 186–201

Preteceille, E. 1973: *La production des grands ensembles*. Paris: Mouton

Rappoport, A. 1969: Housing and housing densities in France. *Town Planning Review* 39, 341–54

18.9.5 Urban fringe

Bauer, G. & Roux, J.-M. 1976: *La rurbanisation ou la ville éparpillée*. Paris: Seuil

Boyer, J.-C. 1980: Résidences secondaires et 'rurbanisation' en région parisienne. *Tijdschrift voor Economische en Sociale Geografie* 71–87

Coulaud, D. 1981: Consommation ou gaspillage d'espace en milieu péri-urbain. *L'Espace Géographique* 10, 180–6

Jaillet, M.-C. & Jalabert, G. 1982: La production de l'espace urbain périphérique. *Revue Géographique des Pyrénées et du Sud-ouest* 53, 7–26

Laborie, J.-P. & Langumier, J.-F. 1982: L'industrialisation périurbaine; une extension de la division spatiale du travail et du morcellement social. *Revue Géographique des Pyrénées et du Sud-ouest* 53, 35–50

L'enjeu péri-urbain; activité, mode de vie, 1987. Paris: DF (DATAR, TRP 83)

Mougenot, C. 1982: Les mécanismes sociaux de la 'rurbanisation'. *Sociologia Ruralis* 22, 264–78

Siran, J.-L. 1978: *Nouveaux villages, nouvelles banlieues*. Paris: Sorbonne

1980 Approche des 'nouveaux villages'. In *Vie quotidienne en milieu urbain* (Actes du Colloque de Montpellier). Paris: CRU

Taffin C. 1985: Accession à la propriété et 'rurbanisation'. *Economie et Statistique* 175, 55–67

18.9.6 New towns and town extensions

Alduy, J.-P. 1979: Les villes nouvelles de la région parisienne. *Les Annales de la Recherche Urbaine* 2, 3–78, with a comment by J.-E. Rouillier, 79–104

Baudelle, G. 1984: *Villeneuve d'Ascq, ville nouvelle; un exemple d'urbanisme concerté*. Paris: Ed. du Moniteur

Chatin, C. 1975: *Neuf villes nouvelles: une expérience française d'urbanisme*. Paris: Dunod

Dompnier, G. 1983: Toulouse – le Mirail and Colombiers Villeneuve; vingt ans après. *Revue Géographique des Pyrénées et du Sud-ouest* 54, 127–43

Goursolas, J.-M. 1980: New towns in the Paris metropolitan area; an analytic survey of the experience, 1965–79. *International Journal of Economic and Regional Research* 4, 405–21

Paquot, T. 1977: Villes nouvelles; une utopie de droit. *Espaces et Sociétés* 22–3, 3–23

Rubenstein, J. M. 1978: *The French new towns*. Baltimore & London: Johns Hopkins University Press

See also 18.5.5 – Urban system: Paris and Ile-de-France region

19 Regional geography

The approach used in this book being entirely systematic, any extended bibliography of regional geography would be inappropriate. For an overview of literature see:

Estienne, P. 1984: France: chronique de géographie régionale. *Annales de Géographie* 93,

369–71 (lists geographical serials concerned with regions and geographical space that appeared for the first time in the preceding ten years, also books and doctoral theses on these themes)

For a detailed regional geography of the regions of France reference should be made to:

Papy, L. (general editor) 1976–83: *Atlas et géographie de la France moderne*, 16v. Paris: Flammarion

✤ Index

ACEAR, 522
administrative geography, 189–202
  agents, geographical 247–68; finance,
    251–4; local and regional government,
    258–62; private sector, 262–5; state
    intervention, 203–23, 254–5, 322–8,
    377–88, *379*
agglomerations, *see* towns
agriculture, 269–330; classifications:
    313–21, *315*, *316*, 317, *320*; employed
    population, 169–70, *169*, *170*;
    European context, 271, 273–5, *274*;
    holdings: 280–96, *281*, *283*, *286*, *287*,
    289, *290*, *293*, capitalist, 284–5, 295–
    6, changing structure, 289–91, *290*,
    classification, 280–5, *281*, *283*,
    consolidation, 244–6, 323–4, 496,
    499, *500*, 505–8, 519, family, 285,
    291–4, fragmentation, 230, 486, 497–
    8, geographical distribution, 286–9,
    286, *287*, *289*, retirement, 282–3,
    283, *286*, size, 280–2, *281*, 497–8,
    supplementary, 283–4, 286–7, *286*,
    295; land use: 271–2, *272*, *274*, 501–
    8, *502*, *504*, abandonment, 503–4,
    changes in, 501–8, 511–15, uplands,

503–4; occupied population, 455–9,
  458; policy: 321–30, education, 325,
  producers' groups, 326, *327*,
  restructuring of holdings, 323–5;
  production: 276–8, *277*, 297–312,
  298, *304*, *316*, *317*, beef, *277*, *298*,
  299, 303, 307–8, cereals, 275, *277*,
  298, 303, 305, *502*, crop production,
  298–9, 301, *502*, ecological
  constraints, 305, fruit, *272*, *277*, 279,
  298–9, *298*, livestock, 9, 275, 299–
  300, 301, 305, maize, 9, *89*, 275, 277,
  277, 305, milk, 275, 277–8, *277*, *278*,
  298, 300, *304*, 305–8, organic
  farming, 279, pigs, 9, *298*, 300, *304*,
  308–9, *311*, *polyculture*, 310–12,
  potatoes, *277*, poultry, *298*, 300,
  regional specialization, 301–12, *302*,
  311, sugar beet, 9, 275, 277, *298*,
  veal, *298*, 300, wheat, 9, *277*, *277*,
  wine, 9, 136, 275, *298*, 299, *304*,
  306–7, *311*, 322, 329; tenures: 314,
  497, rural settlement systems,
  influence on, 467–8, 497–9, share-
  cropping, 314, 322, 471, 497
air transport, 441–2

DATE DUE
